ACADIA
THE SOUL OF A
NATIONAL PARK

Steve Perrin

North Atlantic Books
Berkeley, California

Earthling Press
Bar Harbor, Maine

Published by   and
North Atlantic Books   Earthling Press
P.O. Box 12327   P.O. Box 585
Berkeley, California 94712   Bar Harbor, Maine 04609

Photos and maps by Steve Perrin. Front cover photos: (upper) Jordan Pond and North Bubble from Penobscot Mountain; (lower left) Bald Peak over frozen Upper Hadlock Pond; (lower right) Hiker on the Precipice Trail. Back cover photo: East face, Champlain Mountain

Printed in the United States of America

Acadia: The Soul of a National Park is sponsored by the Society for the Study of Native Arts and Sciences, a nonprofit educational corporation whose goals are to develop an educational and crosscultural perspective linking various scientific, social, and artistic fields; to nurture a holistic view of arts, sciences, humanities, and healing; and to publish and distribute literature on the relationship of mind, body, and nature.

North Atlantic Books' publications are available through most bookstores. For further information, call 800-337-2665 or visit our website at www.northatlanticbooks.com. Substantial discounts on bulk quantities are available to corporations, professional associations, and other organizations. For details and discount information, contact our special sales department.

Earthling Press may be reached at earthling@acadia.net; phone 207-288-8240.

Library of Congress Cataloging-in-Publication Data
Perrin, Steve (Stephen Gale)
    Acadia, the soul of a national park / by Steve Perrin.
        p. cm.
Originally published: Bar Harbor, Me. : Earthling Press, c1998.
Includes index.
    ISBN 1-55643-468-5
    1. Hiking—Maine—Acadia National Park—Guidebooks. 2. Trails—Maine—Acadia National Park—Guidebooks. 3. Acadia National Park Me.—Guidebooks.
4. Perrin, Steve (Stephen Gale)—Journeys—Maine—Acadia National Park. I. Title: Acadia. II. Title
    GV199.42.M22A328 2003
    917.41' 450444—dc21   2003003872

1 2 3 4 5 6 7 8 9 DATA 09 08 07 06 05 04 03

In memory of my parents

P.G.P.

D.M.P.

Porter Gale Perrin
and
Dorothy Merchant Perrin

Their body language
said *Love the Earth*

Summit, Sargent Mountain.

CONTENTS

ILLUSTRATIONS—MAPS vi

ILLUSTRATIONS—PHOTOGRAPHS vii

PREFACE xiii

BOOK ONE—FALL 1

Contents—Fall Hikes 2
Introduction—Fall 4
1 Mansell Mountain loop 5
2 Penobscot Mountain loop 7
3 St. Sauveur & Flying mountains loop 11
4 Around Dorr Mountain 15
5 Conners Nubble & the Bubbles loop 19
6 Sargent Mountain via Chasm Brook 24
7 Pemetic Mountain loop 29
8 Sargent Mountain via the Giant Slide 33
9 Around Jordan Pond 38
10 Beech Cliff & Canada Ridge loop 42
11 Mansell Mountain loop 47
12 Bernard Mountain loop 51
13 Dorr Mountain loop 57
14 Champlain Mountain loop 62
15 Dorr & Cadillac mountains loop 68

BOOK TWO—WINTER 73

Contents—Winter Hikes 74
Introduction—Winter 76
16 Ocean Path 77
17 Beech Mountain loop 82
18 Asticou Trail 86
19 McFarland Hill loop 92
20 Hunters Brook loop 96
21 Sargent & Cedar Swamp mountains loop 100
22 Around Mansell Mountain 108
23 Long Pond Fire Road loop 112
24 Around-Mountain Carriage Road 116
25 Little Harbor Brook loop 123
26 Beehive & Champlain Mountain loop 127
27 Cadillac Mountain Road 133
28 Around St. Sauveur Mountain 136
29 Wonderland & Ship Harbor loop 142
30 Around Cedar Swamp Mountain 145

BOOK THREE—SPRING 149

Contents—Spring Hikes 150
Introduction—Spring 152
31 Hio Road 153
32 Seaside Trail 157
33 Breakneck & carriage roads loop 163
34 Sargent Mountain via Hadlock Brook 168
35 Hunters Brook, Triad, & Day Mountain loop 173
36 Great Head loop 179
37 Little Harbor Brook & Birch Spring loop 184
38 Eliot Mountain loop 190
39 Around Dorr Mountain 194
40 Sargent Mountain via the Giant Slide 200
41 Pothole & Canon Brook trails loop 207
42 Around Lower Hadlock Pond 212
43 Around Jordan Pond 217
44 Sargent Mountain via Deer Brook 223
45 Four trails on Isle au Haut 229

BOOK FOUR—SUMMER 237

Contents—Summer Hikes 238
Introduction—Summer 240
46 Beech Mountain loop 241
47 Parkman Mountain & Bald Peak loop 246
48 Cadillac Mountain 249
49 Schoodic Head & the Anvil loop 255
50 Dorr Mountain loop 259
51 Acadia Mountain loop 265
52 Pemetic Mountain loop 269
53 Norumbega Mountain loop 275
54 Champlain & Gorham mountains 280
55 Penobscot & Sargent mountains loop 286
56 St. Sauveur Mountain & Valley Peak loop 292
57 Western Mountain loop 297
58 Cadillac Mountain loop 304
59 Sargent Mountain loop 309
60 The Bubbles & Conners Nubble loop 314

INDEX 321

ILLUSTRATIONS

MAPS

Sixteen hikes in Acadia National Park
   west of Somes Sound. xxii

Selected trails on Mount Desert Island
   west of Somes Sound. xxiii

Forty-four hikes in Acadia National Park
   east of Somes Sound. xxiv

Selected trails on Mount Desert Island
   east of Somes Sound. xxv

1—Mansell Mountain loop. 5
2—Penobscot Mountain loop. 7
3—St. Sauveur & Flying mountains loop. 11
4—Around Dorr Mountain. 15
5—Conners Nubble & the Bubbles loop. 19

6—Sargent Mountain via Chasm Brook. 24
7—Pemetic Mountain loop. 29
8—Sargent Mountain loop via Giant Slide Trail. 33
9—Around Jordan Pond. 38
10—Beech Cliff & Canada Ridge loop. 42

11—Mansell Mountain loop. 47
12—Bernard Mountain loop. 52
13—Dorr Mountain loop. 57
14—Champlain Mountain loop. 62
15—Dorr & Cadillac mountains loop. 68

16—Ocean Path. 77
17—Beech Mountain loop. 82
18—Asticou Trail. 87
19—McFarland Hill loop. 92
20—Hunters Brook loop. 96

21—Sargent & Cedar Swamp mountains loop. 101
22—Around Mansell Mountain. 108
23—Long Pond Fire Road loop. 113
24—Around-Mountain Carriage Road loop. 117
25—Little Harbor Brook loop. 123

26—Beehive & Champlain Mountain loop. 127
27—Cadillac Mountain Road. 133
28—Around St. Sauveur Mountain. 136
29—Wonderland & Ship Harbor loop. 142
30—Around Cedar Swamp Mountain. 145

31—Hio Road. 153
32—Seaside Trail. 157
33—Breakneck & carriage roads loop. 163
34—Sargent Mountain via Hadlock Brook Trail. 168
35—Triad & Day Mtn. loop via Hunters Brook. 173

36—Great Head loop. 179
37—Little Harbor Brook & Birch Spring loop. 185
38—Eliot Mountain loop. 190
39—Around Dorr Mountain. 194
40—Sargent Mountain loop via Giant Slide Trail. 201

41—Featherbed via Pothole Trail. 207
42—Around Lower Hadlock Pond. 212
43—Around Jordan Pond. 217
44—Sargent Mountain via Deer Brook. 224
45—Four trails on Isle au Haut. 230

46—Beech Mountain loop. 241
47—Parkman Mountain & Bald Peak loop. 246
48—Cadillac Mountain. 249
49—Schooner Head & the Anvil loop. 255
50—Dorr & Kebo mountains loop. 259

51—Acadia Mountain loop. 265
52—Pemetic Mountain loop. 270
53—Norumbega Mountain loop. 275
54—Champlain & Gorham mountains. 281
55—Penobscot & Sargent mountains loop. 286

56—St. Sauveur Mountain & Valley Peak loop. 292
57—Western Mountain loop. 298
58—Cadillac Mountain loop. 304
59—Sargent Mountain loop. 309
60—Bubbles & Conners Nubble loop. 314

ILLUSTRATIONS

PHOTOGRAPHS

Cadillac, Dorr, and Champlain mountains from Gorham Mountain.

Summit, Sargent Mountain. iv
Cadillac, Dorr, and Champlain from Gorham Mtn. vii
Ice, Gilmore Bog. viii
Conners Nubble and Eagle Lake. ix
Mount Desert Island from Baker Island. x

View south from McFarland Hill. xi
Pollen cones on pitch pine, early June. xii
Kurt Diederich's Climb, Dorr Mountain. xiii
Cobble beach near Wonderland and Ship Harbor. xiv
Striped maple leaf and flowers. xv

Hadlock Falls through Waterfall Bridge. xvi
Witch hazel along the Bowl Trail. xvii
Upside-down icicles in Seven Sisters Brook. xviii
Cairn on the Pothole Trail. xxvi
Base of Dorr Mountain Ladder Trail. 1

Hikers on Jordan Pond East Side Trail. 4
Steps across talus slope, Perpendicular Trail. 6
Winding steps on the Perpendicular Trail. 6
Cairn, Penobscot Mountain. 9
Trailhead and steps, Penobscot Mountain Trail. 10

Hiker approaching steps, Valley Cove Trail. 12
Osprey on a snag. 13
Falling steps leading back in time, Valley Cove. 14
Buddha on Cadillac Mountain. 16
The Gorge Trail rising to Pulpit Rock. 17

Pool and plunge on Kebo Brook. 18
Clashing boulder lichens. 20
Conners Nubble from south shore of Eagle Lake. 21
Jordan Pond and Penobscot Mountain. 22
Rock-cap fern. 23

Hiker following the course of Chasm Brook. 25
North slope of Sargent Mountain. 26
Chasm Brook Falls at a wetter time of year. 27
Sargent's summit from north ridge trail. 28
Black chokeberries. 29

Map lichen. 30
Black crowberry. 31
Dwarf juniper with berries. 32
Sargent Brook along the Giant Slide Trail. 34
Hiker follows trail beneath the Giant Slide. 35

PHOTOGRAPHS, *Continued*

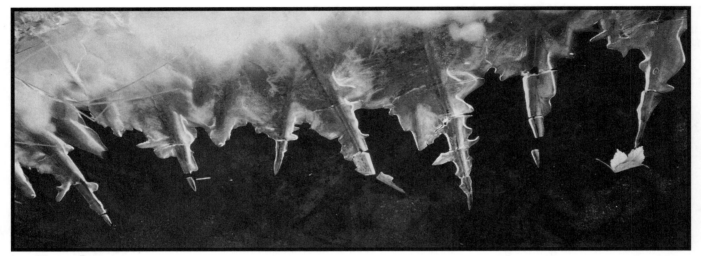

Ice, Gilmore Bog.

Upper end of the Grandgent Trail. 36
Signpost, Sargent Mountain summit. 37
Watershed of Jordan Pond. 39
Jordan Pond East Side Trail. 40
South Bubble from Jordan Pond East Side Trail. 41

Steve Perrin on the Beech Cliff Ladder Trail. 43
Black huckleberry leaves, Canada Ridge. 44
Christmas fern. 45
Base of Canada Cliff. 46
Steve Perrin reflecting on roots. 48

Wine-leaf cinquefoil. 49
Ground pine or tree club moss. 50
Bird silhouette trail marker. 51
Wintergreen and hair-cap moss. 53
Mountain cranberry. 54

Steps on the old Spring Trail. 55
Pincushion moss. 56
Rock slide on Dorr Mountain Ladder Trail. 58
Hiker on Dorr Mountain Ladder Trail. 59
Mayflower leaves. 60

Hiker on the Precipice Trail. 63
Kinnikinnick, or bearberry. 64
Feather moss. 65
Steps, Champlain Mountain East Face Trail. 66
Cadillac Mountain crumbles into the Gorge. 69

Ice on the walls of the Gorge. 70
The canyon of Canon Brook. 71
The Featherbed before freezing over. 72
Raccoon prints in snow. 73
Ice vanes, Cadillac Mountain. 76

Otter Point and the Beehive. 78
Mr. Rockefeller's window on the sea. 79
Male eider diving for mussels off Otter Point. 80
Thunder Hole walkway covered with ice. 81
Christmas fern on the Valley Trail. 83

Ice crystals in the trail. 84
Fox print in thin snow. 85
Red spruce sapling in snow. 86
Asticou Map House. 88
Balsam fir branch decked in light snow. 89

PHOTOGRAPHS, *Continued*

Conners Nubble and Eagle Lake.

Ice on Jordan Stream. 90
Asticou Trail bridge. 91
Deer track in deep snow. 93
Snowshoe hare track. 94
View south from McFarland Hill. 95

Deer prints in light snow. 96
Tree fallen across Hunters Brook. 97
Icicles over Hunters Brook. 98
Fox track. 99
Summit cairn, Sargent Mountain. 103

Cairn with windswept granite. 104
Cairn with wind shadow. 105
Ruffed grouse track. 106
Red spruce garbed for winter. 107
Snow vanes pointing toward the storm. 109

Great Notch Trail. 110
Bridge over Great Brook. 111
Deer track. 114
Fox track on snow crust. 115
Vole track and tunnel entrance. 116

Springtails in fox print. 116
Tumbledown, Jordan Ridge. 118
Waterfall Bridge and icy Hadlock Falls. 119
Hadlock Falls in warmer days. 121
Ice elephants. 122

Ice on Little Harbor Brook. 124
Little Harbor Brook between two bends. 125
The Beehive from Otter Point. 128
Narrow shelf on the Beehive Trail. 129
Pitch pines and iron rungs, the Beehive. 130

The Bowl. 131
Champlain Mountain east face. 132
Red squirrel prints. 133
Sargent Mountain and Bubble Ridge. 134
Cadillac Mountain parking area. 135

Loons on Somes Sound. 137
Northern white cedars in icy stream. 138
Ice in Valley Cove Trail. 139
Tumbled steps, base of Eagle Cliff. 140
Steps over sloping ledge, Valley Cove. 141

PHOTOGRAPHS, *Continued*

Mount Desert Island from Baker Island.

Eider loafing offshore. 143
Headland ledges, broken rock, trees. 144
Cobble beach. 145
Terra incognita on Sargent Mountain. 148
Mayflower, Kurt Diederich's Climb. 149

Ice-covered Hio Road rounds Big Heath. 154
Northern white cedar, tree of life. 155
Tracks of snowshoe hare and coyote. 156
Vole prints in meadow. 158
Red maple tree, Jordan Pond. 159

The Seaside Trail. 160
Fresh coyote prints, claws extended. 161
Ice creepers, my artificial claws. 162
White pine tree, Upper Breakneck Pond. 162
Dorr and Cadillac over Witch Hole Pond. 164

Breakneck Brook. 165
Beaver lodge, Breakneck Brook. 166
Carriage road near Breakneck Ponds. 167
Woods along Hadlock Brook Trail. 167
The snowy course of Hadlock Brook. 169

View west from Sargent's Summit. 170
Sargent's south ridge. 171
Ice on Hadlock Brook Trail. 172
Hunters Brook in spring flood. 174
A bend in the brook. 175

Fallen trees bridge Hunters Brook. 176
A former beach. 177
Spotted lungwort on maple tree. 178
Grouse track on Great Head. 180
Gabbro outcrop on Great Head. 181

Shatter-zone outcrop, Sand Beach. 182
Beehive from Sand Beach. 183
Fox track, Little Harbor Brook Trail. 186
Little Harbor Brook in its maturity. 187
Little Harbor Brook in middle age. 188

Little Harbor Brook in its youth. 189
Trailhead, Amphitheater Trail. 190
Icy trail through woods on Eliot Mountain. 191
Signpost, summit of Eliot Mountain. 192
Spruce cones, cores, and scales. 193

PHOTOGRAPHS, *Continued*

Cadillac, Pemetic, the Bubbles, Penobscot, and Sargent mountains from McFarland Hill.

Kebo Brook flows beneath cliffs. 195
Kebo Brook spills over a mossy boulder. 196
The A. Murray Young Trail. 197
Lodge in Beaver Brook. 198
The Kane Trail. 200

The rocky bed of Sargent Brook. 202
The Giant Slide encased in ice. 203
Sargent Mountain north ridge. 204
View from the Grandgent Trail. 205
Headwaters of Sargent Brook. 206

Feather moss and rock-cap fern. 206
Pothole Trail follows cairns across ledges. 208
Pothole on the Pothole Trail. 209
Pool on the Canon Brook Trail. 210
Canon Brook plunges into its canyon. 211

Hadlock Path bridge over nameless brook. 213
Hadlock Brook runs for Lower Hadlock Pond. 214
Lower Hadlock Pond. 215
Bogwalk on Jordan Pond West Side Trail. 217
South Bubble from Tumbledown Cove. 218

West side trail winds across the Tumbledown. 219
Spruce, birch, and North Bubble. 220
Jordan Pond East Side Trail. 221
Youth Conservation Corps bridge. 222
Cribwork steps, Bubble Gap Trail. 223

Eagle Lake from Jordan Cliffs Trail extension. 225
Eroded section, Deer Brook Trail. 226
Spring shower, Sargent Mountain. 227
Wetlands, Sargent's summit ridge. 228
Rocky upper valley of Deer Brook. 229

Woods along the Duck Harbor Trail. 231
View, Western Head Trail. 232
Volcanic rock with striations. 233
View south from the Cliff Trail. 234
View northeast from the Cliff Trail. 235

Leaf buds on a white spruce. 236
Wood lilies on Sargent Mountain. 237
Blueberry blossoms. 240
Beech Cliff Ladder Trail. 242
Top of Beech Cliff Ladder Trail. 243

PHOTOGRAPHS, *Continued*

Beech Mountain Fire Tower. 244
Steps on Beech Mountain South Ridge Trail. 245
Cinnamon fern. 247
Lady's slipper. 248
Summit of Bald Peak. 249

Pitch pine. 250
Cotton grass, Dike Peak. 251
Featherbed and Dike Peak. 252
Porcupine Islands. 253
Mountain cranberry and reindeer lichen. 254

Schoodic Peninsula from Champlain. 256
Cleft in the ledge, Anvil Trail. 257
Twinflower along the Anvil Trail. 258
Steps, Dorr Mountain East Face Trail. 260
Dorr Mountain summit cairn. 261

Pitch pines in the fog. 262
Pitch pine cone and needles. 263
The Jesup Trail. 264
Acadia Mountain Trail. 266
Kinnikinnick. 267

View south from Acadia Mountain. 268
Pemetic Mountain (Ravine) Trail. 271
View from Pemetic Mountain. 272
Mountain sandwort. 273
Pemetic Mountain south ridge. 274

Beech woods, Jordan Pond Canoe Carry. 274
Cloud lichen. 276
Twining pitch pines. 277
Brown Mountain Trail. 278
Bridge over Hadlock Brook. 279

Beachcroft Trail. 280
Porcupine Islands. 282
Summiteers, Champlain Mountain. 283
Bowl, Beehive, and Gorham Mountain. 284
Log bridge, Jordan Cliffs Trail. 287

Jordan Cliffs Trail. 288
Sargent Mountain Pond. 289
Wood lilies, Sargent Mountain. 290
Sargent Mountain summit cairn. 291
Osprey poised in flight. 293

Eagle Cliff. 294
Valley Cove Trail. 295
Herb Robert. 296
Rungs and ladder, Perpendicular Trail. 297
Perpendicular Trail. 299

View from Mansell Mountain overlook. 300
Goldthread and hair-cap moss. 301
Mansell Mountain. 302
Beech, Mansell, and Bernard mountains. 303
White pine against fog. 304

Pollen cones on pitch pine, early June.

Cadillac Mountain West Face Trail. 305
Pemetic Mountain beyond Bubble Pond. 306
Ledge, Cadillac Mountain West Face Trail. 307
Islands south of Mount Desert island. 308
Red fox of Acadia. 308

Rattlesnake plantain. 310
Sargent Mountain summit. 311
View from upper Grandgent Trail. 312
Sargent Mountain and Upper Hadlock Pond. 313
Jordan Pond Canoe Carry. 313

Bubble Rock. 316
Mountain ash. 317
Conners Nubble. 318
Water striders and their shadows. 319
Hikers on Beachcroft Trail. 320

PREFACE

This book is about the hiking trails of Acadia National Park from one man's experience and point of view. Collectively, these sixty essays make a comprehensive guide to the park, with 65 maps and 266 photographs. Too, they tell the story of one man's adventures with plants, animals, and people he meets along 275 miles of Acadia's trails. They present an informal portrait of Acadia's bioregion through the seasons. These essays are a verbal response to the eloquent, preverbal silence that is Acadia's native language. Or, again, a record of one man's search for sacred encounters in one of the most beautiful regions on the Maine coast.

Acadia: The Soul of a National Park is all of these, and more. It is an ambling meditation on what it means to be an Earthling with a conscience in a time when humankind is laying increasing claim to the homeland of all life on Earth.

As a series of essays, the book shows how I met the challenge of describing sixty more-or-less similar journeys, all with beginnings, unfoldings, and ends, without depending overmuch on formulas and stock phrases. When I started this project in August 1993, I didn't have a clue how to write up a hike. My first impulse was to

Kurt Diederich's Climb, Dorr Mountain.

present my material in chronological order, step by step by step. I soon began to look for themes that emerged from my trail adventures themselves. I approached each hike as it came to me in recollection, helped along by my notes. I enjoyed the writing as much as the hiking, each offering a broad range of challenges and satisfactions. Appreciating the limits of my verbal descriptions, I relied more and more on photographs to catch the flavor of a given trail. At first I had trouble switching between verbal and visual imagery, but soon got the hang of using one to complement the other. Regretting not having taken more pictures on my fall and winter hikes, I went back to fill in obvious gaps. Often, however, I couldn't duplicate the images in my head, so eventually made sure to carry my camera on every hike to get pictures when they were offered. In the end I added maps to give readers a schematic sense of my journey through the park.

How to Use This Book

If you are planning a trip to Acadia National Park in any season, this book will acquaint you with all the major trails, as well as the landscapes, plants, and wildlife you are likely to see at that time of year. There is no better way to prepare for your trip than by picking up a copy of *Acadia: The Soul of a National Park*.

If you are visiting Acadia right now, take this book home with you as a reminder of your stay—and as an aid in preparing for your return.

If you are planning to hike a particular trail, prehike it with me first to find out what to keep an eye out for, and what your options are for returning to the trailhead by an alternate route.

If you have recently hiked a particular trail, compare your experience with mine by reading what I have to say about that same trail. Use these trail descriptions as a refresher.

Many people keep the book by their bedside, delving into it a hike at a time.

If you are looking for a route to a particular destination—a mountain summit, ridge, pond, or stream—read several hikes describing how I got there to find the route that suits you the best.

Dip into the book at random, letting Acadia emerge from its pages by the peculiar logic of serendipity.

And if you want to appreciate the flow of Acadia through the seasons, start at the beginning and go through to the end, using the book as a guide to the local bioregion, its terrain, and the plants and wildlife that live here or pass through.

If you are more a picture person than a word person, use the photographs of Acadia included here for a quick tour of places you can't reach by bicycle or by car.

Why Come to Acadia?

Like spruce trees and red squirrels, we humans cannot help ourselves: we are part of nature, Earthlings through and through. We share the air that other Earthlings breathe, the water that other Earthlings drink, the stored sunlight that other Earthlings eat. We are conceived and born like other Earthlings, and die like them as well. Our every thought is a natural thought, every dream a natural dream, every act a natural act. We are incapable of stepping beyond our natural bounds, of being untrue to nature in any way. Our station is neither above nor below our peers in the natural world; we are with them, fellow passengers on planet Earth. In various forms we have been with them since the beginning. Changing with the times, we will ride with them till the end.

And yet we feel estranged from nature as if we were separated from it by an unbridgeable gulf. Nature is over there on its side and we are here on ours. Having walked upright on Earth for more than four million years, we have lost sight of our place in the natural order of things. Something has made us self-conscious. We have grown preoccupied with our private affairs. We yearn to participate in Earth's ongoing life, but don't remember how. Once blessed with natural grace, we have become awkward and bumbling. The harder we try, the more we go wrong. Instead of rejoining Earth's natural fold, we stray farther afield.

How did we get into this fix? Unwittingly, beyond a doubt. That is, without our wits. Not fully realizing what we were doing, we have come to live in a world of symbols and substitute experiences. We live vicariously through plots and scenarios created by others to employ and divert us. We swim in a flood of

Cobble Beach between Wonderland and Ship Harbor.

speech and music that never stops. We go to sleep to its lull and wake to its rousing call. Money and the economy intercede between us and our home planet. We take our culture in through media that shout for our attention as if their clangor were real and true and beautiful. But in fact it is none of these. It is noise, Samuel Johnson's "busy hum of men" grown to a ceaseless din, which drowns our natural thoughts, replacing flowing lyrics with cacaphony.

The remedy is silence. The silence of ancient times preceding the din of civilization. Imagine a place without engines, advertisements, litanies, talk shows, gossip, hype, numbers, statistics, or symbols of any kind. A place that is what it is without trying to convince us it is something else. A preverbal, presymbolic place. A few such places still exist, though their number is dwindling. Acadia is one of them. Its greatest asset is silence. The silence of the midnight sky, of dawn spreading over the water. The silence of

fog shrouding the Porcupine Islands. The silence of bogs and shaded woods, of still ponds and granite ledges. The silence of moss, lichens, ferns, wintergreen, and kinnikinnick. Acadia does not grab your ear and say, "Now listen to this!" It lets you be wholly yourself. Your ancient self before you learned to talk, and talk, and talk. Your natural, nonsymbolic self. Your self as you know it from the inside, beyond the reach of those who would shape you into something other than what you are.

Acadia welcomes us not as movers and shakers from Away but as peers of its local residents. We are welcome not as the great communicators we claim to be but as members of the silent chorus of listeners and dancers who sway to the living rhythms of clouds, mountains, valleys, and the sea. Acadia releases us to be our natural selves. That is why we come. To leave the world of symbols at home and to rediscover what we are as Earthlings embraced by an Earthling community.

We who share in the present moment of awareness are the vessels of universal creativity. We are the current bearers of the spark ignited fifteen billion years ago when the universe burst into the here and now. Our passions are the embers of that eternal flame. Can we possibly believe we carry that spark in order to amass as much wealth as we can, or to take advantage of our gullible brothers and sisters? Are we here to leave Earth worse off than before? To wage war? To get high on alcohol and drugs? To maim and kill other species? To deplete Earth's resources?

No, we either reinforce the integrity of Earth as a living whole—or we undermine it. The choice is ours: the way of beauty, truth, and fulfillment, or of emptiness, futility, and shattered dreams. We know that is true. Intuition tells us so. Our fifteen-billion-year heritage of strife and struggle tells us so. We yearn to reconnect with nature and with ourselves. To rejoin the creative forces of the universe. To get with Earth's program. To work together for a better world.

The urge to reconnect with nature is, I believe, why we come to Acadia. To recenter our wayward perspectives. To sharpen the vision of who we are, where we live, and what we should be working for. To align ourselves once more with the workings of nature on a regional and planetary scale. Acadia and other national parks can help us restore that vision. That is their promise.

But we have become so immersed in our culture that nature's ways often seem foreign and incomprehensible. We look upon the Acadian landscape to see only the reflected blur of our own myopic vision, listen but hear only the rush of our own whirling thoughts. Whether we come from Portland, Boston, New York, Philadelphia, Mars—same thing—out of our cultural element, we find ourselves strangers in our own land.

Though we read books and watch videos about nature, and study it in school, we are lost when it comes to experiencing the natural idiom of our home planet. We have forgotten our mother tongue, the language people have been born to since our ancestors first walked the Earth. We look at Acadia and have general names for what we see—rocks, trees, plants, flowers, birds—but not specific names by which to move into deeper acquaintance with the rich variety of living beings we meet yet do not recognize as family friends. As a result, we know Acadia in a general way as it might appear on a postcard, but not personally or intimately. Certainly not naturally. Our relationship with Acadia remains stiff, and when we go home again we wonder where the magic was that we seem to have missed.

Striped maple leaf and flowers, early June.

Which is strange, since we think of ourselves as people in close touch with nature—as environmentalists who take pains to recycle cans and bottles, to side with wetlands and wildlife, to worry about global warming and holes in the ozone layer, to feed birds in winter, and take loving care of our pets. Coming to Acadia is like going on a first date; we don't know how to act to break the ice.

Being *Here*

I wrote this book to help people get to know the Acadia bioregion through the seasons. To know it personally. Meaningfully. And above all, for keeps in a relationship with the natural world that will build slowly over the years through the span of a lifetime. No, you can't do Acadia in a couple of hours. Two days or two weeks aren't enough. I have been exploring the park for sixty years, and on almost every

hike I see something I have never seen before, or seen something familiar in a new way. That is why I keep at it: the challenge remains, and so do the rewards. Compared to national parks in the West, Acadia is small potatoes perhaps, but it is bigger than anyone can know inside-out in one life. It is worth the effort to keep coming back. Each time it is a new park offering fresh experiences. The park grows with the years, and our experience grows to keep up with it.

In the end we begin to feel at home in Acadia as if we were born to it, which we were in a former life. We rediscover the unity with nature we once had but lost during our years of self-preoccupation. We get our old selves back again. Our wholeness and integrity. We see that rugged individualism is not self-contained but is based on a sustainable supply of natural resources, a birthright our nation once took for granted, but overspent. To attain global sustainability, every life on Earth must accord with every other life. Personal wealth and power can hardly be seen as signs of success if they threaten the integrity of the whole. To foul or deplete any natural resource—energy, air, water, soil, vegetation, wildlife—is to squander the heritage we were given at birth. Our parents and their parents back to beginning times got us where we are; it is clearly our job to preserve and pass on what they gave us. Or better, to renew what we received in battered condition.

As a sample of the natural world in good working order, Acadia National Park is a living illustration of what the world could be like if we gave up trying to bend it to our will. Natural beauty is an ideal to protect and emulate, not an invitation to possess and control that which is not ours. We come to Acadia to reexperience the good life, the life in which we participate in the beauty and health of our natural surroundings instead of neglecting them from afar.

In these pages I invite readers to join me on hikes into the heart of Acadia, to see and hear what is to going on, to experience the joy of Earthling selfhood in the company of Earthling selves. I share my experiences not that you should think the same thoughts as I do, but that you should follow your own leadings. The reward of being in Acadia is the joy of being *here* and not anywhere else. Being here as *yourself* and not anyone else. Being here *now* and not some other time. Truly *being here,* present to all that is around you. That involves more than just coming to Acadia. It means opening to the wonder and influence of this particular place on Earth. It means letting go of what you know and are familiar with in order to be open to the new and the possible. It means leaving your accomplished, expert self behind and adopting a new, more approachable self suited to the *here* and *now* of this place. It means reaching out to your surroundings, giving them a chance to reach in to you. In to the depths of you, the sacred seat of your identity. If you succeed in doing that—and it takes practice, so be patient—you will find that your visit to Acadia is an occasion for Acadia to visit you. Acadia National Park will meet you halfway. The trick is in leaving your hustling, complex, competent self behind and adopting a stance of simple innocence in which you are willing to receive whatever your surroundings have to offer.

You will start by noticing the most striking features of your setting in nature, but perhaps in a way you have never noticed before, making them seem new and exciting. Then subtler features will enter your awareness and, if you can sustain a receptive attitude deep enough, long enough, you will notice things you have never seen before or

Hadlock Falls through Waterfall Bridge.

even dreamt of. At that point you will have truly arrived in Acadia.

To reach that state of receptivity you have to drop your habitual guard against being surprised by your surroundings—the "been there, done that" attitude that protects us, yes, but isolates us from what is going on around us. To *know* Acadia we have to *give ourselves to* Acadia. If we can wait quietly and expectantly for Acadia to reveal itself in its own way—it will happen, in ways so wonderful we will never forget them.

A Spiritual Quest

Openness, innocence, humility, and surrender leading to revelation, that is what this book is about. When I started out in August 1993, I thought I could write up one hike every week for a year, then get on with my life. The project proved so demanding, however, that I had to take a break

after only three months, so each section represents not only a different time of year but a different hiker as well. I could not hold my temperament or my outlook fixed as if in amber from the fall of 1993 through the spring of 1998, which is how long it took me to finish what I had begun. I surrendered to Acadia each time, but as four different people. Along the way I realized my words needed to be backed up with photographs and, after publishing the fall hikes as a separate volume, with trail maps as well. In these pages the whole project is assembled between two covers—4 seasons, 52 weeks, 60 hikes, 275 trail miles, with maps and photographs—representing a fair portion of my activity through five years of my life. In the meantime I worked as a seasonal employee at Acadia National Park, two years as volunteer coordinator and three years as an assistant, then a writer/editor in the planning office. I lived in park housing during those years, so started my hikes variously from park headquarters on McFarland Hill, from Harden Farm apartments under Kebo Mountain, or from the gatehouse at Brown Mountain Gate.

As readers will discover, I undertook another project at the same time I was working on this book: that of trying to put my spiritual house in order as an extension of my interest in nature. My mother was an active Episcopalian throughout her life; as far as I could tell my father, son of a Vermont minister, was an atheist. While I was growing up, the message I got about spiritual matters was mixed at best. I went to Sunday school to please my mother until I was twelve, then abandoned the enterprise of organized religion as my father had done. At nineteen, while watching the sensuous rise and fall of electrical cables along the track as I was riding to Port Washington from New York on the Long Island Railroad, it came to me as a revelation that God was an invention of creative imagination. Creator, lawgiver, judge, heavenly father, confidant, confessor, fount of abiding love—he (in those days that was the only pronoun that applied) could not exist in the world as I knew it. The Hindenberg had exploded in flames, the hurricane of 1938 hit New England. A second global war had raged during much of my youth, preceded and succeeded by an endless stream of regional wars. Millions were killed in the war, and other millions left homeless to wander about Europe and Asia as if nobody cared. Bazookas, flame throwers, napalm, blockbusters, flying fortresses, buzzbombs, and the great leveler to end all levelers—the atomic bomb—were the stuff of the daily news (newspapers and radios in those days; television hadn't been marketed yet). No God could have suffered the Holocaust or the Second World War, or the Cold War that immediately filled the void created by the so-called cessation of hostilities.

And yet as I grew older I knew that life was not a meaningless exercise in pain and cruelty. There was an orderliness to the way things fit together on the plane of atoms and molecules, of life on Earth, and throughout the universe. I did not construe that order as proof of a grand designer, but there was a kind of dynamic integrity on every plane and throughout the whole that seemed significant, a unity and wholesomeness binding the All as one.

Eventually I came to credit that integrity to two forces acting simultaneously: a restless drive for forms to evolve in response to ever-changing conditions, and a relentless whittling-away by those same changing conditions of forms that could not keep up with the times. The order I perceive results from creation and destruction working as a team on the same flow of universal stuff. What survives is what is left after the two processes have had their way. It adds nothing to assign God the duties of creator or destroyer; the universe as it is accounts for both. What I am left with is a tremendous respect for things as they are in nature, and awe at my being one of the survivors for the time being. This sense of awe and respect is the backbone of my spiritual faith. It holds me erect wherever I go, whatever challenges I meet. For me, faith has no necessary connection to organized religion or consecrated places of worship. I see those as institutional matters, byproducts of the culture we wrap around ourselves to fend off the realization that the universe cares not a whit for us as individuals, no matter how grand a role we play. Whether prophets, philanthropists, or paupers, we all come to the same end. Religion is couched in words, symbols, rituals, and structures; spirituality arises without trappings in preverbal silence.

Beyond being grist for the all-consuming mill of the universe, each of us is a miracle to boot. The odds against our uniqueness are too great for us to be tossed aside as anything less. Each of us stands at the head of an unending line of success. Every one of our ancestors lived long enough to reproduce, no mean feat in a universe that does not hold our survival close to its heart. The spin I place on the fact of my survival is that I have a mission to accomplish, a mission which the universe presented me at birth in the form of a

question: You and yours have gotten this far; now what?

Now what? indeed! This is Mission Impossible with a new twist. Instead of being given an assignment, we are charged with finding an assignment to take as our own. Being compelled to undertake the project presented in this book, I assumed that my answer to some part of that challenge could be found in Acadia National Park. Nobody sent me here but myself. What did I mean to find? That is the

Witch hazel in bloom along the Bowl Trail in October.

question I wrestle with in many of the hikes I describe in these pages. I am looking for the question to which I as one puny Earthling am the answer. That is my spiritual quest, the second project I take some pains to describe in these pages as openly as I can.

The Flow of Acadia

My spirit and the spirit of Acadia come together in my awareness of the flow of the Acadian landscape as I visualize it from my hiking experience. Moving through the landscape, I am aware that everything around me is moving as well. Nothing is fixed for all time. Acadia is a park on the go. Cadillac Mountain granite welled up from the earth as molten rock heated by the friction of colliding tectonic plates some half a billion years ago, attaining Himalayan heights, only to erode year-by-year to its current form, which will not last for long. A series of ice ages assisted that erosion, cutting our mountains down to size with perhaps thirty glaciers, one after another, abrading the landscape, scouring it free of all life. But life has come back each time, nourished by fog and rain blown in from the ocean during interludes between glaciers. Water has flowed across the sculpted Acadian terrain, bearing nutrients to thirsty plant roots. Plants have flowed up from those roots, fed by sweet sap. Leaves, then flowers and berries have flowed from that sap through the seasons. Browsing insects and wildlife have flowed to those green plants and their fruits, followed by predators hungry for tender plant eaters. And people flow to the scene as well, seeking shelter, food, and life in beautiful surroundings. Too, bacteria and fungi flow to Acadia to recycle the bounty of the land and the sea, making organic molecules available to the next generation. The soul of Acadia is revealed in the flow of the landscape hour-to-hour, day-to-day, season-to-season, year-to-year. As visitors move through Acadia they take part in that flow, drawing what they need from it, adding their presence to the whole. The park does not exist apart from us; we are one more species of wildlife caught up in the flow of life through the history of the Earth and the universe. We can no more stay away than blackflies and eagles, lungwort and wood lilies.

When to Hike

Is Acadia a park for all seasons? Yes, no, and maybe, depending on the person and the season.

For people who know the park through personal experience under a variety of conditions, the answer is yes, they can probably get out and enjoy the park at any season, no matter what the weather might be. Even in winter, I find I can always let my legs take me somewhere in the park on Vibram soles, skis, snowshoes, or ice creepers. What I cannot do is set a firm destination—the summit of Sargent Mountain, say, or Bernard Peak—and get there no matter what. I have survived to write these essays by taking into account the conditions that prevail when I go out. People suffer serious injury in the park every year by not anticipating or heeding those conditions. They set their hearts on a particular hike and do not rethink their route when they encounter ice in the trail or, worse, ice in the trail hidden beneath a layer of snow. When I have misjudged trail conditions, I have been blessed with luck, but luck is nothing I can count on to save me. Storms can come up at any time of year, making steep, rocky trails dangerous. Wind is another factor to take into account: am I prepared for that? Summer heat, too, gives me pause. Do I have enough water? What about sunscreen, sunglasses, a broad-brimmed hat? Finicky details, yes, but they can make or break a hike.

In April trails are apt to be icy or muddy. In May the blackflies come out, followed by mosquitoes in June. It can rain anytime, leaving ice in the trail during colder months. Walking over sloping rock on wet lichens is not good for hikers or lichens. Fog can roll in, making the trail hard to find, particularly one the hiker is not familiar with.

The litany of cautions goes on. From the trail's point of view, some conditions cause more wear and tear than others. Many trails in Acadia are badly eroded, a condition caused partly by nature, partly by hikers. We loosen the soil as we go, making it all the more likely to wash away the next time it rains. Soil is thin on every summit, where wind, rain, and boots threaten to dislodge it. In the Green Mountains of Vermont and White Mountains of New Hampshire spring hiking is curtailed to protect trails from harm. Acadia closes its carriage roads when their clayey surface is soft, but as yet the park has no such rule for its hiking trails.

Upside-down icicles in Seven Sisters Brook after a January flood.

Given the condition of many summits and steeper trails, the day of tighter trail-use restrictions is bound to come.

The best (or worst) piece of equipment a hiker carries with her is her on-the-spot judgment. The more experienced she is, the better her judgment is likely to be. The more of a trail novice she is, the less tested her judgement, and the less she knows not to trust it. Acadia is a park for all seasons for those who know how to work with the park for their own safety and the park's well-being. No two winters are alike, so do not think every winter will resemble the one I describe here (the winter of 1995–96). The following winter of 1996–97 was the worst for winter hiking I have ever seen. Trails iced up in December and stayed that way into March. There was no snow to speak of to make skiing or snowshoeing possible. I avoided the slopes all winter, while the year before I was able to hike every week.

When it comes to people who insist on wearing sandals or flip-flops on the trail, most of Acadia is a park for no season at all, as it is for those who don't think to take water with them on a hot day, or those who are physically out of shape. For them, it is best to make a cautious and gradual approach to the park by taking a stroll along Ocean Path, or by visiting Sand Beach, Jordan Pond House, or the visitor center in Hulls Cove. Even the easiest trails have roots and rocks waiting to trip the unwary.

For those who are in reasonably fit condition but don't know where to start because of unfamiliarity with the park, it would be well worth it to visit the park's Hulls Cove visitor center (open from May through October) or the winter visitor center at park headquarters off Route 233 (open 8:00 a.m. to 4:30 p.m. seven days a week from November to April). Doing a bit of groundwork first will make your outing that much more enjoyable.

Acadia can be a park for all seasons simply by adjusting your activity to prevailing conditions. Certainly the park is always alive and beautiful. It just takes judgment and a minimum of gear to find safe and appropriate ways to enjoy it in rain, fog, snow, heat, wind—or the rare, postcard-perfect day. For those who are not prepared to contend with snow or ice, a good rule of thumb is that Acadia is generally safe for hiking between May Day and Thanksgiving. The other five months are apt to present more of a challenge.

Trailheads

Certain trailheads in Acadia give access to a variety of trails from a single location, allowing hikers to put together loops to suit their particular interests and abilities. The magic of loops is that you are always moving ahead, never back over familiar ground (though any trail seems different when hiked in the opposite direction). Here is a list of eight trailheads, and some of the trails that can be reached from them.

◀ Sand Beach parking area, Park Loop Road
Great Head Trail
Beehive Trail
Bowl Trail
Gorham Mountain Trail
Ocean Path

◀ Sieur de Monts Spring parking area, off Route 3
Jesup Trail
Spring Road
Kane Trail
Strath Eden Trail
Hemlock Trail
Gorge Trail
Dorr Mountain East Face Trail
Kurt Diederich's Climb
Dorr Mountain Ladder Trail
Canon Brook Trail
A. Murray Young Trail
Beachcroft Trail

◀ Jordan Pond House parking area, Park Loop Road
Jordan Cliffs Trail
Penobscot Mountain Trail
Asticou Trail
Jordan Stream Trail
Jordan Pond East and West Side trails

Jordan Pond Nature Trail
South Bubble Trail
Jordan Pond Canoe Carry
Deer Brook Trail
Pond Trail
Pemetic Mountain South Ridge Trail
Triad Trail
Day Mountain Trail
and a variety of carriage roads

◀ Bubble Rock parking area, Park Loop Road
Bubble Gap Trail
North Bubble Trail
South Bubble Trail
Jordan Pond Canoe Carry (south to Jordan Pond)
Jordan Pond Canoe Carry (north to Eagle Lake)
Pemetic Mountain (Ravine) Trail
Jordan Pond East Side Trail

◀ Norumbega Mountain parking area, Route 198
Norumbega Mountain (Goat) Trail
Hadlock Trail
Hadlock Brook Trail
Parkman Mountain Trail
Bald Peak Trail
Maple Spring Trail
Birch Spring Trail

◀ Acadia Mountain parking area, Route 102
Acadia Mountain Trail
St. Sauveur Mountain Trail
Man o' War Brook Fire Road
Valley Cove (Flying Mountain) Trail
Valley Peak Trail

◀ Beech Mountain parking area, end of Beech Hill Road
Beech Mountain Trail (East Branch)
Beech Mountain Trail (West Branch)
Valley Trail
Beech Mountain Notch (Defile Mountain) Road
Canada Ridge Trail
Beech Cliff Ladder Trail
Beech Cliff Loop

◀ Long Pond parking area (pumping station)
Long (Great) Pond Trail
Perpendicular Trail
Mansell Mountain Trail
Razorback Trail
Great Notch Trail
Sluiceway Trail
Western Mountain South Face Trail
Valley Trail
Beech Mountain West Ridge Trail

Trail Ratings

Hikers will want to have some estimate of a trail's difficulty before they start out. With the understanding that such ratings are always subjective and need to be interpreted in light of a given hiker's age, experience, and condition, as well as the weather, here is a listing of the trails mentioned in this book sorted by the challenge they present to the fictional "average hiker." Every hiker must use caution and judgment at every step.

◀ Less Challenging Hikes
Alder Trail (from Blueberry Hill on Schoodic Peninsula)
Asticou Trail (from Asticou Map House to Jordan Pond)
Bar Island Trail (accessible from Bridge Street at low tide)
Boyd Road (from Route 3 to Bubble Pond Carriage Road)
Breakneck Road (between Route 233 and Hulls Cove)
Canada Ridge Loop (from Beech Hill parking area)
Carriage roads in general
Cold Brook Trail (pumping station to Gilley Field)
Dorr Mountain South Ridge extension (to Otter Creek)
Forest Hill Cemetery connector to Asticou Trail
Hadlock Path (around Lower Hadlock Pond)
Hio Road (off Rt. 102 at Adams Brook Bridge)
Hunters Brook Trail (first mile from Park Loop Road)
Jesup Trail (from Kebo Street to the Tarn)
Jordan Pond Canoe Carry (Eagle Lake to Jordan Pond)
Jordan Pond East Side Trail (from Jordan Pond House)
Jordan Pond Nature Trail (from boat ramp parking area)
Jordan Pond West Side Trail (from Jordan Pond House)
Jordan Stream Trail (Jordan Pond to Little Long Pond)
Kane Trail (along the west side of the Tarn)
Little Harbor Brook Trail (off Route 3)
Long (Great) Pond Trail (first 1.5 mi. fr. pumping station)
Long Pond Fire Road (off Route 102)
Lurvey Spring Road (Long Pond Rd. to Echo Lake pkg.)
Man o' War Brook Fire Road (off Route 102)
Ocean Path (Sand Beach to Otter Point)
Paradise Hill Trail (from Hulls Cove visitor center)
Pond Trail (Bubble Pond Carriage Road to Jordan Pond)
Seaside Trail (Jordan Pond House to Seal Harbor)
Ship Harbor Nature Trail (off Route 102A)
Spring Road (from loop road to Sieur de Monts Spring)
Strath Eden Trail (from loop road to Spring Road)
Upper Hadlock Trail (around Upper Hadlock Pond)
Wonderland Fire Road (off Route 102A)

◀ Moderately Challenging Hikes
Anvil Trail (Schoodic Peninsula)
Beech Mountain Notch (Defile Mountain) Road
Beech Mountain South Ridge Trail (off Valley Trail)
Bowl Trail (from Sand Beach parking area)
Brown Mtn. Trail (Norumbega Mtn. fr. L. Hadlock Pd.)
Cadillac Mountain East Ridge Trail
Cadillac Mountain Road (a good winter hike)

Cadillac Mountain South (West) Ridge Trail
Cadillac Mountain North Ridge Trail (from loop road)
Cedar Swamp Mountain Trail (a.k.a. Sargent S. Ridge Tr.)
Cliff Trail (Isle au Haut)
Conners Nubble Trail (from Eagle Lake Carriage Road)
Day Mountain Trail (from Route 3)
Duck Harbor Trail (Isle au Haut)
Eagle Lake Trail (from Eagle Lake Carriage Road)
Eliot Mountain Trail (from Asticou Map House)
Flying Mountain Trail (from Valley Cove parking area)
Gorham Mountain Trail (from Ocean Drive)
Great Head Trail (from Sand Beach parking area)
Great Notch Trail (from Gilley Field)
Hemlock Trail (steep but short over Dorr–Kebo ridge)
Hunters Brook Trail (Triad from loop rd. via Hunters Bk.)
Kebo Mountain Trail (from loop road)
Long (Great) Pond Trail (up from Great Brook)
McFarland Hill Trail (from Eagle Lake Road, Route 233)
North Bubble Trail (Bubble Ridge)
Outer Beech Mountain Trail (from Beech Mtn. parking)
Parkman Mountain Trail (off Hadlock Brook Trail)
Schoodic Head Trail (Schoodic Peninsula)
St. Sauveur Mountain Trail (from Route 102 parking area)
Valley Cove Trail (a.k.a. Flying Mountain Trail)
Valley Trail (from Long Pond pumping station)
Western Head Trail (Isle au Haut)

◀ More Challenging Hikes
Acadia Mountain Trail (from Route 102 parking area)
Amphitheater Trail (Little Harbor Brook to Birch Spring)
A. Murray Young Trail (off Canon Brook Trail to Notch)
Bald Peak Trail (off Hadlock Brook Trail)
Beachcroft Trail (Champlain via Huguenot Head fr. Rt. 3)
Bear Brook Trail (a.k.a. Champlain Mtn. North Ridge Tr.)
Beech Cliff Ladder Trail (from Echo Lake Beach parking)
Beech Mountain Trail (from Beech Mountain parking)
Beech Mountain West Ridge Trail (from pumping station)
Beehive Trail (off Ocean Drive near Sand Beach)
Bubble Gap Trail (from Bubble Rock pkg. to Jordan Pond)
Cadillac Mountain West Face Trail (from Bubble Pond)
Canon (Canyon) Brook Trail (from Route 3 to Featherbed)
Champlain Mountain East Face Trail (not much used)
Champlain Mountain South Ridge Trail
Deer Brook Trail (from north end of Jordan Pond)
Dorr Mountain East Face Trail (fr. Sieur de Monts Spring)
Dorr Mountain Ladder Trail (from Rt. 3 south of the Tarn)
Dorr Mountain North Ridge Trail (off the Hemlock Trail)
Dorr Mountain Notch Trail (linking Dorr & Cadillac mtns.)
Dorr Mountain South Ridge Trail (off Canon Brook Trail)
Duck Harbor Mountain Trail (Isle au Haut)
Featherbed Trail (from Bubble Pond Carriage Road)
Giant Slide Trail (from former St. James Church, Rt. 198)
Gorge Trail (to the Notch from loop road)
Grandgent Trail (Sargent Mtn. from Giant Slide Trail)

Hadlock Brook Trail (Sargent from Norumbega Mtn. pkg.)
Jordan Cliffs Trail (to Sargent and Penobscot mountains)
Kurt Diederich's Climb (Dorr Mountain from the Tarn)
Mansell Mountain Trail (from Gilley Field)
Maple Spring Trail (off Hadlock Brook Trail)
Norumbega Mountain (Goat) Trail (from Route 102 pkg.)
Pemetic Mountain Northeast Ridge Trail (from Bubble Pd.)
Pemetic Mountain (Ravine) Trail (from Bubble Rock pkg.)
Pemetic Mountain South Ridge Trail (off the Pond Trail)
Penobscot Mountain Trail (from Jordan Pond House)
Perpendicular Trail (Mansell Mtn. from pumping station)
Pothole Trail (to Featherbed from Otter Creek)
Precipice Trail (Champlain Mtn. from Precipice parking)
Razorback Trail (Mansell Mtn. from Gilley Field)
Sargent Mountain North Ridge Trail (from Giant Slide)
Sargent Mountain South Ridge Trail (from Asticou Trail)
Sluiceway Trail (to Little Notch on Western Mountain)
South Bubble Trail (from Jordan Pond East Side Trail)
Spring Trail (Bernard Mountain from Sluiceway Trail)
Triad Trail (off the Pond Trail)
Valley Peak Trail (from Valley Cove Fire Road)
Western Mountain South Face Trail (from Mill Field)
Western Trail (Pine Hill to Long Pond Trail)
Western Mountain Ridge Trail (Mansell to Bernard mtns.)
Western Mountain West Ridge Trail (off S. Face Trail)

With so many trails to choose from, Acadia is a mecca for day-trippers and day-hikers. The park offers challenge and excitement to suit hikers of every ability, including seniors and children. In summer, most hiking groups are made up of couples or families on vacation.

Keep in Mind

In no particular order, here is a list of trail recommendations I would offer to other hikers. These are not meant to be taken as rules or commandments since I, who have compiled them, have broken many of them at one time or another. I went solo on every hike written up in this book, violating my first recommendation in every case. Some are rules laid down by the National Park Service (dogs, collecting, bicycles, fires), others are informal rules of thumb meant to promote good judgement and a sense of shared responsiblity.

- It is safer to hike with a companion than to go alone.
- Sturdy, supportive footwear is a must on all trails so you won't become a liability to others.
- Do not practice magical thinking in claiming to be in better condition than you are.
- Keep dogs on a six-foot leash and have them under control at all times; better yet, leave pets at home.
- Carry out everything you take with you, including cans, bottles, cigarette filters, and tissues.

- Do not carry out plants, flowers, moss, stones, or other resources visitors come to Acadia to see (eating berries is OK).
- Speak softly; noise pollution can become a distraction on the trail.
- Stay on marked trails to avoid trampling plants.
- Do not ride or carry bicycles on hiking trails.
- Build no fires anywhere.
- Build no designer cairns to clutter the landscape for other hikers.
- Bury human waste at least 200 feet from streams or ponds.
- Be prepared for changes in the weather.
- Take water on every hike so you won't be tempted to drink from pools, streams, or ponds (giardiasis is a potential hazard to your health).
- If you have a cellular phone, pack it for emergency use only.

Maps

The maps I have drawn for each hike are intended as schematic guides only. Their main purpose is to show the route I actually took on a particular hike. They are drawn only roughly to scale, so should not be taken as literal representations of the terrain they depict.

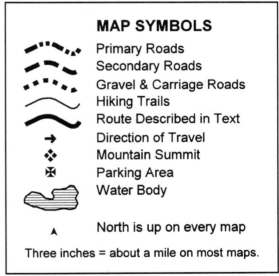

MAP SYMBOLS

	Primary Roads
	Secondary Roads
	Gravel & Carriage Roads
	Hiking Trails
	Route Described in Text
→	Direction of Travel
❖	Mountain Summit
⊞	Parking Area
	Water Body
⌃	North is up on every map

Three inches = about a mile on most maps.

Legend for the maps included with each hike.

Additional Information

Requests for information from the National Park Service about Acadia National Park should be addressed to:

Information
Acadia National Park
P.O. Box 177
Bar Harbor, Maine 04609-0177
(207) 288-3338.

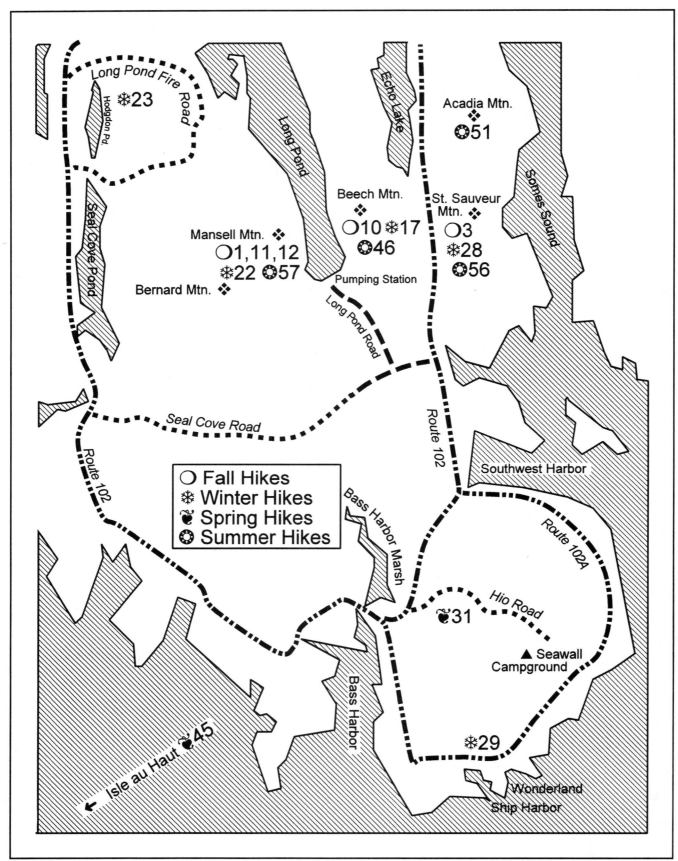

Sixteen hikes in Acadia National Park west of Somes Sound. (Numbers refer to hikes listed in the table of contents.)

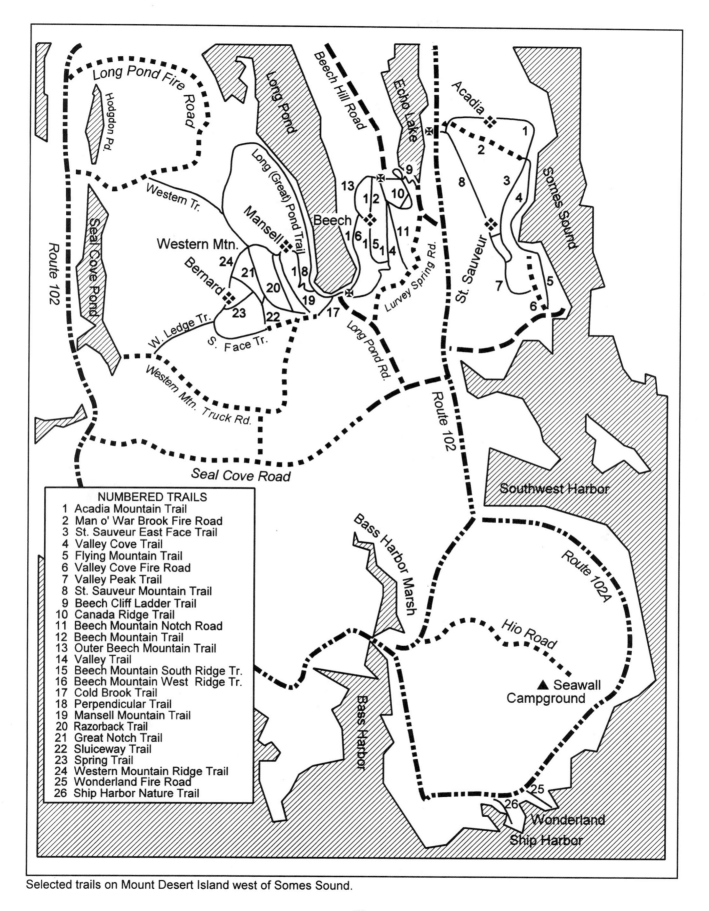

NUMBERED TRAILS
1 Acadia Mountain Trail
2 Man o' War Brook Fire Road
3 St. Sauveur East Face Trail
4 Valley Cove Trail
5 Flying Mountain Trail
6 Valley Cove Fire Road
7 Valley Peak Trail
8 St. Sauveur Mountain Trail
9 Beech Cliff Ladder Trail
10 Canada Ridge Trail
11 Beech Mountain Notch Road
12 Beech Mountain Trail
13 Outer Beech Mountain Trail
14 Valley Trail
15 Beech Mountain South Ridge Tr.
16 Beech Mountain West Ridge Tr.
17 Cold Brook Trail
18 Perpendicular Trail
19 Mansell Mountain Trail
20 Razorback Trail
21 Great Notch Trail
22 Sluiceway Trail
23 Spring Trail
24 Western Mountain Ridge Trail
25 Wonderland Fire Road
26 Ship Harbor Nature Trail

Selected trails on Mount Desert Island west of Somes Sound.

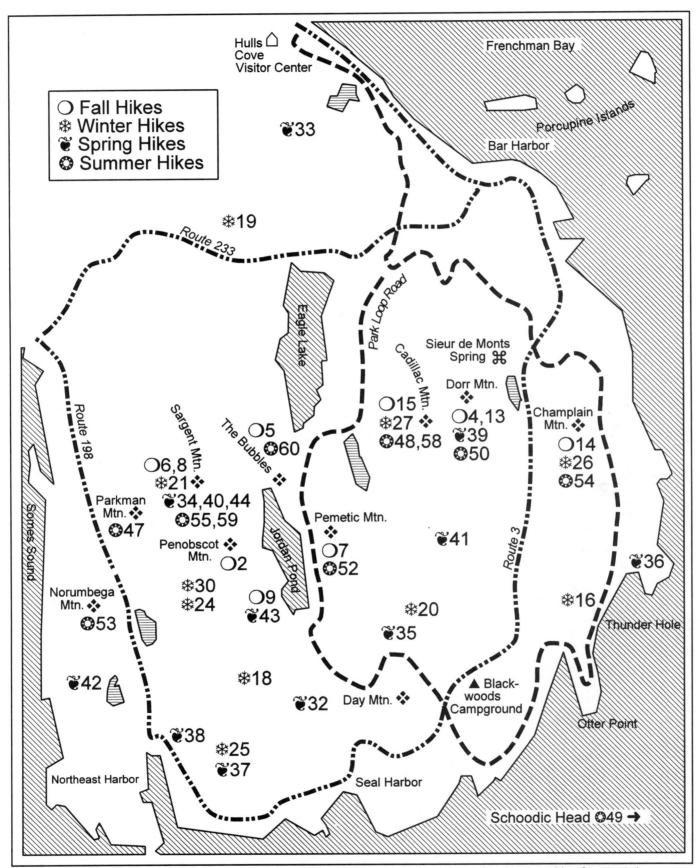

Forty-four hikes in Acadia National Park east of Somes Sound. (Numbers refer to hikes listed in the table of contents.)

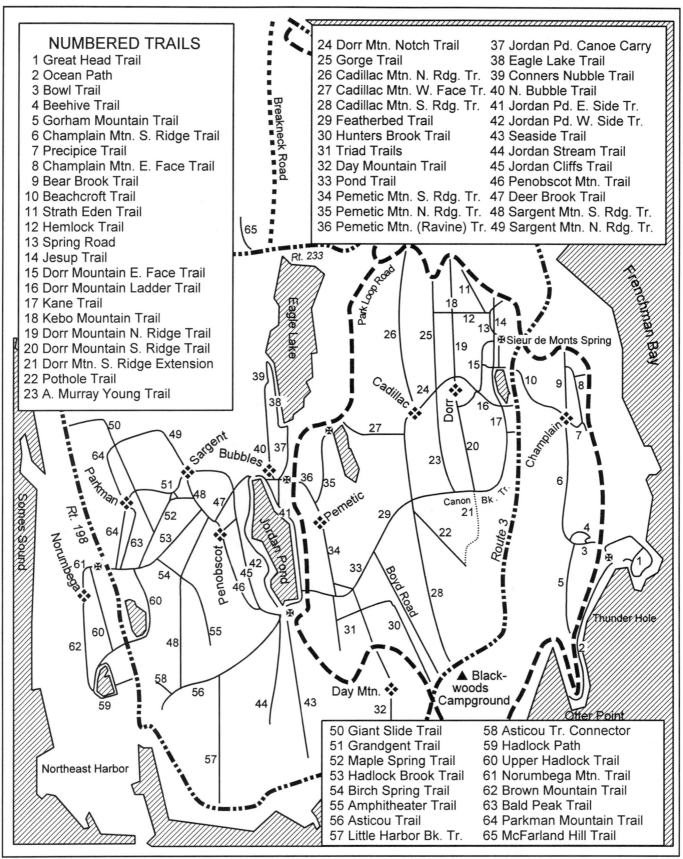

NUMBERED TRAILS
1 Great Head Trail
2 Ocean Path
3 Bowl Trail
4 Beehive Trail
5 Gorham Mountain Trail
6 Champlain Mtn. S. Ridge Trail
7 Precipice Trail
8 Champlain Mtn. E. Face Trail
9 Bear Brook Trail
10 Beachcroft Trail
11 Strath Eden Trail
12 Hemlock Trail
13 Spring Road
14 Jesup Trail
15 Dorr Mountain E. Face Trail
16 Dorr Mountain Ladder Trail
17 Kane Trail
18 Kebo Mountain Trail
19 Dorr Mountain N. Ridge Trail
20 Dorr Mountain S. Ridge Trail
21 Dorr Mtn. S. Ridge Extension
22 Pothole Trail
23 A. Murray Young Trail

24 Dorr Mtn. Notch Trail
25 Gorge Trail
26 Cadillac Mtn. N. Rdg. Tr.
27 Cadillac Mtn. W. Face Tr.
28 Cadillac Mtn. S. Rdg. Tr.
29 Featherbed Trail
30 Hunters Brook Trail
31 Triad Trails
32 Day Mountain Trail
33 Pond Trail
34 Pemetic Mtn. S. Rdg. Tr.
35 Pemetic Mtn. N. Rdg. Tr.
36 Pemetic Mtn. (Ravine) Tr.

37 Jordan Pd. Canoe Carry
38 Eagle Lake Trail
39 Conners Nubble Trail
40 N. Bubble Trail
41 Jordan Pd. E. Side Tr.
42 Jordan Pd. W. Side Tr.
43 Seaside Trail
44 Jordan Stream Trail
45 Jordan Cliffs Trail
46 Penobscot Mtn. Trail
47 Deer Brook Trail
48 Sargent Mtn. S. Rdg. Tr.
49 Sargent Mtn. N. Rdg. Tr.

50 Giant Slide Trail
51 Grandgent Trail
52 Maple Spring Trail
53 Hadlock Brook Trail
54 Birch Spring Trail
55 Amphitheater Trail
56 Asticou Trail
57 Little Harbor Bk. Tr.
58 Asticou Tr. Connector
59 Hadlock Path
60 Upper Hadlock Trail
61 Norumbega Mtn. Trail
62 Brown Mountain Trail
63 Bald Peak Trail
64 Parkman Mountain Trail
65 McFarland Hill Trail

Selected trails on Mount Desert Island east of Somes Sound.

Cairn on the Pothole Trail.

Base of Dorr Mountain Ladder Trail.

ACADIA
THE SOUL
OF A
NATIONAL PARK

O

Book One
FALL

To

Ken and Linda

as they blaze

their spiritual paths

through the glories of this Earth

CONTENTS—FALL HIKES

INTRODUCTION—FALL 4

1 MANSELL MOUNTAIN LOOP 5
From Long Pond parking area (pumping station)
To Mansell Mountain summit, and back
    Up by Long Pond Trail via Great Notch
    Back by Perpendicular Trail
                    4.4 miles, August 28, 1993

2 PENOBSCOT MOUNTAIN LOOP 7
From Pond Trail turnout on the loop road
To Penobscot Mountain summit, and back
    Up by Jordan Pond Trail, carriage road, and
        Penobscot Mountain Trail
    Down by Jordan Cliffs Trail, carriage road, and
        Jordan Pond Trail
                    3.5 miles, September 2, 1993

3 ST. SAUVEUR & FLYING MTNS. LOOP 11
From Valley Cove Fire Road parking area
To Valley Peak and St. Sauveur Mountain, and back
    Up by Valley Peak Trail
    Down by East Face and Flying Mountain trails
                    3.0 miles, September 6, 1993

4 AROUND DORR MOUNTAIN 15
From Sieur de Monts Spring parking area
To the Notch between Dorr and Cadillac mountains,
    and back
    Up to the Notch by Jesup, Kane, Canon Brook, and
        A. Murray Young trails
    Down by the Gorge and Hemlock trails
                    4.5 miles, September 11, 1993

5 CONNERS NUBBLE & BUBBLES LOOP 19
From Bubble Rock parking area on the loop road
To Conners Nubble and North and South Bubbles,
    and back
    Up by north end of Jordan Pond Canoe Carry;
        Eagle Lake, Conners Nubble, and North Bubble
        trails
    Down by South Bubble Trail and south end of
        Jordan Pond Canoe Carry
                    4.5 miles, September 17, 1993

6 SARGENT MTN. LOOP via CHASM BROOK 24
From park headquarters via Aunt Betty Pond
To Sargent Mountain summit, and back
  Up by carriage road and Chasm Brook
  Down by McFarland Trail, bushwhack,
    Chasm Brook, and carriage roads
              7.0 miles, September 24, 1993

7 PEMETIC MOUNTAIN LOOP 29
From Bubble Pond parking area
To Pemetic Mountain summit, and back
  Up by carriage road, Pond Trail, and east branch
    of Pemetic Mountain South Ridge Trail
  Down by Pemetic Mountain North (or Northeast)
    Ridge Trail, returning to headquarters by bike
  4.0 miles (not counting bike ride), October 2, 1993

8 SARGENT MTN. LOOP via GIANT SLIDE 33
From foot of Giant Slide Trail
To Sargent Mountain summit, and back
  Up by Giant Slide, Parkman, and Grandgent trails
  Down by Sargent Mountain South Ridge, Maple
    Spring, Grandgent, and Giant Slide trails,
    returning to headquarters on bicycle
  6.5 miles (not counting bike ride), October 10, 1993

9 AROUND JORDAN POND 38
From north end of Jordan Pond
To south end, and back
  Start from park headquarters on bicycle to Deer
    Brook by carriage road, then by Deer Brook Trail
    to north end of pond and by Jordan Pond West
    Side Trail to south end of pond
  Return by Jordan Pond East Side and Deer Brook
    trails, then by bicycle to park headquarters
  3.3 miles (not counting bike ride), October 16, 1993

10 BEECH CLIFF & CANADA RIDGE LOOP 42
From Echo Lake parking area
To Canada Ridge, and back
  Up by Beech Cliff Ladder and Canada Ridge trails
  Down by bushwhack and old Canada Cliff Trail
              2.0 miles, October 26, 1993

11 MANSELL MOUNTAIN LOOP 47
From Long Pond parking area (pumping station)
To Mansell Mtn. (not quite the summit), and back
  Up by Cold Brook and Razorback trails
  Down by Mansell Mountain and Cold Brook trails
              3.0 miles, November 2, 1993

12 BERNARD MOUNTAIN LOOP 51
From Long Pond parking area (pumping station)
To Bernard Mountain summit, and back
  Up by Cold Brook, Sluiceway, and old Spring
    trails; and bushwhack
  Down by Western Mountain Ridge, Great Notch,
    and Cold Brook trails
              4.0 miles, November 8, 1993

13 DORR MOUNTAIN LOOP 57
From south end of the Tarn
To Dorr Mountain summit, and back
  Up by Dorr Mountain Ladder and South Ridge
    trails
  Down by Dorr Mountain East Face Trail, Kurt
    Diederich's Climb, and Kane Trail
              2.5 miles, November 14, 1993

14 CHAMPLAIN MOUNTAIN LOOP 62
From Precipice Trail parking area
To Champlain Mountain summit, and back
  Up by Precipice Trail
  Down by Bear Brook, Champlain Mountain
    East Face, and Precipice trails
              2.0 miles, November 20, 1993

15 DORR & CADILLAC MOUNTAINS LOOP 68
From Cadillac Mountain summit parking area
To Dorr Mountain, Otter Creek, and back
  Down by Dorr Mountain Notch and Dorr Mountain
    South Ridge trails
  Up by Canon (Canyon) Brook and Cadillac
    Mountain East Ridge trails
              4.0 miles, November 27, 1993

INTRODUCTION—FALL

Hiking is my way of rekindling the flame at the core of my spiritual being. Spirituality, for me, is a reverent awareness of my direct connection to those universal forces beyond myself on which my being depends. It is a deliberate appreciation of sunlight, clean air, pure water, nutrients, and the landscapes they make possible. Spirituality resides not only in houses of worship but flows freely out-of-doors where, in the pre-verbal silence of nature, it affects me all the more. To engage Earth in an unmediated spiritual relationship, I go hiking out my front door, happily located in Acadia National Park on Mount Desert Island in Maine.

The benefits I receive from practicing my brand of footloose spirituality include good health, high spirits, stimulating thoughts, and a sense of being on the forefront of universal creativity. Grounding myself on solid earth, I find beauty around me wherever I trek, and am rewarded by the discovery of meaning and excitement in my life as a whole and in every particular act.

As a writer, I describe my experiences in that part of Earth I know best, coastal Hancock County, Maine, where I work and hike through the seasons. Where I fell in love with the world of nature, and its expression in a beautiful woman.

Hikers on Jordan Pond East Side Trail, October.

Both my life and love are rooted in the ground I walk on. These essays are about that ground as it lives in my experience. About how I am moved as I move about through my homeland on Maine's scenic coast.

Though I have included a map for every hike, what I offer here is more of a hiking companion than a basic guide to the trails of Acadia. This book is meant to complement your own adventures on the trail in Acadia and elsewhere. Every hike is unique. No map can lead anyone else to the territory I describe in these pages because it exists solely in my lived experience. Rather than follow in my footsteps, you have no choice but to follow the leadings of your deepest intuitions and desires.

Fall is one of the best times to be outdoors in Acadia National Park. The air is clear and cool, the landscape colorful until mid-October, then dramatically lit by a low sun. The Gulf of Maine is slow to cool down, holding onto the hard-won heat it gained through the summer. Acadia, surrounded by salt water, cools slowly as well, the season

lingering, seeming to go on and on. Eventually ponds freeze over, the solstice comes, and winter sets in. But the prelude invites hikers to stretch their legs while they can, without having to worry about ice and snow. After Labor Day, families return to work and school, so park visitation eases off. Many retirees take advantage of the lull, and leaf peepers arrive by the busload. Columbus Day weekend brings the park's high season to a close. After that, hikers have the carriage roads and trails to themselves.

I took the fifteen hikes in this section during September, October, and November of 1993, but the same hikes would be equally rewarding in summer and spring. The foliage would be different, the blossoms different, the weather different—but that is true of every hike I take. It is not possible to repeat a hike, even following the same route. Nature is too complex to be taken for granted, just as we are too complex to be the same person hour-to-hour, day-to-day. Fall is a time of remarkable transitions which lend variety to a series of weekly hikes. The cycles of nature spiral onward as they will; it is our job to keep up with them as best we can, opening our experience to the flux of the seasons, pursuing the larger realities that give meaning to our lives. If we disregard the seasons, pretending to wake in the same world every morning, we not only diminish our experience but run the risk of decoupling it from the great round that has ruled the lives of peasants and saints in every culture, in every land, since the human experiment began. If we are not with Earth's program, what program are we with?

The main thing I hope to offer here is encouragement to stay open to whatever possibilities for experience emerge as you move along the trail in any season. If you hike with a companion or in a group, do not let conversation distract you from the wonders on either hand. Hike not so much to get away from somewhere else as to be precisely where you are. Where you are on this Earth is where you are. Take it as an opportunity to discover who you are in that place by interacting with what you find when you are there.

Steve Perrin
Bar Harbor
Fall 1993

1—MANSELL MOUNTAIN LOOP

From Long Pond parking area (pumping station)
To Mansell Mountain summit, and back
  Up by Long Pond Trail via Great Notch
  Down by Perpendicular Trail

4.4 miles, August 28, 1993

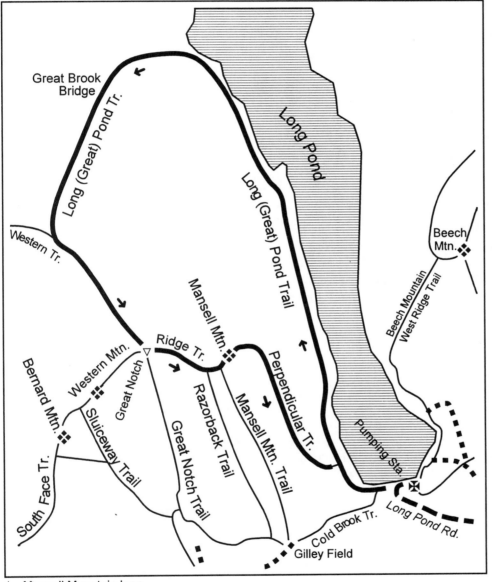

1—Mansell Mountain loop.

vital parts and organs. I wanted to explore a few of those parts chosen at random, opening my life to their life, sharing what happens.

Where to begin? The best loop I could think of: up Mansell Mountain by the Long Pond Trail, down by the Perpendicular. Best because it was fresh in my mind. I would say the same about other trails later on. But it was a great hike, over a trail that most of the way is everything a trail should be. This is the standard by which every other trail in Acadia can be measured. Well, one of the standards.

The 4.4-mile loop from the pumping station at the south end of Long Pond took me exactly five hours. It would have gone faster if I had not taken notes and photographs, or paused now and then to look around at what I call a truly working forest. Not the working forest of the logging industry where trees are harvested as a crop for human profit, but the self-employed woods of Acadia where water and sunlight are shared for the common good of all plants and animals, many hidden from human eyes.

The Long (Great) Pond Trail follows the western shore of Long Pond for a level mile-and-a-half stretch, treading the edge between two worlds, the margin of the pond with water plants and Northern white cedars to the east, steep upland slopes peopled by spruce and hardwoods to the west. I met a woman and an unleashed spaniel, an elderly man peeing in trailside bushes, a couple in a canoe sharing lunch (Pepsi and Pepperidge Farm cookies). A cigarette boat roared up the pond, turned, sped back—end-to-end in five minutes.

Below Mansell Mountain, lichens cover every glacial boulder and chunk of granite fallen from the cliff above. Rocks are alive with a mosaic of green, yellow-green, three different grays, and tufts that seem to sprout from the granite itself. The covering is so dense, I had to peer to find a patch of bare rock. Here is Maine as it was when the glacier pulled north twelve thousand years ago, and these stout little colonies of algae and fungi moved in to get life started again.

Hiking guides give raw facts about a trail: times and distances, elevations, difficulty, and so on, leaving out what you really want to know—the kind of experience a trail might lead to, so you can choose between one and another.

My plan was to hike one of Acadia's trails each week, and tell about it, not simply as a route from here to there, but as a chapter of my lived experience. Acadia National Park is alive, after all, and its trails lead in and around its

The trail pulls away from the pond, crosses a small boggy area filled with moss and New York ferns, then rises gently through woods of birch and mountain maple, with an understory of striped maple. I remembered the woman who called me to ask what could be done about striped maple running rampant in the park. She wanted to wipe it out. As if it were a noxious weed, not an indigenous plant.

Reaching Great Brook with its handsome log bridge, the trail turns south and traverses the north slope of Western Mountain toward Great Notch, which lies between the summits of Mansell and Bernard.

What a trail it is! I mean the trail itself. There is no more solid or better-laid treadway in Acadia. This one is built to last, to endure the slings and arrows of a million footsteps. At least their slams and kicks. Except for the upper reaches of the trail

Steps across talus slope, Perpendicular Trail.

as it nears the notch, it runs on rock and gravel, not fragile soil and roots. The water bars, buried stones and logs which direct water from the trail, are admirable feats of handiwork.

Gaining altitude, I entered thick coniferous woods, among audible signs of red squirrels and pileated woodpeckers. And visible signs of fox. I counted fifteen fox scats along the trail, one white containing fur, one tan, the others blueberry blue—speaking to a summer diet I could relate to. When a passing shadow made me look up through the canopy, I caught a sharp-shinned hawk wheeling just above the trees on the wind.

Not one slug did I see, which suggests how dry it had been. The scarcity of mushrooms told the same story. Many ferns were curled and brown. Yet the woods spoke of hidden water flowing down the slopes. Of plant life rising from that flow. Aside from Long Pond, Great Brook, and Cold Brook near the pumping station, I did not see any surface water at all.

But water signs were abundant everywhere along the trail. Thoreau called the Maine Woods "mossy and moosey." What he meant was wet. Wherever there is life of any kind, there has to be water. So the tall spruces, maples, hemlocks, and birches; their saplings and seedlings; the groundcover of liverworts, ferns, mosses, and lichens; the spiders, ants, mosquito (only one!), frogs, birds, and animals around me—all gave a sense of walking near water the full length of my hike. I could feel it seeping down the slope, unheard and unseen, a nourishing presence wherever I went. In its wake flowed the layers of green hugging the soil. Rising in the understory. Arching overhead in the windswept canopy. All of it was alive; it had to be wet. As I am wet: eighty-eight-and-a-half percent made up of atoms (hydrogen and oxygen) derived from water, true elixir of life. I all but slosh when I move. A wetland on legs. I hike to find my kin. And to find my true home, the place that fulfills me, completes me, and makes me whole—my native habitat. The wooded slopes of Acadia are that. Unravaged, unlike most landscapes in Maine, they are not slated to be cut. Here is a homeland deserving loyalty, love, and respect.

So there I was, in the midst of the woods, ambling along, feeling good about the world and myself. Home again. In my element. Sensing forces that have shaped Mount Desert

Winding steps on the Perpendicular Trail.

Island since the glacier, and shaped the human form since ancestral life was kindled in the primal ooze. Headlong, I met the feelings of wonder and belonging that tell me who I am. There, approaching Great Notch, I knew exactly.

Great Notch on Western Mountain is 3.4 miles from the pumping station by the Long Pond Trail, but only a mile by Mansell Mountain and the Perpendicular Trail. Do not hike up to the notch either way for the sake of the view—not in the usual sense. What you see is woods. Woods. Woods. Better, hike for the sense of being in that primitive place. To celebrate moving step-by-step under your own power. It is not so much a place to get to as a place to *be*. What you are when you get there is what you bring with you. Yourself.

Starting back, I scrambled the 300 vertical feet out of the notch to the summit of Mansell. Looking west over the notch toward Bernard Mountain, there is a view of coniferous woods in good working order. Much of it is old growth, uncut for 100 years, uncommon in Maine. I saw the woods as a shrinking store of Earth's collective wisdom—hard earned, true, inspirational. Worth thinking about.

Past the summit, I met a woman hiking with three lean and smiling children. "How much farther is it?" she asked.

"To where?"

"The Top of Mansell."

"Twenty-five feet."

"Oh, good!" she said.

Dialogue along the trail tends to be brief and self-limiting. Halloos between passing ships.

After skirting a wooded bog with Northern white cedars and sphagnum moss, and turning down my one chance at an extremely hazy view, I followed the Perpendicular Trail as it began its descent, gradual at first, then steeper and steeper.

If you are in shape, and have time for one trail, consider this one. Both up and down. Then you can say you have truly hiked in Acadia and seen what it offers. Here water meets rock under conditions laid down by climate—and Acadia happens! Water rushes down. Life rushes up. You can see the whole drama on the Perpendicular Trail.

Coming down, you see the trail itself winding down the pitch ahead like a serpentine, cyclopean staircase connecting the realm of the gods with that of mere mortals. The thought flashed through my mind that if I were young again, I would pledge myself to the woman of my heart at the crossing of trails in Great Notch. Together, we would descend this grand series of steps and landings to our future life.

To find firm footing on this often slippery Earth, take the Perpendicular Trail.

○

2—PENOBSCOT MOUNTAIN LOOP

From Pond Trail turnout on the Park Loop Road
To Penobscot Mountain summit, and back
  Up by Jordan Pond Trail, carriage road, and
    Penobscot Mountain Trail
Down by Jordan Cliffs Trail, carriage road, and
    Jordan Pond Trail

3.5 miles, September 2, 1993

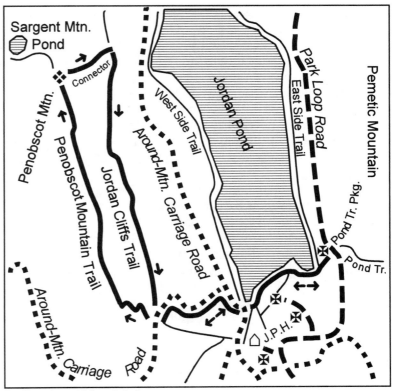

2—Penobscot Mountain loop.

I got off work at 4:30 p.m., changed, packed binocs, water, sweatshirt, and reached the Pond Trail turnout on the loop road above Jordan Pond at 5:00. Maybe three hours of daylight left. Headed down to the pond at a fast clip. Hey, what race is this? Coyote scat in the trail, mostly berries. Almost missed it. Slow down, slow down. Look around. Plastic diaper stashed in the bushes to my right. Sunlight glinting off plastic bag to my left. Keep going, keep going.

Purple asters along the trail. Plumes of goldenrod. September already. What happened to summer? Across the pond, the Bubbles caught the raking afternoon light. One scarlet tree yelled across the pond from South Bubble.

Here was a family walking the Jordan Pond Nature Trail. They stopped at a numbered post. She smoked a cigarette while a boy (who I guessed was her son) read aloud from the trail guide. Voices. Voices all around the still pond. Baby howling. Father shouting, "You don't listen to a thing I say, do you!" Cigar smoke in the air. Met thirty-five people on the trail around the pond. Saw another thirty-four on their way to and from the gift shop-restaurant. Young Asian man passed me, camcorder slung around his neck—seventy people. You have to start somewhere.

A mound of horse manure marked the center of the carriage road bridge over Jordan Stream. Signpost 14: turn left on Around-Mountain Carriage Road loop. Start of the "demonstration mile" showing what carriage road rehabilitation will look like. Lower branches of roadside trees had been lopped off, making them look like cartoon trees, the kind you drew in third grade.

Three hefty cyclists in space suits zoomed down the hill. Then I was alone. No howls. No scolding voices. All clear. It was safe to look around: bracken ferns glowed yellow against the duff, rows of sapsucker holes dimpled a mountain maple, white-pine cone scales decked a coping stone—Mr. Rockefeller's gift to Acadia's squirrels. Flat-topped asters by the road. Everything still. I checked out some brown scat: probably poodle, on a diet of tinned meat. I came to West Branch Bridge, which not only curves but is built on a grade.

Passing the Jordan Cliffs Trail marker, I looked up at Jordan Ridge, buttressed by talus covered with rock-cap ferns. Up there, that's where I'm headed. I began to relax and get into the hike. Thirty-six minutes from the loop road, I reached the Penobscot Mountain Trail.

A woman sat in the middle of the steps leading up to the ridge. I waited for her to lower herself, step-by-step on her fanny, down to the carriage road.

"So that's Penobscot, huh?" she said, meaning, I took it, she did not expect to find it so steep.

"Your basic mountain," I said.

"I tried," she said.

"You have to test yourself," I said.

"Always, always!" she said, and went off down the road.

I followed stone steps up the talus slope, led on by little rectangles of blue paint. Immediately, another world: cliffs, lichens, ferns. Steps laid by giants. The trail does not cut a swath, but seems a natural course through the talus. A pileated woodpecker cried out. That was more like it.

The route onto Jordan Ridge takes you where the action is right away. Suddenly, you are there. Back to reality. Back to basics. Gravity. Rainfall. Sunlight. Alive again, I felt welcomed by every fern, rock, and tree. Nothing else mattered. I belonged.

From a ledge, I looked across at Pemetic Mountain. Touched by slanting light, every tree stood distinct in the clear air. Imagine rooting on such a slope, growing out of a steep cliff. Go for it when and where you can!

Wooden handrail and steep crib-work steps angle up the slope. Someone had worked hard to prepare the way. A small spruce grew into the trail, a few branches cut, the tree itself spared.

On a ledge, four plumes of goldenrod sprouted from lichen-covered rocks, an effect a gardener would strive for. I waited for a man and young girl to pass down, then climbed the last stretch to the ridge. Here was real soil, a forest of striped maple and white birch. And crickets. Standing among the trees, I heard a bell in Eastern Way tolling the rhythm of the swells. It took me an hour and five minutes to reach the ridge. From there the slope rises gradually over solid granite to Penobscot's summit.

All along the ridge, ice-hewn cracks were filled with cinquefoil and black chokeberry, little green rivers flowing across the rocks. Erosion making a bed for life.

Two men came down the ridge.

"Hi."

"Hello."

Last people I would see. For the next two hours, I had the mountain to myself, the known universe as far as I was concerned.

Hiking beside me, my shadow was thirty feet long, stretching to the east. How skinny it was, like the lanky figure of Thirsty Fiber, early trademark of Scott towels. Jordan Pond lay flat and gray in its valley. Beyond, the shadow profile of Jordan Ridge was a whale on the flanks of Pemetic. Behind me, Penobscot Bay and the Gulf of Maine filled with fog. A lone motorcycle whined up the loop road.

Westward, over Cedar Swamp Mountain, the top of Mansell Mountain cut the horizon. I had hiked it five days before, among trees all the way. Here the soil had been scoured to bare rock. Life clung to cracks. A few low pines had taken root, among sparse tundra plants. Luminous green lichens marked the trail, leading me on. I'm coming, I'm coming. Turning around, I saw high ground on Isle au Haut rise out of the fog.

There weren't many signs of wildlife. One bird taunted me from behind, but I couldn't make it out. A bush rustled in front of me. Something made a dash. Your basic gray-brown bird, white feathers edging its tail. Junco.

The shadow of Jordan Ridge may look like a whale, but the ridge itself underfoot was more like a giant brain. Cortex of Earth itself. That is what weathered granite reminds me of. Seat of earthly intelligence. Well, why not? Hiking keeps me in touch with earthy thoughts. Helps me think like a mountain.

By 6:30, Penobscot's shadow was halfway up Pemetic's west slope. Bar Harbor was eating its lobster dinner while I was feasting on sunlight and shadows. Speaking of which, Thirsty Fiber now stretched 100 feet across the ridge. I stopped to eat a few late blueberries, no bigger than peppercorns, but sweet.

The granite knob south of the summit, which gives Penobscot its characteristic shape, loomed ahead. Like a ziggurat or temple built of stone blocks, it is the Angkor Wat of Maine. From the knob, I looked over to Cadillac where sunlight flashed on a line of cars on the mountain road. Two days ago I was just below that road, following a trail abandoned in the 1940s. I could see other old friends. Pemetic, Bubbles, Cedar Swamp, Norumbega, St. Sauveur, Acadia, Beech (setting sun glinting on the fire tower), Mansell, Bernard, with Sargent up ahead. Farther off, Blue Hill. Camden Hills. Schoodic, Black, and Tunk. If I had X-ray vision, I'd see Katahdin on the far side of Sargent. The whole gang was there. Good company.

dan Cliffs. Duck under its branches—and you are there! Abruptly. On the face of the cliff. Granite to your right. Eternity to your left. Every time I round the corner under that oak heading south, I experience one of the great moments of hiking in Acadia. Coming the other way from Jordan Pond House, you attain the cliffs more gradually, asking yourself, "Am I there yet? Is this it?" Coming from the north, you know when you arrive.

Cairn on connector between Penobscot Mountain summit and Jordan Cliffs Trail. Cadillac Mountain and Bubbles to the rear.

At my feet, mountain sandwort, Acadia's hardy subalpine flower, still bloomed. A fan of juniper spread over the rocks. One marbled boulder of schist waited for Old Glacier to make his next move. Be patient, friend, he will.

Six minutes to seven. Penobscot's summit, elevation 1,194 feet. No time to dawdle. The sun dipped into clouds on the horizon. It was time to head down, with all deliberate speed. One look around. One swig of water. Off for the Jordan Cliffs.

Following the line of cairns toward the east (not north toward Sargent and its pond), I headed across the shelf above the cliffs, crossing rocky terrain with trees growing in soil collected in the shelter of the summit. The trail crosses two smoky dikes cutting through paler granite. Then a third. Coming out on the top of the cliffs, I looked over the length of Jordan Pond, silver in the south, dull pewter in the north, across to the Bubbles and Pemetic on the far side. So close I wanted to leap the pond. On the horizon, there was Passadumkeag Ridge, sixty miles north in Penobscot County, where the Union River starts flowing south.

At 7:05, I got to the upper valley of Deer Brook between Sargent and Penobscot. Left, the trail dropped to Jordan Pond. Right, past a sloping rock wall, to Jordan Cliffs. **CAUTION: TRAIL STEEP WITH EXPOSED CLIFFS AND FIXED IRON RUNGS.** The moment of truth was near. I hung a right.

A lone red oak guards the northern approach to the Jor-

The Jordan Cliffs Trail is blazed with two different colors, light blue, and a deeper, more subdued red. Both sets of blazes are freshly painted, so one is not supplanting the other. Two rival schools of thought how best to mark the trail, each bent on outdoing the other. There is really no contest. Hike the cliffs trail in dim light, the blue blazes shine out of the dark and show the way. The red ones, tasteful though they may be, blend with the rocks, quitting when you need them most.

Iron rungs and handholds drilled into the cliffs offer help along the trail. Just when you would like some assurance, there they are. I remembered watching three children scamper over the tightest spot in the trail on an earlier hike, using the iron as naturally as they would the rungs of a jungle gym. They stick in my mind because the woman with them was so beautiful. I saw her for all of ten seconds, but have not forgotten her. Like the girl I saw forty years ago through the window of a New York subway as it pulled out of the station. Inaccessibility fires the illusion of desire. Smoldering yet safe, I survived both times.

There I was on the cliffs, not a good place to hurry. Instead of rushing to beat the dark, I took my time. Memory of the Knife-Edge on Katahdin came to mind. I took in the view. Same line of cars on Cadillac. It was about 7:15. The sunset crowd.

Following the line of blue blazes, holding onto iron or cedar root, whichever came to hand, relying on the Braille method of finding my way by foot, I crept along the cliffs. At one point I realized how awake I was, every sense firing messages at once. Ping-ping-ping, like sonar. Who needs stimulants when you can live like this for free?

Even in the pending dark, I could tell the cliffs trail was well kept-up. Footing was sure, handholds within reach. I came to log steps over a steep place, cribwork. Log bridge over a ravine. That bridge has to be my favorite. It is as simple as they come. Single log spanning a cleft in the rocks, with a difference. This one slopes, is anchored with iron at the upper end, is braced in the middle, and has steps cut into its top surface, with log rails on either side.

I ambled along in the fading light, one section of cliff to the next, unable to make out any but the boldest of outlines. Happy in my own glowing world, I put my trust in the trail makers. Their trail was worthy of the cliff. It is hard to name a trail that at some point does not have a brush with one cliff or another. Trail makers are drawn toward cliffs. Once there, they stick by them. Something to do with the security we feel coming in contact with ancient earth, with the awe that comes over us when we look up at the rock face overhead. We humble ourselves before true majesty.

Seeing Jordan Pond House lit up at the far end of the pond, I saw the fog was about to engulf it. Hurry? If I end up in the fog, so be it.

Trailhead and steps, Penobscot Mountain Trail.

At what I thought was the last stretch of open cliff (I crossed several more "last stretches"), I looked down through the gloom on a great heap of talus fallen from the cliff where I walked. Perhaps the last glacier had wrenched it from the heights, perhaps ice and thaw over twelve thousand years had done their bit. The sight was awesome. Then I heard a cricket chirping behind me. I laughed.

The trail dips down and crosses a stretch of the talus slope, not seeming much like a trail, but doing the duty of one. That is the art of trail making, using natural materials to build a durable treadway that blends with the surroundings the hiker has come to experience. Driving along Route 3, what you see is Route 3. The road consumes the landscape. On a trail you do not have to sacrifice everything to your means of travel.

Hiking in the dark, I realized this was the sixth time I had come this way this summer. I hardly knew the trail at all. Each time had been unique because of differences in time of day, lighting, weather, direction, season, and so on. I kept looking ahead to what I was sure was there, being wrong time after time. Maybe if I take the cliffs trail six more times I will get the hang of it.

Empty gray was all I saw. Particularly under trees. Was I still on the trail? My feet were my surest guide. They could see the trail when my eyes could not. I was not kidding about the Braille method. When in doubt, trust your feet. Do I advise hiking at night? Not for one second. But I refused to feel desperate.

Full moon over Pemetic. What a sight. And stars overhead—Cygnus, Lyra, Aquila! Older friends even than the mountains I met on the summit. But careful, now, do not be fooled into relaxing your vigilance. Friends or no friends, the darkest part of the trail lay ahead. This was no time to ease up and coast.

I could smell the fog. And see the demon eyes of those blue blazes along the trail. One foot in front of the other. That is called strategy. Through an opening, I saw Scorpius rising over Jordan Ridge. Eyes on the trail, dreamhead!

Using a kind of Ninja night walk, I crept along. The worst was near the end when the canopy was solid black overhead. Then down the last slope onto crunchy gravel. Ha, the carriage road!

From the south end of the pond I saw the Big Dipper over Sargent. Polaris over North Bubble. *Dirigo*, says the Pole Star, I lead, I lead. Something led me on that trail. It might well have been a star. Looking across at Penobscot from the Jordan Pond Trail, I saw the shadow of Pemetic cast on its slopes by the moon. Another whale. Moon shadow, moon shadow. Symmetry in all things.

○

3—ST. SAUVEUR & FLYING MOUNTAINS LOOP
From Valley Cove Fire Road parking area
To Valley Peak and St. Sauveur Mountain, and back
   Up by Valley Peak Trail
Down by East Face and Flying Mountain trails
              3.0 miles, September 6, 1993

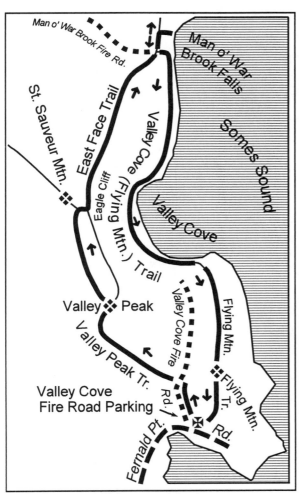

3—St. Sauveur & Flying mountains loop.

The Appalachian Mountain Club guide to the trails of Acadia says you can hike the loop I took on Labor Day in two hours and ten minutes. I took four hours. Some hike to cover the ground, others to dis-cover it. Take our Western heroes. They are all movers and shakers who covered a lot of ground: Odysseus, Huck Finn, Mad Max. Eastern heroes are more contemplative, undertaking voyages of dis-covery. Buddha for one. He found the universe in a lotus blossom, and gave us the eight-fold way. The *way*, not the prize at the end. In the West we go for the pot of gold. In the East they go for the rainbow itself. My hiking style has Eastern overtones. I am more interested in where I am than where I have been or where I am heading.

On today's loop I met a chipmunk and eleven red squir-

rels. A herd of crickets and grasshoppers. An osprey who landed in a snag just over my head. A pileated woodpecker. Seeing the woodpecker was a treat because I hear one from almost every trail these days, but it is usually hidden off in the woods. This one on St. Sauveur Mountain I met up-close and personal.

But wildlife was a fringe benefit. It was where I *was* that made it a hike I will never forget. The loop went up Valley Peak and St. Sauveur Mountain. Down to Man o' War Brook. Back along the shore of Somes Sound and Valley Cove. Over Flying Mountain. A trek of about three miles.

I started from the Fernald Cove parking area on Fernald Point Road (off Route 102 below the Southwest Food Mart), which at that time had room for five cars, but had ten crammed into it on Labor Day. The Valley Peak Trail starts to the left a short way up the Valley Cove Fire Road. A foursome was picnicking out of their van where I picked up the trail (the fire road has since been closed to cars). I wanted to cut the cord that bound them to their tailgate, but could think of nothing constructive to say, so passed by in silence. Immediately I was in thick woods. Beautiful woods. Old and decadent woods. I met only one other couple in the next four hours. It was me and the squirrels, the osprey, the woodpecker. My kind of place.

Starting by a small stream, the Valley Peak Trail rises up the side of a moist sheltered valley, everything covered with liverworts and mosses, through a forest of tall spruces, over ever thinner and rockier soil, onto open granite ledges featuring cedars and three kinds of pine: white, red, and pitch, needles five, two, and three to a clump. Among them a few scrub oak at the northern limit of its range, a true rarity on Mount Desert Island. A great trail for trees.

And grasshoppers in early September. They "fly" like I do in my dreams, throwing themselves into the air and flapping madly to stay aloft. Dream bugs.

Turning to look at the view, I was surprised how near Greening and Great Cranberry islands were. And how close the fog was behind them. Two layers—purple on top, white underneath. When he was a kid, my friend Bob thought there was only one fog that came and went at will. He was sure it was always the same fog. That is why they called it *the* fog. Some days it was in Gouldsboro, other days in Stonington. When it came to Bar Harbor, it was a major event, like the *Queen Elizabeth II* for us now. There it was now as I hiked along, *The Fog, w*ith an escort of twenty vessels, seventeen under sail, three under power.

In half an hour I reached Valley Peak, a spur off St. Sauveur Mountain, elevation 520 feet, about the same as Gorham Mountain. From there the trail winds over ledges, making for a pleasant amble, through terrain so generic I could have been walking on any number of mountains: Cedar Swamp, the Triad, Parkman, to name three. It was a good place to think about trees. About patience. About being rooted in one spot. About making a commitment to a given homeland, come what may. About what that might mean.

And a good place to think about mobility. About animals eating plants, turning carbohydrates into motion. About a species with no true allegiance to any one place. About picnickers choosing the convenience of their van over the drama of the woods.

Four-tenths of a mile beyond Valley Peak the trail splits. The left branch goes on to the summit of St. Sauveur. The right to Eagle Cliff. Eagle Cliff is the place to go. Follow the sign for **MAN O' WAR TRUCK ROAD**. Just past the sign is where I saw a pileated wood-pecker excavating carpenter ants from the base of a snag. I used to pronounce the first syllable to rhyme with pill, until I learned the red crest on its head is a pi-leus, named after the old Roman skull cap. This one had no red mustache. A female, size of a crow, an impressive bird to see close up, banging beak into tree, chiseling deep into ant tunnels, sounding like a camper chopping wood.

Immediately the trail comes out on the brink of Eagle Cliff, the precipitous eastern slope of St. Sauveur Mountain falling away to Valley Cove and Somes Sound. One of the most stunning sites in Acadia for an outing or a picnic. You want spectacular? This is spectacular!

Hiker approaching steps, north end of Valley Cove.

Norumbega Mountain rises out of the sound across the way, backed by Sargent and Penobscot mountains. You feel you are on top of the world because, practically speaking, you *are* on top of the world. Better yet, you are an eagle, eyeing your kingdom by the sea. Struck by how many buoys there were in front of me, I counted. Two hundred, easily. On the bottom of that hole out there, 150 feet down, the rocks must be crawling with lobsters—or had been crawling with them before all those traps were set.

After watching gulls, crows, motorboats, sailboats, wave patterns, clouds, fog, and islands for ten minutes, I headed north along the top of the cliff toward Man o' War Brook. In a few minutes I could see the whole south face of Acadia Mountain, with trees that could not wait till October to turn red. The trail turned steeply down across ledges into woods, and I descended to the thrum of engines out on the water.

From an overlook much lower down, I saw *The Fog*

overtaking Greening Island at the mouth of the sound. Above, an osprey flew into the valley of Man o' War Brook between St. Sauveur and Acadia mountains.

The slope was hard on my ankles. The East Face Trail went down ahead, and down to the right as well. I was wearing my second-string boots because my good ones were drying after I tried to walk on water the day before. My toes hit leather at every step. I made a mental note to make a mental note not to let it happen again.

Above the engines' thrum, I heard an osprey shriek. It seemed wrong, somehow. I tie that sound to low tide when ospreys dive for fish in shallow water. Now the tide was high. I made a mental note to think about that some more. Unlike the fit of my boots, that is the kind of thing I'm likely to remember.

The osprey cried again. A squirrel whirled its ratchet off in the woods. Another squirrel ratcheted back. I passed by mixed patches of cloud and reindeer lichens. Miniature forests. More squirrels. Cone scales along the trail. Witches butter (yellow fungus like wadded bubble gum) on fallen trunks. Four crow feathers melding with the duff.

Dipping into the valley of the brook between the mountains, the trail gets suddenly steep and badly eroded. I had to watch every step. Two red squirrels crossed the trail ten feet in front of me on a leaning birch. Being the less maneuverable craft, I had the right-of-way, but let them pass.

The trail bottomed-out in a lush forest of birch and maple, with an underforest of striped maple, the first wet ground I had crossed since turning off the fire road. The woods had a different feel to them. Different smell. Different sound. The wind in overhead leaves mimicked a rushing stream. I came to a plank bridge over a dry and rocky channel. Fleets of water-striders jockeying endlessly for position. On a root in the trail, a red squirrel munched on a pine cone like a kid on an ear of corn.

Two hours into the hike, I reached my turning point at a sign for **VALLEY COVE** and **FLYING MTN**. But I didn't turn, not yet. I wanted to see where British ships had tied up to fill water kegs from the plunging waters of (what we now call) Man o' War Brook. The water from that brook was reputed to stay sweet longer than water from any other readily available source. I believe it. Acadia's watersheds are so steep, water doesn't stick around long enough to pick up organic matter that would make it go "bad."

On granite steps down to the shore, I met a man who had grown up in Manset, but had not been in that part of Acadia for seventeen years. He and I both wanted to look at the brook cascading into Somes Sound. Talking about this and that, we discovered we had an ancestor in common. Thomas Stanley, who had moved from Marblehead, Massachusetts, to Islesford after the French and Indian Wars. We could not see the brook from the overlook, so went searching for it through the cedars. Soon we found the exact spot we wanted, and stood together on a ledge overlooking the tide (full), and the brook (which was not), lost in our respective reveries about days and ways gone by. After a while he and his wife went back up the fire road paralleling the brook; I headed for the Flying Mountain Trail.

"See you, cousin," I said, realizing I did not even know his name. It was not Stanley, he had told me that. That is all I knew. A man not called Stanley.

From the start I knew the Flying Mountain Trail was made by a different crew than made the east face trail. Stone steps made for good and level footing, not the ankle-bending, toe-jamming jaunt I'd just had. The trail was made by the Civilian Conservation Corps in the 1930s. The men were good at labor-intensive jobs like making trails and, later, fighting wars. Good old CCC. The way led through a dark cedar wood lying between St. Sauveur Mountain and Somes Sound. Past a small stream, the trail crosses a stretch of wet ground on a row of stepping stones. Fir seedlings grew by the hundreds in their parents' shade. Tail straight up, a chipmunk ran for cover. Six old oaks rose from a common hub, perhaps telling the story of a squirrel's cache that got wet some eighty years ago. Seventeen pileated woodpecker holes in a snag by the trail.

More surprises. A dozen big old ash trees, which I come across now and then in the park, but usually not as big, not in such numbers. The slope between mountain and tide got steeper, crowding the trail to the edge of the sound. I

Osprey on a snag.

thought I was going to have to try walking on water again, but the trail pulled back just in time. A caterpillar an inch-and-a-half long wended along the trail, bright green with yellow stripes along its body, with touches of brown between the uppermost stripes.

Coming abruptly to a ledge overlooking Valley Cove, I smelled frying bacon. Here was the *Sunset*, a large powerboat anchored near shore, flying a Canadian pennant. Ahead, the trail wound around the cove under Eagle Cliff, through the talus at its base. Stone steps anchored with iron crossed a sloping ledge along a stark, vertical wall of granite angling toward the cliff. Photo opportunity. Picnic opportunity. Landscape ogling opportunity. Courtesy of the CCC, which had come this way fifty years before and left its mark. Deer pellets on the steps. Cedars were everywhere, neatly browsed six feet above the ground. When I was halfway along the steps, an osprey flew fifty feet above me and landed in a snag ahead.

My senses were on overload. Too much to take in at once. I sat at the upper end of the stone stairway by a huge, jagged block of talus torn loose from the cliff—seemingly held by a white pine blocking its lunge for the cove. I just sat, waiting to find my wits. Having stumbled across this place in all innocence, I found it one of the most dramatic I had seen in months. Slow on the uptake, I let it sink in.

Wits partially restored, I stood and went on. The trail was covered with fallen yellow birch leaves against dark rock. It hooked around the perched block of talus, rose up a short incline, fell away down a rough cliff on the far side in a series of steps which, though crude, made it possible to pass the impassable. Lined with lichens and ferns, the steps led into the damp origins of matter and life itself. This was the way, the original way, back to beginning times. I knew a time warp when I met it. Things were twisting. You cannot be the same person at one end of Valley Cove you were at the other. Something happens along the way. You grow. Irrelevancies shrink. You visit an earlier world and see things in their original light.

Which may sound kinky in a metaphysical sense, but try it. Metaphysics is a two-dollar word for the experience of being in the world. Of feeling alive in a certain place. Of not only being, but being *there*. Where? On the shore of Valley Cove, experiencing yourself in a basic, original way. If you do go, heed this caution: time warps are not for the faint of heart or frail of limb. Body and soul must be ready.

The trail climbs up and down the talus slope at the foot of Eagle Cliff, shaped more by demands of the local terrain than by thoughts for the hiker's ease. User friendly, but not all *that* friendly.

Looking up at Eagle Cliff after three hours of hiking, I saw its juniper-wreathed brow was now lost in fog. The air grew dark. More and more ferns lined the trail. Luminous pink blossoms of herb Robert. A single harebell. Soil clung firmly between boulders. Maples and birches grew up and down the slope. I brushed off a lone mosquito. Stepping out on a stretch of open talus, I felt droplets of fog on my face. The sense of being in at the beginning of things stuck with me—of being called back to Eden.

The view of Valley Cove was as good from the bottom of the cliff as it had been from the top, boats at their moorings now commanding the foreground, Somes Sound as background, with fog for atmosphere. From that low angle, I lost sight of the hundreds of buoys beyond the cove.

Regaining the valley between Flying Mountain and Valley Peak, this time at its northern end, I could have walked back to the parking area along the fire road, but continued on the Flying Mountain Trail to see where it led.

Falling steps leading back in time, Valley Cove.

Winding through tall evergreens surrounded by seedlings, the trail turns rooty and rocky, and gets rootier and rockier as its slope increases. You have to make an assault on the mountain from that side. An aggravated assault. The trail is little more than a channel dug into the soil, exposing a slurry of gravel and rocks held by a tangle of roots. Heading straight up the slope (where water must inevitably rush down), the trail serves as an eloquent example of how not to build a trail.

Things got better on the ledges higher up. Three hours and fifty minutes after setting out, i reached the top of Flying Mountain, elevation 284 feet. The view was blocked by thick fog. I could not see Fernald Cove directly below me. I took twelve minutes getting back to my car, the trail on the south side being cut down to bare ledge most of the way, so in better shape, given several hundred years of wear by hikers, weather, and grazing sheep.

At quarter to seven, mine was the only car in the parking area. The loop up Valley Peak, down to Man o' War Brook, along Valley Cove, and up Flying Mountain—three miles in all—took exactly four hours. That's by my watch. In life terms, I had gone back to Go and started all over again.

○

4—AROUND DORR MOUNTAIN

From Sieur de Monts Spring parking area
To the Notch between Dorr and Cadillac mountains,
    and back
  Up to the Notch by Jesup, Kane, Canon Brook,
    and A. Murray Young trails
  Down by the Gorge and Hemlock trails
            4.5 miles, September 11, 1993

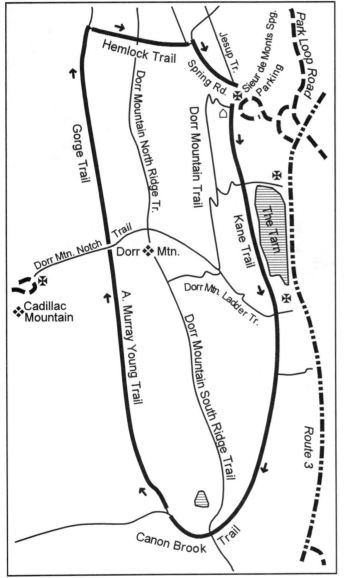

4—Around Dorr Mountain.

What I call the Dorr Mountain loop is a four-and-a-half-mile trail incorporating sections of several separate trails: the Tarn (or Kane) Trail, Canon (formerly Canyon) Brook Trail, A. Murray Young Trail, Gorge Trail, Hemlock Trail, and the Spring Road (former route giving access to the spring). Starting at Sieur de Monts Spring, you can go all the way around the mountain in three hours. Or if you am-

ble like me, it may take twice as long.

Many of Acadia's more famous trails either traverse rocky slopes or run along granite ridges. Sticking to the base of the mountain, this loop is different. Its virtue is in being a valley trail. Falling boulders and water keep you company for much of your hike.

Where there's water, there's bound to be life. But it does not always leap out at you. Bend down. Peer. Be silent. Give the signs a chance to speak for themselves. By the Tarn, two women strode past me without seeing the green frog, marbled orb weaving spiders, and wasps' nest I saw from my perch on a boulder. Give yourself to the trail and it will give itself to you.

In the six hours and eighteen minutes it took me to circle Dorr, I heard crows, crickets, two kinds of woodpeckers, chickadees, and a blue jay. I saw signs of woodpeckers, sapsuckers, beavers, red squirrels, a yellow-shafted flicker, a junco, and a coyote. I kept looking up for hawks, but saw only one, an osprey. I also saw the frog, spiders, and wasps' nest I mentioned, as well as dragonflies, grasshoppers, minnows, water striders, and both a hairy and pileated woodpecker. Then there was the tired and thirsty beagle on a leash. That may not be Teddy Roosevelt's idea of big game, but then I was out for the living, not the killing.

As for plant life, it was wall-to-wall the whole way. I met a lot of island universes, if not in the cosmic sense, in the equally mystifying but more tangible sense of sites where, against all odds, life clings to the face of a cliff or the curve of a boulder without any visible means of support. Aside from asters and goldenrod, not many flowers. But I did see berries! The first thing I did when I got back was rush to the nature center at Sieur de Monts and buy a *Berry Finder* for two dollars. Next time I will be ready. But it will have to be soon, because they are going fast—down the gullets of Acadia's wildlife.

The loop is also a tale of two watersheds, one draining north, the other south. Kebo Brook runs north and east into Cromwell Brook, which runs into Cromwell Cove opposite Bald Porcupine Island in Bar Harbor. The stream between Cadillac and Dorr on the south runs into Canon Brook, Otter Creek, and Otter Cove.

How different two neighboring watersheds can be when they face opposite directions. The Gorge Trail cuts through the watershed of Kebo Brook. The A. Murray Young Trail runs in an entirely different watershed. Hiking those two trails, which on a map look like one continuous line, you pass through two different worlds.

Coming along the A. Murray Young Trail from Canon Brook, I went through mixed woods where no one tree predominated. A little bit of everything, that was the scheme. Maple (red, sugar, mountain, striped). Pine (red, white, pitch). Northern white cedar. A few yellow birch, beech, red spruce, balsam fir. Even in the bowl between the mountains where there used to be a beaver pond, there was a mixture of young trees (add sumac, alder, and pin cherry).

But heading out of the Notch going north into the valley of Kebo Brook, the variety of trees cuts way back. First there was a mix of red spruce saplings coming in among birch, and little else. Then mainly yellow birch. The whole feel of the place was different. The woods opened up. The way ahead was clear. My view was not blocked by stems and leaves jostling for elbow room. Hemlocks began to appear, and a few maples, but that was about it.

Why should a north-facing watershed be so unlike one facing south? Less sunlight, more lasting moisture, cooler temperatures—to name three possible differences. Too, the slope of the trail coming up from the south is less steep than the trail going out of the Notch to the north. Hiking the two trails in succession, I was prompted to compare them.

The Notch itself, where I met the hapless beagle, was a place unto itself. Saddle shaped, it was a very scrubby place, with oak, birch, cherry, and mountain ash vying for space. And harsh, exposed to wind from north and south alike. And wet, catching water streaming down steep cliffs on both sides, releasing it slowly into valleys sloping more gently on either end.

The beagle? I met him as I neared the Notch, with a human couple on a leash.

"Are we hot on the trail of a bunch of kids?" the man asked.

I said no kids had passed that way.

"Is this the trail up Cadillac?"

I told them to go back and take the trail to the left. They made a great fuss over the dog, asking if he were hot, tired, or thirsty. They carried no water. The man picked up the beagle and they went hallooing their way up Cadillac's dry slopes.

To go back to the beginning, parking at Sieur de Monts Spring at 9:30 a.m., I had to decide whether to take the loop clockwise or counter-clockwise. I have been advised to hike into the view, which means you have to know beforehand what direction that is. Wind direction is also a factor, it being easier to walk out of a wind than into one. Slant of sunlight, slope, terrain all make a difference. Looking ahead to lunch (always a factor), I decided to eat by Canon Brook, so voted to go clockwise, and headed south.

It took me an hour and a half to get past the Tarn, a distance no more than half a mile. The trail, set at the foot of a talus slope, was beautiful. The more I looked at that jumble of rocks, the more curious I became about who lived in that place. There is no waste space in nature. For starters, I saw dragonflies, wasps, spiders, and a frog. Good place for insects. And insect-eaters.

Thinking about where those great blocks of granite had come from—up there, the cliffs of Dorr Mountain—I caught myself picturing them falling in the past, or being torn off the mountain by glaciers. But boulders break free every year. The cliffs are still crumbling. A sequence of time-lapse photographs (taken every ten years or so) would show the cliffs eroding decade-by-decade, the talus slope mounding up, fed by a continuous rain of boulders.

Scanning the sky for migrating hawks, I saw none. Minnows swam in the shallows. And leaves of arrowhead and

Buddha on Cadillac Mountain watching over the Gorge.

pickerelweed rose Excalibur-like from the Tarn. Purple gerardia and asters still bloomed along the shore.

South of the Tarn, the Kane Trail passes through beech woods. Many trees were free of the disease that generally infests such groves, inflicting that insidious double-whammy caused by a combination of insect damage and fungus infection. These trees were either too young to be blighted, or genetically resistant.

I had no name for many of the plants I saw. As a botanist, I'm in preschool. And not about to take a class in plant identification. You can pack only so many details into one lifetime. Like foam packing materials, if you cram in too much, they overflow. I looked at a lot of different berries on my hike, admired them all, but did not feel I had to know each one by name.

When I was a kid I did the Boy Scout run, alternately walking and running fifty paces at a time. I hike something like that, now walking a few steps, then stopping to look around. I keep seeing new things, and make progress, too. Watching militant hikers stride by, I wondered what they saw along the way. Imagine hiking Acadia as if it were a map, overlooking everything not shown at that scale.

South of the Tarn, the Kane Trail runs by a series of wetlands in the valley of Beaver Brook between Dorr and Champlain. Ferns and bur reeds to the left, beech woods on higher ground to the right. Beaver lodge with a maple tree growing out of it. Then a couple of beaver dams. Hey, the dams were south of the lodge! That water was not flowing north into the Tarn, it was flowing south toward Otter Cove. I had crossed the divide between watersheds without noticing. I did see dragonflies with glistening wings, coyote scat crammed with berries and hair.

What has coyote scat got to do with anything? How was

The Gorge Trail rising to Pulpit Rock.

I furthering the work of the world? Why wasn't I reading the *Wall Street Journal,* watching football, playing pool? We tall, lanky people are nerve ends of the human world. Sentinels. Our job is to stay alert and observant, to give a warning shout if things are not right. From what I saw, watersheds were flowing. Dragonflies darting. Ferns nodding. Coyotes eating. All was well in my sector.

Passing openings in the canopy, I looked up for hawks. I also scanned fallen logs for turtles. Saw neither. If you do not look you will not see. Keep looking. Seventeen feathers in the duff, all that was left of a junco eaten by a hawk. There was my hawk; my timing was off. I pictured my bones lying in a heap in the trail, hikers stepping over them as I had stepped over those feathers. Beats funeral parlors, lead-lined caskets, embalming. Recycling—oldest process in the world.

Taking over from the Kane Trail, the Canon Brook Trail swings out of the valley and crosses the south ridge of Dorr Mountain. On higher ground I caught a whiff of soil mixed with fallen leaves. Smell of fall. And childhood. But that did not last. Neither whiff nor childhood. I came to the first stretch of granite ledge, and crickets—sound of fall and childhood. At the sign for the Dorr South Ridge Trail, the noon fire horn sounded in Bar Harbor, echoed by the siren in Otter Creek village. Down a gentle slope, I neared the junction of Canon Brook and Otter Creek.

Sitting on scoured granite where creek runs over ledge, I ate my lunch where I have eaten many lunches over the years. No site is more peaceful. The brook trail continues west up the flank of Cadillac to the Featherbed. The one I would take, the A. Murray Young Trail, branches north and heads up the valley between Dorr and Cadillac, passing a plaque on a huge boulder:

IN MEMORY OF
ANDREW MURRAY YOUNG
WHO LOVED THIS ISLAND
WHERE GOD HAS GIVEN
OF HIS BEAUTY WITH A
LAVISH HAND.

Beauty. What is beauty? Firmly seated in the beholder's eye, it is a judgment on experience. A judgment of attractiveness and approval. Sparking an urge to respond—as if beckoned, appealed to, drawn. By what? That which our nature desires. Beauty leads us to what we need and cannot do without. It is our intuitive guide to fulfillment. Opening us to places, people, objects, and actions which, healing us, give us health.

Beauty is an offer of biological well-being. Who can refuse it? It matches our suitability to the world with the world's suitability to us. The welcome is mutual. We are in the right place at the right time. What else can we do but celebrate?

Hiking is a celebration on legs. When we hike the trails of Acadia, we celebrate our luck in being alive and well in this place. Acadia suits us. We are suited to Acadia. Our name for that living resonance is success. God. Beauty. Love.

A small stream was my companion all the way to the Notch, headwaters of Otter Creek. How could one feel lonely in such a place? I heard a soft tapping just off the trail. Hairy woodpecker, probing for insects beneath peeling bark. I saw signs of woodpeckers on other trees. Rows of sapsucker holes. Yawning pits dug by pileated woodpeckers mining heartwood for ants. Too, I saw Buddha sitting on his ledge on the flank of Cadillac, looking so natural he could have been a granite boulder torn from the cliff. I have pictures to prove it.

The trail up to the Notch is the kind we expect in Acadia. A series of solid steps held in place by coping stones on both sides, it offers solid footing for easy going while protecting the landscape on either hand. Crossing the stream, the trail passes under mossy falls, leads along the brim of a forty-foot gorge, and touches on a talus factory where great chunks of stone are even now being torn from eroding cliffs.

I wondered about the influence of women on the men who laid those durable treadways. Were the men being gallant in their way, laying down trails that women in long skirts could manage without mishap? The people I meet in the park are largely couples and families. I would say the sex ratio in Acadia today is 50/50. Women, it is said, bring out the best in a man. We owe thanks to all who helped shape Acadia's trails.

After skirting the basin where twenty years ago there was a beaver pond between the mountains, the trail makes its way through a field of talus fallen from facing cliffs on Dorr and Cadillac. Instead of beaver, I met crickets. Stopping to lean against a boulder, I looked up—and saw my hawk, an osprey soaring over the Notch, climbing a slow spiral, then soaring into the wind and disappearing over the south ridge of Cadillac.

Mountain to the left of me; mountain to the right. The only way through was up the talus slope between them, like fallen walls of Jericho or Knossos. The way seemed ancient. Old as the hills. A monument to cataclysm itself. And through the rubble, one of the great highways of Acadia. A trail that would not take no for an answer.

Amid stunted trees just under the Notch, I met the hapless beagle and his escort. And heard the wind rushing between facing cliffs. From south in summer, north in winter, there was scant shelter in that place.

After five hours, I did not stop when I got to the sign pointing west to the summit of Cadillac, east to the summit of Dorr, but kept going straight, ready to let gravity give me a push.

The most spectacular spot in the entire loop lay ahead. A third of the way down the Gorge Trail, there is one of Acadia's most sacred sites. Best approached from above, it is more impressive that way. Theatrical. Especially after rain when rocks are wet. A great cliff looms on the right. Sheer. Covered with dripping, dark green moss. Facing it, in the middle of the constricted valley, a stone pulpit defies the plunging gorge. Trees all around. Instead of blocking the view, they add to the mood. Why sacred? Holy. Healing. Wholesome. With a natural integrity uniting climate and terrain, promoting life. While there, you know your place in the universe.

Can't stay forever. So on I went, and down, often walking in the bed of Kebo Brook, which is in the same class as Sargent Brook in the valley of the Giant Slide, or the north

branch of Hadlock Brook above the carriage road. Chasm Brook, ditto. The trail along Kebo Brook is exciting the whole way and not to be missed. But I was tired, so hurried on. I merely genuflected to the plaque honoring the woman whose friends had paid for the trail, this time without even wondering who Lillian Endicott Francklyn might have been (see page 195).

I reached the Kebo Truck Road and turned right onto the

Pool and plunge on Kebo Brook seen from the Gorge Trail.

Hemlock Trail through the gap between Kebo and Dorr mountains. Where the trail crosses the Dorr Mountain North Ridge Trail, a field of smooth boulders crowds the slope, like marbles dropped by a kid who's been called in to dinner. No kid in this case, but a glacier called north. Just down from there I saw a pileated woodpecker on a fallen trunk twenty feet to my left. I watched for a minute or so, until she flew into the hemlocks. From there, the trail falls abruptly to a gravel road, the old Spring Road, which leads back to Sieur de Monts Spring through a stand of magnificent hemlocks. It took over six hours to complete the loop. Most pilgrimages take considerably longer.

5—CONNERS NUBBLE & THE BUBBLES LOOP

From Bubble Rock parking area
To Conners Nubble and North and South Bubbles,
    and back
    Up by north end of Jordan Pond Canoe Carry;
        Eagle Lake, Conners Nubble, and North Bubble
        (Bubble Ridge) trails
    Down by South Bubble Trail and south end
        of Jordan Pond Canoe Carry
            4.5 miles, September 17, 1993

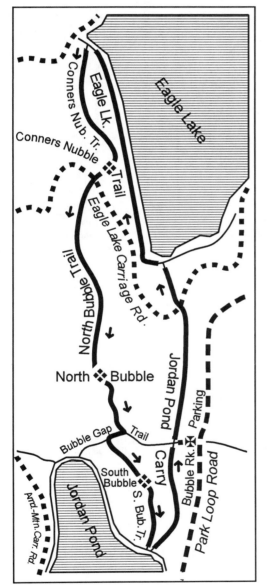

5—Conners Nubble & the Bubbles loop.

Acadia's most famous mountains—Cadillac, Sargent, Penobscot, Pemetic, Dorr, Western, Champlain—are all higher than 1,000 feet. When we hike Acadia, what we generally mean is we hike one of them. But many lesser hikes are equally rewarding. From a lower summit you look not only down and out, but up as well, including higher skylines in your field of view. The effect is of being in the thick of things, surrounded by vistas.

The Bubbles are a good example. Middling peaks at only 766 and 872 feet, South and North Bubbles overlook Jordan Pond and the islands to the south, and in turn are over-looked by Sargent, Penobscot, and Pemetic mountains. From such accessible outlooks, you gain a sense of Acadia's chief ingredients. Wooded slopes. Ponds. The ocean. Islands. Sky.

Everybody hikes one Bubble or the other. Once seen from the shore of Jordan Pond, or even on a postcard, you have to go there. But North and South Bubbles are part of a ridge running between Jordan Pond and Eagle Lake. You cannot claim to have "done" the Bubbles until you have walked the length of that ridge from shore to shore, includ-ing the northernmost hump, Conners Nubble, as well as the one between it and North Bubble. This I call Lost Bubble because it is not named on maps. Piecing together sections of different trails, you can hike the Bubble Ridge Trail as part of a loop, using the Jordan Pond Canoe Carry and Eagle Lake Trail to get back where you started.

I parked in the Bubble Rock parking area on the loop road on a gray and windy day in mid-September, and did the carry and ridge from there. There is not daylight enough after work to do much of a hike these days, so I cashed in some comp time and left work at one o'clock. It took me four hours and forty-five minutes to do the loop, and by the time I got back it was almost dark. A robin escorted me the last 200 feet, flying ahead, perching on roots, chirruping again and again to tell me that gray blur was really a bird. I had spent several hours this summer photographing a robin's nest nearby, and wondered if it could be the same bird. Annoyed at me then, annoyed at me now.

What other wildlife did I meet? Red squirrels, of course, eight in all. Chipmunk. Hairy woodpecker. A bee still mak-ing the rounds of flat-topped asters. Five people—three on foot, two on wheels. Two files of ants crossing the trail, one heading east, one west. A dragonfly over Eagle Lake. And the hawks, of course, but I will get to them.

I heard crickets, crows, loons, and saw three fox scats (two midnight blue, one packed with light-colored fur). Tracks of three dogs and two deer. Feathers of three birds. The usual pileated woodpecker holes.

Scarlet maple leaves decked the trail. A tree on the shore of Eagle Lake had leaves that were half-green, half-red. Goldenrod still bloomed on exposed ridges, and some pur-ple and flat-topped asters. Most had gone by. Eagle Lake was down a foot or so, stranding pickerelweed, arrowhead, and clumps of bayonet rush on gravelly shores. The woods I walked in were still green, yet dry in spite of recent rains.

The Bubble Rock parking area sits on the border be-tween two watersheds. If you pee in the bushes one way, the trickle heads for Jordan Pond, the other way, for Eagle Lake. People tell me how bad the park smells, particularly places with high use and no toilets. They say the park ought to do something about that. Which is right, it should. Meaning the folks who own the park—us. We the people. After all, we are the ones who eat at home or in restaurants, then expect the National Park Service to provide toilets wherever we need them. You cannot separate eating from excreting. They are part of the same process. Rather than blame the park, it makes more sense to put a tax on food and eating at the front end, where the problem starts, to raise money to pay for taking care of events at the nether end of our digestive tracts. [Portable toilets have been placed at several trailheads since this was written.]

The trail up the Bubbles soon crosses the Jordan Pond Canoe Carry linking the two ponds. Thought to be one of the oldest trails on the island, the carry runs downhill both ways through woods still recovering from the 1947 fire. Heading north into the watershed of Eagle Lake, it runs across the stone heap New Englanders call "soil." No wonder they made this into a national park. The former owners were probably glad to unload a lot of junk land on an unsuspecting bunch from Away who couldn't tell boulders from turnips. The land is now given over to beeches scarred by bark disease, birches, maples, hemlocks, spruces, and a host of ferns in wet spots, of which there are many. The carry crosses at least fifteen drainage channels by the time it reaches Eagle Lake. Pemetic's northwestern shoulder drains through these woods.

I ran into several highly vocal red squirrels in this first stretch of the loop, all chattering and scolding. Whether at me or the world I could not tell. One hairy woodpecker battered away at a snag. A loon called out three times somewhere ahead. Here was another of those lush and lively spots the park has so many of. Walking through such places, I come to my senses. Green wakes me up.

Crossing the Eagle Lake Carriage Road, I soon came to cedars, then saw the lake ahead through trees. Taunted by several squirrels from their trails in the treetops, I sat on a fallen log by the shore and ate lunch. Scanning the lake for loons, I saw none. I did see dark clouds scudding over the lake from Cadillac to the east. They formed an intricate, swirling, upside-down landscape mirroring the terrain below. A place I would like to explore, if I could get my hands on the topo maps. A dragonfly darting by brought me back to Earth. From nowhere and everywhere I heard crickets, backed by crows in the distance.

Picking up the Eagle Lake Trail to the west, I headed for Conners Nubble at the northern end of Bubble Ridge. Crossing a plank bridge over a stream running (would you believe creeping?) into the cove at the south end of the lake, I got an X-ray view of the stony soil through which it wound. There were boulders bunched together like knucklebones exposed as if I could see into the flesh of the Earth. Wilderness is anatomical, the body of a thing alive. The wild-deer-ness itself. People used to be part of it, but now pass through as strangers. Motes in the air.

The Eagle Lake Trail skirts the base of Conners Nubble

Clashing boulder lichens.

along one of the best sections of trail in Acadia. The treadway is entirely natural, consisting of cobbles and boulders laid down by the glacier. You go where the stones take you. The route is fairly level and sticks close to the lake shore, but you have to look where to place every step. The hike is worth it. Not so much for the views of Cadillac and Pemetic across the lake, but for the more intimate and intricate landscape of ferns, lichens, and boulders you rub shoulders with as you lurch along.

I looked for tracks on a stretch of sand exposed by the low level of the lake. Dogs in three sizes, and two sizes of deer. A shield lichen on a boulder by the shore was a sunburst in three shades of blue-gray.

Clouds hovered over the summit of Cadillac like hands of a seer over a crystal ball. Descending, they rested briefly on the mountain, then clasped it tight.

Details, details. All I could take in at one time was this lobe of this lichen on this side of this boulder under this tree. The flank of Cadillac was generic, a forest seen from a distance. Where I stood, everything was intricate and particular. It would take a lifetime to start understanding that site. Then there was the part I couldn't see under the boulders. In the soil. Down to bedrock—and within it. What can a passing mote know of that?

Out of my depth again, I moved on, taking pains to make sure of my footing. Idly reaching into the pocket of my raincoat, my fingers felt something like a domino. Pulling it out, it turned out to be a miniature Mr. Goodbar. When had I salted that away? On some unremembered hike a year ago, perhaps two. After eating it, I wondered if I could do that trick again. Ha, Hershey's Special Dark!

After two hours, I reached the sign for Conners Nubble, first step of my way along Bubble Ridge toward Jordan Pond. I turned south into birchy-brackeny woods, and head-

The woods, mostly of beeches with three- or four-inch stems, had an open feel to them. I could see 100 feet to either side. As the trail rose slowly up the ridge, more and more evergreens crept in under the beeches, closing in on the trail. Reaching an outlook from a ledge, I saw rain to the north and west. I would get wet well before reaching North Bubble. Hiking on, I came to open ledge with scrubby pitch pines and gray birches. This was the backbone of the ridge.

Conners Nubble from the south shore of Eagle Lake.

ed up the gentle rise typical of the north slope of glacially carved mountains. In less than twenty minutes I reached the top of the nubble which, at 588 feet, offers one of the truly great prospects in Acadia. There's something to see in every direction. Eagle Lake almost at your feet. Beyond it, over Frenchman Bay, the Black Hills and Lead Mountain in the distance. McFarland Hill to the north. Aunt Betty Pond, Gilmore Bog, and Blue Hill more-or-less west. Then the spectacular part, spread over 180 degrees—Sargent, Penobscot, North Bubble, South Bubble, Pemetic, and Cadillac—my eye at the center of the universe.

The trail off the nubble to the southwest is both steeper and shorter than the approach from the north. I got to the Eagle Lake Carriage Road in six or seven minutes. Oh, oh, cyclist coming. I hung back, letting him pass. I have had too many close calls with speeders to deliberately place my body in one's path.

"Hi," I said as he went by.

He said nothing.

The signpost said it was eight-tenths of a mile to North Bubble. I started across the carriage road, then saw the same cyclist coming the other way. I waited. When he was by, I started again—only to see him coming back! Hikers are worth thirty points. This time I scooted across and ducked into the woods before he had a good run at me. Intuitively I put my hand in my raincoat pocket—Hershey's Milk Chocolate. My luck still held.

"Peep." What was that?

"Squeak, squeak. . . ."

To my left, backed by gray clouds over Cadillac, two birds tumbled in the updraft rising against the cliff on the ridge's east side. One would fold its wings and dive on the other, falling fast as a stone—even faster. They hurtled around one another, spinning, stalling, diving, pulling up. They climbed vertically as fast as they plummeted. I had never seen such aerial acrobatics. Without a catcher, without a net. This was no act.

Peregrine falcons. The silhouette was right, the speed was right, the antics were right, the site was right. One slightly larger than the other, male (smaller) and female. I watched for five minutes as they zoomed in and out of view. They would drop below the cliff together, then come shooting up 100 feet apart. Then duck over to Pemetic for a second, to come barreling back. Space was their medium; they could do anything with it. My word for it was "play," because they looked like they hadn't a care in the world, as if they were flying for joy. Celebrating themselves, the cliff, the wind. More likely they were taking a skills development class, practicing maneuvers they would need for survival. That is what play is, a rehearsal so real it serves as its own reward. Two falcons in their medium of choice; I in mine. At some point they disappeared—I didn't see them go. Turning and heading up the ridge, I put my hand in my pocket, and came up with one last treasure tucked in a corner—Hershey's Krackel.

I lost my cap to a gust of wind. Retrieving it from the lee of a boulder, I put up my hood to clamp it on my head. Clouds were eating away the summit of Pemetic and Sargent, getting lower all the time. Looking down at a dark gray dike crossing the trail, I saw raindrops speckling it almost black.

What are dikes, anyway? Places where the jostling of tectonic plates puts so much stress on bedrock it cracks, then later gives way to molten rock rising to the surface along any avenue it can pry open. The rock cools rapidly, forming crystals so small you need a magnifier to see them (unlike slow-cooling granite, whose minerals have time to form huge crystals). I always notice dikes whenever a trail crosses one, I don't know why. They are important, like lightning, shooting stars, storms, ferns, fox scats, peregrine falcons, things of that order.

Looking at the north ridge of Pemetic, I saw a distinct line where evergreens higher up give way to a lower stand of hardwoods—the beech, birch, and maple woods I started out in. Why that line just there? A sudden change in soil, or is that where the fire burned out in 1947?

The ledges of Bubble Ridge itself are peopled with bright-colored lichens and scrubby trees, the cracks running across them supporting linear communities of black chokeberry and wine-leaf cinquefoil. Acadia is full of places like that, and every time I hike through one, I feel transported to a world apart. The laws are different. There are no rights, for instance. Nobody owes you anything. There is no insurance, no protection, no compensation, no welfare. What you get is what you get. Use your resources better than the next guy, you earn a toehold. If you don't, you don't. That is what it is like in paradise, I thought. Everything up front. No kickbacks. No bucking the line. No pork barrel. No dole.

Beyond the sound of crickets and the wind, I heard an airplane high above the clouds. The picture of an aluminum cylinder packed with hundreds of people all watching a movie filled my mind. I could imagine their paradise; could they imagine mine?

I bent to examine a fox scat on the edge of the trail. Packed with fur: blueberry season must be over. Then I came to another dike running diagonally up the slope, an outward and visible sign of the birthing of this terrain. Stretch marks on the belly of the continent. It began to rain harder. My glasses fogged up. I bent down to peer at something white in the trail. Cigarette butt. The ridge kept mounting, seeming to culminate in a summit, only to lead to another farther on. I remembered another time I was here in the rain, waiting to photograph a rainbow that never came.

I knew I had reached Lost Bubble when I saw the wood-

ed back slope of North Bubble across a dip in the ridge. From where I stood, the drop down the cliff on the Pemetic side seemed enormous. Three hours ago I was down *there*.

Five minutes later I stood by the cairn on top of North Bubble. Coming up the ridge, I had no inkling the view would open that abruptly. Suddenly, there was Jordan Pond. The ocean. Nameless islands cloaked in mist. Mighty Sargent, Penobscot, Pemetic—summits erased by low clouds.

Jordan Pond and Penobscot Mountain from North Bubble.

Jordan Pond was dappled with catspaws, dancing shadows of the wind. Where I was, the wind raced from the east; on the pond, from the west. The Jordan Cliffs stood firm, deflecting the blast down and back, forcing it to retreat in the direction from which it came. I ate a banana in the rain to celebrate my arrival at that splendid place.

Looking toward the Jordan Cliffs, I traced as much of the cliffs trail as I could rough-in at that distance. Then I mentally followed the carriage road lower down. What an audacious thing to do—build a road across a talus slope that steep! I pictured John D. Rockefeller, Jr. scouting the slope with his engineer, the engineer saying, "John, I think we can do it." John D. saying, "Let's go for it!" And they did. I bet each of the Seven Wonders of the Ancient World had its beginnings in the vision of the local John D., Jr.

Hiking over to South Bubble, I retraced one of the most heavily used trails in the park. You can tell that from the wear. And the repair. The trail is in good shape, with new steps and impressive cribwork. The rain let up as I went, and the clouds began to lift. I was overtaken by a wave of joy and well-being. Every hike is a drama staged only once, never to be repeated in the history of the world. You have to be there to catch the loons, the falcons, the rain, the bee landing on that particular blossom. What is Acadia but an invitation to make the most of your gifts in this setting?

Near the top of South Bubble, the trail crosses a dike sweeping in a broad curve across the slope. I think of dikes as running a straight course at right angles to the direction in which the bedrock was stressed. How little I know about such things. I gained the top of South Bubble after almost four hours of hiking. Sitting on a rock, I scanned the surface of the pond for loons, which I had heard as I came along the ridge, but never saw.

As I looked, a hawk came riding the updraft coming off the pond—another peregrine falcon. It swept over my head and veered off toward Deer Brook where I lost it in the mist. There was no point waiting around for anything to top that. I headed down to the pond.

My advice about hiking the South Bubble Trail is—don't, not in the rain. It is a great idea, running a trail straight up that slope and cliff. But the soil along that route is so full of gravel, it makes the footing very slippery. You have to watch where and how you place every step. In the rain, it is even worse. You can always get back to the Bubble Rock parking area via the gap between North and South Bubble.

The line of blue blazes leads to the lip of the drop-off. Looking down, it is hard to believe you are going down there. An iron handhold gets you started. After that, you are on your own. Right off you find yourself squeezing down through a steep crack nine inches wide. This is a trail for those who are slim in the hip. The name of a trail on Mount Monadnock came to mind: the Do Drop Trail, because she do drop, like this one.

After a rapid descent of the cliff, the trail cuts through the talus at its base. Many steps were coated with gravel, so I was careful where I planted my feet. Out of the corner of my eye I saw charred tree trunks from the 1947 fire, and bright red sumac leaves. But I didn't want to break my concentration, so didn't pause to look. Something moving to my right caught my attention—chipmunk nibbling a seed. Then he scooted away.

Dropping through a stand of young birches growing between boulders, the trail quickly reaches the shore of Jordan Pond. Here there was no gentle lapping as there had been at Eagle Lake. This was an ominous roar. I remembered that the elevations of the two ponds are exactly the same, 274 feet above sea level. No way could that be a coincidence, even with dams on both. They must be connected underground. Is that possible? Are their watersheds invisibly linked? If so, it is a good thing George Dorr protected them both back in 1911 when he convinced the state legislature to grant the Hancock County Trustees of Reservations the power to take them in the public interest.

The last leg of the hike was up the Jordan Pond end of the canoe carry, through thick woods which at that hour,

6:25, were surprisingly dark. Along the steady slope, I passed under some truly majestic trees—hemlocks and maples were the ones I noticed towering above the canopy. The rain fell twice, first on leaves overhead, again on the forest floor. The valley Pemetic makes with South Bubble is narrower than the one with North Bubble on the other half of the carry, so the trail skirts a talus slope a good bit of the way. Edging along the valley on the drier South Bubble

Rock-cap fern.

side, it crosses no bridges or bog walks. I have seen squirrels, chipmunks, and woodpeckers here on other hikes, but saw none today.

A smooth shape glowing in the trail caught my eye. Uninflated balloon. To a child anywhere it would have been a treasure. To me it was litter. I put it in my pocket. Later, when I held it up to the overhead light in my car, I could read most of the minuscule lettering: "International House of [too small to read] Restaurants." The balloon was bright yellow, and had pictures of a little boy pancake and a little girl pancake on it.

Ahead of me, a robin chirruped in the gloom—one of the world's great sounds. In the suburbs, it means sprinklers, lawns, and worms. In Acadia it means leaf litter and insects. Here the robin is a canny, wild thrush, living by its wits and hard work. Peering ahead, I saw it perched on a root in the trail. Maybe that was my robin, the one I photographed three months ago on its nest not 300 feet from here. I regarded it fondly. It chirruped and flew off.

At quarter to seven I came out of the woods on the divide between the two ponds. Mine was the only car in the lot.

O

6—SARGENT MOUNTAIN via CHASM BROOK

From park headquarters via Aunt Betty Pond
To Sargent Mountain summit, and back
   Up by carriage road and Chasm Brook
   Down by old McFarland Trail, bushwhack,
     Chasm Brook, and carriage roads
             7.0 miles, September 24, 1993

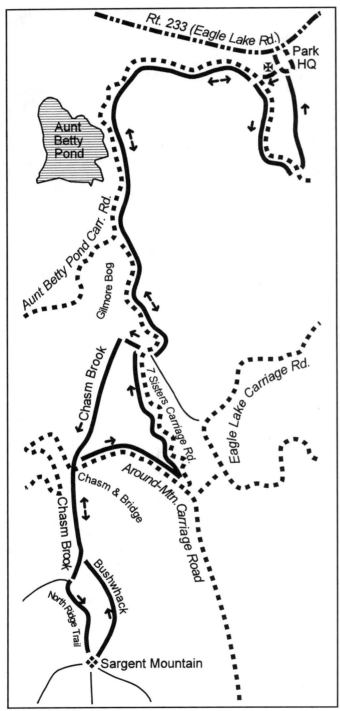

6—Sargent Mountain via Chasm Brook.

Chasm Brook drains the north slope of Sargent Mountain into Gilmore Bog, which flows into Aunt Betty Pond. In the first decade of this century, Waldron Bates built a trail along the brook from Gilmore Bog to the summit. The trail is long gone, but you can still hike the same route using the streambed as a treadway when water is low—commonly August and September. There is a problem connecting to another trail at the point the brook gets too narrow and overgrown to hike. The Sargent Mountain North Ridge Trail runs near, but if you miss it, you have to cut across areas of native vegetation, which in many cases are extremely fragile.

I hiked Chasm Brook by default. My car was in the garage, so I had to pick a trail I could complete in five hours from my apartment on McFarland Hill. I have made it up Cadillac, Pemetic, Penobscot, and Sargent hiking from there, but that was in summer when it was light till nine o'clock. Two days after the autumnal equinox, it got dark by seven. Given my starting place, Chasm Brook offered the most direct route up any mountain within reach. So one beautiful early fall day, Chasm Brook it was.

I did not quite finish in the five hours I allowed. The hike took six hours and ten minutes to cover seven miles. The last half hour was by moonlight flecking my way, and then by flashlight through the woods. It was just over three miles to the top of Sargent via the whole length of Chasm Brook, and more than four miles back by carriage road from Chasm Brook Bridge.

I was in the watershed of Aunt Betty Pond the whole way, from the low point at 210 feet by the pond to the high point at the summit of Sargent, elevation 1,373—for a vertical climb of 1,163 feet, 31 feet less than the hike up Cadillac from Bubble Pond.

Plenty of wildlife at pond level—two squirrels, beaver (or was it a muskrat?), ten ducks, bat, minnows, dragonflies, two hawks, frog, along with signs of sapsuckers and coyotes. On Sargent I saw deer pellets, a porcupine, and three kestrels. In the dry streambed itself I saw only water striders clustered in still pools.

Streams are billed as highways of life—wildlife travel corridors is the term often used. Where, then, was all the traffic? There was me, about twenty-five striders in every pool, and that was it for the entire length of Chasm Brook. The stretch from Gilmore Bog to the north ridge trail was as lifeless as any hike I have made in Acadia. In September, Chasm Brook is a brook in name only. It may run with torrents in April and November, but at the end of a dry summer, it is a river of rocks such as you would find in a Japanese garden. Now it is a pseudo-river. Sham river. Dry river. Dead river. I did not turn over rocks looking for salamanders, or paw through leaf litter looking for spiders, insects, and shrews. Mine was strictly a superficial tally of life that came to me on its own. Either Chasm Brook folk are good hiders, or they were not home when I walked by.

I started out at 1:20 p.m. along the carriage road to Aunt Betty Pond and Gilmore Bog, then down to the end of Chasm Brook by an overgrown trail cutting to the right between Signposts 10 and 11. I had worked at a computer all morning, so felt as the Tin Woodman must have felt when Dorothy first oiled his joints. But in ten minutes I made the transition from work and started noticing a better world than ever hinted at in WordPerfect. How tan the cedars were getting, how yellow the ashes. My first hike after the equinox. Officially fall, and trees were picking up their cues from the changing light and temperature. There's something about the slanting light that triggers my yen to hike. This is a great time to be outdoors, celebrating the gift of mobility. I do not mean wheeled or powered mobility, I mean moving about on two legs. Nothing gives me more pleasure than traveling by Adam's mare.

Reaching the pond in about twenty minutes, I sat on a rock and looked across at Sargent Mountain rising on the far side. There was the valley of the brook I was heading for, a few red trees dotting its evergreen slopes. Two Northern harriers flew over the far shore, ducks splashed near the outlet, and dragonflies stalked back and forth, golden wings glinting in the sunlight. It was warm on my rock and out of the wind. I felt

Hiker following the stony course of Chasm Brook.

as a wasp must feel on a sunlit windowsill this time of year, but my legs would not be stilled. Looking down into the pond as I went on, I saw minnows and a seven-inch fish.

For three-quarters of a mile the carriage road is almost level as it runs next to pond and bog. Lowland, unusual terrain for a park famous for its coastal hills. Taking the left fork at Signpost 11, I went east of Gilmore Bog until the land started to rise and a trail crossed the carriage road, its overgrown extension sloping right. Saplings blocked the way, but it was a trail of sorts, and served my purpose. Beneath a grove of hemlocks at the foot of the slope, Chasm Brook flows into the bog—or would if it held any water. Here was the true base of Sargent Mountain. A good place to eat lunch. It was getting on to 2:30 and I was hungry. I ate my sandwich, and tomato sliced with trusty Opinel knife.

Two brooks join at that point, one coming down from Southwest Pass along the Seven Sisters Carriage Road, the other off the north slope of Sargent—Chasm Brook. I took the fork to the right. The streambed is ten feet wide at that point, wide as it gets. Here was my trail, paved with pebbles, cobbles, and boulders. Mostly pink granite, with other types of rock mixed in. From here to its rise on the upper slopes, the channel is arched by branches of streamside trees. The sky is barely visible during the growing season.

There are no views to speak of. But plenty of things to see. Primarily the streambed itself, the ledges it cascades over, and living walls of rock rising on either side. Now and then the way was dappled with sunlight, until the sun got too low to shine through the leaves.

A lot of trees along the brook had been cut at one time, mossy stumps marking where they had stood. Some fallen trunks serve as charred monuments to the 1947 fire. Even after 46 years, its traces are much in evidence. Here and there a boulder bore signs of a squirrel eating its seedy dinner of maple, oak, or pine. Liverwort had gotten a toehold on every boulder, usually in a shallow depression. From the scouring of the streambed, I could picture how different that serene landscape had been six months ago—how harsh and unforgiving—and would be again.

At one point I looked up and saw the shadow of a damselfly against the translucent gold of an ash leaf. And there were water striders, legs dimpling every pool. Each pool had its resident population of twenty-five striders. I wondered what they ate. There was life in that stream I never saw.

The going up Chasm Brook is easy for the most part. Whenever you need a foothold, one appears. The footing is firm, and except for the upper reaches, not slippery because so dry. It would be another story when wet. Trail maintenance is performed in spring by the brook itself. The few trunks fallen bank-to-bank are easy to duck under or roll over.

Dikes cut through exposed ledge now and then—I noticed four or five. Dikes speak to me of bygone days, so I always pay attention when I meet one. Anything 360 million years old (and probably older) is worth listening to, even if it speaks a dead language. I could see the dikes because their cover of soil had been swept away. No soil—that was it! That is why the stream seemed so barren. It was bare. On sloping ground, soil is what makes water stick around long enough to support plants. This stony swath was an escape route that did not hold water but helped it get away to bog and pond. This streambed was a scar, not a habitat. A gash where water tore the land down to bedrock, leaving what could not serve as either aquatic or terrestrial habitat. Here was no man's land, not successfully claimed by either side.

Charlemagne, Boadicea, or Agamemnon—that bold ruler who dares assume the stony seat of absolute power. Luckily, the chair was not occupied when I approached. I tried it myself, but my frame was too slight to fill its awesome dimensions. When the right person comes along we will know it by the shaking of the ground and darkening of the sun. In the meantime, the throne room is one of Acadia's most hallowed sites.

North slope of Sargent Mountain from Gilmore Bog.

Now and again a low branch swept the cap off my head. I had strung a shoelace through ventilation eyes to tie under my chin when it got windy, but I was not ready to tie the cap on because the visor cut into my view. I let branches play their tricks.

The terrain grew steeper, the streambed narrower, ledgier. The brook falls by a series of sharp drops, which make convenient steps for hikers heading upstream. A rock wall six feet high, looking sheer and impassable, turned out to be terraced so I could climb it with ease. After hiking for two hours, I stooped under another obstacle—an eight-inch cedar fallen across the brook, uppermost branches reaching skyward as trunks in their own right—then looked up and saw the Chasm Brook carriage road bridge ahead. Made of pink granite, it was at home in its surroundings, looking as if it had been dropped in place by the glacier.

Under the arch of the bridge, there was the most dramatic site I would see all day, the chasm of Chasm Brook. Ancient cliff walls twenty feet high, covered with ferns, moss, and lichens, rose starkly in front of me. At first glimpse it looked like a dead end, a geological cul-de-sac. The wall to the left was formidable, but ahead, in the path of the brook where, in other seasons it must cascade twenty-five vertical feet, blocks have eroded away from the cliff. Leaving a huge throne carved in granite, worthy of a new

Though daunted at first, I scaled the throne without trouble. The view from the top was impressive because of the drop, but not as good as that from below where you are surrounded by venerable cliffs. You have to feel properly small to appreciate the grandeur of the place.

The brook levels off above the chasm, looking much as it did lower down, a landscape of stones, pools, and fallen leaves. A fleet of pale green and yellow elder leaves floating in one pool caught my eye. Photograph by Eliot Porter. The striders among the leaves reminded me of outrigger canoes.

Voices from above! One voice, anyway. Looking up through the trees, I saw a row of coping stones to my right, ramparts of the carriage road. Passing cyclist, no doubt. First hint of people in over two hours. Later, I saw tracks of a lone hiker in gravel on the north ridge trail. Size twelve boot like mine. Seekers of solitude, disunite! You have the park to yourselves seven months of the year.

Higher up, the ground slopes more steeply on either side, and the stony channel ricochets between cliffs left and right. First a sixteen-foot cliff looms left, then another much longer one right, covered with a film of green life clinging to damp rock. Kindling images of fortresses and great walls. Brook as moat. I was a passing pilgrim on a journey between sacred sites, pausing to savor the magnificence on either hand. Humble, that is how I felt. Humble stems from *humus*, meaning earth. Cousin to such words as homage, hombre, and human. By derivation, human means Earthling. That is exactly what I was—a child of the Earth. Child of Sargent Mountain and Chasm Brook. That is what Acadia offers, an invitation to return to familial ground.

I kept an eye out for signs the brook had served as a trail in earlier years, but saw no steps, no treadway laid for easy travel. I read in *Trails of History* that Chasm Brook had been one of Waldron Bates' favorite trails. He was the arch trailmaker of them all. How could he have resisted artfully rearranging these stones? If his hand had once been evident here, I saw no trace of it.

Another dike angled across the brook, cracked into a series of plates, then crumbling as grit to be swept before the next flood. As a kid I used to take electrical transformers apart to get at their windings of copper wire. The eroding dike reminded me of the laminated cores of those transformers, built up of layers to prevent the dissipation of electrical energy as heat. Our childhood images shape the world we live in as adults. How will the Nintendo warriors of today see Chasm Brook when they hike it tomorrow? Will they hike it at all?

But for branches, leaves and water striders, I saw few signs of life as I went. The way was reserved for water, and little else. Slow-moving water brings life; spates sweep it away. The residents I met in Chasm Brook had either strong roots or fleet limbs to bear them before the flood.

Chasm Falls at a wetter time of year.

The slope gets steeper, the channel narrower. For the first time I felt I was climbing a mountain. But at the top of that stretch the terrain levels off, and the sense of trekking up a valley disappeared. I came to a series of pools with no water striders. Coming up that steep rise, I had crossed the strider line.

And here was a line of a different sort, a line of stones across the brook. Yes, laid by the hand of man—namely, who but Waldron Bates? The stones were flat and looked deliberately placed, spanning the width of the channel. A trail must have crossed the brook at that point, though there was no sign of it on either bank. I kept going along the streambed, which was now only three or four feet wide, overgrown by elder and mountain ash.

The brook divided and, having taken the left fork on an earlier hike, I kept to the right. Coming to a sort of path, for the first time I left the streambed and followed to see where that faint track might lead. Within ten feet I came to a mound of fresh deer pellets. It was a path for wildlife, not people. I kept on, coming out on a ledge facing MDI High School, and Aunt Betty Pond to the east. Had I really climbed that high? For the first time since basking on the shore of the pond, I felt the warmth of the sun. Along the slope, on the top branch of a dead spruce, a kestrel clung facing downslope into the wind, flicking its tail. Beyond it I saw two other hawks soaring on the updraft.

No sooner had I left the brook than I met terrestrial and aerial life. Finding no trail that way, I went back to the streambed, which had become not only overgrown, but slippery as well. Not much of a trail. But it was my chosen way, so I pushed on through the elders, losing my cap three times, getting hung-up by my pack trying to duck under a branch, pressing on—until I came to a full stop with a stub of a branch pressing into my chest. Message clear, I was licked. Promising to quit in one more minute, I looked around for a way out. Ducking under yet another tree, I saw that others had come before me, breaking branches. Hey, maybe I wasn't so far off. The streambed was no wider than fifteen inches, and overgrown. Wading through a tangle of alders and elders, I came to a grove of maples, and past the maples I could see a ledge. On top of the ledge, silhouetted against the western sky, a cairn told me I had gained the north ridge trail. I knew exactly where I was.

Climbing onto the ledge, I took in the view. The sun stood over the south end of the Camden Hills, its gleam reflected in Penobscot and Blue Hill bays, in visible slivers of Long Pond and Echo Lake, and in Somes Sound off Hall Quarry. Hardwood and Long islands stood out against the glistening water of Blue Hill Bay. Looking upslope, I saw a slightly gibbous moon balanced on the summit. Almost five o'clock. I had been hiking for three-and-a-half hours. It would be dark by the time I got back. Should I quit, or go on? No, I was not about to retreat so close to the summit. I would figure my route from there.

I headed upslope, letting my shadow lead me across

open ledges all the way. Once out of the silent valley of Chasm Brook, I felt space calling from every direction. The brook had only two dimensions, up and down. Here there were three. A kestrel hovering ahead of me made the point. Hawk country. Place where you could soar.

Reaching the 1,373-foot summit of Sargent Mountain after hiking three hours and forty minutes, I sat in the lee of the summit cairn, ate a banana, and plotted my route back to McFarland Hill, watching a kestrel all the while. There was no way to avoid the dark. I would have to stick to carriage roads. The quickest connection was via Chasm Brook. But going down I would pick up the brook lower down, saving time by sticking to open ledges more of the way.

I descended by way of the ruined hut north-northeast of the summit, nothing but a heap of stones today, weathered boards scattered around the surrounding slope. A line of poles marching across the ledges marks some sort of power or communications link with the outside world. Trail phantoms had set up cairns since I had come that way earlier this summer. Standing by the ruins, admiring the treescape lit by low sunlight from behind, I heard a flicker cry out ahead of me. I took it as a reminder not to dally. I crossed the last stretch of ledge, stole a final look at the view, and plunged into the valley of Chasm Brook.

Sargent's summit from the north ridge trail.

Though my route might once have been a trail, it wasn't one now. There were cairns to mark the way, but cairns do not necessarily make a trail. I was careful to step on bare rock where I could, detouring around places where there was none to be found. Even so, I was the enemy. A heavy-footed alien out of my element. I did not belong. The solution is to stay away, or put in a trail protecting the slopes by restricting travel to a treadway built to stand the wear.

In fifteen minutes after leaving the summit I was back in the brook. And there were the steps I saw coming up, crossing the stream exactly at that point. They mark the limit of navigation in the streambed itself. From there down, I saw frequent signs of a treadway laid in the channel of the brook, or next to it for dry footing in the spring. I missed them on the way up because my perspective had been wrong. It is hard to see steps from below. From above, they

stand out. There were too many steps and runs of flat stones to believe they were laid at random by the elements. They had tumbled some over the years, but were still roughly in place. Signs of trail work were particularly clear just above the long cliff, now on my left going down. A flight of moss-covered steps led from the bank into the brook at that point. Up-ended a bit, but steps just the same.

The landscape is what you see from where you are—poet Charles Olson said that. To see all things, you have to go every way, down as well as up. Coming down Chasm Brook, I was sure I saw the handiwork of Waldron Bates, while going up I would have said he left no trace.

At six o'clock, with maybe an hour of daylight left, I reached the Around-Mountain Carriage Road. I confirmed my plan to stick to carriage roads from then on. What's that? A porcupine thirty feet to my left, rolling along among birches and ferns. Young one, to judge from the size. Gliding along with its distinctive rocking gait, it did not seem to be in a hurry to get anywhere special. I watched its slow amble for a few minutes, then ambled on myself.

The winding descent from Signpost 10 along Seven Sisters Brook is one of my favorite carriage roads in the park. Between the Around-Mountain loop and Gilmore Bog, it spans the brook six times, reminding me of a caduceus—serpents twining about a staff. The way seems narrower than some, with trees and ferns bordering it closely on either side. I met two red squirrels in the dusk, and a bat sweeping the road ahead as I passed along.

I heard ducks well before I got to Aunt Betty Pond which, by the time I got there, barely reflected the twilight glow. It was just light enough to make out six pairs of ducks, and a beaver (if that's what it was) swimming along, the ripples of its wake streaming behind.

The rest of the way I followed a ribbon of gray through much darker woods as the carriage road wound up the south ridge of McFarland Hill. I caught glints of the moon flashing through trees, but they were more like fireflies than beacons to light my path. Missing the turn I was looking for, I overshot and took the ridge trail back, using a flashlight to find the way.

○

7—PEMETIC MOUNTAIN LOOP

From Bubble Pond parking area
To Pemetic Mountain summit, and back
  From park headquarters on bicycle by carriage
    road to Bubble Pond parking area, then up by
    carriage road, Pond Trail, and east branch of
    Pemetic Mountain South Ridge Trail
  Down by Pemetic Mountain North (or Northeast)
    Ridge Trail, returning to headquarters by bike
  4.0 miles (not counting bike ride), October 2, 1993

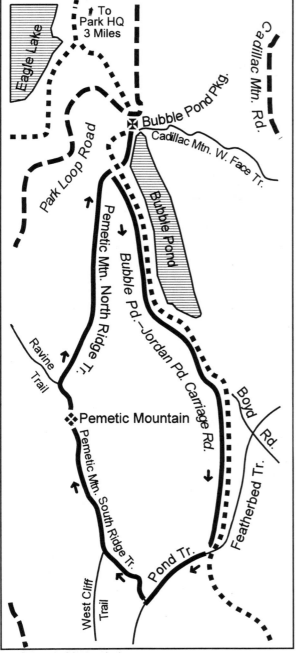

7—Pemetic Mountain loop.

The south ridge of Pemetic Mountain is one of my favorite hikes. The view across Jordan Pond to Sargent, Penobscot, and the dramatic Jordan Cliffs, with Bubble Ridge thrown in for good measure, is as fine as views get in Acadia. The islands south of Mount Desert Island float on the sparkling Gulf of Maine. Eagle Lake lies blue and snug in the north. Cadillac stands watch over Bubble Pond in the east.

But it is not the views that draw me to Pemetic—it is the

Black chokeberries.

mountain itself. Particularly the south ridge. Granite slopes, dikes, lichens, mosaic of vegetation rooted in hollows and cracks. The ridge is not bare or, as Champlain put it, *désert*. Water holes up wherever it can to beat the tug of gravity, green plants testifying to its presence in unlikely places.

Here is one of those original sites where life reinvents itself over and over. A hike up Pemetic will take you back in time to the more primitive conditions prevailing after the ice sheet receded twelve thousand years ago. The climate runs to extremes, and besides a sprinkling of gravelly soil, there is not much else to go on. But that is enough for the hardy plants you will meet on the ridge—lichens, wine-leaf cinquefoil, black chokeberry, blueberry, juniper, mountain sandwort, and other native residents managing to eke out a livelihood on water, sunlight, and air.

The wind from the southwest was fierce that Saturday in early October. I wanted it at my back. Car still at the garage, I biked from McFarland Hill to Bubble Pond, where there was a single van in the lot, and started hiking south on the carriage road at quarter to eight. The loop I took was some four miles long. At a leisurely pace it took almost five hours.

Immediately I met four roving mammals, four unleashed dogs offended by my crossing their turf. They told me so. Overtaking the owners, I mentioned the porcupine I had seen a few days before. The last I saw, all six were headed for the van.

The wind blew up a line of foam along the north end of Bubble Pond. The water was choppy and gray. Across the pond, maples colored the lower slopes of Cadillac in two red bands cutting through the evergreens. Morning glare made it too bright to look up. The scene churned with a steady roar.

It was a time of equinoctial winds and changing seasons. Inflection point between summer and winter. The entire landscape was in transition. Not only spatially as it always is, but temporally. Every day would be different now, as in spring. A leaf blew along thirty feet above the pond. Even trees move this time of year. Where will that leaf be tomorrow?

The carriage road, like all lakeside ways, cuts between two worlds. Cedars, ferns, asters to the east. Boulders and mixed woods on the slope to the west. Landscape in layers, changing with elevation and slope. Transitions, again.

Near the south end of the pond, I looked across at the great blocks of granite fallen from Cadillac's flank. No talus slope on the island is more impressive. Or forbidding. Engineers knew not to squint through transits across such terrain. Look, wheeled humanity, but you can't get there from here.

Beyond the pond, the carriage road rises slowly through overarching woods of beech and birch, out of the valley of Bubble Pond, into the valley of Hunters Brook. An easy walk, good for body and soul. Evergreen seedlings waited patiently beneath the hardwoods on either side. I made a mental note to come this way in fifty years to see how the succession is getting on. Transitions, transitions.

Birds kept calling as I passed through their woods. Chickadees, woodpeckers, blue jays, crows. And somebirds, there are always those—birds I cannot identify. Ahead, a nuthatch flew from the roadway up to the branch

Map lichen.

of a beech, looking like footage of a falling leaf run backwards through the projector.

Not many birds live in Acadia year-round. Those I named do. Along with ravens, juncos, kinglets, grouse, great horned owls, eagles, mourning doves, gulls, eiders, guillemots, loons, and a few others, so familiar, we take them for granted. Chickadees and crows, ho hum. Never met a chickadee or crow I didn't like. Woodpecker either. Or eagle, nuthatch, or loon. First settlers. Seed folk.

Roadside ferns were turning yellow. Royal (by the pond), interrupted, and cinnamon ferns were the ones I noticed. Good-by, chlorophyll; so long, photosynthesis. Food stores closing for the season.

With the Triad looming ahead, the Pond Trail crosses the carriage road, connecting the Featherbed on Cadillac's south ridge with the south end of Jordan Pond. It served as my connector to the Pemetic Mountain Trail. Turning west, I rose toward the gap between the Triad and Pemetic along your basic woodland trail with its treadway of fallen leaves and needles, roots and rocks. Two bikers zipped by on the carriage road I had just left, reminding me of uniformed alien invaders. Martians riding bicycles?

How silent the woods. Not so much an absence of sound as a readiness for anything. Not a lack, something missing, but the medium of possibility itself. Instead of shutting down, I perked up. Silence is an invitation to notice small things in the lee of noise and commotion.

At one point I was surrounded by striped maples, their golds and pale greens lighting the understory in every direction. Overhead, the woods were mixed. Hemlocks, cedars, and spruces joined by sugar maples, beeches, birches. Higher up the gap, lichens and liverworts took over, draping soil and boulders with vibrant green. Evergreen seedlings everywhere. Cliffs loomed through branches to my right, palely mottled with lichens and shadows, reminded me I was heading for higher ground. I moved, and the land moved as well. Nothing stayed the same. Silence flowed with the landscape.

After an hour and a half, I reached the Pemetic Mountain Trail. To the south it leads to the Triad, to the north, the summit. Beyond that, in 2.3 miles, back to Bubble Pond. I turned north toward a stand of tall spruces. In five minutes I stood at the base of the cliff rising to Pemetic's south ridge.

The cliff rises by steep steps, abrupt walls of rock separating narrow shelves holding scanty soils, inviting water to slow its course, plants to put down roots. The effect is of natural terraces covered with life. A hardship environment. Green just the same. The trail winds up the cliff on rock fragments bedded in soil. In spots it is hard to follow, looking not much different from the slope on either side. Blue blazes help tease the route ahead from the general terrain. A sloping dike broke into a series of rough steps. Trailmakers like that sort of thing. Hikers, too.

Just off the trail, a couple of up-ended cedars showed how thin the soil was—six inches or less. How tenuous their grip on life. Small lump of charcoal beneath dangling roots. Souvenir of the 1947 fire? Probably not; it did not burn this far south. Beyond the blowdowns, a three-inch birch limb lay in the trail. Widow-maker.

Requisite twelve-foot cliff, which no trailmaker could refuse. The route angles along its base for more than a hundred feet before scaling it through an easy cleft, attaining the ridge. From here to the summit, the trail follows Pemetic's spine at a steady but moderate pitch. Valley of Bubble Pond to the east, Jordan Pond west.

Crickets! How they love these slopes. In spite of the wind, I heard them all the way to the summit. And didn't see one. The trail went between two clumps of juniper, cinquefoil, and blueberry, a cricket on either hand carrying its part in a rhythmic, antiphonal chant.

At the lower end of the ridge, the West Cliff Trail comes in from Jordan Pond. From there, the trail is in the open. Wind blew straight off the water with nothing to break its force. I put up my hood. From a prospect on the right, I looked into the valley of Hunters Brook, whose floor was peopled with deciduous trees showing green, mottled yellows, oranges, and reds, with ranks of evergreens in bleachers on either side.

Upridge, pockets of huckleberry red stood out against the dusty orange of lichen-covered granite. Those who take the North (or Northeast) Ridge Trail from Bubble Pond, and return the same way, miss Pemetic's finest show this time of year. Narrow cracks run with cinquefoil and black chokeberry. Shallow wetlands brim with stunted cedar, gray birch, spruce, and a variety of heath family plants.

Much as our individual characters tell the story of our lives, the Acadian landscape tells the story of mountain life. Pemetic's mosaic of granite and greenery (much turned to reddery in October) speaks of rains that flood every basin. Snows that blow. Ice that freezes each crack again and again. Winds blasting rock. Sun beating down—day after

year after century after millennium back to the last glacier. What's left is the pattern of life suited to this site, its character telling of hardships overcome. Obstacles surmounted. Trials endured and outlasted.

Looking south over the Gulf of Maine, I saw a field of shimmering gray. The day was totally overcast, making the Gulf, what . . . undercast? One elegant cruise ship was anchored between Bear and Greening islands. Mobile luxury

Black crowberry.

habitat for those who can afford it. Instead of traveling to broaden our experience, we take our comforts with us, ensuring that we are scarcely challenged in our adventures. Cars are modern withdrawing rooms on wheels.

Like a page from a Rand-McNally atlas, a dike covered with map lichen spread at my feet, borders between principalities shown as of October 1993. I wondered if lichens are aggressive, always crowding their neighbors, coveting their possessions, plotting sneak incursions.

The dike zig-zagged up the ridge for several hundred feet, leading to a sloping ledge where, at the base of a step, a cedar sprang from raw granite by adopting the juniper lifestyle—growing out, not up. Silvery stems poked through the greenery, bony fingers, grasping in death at what they most wanted in life. Water. Cut off by drought and frost.

Above the stunted cedar, the trail cuts through a patch of pale granite ringed by loose gravel eroding from the soil, uncovering polished crystals of quartz and feldspar, as if cut by a diamond saw. Here was the mountain naked as the day the glacier left it. Like seeing your baby picture in the paper on your fiftieth birthday.

In a depression farther on, growing out of caked mud, low clumps of mountain sandwort shook fitfully in the wind, a few white blossoms testing the limits of summer. A warbler fluttered to windward from a low spruce, landing on bare ledge. What kind of warbler? The generic, olive-drab kind that comes through in fall, the ones Peterson calls "confusing fall warblers." I recognized it right away.

Strange, how bland Pemetic looks from the shore of Jordan Pond, and how exciting it actually is. We judge a place at a distance, then move on, missing vital details. On top, everything flows. The whole landscape is fluid and on the move. Red leaves run across ledges like water, plunging terrace to terrace. Every glimpse is like a snapshot of a waterfall. You can imagine the thunder.

Just short of the summit I had trouble standing in the wind, so sat near a spray of black crowberry in the lee of a boulder poised on the brink of the slope down to Jordan Pond. A leaf came tumbling tip-over-stalk on the updraft, passing high over the summit and continuing on toward Cadillac. Looking over the pond at Penobscot and Sargent, I sensed the flow of the wind. Flow of the water. Flow of the land. Flow of the glacier that shaped it all. How different the Bubbles looked from their postcard image, not separate mounds at all, but a continuous ridge—a fossilized drop falling sideways from Eagle Lake to Jordan Pond.

Here was one of Acadia's great views. Great because it gives a profile of the flowing landscape with ridges and valleys stretching north and south. Because so active. You can feel the glacier trundling out of the north, grinding mountains and cliffs into boulders, then limping back, leaving the land strewn with debris. The mountains themselves seem to flow, as they once did as molten rock streaming out of the inferno created by friction between colliding tectonic plates. Whitecaps flew on Jordan Pond. To keep from being swept away, I crouched behind my rock.

Moving on as one particle in that fluid landscape, I joined a group of five hovering near the cairn at the top. Make that six—one woman was leashed to a large brown dog. I hung around the summit almost half an hour, looking in every direction. Even up (out of habit), but there would be no hawks today, with the wind from the south.

I passed the turnoff for the Bubbles via the ravine trail, stopping to admire eight amanita mushrooms growing in a clump, a sign of recent rains. Unlike the south ridge, the north slope of Pemetic is largely wooded. The trail leads through trees, with prospects now and then looking over Eagle Lake or Cadillac. At one such overlook I stopped to eat lunch, admiring the west face of Cadillac with its cliffs and fallen boulders. Awesome is the word that applies.

Looking down into the valley of Bubble Pond, I saw a blue jay fly among the trees far below me—just as the noon siren wailed up the valley from Otter Creek. What if jays really sounded like that! On the way down I saw a mushroom lodged in the branch of a spruce, hint of red squirrels.

The trail descends by a series of inclined ledges, the treadway being made of an assortment of needles, rocks, and roots. Entering more open, bouldery woods, I glimpsed a woman's bare bottom as she squatted not far ahead of me. She and her standing male companion were both looking down the trail. Evidently they did not expect any early risers like me to be coming the other way.

The rest of the way to Bubble Pond, the trail is often

Dwarf juniper with berries.

hard to make out from the rocky, rooty terrain on either side. It all looks much the same. You have to search for blue blazes marking the way. Lower down, the spruces get bigger, adding another level to the sense of stepped transitions along the trail.

I met a man who said, "Nice and quiet in here, isn't it?" I replied with a nod.

The trail leads into a striped maple zone, the shrubby trees first no more than a foot tall, then gradually getting bigger along the way until they reached twelve feet or more. Cedars began to show up. And white pines two feet in diameter. In places pine needles spread like a golden carpet across the trail. Then birches appeared. And beeches. One thing led to another. Trails evolve as you go along. The trick is in letting your attention keep up.

I got back to my bike in the parking lot in four hours and forty-five minutes. I had met twenty-one people in that time. There were twenty cars now where only one had been at the start. Biking back around Eagle Lake, I saw an osprey near the dam, and a gray squirrel—the second I had seen in the park that year.

○

8—SARGENT MTN. LOOP via GIANT SLIDE

From foot of Giant Slide Trail
To Sargent Mountain summit, and back
   Up by Giant Slide, Parkman, and Grandgent trails
   Down by Sargent Mountain South Ridge, Maple
   Spring, Grandgent, and Giant Slide trails
                  5.0 miles, October 10, 1993

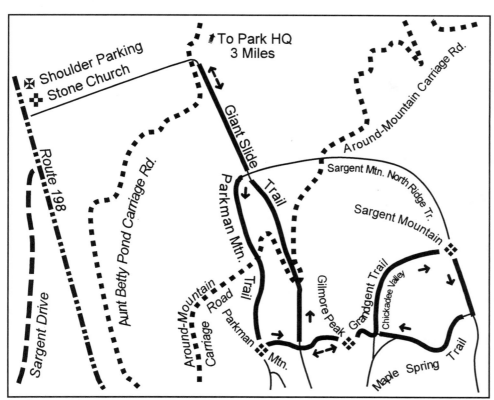

8—Sargent Mountain loop via Giant Slide Trail.

If Caesar could sum up an entire military campaign in three words, I ought to be able to do the same for a five-hour hike. Of my trip up Parkman Mountain, Gilmore Peak, and Sargent Mountain, let me declare, then: unity, variety, gravity.

By unity I mean the peace and harmony that surrounded me, and the sense of belonging I felt. Variety refers to the changing character of the landscape with its alternating valleys and mountains, different habitat areas, its ups and downs. Gravity suggests falling water, falling leaves, the fall of the year, and the force we use to our advantage in hiking or flying—but which in the end draws us all to the bosom of Mother Earth.

My thermometer reading forty degrees, I biked from McFarland Hill to the trailhead where the Giant Slide Trail crosses the Aunt Betty Pond Carriage Road, hiked up the three granite peaks—and down the valleys between them—by a loop between five and six miles long, bringing me back to my bike in a little over five hours.

While biking I saw two squirrels, one gray and one red, but did not see any while I hiked. I did see chickadees and crows, and heard blue jays and crickets. I met twenty-five people (it was Saturday of Columbus Day weekend), with two free-roaming dogs. And I saw an eagle soaring on taut wings around Parkman Mountain, and four hours later, a sharp-shinned hawk in the same place.

I headed up the valley of Sargent Brook, straight for the morning sun. On that golden day, in that golden place, it was my stairway to paradise. Trail maps would say my route was made up of segments of the Giant Slide, Parkman Mountain, Grandgent, Sargent Mountain South Ridge, and Maple Spring trails.

The first things I noticed were leaves underfoot. Maple leaves (red), pine needles (yellow), and cedar leaves (tan). Except for stretches of ledge, the whole route was spread with a Persian carpet of golds and reds. This one was not for sale. It belonged to everyone who hiked or biked in Acadia Columbus Day weekend.

In eight minutes I came to Sargent Brook, the stream which rises in the saddle between Parkman Mountain and Gilmore Peak, then rushes north toward Somes Sound over boulders fallen from cliffs on both sides. The trail in that narrow valley does not pave the route for the sake of human comfort. The treadway has not been smoothed and leveled—or if it has been, ice and water have unsmoothed and unleveled it again. Much of the way is over stones naturally placed, stones with sharp points and edges angling upward.

Sargent Brook was a series of small, jewel-like pools strung together by plunges and falls. I kept looking for skittering water striders, but saw none. Did striders carry spate insurance? The pools were not empty by any means. Floating leaves and needles were lodged behind branches and boulders, creating rafts of reds, tans, and golds. Having left my camera behind, I clicked my mental shutter instead.

Colorful mushrooms pushed up along the trail, spurred by recent rains. Many amanitas had stretched out like eight-inch models of the U.S.S. *Enterprise* painted red, yellow, or white. I passed under a red maple caught with one root in summer, one in winter, half its leaves fallen, half on the bough—every one painted half-red, half-green.

At the foot of the slope where the grade picks up and

boulders stand poised in angry waves, I looked up the valley into a sea of golden pennants, the way ahead flagged with fluttering maple leaves.

How to describe the Giant Slide Trail? It runs in a narrow valley with walls of rock on both sides—on the east smooth and steep, on the west cracked and jagged. A brook runs over the heap of boulders in the middle, sometimes tumbling, sometimes slipping along the base of the cliff. The whole place is full of ferns, mosses, and lichens. And trees—maples, birches, cedars, hemlocks—with yellow leaves waving and falling on rocks and into the brook. The trail, like the brook, bounces from boulder to boulder, and squeezes around or slithers over the bigger rocks.

In three words or ninety-three, it is hard to describe. The valley of Sargent Brook is more dramatic than the Gorge with Kebo Brook welling between Dorr and Cadillac, or, except for the chasm itself, than Chasm Brook. Here is the heart of Acadia—or a chamber of its heart—where gravity pumps the waters of life throughout this wet and colorful land. It is best to see for yourself.

I came to pool after pool, some fed by plunges, some by churning rapids, others by gurgling underground streams. Stopping by the deepest, I watched a gyre of leaves and needles slowly eddy at the base

Sargent Brook along the Giant Slide Trail.

of a cliff, reminding me of stately circus horses wheeling in center ring. And there, in one sheltered bay—water striders (the only ones I saw) waltzing about in that stop-and-go way they have, staging a circus of their own.

At one point the trail leads under a low arch built of three boulders lodged together, quickly sorting hikers into two groups—those who will stick to the trail, and those who won't.

I stopped opposite a slanting thirty-foot cliff to admire two trees, cedar and spruce, growing well up on its face. Their roots must have found a steady water supply somewhere within the rock, but I saw neither roots nor water. Something beyond the trees caught my eye. Dark shape against blue sky. I did not have to look twice—it was an eagle, first I had seen in the park all year. About 100 feet up, it glided on the wind without flapping, from the slopes of Sargent to the north ridge of Parkman, which it rounded,

and disappeared, having been visible for less than ten seconds. If I had not stopped to look back at those two trees I would have missed it. I was reminded of watching for meteors on a moonless night, having a companion call out, "There's one!" but turning too slowly to catch it.

In fifty minutes I reached the trail crossing for Sargent and Parkman mountains. The north ridge trail leads east to Sargent's summit in 1.3 miles, the trail west to Parkman's in 0.7 mile. The crossing is at the entrance to the Giant Slide itself, which forms a tunnel beneath a huge slab of granite let slip from above. I headed for Parkman, leaving the tunnel for my descent.

From the crossing, the Parkman Mountain Trail leads quickly out of the valley of Sargent Brook onto Parkman's north ridge. Heading south, I enjoyed the slow rise through woods into the sun. Now and then I got a glimpse of Sargent's flank to the east, an impressive hillside stand of coniferous trees. Parkman's woods started out tall, but grew shorter and shorter as the trail went up. Trees in the lee of the summit were less than eight feet tall.

Eyes on the trail, crossing through a bright patch of red and yellow leaves spread over the ground, I thought of Plato's allegory of the cave in which people sit back-to the light, seeing reality intimated by the play of shadows across dim walls in front of them. Looking up, I saw the canopy fifty feet overhead glowing with orange light. Fleeting revelation of the world of perfect forms.

Voices ahead. I was nearing the Around-Mountain Carriage Road. The trail led across open ledges with views north and west. Somesville looked like a calendar photo for October. Somes Sound was milky green, a color I associate with glacial meltwater in the Cascade Mountains of Washington. Blue Hill looked closer than usual, due to the clarity of the air. The Camden Hills stood out over Penobscot Bay. In the sky, a decrescent moon aimed like a bow toward the sun. Out in the open, I felt the wind more keenly now. Up with my hood.

Cutting through one last stand of trees, I came out on a granite ridge leading by rounded domes and terraces to the summit, where a crow lifted off, hung in the wind, then glided toward Norumbega Mountain. The scene was back-lit dramatically, bringing out smooth undulations in the rock. Most striking was the deep red color of huckleberry bushes sweeping in layers around the summit. I would not have been surprised to see an old man walking toward me bearing stone tablets, his robes trailing in the wind.

In an hour-and-forty-minutes, I reached the summit of Parkman Mountain, elevation 941 feet. The view opened onto Bald Peak, the Hadlock Ponds, the islands out to Great Duck, and the Gulf of Maine beyond. A couple with unleashed dog was coming behind me, so I hastily turned in a circle, then followed cairns leading down into the valley between Parkman Mountain and Gilmore Peak, where I would pick up the Grandgent Trail for the summit of Sargent, stopping briefly to tap my thermos of coffee while sitting on a ledge out of the wind.

The trail switchbacks easily into the valley, linking summit and saddle, separated by only a few tenths of a mile, but seeming worlds apart. One minute I was turning on a bare and windy granite knob looking over purple terraces onto ever-green slopes, the next I was in the midst of still woods standing at the base of a huge sugar maple, breathing air the color of bright leaves overhead. Two men and three boys with hiking sticks came along Sargent Brook to my left, one boy reading the trail sign, announcing with pride, "We've come 2.4 miles!"

Hiker follows the trail beneath the Giant Slide.

The Grandgent Trail (Grand Gent on the sign), shoots straight up the side of Gilmore Peak over rocks and roots. It quickly comes out on ledges giving a view onto Western Mountain between Parkman and Bald Peak. I reached the 1,036-foot peak itself in nine minutes, stopping to look at Cedar Swamp Mountain from the north, a perspective giving no hint of its long sweep to the south. Beyond Cedar Swamp, I made out Mount Desert Rock and its granite lighthouse tower standing twenty-two miles out in the Gulf of Maine.

Following cairns, it was down again, into a valley for which I had no name. The Germans say a well-loved child has many names. What of a valley that has no name at all?

And yet this is a remarkable place, walled with Northern white cedars and three kinds of maple (red, sugar, striped), with its own wetland and stream. Chickadees chanted the name they gave the place, but I couldn't make it out. Chickadee Valley I will call it, honoring both valley and its bird.

Turning north along the unmarked Grandgent Trail, I was quickly overtaken by the couple and dog I had last seen on Parkman. Asking the dog's name, I was told "Raven." If dogs can be named after birds, why not valleys? Running next to the wetland, the trail stays level, though jagged cliffs loom through cedars to the east. Then it winds up the small stream feeding the wetland, headwaters of the north branch of Hadlock Brook, the trail crossing the rocky streambed a number of times, rising in earnest.

At one stream crossing, a loose, four-foot stick caught against my left boot as I tried to swing it forward for my next step. The next thing I knew, I was falling into the trail, a sharp granite rock aiming for my face at warp speed. Thud. Grate. My tooth bit the rock. Looking into a maple leaf three inches from my nose, I saw a half-inch circle of blood begin to stream down its beautiful shape. *Venery; vagary, villainy!*—which translates roughly: I came; I saw; I fell on my face.

Sitting up, I dripped blood down the front of my blue windbreaker. Taking out first aid kit, I swabbed myself as best I could, trying to assess the damage. Blood flowed from the side and bridge of my nose, which did not hurt, so I took it to be a scrape. I went on, holding a paper towel against my nose.

I'm not clear on details of the trail out of Chickadee Valley to the summit of Sargent Mountain. Along the way I remember passing an old yellow birch that looked like I felt. I think I gave it a sympathetic pat. Within sight of the summit I met a man from the west side of the island who does trail brushing for the park. Wearing headphones, he was heading down the Grandgent Trail. He offered first aid for the "nasty smack" I had taken in the face, but I told him I had it under control. At one point in our conversation I believe he mentioned selling me his wife's car when she found a replacement. He went down, I went up. I also remember passing through tufts of yellow-green sedge growing in mucky soil, the type of plant I would never expect on the summit.

Raven and his owners were sitting next to the summit cairn with another hiker, all looking strikingly earnest. A man in shorts was dashing across the ledges, aiming his camera in every direction. I stared nobly into the distance, waiting to recover my wits. I wish I had a picture of us as a group, six characters in search of an author to script the tear-jerking episode that had brought us together.

As I left the summit along the south ridge trail, I met the two men and three boys who had started up the Grandgent Trail behind me. They had come up the Maple Spring Trail, the way I was going down. I winced at the boys' walking sticks—they looked too much like the stick that had tripped me up.

Mind slowly clearing, I noticed the weathered cedars running along the west side of the ridge, their dry, pointed leaders rising like spires of abandoned churches. At one time there must have been several rainy decades in a row, providing enough water to support them. Or perhaps the trees simply outgrew the shelter of the ridge. As I stood there, four people hiked past on their way to the summit, one in a shiny bicycling outfit. Feeling

Upper end of the rocky Grandgent Trail.

battered and shoddy myself, I turned west at the sign for Maple Spring and started down.

The trail struck across the ridge on a fairly even grade, then descended more steeply. At the change of slope, the variety of plants increased. Here was mountain ash, and a band of gnarled cedars, spruces, and a few maples. The cedars were green, but many of their leaders had died before their time. Feeling drawn to this hard-pressed yet hardy community, I sat on a rock and ate lunch.

Starting down again, I quickly came to the sign at Maple Spring, source of the south branch of Hadlock Brook. Yes, there was the spring, and there was a red maple rising out of the wet rocks below it. Then I came to a bogwalk crossing a wetland filled with sphagnum moss and waving cotton grass among the bones of dead trees. I looked for sundews and pitcher plants, but saw none.

Beyond that, a rocky promontory gave a super view of

Gilmore and Bald peaks, Parkman and Norumbega mountains, Upper and Lower Hadlock ponds. At my feet was a world on a different scale, peopled by lichens, light and dark gray, and bright green. Here was a splendid dike twelve inches wide. Near it a colony of amanitas burst through a clump of blueberry bushes, the largest cap spreading eight inches across. Deep in that microjungle, a cricket chanted its autumn song.

Well-marked by cairns, the trail traverses the slope at an easy grade, offering a stroll through attractive ledgy woods so typical of Acadia. We take pains to preserve endangered species—rightly so—but it is run-of-the-mill places like this that give our region its character, and deserve equal protection. That is what Acadia National Park is all about, protecting the common and ordinary as well as the rare and endangered. It is easy to take such landscapes for granted. Protecting them means saving them from ourselves.

Meeting man and dog, neither leashed, I reentered Chickadee Valley and came (by way of a connector since closed off) to the unmarked junction with the Grandgent Trail. My return route lay on the far side of Gilmore Peak, so up I went a second time. Looking across the valley at Parkman Mountain, I was struck by its tiered terrain. At the base a layer of orange-yellow swept up the slope toward Bald Peak. Then a sharply defined layer of conifer green. Leading to bands of deep red and gray—huckleberry ledges surrounding the summit. Heading into that view, I quickly entered the yellow world of maples and birches in the saddle between the two granite domes. It was downhill from there.

Picking up the Giant Slide Trail, I headed north next to the quiet stream, the canopy yellow above me, the ground yellow underfoot—but waiting in the wings on either side, green spruce and fir saplings taking hold as the next occupants of that site, their motto being, "Ready or not, here we come!"

The beauty of the Giant Slide Trail kept me alert for the fifty-minute hike down to the lower carriage road. Crossing the Around-Mountain Carriage Road, I saw a couple cycling by, the woman looking side-to-side, smiling at what she saw. The memory of her face is one of the beauties I took from my hike. I kept seeing goldthread along the trail, another of the smiling faces I brought back. I do not know why certain plants make me glad, but goldthread always does. Like wood sorrel, Canada May ruby, and gangly fireweed.

Past the carriage road, the trail rejoins the brook—which in the meantime has taken on a new identity. No longer the quiet, unhurried stream it was in the upper valley, it now leaps down its rocky channel making as much noise as possible. Ahead, I saw seven pools in a row, each filled with swirling foam. The valley began to pinch-in, Parkman crowding in on the west, Sargent on the east. At one point their rocky walls were no more than ten feet apart. The stream plunged down the narrow channel left to it, often washing the base of Sargent's great slanting cliffs. The trail led pool to pool, fall to fall, rocky face to rocky face—one wonder to the next.

Sliding down a five-foot rockface, I came to the upstream entrance to the tunnel beneath the Giant Slide, a great slab of granite slipped down on the Parkman side of the valley. There was no way to go but under that slanting arch. Inside, I felt I was in a gallery leading to the center of the Earth. But no, it was not as dark as that. Soft light shone on the walls, and I could see the far end reflected in water ahead. To the strange sound of nylon rubbing against granite, I crept along, soon coming out at the crossing where I had taken the turn for Parkman Mountain four hours before.

Looking up where I had seen the eagle on the way up, I saw empty blue sky—no, I saw a sharp-shinned hawk flapping and gliding into the wind, at about the same altitude the eagle had flown. Perhaps there was an overhead highway up there, winding along the slopes, making the most of air currents to keep travelers aloft. I did not see how it could be a coincidence that the only two hawks I saw all day were flying the same course.

Hunkering through the crawl hole I had ducked under on the way up, I thought that as a gate it was poorly placed. It should be at the start of the trail by St. James Church, to let hikers know what they were in for, giving them a chance to bail out if their frames were too large a caliber. Making it through a second time, I looked down the valley into those waving orange flags, and thought what a splendid trail it was at that season. Fall color and running water turned a great trail into an outstanding one. A blue jay shrieked, seconding that thought.

○

Signpost, Sargent Mountain summit.

9—AROUND JORDAN POND

From north end of Jordan Pond
To south end of Jordan Pond, and back
> Start from park headquarters on bicycle to Deer Brook by carriage road, then by Deer Brook Trail to north end of pond and by Jordan Pond West Side Trail to south end of pond
> Return by Jordan Pond East Side and Deer Brook trails, then by bicycle to park headquarters
> 3.3 miles (not counting bike ride), October 16, 1993

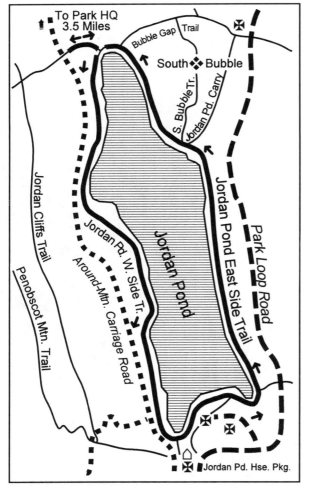

9—Around Jordan Pond.

The outstanding feature of my hike around Jordan Pond was neither scenery nor wildlife, but the people I met along the way. Next to the Cadillac summit loop, the Jordan Pond Trail must bear the heaviest foot traffic of any trail in Acadia. In one round of the pond the week after Columbus Day, I met eighty-six people, some of them twice. Traveling widdershins, I crossed paths with those going clockwise at two different points. Meeting face-to-face the second time, we recognized each other as trail companions, and stopped to compare notes, giving special flavor to the hike.

I spent most of the day on the trail. From the time I left my apartment a little after eight o'clock and returned at 5:20 p.m., it took over nine hours to make the hike. I biked by carriage road from park headquarters on McFarland Hill to Deer Brook, then took the Deer Brook Trail to the north end of the pond. It took six-and-a-half hours to round the pond, a distance of three miles—setting a new personal worst for plodding along at less than half a mile an hour. I had camera and tripod with me, and took seventy-two slides along the way.

I learned right away how hard it was to split myself in two as both hiker and photographer. It is better to be one or the other, not both at once. Since I was serious about wanting to get all the way around the pond, yet knew it was my one chance all fall to complete the watershed slide series I was working on, I adopted two ways of seeing, looking at the big picture as a hiker, and at its parts as a photographer. Using close-up lens only, mounting camera on tripod, I tricked myself into switching back-and-forth between the hiker's overview and the photographer's world of telling details. Like wearing bifocals for the first time, I eventually got the hang of it.

If people spend three-fourths of their lifelong medical expenses in the last six months before they die, the same must be true of the money we spend to keep our cars in good health. Mechanics were still performing emergency surgery on my Pinto, fighting to save it from fourteen years of rusting arteries. To get to Jordan Pond, I had to walk or bike. Strapping tripod to carrier, I biked.

Right off I ran over a squirrel. Coasting down McFarland Hill toward Eagle Lake on Route 233, I saw a red squirrel in the road ahead. I warned it to get out of the way, which it did, scampering to the far side. But another squirrel came out of the roadside bushes directly under my wheels. You know the sickening little jolt you get when you run over something in the road. I have hit pheasants, dogs, cats, and raccoons in my day, and a great many birds, toads, worms, snakes, and insects. Think what America's wildlife population would be if we did not go about culling it on wheels.

Worse than kill the squirrel, I think I only injured it. When I could stop at the base of the hill, I walked back to view the remains. There were none. It had crawled back into the bushes and was nowhere in sight. Continuing on, I kept hearing squirrels scold me from the wayside: "Shame, shame!" is what I heard them say. I could see the headline in the *Sprucenut Gazette*: "Self-styled Environmentalist Maims Mother of Five."

Other wildlife I ran into (not over) on my hike included blue jays, crows, gulls, other red squirrels, robins, juncos, sparrows, and a wren of some sort. I also heard or saw signs of crickets, pileated woodpeckers, sapsuckers, deer, snowshoe hare (a single pellet), and beavers active along the north shore of Jordan Pond.

As for trail acquaintances, two things made it easier to

stop and talk. One was, while making our respective rounds in opposite directions, meeting a second time on the opposite side of the pond. We had the day, the weather, the scenery, and the trail in common. We recognized our kinship immediately. The other was my camera. On its tripod, it made a natural conversation opener. Everyone was out for the sights, many with cameras of their own. Our visual experience joined us as trail brothers and sisters.

There was the woman with binoculars around her neck, hiking with a boy I took to be her son. A natural teacher, she pointed out this and that as they progressed. She showed him my tripod, explaining how it steadied the camera. When we met again, she told me they had hiked the South Bubble Trail that morning, and were now rounding the pond. "We'll be ready for bed tonight," she said.

When I saw two women the second time, I said, "You've come a ways today." "So have you," they said. Stopping to talk, they turned and saw the view at their backs. Taking a picture of it, they thanked me for pointing it out, which I hadn't done.

Three couples I think of in terms of men's caps. Boston Red Sox wished the sun was shining, but settled for atmosphere instead. Dartmouth, with a son in the class of '94, often came to the park in the fall, and was enjoying the mood and muted colors. We had a good chat about Acadia in wintertime. Lobster (cap covered with little red lobsters) explained that when his wife said, "The scenery was better over there," "What she's saying is, there's more color on this side of the pond." I was struck by this last couple's remarks, not because Lobster felt it necessary to translate for Mrs. Lobster, but because I thought the opposite was true.

Another man told me, "You can see that hat coming a long way off," reminding me I was wearing my blaze orange cap, the one I put on in October and wear all through hunting season. For high visibility and long life. Glad to hear that it worked.

Having come full circle, I met a young man sitting on the shore near the beaver lodge, looking over the pond. Which was he contemplating, Jordan Pond or the universe? He said he wasn't ready to work on too big a scale yet. He would work his way up.

The longest talk I had was with a couple at the north end of the pond when I was just starting out. Picking up on the rhythm of his speech, I asked if he were Canadian. "English, actually," he said. From London, his wife from Barcelona. They were staying two days, having come for the fall color.

"We don't have this over there," he said, sweeping his arm in a gesture indicating the foliage on the slopes of the Bubbles. "We've cut it all down."

He asked me to take their picture on the YCC bridge with the birches and maples behind them. What a camera he handed me—auto everything. I took three pictures at different degrees of zoom. If I had one like that, I might have taken ten rolls on my hike, not two. They were out for an all-day hike, and wanted to know where to go. We talked about trails on Sargent and Penobscot. They thought they

The watershed of Jordan Pond from the south.

would check out the Jordan Cliffs. They had knapsacks, rain gear, good boots, and a Phillips map. I figured they would do OK on the misty slopes.

The last couple I talked with, and most endearing, were young hikers coming down the Deer Brook Trail as I was coming up from the pond. They had been hiking all day, having left their car in the Bubble Rock parking area that morning. Taking the Bubble Gap Trail, then Deer Brook, they had hiked up Sargent, then taken a wrong turn and gone down the far side, so had had to retrace their steps. I have not met many people who have climbed Sargent twice the same day. They were tired and sort of spacy by the time I met them, but totally relaxed and full of their hike. It was their spirit I liked, and their eagerness to tell of their experience. She wore a super-size sweater that covered her hands and hung to her knees, he a trim jacket and cap.

We were a very moral group, those who hiked the pond that day, heeding the sign taped to trees along the trail: "Public Water Supply—No Body Contact—No Animals." Our conduct in every instance was above suspicion.

One way to capture the flavor of the hike is to tell what I took pictures of. Plants and their contribution to the soil-building process. Recycling of leaves as organic duff on the forest floor. I photographed yellow striped maple leaves. Tan cedar leaves fallen onto dark soil. Fern blades turned brown. Red bunchberry leaves. Yellow starflower leaves.

Winterberries. And pine needles floating at the edge of the pond. Too good to pass up—the trail cutting through dancing, golden woods on either side. I could not resist rock-cap ferns and rock tripe lichens on boulders around the pond. Deer Brook, the beaver lodge at the end of the pond, as well as a few views of colorful South Bubble looming through haze. I also photographed the one spider I saw, busily wrapping an insect it had snared, as seen against the background of a bright yellow maple leaf. And one ragged purple aster, like the spider, at the twilight of its career.

In *The Songlines,*[*] Bruce Chatwin tells how native Australians sing of terrain they walk through, chanting mythical histories of landforms and their origins. The land speaks to travelers, who sing of the land. I like the idea of looking at the landscape as a kind of notation. Of giving names and stories to places as echoes of the dramas they have to tell. It is a way of showing respect for the land, of accounting for natural features in terms of a walking mythology.

That is what I do when I hike the trails of Acadia—bring the landscape to life in my experience. I know little about how the land really works. What I do is give an account of what I see in terms I can understand. Personally. In a way that accords with my mythology. First I create a basic cast of characters—Water, Sunlight, Soil, Slope, Climate, Gravity, Erosion, and a few others. Who act out my view of history, with colliding tectonic plates, granite plutons bubbling up, scouring waves of glacial ice, water streaming down and down. Accounting for how things come about in the natural world. Soil, plants, and wildlife borrow my voice to tell their stories.

Opening myself to the landscape—that is my idea of hiking. If I give myself to the land—to cedars, squirrels, spiders, and rushing streams—then they share their lives with me in surprising detail. Opening myself means giving attention to my surroundings. It means looking *for*, not merely *at*. For meaning. For stories that tell how nature works. For spiritual insight and fulfillment.

Hikes are lyrical journeys through the landscape of the hiker's mythology. "Songlines" Chatwin calls them. That is what we perform as we hike. Stories of rain and snow falling on sloping ground. Earth cracking and crumbling, creating soil. Water and soil giving birth to plants. Plants nurturing wildlife. Wildlife dying back to soil. Drama of a landscape that is alive. Saga of planet Earth.

A magical trip. Even with few ups and downs. There was so much going on within ten feet of pond level, so much life and activity, I had all the excitement I would have had scal-

* Bruce Chatwin, *The Songlines.* New York: Viking Penguin, 1987.

ing one of Acadia's more glamorous peaks.

The cedars alone were worth the hike. I am susceptible to Northern white cedars. I have a thing for them. An affinity. For their leaves, their bark, branches, roots, and the company they keep. There they were, leaning out over the pond all the way around, foliage dark green set off by tan.

Frederick Goddard Tuckerman, reclusive nineteenth-century New England poet, wrote a sonnet about "Dark fens

Jordan Pond East Side Trail.

of cedar," "mosses wringing wet," and "Remnants of rain, and droppings of decay." He asked why such places so held his heart. He answered himself with a counterquestion:

Is it that in your darkness, shut from strife
The bread of tears becomes the bread of life?
Far from the roar of day, beneath your boughs
Fresh griefs beat tranquilly, and loves and vows
Grow green in your gray shadows, dearer far
Even than all lovely lights, and roses, are?

Sensitive soul. But I agree with him about the calming effect of cedars, and about their positive influence on our affections. What New Englander wouldn't?

At the base of South Bubble there is a plaque to Joseph Allen, Chairman from 1914 to 1945 of the Seal Harbor Path Committee, a "lover of rocks and high places, builder of trails," and "conserver of natural beauty." I'll bet cedar sap ran in his veins, too.

As for the fall foliage, it added a new dimension to the hike. A woman passed me as I was taking a picture, and said, "Look at that yellow!" Exactly. Look at it. It was not there yesterday. It will be gone tomorrow. Color is a dimension of experience—space, time, and color. I spent much of the day drinking it in, storing up yellow for the long, gray, two-dimensional winter months ahead.

The trail skirts the boulders at the base of Pemetic, barely touches those fallen from South Bubble, but hits the Jordan Cliffs Tumbledown full-on as it plunges into Jordan Pond. In that last section it is not an easy trail. You have to stretch your legs to get through it.

Over wet areas, bogwalks of split cedar run between log cribs filled with stones. The longest bogwalks are on the west side of the pond, with only a few on the east. The west side is the wet side, the trail passing over mucky soils much of the way. The bogwalks are a big help. The west side is also the rooty side, the trail often crossing exposed tangles of cedar roots, making for rough going.

By the bog southeast of the pond, the trail goes over a bridge of massive stone steps that must rest on a solid foundation, because they are as firm and level as the day ten years ago when they were set in place. The date 1983 is carved into one of the stones. Looking at the cedars in that bog, you can see the browse line where deer have pruned them in winter.

South Bubble from Jordan Pond East Side Trail.

Another notable bridge is that at the north end of the pond near the beaver lodge. It has log railings and a superstructure, making it look like a model of a suspension bridge. One of the Youth Conservation Corps' good works. Those young workers have improved the Jordan Pond Trail over the years, and the pleasure the trail affords is due in good part to them.

Every time I hike the Jordan Pond East and West Side trails it is different. The trick is to find out which key the trailsong is set in each time. The details will harmonize with that.

Yellow-orange witches butter on downed tree trunks was in tune with the season. A little brown bird I watched gleaning tidbits from the forest duff while I was eating lunch was certainly celebrating sparrow Thanksgiving. The sound of a leaf falling to earth was the stuff of a Zen koan, or haiku by Matsuo Basho. Bright blue Chiquita labels on two brown banana peels stashed behind a log looked like the last blooms of summer. Blue jays endlessly hawking their opinions from soapboxes back in the woods gave autumn its voice, just as whirling yellow leaves, like a chorus of houris, performed the seasonal dance. Holly berries against shiny, dark green leaves whispered of seasons to come. Birches felled by beavers building a winter food supply echoed the same message. Even a tour bus grinding along the loop road on the far side of the pond was part of the scene. Everything fit. All we hikers had to do was let the trail lead us forward as the landscape performed its ritual song and dance.

○

10—BEECH CLIFF & CANADA RIDGE LOOP

From Echo Lake parking area
To Canada Ridge, and back
   Up by Beech Cliff Ladder and Canada Ridge trails
   Down by bushwhack and old Canada Cliff Trail
                    2.0 miles, October 26, 1993

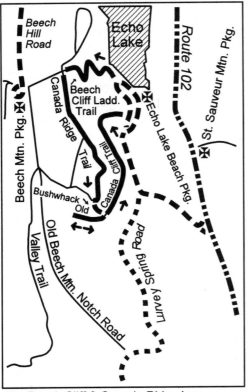

10—Beech Cliff & Canada Ridge loop.

On a clear, windless day in late October, I closed up my camp in Franklin, overturned the *Aurora B.*, my thirteen-foot peapod, stopped mourning the summer that was, and started looking to the winter ahead. My car on the road again, I had wheels, so pitched into chores I had avoided for a month. When they were done, charged with self-satisfaction, I looked for a short hike I could do in late afternoon to reward my good works. Beech Cliff Ladder Trail was just the thing.

The (roughly) two-mile loop from the south end of Echo Lake, up Beech Cliff, along Canada Ridge, and back through Canada Hollow to the parking lot took three hours and twenty minutes. Between lake and ridge, the rise is about 500 vertical feet. The ascent is steep in places, but four ladders (totaling 57 rungs) make it easy. When I got back to my car, I thought I had never had a better hike.

Always on the lookout for wildlife, I saw or heard signs of red squirrels, deer, fox, blue jays, chickadees, and pileated woodpeckers. I met a fly and a gray moth sunning themselves on the ridge. On the way down into Canada Hollow,

I passed two piles of deer pellets, and at the base of Canada Cliff, a single fox scat (midnight blue). Ten feet from the scat, I stepped over a scattering of small feathers where a hawk had eaten lunch.

But wildlife was not the story of this particular hike. Plants were more the issue. By the lake, I started out crunching dry leaves fallen in beech woods, in places six inches deep. Like wading through giant corn flakes in a dream. Higher up the ridge, my route was spread with evergreen needles. The trees themselves often grew to remarkable size. I passed under giant Northern white cedars, white pines, hemlocks, and on top of Canada Ridge, one of the largest pitch pines I had ever seen.

Evergreen ferns gleamed along the way. With overhead limbs bare, they were less overshadowed. Rock-cap, Christmas, and different wood ferns shone on and under the cliffs, festive as bunting on St. Patrick's Day. But that is too airy an image. Ferns sprout from soil. They speak of matters underground. Making do with scant sunlight, they spread from below, rising into dim light bearing good news. Where ferns are, life finds solid support.

Why do ferns affect me so? Their language speaks to me directly. I understand, but I do not know how. I was born understanding them. Is that possible? To feel kinship with marginal wood ferns? Think how long people have lived in the company of ferns—say two million years. It makes sense that we have a gut feeling for such long-standing neighbors. Why else are we drawn to flowers, birds, and butterflies? It is no accident we find them attractive. "Stick by us and you will be OK," is what they tell us, "this is a good place to be." That is beauty's message. A promise of future well-being. Hope for a better life. That, I think, is the whispered secret of ferns.

Besides trees and ferns, other plants that spoke to me include juniper, black huckleberry (its berries may be black, but its leaves are scarlet this time of year), and evergreen lambkill on the ridge and upper cliffs; pink blossoms of herb Robert blooming along the trail in defiance of recent frosts; and mayflower in the woods (leaves, not blossoms), harking not so much back six months as six months ahead.

As for people, I saw but one: a fellow hiker who started ahead of me, going by while I was still in the parking lot. I did not see him again. There was no car in the lot besides mine. Lots of traffic on Route 102, but the collective hum was impersonal, like the wind.

The trail itself is outstanding. Almost too good to be true. What a feat it was to build it, what a dream to even conceive! Yet there it was, taking me across talus slopes to a wall of rock, along the foot of the wall—then up the wall itself via a cleft heading into the sky. The Precipice Trail on Champlain is justly famous, and the Perpendicular Trail on Mansell. But the Beech Cliff Ladder Trail is in the same class. The site is perfect, and the trail lives up to the site. It is shorter than the other two, but packs a wallop the whole way. Length is not the issue; quality tells.

In brief, the Beech Cliff Ladder Trail leads from Echo Lake to the top of the ridge just east of Beech Mountain by way of the gap between Beech Cliff on the north and Canada Cliff on the south. It starts from the parking lot above Echo Lake Beach, elevation 84 feet, and rises roughly 500 feet above that. It is labeled a strenuous hike, but taking its length into account, and its solid construction, I call it easy. It ascends by gentle switchbacks to the cliff, levels off, then shoots up by ladders so quickly you are on top before you have a chance to exert yourself.

With the leaves down, standing in the parking area I could see Beech Cliff through bare branches. Scarlet huckleberry tinted the upper slopes, contrasting with juniper and cedar—a handsome sight. Bright sun raked the cliff, heightening the dramatic effect. The trail starts out as a paved sidewalk, but quickly gets down to business as granite boulders take over the treadway. Valley beeches make way for conifers and ferns on either hand. Crossing into the shadow of the cliff itself, I felt a chill in the air, and was glad to be wearing coat, hat, and gloves.

Zig-zagging up the foot of the slope, the trail crosses several flowing rivers of talus on well-laid steps. Looking up one such rocky flow midstream,

Steve Perrin on the Beech Cliff Ladder Trail.

I wondered what kept the boulders from tumbling. Unseen, gravity jams their edges together, locking them in place. On a different scale, tiny pink blossoms of herb Robert poked between the rocks, their soft colors beaming against gray lichens. I saw one stunted sprig of goldenrod springing from the talus.

The trail quickly reaches the base of a ten-foot cliff, then offers a choice: **SUMMIT** or **OVERLOOK**. (Subsequently, the overlook has been closed off in summer to protect a pair of peregrine falcons that has established a nest on the cliff.) Opting for both—in turn—I first explored the overlook, admiring the cribwork giving onto a granite ledge with a view. Below, the wooded shore of Echo Lake looked largely wild and undeveloped except for the AMC camp nestled among the trees. Acadia and St. Sauveur mountains rose across the lake, evergreen slopes contrasting with the dusty

orange of the beeches in Canada Hollow behind Echo Lake Beach. "Good spot for a cup of coffee," I said to the air, taking out my thermos.

From there to the ridge, the cribwork and supporting walls get more impressive. I would not have been there at all if someone had not paved the way. A whole crew of someones, the CCC workers who built the trail some sixty years ago. What a wonder that project was, spending federal funds on hiking trails, not ballistic missiles! Congress would scoff at such a thing now.

Crossing a steep talus slope, the trail doubles back on a curved stairway of megasteps with railings made from curved logs, Christmas fern on either hand. Running along a wall of rock, the trail leads under an overhanging birch, then on to more steps and more railings resting on more-solid but unobtrusive underpinnings, and beyond that, to ladder number one.

The ladder, a ten-runger, takes you to the base of a forty-foot cliff, the *pièce de résistance* of that stretch of the hike. There are cliffs, and then there are Cliffs with a capital C. This one, dripping with water, reminded me of standing on a dock next to the hull of a huge freighter. It was that big, and I was that small. Looking to the top, I saw a cedar hanging down like a chandelier, and on its gracefully bowed branches, like a dozen dripping candles— icicles.

The trail follows the base of the rock wall, treading the wooded ledge between a row of cedars guarding the plunge to the right and an unbroken sheet of lichens on the left. Lichen wallpaper.

The cliff seems to go, and go, and go. In places it must be fifty feet high. Here is one of those special sites you recognize right away as being beyond the run of everyday experience. You catch your breath out of respect for its still magnificence, as in a great cathedral. A row of bunchberry dogwood at the base of the wall, leaves edged with purple, was the seasonal altar flower. The trail had spiritual overtones, which grew on me as I went along.

Crossing a short stretch of dike, the trail leads to an eighteen-rung iron ladder leaning against the cliff itself, taking you up to a cleft giving access, by way of two more ladders, to the top of the ridge. Midway up the first ladder, I had a flash of climbing up to a haymow as a kid. The feeling was friendly and familiar, with a fringe of excitement. I also glimpsed the scene when the trailmakers decided to take the trail through that eroded gully to the top—one of the great moments in Acadia's history.

What a place! What a trail! Stone steps scale the cleft between poured concrete landings, with steel-cable rails held taut by turnbuckles at either end, the cable supported on iron posts, with ladders rising between landings, first a fourteen-runger, then another of fifteen. I was excited, but not threatened. Before I knew it I was standing on the lip of the cliff, solid granite underfoot, admiring the view out to Greening and Great Cranberry islands, down on Echo Lake, across to Acadia and St. Sauveur mountains. Turning, I saw the fire tower on Beech Mountain through the trees. My lone car in the lot at the base of the cliff tied me to life in another world.

I decided to stay in that spot until I saw a fellow Earthling of one kind or another. A game I sometimes play, stepping out of the role of actor to become a member of the audience. Animals do that all the time, shifting between two modes of awareness, tuning into their surroundings by sniffing, listening, and peering around, then moving on, bent more on covering ground than dis-covering it. With us, once we are on the move, it is hard to stop. We get stuck in the traveling lane.

It was warm in the sun. In three minutes I heard a red squirrel chatter back in the woods, but that did not count. I wanted to *see* one of my neighbors. In the meantime I took out my Phillips map to look for a way down. I planned to head along Canada Ridge, then find a trail into the hollow farther on. The map did not show one. If I were a trail blazer, I would run one down the south slope of Canada Ridge. I had a hunch I would find one.

From my perch, I had no sense of the fall foliage that had dominated the woods in recent weeks. Oak leaves were dark brown, beech leaves more brown than yellow. The green of spruce and cedar ruled the slopes. The herds of leaf peepers had headed for home. It was hard to recall what the fuss had been all about.

Thinking back to the morning when I had closed my camp, I recalled seeing harbor seals, nuthatches, chickadees, blue jays, a swarm of crows, some kind of duck, three eagles, and a great many signs of otter. I had been rowing, and twice passed within 200 feet of an eagle on top of its spruce.

The cry of a jay brought me back to the present, in time to see a chickadee lilt from one spruce to another. Released from self-imposed bondage, I picked up the Canada Ridge Trail, which leads south along the top of the cliff on a tread-

way alternating between fallen needles and lichen-covered granite. I looked for deer prints in sandy and muddy patches, but saw only the treadmarks of hiking boots.

Passing close to a young spruce, I probed for insects among needles on its leader. What I found surprised me— buds set for spring. Here I was clinging to fall, while trees were looking six months ahead. Plans for next year were already off the drawing board. Curiosity raised, I peered

Black huckleberry leaves, Canada Ridge Trail.

closely into a huckleberry bush—and found the same thing. Red buds all along the stems. May would not witness the creation of new growth, but its release. The secret behind miracles is laying the groundwork. They themselves unfold as a matter of course.

Coming to a signpost, I was directed to Beech Mountain parking area by three different routes, but was more interested in the fly crawling up the post. How had it survived recent frosts? Nestled in some blueberry thicket, I guessed. While gazing at the fly, I saw a gray moth rise out of my shadow along the ledge and fly into the light. Eclipsing the sun, I had chilled it. There is something poignant about hangers-on after summer has fled. My heart warms to crickets in October, robins in December. Even to fly and moth clinging past their appointed hour.

Shunning the parking lot, I took the lower trail at the signpost, entering a more wooded section lined with blazing huckleberry bushes alternating with evergreen sheep laurel. The way grew rootier, with black soil and pine needles filling spaces between roots. A generic, typically Acadian trail, which I do not mean as a slur. The story of Everyman deserves to be told periodically, Everytrail to be hiked now and then. Fussing over the rare and special, we run the risk of taking the ordinary for granted—while it is the ordinary that fixes our character. The Canada Ridge Trail is the backbone of Acadia.

Catching glimpses of the ocean from time to time, I saw Mt. Desert Rock over Great Duck Island, looking not like a ship on the horizon as it sometimes does, but like an island in its own right. Baker Island Light was a white dot above the evergreens. Bear Island Light was hidden behind the headlands of Northeast Harbor. As for sails, I saw but one, like fly and moth, on borrowed time.

Near the south end of the ridge, I came to a pitch pine twenty inches in diameter. Standing head and shoulders above its neighbors, its twining branches were covered with yellow needles sprinkling highlights among tufts of green. Each branch was curved to a similar pattern, creating fugal echoes within the whole like elaborate gothic or baroque tracery. Shaped by gravity, sunlight, and wind, a masterpiece of Acadian architecture.

I ate a late lunch at the southern limit of the ridge trail where it bears toward Beech Mountain, the spot I thought I would find some sort of track continuing down ridge to Canada Hollow. Among junipers and lichens on a ledge warmed by the sun, I sat near a fallen white pine still fed by a few gnarled roots—a Stephen Hawking tree which refused to give up. Looking into the tops of trees further down the slope, I watched a red squirrel run up a spruce, thrash about in its branches, then run down again, all with great urgency.

My thoughts ran to communion and spirituality. Breaking bread in the presence of jays and squirrels, I scattered a few crumbs on the ground. I felt a strong connection with that place, by ties running to me and away. Sharing was the theme of the moment, being there with neighbors in peace.

Was there a trail leading down from the ridge? Hadn't I seen a line on one of my maps? If so, I couldn't find it on the ground. Maybe I dreamed it, or just made it up because I wanted it to be there. It did not make any difference whether I had seen it or not. Maps are mythological. The question was, could I find a way across the land itself?

I went back over the ridge trail to see if I had missed a promising turning point. After exploring a couple that did not pan out, I went past where I had eaten to see if such a turning lay beyond, but did not find one. All right, then, I would try my hunch that such a trail would follow the southern end of the ridge. A faint track led through blueberry bushes, maybe that was it. I did not care who made it, wildlife or the CCC. I would follow its lead. The way was steep, but I knew it could not be very long.

Immediately I came to a mound of deer pellets under a large spruce, signature of the trail blazer him- or herself. Then a patch of mayflower leaves. Like Janus, god of doorways, they looked two ways, to past and future both.

Switchbacking down the slope, I followed the lay of the land, not footsteps of a preceding generation of hikers. I was in fairly open woods, the descent broken here and there by minor cliffs and fallen trees. It was easy going, my strategy being to follow the line of least resistance. Trail or no trail, it made no difference. I steered by gravity, tactfully overriding its orders here and there. Halfway down the slope I stopped to survey my surroundings. I was among

Christmas fern with bladelets shaped like Christmas stockings.

friends: cedars, spruces, pines, and hemlocks, with seedlings and fallen branches scattered beneath them. Looking to my right, I saw what looked like a short flight of stone steps rising along the slope in the distance. That is what I get from hiking in Acadia—I imagine steps everywhere.

I checked them out anyway. Walking over, I found myself on a trail traversing the slope at right angles to the course I had been following. They were steps indeed, almost covered by needles and duff. Then I remembered what I had seen on the mystery map: the ridge trail rounded the south end of the ridge, came to a small brook, followed it down a ways, then turned east again and came across the slope—just about here. Not just about—exactly. I had been wrong, but I had been almost right.

To make sure, I followed the faint track west, past another pile of deer pellets, toward Beech Mountain, to see if I would come to the brook. Which I did, the trail turning north along the west bank. That clinched it. All I had to do was follow it the other way, down to Lurvey Spring Road, Canada Hollow, and the Echo Lake parking area.

The trees along the trail had been blazed with an ax years ago, many bearing deep scars now almost buried under crowding bark. How long would it take trees to put on two inches of new bark? At a sixteenth of an inch a year, about thirty-two years. The trail had been abandoned—but not by everyone. Here and there stood a small cairn marking the way. Someone was set on keeping this trail open. Making a loop for ladder trail hikers to take getting back.

Not much of a trail, it kept petering out. Finally I lost it. Looking ahead, I saw what looked like a cairn in the distance, so steered for that. I came to three uprooted spruces and, leading directly down from their bases—a staircase of cut granite, each step covered with liverwort too handsome to step on. Like the Homans Trail at Sieur de Monts, this trail is a museum piece, a relic of labor no longer remembered. I walked next to it, not wanting to mar the soft green of the treadway as nature had refurbished it.

Angling through increasingly dense talus back toward Canada Cliff, the trail wound through boulders supporting gardens of rock-cap ferns, bunches of wood ferns sprouting between them. It followed every turning of the cliff, taking on an entirely new character. At one time it had been as much a feat of engineering as any trail in the park. Steps locked in place with coping stones, it rose and fell with the terrain, dogging the cliff the whole way, sticking close to its heels beneath sheltering hemlocks and cedars. The Canada Cliff Trail, the Talus Trail, the Wood Fern Trail—by whatever name, one of the wonders of bygone Acadia.

Coming across this magical place, picking up the scent of an abandoned dream, I found this part of my hike most stirring of all. It is one thing to find the ladder trail in sound working order, but stumbling across the bones of a trail I never knew existed was like finding the jaws of a tyrannosaur gaping from the walls of a cave. Here I was almost back where I started, just reaching the high point of my day. Coming across an intact run of twenty-four steps plunging down a cleft, I felt I had found the lost entrance to Shangri-la in back of the woodshed.

I found not only a place, but a lost part of myself. I have never written the word "atavistic," but I will use it now. In the sense of recovery of a long-dormant trait. What hit me was how much I belonged at the bases of cliffs. Here was water. Here was growth. Here was health. Here was awe. Here was a profound sense of home. Total and unabashed spiritual union was what I felt. I was a cliff dweller. My people have been living in houses for generations, and I have kept alive a longing for cliffs. Others must have found the same longing among their own baggage. Why else would we build tenements and skyscrapers, places that by rational criteria are unsuited to human pursuits? The World Trade Center is no mere economical use of limited space: it is a harking back to our roots. We are at home in such places. If we cannot find them, we build them.

I was back at the parking area, having come a long way in a little over three hours.

Base of Canada Cliff.

11—MANSELL MOUNTAIN LOOP

From Long Pond parking area (pumping station)
To Mansell Mountain (not quite the summit),
    and back
Up by Cold Brook and Razorback trails
Down by Mansell Mountain and Cold Brook trails
              3.0 miles, November 2, 1993

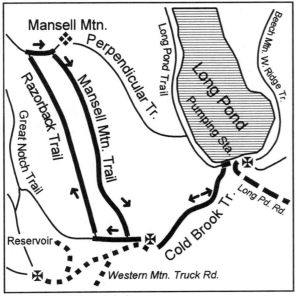

11—Mansell Mountain loop.

For a straightforward hike up one ridge and down another, through woods most of the way, with outstanding views in two directions, I recommend the Razorback and Mansell Mountain trails. You can drive to the trailhead on the Western Mountain Truck Road off Seal Cove Road in Southwest Harbor, or you can walk as I did along the Cold Brook Trail from the pumping station at the south end of Long Pond. From there, the loop is a little less than three miles long. It took me exactly four hours at a leisurely pace, including a half-hour lunch. Being unemployed, my job having ended in October, I decided to employ myself on the lee slope of Western Mountain to see what I could see on a cold, windy day in early November.

The box score for wildlife was not impressive. Robin and hairy woodpecker actually seen. Red squirrels, crows, chickadees, and red-breasted nuthatches heard, along with three unidentified somebirds. Feathers of a grouse (perhaps eaten by a hawk) found. One fox scat (berries, feathers, bones), and one mystery scat found near the grouse. Why a mystery? Looking fairly fresh, the tan scat lay at the bottom of a hole two inches across and three inches deep dug in a spread of moss near the upper end of the Razorback Trail. My guess was skunk. Skunks dig holes. It was the right size for skunk, about half an inch thick, in three pieces. There was no skunky smell to it, but it had rained hard the day

before. Mystery scat, the kind a passing mystery leaves behind.

For plants, the whole route was through woods, both old growth and new. I noticed a few striped maple stems, but having had its two weeks of glory, that tree barely caught my eye. The only fern I saw was bracken, a shabby-looking crew largely brown, bent, and broken. I did notice club mosses in two spots, one group bearing thin upright cones like miniature candles.

And stepping over a tangle of roots in the Cold Brook Trail, at one point I went beyond my usual wish (that they were better protected by soil) to taking them at face value. There they were, roots. Uncovered. Exposed. Laid bare. Their message? Aside from, "don't tread on me," they told me roots are back of everything or, more accurately, under. If you want a root metaphor for causation, take roots. Basis not only of most of the plant kingdom, but of the plant-eater kingdom as well. Including the whole of human civilization. What is a hike but a trek back to basics? A route back to roots? Roots set my mind working, preparing the ground for thoughts later on.

As for people, I saw none. Not even tracks of lug soles, the rain having washed them away. There was one cluster of pistachio nut hulls in the trail, and one cigarette butt, but that was it for people spoor.

What did stand out were streams draining yesterday's rain from the slopes. And views to the south, east, and west. Much of the way down the Mansell Mountain Trail, I headed toward Bass Harbor and the islands south of MDI. The angle of view is different from that on mountains east of Somes Sound. It offers a fresh perspective to hikers more used to views from Penobscot, Pemetic, Cadillac, or Dorr. The islands take on new shapes and align themselves in novel ways.

Near the top of the same trail there is an outlook onto a great many mountains to the east: Beech, St. Sauveur, Norumbega, and between Sargent and Penobscot, the dome of Cadillac in the distance. From the same spot you can also get a new fix on the near islands: Greening, Bear, Sutton, Great and Little Cranberry, Baker.

But the view of views is from the Razorback Trail looking across Great Notch to the old-growth forest on the slopes of Bernard Mountain to the west. The ranks of evergreens are so close you feel you are a bird flying over them. I chose this hike to stay out of winds blowing twenty to thirty miles an hour, but the ridgeline took it full force and sent up a moan that filled the notch. Here are woods the way they are meant to be. Not a so-called "working forest" as a crop to be pulped into coated stock or toilet paper, but a forest employed in its own pursuits, as I was employed in mine. Self-determination. We once fought a war over that very issue.

Water is life's blood to a forest. Trees have a proprietary interest in its flow. What are they but highflying green plants anchored to the soil by two sets of tubes? Their arteries and veins. Bearing mostly water, a pinch of minerals in one batch, sugar in the other. Being low to the ground, mosses and lichens get by without tubes because they get what they need through their skins. But trees are more aggressive in climbing into the sunlight. The price they pay is having to hoist a hundred gallons of water a day to buds and leaves. Over a million gallons of water a year fall on every acre of ground on Mount Desert Island. On Western Mountain many of those gallons flow upward through the stems of tall trees, helping them make the food they need, then evaporating into the air from which they fell.

Yesterday it rained all day. The soil was saturated. Trees had all the water their tubes could hold (if they were not already shut off for the season). In two places along my route runoff was channeled into small streams. I am drawn to running water as I am to the bases of cliffs. Streams excite me. Like a beaver, I am alert to their soft gurgling sound through the woods. I love the glint of sunlight on rills and pools. It is built-in, as basic as an eye for flowers, birds, and wildlife. As a kid I spent hours getting soaked in damp valleys and woods. Name one human settlement not founded on the banks of a river, lake, or spring (or over an aquifer, an underground lake). Take London, a city founded millennia ago on the banks of the River Fleete where it flowed into tidal water. Where is the Fleete today? Commemorated in Fleet Street, of course, beneath which it still flows as a sewer. Tamed to the pipe. Flushing its daily load of waste into the Thames.

The streams I met were fresh from the woods. They were beautiful, with an allure I could not resist. Natural beauty means goodness. That is why it attracts us, so we can share in nature's health and well-being.

Streams speak to my blood, sweat, tears, urine, bile, lymph, my spit and my love juice, to the fluid that bathes my brain, to mother's milk and amniotic fluid. It is no accident water has such a hold on us. We are mostly water ourselves. Counting atoms, more than eighty-eight percent of ours flow from water by different routes. Is there such thing as water magnetism? That is what dowsers pick up. We are drawn to our fluid forebears and kin.

Looking for water is high on my hiking agenda. When I find it I come alive. Water and life go together. Recent floods in the Mississippi Valley had a dire effect on people who claimed the land as their own. But the rivers were doing what rivers do, bringing life to their banks. Silt and water are the food of roots, the makings of our daily bread. In the long run, it is best to let rivers do their thing.

What were the streams on Mansell doing? Flowing from the slopes by the steepest, most direct route. Following the dictate of gravity. Bearing excess water into the valleys. And with that water, particles picked up along the way—minerals, ions, organic molecules. Food for plants, insects, fish, and microbes too small to see. Food for life lower down. Life in the stream. On its banks. In woods, fields, and marshes. To the Gulf of Maine and beyond. Streams are water distributors, sharing one region's excess with an-

Steve Perrin reflecting on roots.

other's dearth. Bearing food for roots. Food for fundamental thoughts.

Aside from Cold Brook emptying into Long Pond, the first stream I came to was the Cold Brook Trail itself between pumping station and trailhead on the Western Mountain Truck Road. A stream by default. Water bars were doing their job draining runoff to the side, but they were overwhelmed. The trail was a series of trickling pools. Stepping along its edges, I helped it develop middle-age spread. It led through mixed woods of birch, poplar, and spruce. Trees on the comeback after being heavily cut some fifty years ago.

The first real stream was a branch of Marshall Brook at the start of the Razorback Trail. Your basic babbling brook splashing over cobbles and boulders on its way to Bass Harbor Marsh. Less than two feet wide, at this point it was more an incipient stream. I stopped to pay my respects.

Another small stream near the top of the Razorback Trail was one of the highlights of the hike. It ran across an exposed granite slope by a rapid series of zigs and zags in a channel so subtle I had trouble figuring why it took the course it did. That it was a set course and not a random meander was told by the thirsty black moss clinging to rocks where it flowed. In one place this upper stream blocked the trail. I detoured, gaining a view higher up. It made seven abrupt turns in falling thirty feet toward Great Notch. The sight of those winding waters filled me with joy. They were not as splashy as Hadlock or Chasm Brook falls, but they were just as amazing. I was hooked by that crooked downhill rush. As if the water enjoyed its snaky plunge, rousing kindred feelings in me. The stream drains the lesser notch west of Mansell's summit, feeding many Northern white cedars along its boisterous cascade.

The hike ran basically up one ridge and down the next one to the east. The Razorback Trail does not run on the wooded crest of its ridge so much as along its western slope. That makes for tricky footing in places where the trail is wet or treads across lichens. It is one thing to head into a slope, another to traverse it at an angle—which the Razorback does. Offering views over Great Notch, but demanding concentration at every step, it is no trail to take when there is ice on the mountain. Why "razorback"? Its upper end meets a sharp ridge giving a razorback impression, perhaps that is the reason. When dry it is by no means the rugged trail its name suggests.

Where the Razorback Trail levels off overlooking Great Notch, I drank a cup of coffee while taking in the view. And mused about root metaphors, those spontaneous, intuitive, and ineffable images propping up our most basic truths. Beyond them, the way is blocked; we cannot explain them. They just are. The Big Bang is one, that cosmic firecracker. Black holes sucking matter into insatiable maws. Scales of justice. Rights of man. Heavenly paradise. All-knowing Creator. They speak of things the way we want them to be, not necessarily the way they are. The sun's never setting on the British Empire was an idea in the human mind, a metaphor, not a fixed truth.

From my granite seat, looking upon the green slopes of Western Mountain, I recognized Maine as it generally used to look. I needed no proof. That is how root metaphors work. As a kind of intuitive shorthand for ineffable truths. To me on that day, in that place, under that sky, having hiked that trail under those conditions—those woods commanded my experience. Such is the power of root metaphors: to seize reality, shape it, and defend it to the end.

The down-leg of the loop along the Mansell Mountain Trail follows a route similar to the up-leg along the Razorback, with the views I have mentioned. But no streams. Another rocky ridge trail, it offers much the same experience as the Razorback, with surer footing, but no glimpses of the woods on Bernard. And no pesky root metaphors.

Stopping at one stony outlook to eat lunch, I sat facing south on a lichen-covered ledge next to a tawny juniper spilling out of a crack filled with reindeer lichens, blueberry bushes, cinquefoil, and a handsome red spruce. The ledge was dry in spite of recent rains. I saw no water anywhere. Surely it was held in that crack. How clever of those plants to grow in the one place water would not run off or evaporate. No, hardly clever. They had little chance anywhere else. They grew where they did because the site stored moisture, letting them hold out between rains. The soil around their roots held water, meting it out over time.

Wine-leaf cinquefoil.

Enabling that hardy crew to endure.

Endurance. What does it mean? Related to duration. Durable. Durance. During. It has to do with lasting for a length of time, not just an instant. With overtones of hardiness rubbed off from duress (which springs from a different root), connoting firmness and steadfastness. Endurance—that is what life requires. The ability to smooth out the wrinkles in our destiny. To span times of scarcity between times of plenty. To carry on between rains. To winter over. To store up supplies. To have strength in reserve. To make it through, no matter what comes.

Endurance. What a powerful word! The plants next to me had it. The right stuff. The wrong stuff makes you vulnerable, dependent on things going your way. Which they may do for a while, but that is sure to change. Grit. Fiber. Backbone. Guts. Depth. Reserves. The strength to spread resources over time. To hold out till things get better (which may take months, years, decades).

I had no idea what it was or how you come by it, but I was sure of one thing. Endurance is necessary to life. Without it you get swept away by the tides of fate. The unstoppable flux of circumstances. Endurance is a sign of character. Character reflects the circumstances we are born to, no matter how adverse. Without character and endurance, unless we live in a hothouse, we wither and die.

Having mulled that line of thought, and eaten my

sandwich, I took one last slug of decaf, and went on. Like the Razorback Trail, the Mansell Mountain Trail winds along a partly wooded granite slope, falling abruptly through spruce woods, then easing off in mixed woods on lesser slopes at the base of the mountain. At one point I stepped over a dike twelve inches wide, which did not look much like a dike because it was light, not dark, more like fine-grained granite than basalt. But it fractured differently, breaking off in angular chunks in a band across the trail, which is how I noticed it.

The trail ends up much like a streambed of smooth rocks. Footing again becomes an issue. Looking down, I saw oak leaves on the ground, the first I had seen. Then bigtooth aspen. Most of the loop is in the company of coniferous trees. Spruce, cedar, pine.

Almost down to the truck road, I heard a red squirrel churring in the distance, then an insistent chirping in front of me. Ahead, on a stub of a branch at eye level, a robin was carrying on, bobbing its tail, flurrying its wings in urgent little gestures, calling all the while. Though it looked full-grown, I took it to be an immature bird soliciting the care of its mother. What in humans we would call an adolescent. I waited to see if mom would respond with a beakful of grubs, but after five minutes went on, driving the robin ahead of me until it sailed into the woods, still pleading.

I have told more how the hike affected me than described the trail itself. That is what experience is like, always filtered through personal interests and concerns. Through our characters. Mine gives a green tint to everything, and is susceptible to quietness, streams, damp soils, and cliffs. Of the trail, what have I left out?

On the pumping station at Long Pond there is a sign, **DANGER CHLORINE**. We add chlorine to our drinking water, then warn against it.

On the edge of the Cold Brook Trail I passed a granite boundary marker, which seemed out of place in the thick of the woods. Every square inch of Maine is owned by somebody. Every bog, swamp, and mountain cliff. There's a deed to prove it. A piece of paper granting title to habitats humans did not create and cannot replace.

Ground pine or tree club moss.

The hairy woodpecker I saw near the marker was digging into a popple snag, tearing out its stuffing with great gusto.

The two ridge trails are roughly a mile long. The link between them at the top and the trail to Long Pond at the bottom add another mile, making a three-mile loop.

Looking up through occasional gaps in the spruce canopy, I saw ragged patches of blue sky, reminding me of a blue shirt showing through worn elbows of a dark sweater.

I take notes on a pad as I go along, though often I cannot read them later when I write up the hike. Till now I have used ballpoint pens, but the three I had along this time did not work. They scored the pad, but did not make a readable mark. Perhaps it was too cold. I remember when ballpoints first came out they were billed as being able to write under water. That claim struck me as strange even then. What I needed was a pencil. I finally dug one out of an inner pocket. Bright red, it was printed **LIZ DOMINICK DESIGNS** in bold white letters. Good for Liz Dominick, she saved the day. The stub gave her address on 6th Avenue in New York.

At one time the Razorback Trail boasted a series of granite steps leading up to its ridge, but they have largely collapsed. Neither of the trails on this part of Mansell are designer trails like the Perpendicular Trail to the east, which bears most Western Mountain traffic. My guess is the steps gave way more to natural erosion than heavy use.

A few metal bird silhouettes mark the trail in places, along with diamonds and painted blazes. I'm always glad to see one of the few remaining birds, an endangered species because they do not reproduce the way they did. Once panted red, they used to be cardinals; now they are bluebirds.

The northwest wind whitened the swells bearing down on Placentia Island. I was surprised to see such a detail at five miles' distance. The same wind coming off Long Pond fairly blew me into the woods at the start of the Cold Brook Trail, and did its best to keep me there when I came out four hours later. It raised massive windrows of pine needles along the south shore of the pond.

A few scarlet huckleberry leaves hung on, but most had

fallen. Sheep laurel leaves were folded along their stems, reminding me of helicopter blades stowed against the wind (an image creeping back from Army days).

Finally, a word about the wooded gap the trail runs through on the western side of Mansell Mountain. Great Notch between Bernard and Mansell is the famous one, followed by Little Notch between Bernard and Knight Nubble. I do not have a name for this lesser one down from the summit of Mansell. Turning east at the upper end of the Razorback Trail, you dip into it immediately. Filled with a stand of spruce, stems like poles raising the canopy high overhead, the gap is a magical place, simultaneously serene and dramatic. The winding stream I crossed on the way up drains what little water it releases to the outer world. Shaped like a saddle, the terrain slopes up east and west, down north and south. There are many such places between the ridges of Acadia. This one is more wooded than most. And like many of Acadia's miniature watersheds, more condensed. Not larger than life, but smaller. Sharpening the experience. Heightening it. Making it more intense.

Bird silhouette trail marker.

○

12—BERNARD MOUNTAIN LOOP

From Long Pond parking area (pumping station)
To Bernard Mountain summit, and back
  Up by Cold Brook, Sluiceway, and old Spring
    trails; and bushwhack
Down by Western Mountain Ridge, Great Notch,
  and Cold Brook trails

4.0 miles, November 8, 1993

Some trails bear names making them sound challenging or exciting: the Perpendicular, Precipice, and Giant Slide trails, for instance. Unlike, say, the Gorge or Beehive trails, which offer equally good hikes, but sound less inviting.

I had long been drawn to the Sluiceway Trail on Western Mountain because of its name. I pictured a mountain stream plunging down a rocky fissure. But what I recalled from the last time I hiked it was a carpet of blossoming wood sorrel spread across the valley leading to Little Notch. I had no memory of water at all. That hike had been in July. Here it was wet November, month of heaviest rain. Time for another go at the Sluiceway Trail.

But the real reason I chose this particular trail was because it cuts across the old-growth spruce woods I had seen last week from the Razorback Trail. Having admired that evergreen slope from a distance, I wanted to walk among its trees. My plan was to start again from Long Pond, walk the Cold Brook Trail to the Sluiceway trailhead in Mill Field, hike up to Little Notch on Bernard Mountain, then over Knight Nubble to Great Notch, and return by the Great Notch Trail, making a four-mile loop in all. That would give me a good taste of those woods.

That was the plan. And it almost worked out. But along the way I developed a serious case of *déjà vu* which led me astray. Stopping to study the woods halfway up the Sluiceway Trail, I saw a flight of stone steps leading away from the trail on the far side of a small stream—and remembered seeing them before, wanting to discover where they led, but sticking to the marked trail and hiking on to discover the spread of wood sorrel in Little Notch. Those steps led up the Spring Trail, which still existed on the ground, but was no longer shown on most maps. For over three years I had secretly regretted not accepting their invitation.

Here was a second chance. On the spot I changed my plans. I would see where they went. So much for Little Notch. If I got there, fine. If not, also fine. I was out to explore the woods, not reach a fixed destination. As it turned out I did get to Little Notch, but by a detour on which I lost the faint track I was following and had to guide myself by the simple principle of heading upslope, knowing I would strike the Western Mountain Ridge Trail at some point. I was not lost, just mislaid for a bit. Wandering around, I got more than my fill of the woods.

To start at the beginning, it was a beautiful fall day—clear, calm, and cold. Cold for November, not February. After a good frost, the temperature had risen to the mid-thirties by the time I set out from the Long Pond pumping station at nine o'clock. Right off I noticed three-inch icicles hanging from a branch over Cold Brook. Then a patch of ice crystals in the trail, oozing two inches out of the soil, bending like glistening question marks. They reminded me of old-fashioned Christmas candy. A more modern image would be bundles of fiber optics. I saw lots more ice during the hike, usually dangling from moss overhanging damp cliffs. Some icicles were fifteen inches long. Pools of water in the trail higher up were skimmed with ice, and in spots runoff had frozen on ledges, making for slippery going.

With leaves off the trees, the lower deciduous woods were flooded with sunlight. Even the evergreen woods higher up were flecked by slanting rays. Eating lunch in Great Notch, I was entertained by fleet patterns of light striking trees, fallen needles, and cliffs on the facing slope. Sitting in shadow, I felt I was watching a light show, the technicians experimenting, never quite getting the effect they were after. Not being fussy, I liked them all.

With the woods more open, groundcover came into its own. Wintergreen leapt out at me wherever I went, its green leaves seeming more potent than usual, the few berries gleaming bright red. Goldthread leaves, too, normally inconspicuous, caught my eye. As did kinnikinnick in places. And mountain cranberry. Most cliffs, boulders, and roots in the ancient parts of the woods were draped with a glowing mantle of liverwort. In the notches, evergreen wood ferns stood out, though many blades lay pressed to the ground.

The ground huggers added to the overall sense of an old-growth spruce forest. But they were bit players. The big old trees themselves stole the show. Collectively and individually. Had they ever been cut? I cannot say, "never." What I know of our forebears' way of life tells me they must have been cut at least once. But not within living memory. Not for a hundred years or more. Which in Maine puts them in the class of primeval forests. Depending how you look at old trees—as venerable first settlers or wastrels—you are bound to have strong feelings on the subject.

It was frustrating trying to find words to describe where I was. Every phrase was too petty or too grand. That is the way with woods. They are both simple and complex. I would look up at a tree and see a million needles. Look at a billion needles fallen to earth and see a fine-woven carpet or tapestry. With no middle ground. No scale to measure the whole. Myriad details or grand generalities, neither catching the feel of the place. I was both Gulliver and Lilliputian, unable to settle on one perspective or the other.

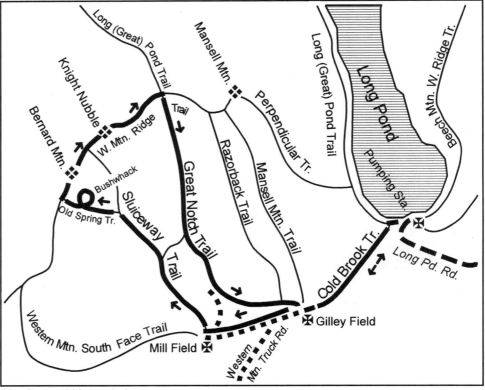

12—Bernard Mountain loop.

Which, after four hours of concentrated effort, led to burnout. I can remember the exact moment it hit, when I was halfway down the Great Notch Trail. I suddenly realized I'd had it with trees. I could not look at one more piece of bark. One more twisted branch. One more sylvan panorama. I switched on cruise control and mindlessly let the trail steer me back to Long Pond. I came to a sign pointing to **RESERVOIR**, which I checked out because it had nothing to do with woods. There it was, backed up behind its dam, a teardrop-shaped pond fifty feet across, some seventy-five feet long. Fed by the combined flow out of Great and Little notches, its water was still and clear. Just what I needed, something besides trees to look at. If I had not turned aside at that point, I might still be wandering in the woods.

Acadia's trails do not just take you places, they wind through habitats all the way. Who lives on the south slope of Western Mountain? The usual crowd: chickadees, robins, nuthatches, crows. Red squirrels were conspicuous inhabitants of those ancient woods. I met them at the base of the mountain, on the way up, and in both Great and Little notches along the topmost ridge. The sprucy slope of Western Mountain is their kind of place. If you are foreign to those parts and need a visa, you apply to them.

Ravens, too, were at home. I heard their throaty croaks and chortles ahead of me, and sometimes walked almost under them, but never saw one of the croakers or chortlers. I did meet a somebird in Little Notch, which in silhouette against the sky looked like a pine grosbeak. I think I could have told if it were a crossbill. I'm not good at bird calls, otherwise I would know for sure. The one scat I saw was on the overlook east of Knight Nubble. Coyote, I will say with mild conviction, planted in July or August. Blueberries and leaves.

Just starting on the Cold Brook Trail, treading on fallen spruce needles packed together to look like fur, I heard a gentle sound in the bigtooth aspens ahead. A downy woodpecker softly tapping at a branch. Then, whit-whit, I saw another downy fly tree-to-tree. Popple is God's gift to woodpeckers. What will they do when the fields and woods have grown to spruce again? But surely there will always be popple in Maine, as long as we keep clearing land and cutting trees. Woodpeckers are assured of easy pickings in our wake—easy pickings. *Wham, wham, wham.* Pounding from a different direction. A hairy woodpecker was banging at a spruce snag, appearing to take joy in making as much noise as she could. Not to be outdone, her male companion hammered an answering beat in a tree almost over my head. What a complex rhythm those woodpeckers built as a quartet. The drums were beating in counterpoint. Was there method in their diddles and tattoos? A message? If so, the gist of it was, there's bugs in these here trees.

Other signs of life included myriad strands of spider silk shining in the sun. Even in deepest woods, a passing ray would glint on a single thread strung between branches or hung on upturned roots, sending a flash into the corner of my eye, making me turn and take notice. It was always single strands, not webs. Some shone with color. A purple sprite dancing along a wafting filament like a blaze in mid air made the woods alive with aerial phantoms and spirits. I was not alone. It is not possible to be alone in the woods.

Then there was the barking. The wind had come up by the time I got on the Great Notch Trail, so it was hard to hear against the overhead concert of sighs. But a bark it was without doubt. A backup beep from the Southwest Harbor transfer station caught my ear. A persistent sound, it got to me now and again, though I generally managed to shut it out. If that sound carried so clearly, perhaps the sound of a barking dog would as well. But the barking seemed to come from the west—the long ridge of Bernard Mountain. I have heard ravens make an insistent kind of barking croak, maybe that was it. Maybe it was a coyote. Or Bowser off on a hunt.

What I did not see was bare cliffs and open ledges, which is unusual for a hike in Acadia. With the best woods in the park, Western Mountain is a different kind of place, with a feel of its own. That was what I was after on this particular hike. And what I found, but do not have the skills

Wintergreen and hair-cap moss.

to convey. The size and spacing of the trees contributed to that feel. So did the shining strands of spider silk. The slopes had something to do with it. And the valleys where they meet. The small streams running through those valleys added to the effect. As did the churring squirrels and yawking ravens. It all added to Western Mountain's distinctive aura, but what it is exactly I am powerless to say. Ineffable. Which only means it lies beyond the conventional use of words, not that you cannot experience it, or it does not exist.

Part of it, too, is the feel of the trail. The give-and-take between hiker and passing terrain. That physical interaction is at the heart of the experience I'm trying to get at. Not just the exertion of putting one foot in front of the other, trudging ahead, but the standing and looking around as well, giving attention to slopes and surrounding woods. The act of hiking combined with the act of attending—that is definitely part of the Western Mountain experience. It is the physicality of the place engaging the physicality of yourself.

I do not have words to describe my experience on this hike. In the woods, what you see is features without individual names. There were no names I could drop, or that others could pick up as being meaningful to them in personal ways. There were big trees and little trees. Near trees and far trees. Straight trees and crooked trees. Trees close together and trees apart. Trees standing, leaning, lying, decaying. Trees draped in a thousand ways with lichens, liverworts, mosses. Trees growing in streambeds, on knolls, on pitched slopes, on boulders. Trees, trees, everywhere, and not a proper term to bring them immediately to anyone's mind the way they struck me when I was in their midst.

It is one thing to say, "I saw a picture of Hillary Clinton on the cover of *Time*," and another to describe that picture to a blind companion who has never seen a photograph, and only knows the First Lady through recordings of her voice. That is what I'm up against. To know Hillary Clinton's face, a blind person would have to touch it. Which is exactly what you must do if you want to know Western Mountain. You have to reach out and stroke it with every sense.

If we lost our stock of labels we would be intellectually lost in the world. William James said that. I was intellectually lost in the woods because I had not been schooled to label the things I saw. Without labels, it is hard to see anything. I was not only blind, but dull as well. Had I been trained as a forester, I would have seen stumpage and board feet of timber. As a hunter, I would have seen spoor. As a priest, the hand of God. We become prisoners of our beliefs and disciplines. It takes a savage (a forest native, from Latin *silva*) to know the woods. No man will ever know them the way a red squirrel does.

Before I give myself totally to the problem of writing about a hike instead of what the hike was like, I will add these details. The geography at the foot of Western Mountain is a little confusing. You can drive to four different trailheads, yet get to every trail from any one of them because they are cross-linked together. The easternmost trailhead is at the end of Long Pond Road off Seal Cove Road out of Southwest Harbor. Also called the pumping station, that's where I started. You can hike either Beech or Western mountains from there.

The other three trailheads branch off the Western Mountain Truck Road, which connects with Seal Cove Road farther out of town (Southwest Harbor) than the turn for Long Pond Road. The truck road forks after a third of a mile, the left fork taking you to Seal Cove Pond, the right fork to the trailheads. That right fork winds around, then forks again in another mile. You can reach Mill Field or Reservoir trailheads by turning left, Gilley Field trailhead by turning right. Gilley Field is where the Mansell Mountain, Razorback, and Great Notch trails begin. The Cold Brook Trail links it to the pumping station. The Sluiceway and South Face trails go up from Mill Field. And from the Reservoir you can easily reach the Great Notch Trail by a short connector. I usually park at the pumping station because I imagine the paved surface of Long Pond Road is

easier on my venerable Pinto than the gravel truck road. From there I can reach Mill Field in less than thirty minutes on foot. (The truck road is closed in winter.)

The Sluiceway Trail starts out as a former woods road heading up a ridge between two valleys feeding branches of Marshall Brook. I could hear water flowing on both sides. The trail immediately takes you into woods, which get better and older as you go. After a gradual rise, the trail runs

Mountain cranberry.

along a stream, sometimes in the bed, sometimes on the bank. The treadway is over broken rock in places, so footing is tricky. Twenty minutes from Mill Field the Sluiceway Trail branches left, the right fork shortly connecting with the Great Notch Trail above the Reservoir. The Sluiceway Trail gets steeper, rockier, and more exciting from there.

In ten more minutes (an hour from Long Pond) I reached serious woods. I won't describe them. I can't. A mingling of cedar, spruce, and white pine, with an occasional birch, these trees had not been cut in a long, long time. I noted pines thirty inches in diameter, a cedar twenty-four. They were a lot older than I was, and could tell wonderfully tall tales. Tales of that site in all seasons and weathers. Tales featuring winds, spates, snowstorms, and ice. Tales we footloose folk will never understand because we cannot imagine committing ourselves to one place for a lifetime. To listen to a tree is to hear the history of a place revealed. Few of us have the patience to hear it through. We would rather know what's doing over the next hill, and the hill beyond that.

The trail heads up a steep rocky gully, then turns for Little Notch. It doesn't look much like a trail at that point. I had the impression not many hikers came that way. In some places it was hard distinguishing the treadway from the untreadway on either side. Twigs in the stream were coated with ice. Pausing to get my bearings at the top of the gully, I felt primal forces swirling around me. That is what these woods are like, a twining of light, water, and gravity, forming a vortex to which I cannot give a name. I remember looking down at wintergreen growing among a cluster of pale green pincushion moss. Looking up to see if I could catch sight of a chattering squirrel, I saw the steps which led me astray. No, that's not right; they did not lead me—I pushed on because I wanted to see where they went. I had wanted to last time, too, but squelched the urge to explore. I had more self-control in those days. Following those steps this time was my doing, not theirs. I was more than just a consenting adult; the first move was mine.

Going to the stream, I found a circle of stones, remains of a fallen cairn. And yes, I could make out a sort of trail heading along the stream to the steps. Where did it lead, that flight of twenty-two granite blocks? I rose to the challenge of finding out. Largely reclaimed by liverwort and fallen needles, it was a genuine trail, not a hoax—the Spring Trail of old. Trees along it had been blazed a long time ago. It led away from the stream, past twelve-inch icicles on the face of a boulder, straight up the steep slope. Up was where it led. Up is where I went.

Steps on the old Spring Trail (beckoning steps).

Once away from the stream, it was not much of a trail. It wound over some pretty rotten rock, making for the worst kind of hiking, especially when wet, which it was. The few steps here and there were slipping down the slope, and saplings did their best to block the way, with the help of fallen trees. But in its day it must have been spectacular. One flight of fourteen steps rises steeply in a double curve past banks of sphagnum moss. I avoided stepping on the carpet of liverwort, not wanting to spoil its effort to take back what belonged to it. The trail belonged to the damp sloping site, not to me. Its proper owner was Bernard Mountain. I was a trespasser from Away.

Which did not keep me from enjoying myself. Here were the woods I had come to find. Heaven. Which turned out to be damper, colder, icier, and more overgrown than I had expected. An old-growth spruce forest, uncut because inaccessible. The site reminded me of the outlet of Wizard Pond on Black Mountain in the Gouldsboro Hills. There, too, old trees had been protected by steep, rocky terrain. On Bernard Mountain I saw pine and spruce thirty inches in diameter, while down below twelve or fifteen inches had seemed large. Many rocks were covered with mats of dripping sphagnum moss, so the site had to be wet. Water on a south-facing slope makes for big trees. Sunlight and damp soil, not fleecy clouds, are the makings of heaven.

Then I lost it. The trail, that is. And in looking for it, lost rapport with my surroundings. Saplings grabbed at my hat from all directions. I fought from one doghair thicket to the next, losing sight of old trees. Up, up, up. I figured I would reach Little Notch where the Sluiceway Trail had been heading when I abandoned it. Coming to an open patch flooded with sunlight, I sat on a blanket of warm spruce needles and gave the woods one last good look. What struck me then was the mingling of different-sized trees. An old-growth forest is no even-aged stand. It is peopled by trees of all ages. That is its strength. No matter what happens, a crew stands ready to fill any breech in the canopy.

If I were a trail, where would I be? I looked in all directions, but found no hint of a track. There was nothing to do but scramble over the tangle of trunks fallen like so many pickup sticks. Excelsior, sort of. The slope leveled off. I was nearing the top. Little Notch, I assumed. Yes, there was the trail along the ridge of Western Mountain. I turned east, heading for Knight Nubble.

Wrong! The next sign I saw said, **BERNARD MTN. ELEV. 1071.** Little Notch and Knight Nubble are east of the summit. I had come up on the west. So much for my navigation skills in thick woods. At least now I knew where I was. There had been a structure on Bernard at one time, still marked by iron bolts set in granite. The view from the summit is trees in every direction. Nearby trees, not those on far slopes. There is a cozy, sheltered feeling to the place, unlike more open summits. I had come to find out about evergreen woods. That is exactly what I had done.

My route down would follow the Western Mountain Ridge Trail to Little Notch, Knight Nubble, and Great Notch, then the Great Notch Trail to Gilley Field, where it ties into the Cold Brook Trail back to Long Pond. I will save the details of the ridge trail for the story of a later hike when, starting from Long Pond, I will do the length of the Perpendicular and South Face trails. For now I will mention the two outlooks, one facing north a little east of Bernard, and one south from Knight Nubble. There is a notebook for comments at Bernard Mountain Overlook. For flavor, I will quote the last three entries:

10/17/93 11:34 AM
Pain, Breathlessness, Fun.
    David Bulger, Manset ME

I could do this 10 more times.
    Mistress Quickly the III

Foggy—But still worth it.
    J. Rotus, SWH

The ridge trail dips steeply into Little Notch, elevation 890 feet, over a route much in need of maintenance at the time of this hike. Roots clinging to the slope were getting worn, and would soon give way. Either a change of route was in order, or a big job of shoring up the fragile trail as it was. There was a lot of ice on the rocks. I watched where I stepped.

The notches along the ridge are the big story of the trail between Bernard and Mansell. These saddles collect water, supporting dense stands of trees. They have a magic of their own. In Little Notch I met a red squirrel, pine grosbeak, and assorted wood ferns. My original destination, this is where the Sluiceway Trail ends. I got there after striking off on a detour of my own making. Now I could get on with Plan A, which was to return by way of Great Notch on the far side of Knight Nubble.

Two tenths of a mile beyond Little Notch, Knight Nubble, elevation 930 feet (or is it 980?—the sign was too worn to tell) is another wooded summit tucked between the major peaks of Western Mountain. It separates Great and Little notches. Passing by a small sphagnum bog through mossy woods, the trail soon comes to an overlook to the south and east. I saw at least twenty boats inshore from the Duck Islands, taking them to be scallop draggers. The view of Mansell from Knight Nubble partially returns the favor for views seen the other way from the Razorback Trail. Pausing to pick apart a scat, I pictured a coyote enjoying the view

Pincushion moss.

while doing its duty by nature.

From the overlook, the trail steers down into Great Notch, elevation 640 feet, by way of a beautifully wooded terrace, and cliffs decked with fifteen-inch icicles the day I passed by. In the notch I had my choice of five split-log benches, and ate lunch beneath a two-foot spruce on a bench facing the sunlit slope of Mansell. There's a box for comments, but the logbook was gone. Picking a scrap of paper off the ground, I read: "Yes, where is the book?" signed, "Libharts, Seal Cove, Me."

The notch hosts a stand of red maples and other deciduous trees, the first I had come across since leaving the lower slopes. I held a conversation with another red squirrel, and spent some time inspecting matted-down wood ferns before heading down the valley between Mansell and Bernard. The hike was about over, though I still had a mile and a half to go. The rest of the way is hazy in my mind because I was not very alert. I'd had my fill of the woods. The Great Notch Trail is a cinch, descending easily all the way to Gilley Field, so I did not have to concentrate on where I was going. I remember yellow birches. Pools of water running into other pools. Moss. The sound of squirrels, and distant barking. In spots the trail is eroded, exposing a jumble of smooth stones. Which came first, trail or erosion? It looked to me like water had not been able to resist following in hikers' footsteps.

There was a heap of seventy-five cigarette butts in the turnaround by the reservoir.

A little worse for wear, I got back to the pumping station after hiking for five hours. Bernard Mountain was in fine shape. Lumbering into my car, I recalled the New England folk mantra, "I pine fir yew and balsam," a saying that once sold millions of evergreen-scented pillows to tourists every summer. Opening my senses to nature, I had let in more stimulation than I could handle. Eye contact with the wild can be dangerous. I had had an overdose, which made me woodenheaded. Trees on the brain. Enough!

○

13—DORR MOUNTAIN LOOP

From south end of the Tarn
To Dorr Mountain summit, and back
    Up by Dorr Mountain Ladder and South Ridge
      trails
    Down by Dorr Mountain East Face Trail, Kurt
      Diederich's Climb, and Kane Trail
                2.5 miles, November 14, 1993

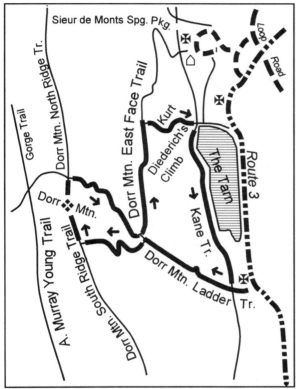

13—Dorr Mountain loop.

With the thermometer reading fifty degrees, this might be my last chance. Trails would be wet, but not icy. Where would I go to make best use of this gift of Indian summer? Easy. Dorr Mountain. The ladder trail. I had climbed the east face of Dorr in winter when it was more bobsled run than trail. I was not up for that kind of hike. But it could turn cold any day. Dorr was my choice for perhaps the last hike under summer conditions. I would go up the ladder trail to the summit, take the Dorr Mountain East Face Trail down partway, then Kurt Diederich's Climb, and finish off with a stroll along the Tarn, for a loop of about two-and-a-half miles.

At my usual stop-and-go pace the hike took six hours between 10:00 a.m. and 4:00 p.m., my speed averaging less than half a mile an hour. But I was out to see what was happening in that part of Acadia, not run a race. Under a layer of thickening clouds, the weather stayed warm. Not many hikers were out. I met only eight the whole time.

What did I find? Always on the lookout for dikes cutting through granite, I met five of those. But most of all I was struck by the life I met on either hand along every stretch of my route. Leaves may have fallen, and tourists migrated to warmer climes, but Acadia's plants and animals were going strong. Harvest season, time of gathering and getting ready for winter. Red squirrels set the tone of the hike. Their signs were everywhere, right to the summit. Nibbled acorns and pine cones, heaped-up maple keys, and pitch pine buds nipped off and strewn beneath selected trees. This had been a great year for oaks. I couldn't remember when I had seen so many acorns. And a great year for red squirrels. They ruled the slopes. I saw nine and heard twenty more. The first thing I noticed when I picked up the ladder trail off Route 3 just south of the Tarn was heaps of chewed acorns on coping stones, boulders, and logs. When the woods changed to pitch pines higher up, I saw nibbled cones and nipped-off buds to within thirty feet of the summit. I met two squirrel cousins, too, Eastern chipmunks, getting ready to hibernate.

Insects were flying wherever I went, more than I had seen for a month. They rose and fell on the air in loose crowds, out for one last fling. Did they know the end of the world was at hand? At wing? If they did, they flitted with abandon and didn't seem to care. Driving back by Eagle Lake, I saw a bat sweeping the airspace over Route 233. Nemesis, meting out justice to all who dared to dance beyond their time.

Crows were out. I saw five fly south over the gorge between Dorr and Huguenot Head. Chickadees, too. And three downy woodpeckers tapping among the birches. At the end of the hike I saw a pair of buffleheads swimming along the Route 3 side of the Tarn, the male in black-and-white finery standing out like a beacon, the female all but disappearing in the reflected shadow of facing cliffs.

A great many birds jeered at me from the lower slopes, but I never located one to get a good look. Warning cries are meant to throw you off, which in my case they did. I would stand for two or three minutes peering into the middle distance where I guessed the sharp peeps came from, but saw only brown oak leaves fluttering on gray branches.

Other creatures I did not see, but saw or heard signs of, were beavers (distant views of their lodge in Beaver Dam Pool); snowshoe hares (blueberry buds cleanly nipped at an angle); pileated woodpeckers (four one-inch holes drilled in a cedar); one noisy blue jay; and a noisier dog, whose prints I found later in wet sand at the summit.

Aside from their nests, which as a rule they do not try to conceal, people signaled their presence in a variety of ways. They hooted at noon from Bar Harbor. Warned of fog by continual blasts from an electronic horn. Sped back and forth along Route 3 in sealed transport modules. Flashed pulses of red light from a beacon on Egg Rock. And sent me birthday wishes by blue balloon (though it wasn't my birthday). Too, there was a lot of honking and shouting on Cadillac Mountain, more bursts of glee and excitement than anything else.

Less effusive than people or squirrels, plants quietly reflected the change of season—the main theme of the day. Birches, beeches, and oaks had shut down for the winter, giving bark, branches, and stems a chance to catch the public eye. Their leaves, along with those of blueberry and huckleberry, were being recycled. Hemlocks, spruces, pines, and cedars—green, but pale on the fringes—added tan and yellow needles to the soil-building cause. Yet among fallen leaves and needles, set off by their glow, a great many green plants were brighter than ever, as if winter was their time to shine. Wintergreen was radiant along the trail, joined by conspicuous patches of mayflower, paler but just as shiny. Sheep laurel leaves drooped as if subdued (reminding me of Pooh's friend Eeyore, or rather his ears), but glowed with a range of soft colors between green and rust. A witch hazel bush next to the trail was in full flower, small yellow blossoms (also with droopy ears) nestling at the base of each twig, beaming as if with an inner light. Ferns thrived on the wet slopes—Christmas, rock-cap, and marginal wood ferns drawing my eye, though in drier parts bracken had gone by.

Rock slide on Dorr Mountain Ladder Trail.

Clumps of moss hung blackly (with touches of green on closer look) from damp slopes and cliffs. Patches of sphagnum moss thrived in seeps. Juniper, kinnikinnick, and wineleaf cinquefoil clung to cracks on the upper slopes. And where nothing else grew, lichens held forth in a variety of colors from olive to iridescent lime. In summer it is easy to take plants for granted, but with fall well under way, every one becomes a miracle. That is how I felt, as if I had strayed into a garden of delight.

A wonder in its own right, the ladder trail is one of the main attractions of that garden, telling of pilgrims being drawn to the living slopes for over a hundred years. Built by Waldron Bates in 1891, and rebuilt by the CCC in 1934, it conducts trampers to the heart of Acadia's typically rugged but fruitful terrain.

The upper portion of the trail has been officially retired, but it still cuts boldly through pitch pine woods on Dorr's granite slopes, tying into the Dorr Mountain South Ridge Trail not far from the summit. You won't find it shown that way on modern maps, but it is there on the mountain, still offering a freelance route to the top. The approved route shown on maps is badly eroded in spots, cutting fifteen inches into fragile soil, and is apt to be slick when wet. If you like hiking through history as well as terrain, read up on the ladder trail in *Trails of History** by Tom St. Germain and Jay Saunders.

The basic plan of the ladder trail is to traverse the steep eastern face of Dorr Mountain along the base of a cliff running at an angle toward the summit. When the way is blocked by hunks of granite jutting out from the cliff, the trail momentarily jogs away from the cliff, scales the obstruction by means of three ladders, then gets back to business hugging the cliff as before. Until it joins the Dorr Mountain East Face Trail at the south end of the promenade along Dorr's awesome east cliff, the ladder trail is stepped most of the way. It is solid and well-laid, letting hikers enjoy their surroundings instead of having to watch their feet.

The trail passes through woods most of the way, even on Dorr's higher, harsher terraces. Starting in deciduous woods of beech, oak, and birch, it ends in wave after wave of pitch pines on the upper slopes where soil is thinner and water harder to come by in dry spells. The shift from deciduous to coniferous woods is not steady or gradual. One moment you are crunching acorns on the steps, the next you are walking on pine needles, then you are back to acorns again. Pitch pines can go without water longer than oaks, so they grow on slopes where soil is thin or held only in cracks. Dorr's upper slopes rise in a series of terraces, not one continuous sweep, so soil builds up in patches interrupted by ledges and cliffs, clinging where it is less apt to be washed away. Where soil is thick, thirsty deep-rooted trees such as oaks take hold. Where thin, more Spartan types like pitch pines have the slopes much to themselves.

Hiking the ladder trail, you pass through a landscape that

---

* Tom St. Germain and Jay Saunders, *Trails of History*. Bar Harbor: Parkman Publications, 1993.

is more like a mosaic made up of discrete groups of plants than a smooth transition from one group to another. That patchy, living landscape reflects the broken nature of the terrain. Here are dripping cliffs covered with mosses and lichens. Here mixed beeches and oaks. Here pitch pines on forested shelves. Here pitch pines scattered along cracks in the granite. Here cedars in the courses of intermittent streams. The landscape changes abruptly, then changes back again, but is far from being random or chaotic. Where there is soil there is water. The amounts of both, together with the prevailing climate, determine the types of plants that will survive in a given place. Conditions vary from site to site like a mosaic or patchwork quilt, with the plants and wildlife depending on those plants changing in a similar pattern.

This becomes instantly clear when you look at a boulder topped with a miniature forest of rock-cap ferns. Where the boulder is flattest, soil is less likely to wash away. Where soil clings, water is held for a longer time over a wider range of conditions. It is no accident that that is where the ferns grow. On the steep sides of the boulder—where water runs off quickly, carrying soil particles with it—you find lichens clinging to bare rock, and perhaps dark patches of moss, but no ferns. Once a few ferns have gotten a hold on top, they capture fallen leaves and needles, aiding the soil-building process, pulling themselves up by their own bootstraps. And if there is a small crack in the side of the boulder, perhaps soil collects there, too, holding enough moisture to support a small colony of plants in that unlikely spot.

Every boulder along the ladder trail, every cliff, slope, shelf, cleft, and ravine is an island of life fitting in with the islands around it as part of the larger mosaic. Life clings where it does by finding what it needs to survive. Cutting steadily up the slope, the ladder trail passes from island to island, from one site to the next, opening the bold pattern of the landscape to view, the bold pattern of Acadian life.

When I hike, I ask questions. Who lives here? Why are things the way they are? Where is this taking me? I was born to ask questions. On my death bed I will exit with a question on my lips: "What next?" Trails, like our lives, are

Hiker on the Dorr Mountain Ladder Trail.

pathways of earthly inquiry.

On the way up, a family of four passed me as I was jotting something in my notebook. Two boys with untied sneakers came first, both carrying walking sticks, both wearing Chicago Bulls jackets. The man asked what I was checking on.

"Everything," I told him, "to make sure it is in good running order."

"That's a big responsibility," he said.

"Basically, I let it alone and it runs itself," I told him.

Seeing he was the only one of the four with a heavy pack, I asked if he volunteered to carry the load, or had that duty thrust upon him.

"You have the responsibility of running this place; I shoulder the gear. We're two of a kind," he said.

I also met a number of red squirrels and chipmunks along the ladder trail. The chipmunks hid and peered at me from under rocks. The squirrels scolded, and set their back feet to quivering, but went on gathering acorns, and nibbling, nibbling. While I was watching one squirrel, an acorn fell from a branch, hit a sloping ledge, bounded into the trail, bounded twice more, and came to rest fifty feet downslope.

The abandoned extension of the ladder trail continues by a little worn track past the point where the trail proper joins the Dorr Mountain East Face Trail. You turn beneath a certain large pitch pine, more on faith than any evidence of a trail. From there to the ridge you are in the company of Waldron Bates. He may have died in 1909, but his spirit still lives in the stones he set in place. This upper section of trail was not reworked by the CCC. You can picture Bates facing the problem of getting up one slope after another, and you can see how he solved it each time. He thought in terms of steps, so laid them straight up a great many bare ledges. And where he did not lay steps, he sometimes lined the trail with huge stones so you could not miss it in fog or dim light. He was the kind of man who set a course and stuck to it. His Goat Trail on Pemetic is like that. When in doubt, go ahead. That settled, the problem becomes merely a technical matter of figuring out how.

Reaching the South Ridge Trail in two hours and forty

minutes, I ate lunch while studying the east face of Cadillac. At first glance it looked much the same as the east face of Dorr, but then I started seeing differences. The steep slopes on Cadillac had pitch pines like Dorr, but many more cedars. The slopes toward Otter Creek were mostly deciduous, with a fringe of evergreens in the valley of Canon Brook and on top of the ridge. I took that to mean there was soil on the more gradual slopes to the south, and where there were cedars, a reliable source of water running down the opposite cliffs. Seeing something blue in a patch of gray birches below where I sat, I checked it out after eating, and found a shriveled birthday balloon draped on a branch. It was a thoughtful gesture, but forty days late. I wondered who could have sent it.

As I was about to set out again, a small fly landed on my left thumb. I thought of the four billion years of earthly evolution leading to that one event. Maybe that was the answer for which everything else laid the groundwork. Two lives coming together, then separating. I could not calculate the vast improbability of our meeting like that, so it had to be profoundly significant. What did it mean? A hundred years ago Waldron Bates laid a trail setting the stage for this one encounter. Thinking back to Vincent Price in the movie *The Fly*, I was struck with the idea that the little fly was trying to tell me something. I listened for its squeaky voice, but heard only the wind in the pines. I wanted it to be Bates himself, asking my help in having his trail restored. If that is who it was, he kept mum about his errand. The fly flew off, and I picked up the ridge trail to the summit, passing a row of four cairns marking the upper end of the ladder trail. If the cairns stay put, you can't miss the turn should you want to go down that way.

I did not pause at the summit other than to note the elevation of 1,270 feet. And to admire the cairn, which seemed larger than when I had seen it last. Perhaps it has reached critical mass and can now sustain itself, or even grow, adding layer upon layer of new stones on its own. I wondered if that heap preserved a cairn at its core, an original pile of stones built by Waldron Bates with the help of George Dorr, or perhaps a ceremonial mound laid down by early

Mayflower leaves.

European settlers. Perhaps by the natives they displaced.

Continuing on through sparse pitch pine woods, the trees no taller than four or five feet, I soon came to the crossing where the south ridge trail meets the Dorr Mountain Notch Trail striking west for Cadillac, and the Dorr Mountain East Face Trail east for Sieur de Monts Spring. Turning east, I went down over a series of bare sloping ledges and wooded terraces by a section of trail showing a great deal of wear. I had been spoiled by the care Waldron Bates had taken to protect the interests of both hikers and the mountain. Here no such care was evident. Not only was the trail wet from recent rain, making it slippery on slopes of bare rock, but it cut through pitch pine woods, digging into the soil as much as fifteen inches, inviting runoff to follow, increasing the probability of erosion.

The upper section of the Dorr Mountain East Face Trail carries a great deal of traffic as one of the most heavily used trails in Acadia. Between the south end of the cliff-top promenade and the summit, it illustrates the problems of building trails in high places. The labor that went into laying down the feeder trails was spared on the upper slopes. Little was done to protect either hiker or habitat. The sole consideration seems to have been reaching the top. Which is perhaps understandable, given how hard it would be getting suitable stones to the site for a solid and stepped treadway. But subsequent wear from boots and runoff has created a hazard to hiker and environment alike. A challenge to a Park Service whose job is to watch over both.

The upper slopes were running with water when I hiked them, the trail holding pools of standing water on more level runs through pitch pine woods between slopes. Maybe the little fly was trying to tell me this needs attention. My thoughts turned to what I would do to repair the trail. In the example of his work just to the south, Waldron Bates had shown how the job might be done. Once singled out as a project, it could be engineered. But the work would be long, labor intensive, and costly. Not the kind of thing park funds are likely to be spent on. Adding restoration of this section of trail to my list of things to tend to tomorrow, I was relieved to reach the solid footing of steps at the start of the long northerly traverse along the lip of the cliffs on Dorr's impressive east face, the stretch of trail I think of as a scenic promenade.

Starting at the link to the ladder trail, I hiked the promenade to where Kurt Diederich's Climb comes in from the north end of the Tarn. The trail is more-or-less level between the two connectors, and is a model of solid construction. Runoff, of which there is plenty, is taken into account, not ignored. Trailside vegetation is respected. And the hiker is given a seemingly endless tour from one prospect to the next, with extensive views over Huguenot Head and Champlain to Schoodic Peninsula, and north to the Black Hills on the mainland, encompassing many of the islands in Frenchman Bay. As I walked north, Egg Rock with its flashing red beacon came out from behind Champlain Mountain to join the Porcupine Islands—Bar, Sheep, Bald, Burnt, Rum Key, Long—and farther-off Stave, Jordan, and giant Ironbound. Not metaphorical islands like those in my landscape mosaic, but places apart from the main.

The view from the top of the cliffs also includes Beaver Dam Pool, around which, ninety-nine years ago, George Dorr built MDI's first bicycle path (now abandoned like so many first things). And, though I generally manage to suppress it, that sprawling industrial complex, the mouse factory known as Jackson Lab, more distended than ever due to recent construction. The lab is a boon to medical research, everyone knows that. And as MDI's largest employer, a boon to the local economy. Burned twice, it has risen from the ashes both times in a tougher, more virulent form. It is also true that with its stacks and roofs and parking lots, Jackson Lab is a blight on the Acadian landscape. It commands the view from both Dorr and Champlain. If the wind is right, you can sometimes whiff its fumes. To avoid being distracted by its foreground eminence, you actively have to suppress it. Which I can do much of the time, but when I suddenly look up—there it is in full view, like the Emperor parading in his new clothes, splendidly arrayed, but stark naked. Like a wart on the end of your nose, or a house on Schooner Head, it draws the eye. How long are we to avert our gaze?

Another structure that caught my eye was one of the culverts built to carry water under the trail. Bridged by a single block of stone six feet long and three feet wide, it looked like a fallen megalith. It must contain twelve cubic feet of granite. Farther along, on Kurt Diederich's Climb, there is another culvert bridged by an even more awesome stone. That one is two feet on a side and nine feet long, containing thirty-six cubic feet. At a tenth of a pound per cubic inch, that is 6,220 pounds. The men who laid those culverts must have been giants. In stature and ambition both.

The long cliff-top avenue is the highlight of the trail system on the east face of Dorr Mountain. I say that as one given more to habitats than vistas. But ambling along on the brink, I got a feel for the openness and exposure of the site that led me to appreciate the character of those who dwell in such places. I was struck by a wave of admiration for pitch pines, spruces, oaks, red squirrels, and chickadees. The native residents of Acadia have what it takes: true grit.

The promenade goes on from one outlook to the next, seeming never to end. And when it does, it merely drops to a lower level, coming out on top of another cliff. I kept meeting red squirrels along the way. Used to scampering through trees, they were at home on the brink. Do they know they own one of the most beautiful sites on MDI? George Dorr knew it. I recognized the setting for his most famous photograph, the one where, hand on flexed knee, he manfully commands this same view (before the building of Jackson Lab).

Where the trail crosses a field of boulders through beech and oak woods, I met a couple hiking up. The young woman trailed a scent of patchouli, which tweaked my nostrils for almost a minute. I liked it best when I could barely make it out.

At the sign for the Tarn, I turned down Kurt Diederich's climb. Mayflower leaves lined the way. Winding steeply down the slope, the trail is stepped in the old manner much of the way. Its construction is classic, preserving an older sensibility. A distilled version of the ladder trail, it features stone steps without the iron. Only half a mile long, it is one of my favorite hikes, and a great way to come off Dorr Mountain. Or come on.

In one section a series of about fifty steps winds steeply in a compound curve between the mountain proper and a hulking wayward spur of granite where a number of hemlocks have staunchly taken root. Stark, damp, and angular, it is striking and rugged terrain, the sort of place ferns and mosses thrive. And hikers pause to refresh themselves. Here is where nature invented cubism long before Braque and Picasso dared mix different points of view in a single painting. Looking up at the site, it surrounds you while, at the same time, you see it in universal perspective.

That is pretty much the story of my hike on Dorr Mountain. Coming along by the Tarn I saw the pair of buffleheads which, next to oldsquaws and hooded mergansers, are some of my favorite ducks. I got back to my car at four o'clock, the sun about to set beyond the clouds, but set long ago on the gorge overshadowed by Dorr Mountain.

○

14—CHAMPLAIN MOUNTAIN LOOP

From Precipice Trail parking area
To Champlain Mountain summit, and back
   Up by Precipice Trail
   Down by Bear Brook, Champlain Mountain
    East Face, and Precipice trails
               2.0 miles, November 20, 1993

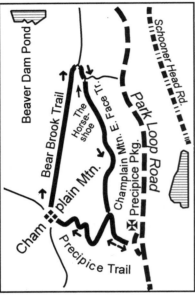

14—Champlain Mountain loop.

Standing back from the east face of Champlain Mountain, you can scan the cliffs, and you will not see it—Rudolph Brunnow's route up the Precipice. *His* Precipice. On *his* mountain. Part of the turf Brunnow commanded eighty years ago from High Seas, his oceanside estate. He knew that face better than anyone, not with his eyes from a safe distance, but through touch, balance, and exertion among the rocks themselves. It was there as a dream. What Brunnow did was carve his dream on the mountain in iron and granite, along the diagonal shelf traversing that formidable wall. Bottom to top—almost. The trick was in bridging the almost. That was Brunnow's gift. Helping us leap from the upper end of the shelf to the top of the Precipice. That leap is the challenge, and the success, of the Precipice Trail.

I hadn't done it in over twelve years, so had largely forgotten what it was like. Some things you should not let slip. Brunnow's dream for one. Keeping it in the back of my mind, I was working up to it. Having hiked Western Mountain three times, I was ready to look farther east. I had hiked Sargent, Penobscot, Pemetic, and Dorr. Cadillac and Champlain were next. Which would it be?

The forecast was what you would expect for November. Showers, wind, and cold. Freezing rain, the season's ultimate weapon against hikers. The slopes would ice up. But

not right away, not till Saturday afternoon. There was a grace period or, as we say now, a window of opportunity—Saturday morning. I woke up at five and knew. Cadillac could wait. The day had come for the Precipice. To see it at work, to find out what, aside from lichen, lives on that cliff.

Peregrine falcons, for one. Everybody knows about them. They are the reason the trail is closed spring and summer, when people feel the strongest urge to climb it. A few think the park should keep the trail open, letting the falcons tough it out. But most regret wiping peregrines out in the East, and are glad to do what they can to get them back, which means forgoing the Precipice April through August. Fair is fair. Getting peregrines back on the cliffs is one of the park's outstanding accomplishments. More glamorous, say, than mending the carriage roads, or giving trees a chance to die of old age.

Beyond peregrines and lichens, who calls these cliffs home? There was a way to find out. I got to the trailhead at seven o'clock Saturday morning, before the icy winds from Canada were due. I would be up and back well before they arrived.

I cannot claim to find cliffside plants and animals more exciting than the trail itself. On the Precipice, the trail's the thing. It not only leads you to that amazing place, but watches over you while you are there. Toeholds and handholds are where you need them. You may have to stretch a bit, but that is all to the good. If the trail was too easy, it would lure casual hikers into spots they might not be able to handle. From the trailhead, the Precipice Trail puts you to the test, making sure those who go on are qualified to make the grade later on.

Ladders are incidental to the Dorr Mountain Ladder Trail and the Perpendicular Trail on Mansell, but they are the essence of the Precipice Trail. Brunnow's genius was in using iron to finish the route nature began. As for ladders as most of us think of them—rungs set between rigid side rails—there is only one on the Precipice. Brunnow's rungs are set in holes drilled into the face of the granite. He shaped them to fit particular walls, cracks, or angles along the way. Trying to keep track as I went, I counted seventy-six foot rungs, set in seventeen separate groups containing between two and nine rungs apiece, including one iron ladder of five rungs. *Trails of History* says there are 183 rungs and four ladders, which must include rungs set as handrails (which I didn't count).

Iron rungs in themselves do not make for difficult hiking. As used in Acadia, they generally make it easier to get out of a tight place here and there. On the Precipice Trail it is where the rungs are set that makes all the difference—places you would not tread on your own. More than a convenience, Brunnow's rungs are the backbone of his route. Where Waldron Bates thought in terms of wedged steps, Brunnow pictured iron. Which may be one reason he bridged the Precipice and Bates did not.

The Precipice Trail has four sections: preamble, traverse, cliffs, and upper shelf. Brunnow's rungs help you get started, and take you over the cliffs at the other end. They play a minor role on the traverse and upper shelf. The reason for installing rungs at the beginning may be to give climbers a taste of what they will face higher up. We are put to the test right off, the trail asking if we are up for this kind of hike, warning the frail, unequipped, and faint-hearted to stay back.

If the trail fails to get the message across, bold yellow signs state it in so many words:

> THE PRECIPICE IS MAINTAINED
> AS A NONTECHNICAL CLIMBING
> ROUTE, NOT A HIKING TRAIL.
> ATTEMPT THIS ROUTE ONLY
> IF YOU ARE PHYSICALLY FIT,
> WEARING BOOTS, AND
> EXPERIENCED IN EXPOSURE TO
> HEIGHTS.
>
> PERSONS HAVE FALLEN AND
> DIED ON THIS MOUNTAINSIDE.

All four sections are exciting in their own way. The first in leading you to the traverse. The second in getting you up on the cliffs. The third in taking you out on them, and then off. The upper shelf is where, ambling through pitch pines to the summit, you congratulate yourself for having done it—the Precipice!

The preamble is a warm-up that gets you into the mood as you near the cliffs. Here is magic. Standing among boulders in birch woods, you look with awe upon those dripping walls. We make fun of yokels gaping at skyscrapers, but here the jaws of urban sophisticates must drop. As awesome a site as any in Acadia, and you are barely away from the loop road. Look at that shimmering fall of water dropping nine feet against a backdrop of damp moss, dripping on a drumhead of matted leaves, spurting out quick-changing rhythms. Whose heart does not dance to such music?

Two rungs, the first set high, in a six-foot wall of granite. You would think they would make it a little easier. You stretch and pull yourself up, muttering about giants, only to get water down your neck from an overhanging drip. The cliffs were gushing the morning I hiked the trail, so that is how I will tell it. Ferns and lichens were in their damp and drippy element.

With an assist from a seven-foot hand rail, you come to the edge of a talus slope, a river of giant boulders rushing down from the base of the cliffs. Ten-foot blocks of granite, the bones of Champlain Mountain. Here is where old cliffs go to die. Sweeping left to right, the view encompasses cliffs, their fallen remains, birch woods at their base surrounding a peaceful meadow, and the misty expanse of

Frenchman Bay—with the *Bluenose* ferry bucking the slate-gray swells as it heads towards Nova Scotia, bow plunging to deck line, rearing, plunging and rearing again.

Blue blazes beckon you up the talus slope, daring you to crawl or leap boulder to boulder, with no steps to make the going any easier. Your reward is a great view of the cliffs. There are two sets, those above the talus, and an upper wall beyond. The trail heads for both. Straight for those granite

Hiker on the Precipice Trail.

palisades, surface scored with cracks and clefts beneath a creneled edge. Straight for peregrine country. I picture falcons screaming overhead in 1914 when Brunnow built his trail.

Scrambling over boulders, you come to another test, a keyhole to squeeze through. And another. In intimate contact with granite, you crawl beneath a fifteen-foot boulder, experiencing the talus from underneath, seeing how stones wedge together. You angle across the field of fallen rock, reaching the base of the lower cliffs. More dripping walls amid woods of birch and oak.

Trees hug the base of the cliff. Two rungs lift the trail onto a ledge where water runs everywhere in sheets over moss, lichens, and liverworts. Collecting in niches. Splashing on slanting shelves and passing hikers without prejudice. The sloping ledge was slippery. A rail of bent pipe looked flimsier than I would have liked, bowing out where

I wished it wouldn't, as if a lurching hiker had fallen against it. Leaning ahead, outstretched arm grasping at niches, I hopped from one more-or-less level spot to the next. Still at ground zero, my confidence gave a shake. Was this a trail I could count on or not? Better to count on myself. In thirty-five feet I came to a dense patch of kinnikinnick. That settled it. A sucker for kinnikinnick, I went on.

Now higher than the trees, the trail looks over a meadow and beaver pond toward Frenchman Bay. Six ducks played tag in the pond, splashing after one another in short bursts, turning, flapping, quacking. I splashed some myself, along the wet trail, now turned from granite to gravel and broken rock. A plank bridge stretched across a chasm, which I crossed, eying the two logs supporting the fifteen-foot span at either end. (This section of trail was subsequently swept away by a rockfall, and has been replaced.) Another sinuous pipe rail ran under Bridal Veil Falls, and some fifty feet beyond.

Down stone steps pinned with iron, up a flight of giant steps, the trail leads to more woods at the base of another cliff. Looking back, I admired the profile of the cliffs I had just passed under. Nine more steps up, hewn blocks fifteen inches on a side. Now opposite High Seas, I had reached the base of the traverse where the east face trail joins from the north, the route I would be taking in a few hours to complete my loop. From here the trail heads in earnest up the cliffs. A sign says it's four-tenths of a mile to the summit. Is that all?

From here the trail rises steadily at a uniform pitch across the cliffs, like the bar of a backwards Z. A few rungs and handholds, but no ladders. Rudolph Brunnow Memorial Highway up the east face of Champlain Mountain. From now on the view is not so much up or along the cliffs as out and down, down, down. Instead of a handrail, the way is lined with trees much of the way, creating a cloistered effect very different from what you would expect. The largest trees were halfway up the Z. Two oaks, one fifteen inches in diameter, the other twenty-four.

"What are you doing here?" I asked the trees.

"Likewise yourself," they shot back.

A river flowed toward me in this ascending reach of the trail, then dashed over the side and went where all good rivers go—down and away to the sea. This one went faster than some, its bed falling two hundred feet straight down. A five-foot wall of rock stymied me for a bit, lower rung almost three feet off the ground. I got soaked getting over that one, first draping myself on the rock, now the bed of a river, before finding a toehold behind me which gave enough purchase to boost myself up.

Squeezing through a narrow gap, the trail goes on, keeping to the same pitch and same heading, until it levels off at about 700 feet. Then Rudolph Brunnow whips out his iron, and the fun begins.

You know the trail has changed gears when you come to a set of seven rungs, followed by a narrow ledge with five handrails, leading to seven more rungs. Made of three-quarter-inch iron, the rungs look solid enough—until you notice two of them are bent down in the middle. I thought of the man Ripley says was buried in a piano case.

Kinnikinnick (bearberry).

Abruptly, I was on the face of the cliff, with no reassuring screen of trees. Out in the o-p-e-n. Exposed to the wind, hearing the fog signal on Egg Rock, and the whumping roar of surf crashing on granite. My senses kicked in all at once. Adrenalin surged. The rules had changed midhike. Up a wet cliff face on the five-rung ladder. Then another eight rungs, leading to thirteen set in a narrow angle in the cliff. Out in the open. Me and the cliff. And Brunnow's ghost.

This must be the hard part. But it got worse. One narrow cliffwalk followed another. I was on a ledge three feet wide, sloping and wet, not a handhold in sight. Creeping along, I saw two handholds ahead. How to reach them? Where do I put my feet? I planned every move. Executed it. Planned the next. Two giant steps. Two pickerel steps. Three butterfly steps with rattail sweeps. One rocking-chair hop. I fit my gait to the terrain, performing whatever steps the cliffs called for. They commanded. I did what they said.

Now and then I would catch an eye-corner glimpse of the view from my cliffside perch, and find myself servant of two masters. The trail demanded attention, but so did the scene I overlooked. Sand Beach and Great Head in the south to the Porcupine Islands. Not able to attend both at once, I gave priority to the trail, but when I felt snug enough, looked at the landscape below. Wetlands and tawny meadows set off by birch woods. I had seen the beaver pond from the base of the Z, but from up here it was joined by a line of five other pools. Runoff from Champlain collected as one long wetland in a meadow between cliffs and the ocean.

They say when facing sudden death, the mind scrolls through the history of a lifetime. There would be survival value in reviewing past experience for anything to help in a crunch. I was not facing death, but my senses were processing a lot of data at great speed. I drank in the view, quaffing it at a glance. It registered in microseconds.

Two oaks growing on the brink. What a view they had. Up two rungs, then along a ledge. . . . Shouts from below broke my concentration. In a quick look I saw two vans had pulled up next to my car, spilling tiny figures. Ten or a dozen, all shouting and dancing about, looking like they had come a long way and were glad to stretch their legs.

A row of eleven handholds took me around a long curving ledge to a rise with three rungs. Onto a shelf. Up three more rungs to another shelf. Then a sloping ledge with a boost from a natural foothold. The lip of the cliff above me retreated as I went.

Standing on a ledge with five handholds, I backed up next to a small pitch pine and scanned the scene below. A falcon's view of the world. Some thrive in high places, others do not. I hate heights. One of my worst experiences was taking the little bubble car to the top of the Gateway to the West in St. Louis, walking to the center of the arch, looking down. Seeing emptiness. Nothing holding me up. Turning, walking very carefully back to my bubble, taking the next ride down. Lighthouses get to me, the kind with winding staircases going round and round and up and up, latticed steps with holes in them so you can see through them straight down. There are hikers like me. Then there are climbers.

Five stone steps led off the ledge, with a killer step at the bottom three feet high. There has to be a way . . . I see, step back and get a boost from that little nub jutting out on the side. The trailmakers had worked economically, making best use of what they had.

A leg-up of one rung, badly rusted, but I had to trust it because I had no choice. Six more rungs onto a tricky sloping ledge with an overhang pushing me toward the edge. No handholds. Good place to crawl. But I would not stoop to that. Stood up, hitting left shoulder on the overhang. I crawled.

Over a step wedged in a crack onto a ledge running thirty feet south. Then another ledge three-feet wide running north. Up seven rungs over a ten-foot wall. North again on a shelf four or five feet wide. Three rungs onto a higher shelf. Not a good place to look down.

As if I had not felt it before, I felt really exposed. Really,

really exposed. The trail leads across the edge of a slab cracking off the mountain in a smooth arc up and over. Without those eight handholds I would not have made it. You commit yourself to doing what you could not normally have done. I pressed on because I had to. Rudolph Brunnow again.

Coming to three stone steps, I was surprised to see them there, supposing Brunnow had replaced such primitive

Feather moss.

technology with rungs of iron (boosting Acadia's Neolithic trail system into the Iron Age). Past the steps, four rungs mounted to a narrow ledge two to three feet wide. Nine rungs ahead. Beyond that, clouds scudding out of the west. This must be the top. A long skywalk, with footholds— long, low bars looking like they would like to catch your toes and trip you up. There were handholds, too. Eleven in a row, around a curving shelf. Then three rungs into a cleft. And with two farewell handholds, I stood on the brink.

Where I was greeted by a yellow sign:

> CLIMBING UP IS EASIER
> THAN CLIMBING DOWN.
> FOR AN EASIER WAY BACK,
> TAKE BEAR BROOK TRAIL
> FROM SUMMIT, LOCATED
> 10 MINUTES AHEAD.

Which I planned to take anyway. I had been down the Precipice Trail three times. Enough for one lifetime. Now I was more into loops.

From the top of the cliffs to the summit, the trail crosses a gradually sloping shelf of smooth granite, with pockets of soil here and there. This is a kinder, gentler habitat, peopled with pitch pines, blueberries, sheep laurel, and occasional oaks. Pine sprigs scattered in the trail told me red squirrels were near. Cairns led up the slope, puddle to puddle in the often flooded trail. Here was a miniature forest of ground pine, the thickest I had ever seen. Coming across nibbled acorns in the trail, I heard the churr of a red squirrel. Climbing three rungs up one last wall, I came to the summit of Champlain Mountain, elevation 1,058 feet. It had taken me three hours to get there.

Clouds hid the horizon in every direction. They boiled over the south ridge of Cadillac, coming my way. Where I was the sun was shining in a clear blue sky. I had been so intent on the trail I had not noticed when it broke through the clouds. But how low it was! Even at ten o'clock. My shadow stretched fourteen feet ahead of me as I crossed the dome of Champlain toward the Bear Brook Trail and the mountain's north slope. I felt a chill wind for the first time, and put down the flaps of my cap. A chickadee flitted ahead of me, and a red squirrel hunkered in the top of a pitch pine. Looking across to Dorr Mountain, I traced the ladder trail and Kurt Diederich's Climb along natural routes set off by the raking light. Where the Beachcroft Trail dives toward Huguenot Head, I continued north, stopping at an overlook to admire Frenchman Bay, and have a well-deserved drink of coffee from my thermos. I had met the challenge of the Preci-pice and felt very accomplished. With plastic cup, I raised a salute to Rudolph Brunnow. Clouds overran the summit, so I cut my break short and went on.

Steps in cleft on Champlain Mountain East Face Trail.

Coming to the brink of Champlain's north ridge, I looked down on Bar Harbor dressed in winter garb, Beaver Dam Pool, and more strikingly, the Jackson Laboratory complex, its more than twenty-five buildings upstaging everything else.

The bald Thrumcap, a naked rock offshore, reminded me of a submerging turtle, domed carapace awash with breakers coming from every direction. The Porcupine Islands looked like a pod of whales heading out to sea, or perhaps some admiral's fleet. No real vessels of any size were on the bay. This was November, not July. The Bear Brook Trail was wet, but the new Vibram soles I'd had put on my winter hiking boots held firm and never slipped.

Thinking how hard the glacier had worked grinding up

that slope in the opposite direction, I easily made my way down through a series of changing habitats, from pitch pine, through gray birch, into spruce, and finally hemlock woods. What struck me was how the outermost layer of granite was peeling off the mountain in great slabs, first cracking, then slipping, to lodge behind some obstruction lower down. Shedding its skin.

The worn sign for the east face trail says simply, **LOOP RD. .3 MI.** I knew I could get back to the Precipice Trail that way. Running along a spur jutting toward the bay, the trail quickly reaches an outlook back onto Champlain itself, from there reduced to a rounded dome, with impressive cliffs in the foreground not visible from the Bear Brook Trail a few yards back. Labeled the Horseshoe on old maps, it is one of those unheralded sites you stumble across—and find your breath taken away. The trail runs along the east rim of a bowl whose far wall is a colonnade of granite pillars. Woods of birch and oak line the sheltered hollow below, edging a swamp filled with red-berried shrubs. I sat on a rock and had a second cup of coffee.

Who lives here? I wondered. In the five minutes I sat on my granite bench, a chickadee called out several times, two red squirrels ran across a log fallen into the swamp, and a blue jay piped from the opposite cliff, filling the bowl with sound.

Heading down off the spur, the trail descends by way of an elegant flight of steps leading from the Horseshoe to the top of a fine talus slope tumbling toward the Park Loop Road. The steps are less grand than some placed by the trailmakers, being constructed of smaller stones—but the flight as a whole is superb. It descends in reverse curves to the top of the talus, where the east face trail branches south.

It took me an hour to reach the Precipice parking lot by a route which edges its way along the base of the cliffs through rocky woods, alternately climbing and descending, over a treadway strewn with leaves of oak and birch, poplar and striped maple. The trail does not show much use, and in places is hard to follow because it blends with surrounding terrain.

The highlight of the east face trail is a run of steps you come across abruptly because hidden by a deep cleft in the rock. A blue blaze leads you to what at first seems like a dead end, it not being possible for the trail to go on from that brink. But it does go on. Almost straight down. Through the narrow cleft, which broadens toward its base. And nestled against both walls, a flight of twenty-four steps rises through the cleft bottom-to-top, or as I saw it, descends top-to-bottom.

Whose signature is revealed by these steps? What genius expressed itself here? Probably Rudolph Brunnow's. High Seas, his seat away from Princeton, is just across the meadow. These steps are well within territory he claimed as his own. But, too, the steps suggest the handiwork of Waldron Bates, of Dorr Mountain Ladder Trail fame, who had headed the Bar Harbor roads and path committee before Brunnow. Whoever laid them, I was glad to follow in the footsteps of him who did.

Heading south after the cleft, the trail becomes a rough path across the rocky slopes with no outstanding features to recommend it. Badly worn and eroded, it offers poor footing in many places. Blue blazes vie with red for jurisdiction, the blues winning out because more freshly painted. Aside from the War of the Blazes, the one thing I did note along here was an acorn stashed behind the lobe of a lichen four feet off the ground in the crotch of an oak. I knew whose signature that was without asking. Deadened to the sight of dripping cliffs by the time I got that far, I barely turned my head when one followed another. The east face trail soon led to the Precipice Trail at the lower angle of the reverse Z, and I retraced my steps the way I had come.

I met two men just starting out, who told me it was their first time up the Precipice. Asked what it was like, I said it gets better and better.

The Precipice Trail is a marvel of psychological engineering, challenging mind and body alike. The first leg of the trail sets hikers thinking how serious they are in wanting to go the whole distance. It lets us gauge ourselves, and make up our own minds. A black and yellow warning sign is one thing, but the trail itself makes us ask what business we have in such a place. It is a self-administered test, scored on a pass-fail basis. Go or no-go. If we remain undeterred by the first slick slope, boulder field, unreasonable rise of rungs and steps, or sight of rickety rails of bent pipe, then there is no reason not to make a run for the top.

Describing other hikes, I have often begun by mentioning plants and animals met along the way. That is my chief interest in the living trails of Acadia. But having given a blow-by-blow account of the trail, I will bring them in here near the end as a sort of appendix. Which is not how I experienced them at the time when each one had my full attention, no matter where I was on the trail.

I was amazed by the amount and variety of plant life clinging to the Precipice. The entire east face of Champlain Mountain is a mosaic of ledges, clefts, and cliffs, each site sprouting with its own kind of life. The Precipice is exposed to the elements, but those same elements—sunlight, water, air—are the very sponsors of life. The limiting factor is soil. Where not washed away, the cliff face is a veritable garden. Species range from lowly lichens, liverworts, and mosses, to lofty pines and oaks. Groundcover thrives. Much of the way, the trail is bordered by dense patches of wintergreen, kinnikinnick, and mayflower. Rock-cap ferns are everywhere, turning ledges and boulders green. I saw some evergreen wood ferns, and a great many tangles of spent bracken. Past the lip of the Precipice, I found the pitch pines near the summit particularly beautiful.

I did not meet many actual or virtual signs of wildlife, and some of those I did meet were not obvious. Holes eaten by insects in oak leaves, or worm tunnels where bark had fallen away from a snag or stump. I have mentioned the ducks and beaver lodge in the wetlands below the cliffs. I saw gulls along the shore, and heard chickadees, crows, and one blue jay. Phantom flocks of chipping birds taunted me from the woods at the base of the cliffs, though as usual, no matter how hard I peered, I never saw one. I did see a red squirrel on the summit, two in the Horseshoe on the east face, and heard several others. A small insect fluttered by me at some point on the trail. The last gnat of summer. I was mindful of the peregrines when I looked up at their nesting site, or down on it from above, and was glad to join the time-sharing arrangement Acadia has worked out with them.

There were eight other vehicles in the parking lot when I got back—two cars, a jeep, two vans, and three pickups. Four were from Maine, with one each from New Jersey, New York, Connecticut, and Massachusetts, representing perhaps twenty-four hikers in all. When, an hour later, it started to rain, I thought of the two men I had met who were making their first climb. I knew it would be getting dark by the time they got back. Now they faced even worse conditions. I felt a strong sense of comradeship with them. Picturing us getting together, swapping stories, I realized what an unspoken bond I felt with everyone who had followed Rudolph Brunnow up the Precipice Trail in the past eighty years. I felt proud to have renewed membership in that widespread society.

○

15—DORR & CADILLAC MOUNTAINS LOOP

From Cadillac Mountain summit parking area
To Dorr Mountain, Otter Creek, and back
   Down by Dorr Mountain Notch and Dorr Mountain
     South Ridge trails
   Up by Canon (Canyon) Brook and Cadillac
     Mountain East Ridge trails
          4.25 miles, November 27, 1993

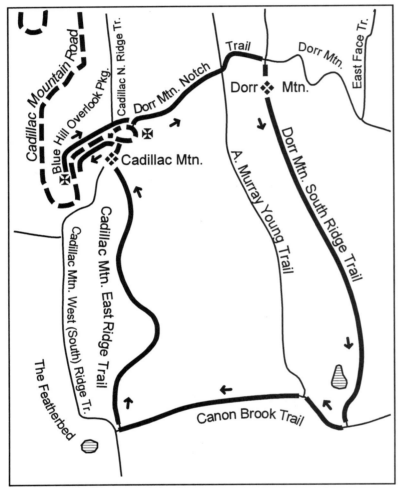

15—Dorr & Cadillac mountains loop.

The Saturday after Thanksgiving I hiked four trails, each with a distinct character, making a rectangular four-mile loop starting at the summit of Cadillac Mountain. I had written up fourteen hikes; it was time to take a winter break after one last outing. I had not done Cadillac yet, so saw that as a good place to stop.

Perrin's last loop turned out to be one of the best hikes I had made all fall. I had not planned it as a grand finale, but that is what it felt like. Four different trails. Four moods. Four different Acadias. There is a reason so many musical compositions are based on four movements. It takes that many parts to fully round-out a whole without one part detracting from the others. Pairs play off against themselves. Threes break down into a pair and an outsider. Fours can at least strive for symmetry, sometimes balancing the tensions between parts so perfectly to produce a work that is both fluid and complete. Boxing the compass with my loop, I ended three months of hiking in perfect union with my surroundings. Which is why I love to hike, and why I have been tramping through Acadia's living terrain these thirteen weeks.

I started out from Blue Hill Overlook on Cadillac Mountain at 8:20 a.m., took the Dorr Mountain Notch Trail across to the summit of Dorr, the Dorr Mountain South Ridge Trail down, the Canon Brook Trail up Cadillac as far as the Featherbed, and the old Cadillac Mountain East Ridge Trail back to my car at the summit. The low point was 218 feet where the trail crosses Otter Creek, the high point the Cadillac benchmark at 1,530 feet, for a vertical climb and descent of 1,312 feet. It took five hours and forty minutes to complete the four-and-a-quarter-mile loop. As usual I went slowly, stopping often to look, listen, and take notes.

The four movements of my *Symphonic Poem for Two Legs* could be titled: "Erosion," "Mountain Life," "Ice and Gravity," and "Acadia before the White Man." The theme played out along the notch trail as it dips between the summits of Dorr and Cadillac tells the story of granite's defeat by the elements. The defining motif of Dorr's south ridge trail counters that initial note of melancholy with a boisterous tale of life on the slopes featuring solos by squirrels, chickadees, crows, and a red-tailed hawk. Next comes the more pensive Canon Brook theme depicting trial by ice and gravity. The final movement is joyful throughout, presenting a vision of Acadia as it was before European settlers possessed its virgin woods and slopes. The overall effect is upbeat and heroic.

Well, no, it did not go exactly that way. But as the hike-to-end-all-hikes (temporarily), it was a good one. Picking up Cadillac's South Ridge Trail just into the woods across the road from Blue Hill Overlook, I headed for the summit, figuring to start at the top and work down. An eight-inch dike crossed the trail, first of the dozen or so I met on my loop. The going was icy in places where seeps had flowed then frozen inches thick. Temperature in the low twenties, I watched where I stepped. Within fifty feet I was in the midst of gnarled, stunted trees, mostly red and white spruce, forming the nearly impassable woods at Cadillac's summit. Driving to the parking lot, you hardly realize those woods are there. But Cadillac is by no means barren or bald.

Heading east, the trail dips into a gully, crosses a fire

road, rises, then comes out of the woods at the actual summit of Cadillac Mountain, as told by the 1856 USGS reference mark set in granite just off the trail, thirty-five feet south of the 1934 benchmark giving the elevation as 1,530 feet (my topo map says 1,528). A rectangular foundation still marked by a few stones shows where the Summit House was built in 1883, with its surrounding porch and observatory. How big was it? Pacing it off, I would say forty by fifty feet. Trying to put myself back 110 years, I balked at the thought of a railroad to the top (also built in 1883, removed soon after), and went on at my own pace in my own time. I took the short fire road back of the gift shop to the parking area where the Dorr Mountain Notch Trail begins.

Seeing a bronze tablet set near the lower promontory at the end of the summit parking area, I went over to read the words honoring Stephen Tyng Mather, 1867–1930, a founder of the National Park Service. "There will never come an end to the good that he has done." I pictured the shadow of his work stretching through time like Earth's umbra in a lunar eclipse. Without Mather and the NPS there would be no Acadia, and the parking lot would be ringed with Summit Houses serving fast food. As I went across the parking lot to the sign marking the start of the notch trail, a blond Cairn terrier bounced out of a car and jumped up on my leg, its four owners all calling at once, "Bonzo," "Bonzo," "Bonzo," "Bonzo." Aside from Bonzo's car there were two pickups parked at the summit.

Pausing at the start of the trail, I looked for Katahdin out of habit—and there it was! hanging over Raccoon Cove in Lamoine, snowy slopes 110 miles distant gleaming with coppery light. But much closer than that, what was wrong with Lead Mountain? A punk haircut sprouted from its usually rounded dome. As I stared, the mountain grew taller and taller. Thinner and thinner. Erupting before my eyes. Similar trees on a mountain farther east began to thin, then disappear. I am used to such looming effects at sea level, especially in winter, when boats and islands get stretched out of shape. Bands of air having different temperatures and densities act like a distorting lens. Lead Mountain began to shimmer, then shrank to normal size. In a few moments the show was over.

The notch trail does its job of connecting the summits of Dorr and Cadillac—but just barely. One of my least favorite trails. Poorly marked, it often seems to disappear like the trees on Lead Mountain, forcing hikers to backtrack to the last cairn or blaze and start again. The problem is partly due to summer visitors rearranging the cairns, seeing them as decorative sculptures rather than trail markers, moving and reshaping them. The terrain itself is difficult because badly

eroded, the trail echoing that decadence. I spent a lot of time trying to find my way down into the Notch. Eventually I got into the spirit of the place, and began reveling in shambles and collapse.

I cannot think of a place in Acadia giving a better overview of the successive stages of erosion. Here are mountains cracking, splitting, falling apart before your eyes. The slope underfoot gives a close-up view of the details, the one

Cadillac Mountain crumbles into the Gorge.

opposite revealing the pattern underlying the whole operation. Emily Dickinson wrote "Dilapidation's processes / Are organized Decays." The west face of Dorr Mountain is a textbook example. The whole story of how a megalith crumbles to boulders, fragments, pebbles, and sand is told in the arrangement of those rocks. We do not need a time-lapse film. The stages are all there. From the smooth brow of the cliff to the talus fallen into the Notch, I could see elemental forces ravaging the landscape, grinding it into soil. The proof was there in the saddle of the Notch below, in woods of spruce and birch rising from the debris.

If mountains did not collapse and resolve into sand, there would be no mineral grains. No spaces between them to hold air and water. No soil. No roots. No birches. Aside from lichens and bacteria, there would not be much in the way of terrestrial life. A mountain's misfortune is our success. Acadia as we know it flows from the destruction of its former self.

Dropping 500 feet into the Notch, the trail then rises to the top of Dorr, regaining about half the altitude it lost on the Cadillac side. There was more ice on Dorr, forcing me to seek alternate routes in several spots. Even with such delays, it took only fifteen minutes to scramble from the Notch to the cairn at Dorr's summit. A hiker in blue was there before me, addressing himself in turn to each direction. We saluted one another but did not speak. Words had lost much of the currency we give them at sea level. Even the wind had lost its breath and was barely discernible. Frenchman Bay was flat calm. No waves crashed against Bald Porcupine, Thrumcap, Egg Rock.

Not pausing at the summit, I started down the Dorr Mountain South Ridge Trail, the liveliest leg of my loop, proceeding through pitch pine woods most of the way, with oaks added on the lower slopes. Squirrel country. I saw two red squirrels and heard at least twelve others. They lived on pine buds above, acorns below. Studying a little nest of cone cores stripped of their scales—and more to the point, of their seeds—I heard a rhythmic whumping sound. Looking up, I watched a crow fly up the ridge twenty feet above the pines, like the rest of us, not speaking. It was if we had a pact of silence, vowing to keep still until we actually had something to say.

A great many ice patches caught the light on Cadillac. Underfoot, the trail wound among frozen pools, surfaces mounded in the center, ice cracked in rays and concentric rings like crystalline roses. The landscape offered plain fare much of the way, pitch pines and juniper being the only plants to spring from fissures in the ridge. After the harsh jumble of rocks in the Notch, this organic order was a great relief. I

Ice on the walls of the Gorge between Dorr and Cadillac mountains.

have always liked the gently sloping south ridge trail, for its beauty more than its ease. Pitch pines and granite. Without soil, little can grow here. The stark simplicity of the landscape stirs me. It is as if bedrock comes to life without having to endure the tedious middle stages of crumbling and decay. Every tree reflects the character of the site.

Chickadees were busy gleaning pine branches for insects. I saw a group of five, another of six, and a third of at least seven, including a golden-crowned kinglet. I saw two more crows, and heard others cawing lower down on the ridge. I glimpsed a beaver lodge in a small pond near the foot of the trail, but thought it was not occupied because I saw no branches stuck in the mud as a winter food supply. Both red squirrels I saw lived up to their name, looking sleek and gingery in new fur coats. At one point, roused by a shrill cry, I looked up to see a red-tailed hawk circling,

circling, circling over Canon Brook. Spiraling ever higher, it rose through the Notch in great, easy rounds, staying in view more than five minutes.

Low on the ridge, the slope increases, and the trail drops into woods of mixed pitch pine and oak. In the steepest part, under a large white cedar, runoff had frozen in the trail, creating a massive fall of white ice. Stepping around it with help from the cedar, I stood at the edge of the ice and looked back. There they were! An endless file of shadowy spermatozoa swimming under the ice. All my life I have been fascinated by that weaving, rhythmic flow in spring and fall when water, with seeming poise and grace, slips slowly through secret channels between ice and a warmer surface of dark rock underneath. In seeing them as giant spermatozoa, am I projecting a male urge to remake the world in my image? I could say they remind me of a paisley shawl. Or, since they seem so alive, of polliwogs in a swamp. But this is no mere fabric design, or dumb squirmy motion. Its hold lies partly in its rhythmic grace and transformations, but more I think in what I will call its purposiveness. Like sperm cells streaming towards their one objective, these agile shapes all slip the same direction. Their separate courses vary, but the thrust of the herd without exception is down and down and down. They are drawn by the same urge that drives the rain, topples cliffs, fells trees, and brings the rest of us in the end to lie down in green pastures.

Crossing a twenty-inch dike, the trail winds through more open woods, oaks now the most common tree. Passing by a small frozen wetland, I stopped to admire leaves suspended in the clear ice, and grasses rising from its surface. I heard more squirrels, crows, and chickadees, and found three scats containing brown fur. A lone hiker overtook me. We agreed the day was warming up. He had hiked up from Bubble Pond on the Cadillac West Face Trail, and was heading back by way of Canon Brook. We had both seen the white swath down the course of the brook, and agreed the trail would be icy. He went ahead. After hiking three hours, I came to the Canon Brook Trail at the foot of the south ridge, and turned west through woods of six-inch beech, birch, and popple overtopped by a few larger white pines.

Passing a frozen seven-foot waterfall, nearby boulders and twigs bulbous and white from the spray, I saw more spermaform shapes, some large as bullheads, creeping past windows in the ice. Just beyond, at the junction of Canon Brook and Otter Creek, elevation 218 feet, the trail bottomed out. My car waited 1,300 feet above me. There was no way to go but up. Jumping the creek, I jumped from Dorr to Cadillac, and began the third leg of my hike.

To reach the Featherbed, a wetland on the south ridge of Cadillac at an elevation just under 1,000 feet, the Canon Brook Trail rises in three stages. First, at a gentle grade through deciduous woods, it leads to the base of the slope proper, Cadillac's granite flank. Then up the bare slope, the exciting part of the trail. And above that, by a long avenue of easy steps past a beaver pond to the Featherbed, a dip in the ridge where runoff collects. The route is near water the whole way, which in August is a definite plus. In late fall the trail is ruled by ice.

Much of the lower slope had been flooded and frozen, and was now icy. Over the years ice had been unkind to the trail itself. A great many stone steps had been wrenched out of place. Some runs were gone completely. Avoiding slippery sections, scrambling where there was no trail, in short order I reached a frozen waterfall eight feet high at the foot of the steeper pitch.

The canyon of Canon Brook.

The midsection of the Canon Brook Trail, steep and often wet, is an adventure at any season. Now it was icy as well, but not completely. There were gaps in the ice where water flowed too quickly to freeze. And a few dry ledges here and there where there was no flow. I decided on a frontal assault.

Low on the slope there is a splendid chute or canyon (for which the Brook is named) where, in season, water rushes headlong eighty to a hundred feet down a deep gouge in the granite. Ahead lay a steep slab of ice which one way or another I had to get by. There were small islands in the slab worn by running water, and I thought I could map out a route from one to the next that would take me across. Keeping center of gravity low, watching where I stepped, and not reaching too far or too short, I hopped from one island to the next as if following the tracks of a great sure-footed cat, soon reaching dry ledge beyond the upper end of the icy slab.

Moving on, I came to a pool on the south edge of the bare ledge where I remembered swimming on one particularly hot hike with a friend. It was frozen this time and looked less inviting. A line of small cairns led away from the pool. The third cairn was locked in ice, which stretched for almost seventy-five feet. A blue blaze on bare ledge upslope showed where I wanted to go. I walked across a pocket of level ice to get to the cairn, which I used as a step to reach a series of ice-free streaks where wet granite showed through. I'm not sure how I did it, but I made it across, aware from time to time of a run of distracting polliwogs beneath the ice, and at one point hearing the noon siren wail up the valley from Otter Creek village. One slip and I would shoot sixty feet downslope into a pile of boulders. I think I willed myself over that stretch. I got to the blaze I was aiming for, and after a scramble on all fours, gained the top of the steepest and most challenging part of the trail. A good place to eat lunch.

Like many lucky Americans two days after Thanksgiving, I ate a turkey sandwich. My thoughts were grave. That is, they ran to gravity. I could not get it out of my mind. From where I sat, I saw three schools of polliwogs wriggling beneath the ice. Three swarms of spermatozoa, lazing in their gravity-powered lust. Gravity. We are born to it, live to it, die to it. It is the medium of life itself. Yet who on Earth celebrates Gravity Day, or drinks to its success? Without that basic tug to work against, we could not dance, hike, or sit in repose eating turkey sandwiches.

A small sound in the woods broke into my dreamlike reflection. Turning, I saw a hairy woodpecker tapping at a birch not far away. Gravity went out of my mind. I went on. The trail headed at an easy incline among leafless trees, following the brook for a ways, then by a long stretch of well-laid steps, it led to the Featherbed, passing a small beaver pond. Were beavers there now? Stepping toward the pond just south of the trail, I stepped on a twig which broke with a snap. A dog started barking ahead, a big dog. A big, big dog. A Weimaraner lunged out of the bushes, eyes glowing, coat glistening with a purple sheen. A man and woman sitting in the trail ahead called it back. Eating lunch by the pond, they addressed the dog, but not me. I had no words to tell them what I thought about people turning their pets loose on the trail. One man's fond Bruno is another's hound of the Baskervilles. Forgetting beavers, I skirted the three of them in silence.

I reached the Featherbed by a long avenue of steps leading through quiet woods, icy cliffs visible on either hand where the ridge seeks lower ground. The wetland was iced over, tall stalks of tawny grass sprouting from its surface. I looked for two dikes I remembered near the trail crossing. Yes, there they were. They had not gone away. Old maps refer to "Great Snake Flat" in this vicinity. I figure the snake is the serpentine dike of gray stone slithering acoss the landscape.

Time to make a decision. Cadillac's west ridge or east? Which would I take to the summit? I had seen the east ridge trail as a dotted line on old maps, but had never been on it. Could I find it? If I could, and it was marked, that's the way I would go. I looked where I thought it would be, and eventually found it. The east ridge trail it would be, to close the loop.

The trail is not hiked much anymore, and the terrain through which it passes has not been disturbed the way the west ridge has been over the years, its soil being worn away, boulders heaped into piles, mountain plants trodden underfoot. The east ridge looks now much as I imagine it did shortly after the glacier receded. Bare granite spread with lichens, and aside from mosses, liverworts, sheep laurel, juniper, and blueberry, not many higher plants have come in. There are some birch and pitch pines, and a few cedars along Canon Brook.

The glory of the east ridge is its wildness. That is why I will hold back details of the trail itself. I had a strong feeling I did not belong there. The vegetation is so lowly and thin, foot traffic poses a real threat. You cannot go there without stepping on living plants, making their lives that much harder. Perhaps uprooting or killing them. I was careful where I stepped, but even meaning no harm, damaged the terrain as I admired it. What I found was a place I had the power to ruin.

Canon Brook drains the basin between Cadillac's two south-reaching ridges. The little soil built up there in the past ten thousand years clings in cracks and dips in the rock. What the landscape lacks in grandeur or magnificence, it makes up for it with stern simplicity.

What grows there belongs there. I saw four red squirrels, a flock of sixteen chickadees, sparse signs of snowshoe hares (pellets and nipped-off buds), and a sparrow's nest woven into a tuft of tan grass.

The upper end of the trail peters out as it meanders through spruce woods toward the summit. I lost myself near the end, just when I thought I was on familiar ground. Eventually I reached a known landmark and steered for my car. Circling through the parking lot, I saw thirteen cars from Maine, Massachusetts, Connecticut, New York, New

The Featherbed before freezing over.

Jersey, Pennsylvania, and Minnesota. Driving down the mountain road, I met another fifteen cars heading for the summit. Late in the season, Cadillac was the most popular spot in the park. As it should be. It gives you a sense of what Acadia is all about, inviting you to fill in the details. Which is what I have been trying to do on my hikes. Today's hike is the last in a series of fifteen made over a period of three months. I look forward to resuming my Acadian journey before long.

○

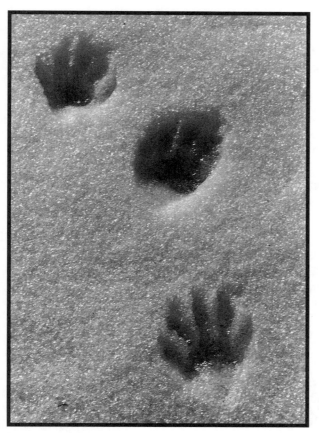
Raccoon prints in snow.

ACADIA
THE SOUL
OF A
NATIONAL PARK

BOOK TWO
WINTER

❄

In memory of

Michael Gale Perrin

February 20, 1959
February 20, 1981

He now, with Orion, strides

across the winter sky

CONTENTS—WINTER HIKES

INTRODUCTION—WINTER 76

16 OTTER POINT TO SAND BEACH 77
From Fabbri parking area on Otter Point
To Sand Beach, and back
   By Ocean Path both ways
                    4.0 miles, December 2, 1995

17 BEECH MOUNTAIN LOOP 82
From Long Pond parking area (pumping station)
To Beech Mountain summit, and back
   Up by Valley and Beech Mountain trails
   Down by Beech Mountain West Ridge Trail
                    3.6 miles, December 9, 1995

18 ASTICOU TRAIL 86
From Brown Mountain Gate parking area
To Jordan Pond by way of Forest Hill Cemetery,
   and back
   By Asticou Trail and connector both ways
                    5.5 miles, December 16, 1995

19 McFARLAND HILL LOOP 92
From park headquarters
To McFarland Hill summit and Breakneck Ponds,
   and back
   Up by McFarland Hill Trail
   Down by bushwhack, old woods road,
     and Breakneck Road
          2.9 miles on snowshoes, December 26, 1995

20 HUNTERS BROOK LOOP 96
From Route 3 between Otter Creek and Day Mtn.
Along Hunters Brook, and back
   Out by Hunters Brook Trail
   Back by bushwhack and the Boyd Road
         2.25 miles on snowshoes, December 28, 1995

21 SARGENT MOUNTAIN LOOP 100
From Brown Mountain Gate parking area
To Sargent Mountain summit, and back
    Up by carriage road; Hadlock Brook, Giant Slide,
      and Grandgent trails
    Down by Sargent Mountain South Ridge Trail
      and carriage road
          6.5 miles on snowshoes, January 4, 1996

22 AROUND MANSELL MOUNTAIN 108
From Long Pond parking area (pumping station)
To Great Notch, and back
    Up by Cold Brook and Great Notch trails
    Down by Long (Great) Pond Trail
          5.0 miles on snowshoes, January 11, 1996

23 LONG POND FIRE ROAD LOOP 112
From south gate of Long Pond Fire Road
To Long and Duck ponds, and back
    Out by Route 102 and north section of
      Long Pond Fire Road
    Back on south section of Long Pond Fire Road
      by way of Pine Hill
          6.0 miles on snowshoes, January 15, 1996

24 AROUND-MOUNTAIN CARRIAGE ROAD 116
Around Bald Peak; and Sargent, Penobscot,
      Parkman, and Cedar Swamp mountains
From Brown Mountain Gate parking area
      counterclockwise on Around-Mountain Carriage
      Road to Jordan Pond, and back
          12.5 miles on snowshoes, January 20, 1996

25 LITTLE HARBOR BROOK LOOP 123
From Route 3 near Little Harbor
To the Asticou Trail, and back
    North on Little Harbor Brook Trail
    South on private carriage roads to
      (Little) Long Pond, then along Route 3
          5.5 miles, February 2, 1996

26 BEEHIVE & CHAMPLAIN MTN. LOOP 127
From Park Loop Road fee station
To summits of Beehive and Champlain Mountain,
      and back
    Up by Beehive, Bowl, and Champlain
      Mountain South Ridge trails
    Down by Bear Brook and Champlain Mountain
      East Face trails, then along the loop road
          5.0 miles, February 9, 1996

27 CADILLAC MOUNTAIN ROAD 133
From Cadillac Mountain entrance gate on Route 233
To summit of Cadillac Mountain, and back
    Up and back on Park Loop and
      Cadillac Mountain roads
          9.0 miles, February 16, 1996

28 AROUND ST. SAUVEUR MOUNTAIN 136
From Man o' War Brook Fire Rd. gate on Route 102
To Valley Cove, and back
    East on Man o' War Brook Fire Road;
      South on Valley Cove (Flying Mountain) Trail;
    Back by Valley Cove Fire Road,
      Fernald Point Road, and Route 102
          5.33 miles, February 22, 1996

29 WONDERLAND & SHIP HARBOR LOOP 142
From Ship Harbor Nature Trail parking area
    on Seawall Road
To Bennet Cove and Ship Harbor, and back
    East along Seawall Road (Route 102A);
      South on Wonderland Fire Road;
      Along the shoreline to Ship Harbor;
      North on Ship Harbor Nature Trail
          2.25 miles, February 29, 1996

30 AROUND CEDAR SWAMP MOUNTAIN 145
From Brown Mountain Gate parking area
To Birch Spring, and back
    Up by carriage road; Hadlock Brook and
      Birch Spring trails
    Down by Amphitheater Trail and Around-Mountain
      Carriage Road
          5.0 miles on snowshoes, March 8, 1996

INTRODUCTION—WINTER

Hiking at any time of year has its challenges—blackflies, storms, heat, wind—but hiking in winter can raise such challenges from inconveniences to severe personal risks. Freezing rain, snow, ice, and cold increase the hazard of any trail. With cairns and blazes buried under snow, navigation becomes a matter of survival. Ice puts the most experienced hiker to the test. An innocent dusting of snow over ice turns the gentlest slope into a bobsled run. The best rule of thumb is not to hike when there is ice on the trail. Since it is difficult to anticipate conditions higher up, that rule translates, when it comes to winter hiking, stay home and read a good book.

The only safe alternative is to know what you are getting into, and be prepared for anything. With modern hiking gear, it is easy to dress for any degree of cold. I use polypropylene long johns; flannel-lined polyester pants; wool turtleneck, sweater, and watch cap; and an unlined Gore-Tex parka (bright red for visibility). For me, that works between 30° and 40° Fahrenheit. From 20° to 30°, I add a thin vest. In the teens, a flannel shirt, and near zero, a wool shirt. Hiking uphill gets your blood flowing, so you feel much warmer than you do in the same gear on level ground. You have to experiment to find what works for you. Carry balaclava, scarf, and extra gloves in a pack of some sort that has room for gear you take off as you warm up. I wear insulated boots with Vibram soles, attaching snowshoes or ice creepers as necessary. Gaiters keep snow out of my boots. I always carry water (which sometimes freezes) and two space blankets.

It is essential to be in top physical shape for winter hiking. The trail will test you in ways you cannot imagine. Let others know where you are going, and always hike with an experienced and trustworthy companion.

The most important piece of gear I carry is good judgment. I try to think ahead, to have an alternate route in mind, to mentally retrace my steps in case I have to retreat. My judgment is not always as good as my intentions. When the trail drives that home, I reassess my situation, then do what seems best under the circumstances.

While winter hiking is a challenge, it also sets the hiker up for a greater sense of achievement and satisfaction than hiking at less trying times of year. If you yearn for solitude and beauty, they are yours on Acadia's winter trails. Winter hiking involves not only your legs, but your senses, mind, heart, and spirit. It stirs footloose reflections on life at the forefront of cosmic creation. If you crave renewal, winter hiking is a robust way to re-create yourself. Spring is beautiful in Acadia, as are summer and fall, but winter adds an edge of excitement that turns a hike into a journey transcending time and space. You become one with your place on Earth, and with the expanding universe. To understand Acadia, you have to know it in the winter months. Only then does the meaning of spring become clear.

Winter's primary lesson is about survival. A surprising number of wild creatures tough it out in Maine when their fair-weather cousins have long since fled to the Caribbean. Imagine living outdoors when the temperature is ten below

Ice vanes, Cadillac Mountain.

zero and the wind is howling out of the northwest at twenty-five miles an hour! Foxes do it; red squirrels do it; eagles do it; chickadees do it; buffleheads and guillemots do it. Without hot cocoa and earmuffs. Without woodstoves and turtlenecks from L.L. Bean. Winter hiking puts me in touch with Acadia's winter residents, if not directly, through their calls, scents, and tracks. The park is alive in winter, peopled by beings having supernatural powers. Every track is proof of their presence. A chickadee in summer is just a lively bird; a chickadee in winter is an exemplar of courage, stamina, and hope. To see where an ermine bounded through the woods, a porcupine plowed a path in deep snow, or a pygmy shrew darted lightly from under a log is to see the tracks of creatures who, like the Cyclopean builders of Mycenae, perform feats surpassing the powers of mere mortals like ourselves. Acadia in winter is home to animals living on a daily basis out in the open at the mythic pitch of angels, trolls, djinn, and giants while humanity retreats indoors to huddle under the covers till spring.

Steve Perrin
Bar Harbor
Winter 1995–96

16—OTTER POINT TO SAND BEACH

From Fabbri parking area on Otter Point
To Sand Beach, and back
By Ocean Path both ways
4.0 miles, December 2, 1995

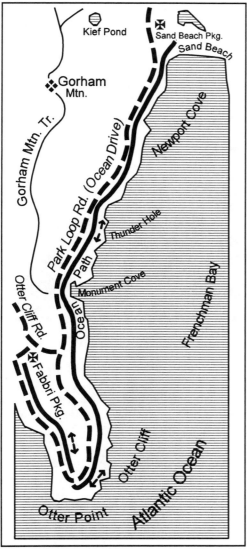

16—Ocean Path hike.

Ducks. That one word summed up my expectations for this hike. It was December now, and Acadia's summer bird population had largely headed south. There would be no sightings of warblers or peregrine falcons till spring. But as compensation for the departure of many locally breeding birds, our waters grant temporary asylum to those hardy northern species that look upon Frenchman and Blue Hill bays in winter as having a southern clime. Ducks. And perhaps a few grebes. Eiders certainly, with a scattering of oldsquaws and others. That's what I set out to see one windy morning after a storm the day before had brought the

first significant snowfall of the season to Mount Desert Island.

The snow had turned to rain as it often does along the coast, and a brisk northwest wind had made short work of drying the landscape. The only reminder that it had snowed at all was Cadillac's whitened dome gleaming against gray clouds. On the summit it was winter; here below, still fall. The temperature was below freezing when I started out from Brown Mountain Gatehouse, my winter quarters at the park. Out in the open, exposed to the wind, the effective temperature was closer to zero. Anyone going for a walk would leave as little skin showing as possible. I donned my new polypropylene long johns, dressed in layers, and drove to the Fabbri picnic area on Otter Point, arriving a little before 8:30 a.m.

The four-mile hike to Sand Beach and back took me just under five hours. The path was level most of the way, so it wasn't the terrain that slowed me down. I kept stopping to gawk at fellow Earthlings through binoculars, and to write down what I saw and reflected on. The reason I write up my hikes is to bear witness to the liveliness of the Acadian landscape at every season. This has become a mission at this stage of my life. I don't ask why; I just do it. If we are taught to look upon the natural world from a utilitarian point of view, the sorry condition of many landscapes compels us now to look from a more sympathetic perspective upon the life that we meet. We stand on the brink of a new age based on the realization that life, the leading edge of universal creativity, is sacred in and of itself. Evolution tells the saga of life's struggle to carry its sacred flame forward to kindle the spark of unknown tomorrows. I am one who values the spark itself—the act of living—over any concept of how it might burn. The *how* is a mystery beyond my grasp. I hike to experience the blaze of life in Acadia now—the only time I will ever know—and to admire the light with which it gleams in my awareness.

I met life in abundance on my hike along Acadia's southeastern coast. Eiders aplenty, 600 at least, diving for mussels close alongshore. And 35 red-necked grebes bobbing on the tide farther out, their compact shapes reminding me of so many gray tam-o'shanters with pompoms rising and falling in a crowd. Herring gulls, of course, surfing on the wind, mooching among eiders, hoping to steal a tidbit brought up from the deep. Crows, many crows, scavenging the black depths of the intertidal zone. And 14 oldsquaws in pairs and threesomes among the eider. I heard the boisterous bugling of others I didn't see. Guillemots dive in these waters year-round, but winter birds are so changed from their summer selves they seem a different breed. I saw two of them fishing solo, black guillemots by name, but ghostly caricatures compared to their breeding plumage of black with an accent of white. I also saw two great cormorants, here throughout the year, but which I don't usually notice in summer when they are outnumbered by their more common cousins with double crests.

Two red squirrels scampered across my path, one on Otter Point, another among the pitch pines as I was approaching Sand Beach. If Acadia were to choose a park mammal, I would vote for the red squirrel over beaver, fox, coyote, deer, porcupine, mouse, vole, or shrew. These feisty omnivores are much in evidence at every season, and even if you don't see one, they often make themselves known by chattering off in the woods. Their lively, bounding gait makes them seem less rat-like than gray squirrels, which I esteem on a par with cowbirds and city pigeons. I also came across two sets of deer prints in the gravel path, one above Sand Beach, one near Thunder Hole. I saw no trace of that arch-moocher, the Thunder Hole fox, who often begs for chips along Ocean Drive in the high season during July and August. A sign posted on the Sand Beach restroom building declares it to be "illegal to feed, harass, or collect wildlife in Acadia National Park," but the wily fox knows most park visitors pay slight heed to posted rhetoric. It makes a pretty good living by depending on the frailty of vacationers hungering for contact with wildlife. That will end badly, of course, when some proffering hand is nipped and the fox becomes demonized. I did see one dog on my hike, running circles on Sand Beach around a sedate man in an overcoat. Signs forbid alcohol, surfing, and pets on the beach, but apparently the dog couldn't read, or didn't care.

Ignoring the many people who passed me in cars, I noticed the twelve I met on foot, including the two who lurched out of a van with Ohio plates, leaned against it to steady themselves against the wind, and peered through binoculars at something out on the water. They weren't dressed for the occasion, so quickly scurried back in and drove off. The other ten people I saw were bundled against the cold, as I was in long johns, wool sweater, vest, and parka. I feel deep kinship with everyone who enjoys the park off-season. In this case their faces were so buried, I wouldn't recognize them later in the flesh without hoods, scarves, and sunglasses, but I valued our tribal connection.

I noticed only a few plants on this hike. Bracken, goldenrod, and fireweed were still much in evidence as brittle husks of their former selves. Neither wholly purple nor green, bunchberry leaves looked bruised and bedraggled. Lambkill leaves hung about their stems like folded umbrellas. I saw several patches of black crowberry on Otter Point, one atop a south-facing outcrop, rust-colored, not green. But cedars, spruces, and pitch pines were holding their own against winter's advance. Poison ivy, which I usually look for along Ocean Drive, I neither saw nor thought of. I was struck by how green the grass still was next to the black asphalt of the road.

The hike took on literary overtones from three bronze plaques along the trail. On the side of the Park Loop Road opposite the Fabbri parking lot, I stopped to read the tablet memorializing Alessandro Fabbri, commander from August 28, 1917 to December 12, 1919 of the U.S. Naval radio station built upon that site. Having been moved to Big Moose Island at the tip of Schoodic Peninsula, the station is long gone, but is described on the plaque as being in its

Otter Point and the Beehive.

time "the most important, and the most efficient station in the world."

At the far end of the Ocean Path, on a boulder at the head of steps leading down to Sand Beach, another tablet commemorates the gift in 1949 of 100 acres of land to the United States of America as part of Acadia National Park by Eleanor Morgan Satterlee in honor of her mother, Louisa P. Satterlee. Where those 100 acres lay I could not tell, but I sent thanks to the donor for her foresight and generosity.

A third plaque is bolted to the granite south face of Otter Point, visible only to walkers along the Ocean Path. It honors John D. Rockefeller, Jr., 1874–1960, contributor of funds enabling the Civilian Conservation Corps (CCC) to extend the Ocean Path around Otter Point sixty years ago. The plaque reads:

THESE GROVES OF SPRUCE AND FIR, THESE GRANITE LEDGES, THIS MAGNIFICENT WINDOW ON THE SEA, WERE GIVEN TO THE UNITED STATES BY JOHN D. ROCKEFELLER, JR. HE WAS AMONG THE FIRST TO SENSE THE NEED TO PRESERVE AMERICA'S NATURAL BEAUTY AND TO SET HIGH STANDARDS OF ENVIRONMENTAL QUALITY. THIS QUIET, DEDICATED CONSERVATIONIST GAVE GENEROUSLY OF HIS TIME, WISDOM AND RESOURCES TO HELP ESTABLISH THIS PARK AND OTHERS FOR THE PHYSICAL, CULTURAL AND SPIRITUAL BENEFIT OF THE AMERICAN PEOPLE.

The plaque is placed at the edge where several different worlds come together: where forested soil gives way to bare ledges; where ledges of granite give way to the variegated rocks of the shatter zone; and where ledges regardless of their composition give way to the ocean. In any weather, at any season, it is a dramatic spot. Undoubtedly John D., Jr. stood just there on many occasions, gazing through his "window on the sea." The plaque is a tribute not to the wealth or acumen, but to the sensibility of Acadia's most faithful friend. That same sensibility is shared by many who live on or visit Mount Desert Island today. It is a sensibility appreciative of life on the edge.

On the edge. That theme kept coming home to me as I followed the Ocean Path. Eiders know all about that: that is where they live. That is where the mussels they depend on for food take hold and thrive. That is where millions of people every year follow in the footsteps of John D., Jr., sharing his view. That is where Otter Point granite lifts out of the shatter zone of older rocks to rise as the new-fledged phoenix from the destruction of the old. Edges, where different worlds come together—that is where the excitement is. The creative energy. And re-creative energy. Edges, where confrontations of opposites give birth to the future of this place.

Where worlds collide, or exist in delicate balance with one another, there is a tension that glows like St. Elmo's fire. That tension sparked John D. Rockefeller, Jr.'s support of great public works. Instead of building dams to harness the energy of the tide, he got people out to discover that energizing tension for themselves.

Three natural landmarks along the Ocean Path testify to the force of surging waves. Sand Beach is made up of grains of pink feldspar, white quartz, and shells of marine animals, grains ground in the mortar of Newport Cove by the rhythmic pestle of tide and surf. Monument Cove is another testament to the energy released along that shore. Resolution of the tension between old granite and older ocean is seen in the shaping of smooth boulders and cobbles from foursquare rock. The cove, difficult to see from Ocean Drive, is one of the wonders visible from the Ocean Path which runs along its rim. I was drawn to go into the cove itself, but could not find a way down from the north, so left that excursion for another day. I remembered how I had done it before, but the route I had taken seemed to have vanished.

Then there is Thunder Hole, one of Acadia's most famous sites, right up there with Cadillac's summit and Bubble Rock. The hole is famous for sending spray high in the air to the accompaniment of a great clap and roar. In July, sandwich in hand, I'd had a ring-side seat at one of its classic performances when swells from an offshore hurricane

pummeled the coast. Old Faithful and Bridal Veil Falls had nothing on Thunder Hole that day. Twelve-foot swells rammed into the gouged-out channel in the ledge and hit squarely home in the resonant cavity at its end. Thrump–splash; thrump–splash; thrump–splash. The crowd loved it, reveling in the tension, energy, and excitement of life on the edge. I loved it, even if my sandwich was damper and saltier than I liked when I got around to eating it.

Mr. Rockefeller's window on the sea.

From the Fabbri monument to Sand Beach and back, my hike was punctuated by peaks of excitement at Otter Point, Otter Cliffs, Monument Cove, Thunder Hole, and Sand Beach. In between there were stretches of spruce or pitch pine woods, and level avenues along granite ledges sloping to the tide. Frenchman Bay was a stampede of white horses fleeing the northwest wind wave-after-wave, but in the lee of Champlain and Gorham mountains the Ocean Path was far less exposed than the open bay. I was drawn by anticipation of seeing what I now describe as life on the edge. I was often surprised by what I actually found. At Monument Cove I saw a fat robin take shelter in the lower branches of a white spruce. Here was a bird on two edges—of the ocean and the seasons at once. Below, in the cove itself, a female common merganser dove within a few yards of the beach. I could see her leap with red feet, throwing herself into the shallow water again and again. On another stretch of cobble beach I saw a trim and compact female harlequin duck, dark brown with white-spotted cheeks, diving much like the merganser. Harlequin ducks winter primarily on the outer shore of Isle au Haut, and are rarities on Mount Desert. This one was on the extreme edge of its winter habitat. A gannet, too, was on the edge of its normal range. In the fall, gannets often push the edge of their deep ocean territory landward, following the fish they feed on toward shore. The one I saw on my hike was a male flying and diving off Otter Point. A powerful, graceful, and beautiful white bird with black-tipped wings and pointed tail, no sight stirred me more. I had given up on seeing loons, but saw one in muted winter dress at last from Sand Beach.

The Ocean Path provided the window looking onto such sights, but my binoculars must be given credit for sharpening my vision. Male eiders with bold black-and-white markings, cap-pulled-low-on-the-nose profile, and group behavior are easy to identify at some distance, but the other birds I saw were more of a challenge. Without binocs, I would have called most of them "ducks" and let it go at that. No teacher has opened my eyes to life on the Maine coast more than my binoculars have. They have given me new eyes. If you want to open someone else's eyes, give them a pair of binoculars and point them toward John D. Rockefeller, Jr.'s window on the world, open year-round.

Another hiking hint is to pack good gorp to feed your inner fires. I've tried many mixes over the years and have settled on the simplest of them all: dates. They will perk up any hike, from Ocean Path to the Precipice. Thinking about them gives me a lift.

The Ocean Path is a smooth graveled surface most of the way, letting walkers tend to the view instead of their feet. On Otter Point it gets rocky and rooty, but footing is rarely an issue. The one bit of drama the path itself provides is in scaling the ramparts of Otter Cliff, the heights being part cliff, part stonework laid down by Mr. Rockefeller's road crew. From below, looking at the curve of granite blocks where Ocean Drive hugs the top of the cliff 60 feet above the waves, I thought I saw Rosencrantz and Guildenstern watching for the dead king's ghost.

Besides the sea, the Ocean Path also looks upon the geological underpinnings of Mount Desert Island. I wasn't looking for rocks, but there they were nonetheless. If you want to study the formation and subsequent decay of the Acadian landscape, visit Sand Beach, Monument Cove, the granite ledges along Ocean Drive, Otter Cliff, and Otter Point, all way stations along the Ocean Path. I won't go into the details of what happened as the result of tectonic collision some 400–600 million years ago when what we know as "North America" was rammed by "Eurasia," but some of the effects are preserved in rocks exposed through millions of years of wear and tear by wind, wave, ice, water, and a series of glaciers. The booklet and maps contained in *The Geology of Mount Desert Island* [*] by Gilman, and others,

---

[*] Richard A. Gilman, et al., *The Geology of Mount Desert Island: A Visitor's Guide to the Geology of Acadia National Park.* Augusta: Maine Geological Survey, 1988.

explain how those geological effects were produced. The shatter zone gives a glimpse of the crunch that took place when molten rock fired by the continental collision rose up under great pressure from the depths to depose crustal rocks already in place. The traces of that tumultuous uprising can be seen in cliffs on Otter Point, Otter Cliff, and the eastern end of Sand Beach.

The tide was high about seven o'clock, low at one-thirty.

Male eider diving for mussels off Otter Point.

On the return leg of my hike, I noticed how much ledge was exposed. Eiders were now feeding among garlands of rockweed hanging into the water at the foot of the intertidal zone. I couldn't see what they were nibbling, but thought they might be plucking periwinkles from among those strands. The bell buoy off Otter Cliff clanged constantly, but the wind blew most of the noise out to sea, so what reached me was a kind of soothing "elevator music" as background to my hike.

As I started out from the Fabbri monument, I walked south along the loop road to pick up the Ocean Path farther out on Otter Point. Immediately I was faced by a large red sign: **WRONG WAY.** I didn't take it personally because it was meant for bicyclists and motorists. Besides, that section of the road was closed for the winter. But later I saw a car speed at a good clip the wrong way between two such signs placed to prevent cars coming down Otter Cliff Road from turning left against the traffic onto one-way Ocean Drive. I wondered if the driver of that car was as immortal as he seemed to think. I felt pretty sure that any folks he might meet driving the right way would be made of ordinary flesh and blood. Here again was life on the edge. My mind took off after that speeding car.

How many times a day do we find ourselves poised between pro and con, right and wrong, before we act? Not consciously so much as deep inside where our personal judgment steers between aversion and desire at every turn. There in that silent cockpit decisions are made whose effects we read only later in the courses we have actually sailed between folly and virtue, evil and good, danger and safety. Seeing that car go against two red warning signs, I knew some temporary desire was overriding the driver's judgment, steering him or her into error. At that moment I saw life clearly as a series of decisions, the self as arbiter between the way of misery and the way of hope. Our journeys are told in such turnings and choice points. The challenge is to go as far as we can, sharpening our judgment through experience, preparing ourselves for more difficult decisions later on. What we find attractive beckons to us, fearsome fends us off. I saw my entire hiking career as a moral journey. Each hike is an invitation to exercise choices making me who I am. I am the pilot who steers this frail craft along the uncharted course that is my life.

As navigators, we trust beacons and rules of the road to guide us on our way. Whenever a system of rules is set in place, a counter-system springs up tempting us to break those same rules. Everyone despises viruses because they don't play by our rules, but we have to admire their success. Around the world, every legally instituted government has its Mafia or drug cartel feeding in the shadows. This is a universal law. To function at all, every system casts a shadow in which rival systems thrive. A shadow is an open invitation, a kind of vacuum asking to be filled.

I have always liked it when people explain how mercury barometers work by saying, "Nature abhors a vacuum." I picture a blowzy Dame Nature throwing up her hands in mock horror at sight of emptiness, wildly gathering up whatever she can find to stuff into it. The charm of the phrase stems not so much from its personification of nature as from the deft substitution of a myth for an explanation. How Greek. How human. Actually, nature adores a vacuum. Any old vacuum. There may be concentrations of matter scattered here and there, but the universe is more than ninety-nine percent pure emptiness. There is far more nothing than something everywhere we look. Life on Earth

Thunder Hole walkway covered with frozen spray.

is the exception, not the rule. We are a minor spur on a tenuous fractal pattern floating in a vacuum more perfect than technology can ever produce. Thriving in the shadow of universal emptiness, we not only live on the edge but partake of its nature. The edge is what we are. Risk taking is as much a part of life as looking through windows on the sea.

Rounding Otter Point on the return leg of my hike, I scanned the horizon through binoculars to see what was happening on the edge of the world. Rather than a placid straight line, the divide between ocean and sky was seething with waves and troughs, looking angry as a cracking whip. One fishing boat was attempting to cross that line, plunging fore and aft, looming like the *Flying Dutchman* as it rose and fell 25 miles out in the Gulf of Maine, a fluid universe bearing no resemblance to the one in which I stood on relatively solid rock. Life on that far edge was as foreign to me as on the moons of Jupiter. Whatever canon of maritime law was in effect out there, I knew it was written in a language I could not read. There before my eyes was life beyond the edge of my familiar little world.

At the end of my hike, walking along the loop road toward the Fabbri monument, I had a clear view of the snow line at 1,400 feet on Cadillac Mountain. Edges, again. Anticipating a hike to the summit later this winter, I thought of the different rules that would apply above and below that line. Icy patches would be obvious below, hidden beneath snow above. I would navigate differently, depending on which side of that line I was on. Our lives inevitably lead us to the brink of one last divide. But the timing of our arrival there depends on our navigational skills. I hope to hike right up on my side of that ultimate edge and present myself as a respecter of natural law every step of the way, willing to accept the consequences of my brief walk in the light.

I got back to my car at 1:15 p.m., having covered four miles of scenic terrain—with digressions that took me miles beyond the further limits of Acadia—in ten minutes short of five hours. Spiritually renewed, I was mortally hungry.

✳

17—BEECH MOUNTAIN LOOP

From Long Pond parking area (pumping station)
To Beech Mountain summit, and back
  Up by Valley and Beech Mountain trails
  Down by Beech Mountain West Ridge Trail
                    3.6 miles, December 9, 1995

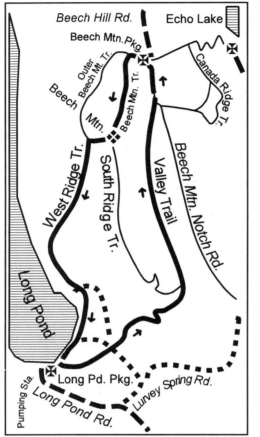

17—Beech Mountain loop.

A special combination of rocks, trees, and ice set this hike up Beech Mountain apart from other hikes I have made. Each ingredient contributed its own distinctive beauty, but it was the mix of all three that fixed the character of the hike. On the Valley Trail I admired the dignity of spruces rising straight and tall against a backdrop of lichen-clad granite cliffs flowing with icefalls and icicles. Between the Beech Mountain parking area and the fire tower at the summit, trailside trees gave me leverage to swing rock-to-rock upslope past icy stretches where footing was hard to come by. And on the way down the ledgy west ridge trail I trod on pine needles the color of red squirrel fur to avoid the trail itself, which was an icy cascade.

It was eleven degrees above zero when I got up at six o'clock. For days the weather report had warned that the first major snowstorm of the season would hit that afternoon. Being my one day to hike all week, I wanted to be out

and back by noon. Time enough to do the Beech Mountain loop from Long Pond, with allowances for gawking and taking notes. On the drive to the pumping station at the south end of the pond, I noticed that Upper Hadlock Pond was frozen solid, Somesville Mill Pond floated a gibbous sheet of thin ice with fifteen black ducks around the edge, Echo Lake was skimmed over, Fernald Cove was solid shore-to-shore, with only Long Pond remaining open. The cold hampered my taking notes—or, more accurately, the heavy boiled-wool mittens I wore against it did. It is hard enough to grasp a pencil through thick wool at the best of times. When my fingers felt as cold as the curled blades of rock-cap fern along the trail looked, it was almost impossible. Holding my pencil like a chopstick, I did the best I could, but struggling to read my notes a few days later, I saw how my handwriting self-destructed as I went. There are secrets in those notes that will never be revealed.

I got to the pumping station at the south end of Long Pond just before 7:30 a.m., and finished the loop at noon as I had hoped. It was 1.5 miles to the parking area at the end of Beech Hill Road, 0.6 miles from there to the summit of Beech Mountain, and 1.5 miles back to the pond by the west ridge trail, 3.6 miles all told. I took four-and-a-half hours to make the hike under icy conditions. Hiking without stopping in summer, the same loop would take an hour and a half.

The hike was a great success, especially the leg from Long Pond to the Beech Mountain parking area, known as the Valley Trail. The trail itself is well laid and solid—a pleasure to walk on. Rocks, trees, and ice offered plenty to look at and think about the whole way. Wildlife, which is one of my principal quarries on this series of seasonal hikes, did not disappoint me. I saw ten gulls, male and female hairy woodpeckers, a female downy woodpecker, and two red squirrels. I heard two more squirrels, two ravens, and one chickadee. Red squirrels were also advertised by piles of cone scales on three different stones, and by three scatterings of spruce tips. I saw only one tree (a yellow birch snag) bearing deep pileated woodpecker excavations. One fox scat lay next to a cairn along the west ridge trail, and what might have been fox tracks ran along a snowy section of the Valley Trail. Closer to the parking area, larger canine tracks followed the same trail, suggesting a prowling coyote or, more likely, a walking dog.

From the fire tower I heard a human voice below me, but thought the sound might have carried a good distance from the base of the mountain. Despite the weather forecast, the day was remarkably still. For half the hike I heard small waves lapping against the shore of Long Pond. Backing trucks insistently beeped from the Southwest Harbor transfer station. A plane went over high above the haze at one point, and the busy hum of traffic on Route 102 bounced off St. Sauveur Mountain's granite flank. Samuel Johnson preferred the "busy hum of men" to the rustic beauties of

Greenwich in his day, but I find that the hum of modern life dulls my senses, so prefer the lull of deep woods. The best sound of all was the crunching of my Vibram soles on frozen snow along the Valley Trail. Through binoculars, I saw two people clad in bright parkas on the Long (Great) Pond Trail on the far side of the pond. When I reached the pumping station at noon, though, mine was again the one car in the lot.

Nothing wakes me up so much as hiking in winter. Crossing icy terrain, my eyes and legs become wonderfully synchronized. There can be no idle ambling along at this season. To turn my gaze from the step ahead might lead to a fall. I enjoy a heightened sense of vitality, and sustain it at all costs. When I find secure footing and pause to look around, I quaff my surroundings in an instant, capturing the lay of the land in the visual equivalent of a sound bite. Deciduous leaves having fallen, vistas are more open than at other seasons. It's like being gifted with X-ray vision, having the power to see mountains and cliffs where before they were hidden. Binoculars, too, help sharpen my seeing. Vowing not to start down from Beech Mountain until I had seen a fellow living creature, I peered into every nearby tree, scanned every ridge and distant slope, gazed across acres of empty sky out to the horizon; only when, after ten minutes, through 10-power binoculars, I saw two gulls flying over the inner harbor at Southwest Harbor some two-and-a-half miles away, was I released from my vow.

Hiking requires vigilance at any season, but in winter that is doubly true. I am doubly awake, seeing with both eyes. The amount of visual information I process at every step expands enormously. Every ripple and shadow on the ice takes on meaning, every island of rock has potential significance. Here is safe passage; here is danger. I am challenged to choose between the two. Every step takes deliberation and decision, step after step after step. Which sounds tedious, but isn't at all. The whole process is exhilarating. I enjoy applying judgment to what my senses tell me. My eyes and legs become such a working team, I wonder if navigation under winter conditions hasn't boosted human intelligence. In his video series, *Canticle to the Cosmos*, Brian Swimme points out that we have lived with industrial-based technology for a scant 300 years, but survived as hunter-gatherers for 3.5 million. Our dress may appear modern, but our bodies and minds reflect skills we need to survive in the wild. Winter hiking takes me back to an earlier stage of my youth. I become young and active again, challenged and alert, brother to the 5,000-year-old iceman recently found in the Italian Alps.

Too, I discover the surroundings which my own buried self prefers in the rocks, trees, and ice along the trail. Can

this be a personal quirk? I feel a deep predilection, an early love for such places. I am meant to be out in the open, wending through a universe of rocks, trees, and ice.

Feeling truly at home, I perk up when I hike. I become another person, wholly alive and alert. I find stark beauty in my surroundings, but it is the radical change in my seeing under winter conditions that opens me to such things, enabling me to find them beautiful. That beauty lies within as

Christmas fern on the Valley Trail.

well as without. I imagine my yen for winter beauty goes back millions of years through a succession of ice ages to the first steps of the two-legged tribe. It has been nurtured since then by the success of my nomadic, hunting-gathering ancestors who recognized beauty when they saw it because it fed and clothed them well. There is strong survival advantage in letting ourselves be drawn by landscapes that meet our basic needs. In those days food, clothing, and shelter grew on trees, or at least in the woods. Natural beauty outdoors in winter invites us to surroundings that give us an edge. That we are alive today is due largely to our ancient folk preference for beautiful surroundings. Attracted to beauty, hunters hunted and gatherers gathered. We are the living proof.

Hiking along the Valley Trail, I was not myself only. Nor was I a mere member of my sex, my particular family, my profession, or any interest group. As a winter hiker I was a scout for a long lost band, a member of the wandering community on which my livelihood depended for millennia. I hike in the winter for the same reason that tourists stream to Acadia in summer—to revive a sense of meaning that has lain dormant since people invented villages, farming, and trade some five thousand years ago, abandoning the wandering life for the sake of crops and property. In our hearts we are wanderers still, no matter how encumbered by goods. In every season, once on the trail we recover a dim sense of our true selves that no amount of civilized culture can bury completely. We yearn to discover the particular beauty that favors the cause of the roving band we still represent in absentia. We are the forefront of the past. It sent us here.

Trail fantasy? Mythic projection? Of course. Like root metaphors, such dreams allow us to approximate the truth. Where once I might have been tracking cave bears or woolly mammoths, I was now on the lookout for hairy woodpeckers, red squirrels, and scats. Thoreau observed how diminished the wilderness of his day was without cougars and wolves. Now we have more chickens and domestic cats in America than people. We scouts are out of a job. But the urge to roam persists, along with the yen for natural beauty. As for the hunting-gathering band itself—fragmented though it may be into nuclear families, and buried under corporations and bureaucracies—it lives in our archetypal longing to participate in functional communities and meaningful social groups. We burden the immediate family with expectations once spread among the members of our roving band. The family cannot persist as the be-all and end-all of social life. It needs help from a larger band if it is to hold together, the sustaining presence of other families and individuals linked by a common yearning and purpose, separated by less formidable walls than bricks and vinyl siding. Walking alone along a snowy path in deep woods, I was amazed how clear the world I had left behind appeared to my rambling thoughts at so small a distance. Not only could I see gulls two miles away, I could see 100,000 years into the past.

Ice kept intruding on my wandering thoughts, bringing me back to the present. Ice underfoot—and underhead if I was not careful. Ice in a variety of forms. Flowing water held in time, it was as diverse as the slopes and surfaces on which it ran. If the Lapps have 500 words relating to snow, ice in Maine deserves half that number at least. In flat puddles on the trail it was smooth as mica or shiny plastic. But plastic is too uniform a substance to suggest the variegated shades and patterns captured within the slick surface itself. Every frozen puddle rendered a unique extraterrestrial landscape in sweeps of translucent grays. Where the water level had fallen away from the picture, leaving a delicate membrane spanning emptiness, the contrast and luminosity of the image were enhanced, making it all the more fantastic. A few years ago I would have shattered these frozen drawings by tapping them with the toe of a boot; now I let them be.

Where water dripped from the edge of a cliff, icicles formed as thick as my arm, typically four to five feet long, like swords or pikes or, in rows, like grinning dragon fangs. In spots the cliffs leered with superior half-smiles fixed on their wintry masks.

Between horizontal and vertical displays, ice assumed a variety of forms reflecting the properties of the sloping surface to which it clung. Where water seeped slowly, it froze in repeated knobs or terraces, creating massive shields with textured surfaces built up layer by layer. Frozen seeps suggested the skin of undulating serpents, clouds of volcanic ash, or wave patterns in thick paint the consistency of

Ice crystals in the trail.

molten white chocolate. As usual, I lack words to describe the natural world with respect and accuracy. Science codes its descriptions in mathematical phrases which, though often elegant, generally fail to kindle the appropriate appreciation and awe. One particularly striking ice formation was a simple ring of frost crystals around the rim of a squirrel hole beneath a large spruce. Was this the frozen breath of the family within? The exhalation of Earth itself? Nothing had broken the circular fringe, which looked like an iris of rime around the depths of a dilated pupil, a hoary Earth eye staring up at the sky.

The Beech Mountain parking area was an excellent skating rink. Beech Hill Road was closed off by a gate where it enters the park, so I was free to perform perfect triple airborne turns without cars to cramp my style. Coming down the Beech Mountain West Ridge Trail, I deferred to the rivers of ice that had claimed that route of descent. I had no choice but to step aside onto the carpet of fallen pine needles through which the slick trail cut like a gash. The carpet was more hiker-friendly than the streaming ice. In small brooks at the bottom of the ridge, icicles hung over the water from every root and stick. Icicles with a difference in being thicker at the bottom than at the top, often spreading out into thin disks just above the flowing water. I have heard such shapes described as upside-down or "Irish" legs.

In the same ethnic vein, I also found an Irish harp in the pond—an arching root hung with lyrical strands of white ice.

The last stretch of my loop ran within five feet of Long Pond where cedar fronds dipping in and out of the waves were rimed with gleaming castanets. The edge of the pond was frosted with ice several inches thick, which smoothed all angles and surfaces, but hardly softened them. Where the trail was made of loose particles of soil, colonies of ice crystals rose like fruticose lichens two or three inches tall. I stepped over them as I would any bed of moss.

Ice is a boon to anyone inter ested in the course water takes in flowing through sloping soil. Much of what I know about wa ter has been told to me by ice. Winter makes watery organs visible. Like the visible man or the visible woman, here is the visible watershed. December is a good month for local hydrolo gists. It helps us visualize vital processes which we tend to take for granted at other times of year. Seepage is both more abundant and more obvious in December than August. On this hike I was very aware of water flowing off Beech Mountain toward Echo Lake on the east and Long Pond on the west. When we go boating, fishing, or swimming, we seldom ask how those waters came to be there for our enjoyment. A winter hike prompts us to ask the question when an answer is more evident.

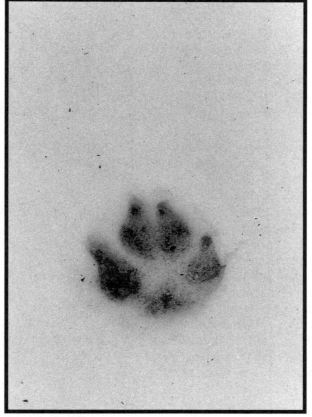
Fox print in thin snow.

The rocks I met on this hike were as spectacular as the ice. If ice is solidified water, mountains are solidified seeps of molten rock. Covered by a flimsy and tattered garment of soil, Beech Mountain is everywhere bursting at the seams, showing great mounds of its outer flesh. At one point the Valley Trail comes up under the looming south flank of the mountain, and from there to the summit the trail is com manded by boulders and cliffs. Even at the very start of the trail on the slope away from the pond, two boulders of schist set the tone of the hike. Dragged many miles by the last glacier, the two great stones will continue their journey when an ice sheet next comes this way. I estimated that what I could see of the first boulder probably weighed eight to ten tons, the second over 100 tons. Farther on, the trail passes around a third boulder fallen from the mountain; I figured it must weigh 250 tons at least. I stopped short of computing the weight of Beech Mountain as a whole. Tak ing a cubic inch of granite to weigh a tenth of a pound, that figure could be derived from an estimate of the volume of rock the mountain contains.

Small stones, too, caught my eye. At several places along the trail the soil had frozen and risen, leaving a stone to peer from its expanded lair. One smooth stone looked like an infant's cranium pressing toward delivery.

The Valley Trail passes un der one impressive stretch of cliff after another, while the Beech Mountain and west ridge trails scale the granite dome of the mountain itself. From the Beech Mountain parking area to the summit, the ascent is largely over brainy granite—granite eroded into cabbage- or cortex- like bumps. The west ridge trail passes over sloping ledge most of the way, so has more the feel of a smooth scalp. Hiking the Valley Trail is like exploring the chambers inside the mountain's brain. This route reveals the in tricate organic architecture sup porting the whole like fitted joinings in a Japanese temple. Every surface is covered with vegetation on one scale or an other. Spruces rise from soil- covered terraces; ferns, moss, and lichens cover the cliffs. Where great chunks of cliff have broken away to form talus heaps below, dark mossy caves are a byproduct of cata clysm. The image of cathedrals rising above catacombs seems not too far-fetched. The drama of the Valley Trail cannot be captured in a simple description. It must be experienced first-hand and first-foot.

My hike led through a variety of forested landscapes. After passing through a stand of pole-like spruce on the edge of Long Pond, I came to woods showing signs of hav ing been cut not long ago, coming back first to popple and birch, giving way in turn to spruce in densely crowded doghair thickets. Fallen birch stems lay rotting on the ground, the remains of a once brief but flourishing stage of succession. By the time the trail reaches the mountain prop er, the trees have taken on a timeless look, as if they had always been there, and intend to stay there forever. Hem locks show up as the trail switchbacks up the first ascent. In the valley east of the mountain, more deciduous trees appear among the evergreens, and in spots they predominate. Pale beech leaves here and there added delicacy and subtle coloring to the landscape. The loop is through woods the whole way. The only place where trees lose their power is at the summit of Beech Mountain on the open ledge south of the fire tower. And even there the view is largely of wooded slopes and islands farther off. The west ridge trail descends through a relatively open forest of red pine, leading to an unbroken ring of Northern white cedar clustered at the edge of Long Pond.

The plants I noticed were wintergreen in the woods, blueberry on the slopes, with a scattering of juniper, lamb-kill, and even kinnikinnick here and there. One wine-leaf cinquefoil leaf rising out of the snow caught my eye as I was looking for a place to set my foot in a particularly icy stretch. Wood and rock-cap ferns grew thick at the base of the valley cliffs east of the mountain, joined by liverworts and feathery mosses.

As for the trail itself—finest kind! Especially the Valley Trail, built sixty years ago by the Civilian Conservation Corps (CCC). The treadway is solid, the grade easy, the route spectacular. At its northern end in Beech Mountain Notch, the trail joins the route of the former road linking Southwest Harbor to Somesville and points beyond. The road can be followed down into Canada Hollow, where it crosses the Lurvey Spring Road, but it is a rocky and icy chute this time of year. The Valley Trail links Long Pond to Mr. Rockefeller's parking lot at the end of Beech Hill Road. In the 1930s, the parking area was built as a significant trailhead for the Beech Mountain area, which it is to this day. The Beech Mountain Trail (Brain Trail) up to the fire tower from the parking area is briefly steep in spots, but in summer offers firm footing on rock the whole way. When ice covered, that climb is definitely hazardous to your health. I succeeded only because I could see the ice. Under a thin layer of snow, the trail would be lethal. The west ridge trail has the straightforward job of getting hikers on and off the mountain between the summit and Long Pond by the most direct route. It has good views of Mansell Mountain across the pond, and is a pleasant if not exciting route. It is more challenging in winter when flooded by rivers of ice.

Back at Long Pond, I realized I hadn't thought of the much heralded storm due to hit at noon, which it was by my watch. The sky was slightly hazy, but above the haze it was decidedly blue. My plan to beat the storm had worked. "Let it snow!" I said to the blue, and drove off.

❄

18—ASTICOU TRAIL

From Brown Mountain Gate parking area
To Jordan Pond by way of Forest Hill Cemetery,
    and back
By Asticou Trail and connector both ways
5.5 miles—December 16, 1995

Red spruce sapling in snow.

During the five hours and twenty minutes I spent trekking along the Asticou Trail in ten inches of new snow, I didn't see one bird or animal, setting a career low for wildlife sightings. Though I did see a great many signs of life, the signers themselves were somewhere else. I heard two peeps from a treetop bird, and saw two snow-filled nests. I saw a chickadee nest hole bored into punky wood high on a birch snag, and pits and tunnels dug by sapsucker, pileated woodpecker, and bark beetle. A dusting of lichen bits under a birch marked one course in a woodpecker's unending lunch. Approaching a carriage road, I saw cross-country skiers glide by, and heard the voice of another already past. One of them called over her shoulder, "I wish I had my camera." Returning from Jordan Pond by the same route, I found three fresh ski tracks in the trail itself. Light snow fell throughout the day, softening my earlier tracks as if they had been made by another being in another time.

Despite the lack of wildlife seen, the hike was as exciting as any I have made in Acadia. I set out looking for animal tracks, and that's what I found. Even if the track makers did hang back in my presence, they left their marks all along the trail. I could see where mice and shrews had hopped in the soft snow, leaving a row of successive body and tail prints at every bound. Here a deer had browsed through a stand of Northern white cedar. There a red squirrel had leapt be-

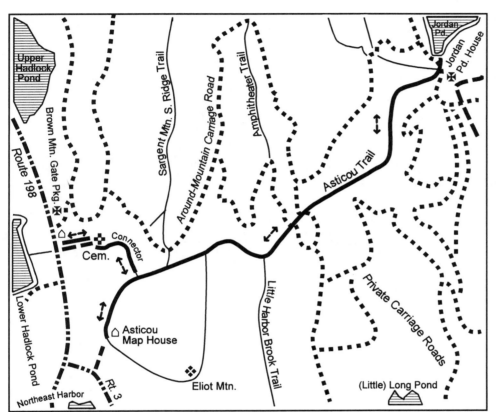

18—Asticou Trail hike.

tween trees. And there, and there. I saw tracks of ten different squirrels where in summer I would not have known one had crossed my path. The most prevalent tracks were of fox. I came across eighteen sets of fox prints from one end of the trail to the other, one set dotting the trail ahead of me much of the way across the valley of Little Harbor Brook. I could not tell how many foxes those tracks represented, but knew I was in the company of at least one, perhaps more.

I could roughly tell the age of a track by the amount of snow fallen on it since it had been made. A few seemed to date from yesterday, but most were fresh enough to have been made the day of my hike, some not long before I came by. Retracing my steps, I found new tracks crossing my earlier ones. Unseen animals were part of my hike all along the trail. Through the pervasive stillness of the woods I sensed the presence of wildlife at every step. Unseen ears were perking, eyes watching, noses sniffing. My trekking gait fell in place as one among many. Acadia is as alive in

winter as in summer, whether we encounter that life or not—as Maine is alive through the seasons, and the whole Earth is alive. When I hike, it is to take part in that living Presence, to join the all-seeing awareness of planet Earth, which I offer as a tentative description of God. In that sense, God is no separate being apart from the rest of us but the sum of our collective wakefulness. Together, we make up the Presence, the divinity of Earth. The One did not create the Many in the beginning; the Many compose the One at this and every stage of the now.

The Asticou Trail cuts a great swath across the valleys of Little Harbor Brook and Jordan Stream between the Asticou Map House (just up from the Asticou Inn at the head of Northeast Harbor) and the lower end of Jordan Pond. Often straight, that swath is twelve feet wide in places, though generally somewhat less, giving the sense of an avenue carved through deep evergreen woods. In addition to the two main streams, the trail bridges eight or nine lesser tributaries, each a gentle reminder to stop and admire the surrounding scene. Though it often inclines up or down, and excepting the brief rise from Little Harbor Brook to the ridge between Cedar Swamp and Eliot mountains, the way is not steep. From either end, it gives immediate and easy access to the living Presence of Acadia.

Crossing carriage roads in three places, the Asticou Trail also connects with several other trails in the south coastal region east of Somes Sound. I passed nine signposts on my hike, directing me to the Hadlock Pond Trail, Sargent Mountain South Ridge Trail, Eliot Mountain Trail, and Little Harbor Brook Trail, among others. At Jordan Stream below Jordan Pond House, one post with eight signs points to the pond house, Jordan Cliffs, Penobscot Mountain, Sargent Pond, Asticou, Amphitheater, Little Harbor Brook, and Sargent Mountain. At the trail's other end, the Asticou Map House displays both the Phillips and DeLorme maps of Mount Desert Island, making hikers feel welcome, inviting them to explore trails they may have missed in the past. I thought that if anyone ever said to me, "You can't get there from here," I'd start along the Asticou Trail and see if I couldn't make it from there.

With ten inches having fallen on open ground, snow made all the difference on this particular hike. Fine and soft, it was the perfect medium to reveal Acadia's presence in the many tracks I have mentioned. The few sounds I heard were muted by the snow, making it hard to judge the distance or direction from which they came. I had a sense of wind blowing above the trees, but never felt it. Somewhere a foghorn whispered, a bell buoy gently tolled. Standing on its banks, I could hear each stream I came to murmur its mellifluous name, but a few steps away I had no sense what that name might be. The sound of the ocean a mile and a half south of the trail seemed to back up the Presence I felt without intruding any character of its own beyond the soft declaration, "I am with you, with you." The quietness of the hike was underscored by the sound of pencil on paper as I made an occasional note.

Every branch of every tree was covered with snow. Every rock and ledge, every tombstone in the cemetery, every stone in its stream, every nest. Nothing was untouched. Every edge and angle was rounded and softened. Acadia had been made more vivid and beautiful by a passing storm. Branches of deciduous trees were hung with contrasting bunting, highlighting their grace and strength. Up-turning beech twigs alternating along the sides of each branch formed baskets filled with long loaves of pure snow. Evergreens displayed their finery each according to its true nature. Needle clusters of white pine were decked in tufts and pompoms; branches of spruce wore soft new gloves, and fir new mittens; cedars set off their lacy fronds with white backing for all the world to see; hemlocks draped themselves in heavy capes which hid their personal charms from casual passers-by.

I began the day by waxing my cross-country skis, but realized that hiking is hiking and skiing is skiing, and it was the sense of immediate contact with nature I was after, not a passing scenic tour. The thermometer reading 26°, I set out from Brown Mountain Gate at 9:40 a.m., took Gatehouse Road off Route 198 to Forest Hill Cemetery back of the gatehouse, then trudged through boot-high snow to the start of the Asticou Trail connector at the park boundary in the southeast corner of the cemetery clearing. That was the last open space I saw until I got to Jordan Pond almost four hours later. I figured the snow would not be so deep in the woods, and generally found the going easy through a depth of four or five inches. The Asticou Trail is roughly two miles long, and I went another three-quarters of a mile in reaching it and going beyond it to the shore of the pond. I covered nearly five-and-a-half miles at an average speed of one mile an hour, going slower than that in getting to the pond, faster in getting back. It was an easy hike the whole way, largely because the snow was full of air, and I had no icy slopes to deal with.

Because the footing was good I didn't worry about where to step, so spent most of the hike looking around at

Asticou Map House.

the panorama I was passing through. Where the trail dips into the valley of Little Harbor Brook I had one glimpse of Penobscot Mountain through bare trees, but other than that the trail offered a close-up view of evergreens covered with snow. Every tree at every age had a distinct personality, so the hike was an unending series of details in white, dark gray, and dark green. A scattering of flakes fell all day from an overcast sky, freshening the wintry effect by timed release. This is how glacial ages begin, I thought, without fanfare, without notice.

Except for the animals whose tracks I saw, I was the first one out on the trail that day. I enjoyed the feeling of being a pioneer on the forefront of civilization's reach into the world. Along with Amundsen, Lewis and Clark, the Cabots, and all the rest, I have my share of the early-bird gene. Nothing excites me more than seeing part of the world in all its freshness and originality as if for the very first time. There is a challenge in making my way through unexplored terrain that grips me particularly. I love the surprise and variety, and the continual reinvention of myself in new circumstances. If you're not the lead sled dog, the view is always the same. I was born a navigator. When I come to die, I think of myself as changing one venue for another, eager to send back reports on the lay of unknown lands and adventures in new worlds beyond.

Coniferous trees grow in such a way to keep their leaders always uppermost. From my vantage point near the ground, I could look at seedlings and saplings near my level and imagine I was witnessing events in the tops of trees seventy feet over my head. Here were roots, stems, branches, and spires fully exposed. Much of the snow had fallen straight down, blanketing the world from above. The smallest seedlings had simply been buried beneath soft caps far too large for their heads. Taller seedlings and saplings—and all mature trees, I was sure—bore white headgear whose design was exactly fitted to the pattern their uppermost branches had formed during the past growing season. Where two twigs extended on opposite sides of a leader, a miter of snow had settled smoothly joining the tips of all three. Where three twigs branched from a leader, a pale tri-cornered hat was set. Other headgear had been tailored in radial designs of four, five, or six points, each more fantastic than the others, each fitted perfectly to the head it adorned. Though I could feel no wind along the trail, I saw good evidence of the southeasterly wind that had brought snow from the Gulf of Maine the day before. The more open stems bore a stripe of white on that side, a telltale vane often three or four inches thick pointing toward the center of yesterday's storm.

Every tree had been subjected to the same natural forces, so shared a family resemblance with its neighbors of every size. Though the specific features of every tree along the Asticou Trail were unique, there was a unity to the whole forest suggesting that at one level it functioned as one simple thing. The principal thrust of the trees was upward toward the light; the principal thrust of the storm had been downward slanting from the southeast. The color scheme was uniform throughout: green, gray, and white. As compel-

Balsam fir branch decked in light snow.

ling as the living Presence I felt along the way, I experienced a sense of harmony and integrity embracing the entire landscape of vegetation through which I walked. It was all of one piece. If not of one plan, it was one result. Here were myriad influences and conditions resolved over time into a singular effect. Fox, squirrel, and mouse were part of it, as I was as well. Our tracks showed up here because the same influences showered on us all, challenging us, but nurturing us in the end. These woods were a world fact, a landscape enduring over time. We are born to them as citizens because we share the same ancestors and line of descent. Again, forcefully, I was struck by the same conclusion: Collectively we are one. One being, one Presence, one wave of extended awareness. I recognize the spruce and the fox because we are children of the one Earth, subject alike to the same natural forces, Earth brothers and sisters. I saw that clearly as the answer to my quest for connectedness with nature. I am as present to these woods as they are present to me. I breathe in what they breathe out; they breathe in what I breathe out. We are made of the same stuff and rise from the same soil. Different manifestations of life's vital spark, we are one genetic idea drawn to separate conclusions.

That is the kind of thing I think about when I hike. I answer Acadia with a peripatetic line of thought reflecting the challenges it presents me with as I go along. I am the

medium in which nature cultures its thoughts, the thoughts of trees and rocks. Solid, yet always changing, these thoughts are like blocks of talus falling from a cliff, like tan needles sifting to the ground. As I went, I pondered ancient questions. Why did the squirrel cross the trail? Clearly, to a squirrel, what I call a trail is more an extended rent in the canopy, which is the squirrel's trail. Crossing my trail, the squirrel is mending its own. Must the fall of a tree in the forest be witnessed to be real? Behavior that does not demonstrably affect me does not seem to exist in my world; a lie is not a lie until found out. If an event is so remote as to have no effect on me, then, in practical terms, I can safely ignore it, as most people ignore the faint light falling on them from the great galaxy in Andromeda, which is undoubtedly real to astronomers. But what about ultraviolet rays which may bring about cancer without our knowing? If ignorance is bliss, it is also dangerous. A tree falling in the woods is a tree falling in the woods, whether we hear it or not. Reality is firmly seated in events, of which awareness gives us a dim and partial glimpse. To solve the mystery of the tree falling in the woods, all we have to do is ask the tree, or the rock it fell upon.

Along the Asticou Trail I kept coming to places I had been before, causing me to remember what happened there on other days and other hikes. I had often photographed these spots, so the experience was like walking into a picture of earlier times with other companions. By Asticou Map House, I remembered the extensive bed of mayflowers now completely buried under snow. A series of hikes from Route 3 along Little Harbor Brook and the Amphitheater to Sargent Mountain Pond came back to me, elicited by one sight of the brook. Here my companion took a picture of me sitting on that knee-like root, though at that time it wasn't covered by eight inches of snow. There I leaned against that fallen tree, resting my boots on that stone in that stream. I can feel what it felt like to take up that posture. On future hikes, spurred by visual cues, I will revisit musings I began this time along the trail. Many trails in Acadia have layers of personal meaning for me built up over the years I have been hiking them. My first hike in the park was on the Bear Brook Trail to the summit of Champlain Mountain when I was four. I can still remember how endless the trail felt, how the summit seemed to recede, how hot I was. Strange, how that trail has grown shorter over the years, how Champlain has shrunk. I often remember particular cairns from earlier hikes. Trail memories are like little piles of stones placed at significant points along the way to guide the hiker in both time and space. Having roamed about the country for years before I came home, I suffer for those who move every couple of years to a new locale, never giving a particular landscape time to acquire a patina of deep-felt significance. On the go as many of us are, we sometimes substitute popular songs for such monuments, letting them take us back when we hear them anew. But that isn't the same as being joined to a landscape where we have planted our feet over the years.

Looking over a choppy Jordan Pond toward the snow-clad Bubbles at 1:25 p.m., I ate a handful of dates which, being frozen, made for a very stiff and chewy meal. Renewed, I hiked back in less than half the time it had taken to reach the pond. Resolved to make no more notes, I tried to come up with a word for the layer of snow that had settled on every branch, echoing and accentuating its reaching curve. Next to tracks in the snow, those white echoes had become the main feature of the hike, yet I had no name for them in my vocabulary. They weren't properly blankets, carpets, mantles, or frosting. They were more like decorative tapes or piping. I invented the concept of snow magnetism to explain their existence, since they seemed far more the product of deliberate attraction than accidental sifting and clinging. Many branches supported furls (bands, bolsters, catchments, pads, pillows) of snow five inches thick, the branches themselves being reduced to mere shadows of the more substantive covering above. Finally I hit upon snow bones and snow ribs to suggest both the curve and whiteness of the phenomenon, and left it at that. That's what I shall call them now, until I can think of a more apt and sprightly term.

The notion of snow magnetism was meant to celebrate the perfect fit and alignment between snow rib and branch. What could have caused so stunning an effect? Surely some exacting plan had been put into play, some painstaking design executed. The perfection of the result seemed to warrant the placing of each flake by a masterful intelligence

Ice on Jordan Stream.

behind the scenes, just as the marvel of life on Earth seems to demand the hand of an awesome creator. Snow magnetism and creationism are two of a kind, handy explanations for happenings that result from the falling away of everything else. Every phenomenon, including life itself, including snow bones, is a temporary event. Those that outlast others and seem more permanent are said to survive. If they're around long enough, we give them names. But in the real world nothing survives. Everything changes and ultimately dies. Based on 20/20 hindsight, change in the less evanescent stages of an event is called evolution. Evolution is a description, not an explanation, just like snow magnetism. Wanting our explanations to be tidy, we get upset when evolution happens in bursts instead of proceeding at an orderly pace. As a description, though, evolution can take such unruliness in its stride. However species change or come into being, that's what happens. What happens, happens—that's evolution. It is an ongoing process, or rather a complex interaction between myriad processes whose orderlinesses are more complex than we can know. Anyway, I like the idea of snow magnetism as an explanation of how snow bones come into being. Tree limbs attract snowflakes just as magnets attract iron filings: voilà, snow bones. I'll work out the minor details on later hikes.

The layering of snow on every branch seemed part of a healing process, like the laying on of hands. The sky had reached down and touched the woods, renewing them and making them whole. When snow bones broke apart and fell, they pressed their shapes into the matrix below, inviting as a tabula rasa, creating a characteristic calligraphy as if a thousand Zen masters had each contributed one stroke. Each dent in the snow caught diffuse illumination falling from above, causing it to glow with inner light, as fox and squirrel tracks glowed. I couldn't read the text, but knew it was profound. From falling flakes, to snow bones, to illuminated manuscript, nothing stayed the same. The landscape was alive and evolving before my eyes.

The stem of every tree along the trail was decorated with lichen filigrees in dark and light green, each a landscape in itself. Wherever I looked, there was order, pattern, and meaning. I studied the first glacial erratic I saw, noting where snow had settled, where pink granite still showed. Predicting that a layer of green life lay beneath the snow, I scraped it away, revealing an intricate underworld of liverwort clinging like an Italian hill town to the granite. Another erratic with hindquarters cloaked in white took the shape of an American bison staunchly standing against a blizzard backside-to.

I kept expecting to see snowshoe hare tracks on the edge of dense thickets where evergreen boughs swept low, providing both cover and browse, but didn't see a single one. On other hikes I've seen such tracks almost everywhere in the park, so was mystified by their conspicuous absence along the Asticou Trail. Perhaps the fox had had a very good year. I did notice that to a large extent fox and squirrel tracks were mutually exclusive. The border between them ran along the high ground joining Jordan Ridge to Mitchell Hill, the divide between the watersheds of Jordan Stream and Little Harbor Brook. Squirrels held territory to the east, foxes to the west.

The strongest of the several strong experiences I had on this hike was the sense of myself as a participant in the very Presence that accompanied me as I went. When I saw the cross-country skiers go by on the carriage road ahead, they did not notice me standing back in the woods, just as I did not notice the fox who surely watched me. My observations added to a more extensive and enduring network of awareness. I was but one sentinel among many. We were all on the outlook, for our individual and common well-being, for the landscape of Mount Desert Island, for the Northern Forest, for Earth, and for the universe. Quakers have a deep respect for the potential for good in every breast, which they refer to as "that of God in every one." Thinking of God as the creation of the collective world consciousness of which I formed a trillion-trillionth part, I turned that old phrase on its head and beheld "that of every one in God." Exactly! Our conscious being adds up to the Presence of God, which subsumes us all. That felt so right, I regarded it as the major gleaning of my hike. The burden of being included in the All is to share in the responsibility of being alert to truth. Being half-awake will not do. Life demands we do our best to be worthy of our common consciousness

which, being that which guides us toward our respective futures, is divine, and therefore God.

I did not know what I was getting into when I started out. Getting back to Brown Mountain Gate at 3:00 p.m., I knew my mortal and spiritual being had entered new territory. I looked up Bruce Birchard's summation of God as the creative and responsive love binding all parts of creation into a blessed community.[*] Yes, the Presence I felt was no

Asticou Trail bridge over Little Harbor Brook [since rebuilt].

disembodied abstraction; it was a palpable embrace. Embracing one another in complex interlacing patterns, we build the structure of the All. Reaching out with love to every possibility of life on Earth, we affirm the common truth that resides in each. Immanuel Kant turned philosophy on its ear when he grounded perception not in the world but in the self, bringing about a Copernican revolution in philosophy. Seeing God as the upper limit of consciousness in which we separately participate, and toward which we collectively and lovingly strive, is part of a similar re-centering move in the universe of spiritual concern. God is a creation of whole Earth awareness, the result—not the cause—of foxes, trees, and snowflakes striving together in truth.

✳

_____

[*]Bruce Birchard, *This Is My Quaker Faith*. Carey Memorial Lecture, Eighth Month 6, 1994. Sandy Spring, MD: Baltimore Yearly Meeting, 1994, p. 13.

19—McFARLAND HILL LOOP

From park headquarters off Eagle Lake Road
To McFarland Hill summit and Breakneck Ponds,
   and back
Up by McFarland Hill Trail
Down by bushwhack, old woods road,
   and Breakneck Road
      2.9 miles on snowshoes, December 26, 1995

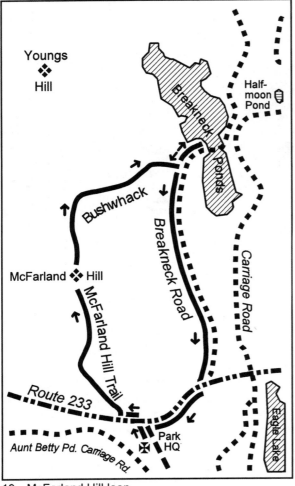

19—McFarland Hill loop.

The day after Christmas, I went looking for hare tracks on the north side of McFarland Hill. Having seen none on the Asticou Trail ten days before, I wanted to set the record straight. Too, I wanted to avoid the crush on Christmas weekend. I have never met anyone on McFarland Hill, which is strange because its south slope looks on one of the best views in the park.

Leaving my car at park headquarters off Eagle Lake Road on the south ridge of the hill, I took a route made up of a variety of seldom-used roads and trails, adding a stretch through trackless hare country which I made up as I went along. With eighteen inches of snow on the ground, it did not make much difference which route I took. I went where my snowshoes took me, first up, then down, then slowly up. Park headquarters sits on a ridge at an elevation of 425 feet. The summit of McFarland Hill is roughly 300 feet above that. The Breakneck Ponds, at 253 feet, are 470 feet lower than the hill, and some 170 feet lower than the ridge. These may seem trifling differences in elevation, but the way was steep enough in places to offer the challenge I was looking for. My strategy was simply to go up to the summit and down to the ponds by whatever way I could find, then return along Breakneck Road to Eagle Lake Road and park headquarters. Running between the south ridge of McFarland Hill and Hulls Cove, Breakneck Road is no longer maintained as a public way, even thought it still owned by the Town of Bar Harbor. In winter it makes a good ski or snowshoe trail. Some ride snowmobiles over it, even between the two ponds where running water reduces the roadbed to a jumble of jagged rocks. The loop I made was a little under three miles long, which took me three-and-a-half hours to complete, with plenty of stops for taking notes and gawking.

The winter solstice past, this was my first hike of the new solar year. The calendar claimed it was still 1995, but it felt like the beginning of Earth's 4,000,001,996th trip around the sun to me. Though summer was on the way, cold weather would hold for a few months yet, time enough for some great winter hikes. Those who know only its summery face might picture Acadia as an eternal-summer kind of place, but it has a wintry face, too, with a more Nordic persona. I may not be fond of winter driving (having skidded off the road in light snow a few days ago, paying $45 to be pulled from a snow bank and $267 for four studded tires), but I love winter hiking. I try to avoid freezing rain, but give most other conditions a try. The landscape is fresh and beautiful; I find it hard to go to work in winter because the call of the trail then is even stronger than in summer. Conditions change so rapidly, you have to seize the moment and get outdoors while they are right; tomorrow it will rain. Worse than our calendar being out of synch with the seasons, our so-called workweek is wholly disconnected from outdoor events. I am torn every time I turn my back on a good hiking day.

With blue skies over fresh snow, Christmas this year was a great day to hike. Two companions and I snowshoed a loop from Brown Mountain Gate to Eliot Mountain and back. The day after was just as good, without the sun. On my McFarland Hill loop I saw chickadees, a crow and a blue jay, hairy and downy woodpeckers, and tracks. Lots of tracks. First there were the prints of the great ribbed paws of a front-end loader in the headquarters parking lot; then, as soon as I started up the hill, fox and squirrel tracks. In the valley between McFarland Hill and Youngs Hill to the north, I found the snowshoe hare tracks I was seeking, and a great many tracks of white-tailed deer. I walked in faint snowmobile tracks on Breakneck Road coming back.

Anyone walking behind me saw the great webbed prints of bearpaw snowshoes.

As for other signs of wildlife, I saw one nest in an oak, pileated woodpecker and sapsucker holes, four beaver-gnawed stumps by Upper Breakneck Pond, a snow-covered beaver lodge in the pond, and evidence of browsing by hare and deer. A sapling bent by a falling poplar had had its bark nibbled off by hares. Along the Breakneck Road, leaves and buds of Northern white cedar, hemlock, and alder had been browsed by deer ambling from one side of the road to the other. I came across two remarkable excavations in the snow, one deep where a fox had pounced at hearing a mouse or vole through eighteen inches of snow, the other superficial where either a bird had taken a snow bath, or an angel touched down. Where the fox had pounced I could see the shape of its head outlined in the deep shaft it had pressed into the snow, and the tunnel its forelegs had dug down to the meadow beneath. There was no blood, so I thought the fox had come up empty-jawed. It is hard to make a living in winter with technology more suited to grassy fields.

The ledgy summit of McFarland Hill is largely open, giving a good view to the northeast over Witch Hole Pond, two beaver ponds, and Half Moon Pond, all iced and covered by

Deer track in deep snow.

snow at this time of year. The Breakneck Ponds lie too close under the hill to be seen from the top. In the opposite direction, Aunt Betty Pond, Gilmore Bog, and a nearby wetland stood out as pale basins ringed by dark gray woods. From almost any elevation, meadows and bogs take on a striking aspect in winter, showing up as landmarks equal to any pond or lake. But the real show was to the south as viewed not from the summit but from the slope rising above Eagle Lake Road and park headquarters on its ridge. Through a veil of snow, Cadillac, Pemetic, the Bubbles, and the combined bulk of Penobscot and Sargent mountains stood firm against all storms and seasons. How grand they loom as seen down that glacial highway along the azimuth that the ice sheet had traveled as it bore down upon them, sculpted them, then, having changed them forever, turned away and melted back to the north. Eagle Lake was a giant white boomerang in the foreground, with a dark oval of

open water showing near Conners Nubble. For this view alone McFarland Hill is worth a hike any month of the year. The first time I climbed it was in thick fog, so I had no idea what I was missing. Oak and birch woods on that slope having lost their leaves, the panorama is more accessible in winter than during the greener months.

I hiked McFarland Hill on a Tuesday when normally I would have been volunteering at the park, but no Interior appropriations bill had been worked out, so the Department of Interior was shut down, the park was closed, and I was free to roam. Blinds were drawn at the park's winter visitor center; no flag was flying from the pole out front.

The McFarland Hill Trail begins on the north side of Eagle Lake Road (Route 233) a short jog west of headquarters where a badly eroded gravel road turns off. [The road has since been graded to provide access to an air quality monitoring site.] Sealed with a snow bank, the road was as closed as the U.S. Government. I put my snowshoes on and scaled the bank where a fox had leapt from the highway not long before. The gravel road is a rutted hillside scar which runs with mud every spring; I avoid it on principle, so climbed out of it when I came to the first break in the alders on the left, as the fox had done. The trail from there is barely visible at the best of times, being more a wildlife track. I angled across the snow in a generally upward direction. In a couple of minutes I turned around to greet the view I knew was following at my heels. Judging from the height of Pemetic Mountain, the ceiling was about 1,000 feet. Clouds shrouded the higher peaks. A light snowfall muted the view, heightening its drama with airy swirls and commotions. The scene generally gets better as you rise, but in this case the clouds thickened and in five minutes the mountains were gone. I got another glimpse higher up where the slope eases onto the summit plateau, but by then the scrim was so heavily whitened, I had to imagine that those shadowy forms in the background were the familiar mountains I knew by heart.

The going was hard, not because steep but because the slope was rendered white-on-white, the even glare making it impossible to tell hummocks from hollows. I blundered my way upslope, pausing often to goad my eyes into seeing what lay before them. I traversed at an angle into open oak woods, then made my way up as passageways opened between the trees. The traditional Quaker phrase, "as way opens" (suggesting clarity will come in its own time to those with the patience to wait) kept running through my mind because, time after time, way did open before me, revealing an avenue I had not anticipated. The opening of such ways became one of the themes of this hike. In thick woods in the valley between the two hills, way opened before me as I kept plodding ahead. The fox patrolling the snowy surface for the vole beneath is guided by a similar faith.

The summit of McFarland Hill is merely the high point of an extended and open plain. The way up may be poorly marked, but the trail across that plain runs cairn to cairn. I knew where I was going and had confidence I was on the right path; still it was reassuring to see those capstones rising out of the unbroken snow ahead. Deer and fox had crossed that plain on their own, paying no mind to the stones. In a landscape of infinite possibility, I made sure to stay on the trail by connecting the dots I could see. The summit plain is wooded east and north, open to the west, partly open to the south. The line at the edge of the plain formed a kind of

Snowshoe hare track.

near horizon, flowing white against gray, broken here and there by a solitary spruce. Trunks of fallen trees silver with age stuck out of the snow here and there, ghosts of forests past. I don't know why, but I love that scrubby, open, ledgy terrain as much as any in the park, even when covered with snow. Perhaps because it is so extraordinarily ordinary. We make a fuss about rarities, but it is the pervading terrain in between that defines them and sets them off. We need them both. Built of loosely fitting stones supporting a straggly stick, the summit cairn at the north end of the plain came as a decided anticlimax. Wherever it announced I was, I was sure I had already been.

From there into the valley between McFarland Hill and Youngs Hill to the north, I was on my own. No trail leads that way. I had a sense from earlier hikes that snowshoe hares would like such a place. As way opened between scrubby gray birch; then balsam fir mixed with birch, oak,

and beech; through a stand of evergreens grading into birch mixed with beech; to the stand of beech on the narrow valley floor, I wound downward between the trees. Stopping to gawk at the feathery structure of a balsam fir branch highlighted by new snow, I noticed the characteristic angle every twig made with its parent stem, and knew I was seeing outward and visible signs of the angle of attachment between dividing cells. Every living feature reflects the process by which it came into being. The motto of Roosevelt High School in Seattle where I graduated long, long ago, was "What I am to be, I am now becoming." As Alfred North Whitehead knew, we live in a world of events, not material things. We grow as way opens, and as way closes behind.

Passing beneath an oak as a hairy woodpecker was lilting *whit-whit* at eye level to another tree, I saw the first hare tracks ahead. Ah, balance restored. After that, I saw them everywhere down to the ponds.

Standing among three- to six-inch beech in the saddle between the two hills, I wondered how long it would be before they bore nuts, and how long after that before bears would discover them. Beeches take fifty years to produce nuts in significant numbers. The black bears of Acadia will become famous long after I am dead. No sight is more beautiful than the pattern of beech stems against a hillside covered with snow. I turned in a circle, admiring the scene around me at every compass point. Tawny leaves clinging to branches here and there added a touch of warmth. In celebration of my reaching the heart of this sacred grove, I ate a bite of fruitcake from a plastic bag in my fannypack.

Just down from where I stood, water seeped out of the slope, forming a clear pool rimmed with snow, headwaters of the brook flowing east out of the saddle into Upper Breakneck Pond. A corresponding pool forms on the west side of the saddle and feeds into Old Mill Brook. I stood at the source of flowing waters, Omphalos, true navel of the universe. I often come across such springy places on my hikes, though I seldom find them listed in the guidebooks. George Dorr seized on Sieur de Monts Spring and made it famous, but it takes hundreds of ordinary seeps and springs to make a national park.

I started following the small brook east toward the ponds, but here and there dense trees or the steep, sloping sides of the valley nudged me into the brook itself, so I sought higher ground, meandering between one bank and the other, much as several deer had done not long before. The deer and I shared the same strategy, letting gravity draw us toward the pond while keeping near the stream. Where a hare had nibbled the bark off a toppled sapling, a deer had turned from a cedar to browse on buds of—what was that shrubby, sprouting bush? Bending down to look at the one clinging leaf, I brought my eyes to focus on the branch inches in front of my face. Clusters of eighth-inch yellow bells hung here and there: witch hazel, which invariably evades me when I look for it, only to emerge out of nowhere like this when I turn to other things. The ribbon-like petals had fallen away, but the sepals hung on in foursomes, bringing a faint touch of yellow to winter woods. Standing up to make a note, I watched a snowflake with six perfect crystal rays land on the blue backing of my glove. No bigger than the witch hazel bells, it was a jewel fallen from the sky. It persisted nearly a minute, then slumped in a heap. Hearing a faint tapping sound, I looked for a downy woodpecker near the top of a clump of birch. Yes, there it was, male or female I couldn't tell. The soft rhythmic sound was the beat of a snowflake's heart.

I came to an orange tape tied around a tree, then stumbled across a woods road that quickened my descent to the ponds. The old road passes through a stand of ten- to eighteen-foot spruce saplings coming back after the area had been cut not long ago. I soon came to Breakneck Road on the west side of Upper Breakneck Pond. A snowmobile had gone by a day or two before. A hundred yards on, the road gave way to the bare, rocky isthmus between the upper and lower ponds, which looked hard on snowmobile runners. Alternately crossing sloping granite ledges and eroding glacial till in flooded ditches, the road remains true to its name. A foot-and-a-half paving of snow might soften the blows a little, but even in winter, riders on any kind of vehicle set out to make a statement by taking the Breakneck Road.

I had seen what I came to see, so took the easy four-fifths-of-a-mile traverse up the Breakneck Road to Eagle Lake Road and park headquarters on the ridge. Now and then I could see the sun hanging low in the sky ahead, a faint disc through racing clouds, giving off more hope than heat or light. The road was lined with larger trees than I had seen earlier on my hike—red spruce, white pine, white and yellow birch, beech, Northern white cedar, and hemlock. In the ditch along the road, alders grew as alders grow—profusely. Two deer had preceded me, dining as they went,

from cedar to hemlock to alder and back to cedar again. They went the whole distance to Eagle Lake Road, browsing on ruminant fast food.

Thinking about the solstice and other quarter days dividing the natural year, I wondered why our culture finds it so necessary to impose an unnatural order on the calendar where a more obvious and sensible one already exists. We do the same in calibrating the Earth. Daniel Webster came

View to the south from McFarland Hill.

up with a scheme for dividing the land into townships six miles square, sides oriented north–south, east–west. A good portion of the State of Maine still suffers from that geometry, which overrides natural boundaries between watersheds. We struggle to administer jurisdictions having no basis in natural law. I had a friend from Greece who came to study in Iowa, convinced by the rectilinear pattern of roads in the Midwest that he would find the seat of rationality at the state university. Walking along Breakneck Road, I found myself in a kind of temporal limbo, with New Year's Day officially a week away—when I knew it had already passed with the solstice. Christmas and New Year's celebrate the same spirit of renewal, which Advent anticipates, yet we go out of our way to deny any link to the sun or the seasons. Why, then, all the candles and lights, the profound sense of good cheer? Seeing the low sun through trees ahead of me, I knew what year it was, and that summer was on its way.

I saw chickadees, a crow, and a blue jay after I had taken off my snowshoes and was walking toward headquarters up Eagle Lake Road. I knew that crow, or one of its brothers, very well. While living in an apartment at park head-quarters, I had often watched the group of five or six crows that held the roadkill franchise on either side of the ridge. From a tree near the crest of the hill where the road makes a curve, they had an unobstructed view both ways. The crows used to play soccer with a tennis ball outside my window at six o'clock in the morning. I remember seeing one of them try to squeeze between the trunk of a tree and two other crows perched on a branch. The newcomer grabbed the branch all right, but couldn't force its way where there was no welcome: it ended up swinging upside-down on the branch, pretending with a stoic grin that that's what it had meant to do all the time.

20—HUNTERS BROOK LOOP

From Route 3 between Otter Creek and Day Mtn.
Along Hunters Brook, and back
   Out by Hunters Brook Trail
   Back by bushwhack and the Boyd Road
      2.25 miles on snowshoes, December 28, 1995

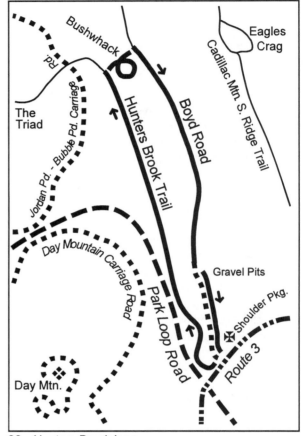

20—Hunters Brook loop.

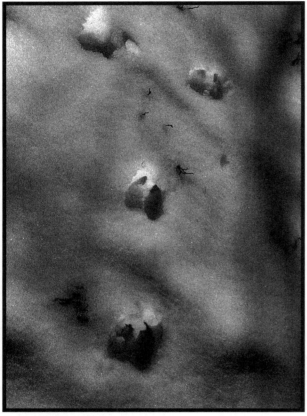

Deer prints in light snow.

I got back to my car at noon-thirty. Giving thanks to Newt Gingrich and his freshmen for giving me the day off, I headed for home.

✳

My previous hike took me to the Breakneck Ponds; this one to Hunters Brook. There doesn't seem to be any obvious connection between the two, but if you look at a relief map of Mount Desert Island, you can see that they both lie in the bottom of the same glacial valley, along with Lake Wood, Eagle Lake, and Bubble Pond. On a heading between south-southeast and south-by-east, the last glacier cut a single groove across the island from what is now Salisbury Cove to Hunters Beach, parallel to a similar groove to the west running from Emery Cove to Seal Harbor where Old Mill Brook, Aunt Betty Pond, Jordan Pond, and Stanley Brook lie today. In a geological sense, the Boyd Road just up from Hunters Brook is a continuation of the Breakneck Road. A hike up Hunters Brook is an extension of a hike by the Breakneck Ponds. Both are excursions into the same glacial neighborhood.

The loop I took this time was made up of two parallel

legs, each about a mile long. Leg one took me along the Hunters Brook Trail to where it crosses the brook a second time just short of the old bridge site. Leg two brought me back along the Boyd Road. I parked on Route 3 south of Otter Creek village at the inconspicuous entrance to the Boyd Road up from the Park Loop Road bridge. It was about a tenth of a mile from my car to the trailhead. From where I abandoned the brook at the halfway point to where I stumbled across the Boyd Road to the east was a little over a tenth of a mile, for a total distance of about two-and-a-quarter miles. I left my car at 9:40 a.m., and got back at 12:50 p.m., giving three hours and ten minutes to the hike. Compared to other hikes it wasn't a long one, but I saw more wildlife tracks in that time than I had seen so far this season.

I followed deer tracks right from the Hunters Brook Trailhead on the loop road. It wasn't hard to imagine why deer had come that way: The first tree I saw was a giant Northern white cedar with sweeping candelabra branches, a sight that must bring joy to the hearts of hungry deer. Their tracks were plentiful near the loop road, becoming scarcer as I went along. Where a tall cedar had fallen across the brook, the top leaves had been browsed, but the section lying over the snow-covered brook had been left untouched. I had deep appreciation for that show of deer common sense. Ice and snow covered the brook in on-again, off-again fashion. Any given stretch of water had a twelve-inch covering here, but was open water there. Neither stream width nor velocity seemed to influence where ice formed or it didn't. The pattern looked random to me. Like the deer, I would not have put my weight on the ice beneath that fallen cedar.

But in another matter of judgment, deer display a devil-may-care attitude. They walk into thickets rife with prickly, eye-gouging twigs with total indifference. They go where I believe they can't possibly go, through the densest undergrowth, where I am unable or unwilling to follow. Of course they do, it's their habitat. But so is the ice-covered brook. I imagine their bodies to be like slime molds, able to pass through the finest screen, re-forming on the other side as if they had met no obstacle at all. However they manage

Tree fallen across Hunters Brook.

to penetrate spruce twig thickets spiked like the innards of an iron maiden, I have great admiration for deer woodcraft and pluck.

I could roughly age the deer tracks by how much snow had fallen into them, or by how much they had eroded into mere dimples in the crust. The obvious distinction was between old and fresh tracks. Fresh ones were the interesting ones. They piqued my awareness, making me look around for taut-eared silhouettes in the distance, or white flags bounding through the trees. Tracks are sacraments of Acadia's eternal, living Presence. Though I never saw a deer or any other animal during this hike, I never felt alone.

Where the streamside habitat becomes more open, which it does as the trail progresses, I saw fewer signs of deer. The canopy is uniformly closed, but the trees are large and well spaced, with few thickets in between. For deer, the going gets easier, the hiding harder. Made up of trees of mixed species and ages, the woods take on an old-growth look. Cedar persists, along with white pine, spruce, hemlock, and yellow birch. Many trees are two feet in diameter at eye level, a few two-and-a-half feet. This is not the primeval Maine woods with white pines five and six feet in diameter, but it is the diminished, twentieth-century equivalent.

My first impression as I passed the trailhead was of great cedars curving out and up over the winding brook. The serpentine airspace above any brook is precious in the woods, and brookside trees do their best to get at the light it lets through. Many succeed and thrive. Others lose their balance and topple across the brook as the bank beneath them erodes. The valley either side of Hunters Brook bears the bodies of the fallen dead. And the standing dead. Even the oldest snag never retires. The woods make room for trees in all seasons of life. Along the brook, the trail passes through a sylvan community in which every member is valued for its unique contribution. No tree is hidden away as too decrepit or infirm. Here are individuals in every stage of vitality and decay, growing at every angle, or left lying in peace. I found a kind of integrity and wholesomeness all around me, a kind of peace rooted in absolute tolerance and acceptance.

One spruce snag near the brook had been reduced to a stub only six feet tall, somehow split top-to-bottom, so that the ancient ruins of a carpenter ant city were fully revealed. The architecture was simple yet grand, based on the principle of radial symmetry, consisting of annular tubes of thin wood separating vertical corridors connected by frequent windows and doorways. I was reminded of pictures of cliff houses in Cappadocia and the American Southwest. Excavations by pileated woodpeckers told me ants were active in many trees, their avian diggings being as admirable as the insect settlements they uncovered. Here were two rival civilizations with a great deal in common: both were highly energetic and advanced in woodworking technology.

A tree fallen across the brook bore a six-inch coating of snow. A red squirrel had hopped across that bridge, leaving a row of double dagger marks from root to crown. The snow beneath several spruces along the trail was covered with a thick scattering of green tips nipped off by the same tribe. I saw five squirrel tracks along the brook, another seven on the Boyd Road. It would surprise me to hike through an area with no signs of red squirrels. As England will fall when ravens fly from the Tower of London, Acadia will be in for bad times when its emblematic, rufous rodent flees its noble woods.

Thin, pale green, branching lichens embellish the bark of every tree along Hunters Brook. In three degrees of fineness, they add another layer of texture to the sensuous woods. Tangles of chestnut-brown lichen filaments soften most evergreen stems. Powdery, crusty green lichens dust trees with the finest texture of all. Every trunk and branch is a miniature kingdom unto itself. Seeing lichens and trees cohabiting on such intimate terms, I wondered if the mutual dependence of tree roots and fungi in the soil might have evolved from the similar arrangement in lichens between algae and fungi. In both cases, one partner produces food by photosynthesis, which it shares with its fungal companion in return for moisture and nutrients. Are trees algae at heart, algae grown tall and old while remaining true to an earlier love? If they did not form a marriage of convenience with mycorrhizal fungi in the soil, spruce trees would play a minor role in the woods of Maine. Whether there is a lineal connection between woods and lichens I cannot say, but they live on familiar terms to this day.

I saw two hare tracks on the Hunters Brook Trail, thirty-one on the Boyd Road. There is little foliage close to the ground in the tall woods along the brook, while the road upslope to the east is growing in with spruce and pine, providing both cover and forage for hare. Colby's 1881 *Atlas of Hancock County, Maine*, shows an R. Boyd living in the vicinity, so I assume the road was named after that family.

It is hardly a road now, being overgrown for much of its length. Yet for another year or two it will provide passage between Route 3 south of Blackwoods Campground and the carriage road by Bubble Pond. Near its Route 3 end, the road widens into a gravel pit where the park has set up a firing range. Beyond that, the way is left to hares and, under their care, will soon be a forest again.

The Boyd Road had become so grown in, much of it

Icicles over Hunters Brook.

resembled a trail more than a road. The treadway was heaped with snow dumped from evergreen boughs close on both sides. In places the snow was four feet deep, forming an alpine ridge through the woods. On an earlier hike following rain, I had gotten drenched brushing past wet boughs. This time walking south into the sun, I was drenched with light. Spruces and pines grew taller and older on the sides of the road, leaving a narrow corridor through young trees between them. The landscape was green, blue, and white. Needles and shadows gave it texture and relief. On the snow itself, animal tracks laced opposite sides of the corridor together. Hare and squirrel tracks predominated, but I did see one line of twin dots where a mouse had hopped across, and just past it, the track of an unhurried fox.

Looking up to gauge the low angle of the sun, I saw the streaking contrail of an aerial messenger far above in the blue sky. Just as I could infer a society of woodland wildlife from tracks in the snow, I could imagine a race of aerial beings inhabiting the clouds overhead. The Sumerians saw sun, moon, and planets moving against a background of fixed stars as angel messengers conveying the will of the gods. "On Earth as it is in heaven," their priests told them. They read the heavenly signs as divine instructions, just as more modern Polynesians based cargo cults on wreckage from ships and planes, which they took to be sent from another world for their guidance. Looking at the great white track in the sky, I empathized with both groups. What message did that higher being have for me? Steady on, it said, your course is true.

Draining the slopes of Cadillac, Pemetic, and the Triad, Hunters Brook has carved a valley through sediments laid down by the last glacier. The Boyd Road runs on top of those same sediments, following the course of a glacial meltwater stream. Hunters Brook is that stream's modern descendant. Winding through its small valley, in places it curves against a wall of fine glacial sediment sixty feet high, showing the depth of its excavations over the past 10,000 years. The Hunters Brook Trail does not follow the brook to its source on either the Pemetic or Cadillac side, nor does it descend to the brook's unceremonious union with the Atlantic at Hunters Beach. At its outlet, instead of rushing to meet the tide, the brook simply sinks into the cobble beach, draining lower down into salt water. An unmarked trail reaches that site from Sea Cliff Drive.

The brook flows on a bed of sand, gravel, and cobble, with blue-gray marine clay showing through here and there. When I walked it, the brook was largely roofed with snow and ice, with a great many skylights exposing the stream and its bed. Those windows came in all shapes and sizes, but were generally rounded and smooth with sparkling interiors—jewels set in the snow. Looking into them, I saw a glowing landscape built up in layers: pink and orange pebbles deep down, translucent waters of the brook itself, and sky overhead reflected in the flowing surface. Where the brook was not iced over but ran in the open, boulders rising out of the water caught snow in mounds, forming marshmallow islands. Logs fallen into the brook were ribbed with snow, and often had icicles of frozen spray dangling underneath. At one point a logjam had formed, damming the brook, raising it three feet on the upstream side. The trail crosses several small tributaries flowing into the main channel, some bridged, some not. Opposite the Triad, a tributary on the Cadillac side has cut its own valley through the bank of sediment on the east.

About a mile from the trailhead, the Hunters Brook Trail crosses the brook in two places. Following blue diamond blazes at the first crossing, I stepped out onto snow over ice of questionable thickness, making it across without incident. In another tenth of a mile the trail crosses back, but here the brook—too wide to jump—was only half iced over. I took the hint and headed east from there through uncharted woods in search of the Boyd Road. I turned off the trail just short of where it reaches an old road and turns west for the Triad.

The first sign of coyote I had along the trail was a brown scat packed with hair lying on top of the snow. Large canine prints merged with deer tracks at that point, the deer coming up the brook, the coyote coming down. From there on, I saw no more tracks of deer; the coyote had the valley to itself. For the most part its track stuck to the brook trail, coming south toward me as I headed north. The track looked fresh, every detail showing clear and sharp. The snow had a light crust which broke beneath the coyote's step, leaving a square edge going in and a sharp point coming out. Made at a steady lope, the prints were deep. Lit by skylight, they shone with a blue glow, forming an azure

Fox track.

chain in the trail ahead. I saw only the one long track, but that was enough to kindle the sense of a mighty Presence in the valley along the brook. What looked like shrew prints sometimes led from beneath a log into the trail, where they met the path of the coyote, though I could not tell which had passed first. Taut between hope and dread, a vibrant tension stilled the air. Fates were in the balance. I imagined the brookside community to be on full alert.

Cutting through woods after turning away from the brook in search of the Boyd Road, I got turned around in unfamiliar terrain. Upright and fallen trees kept me from heading due east as I had planned. Crossing a small wooded wetland on a plateau, I came to a valley cut by a tributary of Hunters Brook. Having just come out of one valley, I did not intend to enter another, so followed along the edge, but got stopped by a dense thicket of trees. I kept trying to get around the thicket, but it seemed to have no end. Only when

I realized that the thicket must be the dense row of trees thriving along the road itself did I thrust my way through (as any deer would have done)—and found myself in the narrow path the road has become. I headed south and made my way as the encroaching trees allowed. Overhead, high clouds of ice crystals shone blue, green, and purple around the sun.

Nearly to Route 3, I came to the gun range in the bottom of a gravel pit which the road cuts across. Seven firing positions face seven target frames backed by a gravel slope. In a gesture of nonviolence, I slalomed through the target frames, weaving a sinuous snowshoe track among the members of that rigid squad. I was surprised to see how many rounds had passed through the angle-iron frames themselves, missing the targets entirely. But then they had been fired by park rangers, not Green Berets. What a sorry commentary on our society that national park rangers now find it necessary to carry guns. Perhaps pistols convey a message of authority more effectively than Smokey Bear hats and badges. But rangers don't just pack pistols, they qualify in marksmanship by shooting at targets on the range. Illegal campers and walkers of unleashed dogs, beware! Rangers mean business. And you curious onlookers, take cover: some of these rangers hit the frame, not the target.

From the gravel pit to Route 3, the Boyd Road is a true road capable of bearing wheeled traffic. It is blocked by a locked gate when the range is not in use. When I hiked it, it was also blocked by snow. Nearing my car, I thought of the tracks I had seen—deer, squirrel, hare, mouse, fox, coyote, shrew. Yes, I had sensed the living presence of wildlife, and the presence of men with guns. Before the park took it over, I'm sure Hunters Brook was true to its name. With foxes and coyotes on the prowl, it still is. The Presence there is equally composed of hunters and the hunted, and always has been. The urge I feel to hike into nature derives from the eternal tension between the two. What we hunt is always free and beautiful, whether we choose to kill it or not. Stopping short of pulling the trigger, I do take careful aim. On this hike, I came back with all the game I could carry.

❊

21—SARGENT MOUNTAIN LOOP

From Brown Mountain Gate parking area
To Sargent Mountain summit, and back
   Up by carriage road; Hadlock Brook, Giant Slide,
     and Grandgent trails
   Down by Sargent Mountain South Ridge Trail
     and carriage road
         6.5 miles on snowshoes, January 4, 1996

The day after a near blizzard in early January, a northwest wind blew across the summit of Sargent Mountain at twenty miles an hour, dropping the actual temperature of minus 10° Fahrenheit to an effective temperature on human skin of 50° below zero. When I reached the summit at noon, it wasn't from modesty that not one sliver of my flesh was showing, had anyone been there to notice.

The six-and-a-half-mile loop between Brown Mountain Gate and Sargent's summit was in many ways a test. My clothing, equipment, strength, and stamina were all at issue, as was my ability to plan a route that would prove doable under harsh conditions. Having spent the storm indoors writing up my previous hike, I was ready to go the next day. The forecast was for cold and wind. I studied old and new maps, making lists of possible routes. My first criterion was to stay out of the wind, but every hike I came up with seemed to avoid the essence of winter, the very thing I wanted to experience. Waking at three in the morning, I reviewed my options while lying in bed. Every one seemed possible—but tame. When I got up at six, my thermometer read four below zero. Where to go? As it had many times before, the summit of Sargent called. A year ago Christmas, sun low in the south, I had made that hike with three friends on a frosty but snowless day. Every twig shining like crystal, the summit had been glorious. Now, three major snowstorms having buried the mountain, what would it be like? I decided to follow the call.

Given the realities of the day, the main consideration was the route I would take. I wanted that wind at my back. Which meant hiking south from the summit on the Sargent Mountain South Ridge Trail by way of Cedar Swamp Mountain. But how to get to the summit? The most protected route would be along the Grandgent Trail. Wanting to avoid the steep slopes of Gilmore Peak, I decided to pick up the Grandgent by hiking the Maple Spring Trail along the northern branch of Hadlock Brook from Hemlock Bridge. OK, that sounded like a plan, but there were problems. Old maps show a trail along the brook all the way to what, on an earlier hike, I called Chickadee Valley, where the Grandgent comes off Gilmore Peak. But the Maple Spring Trail turns off well before that point. Would I be able to make it along the brook past that turn? I hadn't hiked that area for six or seven years, so wasn't sure what shape the trail was in. Another problem was getting through

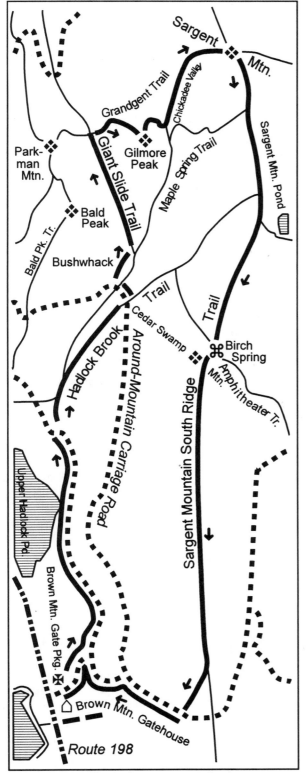

21—Sargent & Cedar Swamp mountains loop.

brook, starting at the north end of Hemlock Bridge. It would be easy to reach the bridge by the Hadlock Brook Trail from Hadlock Bridge on the lower carriage road. Ha!—I had closed the loop in my mind; now all I had to do was close it on forty inches of snow.

I dressed in layers under my parka, adding an additional layer against the exceptional chill—polypropylene long johns, wool sweater, wool shirt, lined flannel shirt. My sheepskin trooper's hat doesn't fit under my hood, so I wore a watch cap over my balaclava, and took a deerskin face mask for the summit. Wool socks, insulated boots, and Austrian boiled wool mittens completed my stylish ensemble. I packed dates, map, camera, two space blankets, extra pencils, water, and a scarf in my fanny pack. As an afterthought, I stuffed in a piece of fruitcake left over from the holidays.

Having hiked on borrowed snowshoes for two weeks, I had bought a new low-end, hi-tech pair which snow and ice would not stick to. They had bindings which wouldn't walk loose, and being narrower than webbed snowshoes, would be maneuverable on steep slopes. Every bit as important as snowshoes, I took my trusty bamboo ski poles; I knew I would need arm and leg power both to get up the Grandgent Trail. As for strength and stamina, I put faith in my record on the trail through the seasons, over the years. Since having been stopped by a narrow band of drifting snow from sliding over a cliff on Mount Monadnock twenty-five years ago, I had paid attention to details of clothing, equipment, and physical condition. When it comes to winter hiking, a lapse in preparation might be fatal—or worse.

My route took me over three very different types of terrain. To gain access to the trails I had chosen, I made use of segments of the park's carriage road system, groomed for cross-country skiing this time of year. Graded for horse-drawn carriages, these roads offer easy snowshoeing. The harshest terrain I crossed was on the treeless mountain ridges where the wind hurled snow into stiff, sculpted drifts, exposing occasional patches of granite ledge. The ridges I hiked were gently sloping for the most part, the chief impediments being drifts, wind, and cold. Out in the open, I hiked with the wind; if I headed against it, I knew I would never make it. The woodland trails I took to reach the ridges were more difficult because they were buried in snow and often steep. The Grandgent Trail rising out of Chickadee Valley was a river of soft snow. I had fallen there on an earlier hike, leaving blood and a chip of tooth on a rock in the trail. I was so groggy from the fall I had no sense of the trail from there to the summit; this time I realized what a scramble the Grandgent is, every step being hard-won. Another difficult stretch was from Birch Spring onto Cedar Swamp Mountain on the return leg of the loop. In that case there was no trickster stream, only a steep, rocky cliff. When you can see what you are trusting your weight to, that cliff is no trouble to scramble up. When two- and three-foot

the rocky gorge above Hemlock Bridge where the brook falls rapidly between steep cliffs. I didn't want to do battle with snow and ice where footing is a challenge at the best of times. All right, I would skirt that narrow gorge by hiking well back from the top of the cliffs on the north side of the drifts dress every possible toehold in a layer of fluff, it is hard to know where to step. Losing the first round or two, I eventually bullied my way to the top.

My Sargent Mountain loop covered a distance of about six-and-a-half miles. It took me four hours to reach the summit, three hours and ten minutes to get back, for a total of seven hours and ten minutes. I half expected to find a **MOUNTAIN CLOSED** sign at the top because of the current government shutdown, but if it was there I missed it. The park superintendent did zip by me on cross-country skis near the end, which I thought was a great way for him to be spending his time off.

The hike unfolded in ten scenes, each with its own subplot and drama. In chronological order, they were:

1. Brown Mountain Gate by carriage road to Hadlock Brook Trail at Hadlock Bridge (1.0 mile);
2. up gently sloping Hadlock Brook Trail through woods to Waterfall Bridge (0.6 mile);
3. Waterfall Bridge by carriage road to Hemlock Bridge (0.05 mile);
4. steep bushwhack through woods to what I thought was the Maple Spring Trail (0.25 mile);
5. rise along what I thought was the north branch of Hadlock Brook to a saddle between two peaks (0.5 mile);
6. steep and snowy ascent by the Grandgent Trail over Gilmore Peak, into Chickadee Valley, and on to the treeless summit area of Sargent Mountain (0.8 mile);
7. exposed summit area of Sargent Mountain, from treeline on the Grandgent Trail at about 1,100 feet to the sign for Asticou above Sargent Mountain Pond at the head of the Amphitheater (0.8 mile);
8. down the Sargent Mountain South Ridge Trail past Birch Spring to the exposed summit area of Cedar Swamp Mountain (0.6 mile);
9. along the gently sloping, wooded south ridge of Cedar Swamp Mountain down to the Around-Mountain Carriage Road (1.2 miles); and
10. the final section of carriage road to Brown Mountain Gate (0.7 mile).

In Scene One, starting at eight o'clock, I hiked the level mile of carriage road in denial that I was actually headed for the windswept summit of Sargent Mountain. Everything was . . . well, calm and unexciting. I noticed a couple of big white pines in the snowy woods, the white expanse of Upper Hadlock Pond through trees, the wooded slopes of Norumbega Mountain across the pond, and the spot where a snowmobile which had been grooming the way for skiers had gone off the road—a great ruckus of tracks showing how hard the driver had worked to get his machine out of the ditch. Early on, I tucked both poles under my arm so I could curl cold fingers inside my mittens. Then I saw a chickadee hanging upside-down from a spruce bough, and a red-breasted nuthatch on a nearby trunk, and things began to pick up. In the corner of my eye I saw a dollop of snow fall from a branch—sideways! It turned into a hairy woodpecker flying spruce-to-spruce. When it landed, it looked larger than life, feathers fluffed against the cold. By the time I reached Hadlock Brook, my fingers were warm and I was getting into the hike. I met the yellow ski-trail grooming machine, headlight aglow, planing the other way on Hadlock Bridge. Machines are the persona we present to the natural world—earthmovers, bulldozers, feller-bunchers, four-wheel drives, tanks, trawlers, jumbo jets. Our diplomatic corps.

In Scene Two I traded the carriage road for a woodland trail at a sign pointing to **UPPER HADLOCK TR.** Within twenty feet I was walking in deer tracks. At first they were old craters from before the last storm; then, at a sign for **SARGENT MT.** on the Hadlock Brook Trail, they were fresh. The Presence was with me. In another minute, I saw tracks where a weasel had bounded across the trail covering two feet at a bound. Long-tailed or short-tailed I could not tell, but I thought of it as an ermine (short-tailed) because I have never seen a long-tailed weasel in the woods. I have often seen ermine in their stunning winter coats chasing after voles, killing one after another, stashing them, going back for more. They're good at what they do. Trim and sleek, they have evolved into perfect killing machines. No, not machines; they earn every kill the hard way, through skill and cunning. No animal on Earth is more vivacious or beautiful. I saw the same tracks twice again farther along on the slow rise to Waterfall Bridge. Deer, too, were with me along the same stretch. Their tracks were everywhere among the many Northern white cedars on both sides of the brook, weaving in and around the trees. The deer kept moving, never stopping to strip an entire branch. Their strategy seemed to be to take only what they needed at the moment, to save the rest for later. Winter was only beginning; the green shoots of May were a long way off. In several places, shrews or mice had hopped, hopped, hopped, leaving tailed body prints in the snow. Where one hopper had crossed my path, I counted sixty-three identical impressions, as if made by a handstamp. Actually, a bellystamp. The woods were fairly open in all directions, making it hard to follow the trail. Markers were scarce. I was glad to see the occasional diamond blaze ahead, a beacon of blue or red.

In an hour and a half since starting out, I came to Waterfall Bridge. Approaching from downstream, I glimpsed the blue ice of the falls through the arch. From up on the bridge, the falls were disappointing, being largely buried beneath a blanket of snow. Memory supplied the shimmering banks of Antonio Gaudi organ pipes I had seen in earlier years.

During Scene Three, I had a good view of Bald Peak looming like a huge scoop of granite-chip ice cream over Hemlock Bridge next door. The hemlocks stood stalwart as ever, but the north branch of Hadlock Brook had withdrawn before winter's white onslaught. What brook, where? The gorge upstream looked bland as a scenic postcard, but I knew trying to get through it would be tricky. The two bridges were scenic in their own right because of the care Mr. Rockefeller's engineers had taken to fit them into their natural settings. Finding such stone-works in Acadia's woods is like coming across a vine-covered temple in the Yucatán.

Scene Four: My adventure begins. Having seen on my topo map what looked to be a shelf above the north side of the gorge, I headed for it through the woods at the end of Hemlock Bridge. The way was steep. Using poles, I became a quadruped in order to make the grade. Immediately, I came to the first fox track of the day, paralleling the carriage road. Farther up, a maze of downed trees blocked my way in every direction. I threaded among them, going over when it was impossible to go around. The gorge was precipitous on my right, the slope steep up to my left. My map had not lied: there was a shelf, but it was densely overgrown and littered with fallen trees. My plan was to rejoin the Maple Spring Trail, and follow the brook to the crossing where the Grandgent Trail comes down from Gilmore Peak. I zigged and zagged where I could, keeping the gorge to my right. Gradually, the high ground I was on sloped down in front—into what I assumed was the valley of the north branch of Hadlock Brook, the same valley I had kept to my right, which was now sweeping around in front. Concentrating on where to place my next step, I never thought that the descent ahead would lead anywhere but to the valley I had in mind. I knew there were tributaries, and an extension connecting with the Giant Slide Trail, but that was abstract knowledge having nothing to do with my current hike. Coming to a valley in the right place at the right angle, I took it for the valley I sought. I had made it around the gorge. On to Chickadee Valley. Excelsior!

In Scene Five I followed the valley up and up, meeting a chickadee and almost meeting a porcupine. The solo chickadee flew lightly from one snow-covered spruce to another, gleaning insect eggs and other delicacies where it found them in pockets of bark. With a body temperature of 104 degrees, and a hyperactive metabolism to match, the little bird had to eat all the time to stay warm, particularly because dinnertime these days was shorter than usual. There was more snow in the valley than down below, ten inches or so, on top of another two feet. Blazes were hard to come by, so I often stumbled across the brook, which gave a flattering imitation of a trail. A bent red diamond confirmed I

was on the right track. After going for a time without seeing a blaze, over increasingly steep and rocky ground, I saw the next blaze ahead on the far side of the brook. Not trusting the seemingly virginal snow to bear my weight, I went in search of a better crossing, but was stymied by great hunks of talus which ganged up on me, blocking my way. Over I went to the other side, my bridge crumbling behind me as if I were Alexander Botts at the helm of a Caterpillar tractor.

Summit cairn, Sargent Mountain.

After that, I saw no blazes at all. This was supposed to be the easy part; the mountain lay far ahead. Pushing upward as best I could, I came to a large tree recently fallen at an angle against the valley slope, tilting its network of roots, creating a cave of dark soil underneath. A single wide track led away from the cave. An unusual track—the animal that made it was much broader than the spread between its feet. Gouging a trough as it went, it had waddled an intricate, feathery-edged rut in the snow. I pictured it sleeping through the storm beneath sheltering roots, then making a foray into the landscape for food. Judging by the freshness of the trail, I had just missed the last porcupine. Looking more closely into the cave, I saw a jumble of inch-and-a-quarter scats like large dogfood pellets. Continuing, I paralleled the deep track a good way until it disappeared among a heap of talus fallen from the cliff on my left. For a time, the watchful Presence took on an almost prickly feel.

The valley leveled off, then gradually declined. I didn't remember that it did that the last time I was here, not realizing that "here" was not here at all but somewhere else. The air was colder now, so I pulled my balaclava over my face, having to break three-inch icicles out of my mustache. Past tracks of a timid shrew that had ventured two feet beyond a log, then scurried back, my way was blocked by a fallen beech. Going around it, I came face-to-face with a branch of witch hazel, its yellow sepals fast turning brown. Looking around, I figured I was home free in Chickadee Valley. Ah, signpost ahead: **ST. JAMES CHURCH RT. 198 2.4 MI.** At right angles: **SARGENT VIA GRAND GENT .8 MI.** Wrong! This wasn't Chickadee Valley. I was caught flatfooted in the valley of Sargent Brook between Parkman Mountain and Gilmore Peak, with the undeniable peak itself between where I was and where I wanted to be. In the dark, lying in bed that morning, I had wanted to avoid scaling Gilmore (one of the park's 1,000-foot peaks) unnecessarily; but now I had no choice.

In Scene Six I did a lot of heavy lifting, more than I had expected. First I had to lift myself over Gilmore Peak into Chickadee Valley, then up to the summit of Sargent Mountain. That was what I came to do; that's what I did. I had traveled about two-and-a-half miles in two-and-a-half hours; I was three-quarters of the way to the top. However steep the way might be, I was mentally prepared. Give me snow, ice, and wind! First, up and over Gilmore Peak—Gilmore piece-of-cake.

Small mammal tracks (shrew or mouse) ran every which way as soon as I turned onto the Grandgent Trail, often twining together in delicate loops and figure eights. It turned out they were the last tracks I saw for the next three-quarters of a mile,

Cairn with windswept granite, Sargent Mtn. south ridge.

except for those of a lone snowshoer who had taken the same route before the last storm, leaving unmistakable Sasquatch tracks on the side of Gilmore Peak. Between those two extremes, I saw no trace of any other creature until I reached the summit. The Presence backed off somewhat, yielding to wind and deep snow. Rising along the steep trail, I trekked through massive drifts swept from the bare peak into surrounding woods. Every step required coordinated effort from arms and legs. I experienced the deeper meaning of "trudge." Any sign of a trail disappeared. Passing out of woods onto the exposed ridge, I stopped to get my bearings. Ahead, I saw patches of bare ledge and ice showing between sweeps of windpacked snow. Turning, I faced the whitened cliffs of Parkman Mountain and Bald Peak, with Western Mountain in the distance caught between the two. Overhead, a low sun

shone through icy clouds opposite a frozen sheet of blue in the north. Exposed to the northwest wind, I was surrounded by blowing snow. The entire slope was on the move. I joined the crowd. Up, up, and up, one step at a time. Avoiding ice and rock, I made my own trail. Two cairns stood on the summit of Gilmore Peak, bleak, like grave markers. Not mine. I wanted out of there. Glimpsing the porcelain dome of Sargent, I thought how lifeless it looked. From the northern of the two cairns, I looked for a marker showing the way into Chickadee Valley; there was none. Over the side I went. As soon as I was among trees, the wind died. Sideways, I did the Gilmore two-step down the steep slope, sending a fan of scurrying snow minions before me. Blue blaze ahead. Back on the trail, I sledded at last into the valley from which, in bed that morning, I had planned to launch my final ascent.

Gilmore having given me a foretaste of the summit, I put on my deerskin face mask. The eye holes sagged because the two straps weren't adjusted right. Taking off hats and mittens to fiddle with the straps, five minutes taught me a thing or two about making preparations in advance. My face finally girded against the wind, hats and mittens back on, hood up, I turned north along the valley floor. It took me an hour to climb the last 475 vertical feet from Chickadee Valley to the summit. What a transition that was. Sunny, windless, sheltered among cliffs and tall trees, the valley seemed almost balmy. It is a beautiful site at any season; under three feet of snow, it was glorious. Every tree cloaked in white, the scene looked more like a valley in the Alps or Colorado Rockies than coastal Maine. The temperature felt cold, but not cruel. Up top it would be different. Getting there, I experienced a revelation. The climb ahead turned out to be one of the best hikes I have ever made. Not easy. Not something I'd be up for every day. But I was focused on what I was doing; I rose above my partial consciousness to become a feature of the scene itself. Like a yellow birch or Northern white cedar, I was in my natural element. A hare or fox looking on would have seen me as part of the Presence in that place. Man making tracks on Sargent Mountain. That is all I was, yet I was all of that. A celebration of one body and its aspirations. Doing exactly what I had set out to do, I became a planetary, a universal, fact. Life doesn't get better than that.

As the Grandgent Trail winds out of the steep valley, it crosses a small brook several times. I fell at one crossing on an earlier hike and, right on cue, I fell again this time. My snowshoes suddenly sank into three feet of nothing, throwing me off balance into the snow. I hadn't intended to make a snow angel, but that's what I did—face down. All things considered, I would rather fall on snow than a rock. The fall was a minor detail, like Icarus taking the plunge in Brueghel's painting. Bit player in a beautiful scene, I was too caught up in the workings of the natural world to mind my own clumsiness. Every step was hard work, but profoundly gratifying. I felt blessed. By whom? Every one of my ancestors for four million uninterrupted years who, without a hitch, had survived by fitting into the landscape. Though they did not know me, they carried me in their hands, in their embrace, in their genes. I am the promise of their lives, one of their gifts to the universe. It is wonderful to experience a sense of that collective effort. If that line of thought seems far-fetched, it does suggest the true experience (which was nonverbal) I had on the upper reach of the Grandgent Trail.

The supreme moment of the hike was climbing out of Chickadee Valley onto the dome of Sargent itself to stand in steep-pitched snow lit by sunlight from a blue and flawless sky. Abruptly, Scene Seven began. I had switched universes. From where I stood to the actual summit, and from there to the turning for Asticou on the brink of the Amphitheater three-quarters of a mile south, I hiked through the spare and windswept arctic kingdom of Acadia's foxes—what I thought of as their mythical happy hunting ground. Along with snow and wind, fox prints were everywhere, radiating in all directions. Some were clear paw prints on the surface, some deep indentations, some raised discs where the wind spared only the snow compressed by their weight. Every square yard was crossed by tracks. The Presence here expanded, incorporating a multitude. Having seen the summit from Gilmore Peak as barren, I had had no premonition of the signs of life I would find. I could not have imagined foxes would be drawn to so bleak and harsh a landscape. Deep snow might have blocked their hunting in the woods, giving them a choice: up or down. Some had chosen the summit where much of the snow had been blown away, leaving what prey there was less protected. That argument hangs on the presence of mice, voles, and hares in such a forbidding place. I pictured a pack of foxes crisscrossing the summit. It didn't seem possible that one fox had made that many tracks.

Unobstructed now, the view was magnificent. To the west, every peak stood out—Gilmore, Parkman, Bald, Norumbega, Acadia, St. Sauveur, Beech, Western, with Blue Hill on the horizon. Upper Somes Sound lay beyond Norumbega Mountain, and I could make out Bartlett and Long islands in Blue Hill Bay. The landscape sparkled and looked brand-new. Upslope toward the summit, drifts in the lee of every bush and stone had been sculpted by the wind into streamlined, futuristic forms. Pink granite and ice

Cairn with wind shadow of driven snow, Sargent Mountain south ridge.

showed through the wind-packed snow here and there. No sign of a trail. The going much easier on packed snow, I went where my snowshoes led. A great many alder twigs stuck out of the drifts, bearing miniature cones hinting at some form of afterlife. I saw cairns to my right marking the trail I was meant to take, but their advice was now moot because I had a clear shot at the summit cairn straight ahead. What a windswept pile that was, crevices packed with white grout, a tumulus worthy of King Arthur himself. After four hours of hiking, I got to the summit at noon. Starting at 260 feet, I had pulled myself up some 1,113 feet by my own thongs. I felt very accomplished. Standing out of the wind behind the topmost cairn, I admired Cadillac and Pemetic to the east; Schoodic, Tunk, and Black mountains north over Frenchman Bay; and the ocean to the south, everywhere swirling with plumes of sea smoke. Hikers in such a situation are apt to feel on top of the world; I was no exception. A few ski tracks persisted in scoured snow around the summit, though I couldn't imagine skiing there with all those stones and ledges on or just under the surface. A reassuring line of cairns led toward the sun along the south ridge, marking the way I was to take in descending from my exalted position.

Thoreau speaks of the winter tracks of fishermen as stitching his town together. On Sargent, that important work was done by foxes. The entire white dome was a network of tracks. Like a longshore current, the wind drove me on, deeper and deeper into the weir of the Presence. I was caught in the spell of the place. My will was driven by a higher will: this is what you must do; this is where you must go. A prompting chill in the seat of my pants kept me in line. Cairns went on before, casting snow shadows in the lee of the wind some ten or fifteen feet long, in which the silhouette of the cairn persisted in grooves and streaks. If I stood still for ten minutes, a similar shadow would stretch before me where the wind, unable to pass through me, would quickly backfill my outline with snow. Every drop and depression on the summit had been caulked and smoothed. Twice I stepped off a hidden drop into two or three feet of fluff which did not hold my weight. I avoided dark patches of bare, often icy, granite. As I went, blowing snow swirled around me and raced on ahead like a younger generation more reckless and sprightly than mine. I walked straight for the sun and its broad, burnished path out to the horizon in the Gulf of Maine. Leaning out of drifts, weathered signs pointed west for **MAPLE SPRING TR.** and then **HADLOCK BROOK TR.** Dipping through deep drifts into trees, then up on a continuation of the summit ridge, I admired the arching backs of Cadillac, Pemetic, and Penobscot all in a line, like a pod of white whales heading into the waves. The fox stitching continued here, too. Where the trail forks at the head of the Amphitheater, east to Sargent Mountain Pond and Penobscot Mountain, west to Asticou, I followed the angling south ridge trail, ending my stay at the summit.

Ruffed grouse track.

In Scene Eight I rode the snowy ridge from Sargent to Birch Spring, then up to the open summit area of Cedar Swamp Mountain, led the whole way by tracks of a guiding fox who knew the trail far better than I did, followed by the wind. Heading between south-southwest and southwest, the trail cut across the path of the northwest wind, which had piled great drifts in the woods and clefts along the ridge. Almost all cairns were buried, making the trail hard to find. Trusting my own judgment, I went astray several times before I understood that the fox and I shared a common journey. Every time I regained the trail, fox prints confirmed my arrival. This was no close-knit mesh of prints but a single, deliberate track, running from the turning for Asticou past the summit of Cedar Swamp. The way was as blustery as the summit had been, the wind hitting not my back but right shoulder. Skirting the drop into the Amphitheater, a deep, wooded gorge between Penobscot on the east and Cedar Swamp on the west, the trail is one of my favorites in all Acadia. Though I had been over it many times, in deep snow it seemed like no trail at all. It was not easy to spot the entrance to wooded sections of the trail, which alternate with open slopes. After I learned to trust my guide, I had no trouble at all. The tracks were recent, made in the past half-hour I guessed, from my sense of how rapidly blowing snow filled every dent in the surface. They led me directly to Birch Spring, where I had a choice of three routes: south into the Amphitheater, north to Hadlock Brook, or ahead to Cedar Swamp Mountain. I voted with the fox for Cedar Swamp. After a hard climb through drifts onto the dome of the mountain itself, I found a pale fox scat on the surface of the snow, which I took to be a blaze showing the way. I had a dim sense of the trail, but the fox knew exactly where it ran. My advice to winter hikers is: know the trail like the reflection of your own face, or have a spirit guide.

Intent on finding my way, I had to break my concentration to take in the landscape around me. The western flank of Penobscot as seen from Cedar Swamp is one of the finest views in the park, rewarding any hike along the Sargent Mountain South Ridge Trail. When I passed, that landscape was made of trees, rocks, snow, sky, and wind, the five winter elements. Once stopped to admire the vista, I had a hard time getting going again. My muscles were trying to tell me something. Out of nowhere I thought of fruitcake, and remembered the piece I had with me, which I ate in short order. Refreshed, I went on, passing among exposed ledges within 200 feet of Cedar Swamp's summit, continuing along the Amphitheater's west rim, overlooking (Little) Long Pond and the islands offshore—Baker, Sutton, Great and Little Cranberry, and the Duck Islands farther out.

Entering woods at the start of Scene Nine, I saw the first snowshoe hare tracks I had seen that day, and continued to see them in great numbers for over a mile down to the Around-Mountain Carriage Road. I had my snowshoes on, they had theirs. This was the hares' kind of weather, their kind of place. I don't know how they make a living nibbling spruce and fir tips all winter, but they survive. Their tracks led from the skirts of one tree to another, occasionally punctuated by pellets of undigested cellulose, which hares do their best to recycle. Tracks of fox and hare did not overlap, as if each respected the sovereignty of the other—which I know cannot be true. Why weren't the track makers on Sargent down here? Were the odds against them so steep that they found pickings on the snow barrens a better bet? I didn't see one fox print among those made by dozens of hares. Being back in cedar country, I did see a great many deer tracks, as I had on the Hadlock Brook Trail. With longer legs than a fox, deer had an easier time getting around in deep snow. On my stroll through these snowy woods, gradually descending all the while, I saw the one set of squirrel tracks I had seen all day, which made me think the squirrel tribe had gone underground for the duration of the big snow. Shrews and mice, being much lighter, still had the energy for bounding across the surface. I saw their imprints in several places on this stretch of trail. I first heard, then saw, a hairy woodpecker high in a poplar. I also saw a ruffed grouse fly across the trail thirty feet ahead. I don't know how grouse fly through tree limbs, but they have that ability, just like deer can penetrate the densest brush. Looking for the grouse's track, I saw that it had more plowed than walked through the snow. I could not explain the difference between this abundant habitat and Chickadee Valley where I had seen no tracks at all, though the cover seemed about the same.

Whether looking into a stand of tall spruce or out over one snowy vista or another, I found the landscape I passed through uniformly beautiful. Even the summit area was beautiful, harsh as it was, as Death Valley or the Badlands are beautiful. Why are we drawn to such austere places? My usual rationale traces beauty to its roots in biological advantage. Why, then, should I be moved to climb Sargent Mountain in the snow? Does my racial intelligence know I will find fox prints in great abundance? It seems the tradeoff in effort and exposure to hazards is hardly worth the attempt. There is wisdom in my genes I do not understand. Perhaps a long heritage of struggle in glacial terrain still speaks to my blood, telling me to pursue beauty—and survival—beyond the walls of my cave.

After separate glimpses east, west, and south of Day, Norumbega, and Eliot mountains, I split off the ridge trail heading for Asticou at a sign reading **GATE HOUSE DIRECT**. The descent is steep for a short stretch; then, passing through a stand of red pines, each branch covered with snow cones on the day of my hike, the trail comes out on the carriage road.

The tenth and final scene of my hike was a tale of return-

ing to the comforts of civilized life. The adventure was behind me. Walking along the groomed ski tracks, a row of snow-capped coping stones keeping me from veering over the outside edge, the trees on either hand seeming to be held back by an invisible wall, I met five skiers in bright colors and was overtaken by a sixth, the park superintendent. A group of three looked to be out on skis for the first time. I thought I detected envy in their side glances at my snow-

Red spruce garbed for winter.

shoes. Stopping for a drink of water, I found it frozen solid in the bottle I carried in my pack. I got back to the gatehouse at ten after three. The temperature had warmed to six above zero. That night I slept ten hours straight.

I will end by reporting my exchange with one of the skiers, a trim young woman dressed in purple, pink, and blue.

"Hi," I said to this colorful person.

"Helloo," she said to me.

"Beautiful Day."

"Yes!"

❄

22—AROUND MANSELL MOUNTAIN

From Long Pond parking area (pumping station)
To Great Notch, and back
Up by Cold Brook and Great Notch trails
Down by Long (Great) Pond Trail
5.0 miles on snowshoes, January 11, 1996

Since my last hike, the Great Blizzard of 1996 had come and gone, Maine receiving only a brief wag of its tail as it bounded out to sea. That storm and the lesser one following on its heels added fourteen inches of new snow, piling our total snowfall for the season some three feet higher than average. Despite the local tradition of snow turning to rain, then freezing, locking the landscape in ice, for now Mount Desert Island was a snowshoer's paradise. Having recently explored the wonders of windswept ridges, this time I wanted an extended woodland hike. Thinking of woodlands, Western Mountain came to mind. Reviewing its many trails, I settled on a loop that would make a perfect snowshoe trail in deep snow: from the south end of Long Pond via the Cold Brook Trail to Gilley Field, up the Great Notch Trail to its end, then north out of the notch along the Long (Great) Pond Trail, which eventually makes its way south along the shore back to the pumping station at the south end of the pond. The virtue of this loop is its easy grade through woods the whole way. Starting at an elevation of 60 feet by the pond, it rises to a little over 740 feet in Great Notch. A mile and a half from the pumping station to the notch, a couple of miles more than that by the pond trail back, the total loop is about five miles long. On a sunny, windless day in midwinter, what could be better? All I had to do was fill in the particulars.

I figure I took 13,200 steps to complete that five-mile loop. At every step the scene around me was focused on my retina in fine detail. I saw how every tree was different from all others; how the snow lay uniquely upon every trunk and branch; how every stand of trees formed a distinct neigh-

borhood unto itself; how shadows on the snow intertwined in patterns of infinite complexity; how the terrain on either hand was never twice the same; how wildlife made brief appearances along the way, giving the changing scene a wild rhythm of its own. If I had made a film of my hike, exposing one frame every step, at twenty-four frames a second it would take nine minutes and ten seconds to run the whole hike—all 13,200 frames—through the projector,

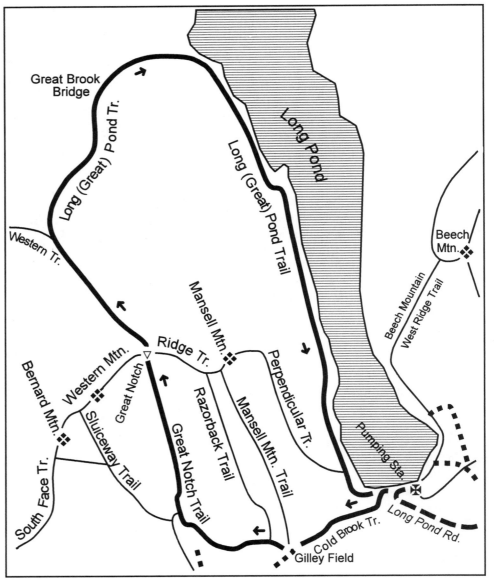

22—Around Mansell Mountain.

where in real time it took me six hours and twenty-five minutes from start to finish. In all its telling detail, the film would leave out ninety-seven percent of the hike. Experience is a matter of being there at the time, there is no way around it. What I experienced on my loop around Mansell Mountain was both complex and simple at the same time. Individual frames stand out against a general impression of the hike as a whole.

I experienced the hike on two levels, general and particular. My mind sifted the infinite combinations of snow and trees into a background of general impressions and possibilities, which emerged as foreground when I stopped to examine one or another of them in closer detail. At times I trudged ahead, intent on finding my way; then I would stop to consider some detail that caught my eye or ear. My sense of the hike, distilled by memory from a boggling number of details, blends snowy woods, stillness, and wildlife, with a sense of progressing through a realm of marvelous possibilities where miracles could occur any moment.

On the Cold Brook leg of my hike, I first met the stillness of snowy woods. With no wind, no trucks, no barking dogs, there was nothing to hear, yet what I heard was the sound of everything at once—the sound of snow lying softly on every surface, trees standing tall, wildlife making its rounds, mountains being mountainous. The loudest sound I heard was the scratching of my pencil as I made a note about the stillness of the woods.

From Gilley Field along the notch trail to Great Notch between Mansell Mountain and Knight Nubble, I walked in the presence of deer on their native ground. Here were white-tailed deer at the northern end of their range practicing traditional deer arts in order to survive in that

Snow vanes pointing toward the storm, Great Notch.

place under winter conditions. Their tracks crossed my way fifteen times. I saw where they had browsed lichens, cedar boughs, and buds buried beneath the snow along Marshall Brook. By the plank footbridge over the brook above the Reservoir, I saw where one deer had bedded for the night in a nest made by its body curled in fetal position under the cover of twin sapling spruce. The perfect imprint of its body and folded legs showed in an oval bowl twenty-eight inches long, twenty-two inches across, in fifteen inches of powder snow. It walked out as it had entered, leaving what looked to be one set of tracks.

In Great Notch itself, snug between two peaks, I saw five chickadees fifty feet overhead swinging upside-down on branches of yellow birch as they gleaned insect egg masses from under the bark. I heard at least three other chickadees calling from nearby trees.

Along the pond trail between the notch and the edge of the pond, I saw tracks of moose, mouse, squirrel, hare, fox, and porcupine. I also saw, in the feather if not in the flesh, a male and a female hairy woodpecker tapping away in a grove of birch.

On the same trail as it hugs the shore of the frozen pond, I saw drifts thrown up by northeast winds off the ice, creating dunes in the trail two, three, and four feet high, beautiful to see but difficult to tramp across. That level stretch was the hardest part of the loop. In one place, balked by massive icefalls in the trail, I walked out onto the pond itself, which I had secretly vowed I would not do, the temptation being great to reach my car at the pumping station by the easiest and most direct route. Except for that brief detour, I stuck to the trail.

Winter woods. That was the medium I traveled through the whole way. Trees to the left of me, trees to the right, an untrodden corridor opening ahead. In places I thought I saw two corridors, or three, equally inviting. Diamond and bluebird blazes gave infrequent help. If there were any cairns along the trail, they had gone into hibernation. I may have strayed here or there, but my general sense of the route from past hikes kept me headed in the right direction. All the way to the bridge over Great Brook on the north slope of the mountain, the sun gave me a gentle push from behind. My lumbering shadow infallibly went ahead.

Up to the notch from the south, the way is largely through an unbroken stand of evergreens. Yellow birches command the immediate approach to the notch, opening the canopy to the winter sky, deep blue on the day of my hike. Spruce saplings line much of the pond trail between the notch and the bridge, creating a riverine trail through banks of dark green. Yellow birches open the trail somewhat from Great Brook to the ridge overlooking Long Pond, while Northern white cedars close it in again for the mile-and-a-half walk along the shore to the pumping station. And, draping every trailside tree, branch, and needle the whole way—a becoming cloak perfectly in keeping with the day and the season.

Soft snow clung to every surface, muting the woods,

invoking the palpable presence of silence. Silence. Sound of the unknown. Of possibility itself. Opportunity for turning inward in trust, for rest and reflection. Invitation to sing whatever song leaps from within, and to listen for other voices singing songs of their own. Embracing everything that is and could conceivably be, silence is the wellspring of existence. Without it there would be chaos, unending and inescapable. Silence is all-pervading order bearing events arrayed like seeds in a perfect fruit. Silence is hope. Silence is expectancy, the birth of all awareness. Silence is the promise of a better world. Silence in the woods is the promise of deer folded upon themselves in sleep, of chickadees calling, woodpeckers tap-tap-tapping. Silence is the sound of one shrew hopping. One squirrel leaping. One hare nibbling. One fox prowling. One porcupine rolling through powder snow. Silence is one hiker turning to watch a veil of ice crystals shimmer as it drifts downward against sunlight streaming through tall trees. Silence is winter woods waiting for spring.

This hike taught me many things. Not little, narrow things, but big, broad expansive things. Things I cannot forget. It was clear to me how we fritter our lives—how *I* fritter *my* life—on trifling details. I have forgotten every fact I so dutifully learned in school, every job I performed at work, every pronouncement I ever made about politics, justice, beauty, truth. Gone, like birch leaves in winter. I am not talking about brain cell death. Forgetfulness is not a failing or a disease. It is a blessing. Letting go of details, we make space for attending to what really matters—the challenge of being at the forefront of the blossoming of the universe, which is where we truly live if we are awake. Each being is one petal in that vast unfolding. Hiking through Acadia, I take part in the flowering of my region. In the creative process itself. The onward flow of life. What I am is not what I know but what I *do*. What I do is my response to the world around me. That is what I have learned, not the dates of battles or the capitals of every state. The sum of my existence is in the skills I have sharpened while hiking along the trail. I have learned to pay attention to things, to listen, to look, to value what I find. And to continue on my way. True, I have for-

Great Notch Trail looking south.

gotten most of what I have heard and seen, but what I retain is a sense of the trail. And a preference—a reverence—for silence. For silence, not commotion. Not for bottom lines, election campaigns, advertising hype, for hullabaloo. The enduring silence of ongoing creation that outlasts all things. They do not teach any such reverence in schools. Yet without it, I wonder if we can truly claim to be alive. To be part of the universal blossoming and expansion. What I have learned on the trail is to value Acadia as a place where deer can curl themselves to sleep and chickadees can sing. Such a place is hallowed. I walk that ground while I can, sharing it with companions heading the same way or crossing my trail, each of us unfolding as Earth itself unfolds.

It is hard to write such thoughts. Hard to invite life to flow through my halting words. Yet what else can I say? What else can writing possibly be about? There *is* such a thing as truth. No one can teach it. It cannot be captured in words. It has to be lived. Truth is something we do, not something we find or are given. No teacher, no relative, no employer, no leader ever told me the way to truth, or how hard such a way might be. Letting go of the past, I am free to go on. My choice is to head into the silence following an urge toward life and creativity. That heading is not the way to truth but as close as I can come to truth itself. If I follow my shadow with eyes and ears open, I can hold my course.

As for the unfolding of the hike itself, there was no sign of Cold Brook or the small bridge at the start of the Cold Brook Trail just past the pumping station; they were buried beneath a huge drift blown off the pond. Up from there, the first slope was swept bare by the wind, exposing the icy trail. I pulled myself up that slope by the palisade of trailside trees. A bend in the trail had stymied the wind; from there to Gilley Field on the Western Mountain Truck Road, the trail was deep in new snow. A fox had crossed it near the bend, and two mice and two squirrels farther on. I heard a chickadee in that first stretch, and what I took to be the hammering of a hairy woodpecker. Rounding the south end of Mansell Mountain, the trail is level and easygoing through mixed woods, providing a link between Long Pond and Gilley Field. In summer you can take the truck road off Seal Cove Road and park at the field, but in winter the closest access is from the pumping station. From the field, you can reach any trail on Western Mountain. That is where the Great Notch Trail starts up.

The notch trail connects with both the Razorback and Sluiceway trails lower down, and with the ridge trail between Mansell and Bernard at its upper end. It starts gradually and makes an easy ascent to the notch, crossing headwaters of Marshall Brook by two simple bridges. Beneath several birches I saw lichen dust spread over the snow by woodpeckers probing for bugs. I heard the no-nonsense tattoo of the hairy woodpecker twice along the notch trail, and saw three delicate tracks of mouse or shrew. Once or twice I heard a gust of wind pass through the tallest trees, and the cracking of the trees in response. Discovering the hollow in the snow where the deer had bedded down, I wondered how well I would fare if I did the same. I could picture the compact form of the deer in the snow, but not my own. Unable to curl into a ball, I would leave too much surface exposed to retain my vital heat. That deer did something I couldn't do. No cute little Bambi, it was a skilled and hardy survivor. Seeing tracks all along the slope, I felt nothing but admiration for those with the drive and talent to make it through a Maine winter outdoors.

Bridge over Great Brook, Long (Great) Pond Trail.

White and glistening, Western Mountain was as beautiful as I have ever seen it. Even covered with snow, its persona or numinous presence was undaunted. The hike took me straight to the spiritual heart of Acadia. Anything that lively and alluring has to be true. I walked in truth and beauty along the leading edge of cosmic creation.

There was one entry for 1996 in the new logbook in Great Notch, dated January 1:

1:30 p.m.
Pam, Mike, & Leah Rae
Over Mansell to Great Notch, down Sluiceway
Happy New Year!
Beautiful Day—blue sky & sunny.

I identified with these fellow seekers whose tracks had been buried by three storms since New Year's Day.

I ate some dates in the notch, telling myself I would save my one blond brownie till I got to the Great Brook bridge. On the way down the Long (Great) Pond Trail out of the notch, I caught a glimpse of Sargent's snowy peak through bare trees. How lifeless it looked, and how far away. Was it only a week ago I was there? Checking my watch, it was ten after twelve. Exactly seven days ago to the minute I had just left the shelter of the summit cairn and was heading down the south ridge trail, my prints mixing with fox prints at every step.

On the down leg of the Long Pond Trail I saw tracks of fox, shrew or mouse, squirrel, hare, and porcupine. Spruce saplings hugged the trail, making it more of a seam than a rent in the woods. Rather than head directly into the valley of Great Brook, the pond trail stays up on the west bank until the Western Trail heads off for the Long Pond Fire Road and Pine Hill, then it cuts into the valley more steeply. I sledded along on my snowshoes, thoroughly enjoying the landscape. From maps I knew there were two private inholdings somewhere along there, but no border crossings told me where they might be. At the bridge, I saw the track of another fox following along the brook, and ate the brownie I had promised myself.

The Great Brook bridge is one of my favorites in Acadia. With a log rail held on four posts on the downstream side, the central two posts laterally braced, it is as simple and sturdy as a span can be. A ribbon of white caulking or toothpaste lay along the rail like a spent serpent, its body draped over each post. I have always assumed the bridge was built by the Appalachian Mountain Club, I don't know why. Perhaps because its design is unlike any other in the park I can think of offhand. From the bridge to the pond, I was in woodpecker country. I saw the two hairies, and lichen dust spread in a dozen places. Within sight of the pond, missing a turn, I lost the trail briefly. From there it was almost a straight shot along the shore back to the pumping station.

A lot of water drains off Mansell Mountain into Long Pond. Including the one over Cold Brook which I could not see because it was buried beneath a drift, on the last leg of my hike I crossed seven wooden bridges and one made of stone (I know because I brushed a foot-and-a-half of snow off each one). The trail also crosses a narrow talus slope, and meets some impressive glacial erratic boulders. I passed under one great gray boulder measuring roughly twelve feet on a side, pausing to admire its smooth features, rock tripe complexion, and the one rock-cap fern leaf curling through the snow on its top. I guessed it weighed some 150 tons. Big Daddy. Down the trail I saw Big Mama out for a stroll with seven of the boulder kids in snowsuits. The trail runs across the steep slope between mountain and pond. In places snow had fallen from branches upslope, forming spirals that rolled down toward the pond, leaving wavering tracks fifty feet long. Cedars on the edge of the pond featured two sets of roots, one for summer, one winter. The winter ones looked like molten glass, sprouting from the trunk fifteen inches above the frozen pond, sending glistening tubers down on all sides. Those tubers told how cold and windy it had been just before the pond finally froze when waves and spray had splashed high on shoreline trees.

I hesitate to mention one other track I saw along the pond trail just north of the notch because it sounds so unlikely. It came out of the saplings on one side, went down the trail thirty feet or so, then went off into dense cover on the other side. It was an old track, made before the last storm, persisting as a set of deep depressions in the snow. Walking down the trail, its stride was the same as mine, about two feet between prints. In size, the track maker must have been on the order of a moose. A moose on Western Mountain in January? I have since found moose tracks and pellets on the north slope of Western Mountain during subsequent winter hikes and have become a true believer in moose as year-round residents of Mount Desert Island. It was either the track of a moose I saw on this hike or of Sasquatch out for a winter stroll.

❄

23—LONG POND FIRE ROAD LOOP
From south gate of Long Pond Fire Road
To Long and Duck ponds, and back
    Out by Route 102 and north section of
      Long Pond Fire Road
    Back on south section of Long Pond Fire Road
      by way of Pine Hill
        6.0 miles on snowshoes, January 15, 1996

I thought long and hard about where to take my next hike, dismissing almost every route I came up with. Scoured by wind, summit trails crossed snow, rock, and ice, requiring the hiker to be prepared for all three. Lower down, trails were stiff with an inch-thick icy crust. Two days ago, Acadia's winter allure had been dampened by rain, which had frozen as stiff as winter sheets drying on the line. Carriage roads were walkable, but I didn't want to compete with cross-country skiers. I had walked up the Cadillac Mountain Road the day before, and several times been unnerved by snowmobiles rounding blind curves. It was Martin Luther King's birthday, and I wanted to honor his memory by being myself, which meant getting out into the park. I wanted to go somewhere I had never been to break new personal ground which, of the choices I had come up with, excluded every trail except Long Pond Fire Road. Unsure what conditions I would find, I decided to give it a try.

What I didn't know was that the fire road is open to snowmobiles in winter, providing access to Long Pond from the west. I didn't meet or hear a single machine, but made good use of the treadway earlier riders had packed nonetheless. Except for the first hundred feet on the northern end of the road, the going was firm the whole way. Testing the crust at the side of the fire road, I sank through six inches or more, my snowshoes punching holes with edges sharp as broken glass. If snowmobilers hadn't broken the crust, I wouldn't have made it. Rounding the southern gate at the end of the hike, I gave silent thanks to all who had paved the way.

Another reason for choosing the fire road was that I'd have no trouble finding the trail. In woods or on bare slopes, winter hiking takes good navigational skills, backed up by a sense of the trail from personal experience. If cars could drive the fire road in August, I knew I'd have no trouble finding my way in January. Snow machines made it that much easier. Except for a short side trip to Duck Pond, I stayed in their tracks, which let me gawk at woods in a part of the park I knew only from maps.

Long Pond Fire Road forms a great semicircle around Hodgdon Pond, the two ends coming out onto Route 102 a mile apart. Parking at the southern end, I made a loop by walking along the highway to the northern end just down from the Pretty Marsh picnic area. Writing about it, I can still taste the fine grit and fumes passing cars blew in my face. Putting my snowshoes on at the northern gate, I found their "mitten-friendly" bindings in a hostile mood. No amount of woolly tugging on stiff straps would make them budge. I took off my mittens and grabbed the wily vinyl with cold hands. The temperature dropped five degrees during the hike, from 17° to 12° above zero Fahrenheit. Snowshoes and mittens finally on, I couldn't wait to get into the woods.

From end to end, the fire road is about four-and-a-half

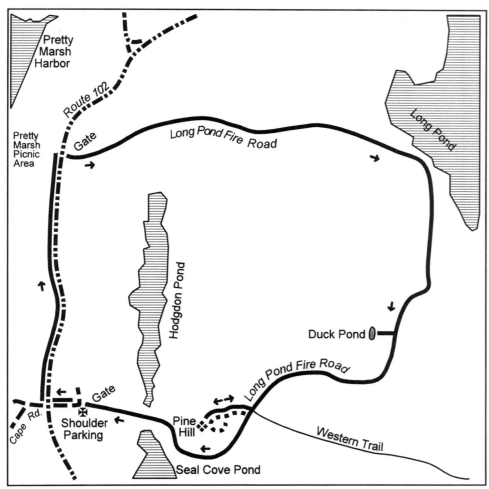

23—Long Pond Fire Road loop.

miles long, with notable breaks at Long Pond (in 1.75 miles), Duck Pond (in 2.5 miles), and Pine Hill (in 3.5 miles). Including the mile along Route 102, and excursions to Duck Pond and Pine Hill, I went six miles in four hours. Elevation along the loop ranges from 50 feet at the southern end of Hodgdon Pond to 250 feet near Duck Pond, the grade along the fire road being a series of gentle ups and downs.

Where cross-country ski tracks went around the gate, I stepped over it on crunchy snow. At the outset, one sign excluded commercial vehicles, another warned me not to speed over fifteen miles an hour. Wading through what felt

like a sea of grit or Carborundum, I didn't think there was much danger of my doing that. In a minute I came to the track of a snowmobile making a U-turn. After that, the going was easy, my snowshoes never sinking as long as I kept to the corduroy ribs the machine had laid down. As for the pregnant silence of winter woods, from start to finish there was none—not as long as I kept crunch-crunch-crunching along on the packed, icy surface. A reveler in silence, I was my own worst enemy. Even when I stopped to gawk, the echoing rhythm of my shuffling gait grated on my ears. I was a stranger to these woods, deaf to the local tradition of mute passage.

I heard chickadees at the start of the hike, and crows near the end. Stopping both times, I saw two chickadees in a tamarack, and later three crows flying over Pine Hill. I also heard a dog bark as I started out, objecting, I was sure, to my noisy parade. I also heard gun shots in the distance from someone else's parade. As for tracks, I came across plenty of those. Several deer tracks right away, then squirrel, hare, and more deer. Fox tracks crossed the fire road in three places, and where the road tweaked the edge of Long Pond, twenty-four snowmobile tracks fanned out across the ice, outnumbering the twenty-one deer tracks I saw. Deer and fox broke the crust, but hare and squirrel barely made a dent. The tracks of lighter animals dated from before the crust had formed. The recent rain had wiped away all tracks of mouse and shrew, the frozen crust supporting their lightfooted excursions without a trace. The snowmobile that broke the first stretch of trail had come along after the crust had formed, its track lined with inch-thick shards of snow where it had dug its groove.

For a mile before the fire road reaches Long Pond, another traveler had gone before me in the snowmobile's wake, leaving a line of clear prints on the endless ladder of crushed snow. At first I took it for a fox, but the front prints seemed a little big, the straddle a little wide. Finding a dark brown scat filled with hair, I suspected it was too large for fox. Coyote and fox would not share the same territory, so the other tracks I thought were fox might have been coyote as well. I will call the track that went ahead of me in the road coyote, the others I saw later, fox. I am not sure who made which track. I do know canids added tang to the Presence I felt on this hike. On Mount Desert Island, foxes fill the spaces between perhaps half-a-dozen coyote territories. Where this hike fit into that geography I do not know. My impression is that I saw tracks of two different canids. One species or two, whoever they were, I was sure they knew all they wanted to know about me.

I looked for woodpeckers in birches along the road, but saw none. From my experience on earlier hikes, that was surprising. I saw only one or two scatterings of lichen dust under roadside trees. There were plenty of birches and snags. Perhaps there were few woodpeckers in the area, or the crashing of my clown feet might have offended them.

On both sides of the fire road, verdant panoramas unfurled in a continuous strip as I went. Anchored at each end by stands of Northern white cedar, with several magnificent cedar swamps between, roadside vegetation set the tone of the hike. I felt like a traveler depicted on a Japanese landscape scroll. The most spectacular thing about this hike was the unending woods on both sides. I had to pay close attention to detect subtle changes from one stand to the next. Here cedar mixed with spruce and pine, there with

White-tailed deer track.

tamarack. Birch and popple put in a show, then mountain maple. The slope of the land was so gradual, the shift from one watershed to the next so unpronounced, the landscape seemed quietly to flow with the road as one seamless forest. But wherever they grow, trees thrive under a limited range of specific conditions. Those conditions changed as I went, from wet to dry, north slope to south, shallow soil to less-shallow soil (never deep), shaded to sunny, with diverse histories of human and natural influence. In one sense, the scene changed with such little commotion that it appeared bland and wholly undistinguished. These trees had been standing behind the door when charisma was handed out. In one sense they were ordinary and uninteresting. And, too, they were the stuff of Acadia, its heart and its strength. The landscape of Maine. The health of our region depends on these woods. They are anything but boring. Maine's motto is *Dirigo*, Latin for "I lead." That is the voice of the pole

star, but it is also the voice of the Maine woods. As they go, so go the rest of us. Our tracks follow the lead of the woods—deer, squirrel, hare, fox, coyote, the rest of us falling in behind, whether by snowmobile or snowshoe, cross-country ski or on foot, ax or chainsaw in hand, or not. If anything is dull it is our perception of the woods, not the woods themselves.

Woods are the waters of Earth come to life. On this hike I crossed six streams, flowing into four ponds, each stream rising in the woods through which I walked. Given air, sunlight, and water, woods spring up. Followed by insects and wildlife. And people. What are we but walking woods? What are woods but water with branches and roots? The woods along the fire road flow as streams flow downslope into Duck and Long ponds, into Hodgdon and Seal Cove ponds. And water, where does it come from? From the firmament, and now this fallen white fundament underfoot. Making tracks in the snow, animals come full circle, walking in the stuff they are made of. Here are the origins of Acadian life.

The primary theme of the winter hike I made around Long Pond Fire Road was the unity I felt between my outer surroundings and my inner self. Everything came together—snow, tracks, woods, streams, ponds, sunlight, and the sky above. Like the little bent figure in the scroll, I played my part in the larger scene, one mote of awareness trekking through the landscape of the universe. You have to go back to the woods or you lose your place. Your ties to the land. To your origins. You forget who you are. You come to believe you are a free agent, an independent being with no ties to anything beyond yourself. You lose your sense of belonging. Your judgment becomes uprooted. With nothing under your feet, what holds you up? You wander and are lost.

I have been that route. Centered on family and work, for years I gave no thought to what holds up the globe of human affairs. Woods, soil, water, sunlight, air—these were nothing to me. I wanted to get ahead, to *be* somebody. Studying science, the humanities, education, I focused on human society and its accomplishments—as if they bloomed by spontaneous generation from human genius itself. I thought nature was a nice place to visit but I didn't want to live there. It was a resort, a kind of sideshow of natural wonders and curiosities. It never occurred to me I was made of Earth, thought its thoughts, saw with its eyes, spoke with its voice, or was in any way responsible to it for the benefits I received, which I took for granted as my deserts for being alive. I saw as a child. Wholly self-centered, I was a child. Reality for me was symbolic, found in art, movies, television, music, and books. I rowed on a rowing machine and ran at the side of city streets. For thirty years, thinking I dwelled in Paradise, I wandered and was lost. One day I woke up realizing I was alone. Looking down, I saw nothing beneath me holding me up. My life was an unfounded dream. That day I might have become a taxi driver or a monk, but instead, for the first time, I heard a voice calling me to witness the miracle of life on planet Earth. The trick to miracles is in recognizing them for what they are, otherwise we let them pass unacknowledged. Another day, oh hum. No, not oh hum, but by golly! How many miracles can we spot before our time runs out?

Fox track on snow crust.

Now paying attention, I explored Long Pond Fire Road for the first time, finding water, air, sunlight, trees, and wildlife in good order. Another day, another walk among miracles. The birth of Hodgdon Brook, for instance. The fire road rounds the south end of Duck Pond and begins a gradual descent into the watershed of Hodgdon Pond. Walking along, I watched water in the ditch beside the road flowing toward Duck Pond until, a few feet farther on, it began flowing the other way in a channel lined with sphagnum moss. Here were the headwaters of Hodgdon Brook. In its birthplace, the brook flows through woods of cedar, maple, and pine into an extensive cedar swamp south of the road, drained by a three- to four-foot-wide channel at its lower end. Crossing the brook in a small valley, the fire road rises toward Pine Hill, which it rounds, coming out between Hodgdon and Seal Cove ponds. Looking down from the bridge over the seven-foot stream connecting the two ponds, I saw swift water continuing its journey from Acadia's woods with one more pond to cross before emptying into salt water in Seal Cove, then joining the farther flood in the Gulf of Maine.

Long, Duck, and Hodgdon ponds were sealed by exact-fitting lids of snow and ice which covered the living waters beneath. I had to imagine the algae, plants, fish, frogs, and turtles that peopled those waters. Snowmobile tracks led anglers onto the ice covering the two larger ponds. Looking onto Northern and Southern necks, the view over Long Pond gives a restricted sense of the island's largest pond. From that vantage point, even Sargent Mountain seems diminished, barely rising above the trees of Southern Neck. Gray poles of dead trees stick out of the shallows at either end of Duck Pond, many having been cut for reasons I could only guess. Perhaps they had warmed parties fishing through the ice in earlier years. Passing close to Seal Cove Pond, the fire road allows only a hint of the pond's existence through a dense stand of Northern white cedar on the slope of Pine Hill. A few icy glints of sunlight through the trees were all I saw.

Pine Hill is a thickly wooded, conical mound rising just east of the juncture between Hodgdon and Seal Cove ponds. On old maps it is shown as a picnic area, but now it goes unmarked, silent monument to the effort to preserve the western side of Mount Desert Island as "the quiet side." Its former status is told by the extensive roadwork leading to the turnaround on top of the hill, including a retaining wall of cut granite, a work on far too grand a scale for a lowly fire road. Making a brief side excursion to see the sights from an elevation of 200 feet, I saw neither pines nor a view of the ponds from my tour of Pine Hill. All was quiet. Three crows flew over, but they held their tongues.

The Western Trail branches off the fire road near the turnoff for the hill, providing access to Western Mountain from the west. It connects with the Long Pond Trail a mile from the trailhead, then rises to Great Notch. The fire road provides a link to no other trails that I know of.

On the side of Pine Hill, a fenced enclosure caught my eye because it seemed so out of place. With open wire mesh hung on sturdy cedar posts, I thought at first it was a remnant from farming days. But then I recognized it as one of the plots the park maintains to study the effects of wildlife on trees and plants. This fence lets hares and squirrels through, but keeps out deer. I have come across other fenced plots near North Bubble, Murphy Lane, and Aunt Betty Pond. On Pine Hill, a falling spruce had tried to leap into the enclosure, but only succeeded in snaring itself in the fence. Coming around the hill, I found a fishing rod apparently fallen from a snowmobile, and farther on, a ten-foot length of rope. I spared the rod but took the rope, adding it to the vipers' nest in my trunk when I got back to my car at 2:30.

❄

24—AROUND-MOUNTAIN CARRIAGE ROAD

Around Bald Peak; and Sargent, Penobscot, Parkman, and Cedar Swamp mountains
Start from Brown Mountain Gate parking area counterclockwise on southern section of Around-Mountain Carriage Road to Jordan Pond
Back by northern section of Around-Mountain Carriage Road
12.5 miles on snowshoes, January 20, 1996

I had long planned to hike the Around-Mountain Carriage Road loop sometime this winter. Now—after a three-day thaw with temperatures brushing fifty degrees, an overnight

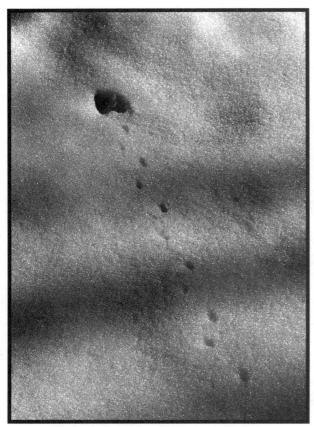

Vole track and tunnel entrance.

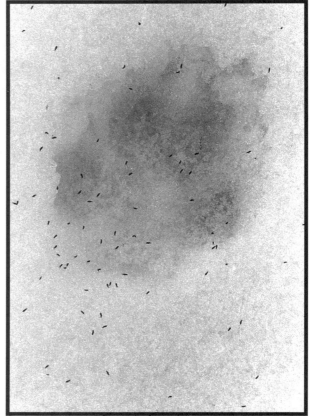

Springtails (snow fleas) in fox print.

rain, and temperatures again below freezing—this was my chance. Slopes and brooks would be rushing with water. An icy crust would discourage cross-country skiers, but my trusty ice creepers would give me the footing I needed. Setting out at 8:15 a.m., I hiked nearly a mile before turning back. The crust was badly pitted with old tracks, making footing uncertain, and kept giving way beneath my weight. I knew I would never make it around that way.

Returning to the gatehouse, I traded creepers for snowshoes, and started again. If they did make a terrible crunching on the crust, the snowshoes kept me from breaking through, and leveled the playing field so I did not lurch side-to-side. My ankles were much happier, but snowshoes were not the ultimate solution. I met long stretches of slick ice, and longer stretches of bare ground, causing me to fall back on Vibram soles to get through the final miles. I completed the eleven-mile loop before dark, with another mile-and-a-half thrown in by my false start and getting back and forth between the gatehouse and Signpost 19 where I started and ended the loop.

As I had hoped, I saw plenty of water. The slopes were alive with it. Every cliff face was dripping, icicles forming before my eyes. Where in summer I might have seen five or six streams barely trickling, I passed seventy-five channels gushing with runoff, and four notable waterfalls. Since childhood, I have been excited by water in every form. Leaky hoses, puddles, swamps, brooks, rivers, ponds, backwaters, coves, bays—I have loved them all. On this hike the mountains held out a promise I couldn't refuse.

Springtime is Acadia's way of welcoming water and sunlight back to the land. The sun was bright all during this hike, and water was everywhere. Though the temperature was twenty-seven degrees and I was on snowshoes, I knew in my heart spring had come. Well, early spring. An adumbration, at least. Sap was flowing in my veins. My thoughts were leafing out. Spring in January is no oxymoron: it is the season of dreams and flaring hopes. Life is the pursuit of better times ahead. Our challenge is to follow the promise, transcending dread all the while. On this hike, Acadia was a land flowing with hope.

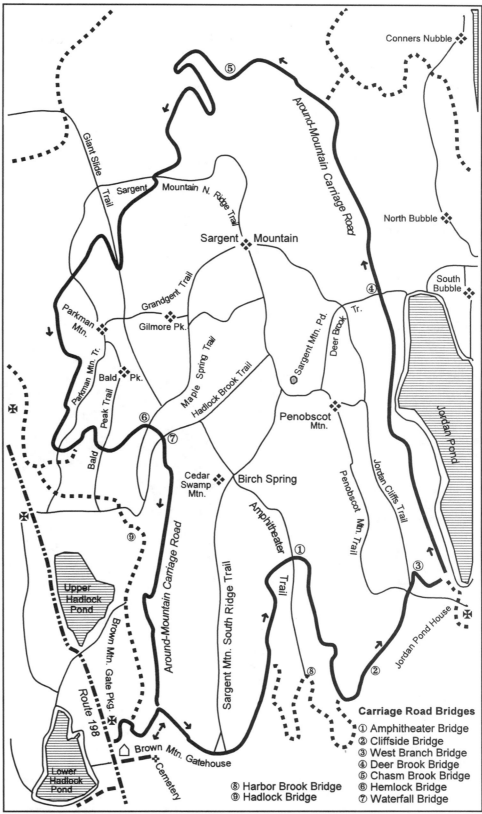

24—Around-Mountain Carriage Road loop.

Carriage Road Bridges
① Amphitheater Bridge
② Cliffside Bridge
③ West Branch Bridge
④ Deer Brook Bridge
⑤ Chasm Brook Bridge
⑥ Hemlock Bridge
⑦ Waterfall Bridge
⑧ Harbor Brook Bridge
⑨ Hadlock Bridge

Not that I don't like winter. My recent hike to the summit of Sargent Mountain was one of the great hikes of my life. I like snowshoeing and cross-country skiing, and seeing tracks of winter wildlife. But winter's charm, like the charm of youth, depends on its being fleet. Who in his right mind likes higher heating bills, icy roads, and shoveling snow? What if we entered a new ice age and this were our prospect for centuries and millennia to come? Perhaps I would take to my cave and draw squirrels and chickadees on the walls, but that wouldn't mean I didn't dream of spring. Even knowing mud season would be delayed for a while, I would yearn for it with all my heart.

My expectations when I started out were that I would see no skiers, no wildlife tracks (the rain having washed them away), and a great deal of water, which is what I was looking for. I did find near the end of my hike that volunteers who groom the park's ski trails had made a noble effort to soften and smooth the surface, with little effect, and that one lone skier had followed the faint track of their snowmobile, slipping and sliding on the unforgiving crust.

As for signs of wildlife, I saw more than I had expected. No tracks of squirrel, hare, shrew, or mouse had survived the thaw and rain, but tracks made by larger animals in wet snow were set in ice. Beyond huge dog prints and scats near carriage road entrances (some people treat Acadia as a federally funded exercise yard for their pets), I saw seventeen tracks of deer, five of fox, and one of coyote. I also found three scats apiece for

Looking up the Tumbledown toward Jordan Ridge.

fox and coyote, which is my interpretation of three scats half-an-inch in diameter, and another three three-quarters-of-an-inch. On bare sections of carriage road, I passed five or six horse scats left from last fall. In the crotch of a birch tree, one robin's nest stood fast against winter winds. A beaver lodge rose above the ice in the valley between Sargent Mountain and North Bubble. In places, my path was strewn with birch seeds, thrown no doubt by the wind, with help from hungry birds. Spruce tips lay in green circles under many tall trees, foraged I thought by red squirrels, though I have never caught one in the act. Perhaps the tips are a byproduct of harvesting spruce cones for their seeds, not an end product yielding tasty buds. I take those circles as an opportunity for future learning.

For actual sightings of fellow creatures, I glimpsed two noisy chickadees, two silent ravens, a male downy and female hairy woodpecker, a pair of black Labrador retrievers with human attendants ("Hi," "Hi," "Hi," we said in rapid succession, and they were gone), two men fishing through the ice on Jordan Pond, and a lone hiker in quest of three companions. Either this last creature was lost or his companions were, I couldn't tell which. Meeting him as I came down from Waterfall Bridge on the last leg of my loop, I told him I didn't think the three other hikers he asked about had passed that way, but he went on none-theless. He carried a backpack stuffed with gear, so I didn't worry about him, even though it would soon be dark. I had trouble assessing what degree of help he might need. He seemed to know where he was going, and given the lightness of his step compared to the heaviness of mine after covering twelve miles, I made only a weak attempt to involve myself in his affairs.

Hiking alone as I do for this series, rarely speaking for hours on end, I realize how much of that hiking takes place in my head. I say I am hiking in Acadia, but the Acadia I hike in lies wholly within the universe of personal, preverbal experience. Writing up these hikes, I face the challenge of describing that inner Acadia in words as foreign to the original trail experience as they are to the outer, objective Acadia, whatever that might be. The stock characters of my experience are not trees, rocks, water, and sky, but phantoms looming in my awareness to which I give such names. Confronting other beings along the trail, whether they are black Labs that silently overtake me while I am ogling the falls on Deer Brook, or a hiker I see coming toward me, I can only assume that their inner worlds, like mine, are a blend of unlabeled images, drives, emotions, ideas, beliefs, expectations, intuitions, memories, and efforts to engage the hidden, objective world, all cut and tailored by a sense of the ongoing situation in which we imagine ourselves to be taking part at the moment. What am I to another hiker; what is another hiker to me? We meet and worlds converge—or more likely pass by.

Tramping along lost in observation, I rarely doubt the connection between the outer world of events and the interior world in my head. Until some conflict suggests those worlds are out of joint, I take them as one in the same.

But when that seamless articulation is upset—by a sudden sound, bright sunlight reflecting off white snow directly into my eyes, or some other event for which I am unprepared—I struggle to set my awareness and objective surroundings in proper alignment again. Writing about a hike has the same jolting effect. Finding words to represent the complex flow of personal experience is a stressful exercise at best. Those phrases do not emerge from the experience itself but are inevitably laid on top of it like white frosting on a chocolate cake. Who knows what darkness lurks beneath silky, glistening words?

Hiking on a carriage road is very different from hiking on a woodland trail, even when few other people are out. The grade is never steep, footing is more-or-less uniform, and the woods keep a discreet and respectful distance on either side. Lichen-covered though they may be, many roadside cliffs are man-made, drilled and blasted from Acadian granite. Engineering works such as bridges, drainage ditches, coping stones, and retaining walls are conspicuous. The way is more cultural than natural, opening the woods to horsedrawn carriages and bicycles in summer, skis and snow-mobiles in winter. Built by John D. Rockefeller, Jr. early in this century, now maintained by the park, the carriage roads of Aca-

Waterfall Bridge and icy Hadlock Falls.

dia are one of the wonders of the civilized world. They are proof of one man's vision, ability, wealth, and generosity. Monumental works in themselves, they enable thousands of park visitors every year to enjoy scenic experiences which, without the roads, many would pass by.

Hiking the Around-Mountain loop gave me a chance to appreciate how carefully Mr. Rockefeller laid out the route. Flowing water played a large part in deciding exactly where and how the road was built. The seventy-five streaming channels I crossed would have overwhelmed the road years ago if ditches and culverts had not been built into the system. Runoff was a threat, but it was also a powerful attraction. I think Mr. Rockefeller must have been one of the arch-watergawkers of all time. It is no accident he built his roads where he did. The Around-Mountain loop crosses Chasm Brook precisely at the falls, just as it does Deer, Hadlock, and Little Harbor brooks. Remarkable as they are

in themselves, the bridges on this loop are sited to allow other water-gazers to share the Rockefeller vision. Separate trails reach those impressive falls by different routes, but the Around-Mountain loop ties them all together for the benefit of all like myself who are drawn to the slopes in full flood.

When brooks are running high, Waterfall Bridge looks onto one of the most stirring sights in the park, as Chasm Brook Bridge does another. The two brooks were plunging full-bore, providing gawking opportunities fully worth the effort it took to reach them. Where the waterfall on Hadlock Brook had been locked in blue ice the last time I came by, now it was tumbling forty feet in a splendid cascade, splashing the broken face of the cliff, freezing into ivory knobs. Chasm Brook Falls was no less dramatic, but in my mind even more beautiful, first falling by three separate streams into a common pool, then twisting left, right, then left again, to plunge into the pool at the base of the cliff, from which it flows under the bridge. Deer Brook put on a good show as well, falling in three chutes of white water, and even Little Harbor Brook made a boisterous splash at Amphitheater Bridge, where a tributary joined the fray.

Though footing was tricky almost the whole way because of the pitted, icy surface, I had to keep myself from taking the Around-Mountain Carriage Road for granted, as I take highways and city streets for granted—until caught up short by a pothole or detour sign. The hiking was almost too uneventful. I reminded myself to look over the edge several times, to appreciate the vast substructure making it possible for the road to cling to the slopes. Like the cherry on top of an ice-cream sundae, the roadway seems to bear little relation to the underpinnings that hold it up—which make up the major part of the loop. Those underpinnings are most evident where the road cuts across the Tumbledown above Jordan Pond, that cascade of boulders fallen from Jordan Ridge. In the Tumbledown the talus was rearranged to make way for the road; in the rest of the loop the rocky roadbed had to be artfully created—mile, after mile, after mile. To reach the level of Hadlock Falls from Signpost 19 near Brown Mountain Gate, for instance, the entire slope for a mile and a half had to be built up at a constant grade, requiring a mountain of rock to be laid in place. I was impressed every time I looked down—all that work, and no cars or trucks! An anachronism now, an anachronism when they were built, Acadia's carriage roads are an aesthetic, not a commercial, enterprise. A labor of love I can relate to, they may not add much to the infrastructure of western civilization, but these roads enable a great many people to make forays into Acadia National Park, where we stand a chance of deepening our appreciation of the natural world, the significance of which, like the underpinnings of the carriage roads, is easy to overlook as we hasten along our paths through daily life.

The Around-Mountain Carriage Road crosses seven bridges, each different, all built of the same granite. In the order I came to them, with the dates they were finished, and the streams they arch, they are:

Amphitheater Bridge (1931)	• Little Harbor Brook
Cliffside Bridge (1932)	• talus slope fallen from the south end of Penobscot Mountain
West Branch Bridge (1931)	• tributary of Jordan Stream
Deer Brook Bridge (1932)	• Deer Brook
Chasm Brook Bridge (1926)	• Chasm Brook
Hemlock Bridge (1924)	• Hadlock Brook, north branch
Waterfall Bridge (1925)	• Hadlock Brook, south branch

Crossing Amphitheater Bridge, I stepped from the flank of Cedar Swamp Mountain onto that of Penobscot. Built on a curve, the bridge complements the heaviness of its stone by supporting its upper course in a way that leaves open spaces beneath them, achieving an almost delicate effect. Cliffside Bridge spans a flowing talus slope on the south end of Penobscot Mountain. It is the most forbidding of the lot, smacking of battlements which, given the hard flood it bridges and the stern cliff to its rear, may not be that inappropriate. West Branch Bridge, though over the smallest stream, is the most graceful, built not only on a grade but on a curve as well. Just up from Jordan Pond House, it sits in a gully near trailheads for the Jordan Cliffs and Penobscot Mountain trails. Deer Brook Bridge may span from Penobscot to Sargent mountains, but only a small stream separates the two peaks at that point. To appreciate this bridge, you have to take the Deer Brook Trail toward Jordan Pond until it crosses the brook lower down. From there you can see the date plaque and twin arches, evidence that Mr. Rockefeller anticipated the McDonald's chain by many years.

Chasm Brook Bridge lies on the north slope of Sargent Mountain where the carriage road starts switchbacking to gain altitude. It is easily missed by cyclists coasting downhill. The falls, set deep in the chasm itself, are easy to miss because they are visible for only twenty feet along the bridge. The two most spectacular bridges on this loop sit in tandem on two branches of Hadlock Brook, separated by a narrow ridge. Hemlock Bridge spans the deep valley of the northern branch, giving a view up the valley of the stream itself, which, on the day of my hike, was rushing headlong down its narrow channel. Whether the stream is rushing or not, this is one of my favorite Acadian views, even though it gives only a hint of the tight canyon just up from the bridge, which can be reached in short order on the Maple Spring Trail. Next door, Waterfall Bridge overlooks Hadlock Falls as I have described. This bridge is worth a visit for its own sake. The builders provided four projecting lookouts giving views of the falls, brook, and bridge itself. The brook runs under the bridge at an angle, and the arch follows suit. After a rain, I like to catch a glimpse of the falls through the arch on the downslope side of the bridge.

The bridges are wonderful works in themselves, but the remarkable thing about them is the unobtrusive way they fit into their natural settings. They look like they were laid down by the last glacier, and seem likely to endure through all eternity—that is, until the coming glacier sweeps them into the Gulf of Maine. In the next interglacial period, fishermen on Georges Bank will drag granite blocks bearing dates from the 1920s and '30s up from the depths, and archaeologists will talk about lost temples built by an unknown Stone Age people on the coast of ancient Maine.

What can I say about the hike itself? It was long. It was hard because of icy footing. Given the length of the loop, I didn't see that many signs of wildlife. But the streams and waterfalls I did see made up for all that. It took no imagination at all to see how hilly terrain influences lowlands below, channeling runoff into wetlands, aquifers, brooks, ponds, and estuaries. Start to finish, the hike was accompanied by the joyous gurgles of life to come. Icicles formed where water dripped and drizzled down the faces of cliffs. Not the great sabers and dragon's teeth of a few weeks ago, these were nubile stilettos and dragon's milk teeth. The most massive ice formations lined the slow descent from Waterfall Bridge to Signpost 19 where, like a row of ceremonial elephants with gleaming domes and pendant trunks, the ice formed a sculptural frieze chiseled in pale jade.

As any circuit must, the Around-Mountain loop meets sunlight streaming from every angle. Their sixteen-foot width cutting a broad swath through the canopy, carriage roads in winter seem to collect light from a low sun, channeling it, heightening its intensity. The sun was a strong presence on this hike, stronger than on any hike I can remember. I started out facing the rising sun, which shone powerfully both from the sky and the white road ahead. In late morning, heading along the valley of Little Harbor

Brook between Amphitheater Bridge and Signpost 21, I faced the same double glory. Rounding the northwest ridge of Sargent at two o'clock, the afternoon sun stopped me in my tracks. Averting my eyes each time, I looked for relief in dark woods to the side, but was stymied by impenetrable shade. In those stretches I plodded along, studying the glazed terrain at my feet, withdrawn into a half-lit world of my own making. Heading away from the sun, I followed in the footsteps of my shadow, peering at the wonders on all sides. On the long north-by-west stretch in the valley of Jordan Pond between Signposts 14 and 10, I often walked in the shadow of wooded slopes on Penobscot and Sargent mountains. Coming down from the high-point along Parkman Mountain, the sun set over Norumbega across the gorge at 3:20 p.m., only to rise again ten minutes later as I rounded Bald Peak.

The low point on the loop is at the south end of Penobscot Mountain, 280 feet. The high point of 780 feet is above the valley of Sargent Brook north of Parkman Mountain, for a difference in elevation of 500 feet, comparable to a Gorham Mountain hike. To keep a strong north-west wind at my back, I approached the high point counterclockwise, which is steeper than going the other way. By the time I got there at 2:15, the wind had died.

Hadlock Falls in warmer days.

Though it passes through mixed woods most of the way, the loop is not closed-in in any sense and offers vistas in every direction. From one point or another, I saw almost every mountain in the park (except those on the eastern shore), as well as the Camden, Dedham, and Gouldsboro hills, Blue Hill, and Lead Mountain. A recently cleared vista on the south slope of Cedar Swamp Mountain looks over Day Mountain, Barr and Redfield hills, and Baker and Little Cranberry islands. That's where I saw two ravens go sailing by against the burnished Gulf of Maine. Through trees, Penobscot was a dappled leviathan. From several natural vistas south of Amphitheater Bridge, the eastern cliffs of Cedar Swamp Mountain looked like a schooner with all sails set before the wind, Eliot Mountain following to the south, a dinghy towed behind. Cliffside Bridge had been recently cleared to reopen a traditional vista over the valley of Jordan Stream onto Pemetic, the Triad, Day, Barr,

and Redfield, all of which rolled like standing waves sweeping out to sea. The Tumbledown looks up to the Jordan Cliffs, and out over Jordan Pond backed by mighty Pemetic, with the Bubbles in profile wending to the north. I think of pond ice as being white for some reason, but the ice on Jordan Pond was dark green and rink smooth, with wide, white bands striping the upper end in concentric swirls. Clearly visible through leafless branches of roadside trees, the slim valley north of the pond between Sargent Mountain and the Bubbles rose up to the opposite ridge in layers—from wetland with beaver lodge, to grass, to a thin stand of spruce, then birch, cedar, granite cliff, culminating in a layer of ridgetop spruce. Angling up Sargent's north slope, the carriage road opens onto views of Eagle Lake and Cadillac, with Schoodic, Black, and Tunk mountains to the north across Frenchman Bay. Gilmore Bog and Aunt Betty Pond lie in the foreground, backed by McFarland and Youngs (hills to some, mountains to others), with Lead Mountain resting lightly in the saddle between. Twisting back on itself, the road heads straight into the slope, providing a full-frontal view of Sargent's northern expanse, impressive as Ayers Rock (if not as red).

Rounding Sargent's north-western ridge as it approaches the high point of the loop, the road got slick, then bare, forcing me to make a decision: travel on snow caught in roadside ditches, or take my snowshoes off. Expecting more snow ahead, I took to the ditch. Blue Hill commanded the view to the west, with the Camden Hills rising on the horizon across Penobscot Bay. Nearer by, Somesville, as always, looked its postcard best. Yes, there was more snow on the road in the valley of Sargent Brook, but it turned icy on Parkman Mountain, and disappeared for as far as I could see ahead. I carried my snowshoes from there. The only stream the around-mountain loop doesn't play up to is Sargent Brook, which it crosses without a glance. You have to know it is there, a flow four feet wide visible on either side of a deep-buried culvert, rising in the gentle valley upslope, quickening its descent in the chute below. On Parkman, the carriage road looks over Hall Quarry and Somes Sound, but with the sun in my eyes, it was hard to tease out Acadia, St. Sauveur, Beech, and Western mountains from the dark mass looming over Norumbega's north ridge. Norumbega blocked the western horizon much of the way to Signpost 19, stretching into what seemed like the longest ridge in the park. Cedar Swamp soon hove into view, another long ridge. Bald Peak reared up behind me briefly as I passed between the last two bridges. For a mile along Cedar Swamp Mountain I followed in the tracks of a fox. Across the valley, the sun stroked Norumbega's back for a while, then set for the last time at four o'clock.

As for vegetation, aside from the 647,996 trees I personally responded to, I noticed sunlight passing through curled leaves of rock-cap fern on a boulder in the Tumbledown, making them shine with an inner light. I came to several clumps of wood fern released from the snow, bowed but unbeaten. Near Cliffside Bridge, two stalks of mullein rose up seven feet tall between the coping stones. Recognizing true survivors, I gave them an encouraging nod. Most drainage ditches were running with water, many lined with banks of sphagnum moss. On the whole, the Around-Mountain loop runs through a landscape of generic carriage road vegetation which seems to stay the same, though it changes at almost every turn. The specific mix of species may change, but the integrity of the scene is an Acadian constant.

Ice elephants.

I passed eleven trailheads and eight forks where the loop connects with other sections of the carriage road system. I had the impression I was touring the heart of the park. On a map of Mount Desert Island, there look to be about the same number of mountains east and west of Sargent, the hub of my hike. I felt as the character played by Jane Russell in the film *The Incredible Voyage* must have felt as she rode her miniaturized submarine through the arteries of the man whose life she was trying to save. Not that I was out to save Acadia, but I was that small, and that close to the core. I carried an experiential map of the park built up over many years, on which I located each landmark, fitting it into a portable model of the landscape. When I first started hiking, I would look at a mountain, island, or pond and ask, "Which one is that?" We learn the local landscape by walking through it, mapping it on the inside of our skulls

as we go. Standing back, we see that all the little maps fit together into one seamless chart. I still carry maps, but rarely refer to them. Some internal loran updates my position on the chart inside my head. That is not a boast. It takes a lifetime to learn the lay of local terrain. Given our modern mobility, most of us carry scraps of old maps of many different places, most of them badly out of date, and not at all helpful in orienting us to the terrain where we are now. I'll settle for centering my life on Sargent Mountain. That way, like Jane Russell in the movie, no matter where I go, I can find my way home.

Though I hiked alone, I didn't feel alone on this hike. As always, I was accompanied by a kind of presence. But this presence was different. More cultivated than wild. A higher kind of Presence, like the one Quakers experience in their silent meetings for worship. Not a god exactly, but a compelling sense of justice, integrity, and truth. I had a strong feeling that I was being guided on the Around-Mountain loop by a powerful force. Every bridge and vista seemed to say, "Look here for something wonderful." The Tumbledown spoke loud and clear: "If I didn't want you here, I wouldn't have gone to all that effort!" The high point said, "See, it was worth every step." This was no random outing. Somebody led me all the way.

Like **PHOTO OPPORTUNITY** signs, somebody knew better than I what there was to be seen. If I had wanted to go my own way, I would have owed an explanation to that higher somebody. Who was it? None other than John D. Rockefeller, Jr. Mr. Rockefeller had strong tastes and beliefs, which he felt driven to share. His was the genius behind the park's carriage roads and bridges. I am his direct beneficiary. But having an unprogrammed bent, and knowing how much richer the park is beyond the carriage road system, I prefer to make my own discoveries, believing that, just as I own my own spirit, my personal experience belongs to me. In *Mr. Rockefeller's Roads*, Ann Rockefeller Roberts writes that just the naming of the carriage roads makes "the wilderness familiar and safe." Exactly! You can't reach wilderness on a Roman road.

Near Amphitheater Bridge, a torrent had rushed down Penobscot Mountain and, coming to the road, was going too fast to turn aside into a mere ditch. It spilled across the road, dumping a heap of debris across the way, a mound of dirty ice containing chips and blocks of stone. Some blocks must have weighed twenty-five pounds. Never underestimate the power of water in flood. Particularly when channelized. Channelization focuses the energy of a rushing stream into a laser beam of coherent water. Look out below! The main theme to emerge from this hike, inspired by so much water draining off the slopes, was the power of channelization. Just as water from umpteen sources is collected and sent rushing down the mountain as one stream, park visitors from across the nation and the world are funneled by roads to Ocean Drive, Jordan Pond House, and the top of Cadillac Mountain, which together form the world image of Acadia. Acadia's system of carriage roads also demonstrates the power of channelization. It takes people where you want them to go so they see what you want them to see. And don't see what you don't want them to trample to death. Acadia's carriage road system is an example of crowd control, which the Park Service is very good at because its primary job is to protect the landscape the multitude has come to enjoy.

Another example of channel power is the upgrading of seeplets into seeps, brooklets into brooks, streamlets into streams, joining them time and again into a complex waterworld supporting plant and animal life in forests, fields, wetlands, ponds and every other wet place, including ocean depths This channeled connectedness joins little powers into a mass movement. Life itself, the most powerful force on the planet, is the gift of sloping terrain, locally the gift of Acadia's wooded and rocky slopes. Hiking the Around-Mountain Carriage Road loop after a rain is a good way to see that power take shape. Not that I'm pushing anybody to do what I did. If it coincides with your plans, fine. If not, fine. You won't catch me herding people around. But if you do have several hours to spend, and feel you should be more tired than you already are, who am I to stop you from channeling your energy into a hike along a carriage road after recent rain or recovering from a three-day thaw?

On this loop I rediscovered the age-old thought that, looking on the upper world of sunlight and wind as our heavenly father, the lower world of dampness and dark soil becomes the mother of all mothers. Plants unite those two worlds by channeling water and nutrients from the soil into the presence of sunlight and air, where that union is consummated by photosynthesis, giving birth to the food that feeds the world. All life stems from that marriage. Religion, which means to connect us to first things, can't do better than that. To channelize our personal powers, we have only to go with the flow of water and air in streams and wind, roots and leaves. Everything else flows from that.

✳

25—LITTLE HARBOR BROOK LOOP

From Route 3 near Little Harbor along
    Little Harbor Brook
To the Asticou Trail, and back
    North on Little Harbor Brook Trail
    South on private carriage roads to
        (Little) Long Pond and back along Route 3
            5.5 miles, February 2, 1996

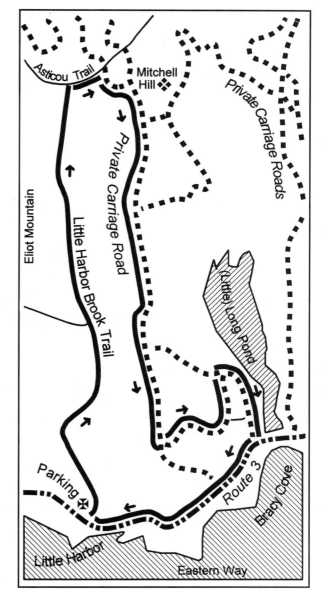

25—Little Harbor Brook loop.

Having crossed many streams on my last hike, this time I wanted to get to know one stream by following it for some length. A dusting of snow in the morning had covered ice and bare ground alike, making rocky, sloping trails hazardous to my health. What I wanted was an easy valley trail along a major stream. I had hiked up Hunters Brook not long ago; this time I chose the Little Harbor Brook Trail from its start at Route 3 (opposite Bear Island) to where it meets the Asticou Trail two miles upstream. The Asticou Trail connects with the carriage road system, which would take me to the south end of (Little) Long Pond. A short jaunt along Route 3 would bring me back to my car, closing a loop of about five-and-a-half miles. That sounded like a good plan, given the uncertainty of trail conditions. In the wake of recent rainstorms, the temperature had stayed below freezing for several days. There would be ice underfoot, but on a relatively level trail, I could handle that. Creepers? Hardly necessary. This was a hike for unassisted winter boots.

Or so I thought. Ice creepers would have been a big help, even on level ground. Beneath a cosmetic layer of new snow, slick ice was everywhere. The gentlest slope was a challenge; steeper slopes were Olympic bobsled runs. I made the whole hike without falling, but only because I adopted the Harbor Brook one-step, a halting, flat-footed shuffle with an uneven gait far short of my normal stride. Because it was so unnatural, that manner of walking took a great deal of attention, distracting me from my surroundings. I wanted to look at the brook, but spent most of my time looking at my feet. Since that view was not

Ice on Little Harbor Brook.

what I had come to see, I divided my attention between the trail and the winter landscape it passed through by making frequent stops to look around. Stop and go, stop and go—that is the story of my hike up Little Harbor Brook. I stopped less often on the carriage road coming back, but my mode of travel was the same, the road being every bit as slick as the trail. The whole hike was a cautionary tale.

One difference between this hike and others I have made is that most of it was on land outside the park. The Asticou Trail crosses Little Harbor Brook just inside the southern edge of the park boundary. It took me two hours and forty-five minutes to reach that crossing, almost all of that time on private land. And shortly after I headed back along the carriage road, I came to twin signs notifying me that the way ahead was on private property. Equestrians and pedestrians were allowed during daylight hours, but motor vehicles and bicycles were taboo. Fine with me.

I didn't need the signs to tell me I was leaving the park. The private carriage road system is groomed meticulously, with no dead or fallen wood left in sight. In places trees have been pruned and thinned far back from the road, creating a more open landscape of bare poles holding up an awning of green branches. Maine has a long tradition of managing its woodlands with a heavy hand. Unlike most, these private woods were groomed not for commercial timber or fiber production but for beauty according to a canon by which dead branches and fallen trees are deemed unsightly. I don't hold to that view, some of my best friends being the worn and scarred elders I meet in the woods. But in a society that prefers its elders out of sight, it does not surprise me when people treat their woods the same way. We garden the landscape for an ornamental effect, just as we put tidy lawns around our homes and trim our hedges.

What did surprise me was how differently these private woods along the carriage road were managed from those along the brook, which are also in private hands. As soon as I mastered the art of walking on icy ground and got down to the brook (which took half an hour when, in summer, it would have taken less than five minutes), I knew I had entered a magical place. Though trees fallen across brook and trail had been cut, their remains, instead of being cleared, were left to return to the soil from which they had risen. The gardening here was done largely by natural forces, creating a kind of unkempt beauty that cannot be matched, much less improved. As soon as I was away from Route 3, I was in a world apart from the everyday world most of us consider real. These woods were left to conduct their own affairs. I am always eager to walk among tall trees, and, with a brook gliding toward the sea, I felt I was passing among an ancient race representing the noble, original inhabitants of the continent. Here business was conducted with an equanimity unknown in the world I left behind. Washington was haggling over the federal budget. Fledgling representatives were flexing their muscles like the young Charles Atlas, as if there were more virtue in that than governing the nation. Along Little Harbor Brook I found what I was looking for in a world as foreign to

Western sensibilities as the far side of the moon. Here was order, beauty, and peace. Yet this was no vacationland, no idle land of escape. Here even the Super Bowl was a non-event. What mattered was that every plant and animal did its utmost, always, and won its share of the prize. The result, the woods taken as a whole, was as democratic a system as I had ever seen. What struck me most was its dignity, with overtones of poise and serenity. I felt as if I belonged there and were in the company of lifelong friends. Which I did, and I was, given my species' long (if forgotten) stay in similar woods.

The Little Harbor Brook Trail is blazed differently than trails in the park. Here are no blue diamonds or woodpecker silhouettes. At one time the trail was marked with orange paint, but that color had faded to a rufous glow on trees here and there. Lettered signs get you started at each end, then you are pretty much left to find your way on your own. In December last year I lost the trail and had to retrace my steps. This time, perhaps because I was following my feet, I had better luck. In several places along the brook, slabs of ice had come to rest in the trail during earlier floods, giving me the choice of going into the brook on one side, thick woods on the other, or over the ice, which in one place stood in gleaming plates like rows of giant shark's teeth. I chose to take to the woods, losing my wool hat each time to light-fingered twigs. The trail generally sticks close to the stream bank, so it is easy to get back on course. One sixteen-foot bridge over a tributary had been washed away, but it wasn't hard finding a way across. Near the end, where the brook takes a long curve to the east, the trail abandons it and heads west. A sign points the way, but from there pathfinding gets more difficult. The woods thin out, erasing any sign of a cleared way ahead. I would stand by the last cut branch I saw, or orange blaze, and scan trees in all directions for similar signs. Once I muttered under my breath, "My kingdom for an arrow!" Other hikers must have been in similar straits just there because, turning, I saw a small pointer nailed to a tree. In a wetland on the park boundary, a single cut branch was the clue I needed to head me in the right direction. From there I saw the wooden bridge I had seen from the Asticou Trail in

Little Harbor Brook between two bends.

December, swept downstream like any piece of woody debris, now lodged against a fence of fallen trees. Just south of the derelict Asticou Trail bridge [since rebuilt], I saw the one blue blaze on the Little Harbor Brook Trail, which announced I was in the park. From there, the Asticou Trail was well marked, and the carriage roads featured signposts at every turn, so the way was easy to find.

With two exceptions, the view on this loop was the woods. Trees, trees, and more trees, with the brook running among them for the first third of the way. Looking back at one point, I saw the east face of Eliot Mountain rising abruptly from the brook. I had never thought of Eliot as being that precipitous, but there it was, snow-clad cliffs contradicting my assumptions. The other viewscape on the loop was at the south end of (Little) Long Pond, looking north over the ice toward Penobscot Mountain, the Bubbles, and Pemetic Mountain farther up the valley of Jordan Stream. I didn't have to hike five miles to get that view, since it is right on the road. Walking along Route 3 from Bracy Cove to Little Harbor, I saw Little Cranberry, Sutton, and Bear islands to the south.

The brook itself drew me to this hike. Having passed so many streams on the Around-Mountain Carriage Road two weeks earlier, I wanted to acquaint one stream at greater length. Higher up in the Amphitheater, the dead-end valley between Penobscot and Cedar Swamp mountains, Little Harbor Brook plunges like any other young stream, but where I walked it lower down, it acts its age and takes fewer risks. Falling 140 feet in two miles, that averages out to a drop of one foot every seventy-five linear feet, which aptly describes the brook I saw. It was largely covered with ice and snow, with open water showing in faster runs and plunges. Some ice windows were smooth, others lined with jagged teeth four inches long. Larger stones in the brook supported glistening rims of ice, looking like white and silver flying saucers skimming the surface. A cantilevered ice balcony all along the bank marked where the brook had frozen at a higher stage. Ice slabs had been rafted onto the trail when the brook was two to two-and-a-half feet higher in recent floods. The shark teeth were four feet higher than the brook, where an ice jam must have backed it up. Winding down its easy valley at the base of Eliot Mountain, Little Harbor Brook flicks this way and that, trail sticking to brook like lynx to dodging hare. Great cedars arch the brook, in places paired on opposite banks like raised sabers. Little Harbor Brook is a close cousin of Hunters Brook, both showing a family resemblance in size, gradual descent, and wooded streamside terrain. I turned hikes along both into loops by returning along roads paralleling the streams on ridges to the east.

For wildlife, I saw two groups of ducks in Little Harbor at the very end of my hike. Two boys were shoveling a section of Long Pond, making a rink, while a woman watched from the bank. I heard crows five different times, and the slow, heavy tapping of a pileated woodpecker at the base of Eliot Mountain as I neared the Asticou Trail. I saw dog tracks on the carriage road, along with tracks of people (sizes eight and eleven), red squirrel, fox, and ermine. On Little Harbor Brook Trail I saw tracks of squirrel, fox, and shrew. I stepped over several tunnels beneath the snow, made by shrews perhaps, or voles. All these tracks had been made since the snow stopped midmorning. A thin layer of fine powder, it was perfect tracking snow. Each print looked like an illustration in a tracking guide. In deep snow, you have to use your imagination to picture what animal might have made such a dent. These were autographs. The ground frozen, there were no tracks from before the snow.

The sun was no more than a wan presence behind dull clouds. Dusted with white, the landscape was everywhere softened, as if rendered in colored pencil or pastel. When I grabbed a trunk for support, I, too, was dusted, like a caroler in an inverted paperweight storm. Upper twigs on several bushes glowed dusky red, trim buds set for the sun to release the green jinni within. In two places mountain cranberry leaves poked through the snow, adding a touch of green and virtual red to the trailside scene. The most notable tree I saw was a red spruce growing ten feet to the side of the carriage road above (Little) Long Pond. Now in thick woods, it must have gotten its start when the land around it was clear; its lowest branches were thick and covered with needles. But some accident had happened to its leader early on, causing its hormones to put Plan B into action. Fifteen feet above the ground its trunk split into two skinny poles, and when they had done that, the lower branches got the order to stop spreading outward and put their energy into reaching for the sun. Defying gravity, the eighteen lowest branches saw their duty and obeyed, over the years bending upward in sweeping curves. The tree now stands like a graceful candelabra placed to light late travelers through evening woods. Equally decorative in their way, a great many snags stand candle-like in the woods along Little Harbor Brook. Each has been filigreed by generations of insects, and further sculpted by insect-eating and cavity-nesting birds.

Along the brook, which was from eight to ten feet wide, I hiked to the steady accompaniment of flowing water ringing with an icy resonance. I saw dark water through holes in the ice out of the corner of my eye, and heard its everpresent strumming at the edge of my hearing. What is the attraction such music holds? Simply, I believe, to give us a sense of the occasion or event. That is what we remember when we hear an old song replayed—where we were, who we were with, what we were doing, how we felt. In the highly vocal world we have created for ourselves, I think we are starved for sounds that are not trying to tell us or sell us something. Sounds that simply are. So that we may simply be, responsive, fully alert and alive to that occasion—as our nature prefers, not as the world commands. Why else do audiences sit for hours in dark halls listening to an infinite variety of meaningless but organized sounds? Cut off from woodpeckers and humming brooks, attacked by sirens and roaring trucks, city dwellers crave contact with ambient sounds that rouse their souls without commercials, warnings, or sage advice. Given the way we bunch together to do our business, the arts give us breathing space, room to be stimulated and alive in our own way. Along Little Harbor Brook, the sounds I heard were the sounds of the landscape singing its song. Crows, a woodpecker, the brook, the wind—each rose from the pervading stillness to add its voice to the chorus of that place. That is my kind of music. To hear it you don't have to buy a CD; go for a walk in the woods. The sound of one running brook is worth all the Stradivari instruments in the world. But if you don't have a brook handy, then a few strings and bits of varnished wood may help make up for the lack.

Since I didn't start till after twelve and it would be dark by five, my game plan for this hike was to get as far along the brook as I could by three o'clock, then find a place to cross the brook and bushwhack up the ridge until I came to the carriage road that would take me back to Route 3. As things worked out, I reached the Asticou Trail at five minutes to three, so I simply went on to the carriage road without having to bushwhack. It took me an hour and fifteen minutes to walk from Mitchell Hill to Long Pond, and another fifteen minutes along Route 3 to reach my car in Little Harbor. With ice underfoot, I completed the five-and-a-half-mile loop in four-and-a-half hours. The section of carriage road leading from the ridge directly to Route 3 was blocked by a **ROAD CLOSED** sign, so I detoured by way of the pond, adding perhaps fifteen minutes to the hike. I could have stepped around the sign, but being on private property, I respected the owners' wishes. It was by their grace I was there at all.

❋

26—BEEHIVE & CHAMPLAIN MTN. LOOP

From Park Loop Road fee station
To summits of Beehive and Champlain Mountain,
    and back
    Up by Beehive, Bowl, and Champlain Mountain
        South Ridge trails
    Down by Bear Brook and Champlain Mountain
        East Face trails, and back along the loop road
                    5.0 miles—February 9, 1996

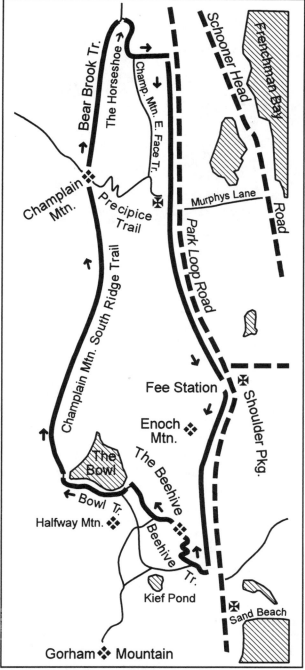

26—Beehive & Champlain Mountain loop.

Though the temperature rose well into the forties by mid-afternoon on the day of my hike, the five-mile loop I made from the park fee station to the summit of Champlain Mountain via the Beehive and the Bowl was no carefree spring jaunt. Winter still ruled the slopes, and was not about to abdicate merely because a little rain had washed away most of the snow. The ground was largely bare, but in many spots the trail was a river of ice. Lying in bed that morning, I had planned on taking a lowland route to avoid the ice I knew I would find higher up. A loop around Jordan Pond perhaps, or from Wonderland to Ship Harbor. But since I had chosen my last three hikes to avoid ice on sloping terrain, I was ready for a ridgeline hike. Steady rain in the night had cleared the woods of snow. The morning forecast was for above-freezing temperatures all day. It would be icy, but I could see the ice and go around it. The trick to winter hiking is to work with current conditions of snowfall, temperature, wind, and ice. I let them have the final say. Seize the moment, they said, go for Champlain!

One way to deal with ice is to wear crampons or creepers. I left mine in the car. The problem with ice gear is that it is no good on bare rock. Rather than keep clamping spikes to my feet—and unclamping them farther on—I opted for Vibram soles the whole way. If I couldn't work my way around an icy patch, I would simply turn back and take an alternate route. The entire east face of Champlain Mountain was oozing white ice, but from the base of the Beehive I saw only three icefalls on the cliffs, and wasn't sure any of them were on the trail. Only one of them was: streaming across a sloping ledge, it commandeered the trail for seven or eight feet, effectively narrowing it, causing me to step closer to the edge of the cliff than I normally would. Holding my breath, I took that step, and another, and another. With a sideways leap across the river of ice, I landed on bare gravel, and had good footing the rest of the way up the face of the Beehive, helped along by iron handrails and rungs.

Meeting ice going up is one thing; coming down is another. On the ascent, having your weight over your lead foot helps you get a sense of the surface, and anchors you in place. On the descent, your lead foot is somewhere out there by itself ahead of your weight, and the first message it sends is likely to arrive as you are shifting your weight onto it—which may be too late to prevent a slip. There is no such thing as a trail for all seasons. Most trails channel seepage and runoff, which freeze where you want ice the least. Between the Beehive and the Bowl, I had to navigate two downward slopes glazed with thick ice. The Bear Brook Trail from the summit of Champlain Mountain to the turn for the Horseshoe and east face trail was slick with ice and damp lichens. The worst stretch of ice I encountered was coming down to the loop road from the Horseshoe and the start of the east face trail. I let the icy trail go its way and found my own way across bare ledges. I never pressed my luck by pretending I was in charge; the icy slopes were in charge, and I didn't forget it.

Which may sound scary, but is actually no riskier than driving from Ellsworth to Bar Harbor along Route 3 at fifty miles an hour, or eating produce grown who-knows-where. Trail ice is a fact of winter hiking, one of life's challenges. It adds a bite to outdoor experience. I meet it the same way every time—with undivided attention. Winter trails whet my navigational skills. Off the trail, I sometimes give myself the luxury of acting first, then examining what I did in hindsight. When I am driven by emotion I do that a lot. Giving in to anger or elation, I act spontaneously, not thinking what I am doing. I learn a lot that way, but after-the-fact. On ice, that may be too late. With ice underfoot, I go slowly enough to be able to keep up with changing conditions so I can plan every step in advance. That's why this five-mile loop took over seven hours to complete. But every step was an adventure, not a chore. I know a woman raised in ice-free Tallahassee who doesn't like that kind of challenge. Raised in upstate New York myself, I wouldn't have lived through childhood if I hadn't come to terms with ice. I fell on my knees, my tail, and my head enough times to give it great respect. And living on a thirty-acre island for two-and-a-half years, going everywhere by trail because there was no other way, I walked on ice three months of the year. Those who live by the trail might well die by the trail. But not if they are careful.

This winter hike had overtones of spring. I could actually feel gravel and clay give underfoot. I smelled earthy smells I had forgotten about. I saw plants I hadn't seen since early December—wintergreen, blueberry, and kinnikinnick. It was a revelation to see all that life reemerge from the snow. Fallen leaves, bent bracken, hair-cap moss, reindeer lichen, and mountain cranberry—it felt like old home week, seeing familiar faces everywhere I looked. I had hiked the same loop last Thanksgiving with three friends, in the first snowfall of the season. Then the ground had been white and views in all directions blotted out. This time, when the clouds briefly lifted, I renewed acquaintance with views I hadn't seen in eleven months.

Light rain was falling from an overcast sky as I started out, with clouds blocking out the top of the Beehive and half the Precipice. As I wound up the cliff into the clouds, I had a series of higher and mistier views of Sand Beach, Great Head, and Gorham Mountain. I never did see Schoodic Peninsula across the bay. Scanning the scene through binoculars, I saw eiders off Thunder Hole, and a loon in winter plumage in Newport Cove. The Bowl was covered by a lid of clouds, which began to lift as I headed

up the south ridge of Champlain. Suddenly I saw a flag of blue overhead. There was Dorr Mountain dappled with snow and ice to the west, with Cadillac over its shoulder, summit lost in clouds. Briefly, I glimpsed Otter Point beyond Gorham Mountain, the Tarn under Huguenot Head. From that angle, the Head looked as much like a beehive as the dome I had just climbed. I ate my trail lunch on the summit overlooking Ironbound Island and the Porcupines in

The Beehive from Otter Point.

Frenchman Bay, but a dark cloud came from the south, cutting off my view. I didn't pay much attention to the view from the Bear Brook Trail on the way down. Not only was I busy studying the slippery lichens at my feet, but I had glimpsed enough of the Jackson Laboratory complex of almost thirty flat-roofed blocks and four parking lots to know there was little that appealed to me in that direction. Sitting on the edge of the Horseshoe, a small wetland surrounded by red cliffs and white birches, I enjoyed one of the best of the park's many pocket vistas. I pledged not to move until I saw some sign of wildlife. After scanning the scene for several minutes, I saw a nest in the crotch of a birch directly in front of me. That was enough of a sign to get me going again. By the time I reached the loop road, conditions were the same as when I started out. But walking under the Precipice, I thought it was the best view I had seen all day. With leaves off roadside birches, I could see every cleft and buttress in the best of Acadia's cliffs. Ice-falls were everywhere, merging with the clouds higher up. I stood in the middle of the road by the Precipice parking area, gawking up at the scene. As I did, a ten-foot icicle let go and skittered three hundred feet down the cliff, breaking into fragments as it went. Granite in a similar fall had put the Precipice Trail out of commission until the damage could be repaired [the trail has since been reopened]. Given the natures of granite and gravity, it is only a matter of time before Acadia's peregrine falcons have the Precipice to themselves.

With so little snow on the ground, I expected wildlife to play a minor role is this hike. Wrong. I met signs of life everywhere I went. There were the usual chickadees, which never stopped singing while I was on the face of the Beehive. And the black-and-gray-feathered remains of a chickadee I found in a disintegrating owl pellet between the Beehive and the Bowl. Past the Bowl I saw a female hairy woodpecker working away at a gray birch, and I heard two other woodpeckers farther on. Twenty-five crows were making a great stir just down from the Bowl. I saw several soar in to join them, and thought they may have been mobbing an owl or a hawk, but they rose in a flurry all at once, then settled down to quiet peace and harmony, ruling out that idea. I heard crows throughout the hike.

Aside from the loon and eiders I saw through binoculars, I saw a lone gull on the Thrumcap, and another flying by High Seas. There was some wet snow left in pitch pine woods on the ridge, preserving tracks of red squirrel, snowshoe hare, fox, and grouse. The grouse tracks looked like a row of asterisks across the trail. I admired the skater who left blade tracks on

Narrow shelf on the Beehive Trail.

the edge of the Bowl, and the hiker who had punched crampon holes in ice along the Bear Brook Trail. Three times I heard coyotes howling across the way on Cadillac's south ridge, each time filling the valley of Otter Creek with deep-throated wails and siren calls. I thought I could make out five different voices, two mature and three young. I saw where hares had nipped off blueberry buds, and deer the bark of sumac and striped maple.

Of all the species I met one way or another on my hike, the day belonged to the beaver. I saw twelve different lodges: one in back of the marsh by Sand Beach, five in the Bowl, three in Beaver Dam Pond, one along Meadow Brook near High Seas, and two along the loop road. The one across from the Precipice parking area didn't look actively used, but down the road a piece a culvert had been dammed right against a beaver fence (installed to keep the culvert from clogging), and fresh-cut trees and branches strewed the area. Since the lodge at this site was built on dry ground, I assumed there must have been a tunnel through the mud connecting the lodge to the miniature pond. Standing quietly, I could hear little piggy noises from under the ice. As I watched, a dark shadow swam through that other world toward the lodge. I have seen beaver lodges in both the Tarn and Kief Pond between the Beehive and Gorham, but saw no trace of them on this hike.

One seamless loop, the hike unfolded in six stages. It ended as it began, on a royal road of asphalt, birches and beeches lining much of the way, their branches hung with drops, with cliffs rising steeply beyond the trees on the west. The road served the double function of prologue and epilogue, both tacked on to round out the whole. In side view as seen from the road, the Beehive looked like a giant sphinx, the trail scaling the badly defaced lips, nose, and brow. The hike properly began with stage two at the trailhead for the Bowl Trail just north of Sand Beach parking area. There the trail does double duty as a stream, serving as an icy warning or, in my case, an invitation. I got across the first several icy stretches by keeping to their margins, to gain the Beehive trailhead where the hike began in earnest. Looking up at the symmetrical dome ahead, I now saw the dark, helmeted figure of Darth Vadar looking down from above. It seemed clear there was a challenge ahead.

The Beehive Trail is one of Acadia's most exciting. A continuous inclined plane, it screws its way up a granite cliff that looks from below to be impassable. Switchbacking in a series of six or seven traverses, it rises steadily and rapidly above the trees, the view getting better at every turn. I tallied twenty-seven rungs and ten handholds that give hikers a needed assist up the steepest pitches. The trail crosses two short bridges, one of wooden planks, the other of fifteen iron rods welded to a length of angle iron, the whole reminding me of a rugged if rusty harp. The middle rods are two feet long, those on either end half of that. Dark green kinnikinnick and pitch pines soften the granite, making a habitat of what otherwise would be a forbidding kind of place. With red stems and green leaves highlighted with straw-colored edges, the kinnikinnick added a festive touch to the cliffs. As a seasonal note, not a single car broke the fishbone pattern of white stripes in the Sand Beach parking area. There is no better way to jump into Acadia than by scaling the Beehive. You will know beyond doubt that you have arrived. If you are subject to vertigo, you can ease your way into the park by strolling along the Ocean Path which starts at Sand Beach.

Stage three took me along the trail from the top of the Beehive to the Bowl, and then around the south shore of that mountain pond to its outlet on the far side. It was along this stretch I first heard the coyotes, and found the owl pellet. I noticed several charred stumps and fallen trunks, memorials to the great fire of almost fifty years ago. In case my gloves weren't wet enough from climbing the dripping cliffs, I dropped one in a puddle as I was wringing the other one out. I went barehanded the rest of the hike. The day was so warm, my fingers never felt cold. Not far from the Beehive there is a scaled-up model in granite of the human brain, which is fairly accurate, given the left temporal lobe isn't quite right. On clear days there is a great view of Champlain, Dorr, and Cadillac from this section of trail, but I saw only clouds, and the lesser sphinx of Enoch Mountain below me through the mist. Fairly level compared to the

Pitch pines and iron rungs on the Beehive Trail.

Beehive Trail, this was surprisingly one of the worst sections for ice. To get down to pond level, the trail descends the north side of a small granite dome just high enough to block the low winter sun. In that section the trail was a cataract of ice. Then, running above the shore of the pond, it crossed a miniature frozen Niagara to reach the bogwalk along the south shore. The planks were buried under mounds of snow swept off the pond, the only deep snow I met all day. The Bowl was frozen white, with a double ring of fox prints around the edge. Birches lay sprawled in every direction on the far shore, calling my attention to a beaver lodge across the pond. Four other lodges clustered in a communal habitation near the outlet in the southwest corner where crows kept diving on tucked wings out of the mist. I saw eight crows, and heard many more in woods below the outlet. Caught in a gray birch, the remains of three yellow balloons fluttered like ragged flags,

signal from a shopping mall in Ohio perhaps, or some other region of outer space. Crossing the outlet brook, I stepped onto the south ridge of Champlain Mountain, opening the next stage of my hike.

Like the south ridges of Sargent–Penobscot, Pemetic, Cadillac, and Dorr mountains, this is one of Acadia's major hiking routes. Heading up-ridge, you face directly into the path of the ice sheet that crept from the Laurentian Plateau not long ago to sculpt these granite hills and valleys. Aligning my steps with the ridge and the course of the glacier, I felt aligned with terrestrial forces that one way or another still control the destiny of plant and animal life on Mount Desert Island. Interacting with the local granite, laying the foundation for modern soils, the glacier determined how water would flow in this terrain, and how life would rise from that flow to this day. "Go with the flow" does not mean take the easiest path, though that is how we generally interpret it. My reading is that it means to line up with the forces that truly shape our lives, the Earth forces that have prepared the way for us and guide every step of our journey. Each of our individual paths is an expression of the power and virtue released into the world when the primal forces of sunlight, water, soil, and wind interact. That is our diet, true source of the energy that carries us on our way. Taken together, like particle tracks, our collective routes trace out the leading edge of universal ferment and creativity.

That thought came to me as a fully developed, if nonverbal, whole as I was watching a female hairy woodpecker tap away at a gray birch next to the trail on Champlain's south ridge while, at the same time, I heard twenty-five crows in a great brouhaha down-ridge and, farther off, a chorus of coyotes echoing from Eagles Crag on Cadillac Mountain across the valley of Otter Creek. It came to me at that moment why I hiked: to seek unity with the forces of nature sustaining every facet and dimension of the Earthling community. Woodpecker, crows, and coyotes gave voice to those forces, which I sensed just as immediately in the sunlight that briefly warmed my back; the water, ice, and snow along the trail; the granite and organic soil nurturing every plant I saw; and the wind with its burden of invisible gases that fires the spirit of us all. I was right where I wanted to be, doing what I most wanted to do. Hiking in Acadia takes me directly to the center of the universe, of which I am a single far-flung atom in search of its soul. That soul is my sense of unity with the powers that be—not with the human pretenders nor the gods they appoint to grace their personal agendas, but the natural powers behind their temporal thrones. Vegetation, wildlife, and sometimes the human version of primate culture, are proof that the universal powers exist. It is our challenge as individuals to acknowledge our unity with those powers. Through that show of respect we give birth to our souls.

Rising above the Bowl, the Champlain Mountain South Ridge Trail is at first badly eroded where, over the years, tens of thousands of footfalls have gouged a furrow through thin mountain soils down to bedrock. That is a problem at higher elevations throughout the park. As the trail rises and soils grow thinner, the problem seems to solve itself, though fragile mountain plants such as mountain sandwort are still at risk. In places the trail swarmed with dark, sperm-shaped rivulets under the ice, all squirming the same direction like line dancers in the festival of world fertility. As the day warmed and sunlight streamed through occasional seams in the cloud cover, the mountain seemed to grow more lively underfoot. Where lower down the

The Bowl from Champlain Mtn. s. ridge; Beehive (l.), Gorham Mtn. (r.).

spermaform drops lolled at an oozy pace, on steeper ledges they raced like a field of Olympic speed skaters competing for the gold. The four natural forces were limbering up. Months of cold weather lay ahead, but here was springtime impatient to show its stuff, even as the scent of wood smoke rose on the wind from Otter Creek. It almost looked like spring in the valley, birch and popple twigs forming a tan mist along the creek, with white pines shining like a green promise in their midst.

Again the image of Darth Vadar appeared in front of me as I faced the steepest rise along the ridge. Ice became less of a problem the higher I rose, so I fairly raced up the trail, arriving on the brow of the ridge as the noon siren wailed from Otter Creek, followed by two hoots on Bar Harbor's noon horn. Where spruce and birch had been common below, here pitch pines dominated the exposed upper ridge, seeming to rise out of solid granite where soil might cling against the wind in shallow cracks, and water run in natural irrigation channels. I saw my shadow for the only time that day as I admired a view of Cadillac with its head in the clouds. I also saw a twenty-four-inch dike of gray stone angle across the trail, the first I had seen in months. Looking across to Dorr Mountain, I could see the ladder trail run up the slope at a surprisingly steep pitch, a thin, straight line of white ice at the base of a cliff marking the

route. The last half mile to the summit of Champlain Mountain was along a gradual rise through stunted pitch pine woods, much of the way on snow sheltered by the bristly trees. Tracks of fox, hare, and squirrel were common to within fifty feet of the summit, which was bare. There were two classes of cairns on this last stretch of ridge. Solidly built of large stones, one not only marked the trail but was made to endure. The others were heaps of small stones thrown together, barely tall enough to rise out of the snow, and seeming likely to slump with slight provocation. Evidently there are two schools of thought about cairn building, one devoted to guiding hikers on their way, the other to building sand castles with whatever materials come to hand.

Reaching Champlain's 1,058-foot summit at one o'clock, I chose a granite seat and ate my lunch looking out over Egg Rock, the Thrumcap, Ironbound Island, and the Porcupines. Two draggers and a lobster boat worked Frenchman Bay. Bands of mist swept across my view, and a dark cloud blocked the sun. Expecting the low traveling clouds to descend on me any moment, I didn't dally. Hearing a faint glup-glup-glup sound, I studied the surface of a frozen pool just north of the summit cairn. Half-round bubbles an inch in diameter were sailing across the pool, the sound coming from their home port near the center, where air was escaping through the ice, building new additions to the fleet. From there I began my cautious descent of Champlain's north ridge on the Bear Brook Trail, which was well-marked with cairns. But cairns don't make a trail, it is the footing that counts. With damp lichens and patches of ice all the way down the north ridge, footing was decidedly an issue on this hike. I briefly registered Kebo Mountain and Great Meadow, Kebo golf course and

Jackson Lab, but gave almost no attention to the view. Footing was my highest priority, so I kept my head down and studied the landscape at my feet. I did notice one seven-inch dike on the way down. The trail began among pitch pines, descended through spruce and gray birch, and reached a small stand of hemlocks where I turned off for the loop road by way of the Horseshoe and east face trail. Giving myself to the trail, I made it down without mishap, though I was uneasy much of the way, which was the price I paid for seizing a one-day opportunity for taking to the slopes. It snowed the next day, masking treacherous ice patches with a layer of bland but deceptive innocence.

Only three-tenths of a mile long, the loop road connector at the north end of the Champlain Mountain East Face Trail passes two of my favorite spots in the park, one natural, the other made by human hand. The Horseshoe is a miniature amphitheater made by a fold in the granite cliff, forming a basin which collects runoff in a shallow wetland ringed by white birches. The wetland was frozen over, but bare twigs and branches lent a softness to the place, which is peaceful at every season. The bird's nest I saw in a birch below my perch on the rim of the cliff was a nest within a nest. I regard the Horseshoe as a sacred site, not in a religious sense, but as a place deserving appreciation and respect for what it is. The ancients sprinkled gods and goddesses among the natural groves of Greece, taming those groves, fitting them into the cultural landscape they preferred. That was their way of showing respect for the natural world while making it accessible to their understanding. Now we can honor a place without tying it to the story of a particular divinity. The Horseshoe on Champlain Mountain has an integrity of its own without reference to any higher scheme. It is what it is what it is. A perfect unity unto itself, it is sacred in its own right, as everything in nature is. Having made it down the slippery north ridge, I sat looking into that hidden wetland and collected my overextended wits.

Below the open end of the Horseshoe, the trail abruptly changes its colors. It becomes evident that great care had been lavished upon it, where above it had been left to fend for itself as a crude route over crumbling and decaying granite. Every one of the eighty-four steps winding down to the talus slope below was laid with great care. The hand of loving trail makers stands revealed. Who did this fine work? Who expressed such passion in placing these stones? Who but Rudolph Brunnow, the man who went on to scale the Precipice—for himself, and for us all. In *Trails of History,* Tom St. Germain singles out this section of trail "as one of the island's greatest accomplishments in trail building." It is a remarkable experience to come onto this eighty-year-old relic from Acadia's early days without warning. It can be reached from above (the way I came on this hike), below, or from the south, but each way it stands as a freestanding treasure seemingly disconnected from the larger trail system as a whole. Here is a sacred site of a different stone, but worthy of as much respect as the Horseshoe eighty-four steps higher up. I sat on Brunnow's seat in center stage amid the blocks of talus he personally repositioned, awed

Champlain Mountain east face.

by his living presence. Descending by another flight of steps along the cliff bordering the talus slope on its northern edge, I quickly left Brunnow's stonework behind. The trail recovers its unkempt nature, giving no hint of the Rudolph Brunnow Memorial Rockwork Theater higher up. The almost nonexistent trail seems designed to keep Brunnow's love a secret. Not easy in dry weather, at this season the last stretch of trail was trying at best. My way blocked by ice, I scampered across sloping granite ledges where I could, reaching the loop road and the trailhead for the **EAST FACE CHAMPLAIN TRAIL** at a quarter to three.

It took me another forty-five minutes to walk back to my car at the fee station. Much of that time I ogled cliffs and the work of a pair of beavers. Clouds had lowered again, draping the route I had just taken in mist. Even so, that route was alive in my experience and would feed my spirit for months to come. Other than perhaps sharing a common origin, what I regard as spiritual experiences have little to do with gods or religious beliefs. I had walked in the presence of sunlight, water, soil, and wind, and celebrated their union in kinnikinnick, coyotes, and owls. The hike had put me in communion with the vital forces on which every life depends. I wanted nothing that I did not have.

❄

27—CADILLAC MOUNTAIN ROAD

From Cadillac Mountain entrance gate on Route 233
To summit of Cadillac Mountain, and back
   Up and back on Park Loop and
     Cadillac Mountain roads

9.0 miles, February 16, 1996

Red squirrel prints.

exceptions, were the same up and down. Those are the facts, nothing but the facts.

I had hiked the same route twice in January under more leisurely conditions. Both times had been on weekends when snowmobile traffic on the mountain road had been

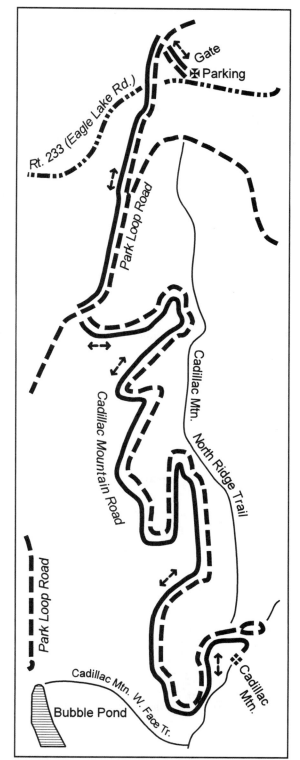

27—Cadillac Mountain Road hike.

I finished writing up my previous hike at noon and was off for the Cadillac Mountain Road within the hour. Sleet, freezing rain, and wet snow were forecast for that evening. The afternoon offered a slim crack of opportunity, which I squeezed through, taking the one mountain route I could think of where eight inches of light snow on a bed of glare ice would not bring my hiking career to an untimely end. I started from the closed gate at the park's Cadillac Mountain entrance on Eagle Lake Road at 12:55 p.m., reached the summit at 3:30, and got back to my car at 5:20 in dim light as snow pellets began to drop from lowering clouds. It was about four-and-a-half miles from the gate to the summit, for a round trip of a little over nine miles. From the gate at 300 feet to the summit at 1,530, the vertical rise was 1,230 feet. My speed averaged two miles an hour, four times faster than my usual hiking rate. Taking the same route up and back, I didn't stop to make notes on the descending leg. I was out for animal tracks which, with a couple of heavy. I decided to take the road only on weekdays after that. Not that I have anything against snowmobiles. At least in the abstract. In the particular, I don't like having to keep getting out of the way of machines going faster than is safe. Some riders are out for thrills more than the beauty of the landscape, and I wonder how much control they have over their machines. I saw enough lone riders speeding into blind turns with no regard for traffic that might be coming the other way to know I didn't want to be in the vicinity when two machines met head-on, or one machine met a skier. Couples riding tandem on the same machine were generally more cautious than singles riding alone. When you care for someone else, you start caring for yourself. Perhaps young warriors and snowsledders act as if they were immortal because they have not yet formed lasting attachments to others. As they grow older, they will slow down, learning to care for those who share the same road, including anonymous hikers by the wayside. Since I didn't have that long to wait, I thought I would avoid the whole issue by keeping out of the way of weekend snowmobile traffic. Opinion, nothing but opinion. I have never been on a snow machine. I don't own one, and never will.

I left my snowshoes in the car because I thought the snow would be light enough to wade through, as it had been on the Asticou Trail in December. I quickly found it wasn't that easy. Well, then, I'd just follow the snowmobile track on the loop road, hoping it went up the mountain. Worse. Much, much worse. Passing machines had compressed the powdery snow into a two-inch layer of butter. Every step I took, I slipped backward three or four inches. Worse than butter: ball bearings on glass. The packed track did turn up the mountain road, so I kept experimenting, trying to find solid footing. After an hour of weaving side-to-side from one track to the next looking for a place to set my boot, I decided this was a day for snowshoes after all. Too late. I adopted the motto, "slog on!" Which I did. The way was hard but not dangerous. I put my legs in compound low and churned ahead.

What was I looking for that got me out on short notice under less-than-ideal conditions? In a word, wildlife. I knew Acadia did not curl up with a good book just because of a little ice and snow. Hare and deer would be working for a living, the fox would be out on patrol. Wee folk—shrew, vole, and mouse—would tunnel under the snow, so I didn't expect to see signs of them. I wasn't sure about red squirrels. They might be light enough to stay afloat on the powder, but I wouldn't be surprised if they found it easier to tunnel underneath. I heard a chickadee and the tapping of one woodpecker. I counted tracks crossing the road: fifty-six hare, twenty-three deer, twenty-

three fox, and five mystery tracks I couldn't identify. How many living beings did those tracks represent? I estimated thirty hare, eight deer, two fox, and four or five different mysteries. One mystery, for example, crept out from under an overhanging ledge, flopped around in the snow for four or five feet, then flopped back under the ledge. What was it? Not a squirrel, but something about that size. A minor mystery, a mystery not yet of legal age. One hare had

Sargent Mountain and Bubble Ridge from Cadillac Mountain Road.

bounded along the road in eight-foot leaps, apparently desperate to get somewhere in a hurry, or to get away from somewhere else.

I actually did see squirrel tracks. One set at the start of the mountain road, five others at the summit of Cadillac Mountain. I took the fire road behind the boarded-up gift shop to the summit near where the Summit House stood in 1883, terminus of the mountain railroad built up the west ridge from Eagle Lake the same year. I dug in the snow for the highest benchmark on Mount Desert Island, which I found but couldn't read because it was frosted with ice. At that altitude I was well into the clouds, with visibility limited to 300 feet. Snow was blowing all around me. Studying nearby tracks, I identified five made by squirrels. Or maybe a singular squirrel. While standing on the benchmark eating my lunch, I saw the little trackmaker itself running along a spruce bough, leaping to another tree. That was the only wildlife I actually saw in the pelt. I told it I had just come four-and-a-half miles to watch it leap. It considered that news in silence. My luck to meet the only Quaker squirrel in the park. I was glad to have seen it because this was no run-of-the-mill rodent, but a notable celebrity. Not only was it the highest red squirrel on Mount Desert Island, it was the highest squirrel on the eastern seaboard of the United States of America, a loftier being than any other coastal squirrel in the fourteen states from Maine to Florida. I dutifully paid my respects as primate ambassador, and headed down. On the descent I noticed a fresh fox track made since I had come the other way. This was a track and a half. Next to the regular sequence of prints was a continuous line of something being dragged in the snow. I saw no drops of blood, but assume the fox was carrying fresh prey in its jaws, leaving an outriding foot dangling to the side.

Remarkable though it may be, I will not describe the mountain road itself because I hiked it more by default than by choice. The slopes were too slippery to take any other route to the top. Coping stones and outcrops cut by steel and explosives do not excite me. Hidden by snow and ice, the treadway was asphalt all the way, marked with twin yellow stripes. I was fortunate in finding most roadworks buried by snow, as if nature had briefly taken back some of what it had surrendered to steam shovels and pneumatic drills long ago. Mr. Rockefeller made my trip possible, just as he was behind the Ocean Path, Ocean Drive, the loop and carriage road systems, and the gatehouse I briefly call home. The Acadia we know today has been largely shaped by his influence. Fearing that paved roads and automobiles imperiled the landscape, he took the bull by the horns and built magnificent roads in a few places to keep lesser roads from being built elsewhere. That was his deal with the devil of inevitable progress. For myself, I would be glad to see the mountain road ripped up and the summit restored to its pre-combustion-engine state. If you can't get to a place on foot, is it wise to go at all? That tells you what a limited world I live in. But it is my own little world, one whose dimensions I have paced off myself. Given the brevity of my stay, it is as much of the Earth as I can hope to acquaint on intimate terms in one lifetime.

The views *from* the road, however, are something else. There are two to the east and northeast, three to the west. Pemetic Mountain lurks to the southwest, the Bubbles and Conners Nubble rise in a sculpted line west across Eagle Lake, backed by the black-belted ridge of Sargent and Penobscot. Black-belted because of the swath of spruce in the valley of Deer Brook between the two. All else is a study in white and gray, like a delicate platinum print. The view to the west grew dimmer as I climbed because of low hanging clouds. In the end it was lost to flying snow and mist. I regained much of it on the way down, Eagle lake seeming more luminous than before by a trick of late-afternoon light. The view to east and northeast was more of saltwater islands than of mountain ridges, the arching dolphin backs of Champlain, Dorr, and Cadillac keeping with the marine motif. At first I could see Schoodic and

Black mountains across Frenchman Bay, but they shortly disappeared as heavy clouds moved in from the northeast. Off Bar Harbor, the five Porcupine Islands stood out like chocolate cookies on a silvery baking sheet. The tidal isthmus connecting to Bar Island was surprisingly broad, and Egg Rock stretched out its low-tide neck like a reclining clam or female goldeneye during mating season. The view stopped at Ironbound, Jordan, and Stave islands,

Cadillac Mountain parking area in winter.

with Schoodic Peninsula a mere suggestion of gray on gray. As I headed south along Cadillac's west flank, clouds crept up behind me, eventually obscuring everything beyond the north end of Eagle Lake. Nearing the summit, I rose into the clouds themselves as snow began reaching toward me from ahead and behind, the approaching storm groping around the mountain to grasp me with cold, wispy fingers. There was no view from the summit other than of nearby trees backed by swirling gray. Wafted from some extraterrestrial archipelago, the only sound was a plaintive foghorn sighing its rote lament.

Though mountain ledges were buried beneath snow, I did see a number of dikes. The U-turn cut deep into the granite at an elevation of 1,000 feet exposes dikes of three different widths (Mamma, Poppa, and Baby) on the inside of the turn, and their extension as one large dike on the outside. In winter the dikes are upstaged by the massive, twenty-foot-high bank of organ-pipe ice lining the cut in hues ranging from lead-crystal white to bottle blue-green. Dark gray rock also showed through on the inside of the curve opposite the interpretive tablet at the first Eagle Lake overlook. This is perhaps a continuation of the same dike exposed in the U-turn farther on. The tablet interprets the "Glacial Landscape" including Eagle Lake and the mountains I have mentioned. It surprised me by stating, "the ice *attacked* from the north" (my italics), which seems to cast the glacier in the role of villain while, in fact, it was innocent of any hostile intent, simply doing what glaciers always do. Another image caught my attention in the sentence explaining the origin of the glacier: "Water evaporated from the oceans, took the form of ice in the far north, then flowed over this region like cold molasses." I couldn't picture cold molasses as the agent responsible for sculpting Acadia's ridges and valleys. I have heard of the Boston molasses flood early in this century, result of a huge storage tank bursting its seams in Boston's North End, loosing a wave of slow-motion molasses which crept down cobble streets to the harbor, drowning at least one person in the sugary tide. For years afterward the streets gave off a sweet, sticky smell. Glaciers flowing like cold molasses? Crawling like a juggernaut or bulldozer is more like it.

The literal and experiential high points of this hike coincided at the summit where visibility was much reduced by clouds and blowing snow. Standing on the granite knob I had bared; wind and frozen crystals swirling around me; tracks of squirrel, hare, and fox punctuating the foreground; the sun an implicit presence above the trees—I felt my substance flowing outward into that elemental scene, as it was flowing inward into me. I felt a strong sense of unity with the landscape I had attained on foot—not a passive, structural unity, but an active, ongoing, fluxing, interactive sense of participation in the wholeness of all things. I was at the center again, where I belonged. The only word I have for that centering, two-way flow is "love." Love is a sharing of equal gifts between lover and beloved, whether they exist on an interpersonal or intergalactic scale. We send valentines bearing the message, "Be mine," but love lies beyond mere possession. It is a freeing rather than a constraining force, more releasing than captivating. "Love" is a sound we utter in certain felt situations, the name we use to refer to the state we find ourselves in—but it is not that state itself. That state of reciprocal embrace can be experienced, but not captured in a name or description. Which does not render it fanciful or inconsequential. Nothing in life has more consequence than being at one with something or someone else. Standing on the highest benchmark on Cadillac Mountain, eating a cookie given to me on Valentine's Day, I was at the center of my lively, swirling universe, and it was at the loving center of me. What I brought back from that hike was a passionate sense of belonging exactly where I was on Earth and in my life.

❄

28—AROUND ST. SAUVEUR MOUNTAIN

From Man o' War Brook Fire Road gate
    on Route 102
To Valley Cove, and back
    East on Man o' War Brook Fire Road;
       south on Valley Cove (Flying Mountain) Trail;
    Back by Valley Cove Fire Road,
      Fernald Point Road, and Route 102
             5.33 miles, February 22, 1996

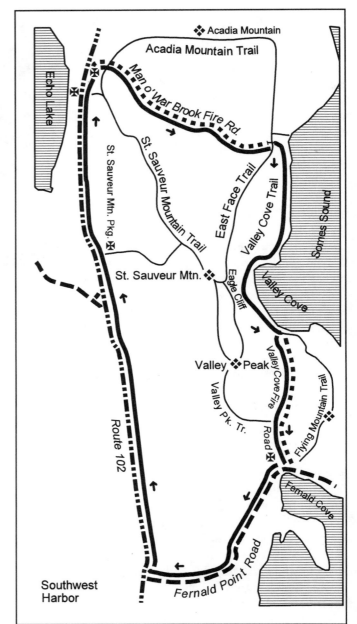

28—Around St. Sauveur Mountain.

The patron saint of foolish hikers was watching over me as I hiked around Valley Cove beneath St. Sauveur Mountain's thawing Eagle Cliff. I had seen two peregrine falcons on the cliff in October, and was eager to find out if a pair might adopt Valley Cove as a nesting site this year. It was early in the season, but most other trails in the park being closed by ice, I decided to check out the cove. What could I lose? Only my life, as it might have turned out.

No, I didn't see any falcons winging along the cliff. It was so rainy and foggy, I never saw St. Sauveur Mountain at all. Cloud-like patches of white ice on the cliff gleamed mistily above the trail, but the cliff itself was just a name on a map. I thought I might hear the falcons if they were there, but I heard only old-squaws and loons, and meltwater coursing over granite. I didn't really expect to see falcons. What I did see and hear fully justified the hike. I include the bugling of oldsquaws among nature's most uplifting music. That gleeful sound (*au-au au'la*, with accent on the third rising diphthong) came out of the fog for an hour and a half, giving me a boost when I needed it most. I saw eight oldsquaws swimming 150 feet from shore, their jaunty appearance giving shape and color to the spirited call coming out of the fog. I could make out the males' elegant tail feathers and, through binoculars, the feathering of both sexes in black, rich brown, and white. I also heard the truncated call of a loon, a sort of abrupt bark, and saw three loons in winter dress (white breast, dark-brown head, light-brown back) close to shore. One loon and a female red-breasted merganser were fishing in Valley Cove, peering down like snorkelers, then diving. While conducting my falcon watch standing for twenty minutes at the north end of the cove, I saw a red-breasted nuthatch land in a snag ten feet below me, quickly joined by three chickadees lilting through nearby cedar branches. I also heard a fuss of crows from across Somes Sound. Most amazing of all, while scrambling off-trail across talus below Eagle Cliff, I was passed by a gossamer insect fluttering on long wings. Having dropped my gloves in a puddle while getting out of the car, my own wings were incapable of moving with such dexterity.

My plan was to reach the base of Eagle Cliff in Valley Cove by starting along Man o' War Brook Fire Road from Route 102 south of Ikes Point, then picking up the Flying Mountain Trail (which I call the Valley Cove Trail) heading south through woods between the base of St. Sauveur Mountain and Somes Sound. I would return by the Valley Cove Fire Road, then by Valley Peak and the St. Sauveur Mountain Trail. I picked this loop because I knew it would be icy on the slopes, and wanted a fairly level trail leading to a place where I could bail out if I had to. I could have parked at the Valley Cove parking area, but started at the other end of the loop instead because, expecting to meet ice, I would have better traction hiking up the steepest slope rather than down. The highest point on the first leg of the

loop was near the beginning of Man o' War Brook Fire Road at about 200 feet. From there the hike would descend to a few feet above the high-tide line in Somes Sound. It was about two-and-a-third miles to the cove, and would be somewhat longer coming back, depending on the route.

Three days before, eight inches of snow had covered the ground, but it was gone, washed away by a day of rain. It was still raining as I started out, and rained off-and-on

Loons on Somes Sound.

throughout the hike. The temperature was forty-one degrees. I had low expectations for finding tracks and other signs of wildlife. In the first five minutes I saw a set of deer prints in wet snow. The ground was largely bare, but all along my route I saw where deer had browsed the bark and leaves of fallen cedars. Fox prints survived in four places, one set looking like a row of marshmallows set on top of the snow (the weight of the animal having compressed the snow, making it last while the less-dense snow around it melted away). Near a bogwalk on the cove trail there were four-toed prints that looked like woodchuck, perhaps just come out of hibernation. Collapsing vole or shrew tunnels ran every which way across snow at the foot of Man o' War Brook Fire Road. I saw one hare pellet and two soggy canine scats in Valley Cove. And the usual pileated woodpecker drillings. Near the shore I found an open but unbroken blue mussel shell on a stone in the trail, and later a shard of lobster claw. Pale and weathered (and not very digestible), the claw was perhaps a source of calcium carbonate for some desperate scavenger, but I cannot guess what the mussel shell was doing in the trail, or how it got there. Gulls break mussels open by dropping them on ledges and rocks. The living animal was missing inside, but the shell was in mint condition.

I feel at home walking through wet, green woods. The snow almost gone, I was on more familiar ground than I had been all winter. The trees along this hike are tall and splendid, but it was the ground cover beneath the trees that caught my eye. Beneath Eagle Cliff I came across three saxifrage rosettes as I was hurrying across a slope of fallen rock. I noticed them gladly, but did not stop to give them the admiration they deserved. I saw several miniature forests of ground pine, and sprigs of white-veined partridgeberry leaves hugging the soil. A single partridgeberry gleamed spectrum-red like a hanging drop refracting the rising sun. Without warning, berried juniper erupted in thick clumps, and rock tripe sprang out of granite. Blueberry twigs were everywhere sunlight could reach, and wintergreen where it couldn't. Luminous green ferns blazed my way. Here spinulose wood fern spread across a pile of fieldstones now buried among trees, there marginal wood fern lay relieved of its burden of snow and ice. The talus slope at the base of Eagle Cliff in Valley Cove was decked with rock-cap fern as if winter had never been. The wet, green woods themselves stood above the rest of us, quietly gathering strength for the push into spring. Along with living spruce, hemlock, fir, cedar, pine, birch, maple, ash, and oak, I was struck by the many snags among them drilled through with holes made or used by insects, birds, and mammals. Old forests never die, they just recycle themselves. The group of six large oaks growing in a single clump as if risen from a squirrel's cache of nuts—the ones I mentioned in describing an earlier hike—had fallen outward to occupy a circle well over a hundred feet across, each trunk the spoke of a giant wheel.

During the hike I thought of renaming this book *The Slippery Trails of Acadia*. I didn't complete the loop I had planned after all. When I got to the trailhead for the Valley Peak Trail on the Valley Cove Fire Road, I passed right by and came back by walking at the side of Fernald Point Road for a mile, then along Highway 102 for more than a mile in the rain, taking a route I would normally do almost anything to avoid. I have seen my life quota of beer cans thrown into ditches and over embankments. Hiking two-and-a-quarter miles in the park, and over two miles along public roadways, I ended up making a loop of five-and-a-third miles by the time I returned to the entrance to Man o' War Brook Fire Road where I had parked.

A northern winter does not easily pass its crown to spring with a cheery, "Have a nice day." It stalks off after making sure every one of its subjects has had been tried by snow, ice, and cold. Or, by a different metaphor, no matter how many times winter gives birth to spring, each confinement is as difficult as the first. As a mother's pelvis

puts a limit on the size of the children she can successfully bear, the rigors of winter put a limit on life's ability to revive when the trial is over. Every winter takes its toll. Trees are snapped like twigs; soils washed away; rocks broken into fragments; life itself is drowned, starved, and frozen. Winter is both precursor and leveler. Survivors are likely to have the grit to pick themselves up and start again. As a hiker, I do not fear winter's snow or cold so much as

Northern white cedars in an icy streambed, St. Sauveur Mountain.

its ice. Smooth, sloping ice running with meltwater is the biggest challenge I meet on the trail. Strapping spikes on my boots provides better footing, but creates another problem when I meet open ledge farther on. There is no simple solution to hiking on trails with rock and ice intermixed other than to stay home and bake cookies. Having committed myself to a project requiring one hike every week for fifteen weeks, when the day comes and I am free, I hike. My strategy is to select a route suited to whatever conditions prevail on that day. Which works as long as I can guess what those conditions might be. When I guess wrongly, I sometimes find myself in a fix, as I did on this hike. I tell myself I can always turn back, or find my way around, but turning back is sometimes as bad as moving ahead, and going around is seldom easy. Every time I considered my options, I told myself the worst was behind me; it's got to be easier from now on. It never was.

I deliberately picked a route I remembered as being relatively level. Strange, how memory can play such tricks. Coated with ice, even relatively level stretches of trail become treacherous. Since I expected some ice, but felt I could always work around it, I left my sturdy ice creepers on a shelf in the entryway to my apartment. Parking by the gate at the start of Man o' War Brook Fire Road across from the Acadia Mountain parking area on Route 102, I had to try three times before my studded tires got enough of a grip on the ice to let me back in. There was a message there I failed to pick up. Immediately inside the gate the road was paved with streaming white ice where a brook draining the northwest slope of St. Sauveur Mountain had flooded in its drop to Echo Lake. Northern white cedars rose out of the ice, which spread thirty feet either side of the (normally) three-foot brook. Again, I ignored the warning, slip-sliding over the ice to find the perfect spot from which to photograph that icy scene. This is the worst spot on the road, I told myself, it will get better. Which it did right away. Finding sure footing along the edge, I walked up the slight rise into woods that gave me a warmer welcome than the ice had managed to do. Ha! Deer prints in four inches of wet snow. I was in my element now. A snowshoer, two skiers, and several walkers and dogs had gone before me in recent days, leaving raised tracks in the now melting snow. I passed several white pines thirty inches in diameter, and a great many yellow birches and white cedars. Two years earlier I had studied the valley of Man o' War Brook, crossing it swamp-to-ridge and end-to-end. I had found deer antlers gnawed by coyotes, including a skull with antlers attached, which I left for gnawers yet to come. Unusual for Mount Desert Island in that

Ice in Valley Cove Trail.

it drains west-to-east across the grain of the glacier, this small watershed rises through largely coniferous woods on the southern slope, but into red oak woods on the sunnier, opposite side. The fire road runs parallel to the brook along the axis of the watershed toward the receiving marine waters of Somes Sound. I knew this quiet terrain in all seasons, and loved it for itself, overlooking its icy faults.

Man o' War Brook Fire Road is ditched on the uphill (south) side, with several corrugated metal culverts placed to carry runoff under the road toward the brook. In theory this keeps the road from being flooded, but in practice when the culverts are blocked by leaves or ice, as I found three of them were on this hike, the road gets flooded anyway. And badly iced. The fire road was slick unto impassability, and the streaming woods on either side were not much better. Unable to cross the icy road, I took to the downhill woods and, bracing boots against trees, stumps, rocks, and roots,

made my own path through the woods across the streaming slope past the first blocked culvert—only to come to another, and then another, each making the woods as icy as the road above. It took time and cautious attention, but I made it down to the turnaround at the end of the fire road after an hour of slippery travel, wondering in the back of my mind how, if I had to turn around, I would ever get back. Same way I got down, I said cavalierly, and went on.

I always pay my respects to the Robinsons' apple trees by the trailhead for ACADIA AND SAINT SAUVEUR MOUNTAIN TRAILS. On the hundred-year-old, hand-drawn Colby map in the Northeast Harbor Library, the Robinson place, snug between Robinson Mountain (now called Acadia) and Dog Mountain (now St. Sauveur), is labeled, "The Hermitage." I can believe it. How would anyone have gotten up or down that icy road in February, March, or early April? If the Robinsons went anywhere during ice season, they must have gone by boat. Apparently Mr. Robinson couldn't work, or died young, because his wife was not able to support the children who, according to Robert Pyle, the Northeast Harbor librarian, were placed with neighbors. The town saw to it that Mrs. Robinson received training as a seamstress, a skill enabling her to gather her family about her again. There are still piles of fieldstones in the woods, and the few apple trees marking the Hermitage site, the dooryard flooded with a large pond of slick ice on the day I came by. Instead of livestock, there were only shrews or perhaps voles in the vicinity, as told by the network of tunnels in the field of wet snow past the end of the road.

Down almost to Somes Sound, I was sure the footing would get easier on the level trail ahead. I seemed eager to delude myself at every step. I knew I would never make it to the falls at the outlet of the brook, so resolutely started along the trail to Valley Cove. First there was the matter of crossing the icy ledge at the start of the trail. Getting up the few steps onto the ledge was no harder than getting down on the far side, or crossing the frozen top—and certainly no easier. I noted shield lichen, reindeer moss, and blueberry twigs, but kept my eye on the ice underfoot. When necessary, I am an extremely vigilant hiker. I let the lay of the land, not my urge to push ahead, determine my next step. If I get myself into predicaments, I also get myself out. Attending to detail, and moving by small steps, so far I have gotten myself out of most scrapes, accepting a helping hand when one has been offered. The result has been a kind of confidence based on past experience, which may or may not be equal to future scrapes I can't yet imagine. Once decided on a course, I stick to it until baffled by forces greater than my own. I did get up onto the granite ledge, across it, and down the other side, its size seeming a great deal larger than I remembered. At one point I used the flat top of a three-and-a-half-foot dike in sidestepping the wicked slippery trail. From there I hopped root-to-root to the edge of the small brook flowing toward the sound from a saddle on St. Sauveur. This was no babbling brook; it was dumb, making no sound at all. With a bed of neither stones nor gravel to rile its fall, it fled swiftly over smooth, white ice—as I imagine a ghost brook would travel on Avalon or Olympus. After that, a bogwalk in eleven sections offered the best footing on the hike. A woodchuck roused from his long sleep had found that ice-free and level bridge before me, its twin split logs offering passage as inviting to him as to me. After that it was trail ice veined with roots again, and

Tumbled steps at the base of Eagle Cliff.

much slower going. The splayed group of six oaks had fallen across the trail in two places, causing me to duck. I gazed on their ruin with a sense of reverence tinged with regret, the kind of feeling burial grounds stir up in an aging breast. I stepped off the trail to photograph a downed cedar browsed by deer, which lay next to a heap of fieldstones cleared by the Robinson family, the heap long outlasting the grown-up field. There would have been morning sun on the site, and plenty of moisture flowing from St. Sauveur, but only a coarse, gravelly soil which would let moisture quickly slip away. Better a national park than a hardship farm.

The trail runs parallel to the shore of Somes Sound, making it possible, while walking in deep woods, to overhear loons and oldsquaws at their revels. If a thing misplaced in time is called an anachronism, what is a thing mistimed in space called? Anatropism (from Greek *topos, place*) is one term for such a faulty arrangement. How about

oldsquaw-in-the-woodsism? How strange it was to hear bay sounds among the trees. Thinking about oldsquaws from a fresh perspective, I was struck by the ethnic slur inherent in our name for that duck, which mocks the "babble" of elderly female Native Americans as overheard by uncomprehending foreigners. Another name for this duck is old-wife, which is just as bad. I think we should settle for long-tailed duck and let it go at that.

Nearing the shore, the trail runs by a small clearing offering a first look at the sound. I could see for about two hundred feet in the fog, far enough to make out the ducks I have described, and a loon swimming closer in to shore. Past the clearing, outcrops of ledge push the trail nearer the shore, channeling runoff at the same time, which when frozen seals the trail in massive falls of ice. Salt water on one side, ice running across the trail and upper slope, the way seemed blocked by Scylla and Charybdis. I went up the steep slope looking for a way through, but met more ice, and more ice again. Up. Up. Finally I got above the seep that was the source of the ice, and came back to the trail at the northern end of Valley Cove after two-and-a-half hours of hiking.

The cove was deep green, ringed by talus slopes red at the tideline, quickly shading to lichen-gray above. Other than the talus, the sound of dripping water, and the gleam of ice patches through the mist, there was no evidence of Eagle Cliff. The scene was as beautiful as it is at other seasons, so I gladly stood for twenty minutes waiting for a sign—any sign would do. Instead of falcons I heard from chickadees and a nuthatch. I admired the twenty-three steps pegged with iron that crossed the sloping ledge at the foot of a vertical wall of granite, then headed around the cove. The steps were the easy part; where they left off at the upper end, there was still an eight-foot stretch of sloping ledge to cross. Wet sloping ledge. Then a drop of four feet onto another streaming, sloping shelf. I picked out my footholds in advance, braced one foot and led off with the other, hitting my mark with both strides, then let myself down onto the last shelf. Rounding a huge lichen-clad boulder itching to resume its journey to the bottom of the cove, I came to the lip of the mossy, licheny, ferny, cedary, misty, damp and dripping depths I think of as the source of Acadian life. I felt a thrill to be here again, even though I was paying more attention to my footing than my surroundings. The mossy cliff near the steps leading down was not green but iced along its length in white, with a waterfall flowing down its center. The way down was more a jumble of rock than a graded series of steps. Marginal wood fern gleamed with local color, and water running and splashing in the mist filled the air with regional folk tunes and dances. I took a minute to photograph the waterfall and steps leading up from that original place, then continued on.

From that low point, the trail ascends to the base of Eagle Cliff by a flight of about a hundred steps. In October I had seen falcons from the top of those steps, and thought I would pause there again to give them one more chance to materialize out of the mist. Mounting toward the base of the cliff, counting steps as I went, I had reached step seventy-eight when I heard a sound above me, the faint crack of something letting go. Suddenly a great icicle plunged into the trail at the top of the steps, smashed into a thousand cubes and shards, which hurtled out and down across the talus, spraying the slope with 350 pounds of shattered ice. Here I had been concentrating on danger beneath my feet while an even greater danger lurked out of sight overhead. I had had a rendezvous with that bolt of ice, but missed my appointment because I had taken one picture more than I had intended to. Completing my tally of the steps by eye rather than foot, I examined the range over which the shards had exploded, mapping out a route just beyond its edge. Then I took off across the talus, noting unfamiliar ferns and flying insects and buds big as chickpeas greening before my eyes as I passed without slowing or stopping. The way was steep and slippery across small chunks of granite smashed much as that icicle had been smashed, the entire slope tilted as such an angle it seemed likely to slump if slightly disturbed. There was no way to walk gingerly, so I scrambled across the base of the cliff, soon finding my way blocked by trees and thick shrubs. The way seemed steeper below than above, so I regained the trail—barely a narrow cow path filled with ice and snow at the base of an icy cliff rising into the mist. I tried to gauge the stability of every ice formation I could see, but didn't have the knack. All of it looked like it could fall any instant. I didn't belong there, but that's where I was. The Presence I felt was mad because I had missed my appointment. I did what I had to do. I got out of there.

Eventually the trail crosses a slope of huge blocks of talus, and moves down and away from the cliff. I relaxed and looked out to discover a loon and merganser fishing the deep, green waters of the cove. The trail was no less icy than it had been, but by now I was used to it and had an assortment of silly walks to meet every challenge. I peered at two canine scats disintegrating in the rain, thinking they looked about right for coyote, though they may have

swollen somewhat. I though the going would get easier when I reached Valley Cove Fire Road, but the whole turn-around was a slanting rink of wet ice, so I had to find my way around it through dense undergrowth. Crossing an eight-foot stream of meltwater on a fallen log, I edged my way along the road, passing the trail for Valley Peak without regret. I came to Fernald Point Road, which in a mile connects to the state highway, which in turn led me

Granite steps across sloping ledge, north end of Valley Cove.

back to my car. The hike took me five-and-a-half hours, and though it had not gone exactly as planned, it was a hike I will never forget.

✳

29—WONDERLAND and SHIP HARBOR LOOP

From Ship Harbor Nature Trail parking area
    on Seawall Road
To Bennet Cove and Ship Harbor, and back
    East along Seawall Road (Route 102A);
    south on Wonderland Fire Road;
    along the shoreline to Ship Harbor;
    north on Ship Harbor Nature Trail
             2.25 miles, February 29, 1996

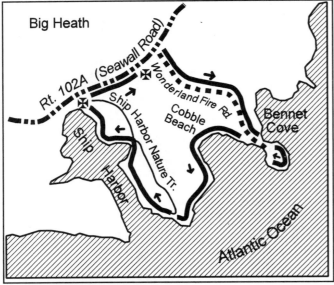

29—Wonderland & Ship Harbor loop.

When I am up for a certain kind of hike, Acadia never lets me down. With granite peaks and wooded slopes, wetlands and valley ponds, sandy beaches and rocky shores, water both fresh and salt, it has whatever terrain I want—and wildlife to suit. After my last hike, I'd had it with ice! Where was footing I could trust? I wanted a hike where I could look at something besides my feet. It had rained the day before, then frozen, so sloping routes were out. With snow long gone, there would be no tracks. To look for wildlife, I thought I would hike along the shore. Wonderland was just the place, and Ship Harbor, with the shoreline in-between thrown in to complete the loop. This short hike was so eventful, I never regretted not seeing winter signs of fox, hare, or squirrel. What I did see more than made up for the absence of my regular hiking companions.

I got to Ship Harbor Nature Trail parking area on Seawall Road at eight o'clock on a clear and blustery winter morning. The temperature was twenty degrees which, because of the northwest wind, felt like ten below zero. After walking east along the highway at the edge of Big Heath, I took the Wonderland Fire Road south to the shore. I explored Bennet Cove, walked west along the seawall beach at the head of the next cove, around the next point to

the entrance of Ship Harbor, then walked north on the nature trail along the harbor, reaching my car at ten minutes till noon. The total distance was only two-and-a-quarter miles—less than the loop around Jordan Pond—but there was so much to see I didn't average much more than half-a-mile per hiking hour. I had camera and binoculars, so spent a lot of time peering through each.

If you don't own binoculars, do yourself a favor and get a pair. Tell friends and family what you want for your next birthday. The miniature ones are hard to see through; go for a pair that magnifies between seven and ten times, with a lens diameter between forty and fifty millimeters (7x40 to 10x50). They will change your life. Particularly at the shore where so much happens in the middle distance. A pair of 8x (the x stands for power of magnification) binocs does for your eyes what a 400mm lens does for your 35mm camera. When I say I saw such-and-such a duck, I saw it through binoculars. That's how I know it was a red-breasted such-and-such and not a lobster buoy.

The rocks I saw on this hike were different from those on other hikes. The granite was pinker and finer-grained, suggesting it had cooled faster than, say, Somesville or Cadillac Mountain granite, producing smaller crystals with a more delicate texture. Great ledges of granite dipping into the tide dominate the shore at the seaward end of both trails, with blocks of the same rock piled by waves in heaps on higher ground. These blocks reveal the stress this granite has known over the years—from forces such as storms, glaciers, and the collision of tectonic plates, producing joints (cracks) in the ledge, which eventually cleave, splitting the ledge into building blocks. This is how rock reproduces itself in ever-more-compact form, assuring its lineage will go on in future generations of boulders, cobbles, pebbles, gravel, sand, silt, and clay, eventually to be drawn into the Plutonic underworld, from which it may be reborn as solid rock in some future life. Wonderland granite did not form on the surface where we see it now, but welled up into Earth's crust more than 360 million years ago, where it cooled over hundreds of thousands of years. Only recently has it come into the light, currently exposed beds having been stripped clean by the glacier a few tens of thousands of years ago. The older volcanic rock into which this granite intruded is visible at two places along the loop: in a fragment on the Wonderland shore at the western lip of Bennet Cove, and along the section of the nature trail overlooking Ship Harbor. It is hard to picture volcanoes in Downeast Maine, but they were here 400–600 million years ago, spewing out gas, ash, and rock, fired by tectonic collisions. As a result, this gray rock, called tuff, fell out of the sky, building in layers created by a series of volcanic eruptions. Today it forms much of the bedrock between Bass Harbor and Little Cranberry Island.

Do rocks make a difference in our lives? Wonderland granite certainly made a difference to passengers immigrating to William Penn's "holy experiment" in the province of Pennsylvania on board the *Grand Design* in 1739. The ship struck Long Ledge, the prominent granite bar just off Wonderland, and although many survivors reached shore, they soon succumbed to hunger and cold. I saw nine great cormorants stiff as statues on one end of the ledge, looking like professional mourners, or perhaps undertakers awaiting the next ship. Largely wooded, with less dire connotations, other rocks spread across the horizon from Great Cranberry Island in the northeast, to Great and Little Duck islands in the southeast, and Great Gott and Placentia islands backed by Swans Island in the southwest. These islands looked like harmless, floating flapjacks to me, but through binoculars I could see great waves sending up spindrift along their windward shores. A dragger, trawler, and lobster boat were out in those waves beyond the cormorants patiently waiting on their ledge.

Although walking along the rocky shore was one of the novelties of this hike, the inland portions of the loop passed through familiar woods and wetlands which I found every bit as beautiful. Along Seawall Road (Route 102A), a break in roadside trees gives a glimpse over a small lobe of Big Heath, a vast peat bog draining into Bass Harbor Marsh through Adams Brook. Acadia's trails generally steer clear of bogs out of respect for their fragility. Built on a foundation of sphagnum moss and peat, bogs present a more open landscape than the woodlands we are used to. It was good to be that close to one, even if I didn't see sundews or pitcher plants.

Ten feet wide, the Wonderland Fire Road winds across a coastal plain dominated by alder, fir, and spruce, with ground cover of moss, ferns, lichens, bunchberry, and sheep laurel along the way. Rising onto a low granite dome devoid of soil, the road passes into an open area where only pitch pines can find enough water and nutrients to grow. The area looks like a carefully tended garden, but the gardener in this case is the landscape itself. The Ship Harbor Nature Trail passes through similar terrain, with numbered posts keyed to a printed guide available from rangers in Seawall Campground when the kiosk is open. The most spectacular plant I saw along the nature trail was a humble pussy willow beginning to sprout tufts of gray fuzz. Walking along the shore between the two trails, I saw tangled thickets of rugosa rose, lichens looking like splashes of bright orange paint, and a fallen spruce whose roots had found enough water to grow in a mound of smooth cobbles.

Of all the plants I saw on this hike, the ones that excited me the most were the ones twisted together with other forms of wreckage at the high-tide line as wrack from the gardens of the sea. I recognized dulse, kelp, rockweed,

sponges, marsh grass, mussels, and sea urchins, but saw a variety of life forms I had never seen before. Running through the knotted mass were snarls of bright-colored rope and warp mixed with feathers, sticks, bones, bait bags, gloves, boots, rain gear, and other debris. Sea spoor. Scats passed largely undigested through the bowels of the Gulf of Maine. I don't know why it fascinated me so, but I had to scan every foot of it to see what story it might tell. It spoke

Eider loafing offshore.

to me of a world I would never know firsthand, and adventures others had had, but I never would. I stood on one side of an invisible barrier, the Emerald City lay on the other, with no Yellow Brick Road in between. Transitions are always the hard part. It takes more than clicking your heels together to find the source of that splendid wrack. The ocean had the energy advantage. To enter its realm meant going against currents, waves, and wind. It could send emissaries to me, but beyond skipping flat stones, I was unable to reciprocate.

Visually, the vertical transition from woods to salt water didn't seem that much of an obstacle. Here was the tide line, here hanging strands of rockweed, above that dark granite tinged with green, then pale granite, piles of granite blocks, then shoreline trees. Looking across the small cove separating the granite headlands of Wonderland and Ship Harbor, the vertical distance from tide to trees looked no more than twelve to fifteen feet. So near, and yet. . . . Life began in the sea, then took three billion years to bridge that slender gap. No wonder I have curiosity about, and respect for, that black and tangled wrack offered up by the tide. Mixed with recognizable plastic artifacts, here are traces of ancient forests and beings that lived before the first plant took root on land, before the proto-blackfly sprouted wings, before curiosity drove the first parent of all primates to bite the first apple. Gawking at tangled seawrack, I am gawking at relics from my distant past. Who expects to find those in a national park?

The best display of seawrack was on the cobble seawall beach between the two granite headlands. Larger than pebbles, smaller than boulders, cobbles are stones two-and-a-half to ten inches long. Polished by tumbling against one another when pounded by waves, they are often oblong in shape, smooth, and surprisingly beautiful. Massed together, their various sizes and colors meld into a texture as harmonious as anything in nature. The beach between Wonderland and Ship Harbor is a classic example. Winter storms pound the cobbles with more energy than usual, throwing them up and back, creating a storm ridge or seawall rising eighteen feet above the coastal plain. Where roads have been built along the shore behind these barriers of stones (as at Seawall and Bracy Cove), drivers often find cobbles thrown like so much gravel into the roadway during winter storms. While boulders stay put, cobbles adjust to your weight when you walk on them, providing a firm but pliant surface in which footprints register as miniature craters. I could see where others had crossed the berm ahead of me, piling stones, poking sticks, pulling on knotted ropes. The finest construction was a double throne built on top of the storm ridge in the center of the beach. Pale, smooth boulders lugged from lower on the slope had been stacked so two people could sit side-by-side and survey the cove as monarchs of that narrow realm. I tried the larger throne, but was rejected as an oversized pretender. Garlands of black and twisted wrack draped the cobble ridge, which I insisted on examining in fine detail. It is a good thing I came along when I did; the position of wrack inspector was open, and applicants were scarce. I did my best to uphold the standards expected of me and, if I do say so, handled myself professionally and with great credit. If I hadn't been there, who else would have noted that yellow-banded lobster buoy or those six twisted wire traps?

I was struck by the difference between how the granite headlands and the cobble beach had received the thrust of the waves. The beach literally rolled with each punch, coming back for more. It dissipated the energy hurled upon it by piling itself into a ridge, rebuilt in every storm. The inflexible granite had no recourse but to crack under pressure, letting blocks be torn away and later be pushed farther landward with the thrust of every wave, exposing raw ledge to the onslaught. As a result, the granite broke up and retreated in disarray, while the beach of small stones stood its ground season after season. In a snapshot, the beach would look punier than the mighty ledge, but in a time-lapse film made over a span of centuries, that impression would be reversed.

Other than dog and horse prints, and one soaring gull, I neither saw nor heard signs of animal life along the highway or the Wonderland Fire Road. But when I reached the shore, I saw birds in every direction. Hundreds of birds. Sixteen eider were diving off the granite headland; crows were landing at the edge of the receding tide and scavenging in the rockweed; like origami ornaments,

Headland ledges, broken rock, and trees east of Ship Harbor.

dozens of gulls were hanging in the sky and, through binoculars, I saw a dozen dozen sailing before the wind farther out; and nine great cormorants formed a dignified line on Long Ledge. Two mourning doves flustered off as I approached Bennet Cove to the east, four buffleheads swam and dove together, and twenty-five black ducks flew in low, landing around the next point.

Looking toward Seawall picnic area, I saw hundreds of gulls abruptly scramble into the air, joined by the ducks that had just landed. Looking higher for the cause of that alarm, I saw an eagle soaring above the sudden riot of whirling birds. Seeing it head-on with outspread wings bristling at the tips, I watched the eagle dive into the flurry, turning its head left and right, looking for a vulnerable target, but finding none. As it flew in my direction, I could make out its markings through binoculars: white tail edged with a dark band, light belly and mottled underwings, dark head—an immature eagle in its second year, with three years to go before achieving the distinctive plumage of maturity. Over the far side of Bennet Cove, the luckless hunter began to spiral higher and higher, in a few minutes becoming a restless speck pacing against racing clouds. Turning aside at the call of a nearby crow, I lost track of the eagle and could not find it again.

Thousands of periwinkle shells lay strewn among the

boulders at the upper end of the granite ledge, accented by shards of blue mussel shell. Two birds fished in the cove between the two headlands, a female common merganser and a more active guillemot, its coloring a mottled gray halfway between winter white and summer black. I found a single hare pellet at the far edge of the cobble beach. One-hundred-and-twenty-five eiders were diving off the next point, with eight oldsquaws diving and trumpeting in rougher seas farther out. Looking large as a goose, a loon fished the waters at the entrance to Ship Harbor, and inside the harbor four buffleheads and a female goldeneye dove in the shallows. It was a great hike for birds.

The park abounds with life at every season; you just have to seek out places where you are most likely to find it. Keeping eyes and ears open, I usually manage to find some

Cobble beach between Wonderland and Ship Harbor.

sort of wildlife, though not necessarily what I've been looking for. More than just a place, Acadia is an ongoing *event*. When I hike, I take part in that event. A *place* might conceivably look the same when revisited, but an *event* unfolds differently every time. If the park stays the same in any respect, it stays forever new. Over familiar ground or fresh terrain, every hike is unique. And every hike is renewing, inviting all who love the park to celebrate Acadia's continual rebirth.

❄

30—AROUND CEDAR SWAMP MOUNTAIN

From Brown Mountain Gate parking area
To Birch Spring, and back
    Up by carriage road; Hadlock Brook and
        Birch Spring trails
    Down by Amphitheater Trail and Around-Mountain
        Carriage Road
            5.0 miles on snowshoes, March 8, 1996

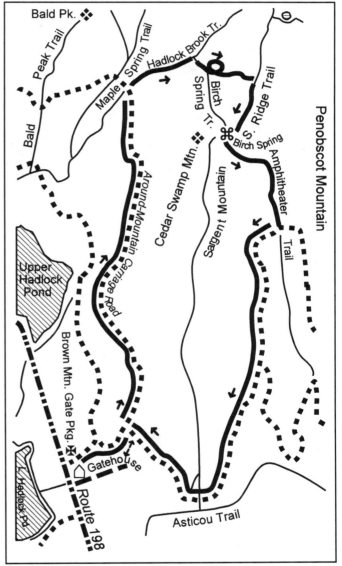

30—Around Cedar Swamp Mountain.

On my last two hikes in February, the ground had been largely bare; now, in March, Acadia lay buried beneath two feet of fine snow. On the day of this hike, a strong northeast wind was blowing moisture in from the Gulf of Maine. It was snowing, and would go on snowing into the night. Falling snow makes the wind visible, revealing hidden patterns in moving air. Hiking through this storm, I felt as if

I were moving through the mind of God, watching his thoughts and emotions flow and take shape. There is precedent for that feeling in the story of the Sky-Father and Earth-Mother: Cretan Zeus; Thor with his hammer; Hadad, Baal, and Yahweh as storm and weather gods who spoke in the thunder. As depicted in Psalm 18 (King James version):

The LORD also thundered in the heavens, and the Highest gave his voice; hail stones and coals of fire.
Yea, he sent out his arrows, and scattered them; and he shot out lightnings, and discomfited them.

Acadia received the blowing snow with grace, storing it for later use. The landscape was smooth and white, every tree and ledge adding to the beauty of the scene. In his story "The Dead," James Joyce used the image of snow covering the earth to suggest bleakness and despair, but in nature snow is more aptly depicted as the procreator of spring. I saw few signs of wildlife, but that didn't matter. I was witnessing the union of sky and earth, the sacred marriage from which every plant and animal springs in its time. In the beginning was the storm, covering the Earth.

On this last of my winter hikes I wanted to experience the storm while keeping away from exposed ridges. I knew the going would be difficult even on snowshoes because the snow was so soft and deep. I chose a relatively sheltered route, hoping trees would intercept much of the falling snow. I started from the gatehouse at five minutes to eight, walked the ungroomed carriage road to Hadlock Bridge, picked up the Hadlock Brook Trail, which I followed by way of Waterfall Bridge to the turning for Birch Spring. Heading between Sargent's south ridge and Cedar Swamp Mountain, I eventually found the spring. From there, I took the Amphitheater Trail into the valley of Little Harbor Brook as far as Amphitheater Bridge; then, bailing out of my original plan to continue on to the Asticou Trail, I completed the loop on the Around-Mountain Carriage Road, arriving at the gatehouse at five after two. Even on snowshoes I sank in ten to fifteen inches at every step, giving my thigh muscles a good workout. On bare ground, it takes me half an hour to get from Amphitheater Bridge to the gatehouse; this time it took three times as long. On that last leg I started out resting every hundred yards or so, then cut that to fifty, then twenty yards.

Planning the hike, I thought it would be hard getting up to Birch spring on the relatively open Amphitheater Trail, so chose to go the other way, approaching from the north through thicker woods. At an elevation of 820 feet, the spring lies 600 feet above the gatehouse. I ended up going higher than I had intended, adding 100 feet to the vertical climb, comparable to a hike up Beech Mountain from Long Pond. It took me a little over six hours to cover the snowy five-mile loop. By the map, the loop is half a mile shorter than that, but I ended up mislaying the trail for a bit, putting in some extra wandering through terra incognita on the side of Sargent Mountain before I found it again.

Being open to the sky and not yet groomed for cross-country skiing, the carriage roads demanded a good deal of slogging at the start and end of the hike. Under trees, the snowfall was less, but the going no easier on uphill slopes. Wind sweeping over the lip of the Amphitheater dumped great drifts on the Amphitheater Trail, burying cairns and boulders, filling the valley of Little Harbor Brook. I had hiked that section of trail many times, but had never seen it like this. The way was unrecognizable. I switched on my automatic pilot and navigated by a combination of intuition, imagination, and bull-headedness. Next to Little Harbor Brook, from what I could see, there was no place to walk along the steep, snow-covered slope. Three or four feet straight down there might have been a trail, but the valley is so narrow in places that brook and trail disappeared. If I hadn't known the terrain, I would have been stymied.

Why did I go out under such trying conditions? To conclude this series of winter hikes, I wanted to experience winter itself rather than its aftermath. Days were lengthening; sunlight was getting stronger. The spring equinox was a week and a half ahead. This storm blew in off the Gulf, giving me one last chance to see what winter was all about. Offering me one last fling. I said yes, and threw myself into the storm. For me, hiking is less about reaching a set destination than making the most of my experiences along the trail. I yearned to meet the spirit of winter halfway.

Yes, spirit is the right word, from Latin *spirare*, to breathe. With our first yelp, the spirit enters into us; at our last gasp, it departs. In between, we breathe in and out every minute of our lives, as every animal breathes. As trees and plants breathe carbon dioxide in, oxygen out. The air made visible by blowing snow, I could see the spirit I drew from the Acadian landscape, the fuel that fires my blood. It is commonly held that spiritual matters are best dealt with in houses of worship, but I prefer to face them out in the open, away from rituals and creeds. In my view, spirituality has little to do with organized religion or belief in God. It is more fundamental than that, more ineffable. Every religion defines God in its own way, then claims a special relationship to that which it has defined. People create gods, not vice versa. Air, sunlight, water, and soil simply *are*. It is *they* who define *us*. Without that definition, we would not exist. Spirituality entails getting back to basics. Back to considering the elements on which life depends—on which I personally depend—with due wonder, respect, and thankfulness. That is why I revere sunlight, streams, rocks, plants, and wildlife. That is why I go out in winter storms. If I did not, I would run the risk of taking the natural world for granted as if I owed it nothing or, worse, as if it owed something to me: sustenance, perhaps, riches, or even success.

Each hike is an event in my life process, another inch of clay added to the coil of my ongoing experience circling round and around the fullness of my deep-breathing spirit.

As every coil of clay adds depth to a pot built spiral upon spiral, every year of my living adds depth to that experience. Starting with my first breath, I began a year of experience which wound upon itself, as a potter winds a small spiral of clay when starting a coil pot. In my second year, with every breath, I added to my experience, expanding the small coil I had begun. I did the same in succeeding years, until I had a broad base that supported more ambitious endeavors. After that, I began to build up and out, creating first a small plate, then a shallow bowl, which became deeper with the years. With every round, my experience grew bigger and stronger, yet it followed the same spiral pattern set in my first year. I did not know what sort of life I was building; I merely extended what I had begun. With every breath, the bowl of my life grew wider and taller. Then it began to climb upward, resembling more a vase than a bowl. And then, year after year, coil after coil, it began slowly to close on itself, creating a more fully rounded shape, narrowing the small hole at the top. When I whisper into it, that opening sends back echoes of every breath I have taken, every experience shaping my life, seeming to breathe with a life of its own.

The most wonderful thing about it is that the vessel of my experience has a center which I didn't know I was building into it as I wound the coils of daily living on which I was so intent. That virtual center is as real as the clay of my life. It is the essence of the pot itself, the spiritual focus of my life's silent breathing. Every person has such a center, as does every being on Earth—moth, newt, and weed. Each builds the spiritual core of its existence as it winds the coils of its life minute-by-minute. Each center hums uniquely, adding its resonance to the spiritual voice of the Earthling community. The wind is the sound of that soft breathing in unison, the sigh of the communal Earth spirit. Every flake of snow in a great storm is the crystallized breath of one Earthling spirit. To go into a storm is to share in the communal inhalation and exhalation of Earth's spiritual life. Rather than ask, why go? it makes more sense to ask, why doesn't everyone go?

If these images seems far-fetched, I can only say that they seem less far-fetched than the idea of a supreme being who created heaven and Earth (out of either chaos or emptiness) and now watches over their day-to-day operations. As I see it, life gives us a chance to join in the ongoing creativity of the universe. Not here by design, each of us descends from a long and honorable line of survivors. We can talk about our deepest beliefs—which are truly ineffable—only in terms of images and symbols laid upon them from outside. Metaphor does for those beliefs what snowflakes do for air. They let us tell the story of that which exists beyond words. We should not make the mistake of thinking that, because a truth is ineffable, it is not real. If words are not up to describing the world of the spirit, that says more about the inadequacy of language than of the spirit. My aim here is to suggest the silent breathing of one crystalline flake in the wind.

Aside from spirits, I did see direct evidence of wildlife on this hike. Insect tunnels were engraved on every snag, and tunnel entrances had been drilled into the bark of many living trees. I saw a dozen nesting cavities of woodpecker and chickadee. A fox had crossed the carriage road an hour before I came by, leaving a set of prints which were fading by the minute. Another set of fox prints was preserved near a cairn on the Amphitheater Trail, the wind having swept away the fine snow that had buried the frozen track. I saw one dusting of lichen bits under a birch where a woodpecker had recently dug for bugs. On the Amphitheater Trail, I thought I heard the burbling of purple finches, but took that as an illusion having more to do with my wearing a hood than any actual birds. As for living creatures, I saw only one gray bird dart into the wind like a rocket and, in the last five minutes of my hike, two couples skiing the carriage roads.

Coniferous trees along my route were made more slender by the weight of ten inches of snow on their boughs. Every branch of every deciduous tree bore a bone-white rib along its length. The bark of yellow birches glistened, of red pines glowed with purple light. Beech leaves fluttered in the wind, sheep laurel twigs sticking out of the snow never stopped shivering. Getting occasional glimpses of snow blowing through a receding landscape of spruce and white pine, I thought I had never seen anything more beautiful. Lichens adorned every tree and branch. I passed through several stands of mature trees, and was struck by how each stem was set off by the white behind it, making it notable as something in itself, not merely as a support for higher things. Stems convey sap between roots in damp soil and leaves in sunlit air. They open up the woods, making way for life in the understory and on the ground. If it weren't for such stems, we would have to fight our way everywhere through thickets of green shrubbery dense as alder swamps.

The three streams I came to—two branches of Hadlock Brook, and Little Harbor Brook—were buried beneath mounds of snow. In a few places I saw clear water running over red granite chips, but generally the streams were as white as their banks, which were as white as the sky. When the temperature next rises above freezing, as was forecast for the following week, every stream in Acadia would come into its own. Then Hadlock Falls would break its chains and send the snow and ice that have held it down fleeing for refuge in the sea. The three carriage-road bridges I saw—Hadlock, Waterfall, and Amphitheater—looked magnificent, every stone picked out in white. They wore the snow like time itself and looked as ancient as the cliffs.

Strung between two sections of carriage road, the route between Hadlock and Amphitheater bridges along the Hadlock Brook, Birch Spring, and Amphitheater trails was the central feature of this hike. It is a great way to get out in a storm without being overwhelmed. There are steep stretches up and down, but they are not that long. The crucial turn is indicated by a sign for **BIRCH SPRING** on a post [replaced by a trailhead since I made this hike] along the Hadlock Brook Trail up from Waterfall Bridge. I dug it out of the snow to make sure. It is three-tenths of a mile from there to the spring. Up and over, I said to myself.

A funny thing happened on the way to the spring: I got lost. Not far beyond a blue diamond blaze, I came to a great fallen tree—and the trail disappeared. I circled left and right, but came across nothing that looked like a trail. I went back to the blaze and started again. A root of the fallen tree had been cut, so I knew I was on the trail at that point. The roots had been exposed for a long time, so the downed tree was not the problem. I had taken the trail last fall: it was there, I knew it was. Less than a quarter mile to go, how could I miss the spring? Up and over.

I went on through impressive woods, making my own trail, looking for the wetland I remembered the trail running past on a shelf between Sargent and Cedar Swamp mountains. I wound among fallen trees which, buried in snow, were not hard to get around. A cliff blocked me at one point, but a sort of shelf ahead on the left looked promising. The trail would be on the far side of the shelf, so I tried to get through that way, but was blocked by dense undergrowth. Instead of a wetland, I stood in a forest of mature trees. I knew two things about it: it was beautiful, and I had never been there before. Which mountain was I on, Cedar Swamp or Sargent? I had no idea. I am having an adventure, I told myself; enjoy it. I knew the spring was above me when I lost the trail, so my plan was to keep going up. If way didn't open on the left side of the shelf, I'd try the right. I backtracked, then approached the shelf again, this time finding myself among tall trees on a terrace stretching along the base of a steep slope.

I always get excited when I explore new terrain, even if I don't know where I am. I was Charles Darwin making a foray into the jungle from the deck of the *Beagle.* A phrase from my favorite paragraph in *Walden* rose to the surface of my mind: ". . . not till we are completely lost, or turned around, . . . do we appreciate the vastness and strangeness of Nature." I looked on my surroundings with new eyes, as if I had never seen anything like them before. Snow blowing through the woods made them even vaster and stranger. I was meant to lose the trail so I could experience Nature with a capital N. Thoroughly enjoying myself, not caring that I was lost, I followed the shelf to its far end, where I saw a snow-covered stretch of open ledge above me to my left. Maybe I could get a view from up there to tell me where I was. Scrambling up through loose snow, I

found—no, no view, but there was a stone that seemed to float on a drift of snow, which I thought might be the capstone of a cairn. Digging beneath it, I found a three-foot heap of stones. I was somewhere at least, even if I didn't know where. Knowing the way of trail builders, I assumed one cairn was bound to lead to another. Looking in all directions, I found nothing. The terrain gave no hint where a trail might lie. Circling, I inspected every tree, and found

Terra incognita on the flank of Sargent Mountain where I got lost.

one branch that had been cut. Heading in that direction, I came to a rising expanse of snow beyond which, when I had trudged to its summit, I saw the most awesome sight I have seen in all Acadia—a great mountain ridge rising out of a deep gulf across which snow was streaking horizontally, misting and mystifying the air, creating a scene of unanticipated magnificence. Click! I knew exactly where I was: on the south ridge trail of Sargent Mountain overlooking the Amphitheater and, beyond it, the splendid west face of Penobscot Mountain. The transition from being lost to being found was so abrupt, the scene, which I had witnessed under less dramatic circumstances many times, had an aura of spiritual significance. Painted in shades of white and gray, here "the vastness and strangeness" of Acadia rose before me, rendering me as small as I have ever felt. After ogling the scene for several minutes, I headed down toward Birch Spring, passing the first blue blaze I had seen in over an hour. At the spring I connected with the Amphitheater Trail and continued the hike as planned.

I had other visions along the way of Bald Peak and the cliffs on Cedar Swamp Mountain, but none came near the one I had at the high point of the hike. What better place to end the telling of these winter tales?

❊

Mayflower, Kurt Diederich's Climb.

ACADIA
The Soul
of a
National Park

Book Three
SPRING

To Jesse

Wherever he goes,

his footsteps trace

the leading edge

of universal creation

CONTENTS—SPRING HIKES

INTRODUCTION—SPRING 152

31 HIO ROAD 153
From Route 102 north of Adams Brook Bridge
To Seawall Campground, and back
  By the Hio Road both ways
4.0 miles, February 26, 1997

32 SEASIDE TRAIL 157
From Jordan Pond
To Seal Harbor, and back
  By the Seaside Trail both ways
3.8 miles on ice creepers, March 5, 1997

**33 BREAKNECK &
  CARRIAGE ROADS LOOP 163**
From park headquarters off Route 233
To Hulls Cove, and back
  Out by the Breakneck Road
  Back by park carriage roads
5.4 miles on snowshoes, March 12, 1997

**34 SARGENT MOUNTAIN via
  HADLOCK BROOK TRAIL 168**
From Norumbega Mountain parking area
To Sargent Mountain summit, and back
  By the Hadlock Brook Trail both ways
4.0 miles on ice creepers, March 19, 1997

35 TRIAD & DAY MOUNTAIN LOOP 173
From Route 3 near Blackwoods Campground
To the Triad and Day Mountain, and back
  Up by the Hunters Brook Trail and bushwhack
  Down by the Day Mountain Trail and bushwhack
4.0 miles on snowshoes, March 26, 1997

36 GREAT HEAD LOOP 179
From Sand Beach parking area
To Great Head, and back
  By the Great Head Trail and Sand Beach
2.0 miles, April 2, 1997

**37 LITTLE HARBOR BROOK &
BIRCH SPRING LOOP 184**
From Route 3 at Little Harbor
To Birch Spring and Cedar Swamp Mountain,
and back
Up by Little Harbor Brook and Amphitheater trails
Down by Cedar Swamp Mountain, Asticou, and
Little Harbor Brook trails
6.5 miles, April 4, 1997

38 ELIOT MOUNTAIN LOOP 190
From Brown Mountain Gate parking
To Eliot Mountain, and back
Up by Forest Hill Cemetery connector, Asticou
Trail to the Map House, and Eliot Mountain Trail
Down by Eliot Mountain and Asticou trails, and
Forest Hill Cemetery connector
2.7 miles on ice creepers, April 9, 1997

39 AROUND DORR MOUNTAIN 194
From Sieur de Monts Spring
To the Notch between Dorr and Cadillac mountains,
and back
Up by Spring Road, Hemlock Trail, and
Gorge Trail
Down by A. Murray Young, Canon Brook, Kane,
and Jesup trails
5.0 miles, April 16, 1997

**40 SARGENT MOUNTAIN via
GIANT SLIDE TRAIL 200**
From St. James Church on Route 198
To the summit of Sargent Mountain, and back
Up by Giant Slide and Sargent Mountain North
Ridge trails
Down by Grandgent and Giant Slide trails
5.6 miles, April 23, 1997

**41 FEATHERBED LOOP via
POTHOLE TRAIL 207**
From Canon Brook parking on Route 3
To the Featherbed, and back
Up by Canon Brook Trail, Dorr Mountain South
Ridge Trail extension, and Pothole Trail
Down by Canon Brook Trail
5.0 miles, April 30, 1997

42 AROUND LOWER HADLOCK POND 212
From the pullout on Hadlock Pond Road
To the far side of the pond, and back
Counterclockwise around the pond by the
Hadlock Path
1.3 mile, May 7, 1997

43 AROUND JORDAN POND 217
From the boat ramp parking area
To the north end of Jordan Pond, and back
Clockwise around the pond by the Jordan Pond
West and East Side trails
3.0 miles, May 14, 1997

44 SARGENT MOUNTAIN via DEER BROOK 223
From Bubble Rock parking area on the loop road
To Sargent Mountain summit, and back
Up by Bubble Gap and Deer Brook trails, and
Jordan Cliffs Trail extension
Down by Sargent Mountain South Ridge,
Deer Brook, and Jordan Pond East Side trails,
and Jordan Pond Canoe Carry
4.6 miles, May 21, 1997

45 FOUR TRAILS ON ISLE AU HAUT 229
From the town dock
To Western Head, and back
Out by Duck Harbor and Western Head trails
Back by Cliff, Duck Harbor Mountain, and
Duck Harbor trails
13.5 miles, May 27, 1997

INTRODUCTION—SPRING

The Gulf of Maine acts as a great heat reservoir in the fall to keep temperatures on Mount Desert Island relatively mild almost till Thanksgiving; in spring it has the opposite effect, fighting the influence of longer days and a higher sun, keeping temperatures cool until Memorial Day. Fall in Acadia seems to go on and on, while spring never comes.

The spring of 1997 is a case in point. On the first ten of my fifteen spring hikes—made between February 26 and April 23—snow and ice were major factors to be dealt with. I could have made things easier on myself, but my program called for walking along streamside trails to witness snowmelt and runoff from the slopes firsthand, so I deliberately chose shaded valley trails where ice was sure to linger long after sunnier slopes were clear. I had hiked many of Acadia's ridge trails the preceding summer, so the time had come for the cooler valley trails. I got exactly what I asked for, a closeup look at winter flowing off the land, soaking the soil, preparing the ground for spring.

Four hikes in this group cover relatively level ground because, on the day of my hike, steeper trails were made unsafe by ice. I held the Hio Road near Adams Brook Bridge, Seaside Trail from Jordan Pond House to Seal Harbor, Great Head Trail east of Sand Beach, and Eliot Mountain Trail in reserve for use when steeper valley trails might shorten my hiking career. Two other trails rounded ponds recently freed of ice—Lower Hadlock and Jordan ponds. I saved trails on Isle au Haut for a grand finale to end not only this series of spring hikes but my project of hiking the living trails of Acadia at every season, making sixty hikes in the fifty-two weeks of the year. I had planned to end with a last hike up Sargent Mountain, but changed my plans because the Isle au Haut mailboat only made one trip a day when I was free to hike. I took a day of annual leave on a Tuesday when the boat made both morning and late afternoon trips, squeezing an eight-and-a-half-hour hike between boats.

Three of my spring hikes took me to the summit of Sargent Mountain by different routes, giving me more hikes on Sargent in these essays than any other mountain in the park. I hiked Sargent twice in the fall, once in winter, and twice again in summer, for a total of eight hikes to the summit out of sixty hikes. If that suggests to you that Sargent is my favorite destination in Acadia, I would have to agree. It is not the summit itself that draws me so much as the opportunity to choose from such a variety of routes, each challenging in its own way. I have never found the summit the same on two different hikes, even if made only days apart. The south fork of Hadlock Brook is as different from Sargent Brook as the north fork is from Deer Brook. The Penobscot Mountain, Jordan Cliffs, Grandgent, and Sargent Mountain South Ridge trails all have distinctive flavors of their own. Even the Chasm Brook Trail, which is no longer much of a trail to speak of, is different from the others. So, yes, Sargent Mountain is my favorite because it has so many facets to its personality. I could hike it every day for a month and find it different each time. The three hikes to the summit I made this spring place emphasis where it is deserved.[*]

For the record, although I have made a point of hiking in Acadia every week of the year, I want to state that people who are unfamiliar with the park and its trails should restrict their hikes to the season between May Day and Thanksgiving when they are unlikely to run into snow or ice on the trails. Compared to parks in the Sierras or Rockies, Acadia may seem a genteel, New England kind of place, but it has another side to its character in winter and early spring when even the gentlest slope can be a hazard to the unwary. I chose my winter and spring hikes carefully if not always wisely. Several times I had to abort a hike to fetch my ice creepers, and other times I should have but didn't. I make a day-by-day study of trail conditions throughout the year. Visitors coming to the park cold without that kind of overview are apt to make wrong assumptions about trails higher up based on conditions at sea level. A few hundred feet of elevation can drop the temperature sufficiently to turn fog or rain to ice. It is worth repeating that I ran into ice on two-thirds of my spring hikes (taking spring as running roughly from March through May).

With that caveat, there is no more exciting time to hike in Acadia than in the months when winter slowly relinquishes its hold and summer creeps in. The first buds, first leaves, first flowers—they finally do arrive, making the long siege worth it in the end because without thawing snow and ice to dampen the soil, summer wouldn't amount to much. First buds lead to first birds—thrushes, palm and yellow-rumped warblers, phoebes, ospreys, peregrines, and the troop that follows. To watch an Acadian spring unfurl is one of the joys of a lifetime.

Too, I have known grumpiness at spring's balky advance. It is a joy when it comes, but why does it take so long? My impatience flares in a few of these essays, sometimes vented at the imperfections of my fellow man. Spring is blameless after all, so human weakness offers a handy surrogate for the cause of my frustration at the season's refusal to come when I call. I end these fifteen hikes with Canada May ruby about to bloom, along with starflower, pin cherry, and lady's slipper in the woods, and lilac in town. Right on schedule, my soul recovers and blooms with the rest.

Steve Perrin
Bar Harbor
Spring 1997

---

[*] In years when peregrine falcons nest on Jordan Cliffs, the Jordan Cliffs Trail is closed until fledglings have safely left the cliffs. TRAIL CLOSED signs are posted at each end of the trail.

31—HIO ROAD

From Route 102 North of Adams Brook Bridge
To Seawall Campground, and back
By the Hio Road both ways
4.0 miles, February 26, 1997

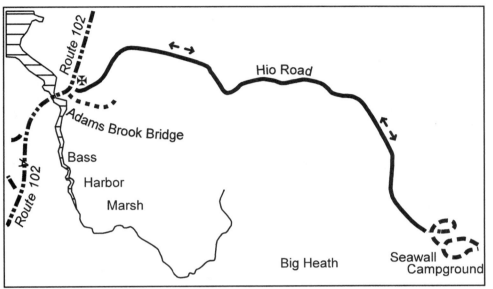

31—Hio Road hike.

Driving south on Route 102 from Southwest Harbor toward Bass Harbor, about where Bass Harbor Marsh first comes into view, I turned left into the gated entrance to the Hio Road just up from Adams Brook Bridge and parked next to a glittering Budweiser beer can tossed into the bushes. Switching off the motor, I heaped my camera bag onto my lap, and my fannypack on top of that. I sat briefly, contemplating the start of my last series of hikes. I had spent much of the winter drawing maps and taking photographs to go with the forty-five hikes I had already made. In only three months—fifteen hikes from now—my manuscript would be done. Then all I had to do was wave my magic wand and turn those words into a book. I looked forward to the hikes, but dreaded the detail work that went with them. To nip that line of thought, I pushed the car door open and stepped onto half an inch of powder snow fallen during the night. Damn the details—onward and upward!

Well, not upward exactly; the Hio Road is pretty flat. It skirts the northern edge of the marsh drained by Adams Brook, so isn't more than seventy-five feet above sea level at any point. As roads go, it is far more than a raw track through the wilderness, in places being built on a raised bed well above the wetlands on both sides. About twelve feet wide and two miles long, it was an ambitious project in its day, requiring load after load of gravel to keep its travelers' feet dry. Now it runs just inside the park boundary around Bass Harbor Marsh and Big Heath. The park calls it a fire road, lending stature to a lane that now goes from Here to

There for no reason at all. Gated at both ends, it is open to snowmobiles in winter and foot traffic year-round.

Hio, a peculiar name. I asked Ralph Stanley where it came from. He said the road is named for Hio Hill, the 170-foot rise toward Southwest Harbor, and the hill was named for Ohio Gros who lived long ago where Mount Height Cemetery is now. He cited Mrs. Thornton's book as the source of his information.*

I selected the Hio Road for the first of my springtime hikes because, though I knew it would be icy like every other road and trail in the park, it was the flattest route I could think of. The dusting of snow in the night covered ice and rock alike, making footing uncertain and dangerous. I carried ice creepers in my fannypack, but never used them. The road was slick but not slippery, partly because it is so flat, partly because I had learned to plant my feet as if the world were glazed with ice, which it had been from late December until now. Last winter was the snowiest winter I could remember, this the iciest. People had had their driveways plowed a dozen times last year, not once this year. Poor plowers. Poor skiers and ski renters. Poor winter hikers. Acadia's trails were deadlier this winter than I've ever known them. Not accepting limits placed by nature on his winter recreation, one man slipped and fell thirty feet, taking the last hike of his life on Champlain Mountain. But a quick look at the slopes told the story, you didn't have to get out of your car to know every trail would be seized with ice. Judgment. That is the one essential piece of gear every hiker must carry. Judgment told me to stick to the Hio Road, and I did as I was told.

Except for a couple of stretches, the road was covered with snow and ice while the woods on either hand were bare. By making forays left or right I could leave winter behind and enter early spring. Early, early spring. This pregnancy didn't show yet, but expectancy was in the air. In my head, at least. Mountain cranberry leaves stood pert and green on the margins of the Hio Road as if it were spring. Lambkill still suffered its wintry droop, but it was nothing a good dose of sunlight couldn't cure. A change of climate would be good for wintergreen, too, which looked unkempt and be-

---

* Mrs. Seth S. Thornton, *Traditions and Records of Southwest Harbor and Somesville, Mount Desert Island, Maine.* Bar Harbor, ME: Acadia Publishing Company, 1988. Originally published 1938. See page 182 for Ohio Gros.

draggled, like other sufferers of cabin fever. Patches of moss shone green and bright all along the way, mostly sphagnum, with pincushion, feather, and hair-cap mosses adding variety. Goldthread carried on business as usual in a few places, not seeming to care what season it was. The same for reindeer lichen on higher ground, and spotted lungwort lichen on maples by the side of the road. Leaf litter, released only last week from its stretch in the icy lockup where it had done time since December, showed signs of drying out. As tan as if it had spent the winter in Key West, the fallen litter glowed with a purple hue. The only fern I saw was last year's bracken, bent and broken, but gleaming with a renewed, coppery glow.

Ice-covered Hio Road rounds Big Heath.

The one sure sign that convinced me winter was not over yet was a number of great boulders still hibernating, moss-furred bodies curled on themselves, extremities gathered in close to conserve body heat. I must have seen three or four of these great beings, which geologists call glacial erratics, but which have become so much a part of the Acadian landscape after 12,000 years, they deserve to be acknowledged as natives. Most of our so-called natives trace their origins back a couple hundred years at best.

Start to finish, the Hio Road passes through thick woods on both sides—largely red spruce, with balsam fir, white pine, white birch, maple, and Northern white cedar mixed in. Sticking to higher ground in a neighborhood where wetlands predominate, the road winds along an upland edge on the verge of boggy, swampy ground. Scrub-shrub swamps were still frozen, inviting me to go skating among alder and maple poles sticking up through the ice. I slalomed among them, enjoying one last chance to trespass without offending summer residents. I also slid out on a frozen pond that shone through the trees as a white line a hundred feet north of the road. When it thawed, it would not advertise itself so boldly. In another few weeks I would have passed it not knowing it was there. About 120 feet long and 60 feet wide, with grassy edges surrounded by woods, it was a perfect rink for me to polish turns and glissades, my last run-through before trials for the winter Olympics.

It wasn't only ice that drew me aside but the woods as well. I love being in the midst of standing and fallen trees, walking among them as I would a group of old friends. I must have known them in a former life. I am sure we share a good number of genes in common, making us members of the same Earthling clan. In quieter moments I assume the character of a red spruce, my hair hanging with cones, roots binding me to the Earth. Acadia offers us communion with our fellow selves, those widespread parts of our being we cannot live without. Life without spruce and Northern white cedar is unthinkable. Any form of government in which they do not have full standing as peers only pretends to be a democracy. True democracy requires representation for all life in the region, not merely one species that presumes to speak and act for all. To treat woods and swamps as lesser forms of life—as natural resources to be managed by us for our exclusive use—is to cut off our arms and legs, to smoke out our lungs, to sell our livers to the highest bidder. Without them we would not be here or anywhere. I ask spruce and cedar how they wish to be used. I listen to what they say. Their answer is unambiguous: their highest and best use is to strive for perfection and success in whatever settings they find themselves, under whatever conditions prevail. Their destiny is *their* destiny, not ours to decide on their behalf. Comes the revolution, spruce and cedar will have their day, and humankind will beg forgiveness for keeping them downtrodden all these years.

At one point a small stream draining the south slope of Hio Hill crosses through a culvert under the road in the midst of a small cedar swamp, the trees forming a canopy over the road, which tunnels beneath their branches as through an arbor. Slender, cut-granite slabs do double duty as guardrails keeping hypothetical vehicles from slipping into the stream and as benches for travelers who wish to linger in that green vicinity. Northern white cedar is not only a beautiful tree, but it has changed the course of history. High in vitamin C, tea made from its leaves warded off scurvy in Jacques Cartier and his crew when they explored the Gulf of St. Lawrence in 1535. Indians had shown them that a drink made from cedar leaves cured and prevented the disease, a deficiency stemming from sailors and explorers eating a restricted diet during long voyages and periods of winter confinement. In gratitude, the French later ennobled the common "new world" tree with the grand Latin name *arborvitae*—tree of life.

Tree of life. Was honor ever more deserved or rightly given? And yet it acknowledges only a smattering of all that cedars do for us—a smattering of a smattering of the debt we owe trees and the kingdom of plants. Tree of life, indeed. Without trees and plants we would have neither arms nor splendid eyesight, lungs nor food to eat. We would not be here or anywhere. We would not *be* at all. The Hio Road is a road back to the roots of our being through aisles of kindred Earthlings, every one a soulmate, a tree of life every one.

Aside from the sleeping boulders and a few outcrops, there are not many rocks to be seen on the Hio Road. This is a lowland trail, a trail of wet land and dense vegetation. Roadmakers cut through only one ledge beyond the stream crossing, reducing the grade to what a team of oxen could easily manage with a full load. A glance at the cut tells you it is not granite, but nothing announces that these are volcanic rocks, rocks that melted and flowed when Eurasian and North American rock rafts collided 400 million years ago (or 600 million years ago, or a billion years ago—geologists are not sure of the date), raising mountains high as the Himalayas, which were cut down a few inches a year by wind, water, and ice for years-after-millions-of-years, leaving Acadia's gentle coastal hills of today.

Volcanoes in Acadia! The thought boggles the mind. Continents careening against one another, smashing head-on, sheets of rock crumpling, twisting, bending downward to be melted by earthheat and friction, to be sent streaming toward the surface to erupt and spread, creating new land from the wreck of old, new ocean floors from recycled sand and silt. Rebounding, Eurasia and North America are still spreading apart, the Atlantic widening every year as it has widened for perhaps 180 million years when the rock rafts making up the supercontinent Pangaea split, first into Laurasia north and Gondwana south, then further divided into the continents as we know them today. The Hio Road brings you into contact with events that took place before dinosaurs were invented, before even fins flicked at the leading edge of creation. And yet nothing draws attention to the story. The mute stones do not boast of their lineage. Humans did not put the picture together until thirty years ago when the pieces fell into place. Read the two-page summary, "Geology of Maine's Shores" in the *Golden Guide to Acadia National Park and the Nearby Coast of Maine* to understand how much we have learned since 1968 when that account was published. Until thirty years ago, geology just happened. This, then this, then this, with no rhyme or reason. Geologically speaking, with a single spark, tectonic plate theory put an end to the Dark

Ages. When similar light is shed on the interdependency between all living beings with enough intensity to illuminate the mind of humankind, the Cenozoic Era will set and what Thomas Berry and Brian Swimme call the Ecozoic Era will dawn, ending the night we now mistake for enlightenment.[*] A revolution in understanding and thought will change the world more than any mere tectonic collision ever could.

It struck me once again as I walked the Hio Road that it is

Northern white cedar, tree of life, in a swamp on the Hio Road.

not possible for a conscious being to be alone in the natural world. We know too much to claim to be free and independent of all others. We are part of them and they of us. By ourselves we do not exist. We exist solely as creatures of this Earth and of its universe. That is what human literally means—Earthling, of the Earth (Latin *humanus,* from Indo-European *dhghomon*, Earthling, Earthbeing, from the root *dhghem-*, Earth). How we have struggled to prove we descend from some other origin, preferring to believe we were fashioned by one divinity or another, or descended directly from the gods, while all along we are children of the universe, direct descendants of supernovas, galaxies, and the great-grandparent of us all, the gleam that ignited the Big Bang. The parentage of that divine spark we cannot guess. The universe happened. And goes on happening. And as it goes, each of us happens as a microparticipant in the process of unfurling. Universe stems from Latin *universum*, one turning. Like it or not, we turn with the whole because we cannot be cut out of it. It is we and we are it. The Hio Road not only stems from intercontinental collisions but from the source of everything that is and everything that ever can be.

---

[*] Brian Swimme and Thomas Berry, *The Universe Story*. San Francisco: Harper San Francisco, 1992.

The Hio Road is where Earthlings walk and come together in communal consciousness, sharing their experience and their being. Take a turn north of Adams Brook Bridge and you are there. In the thick of things. In the universe as it reveals itself to you and through you. If you aren't there now, and feel you haven't been there—go. Get with the universe, the Earth, the Hio Road, and most of all with yourself.

Aside from trees, plants, rocks, and universal thoughts, I had a lot of company on the Hio Road. Virtual company for the most part, company I could see in my mind's eye but could not see in flesh or fur. The snow kept a perfect record of the tracks of all who stepped upon it. I saw fifteen red squirrel tracks, five hare tracks, a tangle of deer tracks, one coyote track coming along a tributary of the Hio Road, one large vole (?) track, and several other signs of animate life. I didn't see a single chickadee or woodpecker; the only wildlife I actually met was a red squirrel in the sprucy offing somewhere which I heard but did not see. Mounds of spruce-cone scales also spoke of red squirrel activity. I saw a gaping ten-inch-diameter hole some thirty feet up in a snag which I thought might have been gouged by a pileated woodpecker or other large cavity-nesting bird. Blueberry twigs in several places had been nipped by hares. As for scats, I saw one large mound of frozen horse dung in the road, and four coyote scats wound with white hair, seed husks, and in one a twisted, white plastic bag.

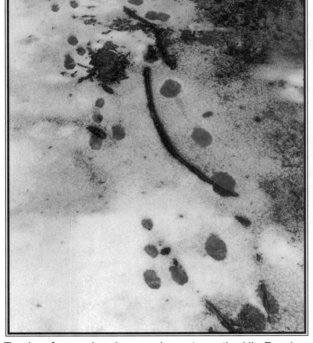

Tracks of snowshoe hare and coyote on the Hio Road.

After inspecting one of the coyote scats, my mind on earthly things, I looked up—into the large round eye of a horse that had come up to me while I was bent down in the road. Wildlife Tracker Caught Off Guard by Galloping Quadruped. Black helmeted, dressed in red, a young woman sat astride the horse. Head turned aside, the horse held its great eye fixed upon me.

"It's OK, he hasn't been ridden in a while," the young woman said, "he won't hurt you."

Why was I surprised she spoke English? Horse and rider came upon me so unexpectedly, they might well have beamed down from an orbiting spaceship. My attention on the horse, her words seemed to come from him. No wonder the Greeks believed in centaurs. I waited for the talking apparition to pass, then continued on my way.

The only other creature I saw was a striding biped in big boots and fluorescent green hat.

"Good day for a walk," he said, overtaking me.

"Not muddy yet," I said, mud being on my mind because I had been looking at tracks made last week when the road was soft.

"Won't be long now," he said, not slackening his stride.

Later, I met the same man returning from wherever he'd been.

"You're getting there," he said, seeming to know where I was going.

Having noticed tracks in frozen mud like the ones he now made in snow, I said, "You've been here before."

"I come out every day," he said. "Try to, anyway."

And he was gone. I would like to have talked with him about his experiences on the Hio Road, but exercise and fresh air were what he was out for, not engagement. I was allowed only those two terse exchanges. What if every conversation were that short? Opening, response, conclusion—one, two, three—then move on. The world's business would get done by a series of microdialogues. Emily Dickenson would be good at that. Shakespeare, too. Schools would change radically, having to teach substance and precision. Class, I want you to write a fifteen word composition about the industrial revolution by tomorrow morning. That would be much harder than taking fifteen hundred words to say the same thing. Think of the paper we would save, the filing, the time, the money. We would have six seconds to get our message across. So much for oratory, lectures, sermons, diatribes. We would have to be brief and upfront, always. On our toes. Quick-witted. Alert. Awake. Receptive. Responsive. Keen. Eloquent in a wholly new sense.

It took me two hours and fifteen minutes to walk the two miles from Adams Brook Bridge to Seawall Campground at my usual, note-taking pace. In the same time, a world-class runner could complete a marathon. It would take me thirty hours to go the distance. But think of the story I could tell when I crossed the finish line, if I ever got there. We crown the least observant among us with laurel leaves, yet what do they contribute to our betterment? The tortoise knows the lay of the land better than the hare. Who cares how long it takes to go the distance? She who gets most from her journey deserves the prize. Many that are first shall be last; and the last shall be first.

The weather cleared as I went along, the sky turning from gray to blue in the course of three hours. The road ahead was hatched with streaks of sunlight, tentatively at first, then brighter and bolder. It was as if the season changed as I walked, winter giving way to spring. The day grew warmer and more luminous. Animal tracks stood out in sharp relief. At Seawall Campground for twenty feet the road turned soft; water stood in the tracks of earlier passers-by. But the Hio Road knew the warming trend was not official. The frozen ground remembered what season it was. On the way back my own waffle prints went ahead of me like Ariadne's thread.

It took me forty-five minutes to cover the same distance that had taken two hours and fifteen minutes going out. As a rule of thumb I have always said my normal hiking pace is three times faster than my note-taking pace. In this case, three-and-a-third times faster. Dividing the time it takes me to complete a hike by three gives a rough estimate how long someone else might take to do the same hike.

When I got back to my car, I picked the Budweiser can out of the bushes to recycle. By Maine's bottle deposit law, I will get a nickel for my trouble. But the hike itself was my reward for going the Hio Road out and back. If a journey is not its own reward, it is probably a waste of time. Laurel wreaths don't tell the whole story any more than empty beer cans do. I'd say the two are worth about the same, a nickel apiece.

ℰ

32—SEASIDE TRAIL

From Jordan Pond
To Seal Harbor, and back
  By the Seaside Trail both ways
      3.8 miles on ice creepers, March 5, 1997

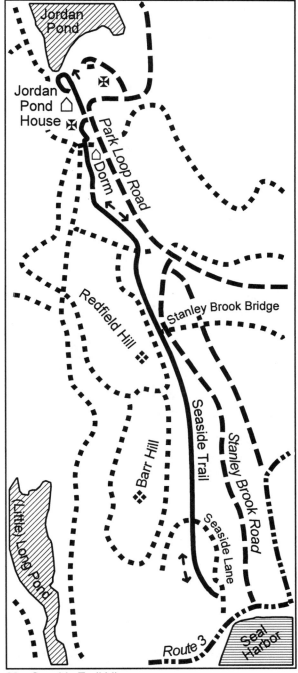

32—Seaside Trail hike.

I met animal tracks but no fellow hikers in the three-and-a-half hours I spent going from Jordan Pond to Seal Harbor and back via the Seaside Trail. For good reason. Four inches of new snow covered the ground, putting a deceptively innocent face on any ice that lay below. Every trail in the park would be treacherous. That is why I selected the Seaside Trail, figuring its easy grade would make ice a nonissue. I got away with that strategy last week on the Hio Road, but not this time.

I backed into the driveway to Jordan Pond House at 9:30 a.m. The parking area is not plowed in winter, so I left my car just off the Park Loop Road, which is plowed only from the junction with Stanley Brook Road to the boat ramp parking area at the south end of Jordan Pond. My plan was to check out the pond, then head south for Seal Harbor.

Being the first one out after a snowstorm is one of life's greatest joys. With roads and walkways erased, there are no rules governing where you can go. The world has been made anew, and you are the first to witness its beauty. Usually, creatures of habit that we are, we get out the snow shovel and start remaking the world as it was. But if we resist that urge and give in to the wonder of the moment, we find ourselves made anew as well, as we were as children awakening to a day when school was called off because of a storm. I remember lying in bed without opening my eyes, listening for sounds from the outside world that would tell me what kind of day it was. Better than the scrape of shovels or the whump of loose tire chains clattering against fenders was the eloquence of a town muffled beneath a foot of new snow, the news conveyed by absolute silence. I did not have to look out the window to know a revolution had swept over the world in the night, and I had been dubbed emperor while I slept.

That is how I felt wending my way across lawns and fields to Jordan Pond, which was an endless meadow of white broken only by a single forest-green fishing shack well out from shore. Jordan Ridge formed the western, Pemetic Mountain the eastern, and the Bubbles the northern boundary of my domain. I had looked out from the south shore of the pond dozens of times over the years, but had never known it as still as this. There was no icy wind blasting out of arctic Canada, no wet wind blowing in from the Gulf of Maine. The only sound was the pouring of the pond into Jordan Stream at the outlet, a rolling, soft fluid whisper. Dusted with snow, the spruce and cedar on the slopes stood as separate

Small prints in meadow below Jordan Pond House.

individuals gathered in some great assembly. At the center of attention, the Bubbles looked radiant and womanly in a train of new lace spread the length of the pond.

I do not need to resort to fantasy to find nature attractive. The more I set aside my own thoughts, the freer nature is to be itself. When we project our limited impressions outward, we risk doing violence to the world. We find old men in the mountains, and if we do not find them, we sculpt them there.

Mount Rushmore is not so much a monument to four presidents as a fragment of our psyche inflicted on the Dakota Hills. When we are tempted to remake nature in the image of our own idols and demons, we stand to learn something about ourselves. To see the Bubbles as magnificent breasts gives us an opportunity to claim one of the images that shapes our perceptions. Once called the Bubbies, those twin peaks have reminded people viewing them from the south end of Jordan Pond of larger-than-life breasts for hundreds, perhaps thousands, of years. We look at one thing and something else comes to mind by an unconscious neural link searching for relevance. Seeing *as,* that is the basis of metaphor, which we don't learn in school but pick up as a means of making the most efficient use of our experience. Why? Because the universe wants us to keep our priorities straight. Our genes will be more likely to survive. We see lakes in the desert for the same reason, using mirages to keep our deepest desire at the forefront of conscious awareness. To go out and actually dig an oasis in the desert—as at Las Vegas—is something else again. To turn such a vision into reality diverts water from sustaining habitats in more suitable places. So we can gamble and play golf where we never did before. When the street thug points a gun at a rival gang member and pulls the trigger, he kills the projected image of the rage in his head due to his own sense of inconsequentiality—but he does nothing to better his condition in the world. Seeing mountains as breasts, or vice versa, tells us more about how we see the world than about the world itself. Metaphor helps us take responsibility for our own perceptions, reminding us that the perceiver is always part of the act.

Celebrating the Bubbles in their fine gown of white lace, I celebrated the bubbles in my head which float from thought to thought. I love my bubbles and hope I will never lose them or mistake them for attributes of flesh-and-blood women, women I will get along with better if I appreciate their actual virtues instead of those I thrust upon them for reasons of my own.

I chose to hike from Jordan Pond to Seal Harbor in order to cross the full width of the earth dam between the pond and the ocean. The dam exists today much as the last glacier left

Red maple tree overlooking Jordan Pond.

it. At the south end of the pond where Jordan Pond House sits on its rise, the glacier left an end moraine of unsorted stones ranging in size from particles of clay to great boulders. Farther seaward, a delta fanned out from the melting ice, streams depositing sand and clay in a shallow inlet of the sea, which was several hundred feet higher then than now (or, more exactly, the land was several hundred feet lower relative to the tide-line of today). Lower still, the glacier deposited a mixture of fine-grained sediments on the deeper floor of the sea in relatively calm water. The Seaside Trail crosses from end moraine to the calm-water deposits, passing over one edge of the sandy delta between the two. The story is told two ways, by the gravel pits where the glacial treasure is still mined, and by the deep-rooted forests that thrive on the thick, well-drained soil of moraine, delta, and sediment alike. For an easy walk among tall trees, the Seaside Trail is an excellent choice. As you go south, think of yourself

walking across the sloping floor of an ancient sea away from the foot of the great ice sheet that blanketed Acadia 12,500 years ago. From an elevation of 297 feet at Jordan Pond House, the trail drops some 250 feet to within 40 feet of the modern high-tide line in Seal Harbor. On the return, you will regain those 250 feet almost without realizing you are walking uphill.

Through woods for about one-and-three-quarters miles, the trail passes just behind the dormitory used in summer by Jordan Pond House workers, then next to a private stable outside the park boundary, and before reentering the park, under the west arch of Stanley Brook Bridge which links the carriage road loop around Day Mountain with the carriage roads around Barr and Redfield hills. The bridge has three arches, one for Stanley Brook, one for Stanley Brook Road, and one for the Seaside Trail. It fits so naturally into the terrain it might well have been set down by the glacier.

From bridge to Seal Harbor, the trail runs a straight course through tall red spruce, balsam fir, white pine, birch, and maple. You know you are near the end when the woods take on a groomed look, seedlings and saplings having been cut away to create a park-like effect. In Seal Harbor the trail ends at a gravel road (Seaside Lane) leading to the highway and the beach beyond. Looking south along the road, I caught a glimpse of salt water. I didn't have to walk in the waves to complete my journey. Mentally if not physically, I had fully crossed the glacial ramp between Jordan Pond and the ocean. What turned me back was the sight of a fire hydrant at the end of the trail, looking like a squat and saucy Lilliputian with a helmet on his head. In his veins, courtesy of the Seal Harbor Water Company, ran the waters of Jordan Pond. I hadn't come that far after all.

The trail crosses a gravel road about where the grooming begins, and just off the trail a great boulder bears a plaque honoring Edward L. Rand, whose name appears with that of Waldron Bates and Herbert Jaques on the first path map of Mount Desert Island east of Somes Sound, issued in 1896. The plaque reads:

TO THE MEMORY OF
EDWARD LOTHROP RAND
IN GRATEFUL RECOGNITION OF
HIS PIONEER SERVICE AND LABOR OF LOVE
IN MAKING KNOWN
THE FLORA OF MOUNT DESERT
AND COMPILING MAPS OF
WOODLAND AND MOUNTAIN PATHS

Rand and Redfield listed nearly 1,500 plants in their book, *Flora of Mount Desert Island, Maine,* printed in 1894. Edgar T. Wherry mentioned 591 plants in his book, *Wild Flowers of Mount Desert Island, Maine,* published in 1928. These are men of legendary repute, setting standards few but the most ardent botanist will approach today.

The Seaside Trail is a great walk—if it isn't too icy.

Boosted by my experience on the Hio Road the week before, I left my ice creepers at home. It is almost spring, I told myself, I won't need them—forgetting that ice is the very herald of spring in Acadia. I started bravely enough, slipping and sliding on the frozen treadway covered by four inches of snow. I made it to the start of the trail just south of Jordan Pond House where the trail to the dormitory enters woods beyond the parking area. The night-lights mounted on logs for the benefit of staff returning after dark looked like stiff little R2D2s in parade dress with white caps. The trees overhead hurled great clots of snow into the trail, creating an array of craters reminding me of prints made perhaps by drunken hares dancing wildly on their toes. In self-defense, I put up the hood of my parka, but soon took it off because I felt isolated from my surroundings. I wore my watch cap the rest of the way, taking only one direct hit which wet me, notebook, and camera case with one load of icy shrapnel. Halfway down the line between the lights, I heard a woodpecker drumming on a resonant limb far in the woods—a sure sign that spring was in the offing. That sound thrills me like the call of wild geese, speaking to some primal hormone that flows in my blood. The shadow of an unseen bird raced ahead of me in the trail as if supporting the woodpecker's proclamation.

The Seaside Trail.

At the carriage road opposite Jordan Pond Gate, I turned west around a sign listing the rules of carriage road use. As I remember them: thou shalt not ride or walk on the left; thou shalt not pass without warning; thou shalt not speed; thou shalt not alarm horses; thou shalt not walk dogs unleashed; and thou shalt not ride (horses or bicycles) off road—words to that effect. In fifty feet I turned south behind the dormitory onto the Seaside Trail proper. A fallen spruce blocked the trail, but a sign bolted at eye level to a tree pointed to **SEAL HARBOR**, and another a few feet farther on clinched the message with a terse **SEASIDE**.

I skated past the dorm with its parking area into tall woods, heading directly toward the sun, which lit up the falling clots of snow like comets pelting the Earth. Overhead a bird trilled a heartening note, but it didn't make the trail any less slippery. I stuck it out for twenty minutes, almost falling several times, my feet compressing snow into crude

skates which took my feet where the ice wanted them to go. I tried walking on the edge of the trail, but that was just as icy. After twenty minutes of determined labor, my feet suddenly twisted sideways, my arms flung wide, and my pencil flew twenty feet into the woods. I knew when I was licked. Turning around, I exited via the dorm parking area, got in my car, and drove back for my creepers, taking fifty-five minutes to cover twenty-three miles. Parking again in the blocked-off entrance to the dormitory, I strapped on my creepers (the real kind with spikes under both ball and heel, the only kind to get) and made a fresh start.

The same thing happened again. Snow clumped on the bottom of my creepers so the spikes couldn't get a grip on the ice. I slipped as badly as before. It wasn't supposed to be like that. Now what? I tried planting my feet with determination, but that just packed the snow all the more, making the footing slipperier. I had to walk without getting snow under my creepers. How was I to do that? If you can't walk, shuffle. That's what I did, the Seaside shuffle, all the way to Seal Harbor and back, never lifting my feet above the snow, pushing the snow ahead with my toes, keeping the spikes no more than an eighth of an inch from the ice. Sounds dumb, but it worked. I never slipped once, thought the trail was slick much of the way. And by clearing the snow from the ice with my boots, I had an easier time on the return, being able to take normal steps, giving my spikes a chance to dig in the way they were meant to.

While I was battling the ice for control, I couldn't take my eyes off my feet, so didn't see much of the landscape around me. Once I got the hang of the Seaside shuffle, I began to look around and enjoy the hike. I saw mountain cranberry and wintergreen leaves poking through the snow, a patch of ground pine (tree club moss), and hair-cap moss. Scale moss (three-lobed bazzania) dripped from its perch on top of a cut through the only ledge I saw from the trail. Many tree stems were wrapped with a layer of lichens, bright green lungwort being the most conspicuous. Bracket fungi (conks) each bore their burden of snow like white epaulets. Several dead trees sprouted miniature fungal fans with striking bands of light and dark earth tones.

But it was the trees along the trail that got most of my attention. Not so much as individuals but as corporate groups. Woods. The primal northern coniferous forest. Aftermath of the great Laurentian ice sheet. Currently, the leading edge of ongoing creation in these parts. That's where the Seaside Trail took me—to the heart of the bioregion, much of it in private ownership at the time. Great forests of birch, hemlock, and white pine have had their time in the sun. Since the 1700s, about the time European settlements took hold in the region, the red spruce has reigned supreme. Maine is miscalled the Pine Tree State; the most noble white pines were felled and taken out long ago. The growth of red spruce is now the highest and best use of much of the state. Not because paper companies say so, but because the local climate, soil, and terrain say so. The so-called old seed folk were latecomers; the old seed trees were here long before they shipped in. To meet a true native, walk up to a red spruce and introduce yourself. Then listen to what it has to say. That would be oral history worth writing down. Spruce can live 300 years. Think of the storms their branches can recount, the floods, the droughts, the wintry blasts, the nestlings fledged, the insect swarms, the starry nights. The saga is written in their rings, one sentence a year, to be told only upon death. Walking among these silent annalists, I could only guess what their groans and sighs meant to convey. Their body language was more eloquent, telling of the decades of struggle and perseverance it took to lift the canopy to its present height at ten to eighteen inches of growth a year, every season a challenge met and overcome, every year a triumph of coniferous will.

To walk the Seaside Trail is to walk among genius. What else does it take to lift water and nutrients out of the soil to a height of sixty or ninety feet; to combine it with carbon dioxide extracted from the air to produce sugar by a sustainable, solar-powered process giving off oxygen and water as byproducts; and then to distribute that vital food throughout a massive body to support every life function including growth, repair, defense, and reproduction? Could any of us do the same? Could Mozart, Plato, or Leonardo? Genius, like I said.

I encountered several signs of animal life on this hike, of creatures not rooted firmly to glacial deposits but able to move freely among the trees as direct beneficiaries of the standing tribes. I heard the woodpecker love song as I said, the trilling bird, and calls of chickadees, nuthatches, crows, ravens, mourning doves, and a red squirrel or two. I saw the fleet shadow of a spirit bird, and twice the corporeal shadow of a raven flying across an opening in the canopy, conversing with a stationary raven I took to be its mate perched on the far side of Stanley Brook. Ravens are gregarious and talkative birds, but this conversation had the added zest of a love affair. In Maine, ravens typically lay eggs the last week in March, so that interpretation is not far-fetched. Love is blind to the present because its gaze is on bringing the future into being. I took the amorous raven overhead as a sure sign of spring. Springtails (snow fleas) confirmed that reading, hopping about on the trail in their own wild rite, bodies painted blue, massing by the thousand. Passing under Stanley Brook Bridge a second time, I met an insect trying its wings in the chill air, not exactly whizzing but staying aloft. Once the lesser winged tribes take to the air, the greater are upon them. Warblers and blackflies go together, like bluefish and pogies.

New snow on the trail recorded the imprint of everyone who had come that way in the past twelve hours. I saw one squirrel track, three snowshoe hare tracks, six vole tracks (in the meadow by the pond), and a mile apart, the track of coyote and fox. The fox had walked in the trail for only a few feet, the coyote had slowed from a gallop to a trot over the course of several hundred feet. On the return leg of the hike I saw where a more recent coyote track ran in my own for a considerable distance. I had been followed without knowing. The Presence had been keeping an eye on me, seeing what I was up to. This tracker had been tracked.

Ravens will be ravens; snow fleas, snow fleas; coyotes, coyotes; people, people—each answering in its own way at every moment the force that drives the keen, creative edge of the universe through us, carving out our destinies. Acadia is the place where I am most aware of that edge. I am not *on* it so much as *in* it. It is what I am. I am that edge personified—the universal force shaped and given life. No, not *given* life, as if I were somehow separate from it. I *am* life,

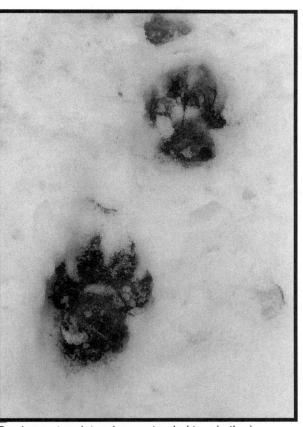

Fresh coyote prints, claws extended to grip the ice.

the living presence—as coyote and raven *are* life in their own ways. Together, we are the origin of the universe in modern guise. We are the energy, the force, the presence, the leading edge. Here for a time, then left behind as others bear the edge forward, and forward, and forward without stopping. Our job is to keep the creative edge sharp and bright as a woodsman's axe. The force doesn't make us; we hew ourselves. For the moment, we *are* the universe, bearers of

another can best be said in language that goes from heart to heart without being put into words at all. Acadia brings out that ability in us, letting us share in the presence of springtails and coyotes, be in their world, live on the same planet they do as equal brothers and sisters under the same gleaming star.

Ice creepers, my artificial claws.

White pine tree near Upper Breakneck Pond.

its creativity and forward thrust. Peers, every one. When we meet, a spark of recognition jumps between us. I am with them, they with me—children of the universe.

When I hike I take part in a higher order of consciousness. Not that I think more elevated thoughts, but new thoughts appear in me that I never had before. Acadia affects my mind, enlarging it, giving it depth and a broader scope. It is a new person who thinks these thoughts and shares in these experiences. That is what Acadia does, it renews us, extending us into the natural world where we experience new things, and old things in new ways. We become natural ourselves, understanding natural language and natural signs. Nature speaks. We understand. We were born to this exchange. This is our native tongue. Earthspeak, the Earthling language. Spoken on every continent by every tribe. It makes our everyday chatter among ourselves seem like the buzzing we ascribe to insects. What we really have to say to one

33—BREAKNECK & CARRIAGE ROADS LOOP

From park headquarters off Route 233
To Hulls Cove, and back
   Out by the Breakneck Road
   Back by carriage roads
        5.4 miles on snowshoes, March 12, 1997

Here it was almost spring, and winter was digging in its heels. It had snowed every other day since my last hike a week ago, stifling the hopeful reemergence of mosses and low plants under a thick shroud of white. Ice hidden beneath a foot of snow made mountain trails dangerous. I wanted yet another relatively level trail to see me through this time of trial. How about Great Head? Icy. Eliot Mountain? Icy. The Breakneck Road? Icy, but so what! It was the level hike I was looking for, making a loop by returning on the Witch Hole Pond Carriage Road, giving me a tour of seven ponds in four hours. We had had so little snow till now, I had given up on snowshoes for the winter, but they turned out to be the perfect footwear for mid-March.

The Breakneck Road runs north–south for two-and-three-quarters miles between Eagle Lake Road (Route 233) and Route 3 in Hulls Cove, passing through park land the whole way, except for the road itself which is not a park road. The slender right-of-way is still owned (but not maintained) by the Town of Bar Harbor, a gash of mud, gravel, and ledge that appeals to the owners of all-terrain vehicles and snowmobiles. The name says it all. But paved with a foot of new snow, it is an inviting lesser byway that gives access to over two-and-a-half miles of the park. The road starts off the north side of Eagle Lake Road at the top of the steep incline up from Eagle Lake, and ends by the General Store in Hulls Cove, passing the Tool Barn on the way into town.

I made my outing into a loop by bushwhacking from the Breakneck Road to the trail connecting the park visitor center with the Paradise Hill Carriage Road. I was prepared to go all the way to Route 3, then walk along the highway to the start of the Paradise Hill Road, which would take me to the connector. But the beaver pond near Hulls Cove was frozen, giving me an easy way to cross Breakneck Brook without having to go all the way to the highway. I followed the carriage road south almost to Eagle Lake, bushwhacking again to regain the Breakneck Road, avoiding a steep uphill stretch of Eagle Lake Road.

I had worked till noon, eaten lunch, then started out, my mind still on workish things. Carrying snowshoes, I walked from park headquarters to the unmarked southern end of the Breakneck Road, merely an opening in roadside trees. Testing the snow, I sank in eight inches. Snowshoes it was. I put them on and started out, not knowing what I was looking for. As always, the park made the transition from work to the here-and-now easy. A blue jay called, then a chickadee—and I was there, my brain keeping up with my feet for over four

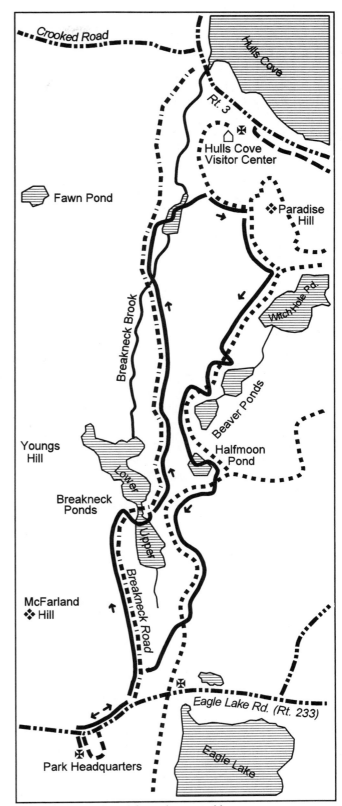

33—Breakneck Road & carriage road loop.

hours. I hadn't planned it that way, but the loop gave me a good tour of seven ponds, all frozen, all crossed with fox tracks, containing nine beaver lodges in all, each looking like an igloo woven by a work crew of Fiji Islanders. Surrounded by spruce and white pines, frozen and covered with snow, the ponds gleamed like moonstones in a setting of jade. Most were crossed by a single set of fox prints linking several beaver lodges, the prints passing over the tops of the lodges, which I was sure the fox marked with its scent. There were two lodges in Upper Breakneck Pond, three in the pond on Breakneck Brook near Hulls Cove, three in Witch Hole Pond, and one in a beaver pond flowing into Witch Hole Pond. There were probably others I didn't see. The upper beaver pond above Witch Hole was dammed by a graceful thirty-foot span of branches and twigs which the Bureau of Reclamation would be proud to take credit for. The beavers had modeled their dam on the rainbow's arch, curve pointing upstream, ends solidly braced on either side against higher ground.

The temperature hovered at 25° during the four-hour hike, a cold northwest wind adding a bite of its own where it swept over the ponds. The sky was a cloudless dome of blue. The clarity of the air was stunning. Dorr and Cadillac mountains three miles away seemed to loom over Witch Hole Pond undimmed by haze or fog. Admiring that view, I saw an eagle gliding into the wind, soaring without flapping from the slopes of Cadillac to the middle of the pond, above which it slowly spiraled upward toward the apex of the blue dome. Two women on skis came by, distracting me from the bird.

"Icy," I said, stating the obvious, having noted the glaze in carriage road ski trails.

"The way I ski," said one woman, "it doesn't matter."

As they passed north I tried to find the eagle again, but it had dissolved in the seamless blue sky. Later, the same women overtook me near the end of my hike.

"You got your exercise today," I said, standing aside to let them by.

"Now for the hot tub!" the same spokeswoman said.

I thought that was it for fellow travelers, but in the last few feet on the Breakneck Road near its southern end I met a youth and child riding a three-wheeler, the child astride the gas tank, wedged between the youth's outstretched arms. They were covered head-to-toe in warm clothing, only the glint of their eyes hinting at the life within. The driver stopped and peeled back the flap protecting his face from the wind.

"Did you go the whole way?" I think he said over the idling motor.

I nodded, not wanting to shout.

"How long will it take, two hours?"

Not knowing how fast he could go, I shrugged.

"The road is washed out in two places," I shouted.

The youth nodded as he refastened his flap, and they were off, snarfing their way through the snow as through clouds of stiff meringue.

If gods were delivered by machines these days as they were in old plays to make the plot work out, they would come on three-wheelers. Castor and Pollux would arrive in one-piece snowsuits, whip off their masks and say, "Hey, little lady, you look like you could use some help," then proceed to save the heroine's day. Delivered by stage ma-

Dorr and Cadillac mountains over Witch Hole Pond.

chinery, gods help us make things work out the way we want, or if they don't, to help us keep trying with grace. We can't seem to go it alone; we need their aid to put things in order. So when we ask their help—Shazam!—they come, just like that. Gods are a means of pulling ourselves up by our bootstraps, a metaphorical trick of the mind empowering us to do the impossible and bear the unendurable. When we meet them face-to-face, they turn out to be a kid and his brother on an ATV. Appearing out of nowhere, surely they have a message for us.

We have a saying, "Don't kill the messenger," meaning don't blame the bearer of bad news for the events he relates. That makes sense. But it is strange we don't have a comparable saying, "Don't laud or love the messenger," reminding us not to credit the bearer of good news as its author, which makes equally good sense. We are particularly susceptible to messengers bearing glad tidings. That is how we have survived the past 35,000 years through an ice age that tested the mettle of every creature on Earth. By painting cave images of the gods who brought game; by carving figures of sky gods and earth goddesses, by inscribing the words of gods who spoke our native tongue, and the stories of prophets who showed us the true road of life—we have shown our love for the messengers who brought news about how we should live and how we should die.

The Sumerians saw the planets moving across the night sky as messengers or, as we would say today, angels (from Greek *angelos*, messenger). The Sumerian gods in their heaven among the stars made their will known to humankind through messages coded in planetary positions and relationships, a belief preserved in the teachings of modern astrology. Patterning their lives on the dictates of the luminous gods, the Sumerians saw the good life as lived on Earth as it is in heaven. The stars and planets were the shapers of their deep beliefs.

The shapers of my beliefs are the spruce tree, the mountain cranberry, the wood fern, the snowshoe hare, the fox, the chickadee, the mountain spring, the north wind, the rain, and the sun. I revere the damp soil beneath my feet and the sky above my head, comets and galaxies, hydrogen atoms and ladybugs. They bring the same news: planet Earth still spins on its axis, the seasons progress, the universal force that kindles life in our diverse bosoms—and the complementary force that douses it every time—are all in good order. The sun will set tonight and rise tomorrow. The cycles of life continue. New beings will rise as others fall. The great dance will go on.

That seems a large thought to squeeze out of a small apparition, which the abrupt appearance of two boys on a three-

Breakneck Brook.

wheeler certainly was, given my state of mind at the time. The key element was surprise. I was not expecting to meet any such machine. Full of my hike, I was caught off guard, so my mind compensated by speeding up and trying new channels. It made sense at the time, under circumstances I cannot now re-create.

Other signs and visitations I received on this hike included crow tracks in the snow, dog tracks near Hulls Cove and along the carriage road, seven fox tracks, three snowshoe hare tracks, eleven deer tracks, nineteen red squirrel tracks, and the track of a single porcupine waddling through hip-deep snow (gauged by its hips, not mine). Then there were the rooted apparitions of which white pine, spruce, and white birch stood out among alder, balsam fir, tamarack, hemlock, Northern white cedar, red pine, pitch pine, aspen, beech, gray birch, maple, oak, and ash. Their unassuming presence was sufficient to nurture my faith. The birches stole the show, sunlight striking their bark, making it gleam across the ponds. In summer they are overshadowed by their own leaves, but in winter their white bark comes into its true glory. Even gray birches looked beautiful, many of them bowing in graceful arches, brought low by the burden of snow caught in their twigs. Dark spruce and fir saplings rising in the midst of the glowing stand told me the birches' winter glory was not without end. They have their day in the sun, then in thirty years will be gone when the evergreens overtake them. They were born of the great fire that swept this part of Acadia in 1947. Birches are the living memory of that blaze. But not for long; nature is quick to forgive and forget.

The white pines surrounding the ponds and wetlands along my route looked god-like, indeed. Reaching over and crowding out other trees from the shoreland, they co-opted the sunlight, their branches thriving under ideal conditions.

Even the snags sticking up in the wetlands I passed looked regal and magnificent. Standing dead trees are common in wetlands, particularly where beavers dam the outlet, raising the water level, cutting off air from living roots. Every pond has its share of standing and fallen poles, blasted smooth by the wind, bleached by the sun. I saw several nesting holes carved out by little wanderers in need of shelter. The gods help those who help themselves. That is the essential wisdom at the core of every religion. Allah watches over all, but even so I will tie up my camel for the night.

I saw no signs of moss, ferns, or other lowly plants. A few lambkill and huckleberry twigs poked above the snow, but their day was yet to come.

The ponds I came to on this loop were, first, Upper and Lower Breakneck Pond, then a beaver pond on Breakneck Brook near Hulls Cove, Witch Hole Pond, two more beaver ponds, Halfmoon Pond, and the Breaknecks again on my return. The Breakneck Road crosses the treeless neck separating its two namesake ponds, the culvert there no longer doing its job, so the road passes through a ten-foot ford where the water was eight inches deep. The ponds being frozen, I detoured around the ford on the ice. My maps show both ponds as having the same elevation, 253 feet, but clearly the upper one was higher by a foot or two, a quick-flowing stream running downhill between them, south to north. A quick-flowing stream of cold air ran the other way, the two ponds lying along the axis of the northwest wind as well. I didn't dally out on the ice, but the view across the open expanse of white on each pond kept whispering for my attention. The clearness of such winter views makes them seem wholesome and refreshing. I drank in the view to north and to south, with a shot of wind for a chaser, then went on.

The road heads on through red and pitch pines, then heads into the valley carved by Breakneck Brook on its rush to Hulls Cove, the descent slow at first, then dropping rapidly to the brook, which the road crosses at a second, wider ford where the stream leaves its narrow valley and enters a floodplain about a mile south of the cove. Highlanders may have less fertile soil, but lowlanders run the risk of frequent floods. Witness recent events in Ohio and Kentucky where floodplain dwellers got their feet wet up to their necks. Beavers had dammed the lower end of the plain, creating a pond where three of their lodges hove above the ice. The pond crowds the road to the side of the valley, where it passes between water on the east and rocky outcrops on the west. Again, the view across the pond was strikingly beautiful, the field of pure snow on the pond leading across to a stand of white pines whose needles glistened like green fur. Not wanting to walk along Route 3, and not knowing if I could cross the brook farther on, like the fox before me I took a shortcut over the ice to the northeastern shore and, like the fox, checked each of the three beaver lodges in turn. I didn't see or hear any signs of beaver, but I felt a beaver presence which, along with the presence of hibernating chipmunks, skunks, woodchucks, and others would soon animate the park not as a mere idea or possibility but as a famished reality. Nothing about the scene specifically suggested spring, but spring was latent in the angle at which sunlight fell on the snow, and I knew the entire scene could change in a week.

Witch Hole Pond is 100 feet higher than the beaver pond on Breakneck Brook, elevation I gained along the connecting trail rising across the slope of Paradise Hill northeast of the pond. I couldn't see the trail until I came across it in the woods, but I knew it would be there. **GABE** and **MARGHERITA** had been there before me, scratching their names beneath a heart on a trailside birch in 1993. **AIRIKA** (or her admirer) had cut her name in capital letters on the next tree up the slope. The connector leads to Signpost 1 on the carriage road system, which offered me a choice: **PARADISE HILL** or **EAGLE LAKE** and **WITCH HOLE**. I turned south toward Eagle Lake. Passing a snowy wetland on the west, I came to Signpost 2 where again I chose **EAGLE LAKE**. That stretch of carriage road runs along the western side of Witch Hole Pond, and opens onto a view of Dorr and Cadillac

above the wooded southern shore. That's where I saw the eagle and first met the two skiers.

As I was surveying the frozen pond, my mind stumbled across the memory of the commercial slogan, *the pause that refreshes.* A strange thought for such an uncommercial place. My refreshment didn't cost me any intake of caffeine, calories, or chemicals, and the exercise I put into my excursion did me more good than reaching for a soda. From an

Beaver lodge, pond on Breakneck Brook.

advertising executive's point of view, Acadia in maple sugar season would be a menthol cigarette kind of place. Imagine being fooled into thinking you could share in the allure of Acadia by fouling your lungs with smoke. Again, we trick ourselves into loving the messenger who brings us the pretty ads, getting hooked on caffeine, nicotine, and alcohol as a result, making billions of dollars for the messenger companies while impoverishing ourselves, our families, and all of society. Ruled by business and industry as we are, we fulfill Adam Smith's vision of a nation governed by shopkeepers in which all the people are raised up to be customers. That has become the American dream, the dream of all industrialized nations, and is fast becoming the dream of nonindustrialized nations as well.

The next two ponds I came to were small wetlands draining into Witch Hole Pond from the southwest, white oases surrounded by dark evergreen woods. The second with its beaver dam and lodge held an impressive forest of dead trees killed by water rising behind the dam. Even in death many of the trees stood tall and straight as they had in life while others leaned toward the pond and some had fallen into it, creating a stark shrine to what might have been in drier days.

Halfmoon Pond anchors the stream along which the other ponds are strung, springs keeping it full to overflowing. It is a compact gem of a pond—small, round, and surrounded by woods, notably on the south. Carriage roads run near it on north, east, and south, leaving it open to the west facing Youngs and McFarland hills. It was iced over like the other ponds I came to, creating a circular white dial on which tall poles on the south cast their shadows for those who would tell the time. My watch had stopped that morning, and my first thought had been to buy a new battery after work, or a new watch if necessary. I felt I needed a watch when I hiked.

Carriage road near the Breakneck Ponds.

But then I thought about that. Why did I want to import Eastern Standard Time into Acadia? What difference did it make how long it took me to get from here to there? Did I care? Did anyone else? So I put off getting a new battery, noting only the time I left my apartment at park headquarters and the time I got back. I could see the sun getting lower as I went along, providing an unconscious sense of the hour if not the minute. Certainly not the second. Walking out onto the face of Halfmoon Pond, I could tell exactly what time it was—the only time of any importance—*now,* the only time it ever is. Every hike I have ever taken has been in the now, the intersection of my reality with the reality of Acadia—that's where the action is. Occasionally I slip into other time zones and live on others' time, but not for long. Without a TV I don't rush home to catch the opening of any show, or time my bodily functions to coincide with commercial breaks. I run by local time always, which is never slow or

fast, local referring to the locus of my consciousness, whether dream, illusion, reminiscence, anticipation, or perception. It all happens in the here-and-now, which no watch can ever capture or measure off.

I started to cross Halfmoon Pond to avoid going around by carriage road, but some intuition warned me not to, so I turned for the nearest shore and went round from there. After the coming thaw my route would be boggy and impassable, so I enjoyed my version of walking on water while I could. Regaining the carriage road on the far side, I soon saw Lower Breakneck Pond through the trees, then the upper pond, the first I had come to heading north earlier on. Continuing, after the carriage road crossed a small stream draining into the Breaknecks, I bushwhacked upslope among mixed woods, glad to be off the beaten path again. Coming to Breakneck Road, I met the ATV riders, then walked up Eagle Lake Road to park headquarters, completing my loop four hours after I started, though my personal clock, which had stopped at now, said it was the same time I had started out.

❦

Woods along the Hadlock Brook Trail.

34—SARGENT MOUNTAIN via HADLOCK BROOK TRAIL

From Norumbega Mountain parking area
To Sargent Mountain summit, and back
By the Hadlock Brook Trail both ways
4.0 miles on ice creepers, March 19, 1997

It was taps for the winter of 1996–97. Tomorrow was the vernal equinox. Where could I go to pay my last respects? Where else?—the summit of Sargent Mountain, Acadia's second highest but most sacred peak. Sacred because most exposed to sunlight, starlight, storms, and the elements, yet not visited by a human horde because it can't get there by car. To stand next to the great cairn at the top is to stand at the navel of the universe. Here is the crux and measure of Acadia, the standard against which all other places in the park are gauged. To hold up in comparison to Sargent is to rank high among Acadia's holiest places. What better site to say farewell to winter and welcome to spring?

The Hadlock Brook Trail is the most direct route to the top. Starting from the Norumbega Mountain parking area in Brown Mountain Notch on Route 198 above Upper Hadlock Pond, the trail follows Hadlock Brook much of the way up, tying into the Sargent Mountain South Ridge Trail half a mile from the summit. It is close to two miles long, making a four-mile trip to the summit and back. Hadlock Falls and Waterfall Bridge are landmarks three-quarters of a mile from the start. Above the bridge, the trail follows along the brook, rising steeply in places, then leaves the brook behind to make a direct assault up the ridge. The trail gives access to the network of trails on the western side of the mountain—the Parkman Mountain Trail, Bald Peak Trail, Maple Spring Trail, and Birch Spring Trail—each offering its own variant route to the summit.

Rising through the watershed of the Hadlock Ponds, the Hadlock Brook Trail gives the hiker a close-up view of the local bioregion at work. Until it gains the ridge, the trail passes through a heavily wooded valley. Near the pond, Northern white cedars thrive in a damp outwash plain deposited at the foot of the last glacier. From there the trail rises through mixed woods clinging to thin, rocky soil up to the wind-stunted spruce hunkering for protection below the ridgeline. Red spruce predominate, mixed with white pine, maple, birch, beech, and a variety of other trees. In winter the woods have an open look, sunlight shining through where it would be blocked by leaves from late spring until early fall. From ground level, the trees look tall and dignified, each holding its head erect, forming a collective canopy of needles and branches seventy feet overhead.

When spring really comes, the trees will be the first to get the news, letting it gradually filter down to the commoners below. The watershed is built in layers—bedrock, thin soil and roots, ground cover plants, straight stems, and the high green garden where air and water are wrought into sugar by means of energy supplied by the sun, creating a habitat for myriad bacteria, fungi, insects, spiders, amphibians, and the occasional mammal. Without water seeping downslope

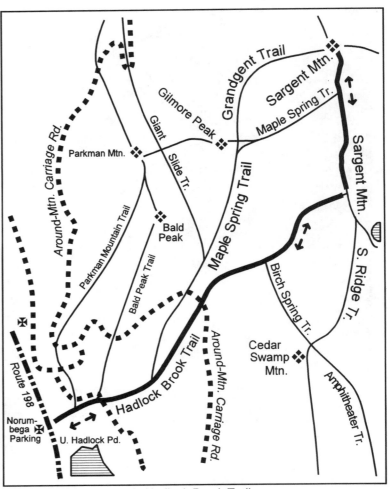

34—Sargent Mountain via Hadlock Brook Trail.

through the soil, the entire enterprise would collapse. The valley terrain keeps a trickle of moisture available to roots through the growing season, giving trees sufficient time to work the magic of photosynthesis. Hadlock Brook carries off what excess water the trees can spare, supporting life in the ponds below, and the town of Northeast Harbor beyond.

Whether as microbe or salamander, striped maple or haircap moss, to reside in the watershed of the Hadlock Ponds is to share the ways of the local bioregion, the lifestyle of planet Earth here and now. A trek along the Hadlock Brook Trail gives hikers a chance to see local stylists at work, putting Earth forces to communal use. Climate, terrain, precipitation, bedrock—all play a role in the process, producing life suited to this place in this clime. Here is nature's local idiom in daily use, a maritime dialect of the northern mixed forest that stretches in the U.S. from New England through northern Michigan and Wisconsin to northeastern Minnesota. Bioregions are places where a particular lifestyle predominates because it is best suited to local conditions. In Acadia the prevailing style is that of the northern hardwood-spruce forest. To see what that looks like, hike the Hadlock Brook Trail at different times of year. The landscape will look familiar to New Yorkers and New Englanders because it is similar to landscapes found throughout much of the region. We have taken in its style from our earliest days, if not in mother's milk, in grandfather's maple syrup and grandmother's blueberry jam.

In nature, style is the essence of survival. Each individual's style is suited to the style of its favored habitat. Warblers eat insects; they thrive where insects abound. Sparrows typically eat wild fruits and seeds of weeds and grasses; they thrive where fruits and seeds abound. Home is where we thrive, where our personal style reflects the style of our surroundings. Anywhere else we are out of our element and don't feel like ourselves. That the universe makes sense to us at all is due to our finding a niche within it that feels like home, a niche where we are rewarded for

The snowy course of Hadlock Brook.

being who we are. Everywhere else we are at risk, our style clashing with unfamiliar surroundings. Sanity stems from being where we belong; insanity from being out of place. How terrible to possess a personal style that has no counterpart in the natural (or cultural) world, to be an outcast forever, to have no place that feels like home. If we can find no unity or logic in the world around us (that is, nothing that reflects the unity and logic of ourselves), we are homeless and lost. That is what war or the sudden loss of a loved one does to us in turning our familiar dream of reality into a nightmare where nothing will ever be the same again. Peace restores us to our dreaming if not to our former dream, to the state in which our surroundings seem welcoming and familiar, helping us to accept the fact that we are who we are.

French philosopher Marcel Merleau-Ponty saw perception as a form of communion between our bodies and our surroundings, a primal faith placing us in the world as in our native land. The reason we make sense of the world is because it reflects our sensory explorations while we in turn reflect its possibilities of discovery. If we find order around us, that is because we are born of that same order. To come into the world is to join the Earthling order that created us and gave us life. We habitually screen ourselves out of our perceptions, but we are at the core of our earthly experience—and Earth is at the core of our core. To walk through the watershed of the Hadlock Ponds is to walk through the bioregion from which we have sprung as naturally as cones spring from the branch of a white pine. What nurtures the pine nurtures us; what threatens the pine threatens us. We belong to one community, one habitat, one bioregion of the Earth. We and the pine are of the same stock.

The ridge to which the Hadlock Brook Trail leads belongs to another bioregion altogether. Subalpine, it is peopled not by stately spruce and maple but by stunted sheep laurel, blueberry, huckleberry, and their ilk. Where tall trees on the slopes moderate the harshness of the climate, plants on the ridge are exposed to extreme daily and seasonal conditions. It is a wonder anything survives there at all. Snow on the ridge was about two feet deep, except where it had been scoured down to bare granite by the wind. The snow was packed and rippled, smoothing the terrain, inviting hikers to stray off the trail marked by cairns. The crust held my weight for the most part, giving way every ten or twelve steps, pitching me down and forward when one foot would drop eighteen inches without warning. Occasionally I fell, instinctively thrusting out my arms, punching two holes in the snow, spraying icy crystals up my sleeves and down my neck.

Twigs poked up through the snow in a few places like bony fingers through a dungeon grate, pleading not for alms but kinder treatment from the weather. In one place I almost stepped on a quaking stem with three empty seed capsules sticking out of the snow, remains of what I felt sure was a wood lily like those I had seen in late July and early August scattered across the ridge. Both memorial and harbinger, the hardy little stalk lived in my experience as well as in its mountain setting, an example of exactly the kind of perception Merleau-Ponty was talking about, the outer arousing the inner, the inner reaching out in anticipation of the outer, together building a conjunct reality that would not exist without either. "The sensible gives back to me what I lent to it," Merleau-Ponty wrote, "but this is only what I took from it in the first place."*

The cairn on the summit of Sargent Mountain might well mark the burial of some ancient warrior-king or beneficent queen from whom we as a people trace our line of descent. It stands like a barrow against the horizon, a monument to our heritage, lest we forget. It is our local version of a pyramid, built to anchor humankind to something solid against our drifting on the gyre of life experience. The universe has many centers and this is one, a kind of benchmark to help us orient ourselves to the local scene. When I reached it, I looked around for signs of human life, but didn't see another soul, not even a rising column of smoke. Mountains and islands, the deep blue Gulf of Maine, sky above, snow and granite at my feet, but nothing moving, nothing to deny my sense of being alone on Mount Desert Island, alone in Maine, alone on Earth and in the universe. Alone, yes, but not lonely. Not empty. I was full to the brim.

In unspoken, preverbal form, an incipient thought kernel welled up in my being, "I own all this." Sensing the absurdity of such a conceit, I immediately corrected myself: "All this owns me." Not in so many words, but felt in the part of my experience from which the urge to speech originates. I felt I was a creature of my surroundings. The sun was dropping toward its rendezvous with the horizon due west of where I stood; the gibbous moon was rising above Pemetic and Cadillac in the east; comet Hale-Bopp was coursing unseen in its great ellipse around us all. Standing next to the summit cairn, I was at peace with the universe.

"Hail, Hale-Bopp," I said to the unseen wanderer in the northern sky, the only words I spoke throughout the hike.

I listened for an answer but heard only the wind.

Ownership. How did such an idea originate in a universe made entirely without benefit of private property? How did one creature like myself dare to claim a thing or place as his (I was sure the urge to possession arose in a male, not a female stream of consciousness) alone to enjoy and rule? There are no fixed boundaries in nature, no deeds, no titles, no claims. Well, claims of a sort in the territories defended by nesting birds, coyotes, and many others. And traditional routes of migration might be seen as a kind of property serving as a right-of-way. And mating for life, which a few

*Maurice Merleau-Ponty, *Phenomenology of Perception,* translated from the French by Colin Smith. London: Routledge & Kegan Paul, 1962, page 214.

species might actually do, represents a sort of mutual commitment akin to ownership. But with us such rudimentary forms of ownership are developed to a degree that seems to parody the underlying idea of making a commitment to care for and defend, for instance, a certain place in exchange for its use in limited ways. We have divided the Earth into *private* property, property ruled for the exclusive benefit of one member of one species. Imagine one man owning Sar-

Looking toward Western Mountain from Sargent's summit cairn.

gent Mountain and everything on it. One man owning a watershed or a bioregion. One son of Earth owning a part of Earth itself. One living being owning a living corner of a universe that made him everything he is.

As far as I can tell, the notion of private property is rooted in the drive to get away with what we can while nobody is looking. It is an invention of those who have taken something by force and wish to prevent others from taking it back. The framers of the U.S. Constitution were landed gentry, men (again) who framed the document to perpetuate their personal estates and self-interest. To this day our courts defend that same self-interest, now spread as a seemingly inborn right of certain members of our species in many parts of the world. We say we have a right to private property that no person and no state can take away from us. Yet I can find no justification for claiming any such right. No god would be so foolish as to give away what she did not possess in the first place. Any state granting such a right would at one stroke divide its citizens into the haves and the have-nots, into a propertied upper class and a landless underclass. War and its civil equivalent, politics, are the basis of our taking the land. Private property is the fruit of mayhem and the seizure of power. We have crafted a system of justice that maintains property in the hands of the powerful and the ruthless while the meek do without. Ownership violates the inherent innocence of the Earth. In its name we strip the land, mine it, cut it, pluck it, have our way with it until it is exhausted, then turn to other ventures that will yield to our lust.

Overstated? Heavy-handed? I've barely begun. The little thought kernel that erupted into awareness on Sargent Mountain is so central to my life experience that it bears on almost every other thought I have ever had. Our so-called free society is based on our tyranny over the land and its native inhabitants. Seldom do we temper our notion of ownership with a sense of responsibility to do well by that which we claim. We do what we want with our land, not what is best for it. Few of us know the true value of what we have—the value on a global or universal scale. All evidence points to the scarcity of life in the universe. We on Earth are the exception, not the rule. Our brother and sister Earthlings deserve love and respect, not cruelty. We owe it to all of them, everywhere—to every plant and animal in every habitat throughout the Earth. To own property in any true sense requires that we protect the interests of all who enjoy its benefits now and stand to enjoy them hereafter. Ownership is less a right than a privilege entailing clear obligations to let others lead their own lives. Live and let live is the law. If you can't sustain it, don't take it. I am for abolishing private property and restoring self-rule to Earthlings of every sort. That is how the Earth was governed until we came along. That is how it will be governed after we are gone. To pretend to the right to control even one square inch of land is not only pretentious but absurd. If we do not surrender to the wishes of the land, we are not long for this world. With a projected population of 9.4 or more billion in the coming century, we will be hard-pressed to come up with a flattering metaphor to describe our success. Think of all those mouths to be fed, of which our children will be a decided minority. Now is the time to release our grip, our pretension to the throne of Earth. We are born to contribute to the common wealth, not deplete it. The first thing we need to do is surrender what we have taken for our exclusive use so that every being has her share. Forget stewardship; we will never know enough to make decisions on behalf of others we do not know or care about. Forget central authority, ditto. Delegate authority back to the bioregions where it was when we came on the scene. Earth thrives without benefit of our control; it dies when we take charge. If we haven't learned that by now we haven't learned much to speak of. Colonialism is dead. Free the Earth from human control. One tribal perspective is not enough. Life is a communal venture. We are in this together. With freedom and dignity for all. Amen.

That in crudely exploded form is the ineffable thought kernel I experienced by the cairn on Sargent Mountain on the last day of the winter of 1996–97. It came to me in a flash, entire and complete. I recognize the truth when it descends upon me like that. So much for the myth that I can own what I behold. So much for the myth that I can improve what I "own," or that it needs improvement in any way. So much for the myth of highest and best use. What I do own is my obligation to participate in the universe as an equal of every other citizen. I am one of the players, nothing more. I and my

Sargent's south ridge.

kind don't make the rules for others to follow. That is the truth I brought down from the mountain.

The view from the summit is magnificent any time of year, but in winter the landscape of evergreens and snow centered on Sargent Mountain is particularly beautiful. The Dedham and Gouldsboro hills to the north; Pemetic and Cadillac mountains to the east; Western Mountain, Blue Hill, and the Camden Hills to the west; and the spread of islands toward the horizon at the end of the Earth to the south— Baker, Little Cranberry, Sutton, Great Cranberry, Little Duck, Great Duck, Great Gott, Little Gott, Black, Long, Swans, and all the rest, including Isle au Haut, seaward extension of Acadia National Park where I hoped to make a springtime hike a couple of months from now—what a splendid universe to inhabit and explore! I knew how lucky I was to be alive and well at its center. All this was mine, not to own, but to gawk at and appreciate during the brief instant I could share in its life.

I saw only one fox track on the ridge, which didn't surprise me because the myriad tracks I had seen in January a year ago had an aura of myth or dream about them by now. I saw another track near Waterfall Bridge on the way down where a fox had passed since I had come by on the way up. Other tracks I crossed included those of eight red squirrels, six deer, a snowshoe hare, and a ruffed grouse. I saw insect tunnels exposed where bark had fallen from a snag, and nibbled spruce cones and scales where a red squirrel had eaten its lunch. I heard a crow near the highway and two croaks from a raven high on the ridge. That was it for wildlife. I didn't personally meet any creatures on the hoof or on the wing.

It is not possible to hike in Acadia without seeing lichens. In one small bare patch at the base of a Northern white cedar I saw a spread of reindeer lichen among wintergreen and sheep laurel plants. The exposed knobs of granite on the ridge were covered with lichens in grays and greens. Most tree trunks bore their share as well, some maples sprouting showy, bright green lungwort epaulets. Between the highway and the ridge, trees were the dominant life form. The trail passes intimately among them, the traveler feeling small and insignificant in their shadow. Several times I was struck by the intricate pattern of light and shade that stretched ahead of me where dematerialized trunks, twigs, and branches projected by the sun fell against the snow. It is a miracle we can navigate under such conditions, the terrain looking tangled and confused unlike its normal self. How do we do it—tell shadow from substance? It takes a lot of brain power to tell them apart. But then, think of squirrels leaping within the shadowy canopy, and birds alighting from the sky, grasping the branch and not the shadow. We know the difference because if we didn't we wouldn't be here to tell the tale. Our nervous systems do it automatically without invoking consciousness. That in itself is a miracle. Such is life.

Ice on Hadlock Brook Trail.

For its part, the snow smoothed out the trail, making the going easier than I expected. The treadway was soft and forgiving, cushioning every step. Much of the hike was a matter of slogging ahead. I slid back some going up, but coming down I turned that to an advantage, skiing on my soles even with ice creepers on. The creepers were a big help, grabbing ice when my boots got within reach. Without the recent quilt of snow, the going would have been treacherous in spots. It was bad enough near the pond where meltwater had frozen into rivers of ice across the trail. Slick and shiny, these stretches ranged from twenty to sixty feet across. As it turned out, they were one of the few hazards I met. The worst was a frozen seep just up from the lower carriage road where the trail itself was the bed of a steep river of ice. I kept to the side where fortunately there was enough snow to get me past. On the summit I avoided ice and granite by keeping to wind-packed snow, which covered ninety percent of the ridge.

I got lost a few times because the trail was hard to tell from other inviting avenues leading between the trees, but never very lost. When I was unsure, I looked for cut branches and blazes, and always found them within minutes. Cairns sticking up through snow led the way on the ridge. The worst that happened to me was I lost the trusty blue pencil I had carried on many of my hikes. It was the perfect tool, reliable in wet or cold. No circuits to fail, no moving parts. I kept it tucked under a clip on the notebook hung around my neck, but once I missed tucking it in just right, so it took off on its own. I went back to look for it, but it had burrowed into the snow and was gone.

Hadlock Brook was a cheerful companion for much of the hike, chuckling its low chuckle under the ice, which resonated with it, smoothing it, adding a richness of its own. I seldom saw open water, and when I did it looked almost black against the snow. The banks were smooth on either side, clearly marking where the brook was hiding. In a few places the brook had overflowed in recent days, rising above the ice, plowing a higher course through six inches of new snow, leaving a serpentine track. The brook, and the trail along with it, winds around behind a nameless spur east of Bald Peak. Where the brook heads for its rise in Maple Spring, the trail puts the spur behind and heads up the ridge. That is the steepest section, but the terrain changes so quickly, and there is so much to see, it goes by in a flash. I came to a boulder near the trail where I remembered having a picnic in August when I led my partner along the same route to see the wood lilies I had found in bloom the day before. We ate our trail lunch by the boulder, looking out toward Western Mountain and the granite shoulder between us and Bald Peak where turkey vultures were soaring. Not looking for the spot, I heard it call out to me as I passed. I recognized it immediately, even under two feet of snow. Every trail has taken on an aura of familiarity which shines on me as I come by. While I am on the trail the trail is in me as well. The terrain becomes personalized. That is the way with habitats. They become extensions of ourselves, as we are extensions of them. We do not live in a world of things but in a world of experiences. Taking an image from Merleau-Ponty, experience stands in the wake of our subjectivity, affording us a glimpse of the natural world through our personal history.* A good chunk of Acadia now stands in the wake of my subjectivity, as I stand in the wake of Acadia.

I took a little over two hours to reach the summit cairn, and less than an hour and a half to get back, taking three-and-a-half hours all told to cover four miles. If it was indeed the last day of winter, winter didn't seem to have gotten the word. In men's calculations the seasons may have reached a turning point, but Sargent Mountain and Hadlock Brook didn't care a whit about that. Nobody was going to tell them when to thaw and rush by the numbers. As far as they were concerned, the season was neither winter nor spring; it was what it was. When the time came, they would do what they had to do to catch up with the sun. For the time being they were content not to hurry. That is the story of spring in New England. Don't look for it until it comes.

35—TRIAD & DAY MOUNTAIN LOOP
From Route 3 near Blackwoods Campground
To the Triad and Day Mountain, and back
  Up by the Hunters Brook Trail and bushwhack
Down by the Day Mountain Trail and bushwhack
     4.0 miles on snowshoes, March 26, 1997

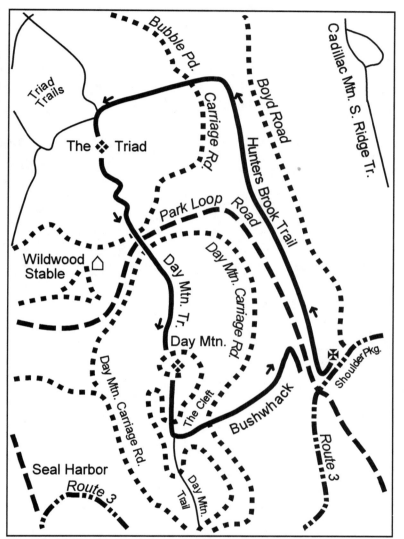

35—Triad & Day Mountain loop via Hunters Brook.

While driving from park headquarters to the Route 3 bridge over the Park Loop Road west of Blackwoods Campground, I saw a chickadee fly across the road in front of me, a crow with a twig in its beak, two pileated woodpeckers (one on McFarland Hill, one near Sieur de Monts Spring), and an eagle circling south of Day Mountain. Spring was in the air if not on the ground, which was covered with ten inches of wet snow. It had snowed in the night, then rained much of the morning. Every stream in the park was in full spate. Of the streamside trails on my list of spring hikes, the Hunters Brook Trail seemed the most doable. I parked by the guardrail before the bridge at 12:30 p.m., scrambled down the

---

* Paraphrased from Maurice Merleau-Ponty, *Phenomenology of Perception,* p. 325.

173

slippery slope to the loop road by holding onto wet branches (soaking my gloves, which I took off), crossed over Hunters Brook, put on my snowshoes, and was off.

The first thing I noticed was the roar of the brook. Instead of its normal, quiet gurgle, the brook was rushing full-bore over a series of falls with great splashing and commotion. That roar was the soundtrack of my hike for the next two-and-a-half hours. If any birds sang, their subtle notes were drowned in the onrush. All I heard was the incessant clamor of water racing headlong to meet the tide.

There were two brooks, actually, one on top of the other, with a layer of ice in between, forming a double-decker. Before the rain, the brook had been completely frozen over. Runoff from the rain had nowhere to go but up. It overflowed the ice, converting the former ceiling to a floor. I never saw the clay and gravel bottom I knew lay underneath.

Ten to twelve feet wide for much of its length, the brook was often obstructed by logs, boulders, or ice, sometimes narrowing to a chute three or four feet wide, through which the water shot like a millrace. Above the first such constriction I came to, the thwarted water formed a great whirlpool above a dam of logs. I watched a large cake of ice spin around in that gyre, wanting to see how it would manage to break free—which it didn't in the five minutes I took up its cause. If it couldn't muster enough radial force to spin out of the water's grip, eventually it would melt and join forces with its tormentor; but that would take a long time, the water being little warmer than the ice.

The brook was flooded with energy, affecting me with excitement bordering on agitation. It was not possible to remain calm in its company. It kept telling me to go, go, go, go, without telling me where or why. Motion was of the essence, it didn't matter whether linear or spiral. Slack-jawed, I kept ogling the torrent without a thought in my head. My route being upstream, the brook seemed to rush against me all the faster, largely in long straight runs, then careening four or five times against the steep eastern bank. Where the brook had brushed the snow away, hair-cap or sphagnum moss gleamed in the strong overhead light that shone between the avenue of trees lining the bank on both sides. It was still winter in the floodplain, but the brook itself was in midleap toward spring.

Compared to the agitated brook, life in the floodplain seemed calm and stiff. I saw one swollen bud with erect donkey ears on either side that would soon turn into leaves, but that was the only hint I saw that some great work was under way. The stems of trees rose high overhead, but they didn't do anything or go anywhere except up. Spotted lung-wort lichens clung to their maples, looking like corsages that would squirt you when you bent down to sniff them, but they were out of squirt juice so they just sat there while the brook roared with juice. Friends had seen three robins earlier in the week, but I hadn't seen any robins, and I wasn't seeing any by Hunters Brook. I trudged along through the slush while the brook lithely danced the other way. I forced myself to pay attention to the trees—cedar, spruce, fir, pine, hemlock, ash, maple, birch, some of them thirty inches in diame-

Hunters Brook in spring flood.

ter—but the brook kept distracting me like a child: look at me, look at me, look at *meee!*

Many trees had fallen across the brook, spanning the flood with snow-covered bridges, or damming the brook, making it pour over and under their trunks. One dam was three feet high, the brook breaching it in flying, translucent leaps. In another place the brook spread into two channels fifty feet wide, then came together again where the roots of a fallen tree constricted the channel to a width of three feet, the torrent rushing past leaving only a few standing waves in its wake as a reminder of its passing.

It was impossible not to be caught up in the excitement of Hunters Brook. I flashed on being a kid spending Saturdays in late March damming runoff streaming down the hills in Hamilton, New York, using twigs and stones to divert the flow, getting sopping wet—but loving every second. No wonder baptism has such religious significance. If watering seeds releases their magic, think what sprinkling people must do. Spring runoff released me as a child, and still releases me today, causing my spirit to sprout and turn green. Life everywhere depends on water. No wonder it brings out our best.

Beauty is clear water flowing downhill in spring—three inches wide or thirty feet, it makes little difference.

The brook turned my mind into aphoristic channels, I was powerless against its spell. Phrases and images came to me on the soft air.

Beauty is a stream brushing against a bank, baring sphagnum moss beneath the snow.

Beauty is sensing the same driving force in all Earthlings that you feel expressed in yourself.

Beauty is a red spruce sapling, twigs hung with silver drops, each drop containing a capsized universe.

Beauty is two valleys coming together, their brooks twining and going on as one.

I kept imagining I heard bird calls against the background of the brook. Looking up, I never saw a bird.

I expected the rain to have wiped out what animal tracks there may have been, but right away I came across fresh deer tracks in a pool of slush. I saw eleven more deer tracks, most of them on the slopes of the Triad and Day Mountain. I saw three snowshoe hare tracks, five squirrel tracks, and five fox tracks later on, some merely faint traces, some fresh (made after the rain had stopped). I saw two grouse tracks, one identified by a tan pellet along a row of faint indentations, the other like a line of stars (or grappling hooks) in the snow. On top of Day Mountain the snow had melted in one place to expose a network of vole tunnels running hither and thither in a maze. It looked far more complicated than necessary for small animals to get from here to there. Perhaps it was designed to foil any fox or ermine that might stumble onto that snowbank civilization.

Once while I was writing a note on the pad hung around my neck, a tiny gray insect a sixteenth-of-an-inch long descended on the damp paper, folded its wings, and thrashed its antennae this way and that in search of some meaningful encounter. How could two such minute beings ever find each other in the vastness of space? The temperature barely 40°, here was one already on the prowl, a lone scout probing the heavens for signs of intelligent life, a category from which I, lacking proper feelers, was exempt.

Much of the south slope of the Triad and north slope of Day Mountain had five-o'clock shadow from the horde of springtails that overran the snow. I watched them hop around for a time, finding neither rhyme nor reason in their flippant ballet. Maybe they hopped to keep warm. If so, they must burn a lot of microcalories in the process. What do they eat? Pollen grains, I am told, too small to see.

I heard a crow on the Triad and a mourning dove on Day Mountain. After the great buildup, the only bird I actually saw was a solo raven flying over the summit of Day Mountain. Other signs of animate life I came across were cone scales scattered beneath three spruce by red squirrels in the topmast rigging and, like crumbs around a highchair, bits of bark and moss spread beneath a birch snag where a woodpecker had snacked on bugs.

The Hunters Brook Trail is really two trails, one that

A bend in the brook with a natural bridge.

follows the brook for more than a mile, and another that leads up the east slope of the Triad, their total length making a hike nearly two miles long. The question is, once on the Triad, do you go back the same way? There are a number of options. I planned to descend the south side of the Triad to the carriage road bridge over the loop road. The bridge connects the carriage road around Pemetic and the Triad to the Day Mountain Carriage Road loop. From there I could walk back along the loop road to the start of the Hunters Brook Trail, or go on to Day Mountain. From Day I could reach Route 3 or bushwhack down the east flank to avoid having to walk along the highway. I would decide at the carriage road bridge whether to go on to Day Mountain, and at the summit what route to take back.

I bushwhacked in two places, once at the north end of Hunters Brook, and again on Day Mountain. The Hunters Brook Trail crosses the brook twice before it heads west for the Triad. In summer there are convenient stepping stones at both crossings, stones now under two feet of water and a layer of ice. The trail crosses the brook because the brook sideswipes the steep western slope of its valley, leaving no room for a trail on that side. If you can't go on, cross over. If you can't cross over, then what? I tried to push ahead on the western bank, but the brook being in full flood, I was stymied. The thirty-foot bank was too steep and slippery to attempt. I backtracked to a ridge where, with a lot of green belays from tree stems and branches, I pulled my way up.

The top of the bank was a level plateau covered with thick woods. I figured it was the top of the glacial outwash deposit where the glacier had poured sand into the (then higher) ocean. Seeing how much of that deposit Hunters Brook had since carved out in its rush to the sea, I found new respect for that seemingly quiet and modest stream. The soil being thick, trees thrived on that outwash plain, making the going difficult. I forced my way along the top of the bank through dense undergrowth, keeping my eye on what I could see of the winding brook, and eventually came to a place where I thought there was room enough down below to reconnect with the trail after its return to my side of the brook. I went down the slope, often sliding because the snow was so saturated with water, holding onto trunks and branches where I could. A rushing tributary coming off the Triad blocked my way. I climbed up along the tributary and once again came out on top of the outwash deposit, this time on the old road that once tied into the Boyd Road and continued up the valley to Bubble Pond. The road is no more, its bridge washed out long ago. The trail follows Hunters Brook to that road, then turns west for the Triad. I followed the road east to get one last glimpse of the brook, then headed west. It took me three hours to cover the first mile—what I figured would be the easy part of the hike.

From the washed-out bridge on the old road, the Hunters Brook Trail immediately starts rising toward the Triad. The sound of the brook receded as I went, to be replaced by the gurgle of a small tributary flowing next to, and sometimes in, the trail. The small stream flowed beneath the snow, which muffled its outcries to a soft but steady babbling. The trail was slushy in places, and would get worse before it got better as the snow continued to melt. I soon came to the carriage road connecting Bubble Pond and the Eagle Lake loop with the south end of Jordan Pond. The road had been groomed for cross-country skiing, but rain had wasted that effort. A trailhead on the other side pointed me in the right direction: **TRIAD-HUNTERS BROOK TRAIL; THE TRIAD .5 MI.**

The trail then follows a small valley toward the west, first at an easy grade, then steeper, and steeper still, following the small tributary that enters Hunters Brook below the old bridge. The trail leaves the thick glacial deposit behind in the valley and enters a scrubbier landscape supported by what little soil manages to cling to steep granite. The transition is gradual but clearly marked by trees that shrink from seventy to thirty feet in height. The sun beamed through a break in the clouds and I headed up the slope straight toward it, climbing its rays like a ladder. The woods opened up as the way became ledgier under the snow, giving me a glimpse of

the south ridge of Cadillac on the far side of the valley. Deer tracks crossed the slope I was on, some reduced to mere dimples by the rain, others punched into the slush after the rain had passed. The distant rush of Hunters Brook mingled with the sound of wind in the trees; I could briefly tell the two strains apart by the direction from which they came. Then a stillness settled over the landscape and I was startled to hear the sound of my pencil scribbling on my notepad.

Fallen trees bridge Hunters Brook.

Birds could now safely declare themselves without competition, but they remained mute. They were as quiet as the hare, deer, fox, and grouse tracks I crossed on my way up the Triad.

Trying to write clearly on wet paper, I wished I didn't need to take notes but could merely wait for my trail experiences to pour from an infallible memory at my bidding. I thought of China's premier and most prolific novelist saying that if words didn't come tripping off your tongue onto the page, you should take up another line of work. I am a plodding writer and I am here to tell the world it is OK to be slow if you love what you do. So what if her words go down like bubbly soda and mine like dumplings or cobblestones! The world has room for both styles, and for every gradation in between. Fluency isn't everything. I love to wrestle with words, to match wits with them, to shape and reshape them, to fully engage them as they fight their way into the open. Writing is like hiking. If I knew beforehand where the journey would take me, why make the effort? The way can be steep or obscure. That is part of the story. Writing, for me, is being myself under whatever conditions prevail at the time. It is an engagement between me and planet Earth to see what we can concoct between us. If I need to take notes, that is the price I must pay. Scribble away, notetakers, and let the smooth-talkers burble among themselves.

The trail soon eases off after a brief climb and connects with another trail coming up the gap between the Triad and Pemetic. At the junction I turned south and followed the easy grade to the cairn at the summit. The view north and south is through trees, but open to the west, giving a striking view of Sargent and Penobscot, Cedar Swamp and Eliot, with Western and Beech mountains on the horizon. Cliffside Bridge and the Around-Mountain Carriage Road stood out at that distance. Soon they would be hidden beneath leaves. Isle au Haut loomed over Manset to the southwest. Nearby, a crow called three times. I kept looking up, but saw nothing. I ate a few dates and dried pears, turned south, then headed toward the Duck Islands just visible above the trees.

The Triad and Day Mountain are two of Acadia's middling peaks, which offer some of the best views in the park. These two are closer to the waters south of Mount Desert Island than most, making the islands look more imposing than they seem from taller peaks to the north. Day Mountain is tamed by a carriage road which winds its way to the top, but the Triad, though crisscrossed by trails like a hot cross bun, feels much wilder and woollier.

Day Mountain soon came into view, a gray dome in the foreground, backed by a clear view of the Cranberry Islands, Sutton Island, the Ducks, with Seal Harbor to the side. The trail started down in earnest across ledges strewn with great boulders. Here I saw fresh fox prints and wall-to-wall snow fleas. My snowshoes have claws and grips on the underside, but even so I kept slipping more than I wanted to. The wet snow itself slid, not my snowshoes. Once started downhill, my legs didn't want to stop. Rather than crash into a tree, I turned at right angles to the slope and stepped sideways—that seemed to work. I soon ran into even wetter snow and ice where a small stream drained off the slope, commandeering the trail much of the way down. I stayed as near the trail as I could, slaloming through open beech woods, backtracking when I came to ice, taking an alternate route. I saw the white surface of the carriage road below, and soon jumped onto it from a retaining wall. I was about a hundred feet east of the bridge across to the Day Mountain loop near Wildwood Stable.

A former beach now 200 feet above sea level.

Not wanting to take the loop road back at that point, I decided to go on to Day Mountain. I crossed the bridge and started up the Day Mountain Trail through spiny and spindly woods. Icy in places, the trail did its job of taking me the 0.6 mile to the top. I thought of myself going with the glacier as it crept southward inch by inch, mile by mile, from the Laurentian Plateau to Georges Bank. Coming by in earlier days, it had smoothed the way for me and those who had blazed the trail. It is an ordinary trail, through an ordinary landscape, rising in one direction at a moderate grade. Over and over, a mourning dove sounded its pitiful lament somewhere ahead. I took twenty minutes to reach the final curve of the carriage road and the summit just beyond. The view from Day Mountain is much the same as from the Triad, though the top is more open, looking also toward Cadillac and Champlain in the northeast. Here the raven chuckled as it glided by, and I saw my bird at last.

The second bushwhack on this hike was longer than the first, down the Cleft in the east flank of Day Mountain to the loop road where it crosses Hunters Brook. It was 5:00 p.m. when I got to the top of Day Mountain. The sky had clouded over again, sunbeams flooding behind Western Mountain showing where the sun would set before long. Not wanting to walk along Route 3 back to my car, I decided to follow the Cleft more or less east–northeast through the woods. I knew I would come either to Hunters Brook or the loop road if I kept to that heading, so I wasn't worried about getting lost. I would enter the Cleft after a short descent toward the south on the Day Mountain Trail. There was no sign of the trail at the summit; if I hadn't known where to go, I might not have found it. Again, I headed toward the Duck Islands, letting my feet lead me where they would. Eventually I came to a cairn, confirming my route. The trail soon crosses an open ledge with a fine view to the south and west. Then it dips toward the Cleft, a dent in the east side of Day Mountain. The upper slope of the Cleft is extremely steep if not vertical, but there is a smooth, gradual drop that starts between Day and the outriding hump to its south. The wooded point of access is narrow, but easy to find. From my former explorations I thought it would be an easy grade posing no problem on snowshoes. There was bound to be a brook taking the shortest route down to Hunters Brook, but I could walk to the side of that. I figured the distance I had to go at something less than a mile.

I didn't have a compass, but knew the terrain well enough that it gave me all the directions I needed. I walked through the open woods in the Cleft down to the carriage road encircling Day Mountain. Crossing that, I entered territory I had never been in before. Yellow birch and beech were the dominant trees. I didn't follow the slope down like runoff would, but traversed it at an angle calculated to take me to the loop road, not Hunters Brook. I stepped over several downed trees, seeing blades of Christmas fern beneath one of them. The open deciduous woods gave way to denser coniferous woods, cutting visibility to less than forty feet. Coming to a field of smooth boulders that dimpled the snow, I knew I was crossing an ancient beach where the ocean had transferred its surging energy to the land in days when the glacier depressed the shoreline, giving the ocean access to ground which today is two hundred feet above sea level. The slope eased and the trees grew taller, evidently rooted in deeper soil. Under several tall spruce I saw mountain cranberry leaves coming out of winter hibernation.

Spotted lungwort on a maple tree.

I like navigating on my own through woods, being able to go in any direction, but picking one I believe will take me where I want to go. It reminds me of rowing, of being free to go where I want, each point of the compass being as good as any other, but sighting on one tree or point of land behind me which I figure marks the back azimuth of my true course. I am sure the challenge of land navigation spurred the development of our brains, enabling hunter-gatherers to find their way from one grove or spring to the next, and nomads to return to pastures they had known years before. To me, city streets running at right angles are a trap preventing me from using my native skills. They take the joy out of getting around. Getting *around*—reading the terrain and using its flow to advantage. Who cares about getting asquare?

To finish an earlier thought, writing is a lot like finding your way through thick woods. There are as many possible words and phrases to choose from as there are points of the compass, but you select the one combination that matches the direction of your thoughts and feelings, trusting it to carry you through the wilderness of all possible utterances. Your heading is *your* heading and no one else's. To be who you are, you have to go your own way. Let others drive in grids or mill around in confusion because they have not learned to trust their internal guidance systems. If you fear walking in unknown woods, you are not afraid of the woods but of yourself. You have not yet found your inner sense of direction. The only way to find it is to break free of society's conventional coordinates. Not merely in a figurative sense, but literally. You have to get lost. That is, lose your social orientation. In finding your way again, you will find out who you are and where you must go. Leave your wheels in the garage. You have to go on foot, under your own power, feeling your way at every step, working with the terrain, not against it. Ask the Earth where it wants you to go; after you learn to read its signs, it will tell you, just as your heart will let you know what it wants you to write after you learn to read its signs.

Lower down the slope I came to a field of great boulders, some taller than I am. This was the most dangerous part of my trek because the crevices between the boulders were hidden beneath snow. I tested each step, winding among the stones with care as if they were great eggs, but it was my legs I did not want to break. Was this another beach where the ocean tumbled and roared 10,000 years ago? It had the feel of a proto-beach where chunks of raw granite were to be ground into cobbles, but the work was interrupted by Earth's recovery and the tide's retreat, leaving the workshop in shambles.

The one thing I wanted to avoid was a thawing wetland between me and the brook. I didn't think there was one, but I wasn't sure. I came across large stretches of ice running with meltwater, but they were no Nine-Mile Swamp. It was rugged terrain, but nothing my snowshoes couldn't handle. Thick coniferous woods gave way to open deciduous woods free of boulders. I crossed a tributary of Hunters Brook, then another, reentering another stand of evergreens. Through the trees I saw what looked (and sounded) like a large brook below me, with a streak of white on the far side which I took to be the Park Loop Road. I walked above them on a ridge, expecting the brook to disappear under the streak. It didn't, so I went down to investigate. The brook turned out to be drainage running along the west side of the loop road, the roar I heard coming from Hunters Brook off in the woods on the far side of the road. I found a narrow place and jumped across, finding myself on the loop road 300 feet above the Hunters Brook bridge and the trail where I started. It was five minutes to six.

Five minutes later I was at my car on Route 3. I had taken five-and-a-half hours to make the four-mile loop. Checking elevations on a map, I had climbed about 620 feet to the top of the Triad, and another 320 to the top of Day Mountain, for a total climb (and declimb) of 940 feet. The sun had set and clouds darkened the sky.

The equinox past, this was my first hike of official spring. Now the sun would rise north of east and set north of west, days would grow longer and nights shorter, and the temperature would slowly rise, even though hobbled by the cold waters of the Gulf of Maine. The sheep laurel (lambkill) rising through the snow all along the trail would return to life, lifting its leaves to the sun, turning water and air to pink blossoms in time for the solstice in June. The spring equinox is one of life's major inflection points, inviting us to turn our thoughts from the winter that was to the birth (no matter how labored) of the summer to come. What the raven said was, "Have hope, have hope," a far cry from, "Nevermore." The winter of the mind had been laid to rest. The sap of the Earth was in full flood. Spring, the season of possibility, was overtaking Acadia.

❧

36—GREAT HEAD LOOP
From Sand Beach parking area
To Great Head, and back
  By the Great Head Trail and Sand Beach
2.0 miles, April 2, 1997

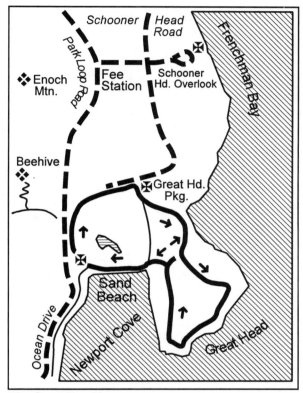

36—Great Head loop.

I felt dumb getting lost on the Great Head Trail, one of my shorter hikes. Not once but twice! The problem was that the April Fools' Day blizzard the day before had obscured the treadway and the painted blue blazes that marked the trail. Mount Desert Island had been swiped by the outer edge of the storm. Where Boston got two feet of snow, Bar Harbor got four to five inches. The day after, the temperature reached 40° Fahrenheit. The snow was melting, but in places it was still two or three inches thick, enough to bury the trail so it blended with the surrounding terrain. Guessing at the route, once I found myself on top of a cliff where the trail evaporated beneath my feet; a second time I regained the trail, but the wrong trail, and wound up tracking bootprints I had made two hours before. I backtracked both times and found where I had gone wrong. I went about three-tenths of a mile out of my way, but was doubly rewarded for my trouble with a spectacular view of the Beehive over Sand Beach with seaside cliffs in the foreground, and a scramble over granite into wintry birch woods.

The blizzard had hit after a five-day thaw. With the ground almost bare, I was looking forward to a mountain valley hike; but when the snow came, I picked a less challenging route. Looking over my list of spring hikes, I realized I kept putting the Great Head Trail off for a later day. Confronting my prejudice, I asked myself, why? Images of a wet and rooty trail came to mind. There were some stretches I actively disliked. But the ground was still largely frozen, so that would solve the seepage problem. And snow would cover the roots. I'll give it a try, I told myself.

In retrospect, I have dismissed the Great Head Trail unfairly. It is a particularly Acadian trail, exposed to the same winds Frenchman Bay is exposed to, crossing through three kinds of woods—white and red spruce, popple and birch, scrubby pitch pine—over four kinds of rock—granite, shatter zone, gabbrodiorite, Bar Harbor formation. It offers splendid views of Acadia's three easternmost peaks—Gorham and Champlain mountains, with the Beehive in between—and the tan expanse of Sand Beach. It takes you to the edge of the bay where you are likely to meet creatures more at home in a marine habitat than on land. Whatever the weather, Great Head will put you intimately in touch with it. I had thought of the trail as a minor hike only a mile and a half long, yet it took me four hours to complete the loop. I was wrong; it is a wonderful trail.

Grouse track on Great Head.

What surprised me most was the variety of wildlife signs I met along the way. I heard robins (three chirps to a phrase) and crows; saw gulls, robins, crows, eider, a guillemot in breeding black, and a loon; and saw tracks of ten different animals. When I had lost my way, I brushed against a white spruce which held a pellet of ground feathers and small bones on a branch at eye level. Thinking crows and gulls would be unlikely to eat a small bird, I pictured an owl or hawk regurgitating the loose casting. Walking along the top of a cliff overlooking Newport Cove, I saw a sea urchin in the trail, or at least the bristly shell of one, eaten out by a gull.

The eider were in rafts in the lee of Great Head out of the wind which was sweeping the bay from the north. They were actively feeding, using half-spread wings as diving planes to carry them to mussels growing on the rocks below. I counted 125 of them in three groups, with a few individuals here and there. Now and then I could hear their soft mewing and clucking. I took my binoculars on this hike, which gave me a closeup view of their ghostly forms diving beneath the waves at the foot of ocean cliffs. Several eider swam near Old Soaker, the ledge south of Great Head. The one loon I saw was out from the ledge, rising and falling on the waves. It was carried into view by one great crest after another, then swallowed by the succeeding trough. Low in the water, it reminded me of pictures of nuclear submarines, an unhappy image to project on an innocent bird.

I was saddened to think this might be my last tracking expedition till next winter. The blizzard was a gift out of the blue, giving me one last chance to see who had used the trail before I came along. Because of recent forty-degree days, and the trail's location at the edge of the bay, more animals were up and about than I had noted on earlier hikes. I saw two deer tracks, four coyote (maybe fox) tracks, three mouse tracks, eighteen red squirrel tracks, twenty-one snowshoe hare tracks, one beaver track (from the inlet stream toward the lodge), and the track of one weasel (maybe mink; a bounder at least). Some of the prints had spread as they melted, so I could only be sure of the most recent ones. Crossing the stream feeding the wetland back of Sand Beach, I saw a great beaver lodge south of the trail, and many trees felled by gnawing determination. The branches had been taken for food, leaving only the delimbed torsos lying on the ground like so many marble statues after an earthquake.

I saw three different grouse tracks, four crow tracks, and three robin tracks (smaller than crow, bigger than junco). Nature was on the hop if not the march. The pace of spring was picking up. Peregrines were back on the Precipice and Beech Cliff. Warblers were heading north, keeping up with insects roused by warmer days. Harbor seals were back on their ledges, herons on their nesting grounds. Ready or not, it was happening, as it has happened ten thousand times since the glacier went north, releasing its icy grip on the land. I grudgingly overcame my prejudice against the Great Head Trail, letting my heart thaw, opening myself to the onrush of spring.

The trail was wet in a few places, but the stretch I remembered as being the worst was shaded from the sun, and so still locked in ice. Birch and spruce roots were under snow for the most part, so boots were kinder and gentler to the trail, and the trail was kinder and gentler to passing feet. It is the stretch from the Great Head parking area to the outer bluff that is apt to be wet, and that is only a small segment of the loop, much of which passes over rock.

I took the Great Head Trail clockwise, starting and ending at the Sand Beach parking area. A trailhead at the north end of the lot directs hikers **TO GREAT HEAD TRAIL AND PARKING AREA**. The route runs north parallel to the loop road for a short way, connects with an asphalt path running on the bed of the old extension of Schooner Head Road, which dips down to the marsh inlet, then rises, joining a gated service road maintained by the park. The road leads through an alder swamp to the Great Head parking area, where the Great Head Trail proper begins. The trail turns south then shortly forks, the right fork leading to **SAND BEACH**, the left to **GREAT HEAD**. The left fork dips through spruce and birch woods to the head of a stony beach, then rises slowly through woods, passing another connector to **SAND BEACH** on the right, continuing south to the top of Great Head, elevation 145 feet above mean high tide in Frenchman Bay. The trail goes on, dropping to the south, rounding the head, then slowly climbing northward to high ground overlooking Sand Beach.

Gabbro outcrop on Great Head.

There are two routes from there, one leading back toward the Great Head parking area, the other dropping steeply to the eastern end of Sand Beach. Crossing the beach, the trail rises by gray granite steps to the Sand Beach parking area, where I began. I figure the loop is about a mile and three-quarters in all, which I stretched to two miles by getting lost.

Like the head of a frog with protruding eyes, Great Head has two knobby humps of equal height. One hump overlooks Frenchman Bay on the east, the other Newport Cove and Sand Beach on the west. The trail passes over both humps, falling to seventy feet in between.

The eastern hump is made up of three kinds of rock: shatter zone, gabbro-diorite, and Bar Harbor formation. The western hump is largely granite. Rock in the shatter zone contains fragments of older rock floating in an intrusive flood of granite. It looks a little like rocky road ice cream, or chocolate chip. Gabbro is a dark gray rock that looks like basalt. It flooded up from the depths when "North America" collided with "Europe" 400–600 million years ago, in the days when rock melted and flowed from the heat of the crash. Later on, granite, made of a different combination of minerals, bulged up in much the same way. Rock of the Bar Harbor formation forms the eastern edge of Great Head. It is older than gabbro or granite, being laid down in the ocean as sediment flowing off of the proto-continents. Dark gray gabbro and pink granite form similar knobs, giving character to their respective humps on Great Head. Sinking their roots into joints in the rock, pitch pines grow mainly on the granite hump, which is how I first realized what kind of rock lay under the snow. A loop of Great Head provides one of the best geological tours on Mount Desert Island. I took pictures of shatter zone rocks bared at the extreme eastern end of Sand Beach. The same rock forms the shore on the outer side of the head where the trail nears a stony beach. Sand Beach is another glacial remnant, deposited in the ocean by streams flowing under the ice, now mixed with the broken shells of marine animals.

Lifting above the surrounding terrain, the two protuberant knobs on Great Head overlook Frenchman Bay and the eastern edge of Mount Desert Island from Otter Cliff in the south to the Precipice on Champlain Mountain and the Porcupine Islands farther north. Flanked by Gorham and Champlain mountains, the Beehive is the centerpiece of the vista, rising steeply and, when backlit by a lowering sun, darkly from the coastal plain. Its terraces accented by snow, the Beehive looked like a great Mesoamerican temple oriented toward the rising equinoctial sun. Facing east, the view is over Frenchman Bay to Schoodic Head and its peninsula. On this hike, the bay frothed with whitecaps surging before the north wind, its typical winter look. I tried to picture life on Egg Rock in the days when the lighthouse was manned. There was not one twig on that small island to break the blast. We romanticize the noble keeper, but his life was far stricter than we can imagine. The blinking red eye said it all: "Beware." I found it far easier to hike with the wind than to stand against it. Ranging between twenty and thirty miles-an-hour, the blast made the temperature feel more like twenty than the forty my thermometer claimed it was.

From the granite western knob, Great Head is seen to be covered with trees in three different bands: pitch pine on the west, spruce on the east, and popple-birch in the center. The effect is both dramatic and beautiful. Spruce and pitch pine are the hardier species, withstanding extremes of wind and temperature better than the hardwoods, which seek shelter between the two ridges. Did I fool myself into thinking that a reddish hue colored the upper branches of that swath of birch trees? It looked to me like sap was beginning to run beneath those inscrutable white facades.

The blazing of the Great Head Trail is halfhearted at best. Or two-hearted. Blazed with both red and blue paint, it makes one wonder what the difference might signify. In this case nothing at all beyond the age of the blaze, and the possible temperament of the blazer. Red paint was commonly used before the park standardized on blue as being the more durable and visible color. If some dedicated band of trail phantoms keeps the old tradition alive, it is clinging to an empty cause defeated in a fair contest. The worst thing about the blazes is that they were made from the point of view of a hiker traveling counterclockwise about the loop. There is little to tell hikers going the other direction where to go. When blazes are covered by snow, there is nothing to guide travelers one way or the other. I can't blame anyone but myself for getting lost, but the trail blazers didn't make it any easier to get found again.

The reason I got lost was because I was busy keeping track of so many other things besides the trail. Crows were flying, waves crashing, eiders diving, tracks leading in all directions, I had too much to do to keep my eye on the trail. It is a wonder I didn't lose my way more times than I did. Snow on the trail didn't help matters. Coming to the brink of an abrupt fifty-foot drop-off into Newport Cove, even in my distracted state I knew enough to turn around. The maze of pitch pines on the western knob would have been a cinch to navigate if the blazes had been showing. With them whited-out by the snow, it was a real challenge, there being nothing to indicate which avenue the trail followed between the trees. It was too bad I got off the trail where I did, missing a trail-

Shatter-zone outcrop, eastern end of Sand Beach.

head where the trail splits in two. When I got back on the trail, I picked up the wrong branch, having forgotten its existence. I went on to its junction with the trail I had taken earlier south from Great Head parking area. At least I knew where I was, which didn't happen to be where I wanted to be. Backtracking, I saw where I had gone wrong, and went right the second time.

Aside from the trees I have mentioned, I also saw lamb-kill, pincushion moss, reindeer lichen, crusty lichens in three colors (light gray, bright green, deep orange), and pale green boulder lichens. White spruce, sunlight-loving cousin of red spruce, thrives on the exposed ledges. In spots it was the dominant tree. Many birches still bore a vertical white stripe that told which way the blizzard had blown the day before. Along the maintenance road south of the Great Head parking area I saw several apple trees near the open meadow once used for research into the effects of ozone on native plants. The road passes through an alder swamp just north of there.

The trail from the granite knob to Sand Beach is fairly steep. Covered with wet snow it was an invitation to disaster. I made sure of my footing before I put weight on a forward leg. Even so, I slid down greased granite in a number of places, there being no other way to go. I always find it easier to climb up slick rock than to climb down. The danger comes in not keeping your weight over your feet. I had stayed away from Great Head for six or seven years, so had forgotten the lay of the land. Had I remembered, I might have taken the loop the other way around.

Above Sand Beach, the trail passes by what looks to be a great millwheel six-and-a-half feet across lying on its back. What local stream had the energy to turn such a massive weight, even when trained through a series of gears? It looks like the stone just rolled over and said, "No farther!" I've heard that the great stone was recovered from a shipwreck on Baker Island, and was brought to Great Head as an ornament, not a working wheel. The other stone artifact on this hike is now a heap of rubble on the eastern knob. Built eighty years ago as a tower with a view, it has reverted to an earlier state. A plaque commemorating the gift of Saterlee

Field to the National Park Service stands on a low boulder by the stairs to Sand Beach, a memorial to the family that once owned the land and built the tower.

I met four people on this hike. One couple I knew from two intertwining tracks leading south from the Great Head parking area. The smaller set of prints did a lot of slipping and sliding on the ice beneath the snow. When I met the track makers on their return, I asked if it was windy ahead.

"Windy?" mused the maker of the larger prints. "Yes it is. It is very windy up there."

Having considered his answer, the track maker spoke like an oracle. His answer confirmed what the trees had tried to tell me already. I took him at his word.

The other couple was strolling on Sand Beach when I reached the end of my hike. I was preoccupied and they were preoccupied, so we left one another in peace.

Crossing the beach, I remembered how hard it was to walk on the sands of Cape Cod. Give me a trail of solid rock, something firm I can press against. Nauset Beach is a trail from hell which crumbles when you step on it and stores heat to scorch the soles of your feet. The faster you run, the slower you go. I'll take gabbro and granite over sand any time.

Having completed my hike, I thought back on the wildlife and signs of wildlife I had met.

I heard:
    robins
    crows

I saw:
    robins
    crows
    gulls
    eider
    a loon
    a guillemot

I saw signs of:
    red squirrels
    snowshoe hares
    a canid (probably coyote)
    mice
    a beaver (track, lodge, stumps)
    a weasel
    robins
    crows
    ruffed grouse
    a hawk or an owl (casting)
    a sea urchin

Aside from plants, I had come in contact with fifteen different Earthling tribes. Adding people to that list makes sixteen. In summer, park visitors commonly want to know where they can go to see wildlife. They are often disappointed to discover that Acadia's wildlife is not gathered in one spot waiting to be ogled and photographed. Many visitors leave without having what they consider to be a wildlife experience. Others are glad to have seen gulls and cormorants up

The Beehive from the eastern end of Sand Beach.

close, a cloud of chickadees in a nearby tree, or a raccoon raiding a garbage can. How many notice the blueberry buds nipped by hares, cedars browsed by white-tailed deer, spruce cone scales on coping stones, fox scats in the trail, a beaver lodge in the pond, or the myriad insects hovering around Acadia's vegetation? It is not possible to enter the park without encountering wildlife one way or another. It is not a question of where to go but of what we can see where we are. The trick is in opening our eyes to wildlife. In meeting it halfway. If I look for it, I will find it. Maybe not right away, but eventually, once I have learned to read the signs, to sniff the air, to hear the faint rustle in the bushes.

The snow on Great Head was a gift in bringing the presence of wildlife to my attention. On dry ground I would not have known a beaver had recently crossed my path or ruffed grouse had crossed it in three different places. But still I would have seen the robins and crows, the guillemot and loon, eiders and gulls. I would have found the casting full of chopped feathers and bones, the empty sea urchin shell, and spruce cone cores and scales where a red squirrel had nibbled the seeds. I would have seen the beaver lodge, the gnawed trees, and the runway up from the inlet. I would have felt the Presence nonetheless, not as strongly as brought out by the snow perhaps, but every bit as convincingly.

I am a seeker of patterns in my surroundings. I have been

since childhood. I sort my experience in different ways to see how it will arrange itself. Pattern is never accidental. It is a kind of order revealing regularity in repeated events. When I taught learning-disabled children, I noted every reading or spelling error they made, then looked to the patterns I found in those errors to tell me where they were having trouble. A hundred errors might fall into four or five classes. By not harping on the errors individually but remediating the cause of those clusters of related errors, I could magnify the effect of my teaching and a given child's mastery of language. Where conventional teachers might see only dysfunction, I saw every child taking a systematic approach to learning—a misguided approach for some reason, but a systematic one. By tracing the misguided approach to its source (perhaps a perceptual deficit or a difficulty distinguishing between similar signals), I could almost always mitigate or rectify the outward and visible disability.

How does that connect to a hike on Great Head? When I enter Acadia I ask what it is trying to tell me. I look for patterns of meaning. I don't wait for a deer to leap across the trail ahead of me, I ask where deer have already been. I look for signs in browsed vegetation, for clumps of pellets, for tracks in gravel, sand, mud, or snow. By keeping myself open, I always find something. A casting at eye level in the branches of a white spruce perhaps, or a pattern of chips beneath a particular tree. By listening to Acadia, I hear it whispering to me in a language I can often translate into my own native tongue. We speak the same basic language. The universal language of Earthlings everywhere. It conveys our mutual presence to one another. As surely as I note canid tracks in the snow, fox and coyote note my tracks and my scent. They keep tabs on me because their safety depends on knowing where I am and what I am up to. It makes a difference whether I am a tree hugger or am out for their pelt. Or whether I am walking Bruno and Fritz, my faithful Weimaraner companions.

I got back to my car in just under four hours, having hiked a loop about two miles long. I felt I had been to Acadia and interacted with a real place on Earth. I carried away a sense of its presence as a habitat where native Earthlings roam in comparative freedom and safety. Like so many runes, the signs I had seen spoke that message. I carried away a deep sense of stillness.

ꙮ

37—LITTLE HARBOR BROOK & BIRCH SPRING LOOP

From Route 3 at Little Harbor
To Birch Spring and Cedar Swamp Mountain,
    and back
    Up by Little Harbor Brook and Amphitheater trails
    Down by Cedar Swamp Mountain, Asticou, and
      Little Harbor Brook trails
          6.5 miles, April 4, 1997

The media have been abuzz with conjecture about the group suicide of thirty-nine members of the Heaven's Gate community in California last week. The members apparently shared a belief that they could transcend the hardships of life on Earth by moving on to a more perfect existence in some other region of the cosmos. The group seemed to appeal to people who had trouble accepting and managing their sexuality. Instead of killing their spouses, rivals, or ex-lovers as thousands do every year, they chose to kill themselves. Group members have been made the object of public pity verging on ridicule by commentators using the sad occasion to advance their superior beliefs. But I wonder if belief in a god who died to take our sins unto himself and physically rose to heaven is in fact better informed or in any way superior to what the Heaven's Gate members believed. Are fighters in an Islamic holy war actually assumed into heaven when they die as they maintain? Can any group establish an exclusive covenant with a god that sets it apart as a chosen people among all beings on Earth? I view those who sacrificed themselves in California as no more foolish or gullible than the rest of us. They illustrate the universal truth that we make the worlds we believe in to suit our personal fears and desires.

What kind of world *do* we live in? Is life a trial or an opportunity? Are we working off our former sins, or suffering now in preparation for a future life of ease? The Heaven's Gate drama gives us a chance to review our own beliefs and put them in modern perspective. For myself, I believe my ancestors have given me the opportunity to develop my awareness as broadly and deeply as I can within a finite span of time. I get the one chance, then pass that same opportunity to those who come after me. This life is all I can know of heaven. Am I here to consume the beauty of the Earth, to despoil that beauty, to prevent others from sharing it with me? Am I here to inflict pain and suffering on other beings, to raise myself up at their expense, to set myself apart as their superior? No, no, no, no, no, and no. Given my unique combination of strengths and weaknesses, my task is to participate in the creative unfolding of the universe as best I can, and to help others do the same, those who are with me now and those who will follow. All of us are flawed; all of us are perfectible to some degree. Our job is to do the best we can with what we have in the time allowed. To do that, it helps to imagine what a more perfect world

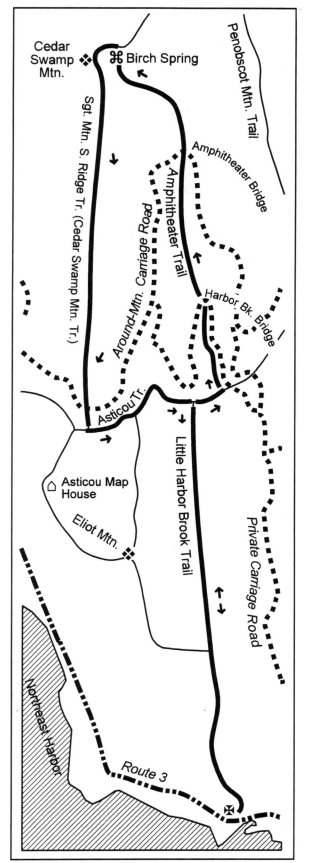

37—Little Harbor Brook & Birch Spring loop.

might look like, and then to work to make that vision a reality. To do anything less is to squander the wealth Earth invests in maintaining us. We act not for ourselves alone but for the Earthling community. Every day we wake to the opportunity of doing what we can; every night we lie down one day closer to the realization of our dream. As Earth whirls its crazy corkscrew course through space, we have the privilege of going along. In the end we ask ourselves whether Earth is worse off or better off for our having taken that ride. Whatever our answer, we serve as examples to others, to improve upon or emulate. Either way, if we have done our best, we have lived as happily as we are able in our time.

This line of thought may seem tangential to the story of a hike up Little Harbor Brook to its headwaters at Birch Spring, but I see that journey as one stage of my life's journey, and its progression as one episode in working out my mission to join with Earthlings everywhere in appreciating Earth's perfection in the here and now. To walk the watershed of Little Harbor Brook from the ocean to the rise of one of its tributaries is to walk backwards through history from the death of a brook in the arms of the sea to its humble birth at the foot of a steep mountain cliff 800 feet above and only three miles inland from its salty release. Here was Heaven's Gate, indeed, opening not onto some mythical kingdom of God, but onto the fertile slopes of planet Earth. Here every drop of surface water is compelled by gravity to follow the dictates of the local terrain as it races toward its appointed union with the sea. The brook spans a small bioregion on the verge of resurrection as snow and ice melt to flood the soil with the essential fluid no plant or animal can do without. We are all children of the waters of Earth. This hike was a celebration of those waters in general, and an appreciation in particular of that portion of them conducted to the sea by the channel of Little Harbor Brook in Mount Desert, Maine.

Much of the brook lies on private land outside the boundary of Acadia National Park. The owner maintains a trail that runs next to the brook from Route 3 almost to its junction with the Asticou Trail a mile and three-quarters north of the road. The trail was in excellent shape, having recently been cleared of blowdowns and crowding undergrowth. Trail workers had inscribed their initials with chainsaws in stems they had cut, **AT** in one, **LT** in another. Aside from J ♥ T scratched in a stump, those, and a few peanut shells dropped in the trail, were the few signs I saw that humans had passed that way. The only tracks on the Little Harbor Brook Trail were those of squirrel and hare, fox and deer, muskrat and raccoon, weasel and grouse. At the bridge where the Asticou Trail crosses the brook, I saw a few dog and hiker prints and, farther on, a faint ski track along a section of carriage road. I didn't see any people in the six hours and fifteen minutes I was on the trail.

From the upper end of the Little Harbor Brook Trail (or simply the Harbor Brook Trail) I followed the Asticou Trail east a short way to the first carriage road it crosses, where I turned north along the carriage road, descending to Little Harbor Brook Bridge. The Amphitheater Trail begins on the north side of the bridge at a trailhead which reads:

AMPHITHEATER
TRAIL
BIRCH SPRING
1.4 MI/2.2 KM
PENOBSCOT MT.
2.2 MI/3.5 KM
SARGENT MT.
2.6 MI/4.2 KM
↑
ASTICOU TRAIL
.3 MI/.5 KM
JORDAN POND
.9 MI/1.4 KM
→

From the bridge, the Amphitheater Trail rises gradually toward the north along Little Harbor Brook to Amphitheater Bridge, then more steeply up the valley between Cedar Swamp Mountain on the west and Penobscot on the east to a turn to the west, from which it rises rapidly across ledges to Birch Spring and a junction with the Sargent Mountain South Ridge Trail. As hinted by the old sign on Route 3 at the beginning of the Little Harbor Brook Trail, **JORDAN MTN. VIA AMPHITHEATER 5.3 K**, the brook and Amphitheater trails used to run in a straight line through the Amphitheater (the closed valley between Cedar Swamp and Penobscot mountains) almost to Sargent Mountain Pond. The trail no longer continues past the turn for Birch Spring, though I once followed its former course in March across soggy ground and made it to the summit of Penobscot (formerly Jordan) Mountain. The wet ground is not stable enough to support a trail, and I do not recommend trying to retrace the old route at any season.

From the harbor to Birch Spring, the brook rises very gradually to Little Harbor Brook Bridge, then somewhat more steeply to Amphitheater Bridge, and more steeply still to the turnoff, where a small tributary rises rapidly to the spring. Approximate elevations along the way include:

Route 3	20 feet
Asticou bridge	110 feet
Amphitheater Bridge	370 feet
turn away from brook	500 feet
Birch Spring	820 feet.

Above the spring, the Cedar Swamp Mountain Trail (a continuation of the Sargent Mountain South Ridge Trail) rises to 900 feet, skirting the 942-foot summit.

On the return, I followed the Cedar Swamp Mountain Trail past the Around-Mountain Carriage Road to the junction with the Asticou Trail, which I followed east to Little Harbor Brook, retracing my steps south along the brook. I

had thought of crossing Eliot Mountain, but didn't reach the Eliot Mountain Trail until 5:10 p.m., when I didn't want to risk losing my way on a trail no one had been on since the blizzard. I had done the trail on snowshoes with friends on Christmas Day 1996, and knew how hard it was to follow the seldom used route.

Details, details! What about the route itself? The trip to Birch Spring up the valley of Little Harbor Brook is one of

A fox leads the way along Little Harbor Brook.

the finest hikes on Mount Desert Island. Especially in early spring when the upper brook is feisty and full of froth. The middle reach (between the two carriage road bridges) is through largely deciduous woods, so has an open feel to it unlike many of Acadia's brooks which run through more constricted valleys with close, coniferous woods. The hike is also good after a downpour in October and early November. The brook is the centerpiece of the hike, so in drier seasons the trip is less spectacular. I love to watch the brook get younger and younger as I go along, starting as a stately stream that has seen it all by the time it goes to its salty reward, getting trimmer and more energetic as the valley rises more steeply and the bottom gives way from smooth sand to gravel, to pebbles, to cobbles, to rough-hewn boulders torn from the cliffs above. My mood follows the example of the brook, from serenity, through the seasoned competence of middle age, to the jounce and bounce of youth. The change from age to age is subtle, as it is in life. The channel narrows, from eleven or twelve feet, to nine or ten, to eight, to six, to three or four. The noise level increases from a gliding murmur to a bouncier purl to a vehement splashing to an impatient, bounding and rushing roar. Excitement rises from start to finish. At least to the turn away from the brook. From there you know the tributary is nearby, but a stream in its infancy doesn't have the lung power to assert itself as loudly as it does in adolescence.

No other hike on the island encompasses the full life story of a brook as this one does. The Hunters Brook Trail opens up the later stages in the development of a similar brook. The Gorge and Giant Slide trails present excellent pictures of brooks in their youth, as do the Canon (Canyon) and Hadlock Brook trails. If pursued far enough, the Giant Slide Trail reveals a brook in its infancy. On this hike, by patching together a number of different trails, I saw the full span of one brook's history spread before me as I walked.

Except for the summit region of Cedar Swamp Mountain and the slope leading up to the spring, the entire route is through woods. If you want to touch a variety of trees, this is the trail for you. The Little Harbor Brook Trail leads through tall mixed woods with maples and Northern white cedars along the brook, and great white pines and yellow birches thrown in among the usual spruce, fir, ash, and white birch. The Amphitheater Trail leads alternately through deciduous and evergreen woods. The Cedar Swamp Mountain and Asticou trails run through mixed woods most of the way. It was snowier in the woods than in the open, but bare spots were beginning to appear, with mosses, ferns, and other ground-cover plants standing tall in the dwindling layer of white. When had I last seen partridgeberry leaves? Beechdrops? Mayflower leaves? There they were, as if they had been there all the time and I had overlooked them. I have seen mayflower blooms on Dorr Mountain as early as April 17th. That would be two weeks away! Was it possible we could move that quickly, with so much snow on the ground? Stay tuned to this station for further bulletins on this story as it develops.

The box score for tracks on this hike includes:

Red squirrel	46
White-tailed deer	19
Snowshoe hare	16
Red fox	13
Ruffed grouse	4
Robin	2
Vole	1
Ermine	1
Muskrat	1
Raccoon	1

On my return along Little Harbor Brook I saw two sets of fox prints overstepping those of my Vibram soles. I saw several

bird tracks I could not identify. I heard two red squirrels, two red-breasted nuthatches, two crows, a robin, and a hairy woodpecker tapping away at a birch. I heard what I thought was another woodpecker just off the trail, tapping in phrases of four regular beats. Scanning a snag in that direction, I saw no chips flying and no banging bird. I heard the sound again—behind me. I turned, but again saw nothing. Then again nearer, at my feet. Under my feet! Looking down, I

Little Harbor Brook in its maturity.

saw not a bird but a sheet of ice, with a trickle of black water coursing beneath it. Somehow air trapped under the ice was making that sound as it was released, tapping four times, pausing, then tapping again. Like coded signals relayed cell to cell in prison, the message was that someone under the ice wanted to get out. Spring was patiently tapping out its intentions, giving us a chance to join the big break when it came.

By far the most exciting sound I heard was the cry of Canada geese flying low over Cedar Swamp Mountain from west to east. Looking up, I saw a group of twenty-six geese forming a lopsided V, twenty-two on one side, four on the other. More a ✓ than a V. I watched them fly in a ragged line across the island, then well out over Frenchman Bay almost to Schoodic Point. Cries from a second flock distracted me, a group of twenty following the same course. When I got out of my car at the start of the hike, the trees were filled with burbling and trilling birds, which I thought must be juncos, one of Acadia's most common species, or perhaps purple finches. If they were juncos, their concert was anything but common. I hadn't heard such glorious music since last July when hermit thrushes put away their flutes for the season. I saw two juncos gleaning near the brook at the start of the hike, and assumed they and their kin were the music makers.

I was almost as thrilled to see a lone winter wren as I was to see the geese. It was hopping among woody debris caught behind a rock in Little Harbor Brook. I saw it twice (perhaps the same bird) in the same place, once at the start of my hike, again at the end. There were insects in them thar branches, and the perky little brown bird with its saucy tail was out to get 'em. I did see three flying insects hovering over a small stream, but it was early for the flying horde. Snow fleas were out in force on Cedar Swamp Mountain, hopping around on the snow. I counted 1,658,449 of the little dancers in one short stretch of trail before I had to move on. I smelled fox scent twice in two widely separated places, and saw four scats containing white hair and crunched bone, three on Cedar Swamp Mountain, one on a stone near Little Harbor Brook. Snowshoe hare is a staple in the fox diet during winter. I saw several recent excavations dug by pileated woodpeckers, one a series of seven holes drilled one above another. It was a good

Little Harbor Brook in middle age.

hike for wildlife seen, tracked, heard, and sniffed.

It was a good hike for bridges, too. Amphitheater Bridge is an Acadian classic, built overlooking a cascade that was fairly gushing with meltwater. The Amphitheater Trail runs under the arch in gaining access to the upper valley. Little Harbor Brook Bridge, like Hadlock Brook Bridge, is one of the minor spans in the park, but it is as solid and well-built as any other. I crossed several snowy bogwalks, and two plank bridges along Little Harbor Brook. My favorite was the log bridge where the Asticou Trail crosses the brook, which is twenty-six feet wide at that point. It is made of two spans resting on a granite pier set midstream, with railings on both sides. The last time I came by the bridge had been washed out by a flood and was on its side among a tangle of trunks and branches. Rescued and restored by the park's trail crew, it is a magnificent sight to see in the middle of the woods where such an elegant structure comes as a total surprise.

The Hadlock Ponds and (Little) Long Pond were still frozen over, as was much of the route I followed on this hike. The climb up the side of the valley to Birch Spring would have been impassible if the temperature were below freezing. As it was, the ice was turning rotten and offered a tooth which gave some degree of traction. The descent along Cedar Swamp Mountain was icy in many places, and I accepted help from a great many trailside trees. The descent toward Little Harbor Brook along the Asticou Trail was much the same. By far the iciest stretch was the scramble onto Cedar Swamp Mountain from Birch Spring, which came as no surprise. The trail climbs steeply up a rocky cliff, following the same route water takes in plunging down to the spring. The ice builds to great thickness as winter wears on and daytime thaws alternate with nightly freezes. It is a tricky spot at any season, but in early spring is apt to be particularly challenging, every hiker being put to the test. Which it was, and I was. I willed my way up, climbing with foot, hand, and fortitude.

Cedar Swamp Mountain overlooks the Amphitheater onto the western flank of Penobscot Mountain, which floats like a whale on the horizon. Flecked with snow streaks, it reminded me of a seal pup shedding its white birth fur. From the other side of the ridge lower down, the Cedar Swamp Mountain Trail looks over Lower Hadlock Pond, Norumbega Mountain and, across Somes Sound (of which only the entrance can be seen), St. Sauveur, Beech, and Western mountains. As on several of my recent hikes, the sky had clouded over by the time I got to the top, with sunstreamers pouring over Western Mountain against a salmon-hued horizon. Eliot Mountain looms south of Cedar Swamp, like a giant green pumpkin.

I saw one cairn on Cedar Swamp Mountain that looked the same now as it must have looked fifty or seventy-five years ago. Furred with gray lichen, it had been welcomed back by nature as one of its own. Built of four stones—two spaced apart on the bottom, a larger stone bridging them, topped with a smaller stone in the middle—it was an example of harmonious and timeless design. A cairn for the ages. I was struck by how few cairns are left to mature at their own pace. Hikers keep fiddling with them, adding stones, rearranging them, moving them, making them ugly, silly, and unstable. Why can't we leave them to do their job in peace? We seem to have to leave our mark on the trail to show that we have passed that way. We carve our initials on birch and beech, and pile up stones as monuments to ourselves. I changed the world; therefore I am. But if everybody does it, the trail loses its natural character and begins to reflect the whimsical urges of its occasional users. There are times when we need not assert ourselves, or when we assert ourselves best by leaving things as they are. I would like to see Acadia's cairns restored to a basic design carefully made, then respected as reliable guides for thousands of hikers over hundreds of years. We all could take pride in cooperating in that effort. I left the world as I found it; therefore I am.

The route I took on this hike is fairly well marked except where the Little Harbor Brook Trail crosses from private land into the park south of the Asticou Trail bridge. There seems to be a no-man's land where the trail disappears for about 100 feet. I was as unsure where to go this time as I was the last time I hiked the trail. I kept heading north, soon spying a blue diamond nailed to a tree. Between the two carriage road bridges, the Amphitheater Trail crosses the brook several times on stepping stones. When the brook is

Little Harbor Brook in its youth.

in full flood, some of those stones are submerged, making crossings difficult. Several times I had to invent an alternate route in getting across. The valley is full of small boulders in that stretch, so any problem there may be is only temporary. The trail looks like it doesn't get much use, probably because it is not readily accessible by car, and perhaps because it doesn't lead to any popular destination. Even so, I hike it every spring because it is what it is, a brookside trail through open woods. It passes a remarkable chute where the brook cascades between granite walls only two-and-a-half-feet apart, making beautiful mountain music in its plunge.

The notion that the brook was a musical instrument powered by water came to me several times during the hike. Every time I heard a different note, I considered the instrument that made it. Sometimes it was a great water organ, sometimes a water cymbal or flute. The sound did not fit well into the usual sections of percussion, strings, wood-

winds, or brass. It was in its own rockwater section, sometimes muted with snow and ice, sometimes blaring, sometimes soft and euphonious. What was this music that it should affect me so? I often found myself listening to the streaming water without a thought in my head. Without a verbal thought, at any rate. The sound was preverbal, coming from a source older than song, older than language. Perhaps we listen to music to be taken back to that time. Opera sung in a language we don't understand always seems an enigma. It is the drama that grips us, the music that stirs something basic within. We long to do away with words, to go back to a time when we didn't need them to communicate directly with our companions and surroundings, when others knew our minds without our having to ask, "Do you know what I mean?"

Rather than sit in a dark concert hall trying to stifle a cough until the end of a movement, I choose to take my music straight in the open air. The drama, beauty, and excitement of much of our music seem often effete, empty calories for the mind without food for the spirit. We praise the composer and his interpreters as minor gods, but their works are more clever than divine. If music wells from an urge to herald the sacred, we seem now more intent on tooting our own horn. Outdoors, I know exactly what the wind and the stream mean without having to ask. They speak to me—to my soul, the part of my communal self that has nothing to do with words.

The Little Harbor Brook and Amphitheater trails led me to the oldest concert hall of all, the natural amphitheater where music can be heard for what it is, the voice of the Earth. We know it right away when we hear it. It stops us in our tracks. We have no choice but to listen, to take it inside us as the nourishment we are starved for by a diet of symbols which stuff us without feeding our souls. At last we have gotten somewhere. Once there, it is not possible to go back unchanged to the urban environment where we started out. Having heard the Earth sing, we hunger to hear it again.

❧

Trailhead, Amphitheater Trail, at Harbor Brook Bridge.

38—ELIOT MOUNTAIN LOOP

From Brown Mountain Gate parking area
To Eliot Mountain, and back
   Up by Forest Hill Cemetery connector, Asticou
      Trail to the Map House, and Eliot Mountain Trail
Down by Eliot Mountain Trail, Asticou Trail, and
    Forest Hill Cemetery connector
        2.7 miles on ice creepers, April 9, 1997

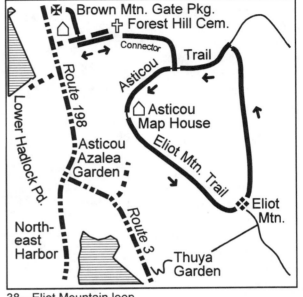

38—Eliot Mountain loop.

A brief snow squall hit at 8:30 a.m., and the daytime temperature peaked at 25° Fahrenheit, setting a new low for the high temperature on April 9. It had rained earlier in the week; I figured the snow would be gone by now. The peaks were largely bare, but in the woods trails were avenues of snow and ice, creating the worst hiking conditions of the year. April in Maine can be such a trial. The cold waters of the Gulf of Maine keep wooded coastal areas locked in ice after the sun is well up in the sky. Equinoctial winds chill the air even more. Mainers have three options: stay indoors, tough it out, or suffer the duration in Bermuda.

I started this hike twice, the first time without ice creepers. Parking in the lot north of Brown Mountain Gate on Route 198 up from Northeast Harbor, I took the trail through the woods behind the gatehouse, where a flitting shadow alerted me to a hairy woodpecker on a birch twenty feet over my head. While watching the woodpecker, I saw a red-breasted nuthatch gleaning tidbits from the bark of a nearby spruce. South of the gatehouse, I followed Gatehouse Road back to Forest Hill Cemetery. In the southeast corner of the cemetery I picked up the connector trail that ties into the Asticou Trail. Ties in, that is, if you have brought your creepers. It didn't take me anywhere at all on Vibram soles. After forcing the issue for about a third of a mile, I got the message. Mind may triumph over many things, but I doubt it ever gets the best of ice. Why hadn't I put my creepers in the car, just in case? Ice on the level is one thing, but when it slopes up or down, you go where it takes you, not where you want to go. I gingerly backtracked to my car, drove to my apartment at park headquarters, got my creepers and a file to sharpen the points, arriving back at Brown Mountain Gate an hour after I started the first time. My false start added 0.6 mile to the overall distance, raising it to 3.3 miles.

I saw two robins back of the gatehouse, and this time I noticed the pink granite gravestone set in the ground where the connector heads into the park:

A FISH MONGER EXTRAORDINAIRE
"SNICK"
SHELDON LEROY DAMON
APR. 15, 1933–OCT. 18, 1995
WHO HAS MORE FUN THAN PEOPLE

As I was passing through the cemetery a third time, I saw my first turkey vulture of the year rocking on its brittle dihedral in the gusty wind. It may have been winter on the ground, but in the sky it was spring. Being an earthbound biped myself without a dihedral to carry me through the air, I strapped on my creepers and walked past the orange **US BOUNDARY NPS** marker into the April woods with new-found confidence. This time I noticed pincushion moss, hair-cap moss, wintergreen, and mayflower leaves along the trail. The creepers on my feet gave me new sight in letting me look beyond my next step. Where before I had looked for rocks and roots to walk on, now I had to remember to stick to ice. Creepers require adopting a counterintuitive mindset. And when I took them off on the ledgy summit of Eliot Mountain, I had to think again whether to step on ice or rock.

Once I began to work with the ice rather than against it, I took joy in being in tall spruce woods once again. Getting a whiff of fox scent clinched it; I was back among friends. This is where I belong, I told myself, in the lap of nature, our true storyteller and master teacher, as opposed to that other place where we seem to get so many basic things wrong because we live at such a psychic remove from the natural world. How ironic it is that in writing up these hikes I reduce nature to symbols, belying its immediacy, intricacy, and beauty. I would rather have people go take a hike than sit indoors reading about me taking a hike. Hiking clears the head, while reading often clouds it with other people's notions and ideas. We have to keep asking, is this the best use of our time? Hiking is the highest and best use I have found yet for mine. It puts me in touch with life's funda-mentals—rocks, soil, ferns, mosses, lichens, trees, fresh air, clear running water, and the Earthlings who accompany us on our journey around the sun. We often pretend that the economy is the basis of life, or ownership and the control of wealth, or free trade, or a legal system founded on the right

to own property. In the woods, none of that matters. There are no lawyers in the woods, no capitalists, no entrepreneurs. Our professions and job specialties have no meaning there. We are included among the ranks of Earthlings ourselves, proud sons and daughters of the third planet from the sun, our homeland amid the universal flux. Money and language lose all meaning in the woods. Without them to color our thoughts, we see who and where we are, perhaps for the first

Icy trail through woods on Eliot Mountain.

time in our lives. What if we never found out? What if Snick Damon went through life believing that a fishmonger was what he was, mistaking what he did for a living for his identity? We are so much more than the labels we stick on ourselves suggest. A walk in the woods without those labels lets us begin to appreciate the vastness we are under the skin. We are extensions of the vastness of Earth, which in itself elaborates the possibility of the universe. We are children of the universe up and walking on two legs, direct descendants of supernovas, galaxies, and the seething plasma of pre-atomic particles we call the Big Bang, cosmic spark that kindled the fires of life. We are universal beings, as natural as spruce cones and granite. Yet we scorn our brute selves, taking heavy (the root meaning of brute) in a negative sense, while it also means weighty and venerable, as in gravity and guru (derived from the same root). How can we expect salvation if we never embrace our weighty, natural selves, biological-geological-cosmological miracles that we are? Salvation awaits us outdoors where we are as natural as the sun and the rain, our godparents in the sky who give us every opportunity to be all that we can be.

My springtime thoughts were ponderous. Where was the lightness of being I usually experience on the trail? My body was impatient for spring to declare itself. Now, not some indefinite time in the future. Why was it holding back when I was so ready to receive it? The fever of yearning was getting to me. I was full of philosophical grumblings and complaints. There was nothing to do but sweat it out, to keep hiking and hope that time would heal my mood. Struggling to reach out to the world, I was stuck for now in my head.

The park's trail crew had been clearing the connector trail between the cemetery and the Asticou Trail, cutting back saplings that were crowding the trail. My way was strewn with Christmas trees, just in time for the April holiday season. By the side of the trail I also saw mountain cranberry, goldthread, and sphagnum moss beginning to thaw from the ice. How hardy can you get? They were green and ready to get back to work as if winter had never been.

Even with ice creepers I found sloping ice a big challenge. I planted my feet firmly, making sure the points got a

Signpost at trail crossing, summit of Eliot Mountain.

good grip. Going down felt less secure than going up because I didn't have the leverage to sink my claws into the ice. I accepted help from wayside trees, which were always ready to give a hand. There are no major slopes on the route I took, but when slicked with ice the trail is plenty steep enough. The low point was at Asticou Map House, about 215 feet; the high on Eliot Mountain at about 460 feet. The vertical climb and descent was only 245 feet, but with ice underfoot, that was about all I was up for. A hike like my last one up the valley of Little Harbor Brook to Birch Spring would have been out of the question.

Most of this hike lies on private land outside the park. The connector is just inside the boundary, but the leg of the Asticou Trail to the map house is outside, and the Eliot Mountain Trail is outside as well. Development is starting to creep up the hillside above the Asticou Inn, another lot having been sold last year. The operative rule is that if land

can be developed, sooner or later it will be developed. Given real estate values on Mount Desert Island, it would be unreasonable to expect otherwise. I hike Eliot Mountain while I can. The last time I was here was on Christmas Day 1995. That was a snowshoe hike along the same route with my partner and a friend. Cairns were buried then under several feet of snow. We had trouble finding our way back along the edge of the drop toward Little Harbor Brook, but by brushing snow off of suspect heaps, we uncovered enough cairns to confirm we were on the right track. It was a great way to celebrate the triple event of solstice, Christmas, and New Year's Day—truly one and the same occasion—at a single swoop.

The route is fairly level between Brown Mountain Gate and the map house. From there it rises gradually, grows steeper, then levels off again on the wooded summit ridge. The virtue of the Eliot Mountain Trail is not its challenge but the spruce woods through which it leads. Old woods. Tall woods. Woods as true as the Earth. This is how coastal Maine is supposed to look. How it did look some 230 years ago when an exotic species from Europe imposed a new canon of beauty on the "New World" based wholly on extraction of natural resources. As long as logging was done in winter with axes and oxen, the woods were a match to human consumption, but when skidders were brought in about 1965, and behind them the entire apparatus of industrial forestry, the exotic species got the upper hand and the woods were doomed. Now the woods on Eliot Mountain are an anachronism because they have not kept up with the times. They are a marvelous example of the possible, but fall far short of the cornucopia humankind would have them be. Their miracle simply isn't good enough for us. We want woods truly worthy of our machines and the appetite that drives them. I am sure these woods were cut once or twice early on, but now they are a good example of old growth, trees growing for their purposes, not ours.

Beauty is spruce woods, green seedlings and saplings gathered at the roots of the old ones.

The way through the trees was strewn with cone scales

where red squirrels had scattered their litter to be recycled in the duff on the forest floor. In the woods those scatterings were the prime sign of spring. I heard one squirrel, and saw another, but must have seen the work of twenty-five or more. I heard a raven, too, another aborigine, and soon saw its black form spread against the sky just above the sprucetops. I saw two scats packed with fur and fragments of bone, deer pellets, hare pellets, one set of fox prints, and the workings of pileated woodpeckers over the years. I saw one chickadee and knew that where there was one, there must have been ten that I missed. As for people, I saw the tracks of one person on Eliot Mountain, and another two or three on the Asticou Trail.

Spruce cones, cores, and scales on ice in the trail, the work of red squirrels.

The summit ridge of Eliot Mountain is broad, wooded, and relatively flat. It offers no breathtaking views other than onto trees and more trees. Through one opening I caught a glimpse of the white monument on Bunkers Ledge south of Day Mountain in Eastern Way, and through another the forms of Penobscot, Pemetic, and Cadillac mountains, with the Triad and Barr Hill to the south. You don't go to Eliot Mountain for the view; you go to be where you are, in spruce woods. There isn't much to tell you that you have reached the top, no mountainous cairn, no expanding vista on the far side. There is a trail junction marked by a signpost:

JORDAN POND [north]
LITTLE HBR. BROOK [southeast]
THUYA GARDENS
ASTICOU TERRACE [southwest]
MAP HOUSE
ASTICOU [west].

I saw a few clumps of rusty juniper on open ledges, and lots of reindeer lichen growing in island-like clumps. The sun had disappeared behind clouds by the time I got to the summit, which seems the normal course of events at this time of year. The wind chilled the air, which my internal thermometer put at zero. I looked around the summit ledges for ten minutes, poking here and there, but soon yearned for the cover of the woods, so headed north toward the junction with the Asticou Trail where it dips toward Little Harbor Brook.

I hadn't noticed many Northern white cedars on the way up, but there were a lot of them along this leg of my loop. The trail leads on through old, sometimes decrepit (that is, natural) woods. Stretches of ledge creep in now and then, to be gradually crowded out by trees as the soil grows thick enough away from the summit to withstand the forces of erosion. Dropping slowly, the trail enters the wet area between Eliot and Cedar Swamp mountains, the ice as unrelenting as it was coming up the west side. I put my creepers on again and made the slippery trek without mishap, though it was no easy jaunt. Having to concentrate on my footing, I didn't get to gawk as much as I wanted to. There were a lot of pileated woodpecker excavations on that stretch of trail, which was near where I had seen the bird itself the past two years.

A little over an hour since leaving the summit, I reached the Asticou Trail where, five days before, I had declined an invitation to return to Little Harbor Brook over Eliot Mountain. There had been much more snow then, and much less ice. Maybe in another week the ice would be gone. When that happens, I will officially announce it is spring.

I punched my way along an icy stretch of the Asticou Trail for twenty minutes, catching a glimpse of partridgeberry leaves at the turn for Sargent Mountain by way of Cedar Swamp, then picked up the connector to the cemetery. I took off my creepers near Snick's grave and got back to my car in a few minutes, after seeing a squad of ten robins digging under leaves in the thinned woods below the cemetery. The trail used to lead through those woods, but that section is now gone, many blazed trees having been felled. It took me four hours to go the loop, including an hour going back for the creepers I might have brought with me. It was time well spent, considering I had been all the way to the front lines of universal creation and back.

What we humans call creativity is often not that at all but a random assault on the possible. We figure if we do every imaginable thing in every conceivable way, something is bound to work. Civilization is the sum total of our collected efforts, without a center, without a sense of purpose or direction. Nature always starts from the baseline of existing conditions and works from there, allowing conditions as they subsequently develop to shape and edit the project, to nip it in the bud or bring it to fruition. Humans rarely have the courage to put their work to any true test, but push it for all it is worth in the shelter of their minds and institutions. Nature fits its works to actual conditions prevailing at the time; people deny those conditions, doing more what they can get away with. Untested by natural forces, human creativity goes off in all directions like a display of fireworks, with effects every bit as lasting. One spruce tree on Eliot Mountain is a far better use of Earth resources than all the compact disks, bottled sodas, and T-shirts produced by humans around the world. I know, I have consulted the red squirrel, the raven, and the chickadee, learned critics in their fields. The difference between a spruce tree and a compact disk is in their respective technologies; one is sustainable, the other is not; one is recycled, the other thrown out. What a waste of the universal stuff it is to develop complex products that end up in the dump without bringing benefit to subsequent generations of users. We live off the Earth instead of on it. We maintain we are a higher species that does not need to live by Earth's rules. Earth has an answer to that: Wait and see. In shaving away unwarranted complexity, Ockham's razor applies to us. We should tape Shelley's "Ozimandias" to our bathroom mirrors. We know what works from observing the natural world that surrounds us. Rather than heading off on whatever tangent appeals to us at the moment, for whatever reason, we would do better to follow Earth's game plan of following the simplest, most obvious course for the most basic reason. There is more wisdom on Eliot Mountain than in the collected works of all the world's economists, more business acumen than possessed by the faculties and graduates of all the world's business schools. If you want a seminar or conference on the latest in creative *and* sustainable survival techniques, there is an ongoing session just up the slope from Asticou Map House. You may not recognize it at first, but that is where true economy is taught.

Driving to Brown Mountain Gate, I had passed by Upper Hadlock Pond, which was covered by a solid sheet of white ice. Driving back on Route 3 counterclockwise around the island I passed by the Tarn, which was all open water without one cube of ice. Word is leaking out that spring is here, or if not actually here, can be heard rattling at the gate.

39—AROUND DORR MOUNTAIN

From Sieur de Monts Spring parking area
To the Notch between Dorr and Cadillac mountains, and back
Up by the Spring Road, Hemlock Trail, and Notch Trail
Down by A. Murray Young, Canon Brook, Kane, and Jesup trails

5.0 miles, April 16, 1997

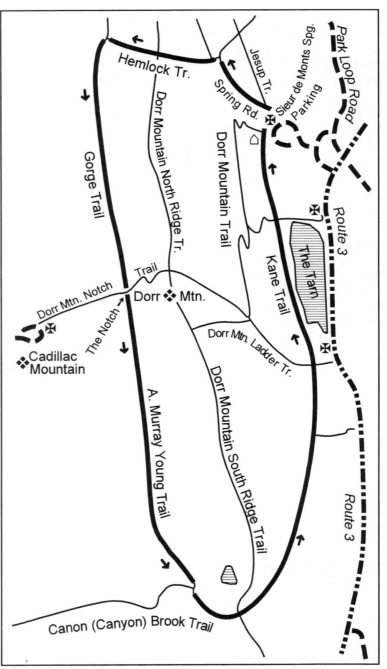

39—Around Dorr Mountain.

Acadia's south-facing slopes were bare of snow and ice, but great patches of white still showed on those facing north. The ice on Eagle Lake was going but not gone. I had two north-facing valleys on my list of spring hikes, the valleys of Kebo and Sargent brooks. I knew they would be icy. But I wanted to hike along the brooks while they were still running with meltwater. Could I make it up either one?

Three days earlier I had made a trial run along the Canon (formerly Canyon) Brook Trail as far as the junction with the A. Murray Young Trail coming down from the Notch. So much water was streaming off the mountains, I couldn't follow either trail beyond that point. The trails themselves were flooded in many places, and where they crossed their respective brooks, boulders that might have offered footing on drier days were submerged in swift flowing water. That was Sunday. By Wednesday the torrent had subsided, so I knew water would not be a problem. But what about ice in those north-facing valleys? There was only one way to find out. I decided to make a loop around Dorr Mountain to compare conditions in the north- and south-facing valleys leading up to the Notch.

I had hiked the same route several years ago in the fall (see Hike 4) going clockwise around the mountain; this time I decided to go the other way, hitting the northern valley first, then the southern. I made a circuit from the Sieur de Monts Spring parking area comprising sections of the old Spring Road, Hemlock Trail, Gorge Trail, A. Murray Young Trail, Canon Brook Trail, Kane Trail, and Jesup Trail. I started at 1:00 p.m. and got back to my car about sunset at 7:10 p.m., taking a little over six hours to cover the five-mile loop. Yes, I made it up along Kebo Brook and, yes, it was icy. The northern valley was still locked in late winter while the southern valley had eased into early spring. I had to watch every icy step going up to the Notch; coming down I took solid footing on dry rock for granted and could eye my surroundings as I walked. It was a beautiful spring day, the temperature about 55° when I started, 45° when I got back. The shaded parts of the valley of Kebo Brook felt a lot colder.

I knew I was pushing it, but my eagerness to see Kebo Brook flowing with meltwater spurred me on. At one point in the constriction near the memorial plaque to Lilian Endicott Francklyn on the Gorge Trail, I was faced with a blue-white wall of slick ice. There was no way I could scale that wall; I had to scramble up a steep slope through a doghair thicket to get around it. Knowing the valley widened out after that, I guessed that would be the worst ice on the trail. It was. My suggestion would be to stave off the urge to hike the Gorge Trail until mid-May at least. I was too impatient to take my own advice. The Giant Slide Trail would be worse, particularly where the trail ducks under the Giant Slide itself through a dark tunnel where ice would hold out even longer.

I passed four memorial plaques on this hike which lent it literary overtones. Lilian Endicott Francklyn has become a fabled figure in my mythology. I know little about her other than what I have read on her plaque:

IN LOVING MEMORY OF
**LILIAN
ENDICOTT FRANCKLYN
1891–1928**
THIS TRAIL IS ENDOWED BY
HER FRIENDS.

Kebo Brook flows beneath cliffs in the Gorge.

She lived for thirty-seven years, and had friends who loved her. The setting of the plaque tells the rest of the story. She was sensitive to natural beauty. Those who read the plaque on the Gorge Trail face toward a dramatic plunge of water over granite into a slowly revolving pool. Lilian, we are with you in spirit. Beauty is all that matters. What more intimate moment can we share than to stand where someone else has stood and see what they must have seen?

I met a party of five youths in T-shirts hiking down the Gorge Trail, four boys and a maid with a gold ring through her eyebrow. A dachshund came trotting at their heels. They were slipping and sliding on the ice and wet snow. The boy in the lead said something about it being easier going down than going up. I shouted back above the roar of the brook that it got worse down below, but I don't think he heard me. They stopped to throw snowballs at each other, and seemed generally frisky and carefree. Watching them for a time, I saw the girl slip in one spot, plunging four feet sideways toward the brook. I suspected they would have a harder time getting down the wall of ice ahead of them than I had had getting up. Every generation begins the world again, starting from scratch. Whether we feel freed by it or condemned, each of us must live her own life. Different lives, different experiences, different worlds. We may appear to walk the same course, but it is a different course for each of us. We are so much flotsam on the tide, carried along by universal currents playing themselves out in our lives, with no way of knowing what shore we will wash upon, if we wash upon any. A strange thought for the valley of Kebo Brook, but I could incorporate these fellow hikers into my world no easier than I suspect they could incorporate me into theirs. Untamed Youth meets the Abominable Snowman. Wildlife indeed, on both sides.

Wildlife on all sides. It was a great hike for birds. Leery of ice, I set out to see Kebo Brook in action, but kept getting distracted by singing and flying Acadians who cared not a whit about snow and ice. What little was left was moribund. Winter had had its day; this was spring. Get with it, I was told at every turn. Start-to-finish, life returning to Acadia was the story of this hike, not some trickling brook or leaking pile of ice.

Kebo Brook spills over a mossy boulder.

From the wide, graveled surface of the old Spring Road running north from the Sieur de Monts Spring parking area, I saw, in the order of their appearance, a blue jay, two water striders, a female downy woodpecker on a birch, eight juncos hopping and scratching in the road ahead, a white-throated sparrow and a song sparrow in wayside shrubbery, and an Eastern chipmunk scurrying through the leaves. I took my binoculars with me, so had a good look at them all. It is easier to see birds at this time of year before poplars and birches leaf out. The road runs through deciduous woods on the east side and hemlocks on the west, skirting the outer fringe of Great Meadow. It bends northeast and crosses through the meadow toward Bar Harbor, its course interrupted by the loop road and Kebo Valley Golf Course, then goes on to Ledgelawn Avenue as a track through the woods.

Where the Spring Road turns for the meadow, the Hem-

lock Trail heads west over the saddle between Dorr and Kebo mountains. It rises steeply up a slope through hemlocks, then passes at an easy grade through oak woods, to link up with the Kebo Mountain Road and the Gorge Trail. I met a shaggy dog (part collie, part juniper bush) coming down the Dorr Mountain North Ridge Trail, its pink tongue hanging out to catch the breeze. Without a sidelong glance, it crossed in front of me and went straight on at a steady trot toward Kebo Mountain. I saw several gray moths fluttering about rocks in the trail and various gnat-sized insects hovering in the sunlight above the small brook draining the saddle into Great Meadow. Deer prints showed clearly in a stretch of sandy soil, but what caught my attention was a strange-sounding crow in the bushes north of the trail. No, not a crow . . . a frog tuning its mouth-harp, twang after twang. It sounded like a green frog, with a difference, each note richly embellished, but not enough to mask the basic frogginess underneath. Comes the next rain, all frogdom will burst out in song. This one was warming its vocal cords for that great event. The Hemlock Trail passes by a forty-foot vernal pool, frozen now, a crescent of open water showing around the north edge. From there the trail dips down in short order to the old Kebo Mountain Road and, next to it, Kebo Brook.

What struck me about the brook was its color, a deep orange red from the gravel it flowed over, chips off the old block of Cadillac Mountain. The Gorge Trail starts at the loop road bridge between Cadillac and Kebo mountains, then rises through the rocky valley to the Notch between Dorr and Cadillac. From the Hemlock Trail, the Gorge Trail starts out as wide as the old Kebo Mountain Road, but soon narrows to a slender track clinging to one side of the valley or the other above the brook. There was thick ice in the road, punched with cookie-cutter holes in shapes of popple, oak, and maple leaves. Fallen onto snow that turned to ice, the leaves had become trapped. Absorbing sunlight faster than ice, they sank straight down, melting out hollows having their shape. Some were six inches deep, the excavating leaf having dried and blown away, leaving its life-size hallmark in the ice.

The treadway of the Gorge Trail is well laid with flat

stones, making the going easy for the most part. In places the trail runs in the bed of Kebo Brook, making for easier passage in August than April. The valley constricts in three places, adding the drama of crumbling cliffs to the trek. The brook is full of rocky plunges and pools, providing background music to spring hikes, and hikes after rainstorms in summer and fall. I heard one chickadee over the sound of the brook, a brief solo that soared above the boisterous chorus.

Below the Notch, a pulpit of rock rises midvalley across from a sheer, forty-foot cliff on the Dorr Mountain side. A hoary yellow birch rises next to Pulpit Rock. Gazing into its gnarled branches, I saw five turkey vultures soaring north overhead, emblazoned on a field of blue enamel. At my feet, I saw green wood ferns pressed flat by the snow, downtrodden perhaps, but not beaten. I also saw feather moss, and almost to the Notch, hair-cap moss, mountain cranberry, and reindeer lichen.

The Notch Trail connecting the summits of Dorr and Cadillac crosses the Gorge Trail in the Notch, the saddle between the two peaks. On the axis of the streams draining north and south, the so-called Notch is a summit having an elevation of 1,030 feet, 960 feet above Sieur de Monts Spring. With walls of crumbling rock east and west, and views of the horizon north and south, the Notch is the Charing Cross of Acadia, the Broadway and 42nd Street. No one hikes to reach the Notch itself, it is a place you pass through in heading for somewhere else. When Cadillac Mountain was called Green Mountain, the Notch marked the midpoint of Green Mountain Gorge, the round-bottomed valley scooped out by the glacier that is one of the trademarks of Acadia. Before the auto road (Cadillac Mountain Road) was built, the Gorge Trail and the north ridge trail made a popular loop between Green Mountain and Bar Harbor. The trail link to Bar Harbor has been broken. The Gorge itself is split in two, the Gorge Trail running up to the Notch from the north, the A. Murray Young Trail from the south.

Heading through the small birch and spruce woods in the Notch, I picked up the A. Murray Young Trail at the crossing and headed for Baker Island and points south. Passing beneath Buddha sitting on his ledge overlooking the valley, I paid my respects. Having sat there so long, he now looks like

The A. Murray Young Trail drops out of the Notch.

nothing more than a pile of rocks. What do you say to Buddha when you meet him face-to-face? I gave him a one-handed round of applause and let it go at that. A coppery sundog showed above the squat form sheltered on its ledge beneath the rim of the Gorge on the Cadillac side. (Buddha is best seen from farther down the trail.)

The A. Murray Young Trail crosses steeply through boulders dropped from the cliffs above, then comes out in a broad valley where Dorr and Cadillac step back, leaving a basin between them which I call Beaver Hollow after the rodents I found resident there in the early '70s. The trail remembers them too, skirting their former pond with respect, thought it has now shrunk to a brook. Insects were warming themselves above those south-facing slopes. I saw a phoebe in a striped maple grove dart out again and again to pick off the little sunbathers one-by-one. I heard a raven somewhere on Cadillac, and saw a crow drop down the valley toward Otter Creek. Looking back to admire the Notch, I saw two turkey vultures circling above the cliffs. A downy woodpecker tapped at a birch near the trail. Robins raced among the leaves, gleaning tasty morsels exposed by retreating snow. On the southern edge of Beaver Hollow I saw two hermit thrushes sitting side-by-side on a low branch. Through binoculars, I saw one fly off, then the other. That clinched it: spring had officially arrived. In the south end of Green Mountain Gorge at any rate, if not in the north. Near the bottom of the valley I saw two more hermit thrushes silently flitting through the woods. Can eyes be glad? Mine certainly were. They welcomed those birds back to their breeding grounds once again, though the birds were glad in their own right to be back where they belonged.

The A. Murray Young Trail follows along the headwaters of Otter Creek from their rise in the Notch to their meeting with Canon Brook coming off the east flank of Cadillac Mountain. It is a classic Acadian trail with impressive woods, rocks, and falling water. The treadway is laid on stones and ledge the whole distance, giving solid footing for the gradual 1.2-mile descent from (or rise to) the Notch. Like the Valley Peak Trail, it is a good trail for trees. White and yellow birch, Northern white cedar, red and white pine, red spruce, balsam fir, and hemlock stand out in my mind from this hike. There are alders in Beaver Hollow, and many ferns near the brook. The trail crosses the brook several times in places where I could follow it on this hike while last Sunday, with the water fifteen inches higher, I could only stand and gawk from the bank. The brook plunges unevenly down the valley, the trail following a more sedate route to the side. Brook and trail come together lower down near the stone plaque to Andrew Murray Young set in a huge boulder facing over the water:

IN MEMORY OF
ANDREW MURRAY YOUNG
WHO LOVED THIS ISLAND
WHERE GOD HAS GIVEN
OF HIS BEAUTY WITH A
LAVISH HAND.
1861–1924

Beauty is the face of the cosmic force that drives the world. We know it when we see it, our true ancestor whose blood flows in our veins and in our children's. Our job is to admire it while we can, and to carry it forward so the work of the force, which is never finished, will continue. Lilian Endicott Francklyn saw the face of the universe in Kebo Brook; Andrew Murray Young saw it in the headwaters of Otter Creek. They remind us to be on the lookout for it in our own lives, and to dedicate ourselves to it when we find it.

Last Sunday I had seen three white mayflower buds beside the trail above the junction with the Canon Brook Trail. I wondered if they had opened since then. No, they looked the same, about to bloom—but not yet. The cosmic force works at its own cosmic pace. Who am I to ask it to schedule its doings for my convenience? I still have mayflowers to look forward to in coming weeks.

The worn ledges where the waters coming off Cadillac and Dorr rush out of the Gorge and head for Otter Cove are my favorite picnic spot in Acadia, whether the waters are rushing or not. You can't get there by car, so the only sounds you hear are natural sounds, the sounds of the local cosmos at work. On Sunday, my partner and I ate our sandwiches on what little dry ledge the brook left us. I had never seen the brook so high or so swift. The cosmos was rushing full bore to get Acadia ready for spring. The brook frothed east, then west, then east again, roaring as it went. Spates don't last long on these steep slopes, so you have to enjoy them while you can. On this hike the water swept with grace through the channel across the granite ledges where on Sunday it had bolted pell-mell. At the ledges I picked up the Canon Brook Trail and headed around the south end of Dorr Mountain toward Beaver Brook Valley on the other side.

Where the trail in the Gorge is up and down, the trail around to the east side of Dorr Mountain and on to Sieur de Monts Spring is relatively level, falling only 148 feet between the picnic ledges and the spring. Up from Otter Creek

the trail passes the outlet stream from a beaver pond higher up on Dorr, the stream spilling over an abrupt drop in a fine fall of water. The trail soon meets the Dorr Mountain South Ridge Trail coming off the mountain and continuing on through woods to the swimming hole on Otter Creek lower down. From that crossing the Canon Brook Trail drops into the valley of Beaver Brook, a tributary of Otter Creek that rises south of the Tarn. The long ridge of Champlain loomed

Lodge in Beaver Brook off the Canon Brook Trail.

ahead through the budding trees. On this section of trail I heard a ruffed grouse whir off into the undergrowth, and heard chickadees, and robins all along. Watching a pair of chickadees, I noticed a brown bird with them hawking insects from the bark of a birch. I knew immediately what it was, and used my binoculars to confirm my guess—a palm warbler, as pretty a sight as the cosmos presented me with all day. I had made a lanyard when I was in fifth grade using brown and yellow gimp, and those were the colors of this bird's breast, warm brown speckles against a background of yellow, the brown echoed in a cap on its head. The warbler stuck with the chickadees as they moved tree-to-tree through the woods, passing less than twenty feet from where I stood. A noisy hairy woodpecker tapped away overhead, soon joined by another who came on whumping wings, and then a third, all making a great racket of chinks and shrieks. A downy woodpecker tapped gently away on a nearby birch, unmoved by the commotion around her. Two robins flew by, my head swirling this way and that to keep track of the cosmos in action around me. I had been all set to mourn the passing of tracks in the snow, but here the woods were alive with birds, so I canceled the black band and long face and left the mourning to that bird I heard calling so forlornly in the distance.

The trail parallels Beaver Brook, which, with gnawed poles strewn this way and that, was aptly named. I saw two beaver dams and two lodges, and in one swollen wetland behind a dam, Paddy himself. He dived without making a sound just as I heard a slow, heavy drumming from a silver snag off the trail. I knew who made that sound, but scanned the snag through binoculars to make sure. The drummer was on the far side, so I couldn't see him. He drummed again, and this time was answered by a series of sharp, staccato cries from near Huguenot Head. Then the drummer flew to a neighboring snag, showing off his bright red mustache and pointed cap, as fine a specimen of pileated woodpecker masculinity as I have seen. He clawed his way up the trunk, cocking his head to one side then the other, listening, listening—perhaps for insects, but more likely for a further response to his drumming. Not forty feet from me, he was so caught up in his cosmic whirl that I was no more to him than a gnat sunning itself above a brook. Looking up at the woodpecker, I saw a marsh hawk over his shoulder coasting down the valley on outstretched wings. A blue jay called from across the brook, and a downy woodpecker tapped a sharp tattoo that sounded like a string of miniature firecrackers going off. I left the pileated woodpecker to his business, and he saluted my departure with a long series of clucks like a clock winding down. In the next pond I watched a pair of wood ducks take off and wing down the valley.

The Canon Brook Trail turns east toward Route 3, crossing the brook on a former beaver dam which last Sunday had been unpassable, but was now dry and firm. The Kane Trail continues on from that turn, though there is no sign to that effect. The upper reaches of Beaver Brook are full of snags toppled every which way into the mucky soil, their roots upended as graven tableaus of serpents writhing above the water. The trail passes through birch woods, crosses the divide between the watersheds of the brook and the Tarn, then crosses the start of the Dorr Mountain Ladder Trail, to continue along the western shore of the Tarn.

The Tarn, of course, isn't. A tarn, that is. A tarn is a deep, high mountain lake formed by a glacier. This one sits in a glacial valley all right, but is no more than six feet deep at any point. It is more a mud hole or a slough. George Dorr had a way with words, particularly when he wanted to put his personal spin on things. Tarn or no tarn, a great blue heron flew slowly from the south shore toward the north, and a pair of black ducks drifted over the surface. The Kane Trail winds among the talus blocks fallen from Dorr's east face, as fine a walk as the park has to offer, caught as it is between cliffs and the Tarn, with Huguenot Head rising starkly beyond. Pay no attention to those cars whizzing by on Route 3, you are where their occupants wished they could be. The start of the Kane Trail is fittingly marked by a plaque set in a boulder:

IN MEMORY OF
JOHN-INNES KANE
A MAN OF KINDNESS WHO
FOUND HIS HAPPINESS IN
GIVING OTHERS PLEASURE
1913

Behind Mr. Kane I see the cosmic force smiling approval at his good works. We are not here for ourselves but more to keep the force alive in others so that they may thrive in their own ways. Thank you, Mr. Kane, for a gift that has spanned most of the 20th century. I hope it goes on to affect the lives of people coming to Acadia a hundred years from now, and a hundred years after that.

Kurt Diederich's Climb starts up at the northern end of the Tarn, another of Acadia's classic hikes. I will take it shortly in pursuit of mayflowers which bloom along its upper reach. The Jesup Trail begins there as well, leading north past Sieur de Monts Spring to the loop road where Kebo Street comes in. This trail, too, has its plaque:

IN MEMORY OF
MORRIS K AND MARIA DE WITT JESUP
LOVERS OF THIS ISLAND
1918

Lovers of this island. Who among us is not? But to endow a trail seems a particularly fitting expression of that love because it enables others to share it in their own way. Again, the cosmic force is at work through the Jesups as through Mr. Kane, A. Murray Young, Lilian Francklyn, and all who remember them by hiking the trails built in their names.

I walked the Jesup Trail only as far as the parking area at Sieur de Monts Spring, leaving the walk through birch woods and across Great Meadow for another day. What a hike it had been, far surpassing my expectations. Could I make it up the Gorge Trail? I could, indeed! But that seemed a minor matter compared to the birdlife I had met on my route. I had heard a frog and eleven different birds, seen eighteen bird species, a beaver and a chipmunk, numerous insects, and the print of a deer. The birds I had seen were:

great blue heron	blue jay
black ducks	crow
wood ducks	chickadees
turkey vultures	hermit thrushes
marsh hawk	robins
hairy woodpeckers	palm warbler
downy woodpeckers	white-throated sparrow
pileated woodpecker	song sparrow
phoebe	juncos

The cosmic force was out in strength, and I was one of its beneficiaries. As are we all, though we sometimes let it slip from our awareness. The four plaques I had seen served as fitting reminders that love, kindness, and beauty are no accidents. They are gifts from the universe to us, and through us, to others. What are we to do if not distribute those gifts as widely as we can so that all can share our good fortune in being able to walk the Earth at our own pace in the time we

The Kane Trail runs along the Tarn at the base of Dorr.

are allowed? There it is, happiness, staring us in the face. Ours for the reaching of our arms and the stretching of our legs. If we lack for something else, I cannot imagine what it could be.

As happens every year, I was amazed to discover how a good dose of springtime is a sure cure for the blahs and a sour mood. Spring fever is a misnomer; it is actually yearning-for-spring fever. When spring finally comes, the fever is gone.

❧

40—SARGENT MOUNTAIN via GIANT SLIDE TRAIL

From St. James Church on Route 198
To Summit of Sargent Mountain, and back
  Up by Giant Slide and Sargent Mountain North
    Ridge trails
  Down by Grandgent and Giant Slide trails
                5.6 miles, April 23, 1997

While much of Acadia is bolting headlong for spring, the valley of Sargent Brook is holding back, saving its strength for a last-minute sprint. By the solstice things will even out, but for now, tucked in its north-facing valley between Sargent and Parkman mountains, Sargent Brook seems set on savoring winter as long as it can. A week ago I saw eighteen bird species on my tour around Dorr Mountain; this week on Sargent Mountain I saw only two species, American robin and ruffed grouse. I heard six other species: blue jay, chickadee, red-breasted nuthatch, raven, mourning dove, and what I shall call a warbling vireo.

Hearing the vireo made up for missing the variety of birds I had seen last week. This one let loose one of the most thrilling bursts of heartfelt song the universe has yet composed. A pure ode to joy, it radiated from the shadowy branches of a red spruce out to the galaxies spinning overhead. Earthlings make no finer noise. It captured the sizzling energy of electrons in vocal form. I heard it more with my innards than with my ears. It burst forth as I was bushwhacking out of Chickadee Valley up the east side of Gilmore Peak. I was about to jump from one boulder to another when that song rang out from the spire of a small spruce ten feet ahead. There is no way to prepare for such an auditory eruption. Suddenly it is there and you are in it, wholly immersed. I was overtaken and taken over as if I were the singer and the song was my song. It *was* my song. I recognized it right away. The song I would sing if I had the throat to make such a noise. A universal bursting forth of uncontainable love. Not love directed at an object but love given freely to the cosmos at large. Love that celebrates being here in this place, aware and alive. I peered into the tree from which the song had rung out but saw no shadow or silhouette of any bird. Had I imagined the outburst? My life experience isn't rich enough to make up such a thing. I had heard it all right. While climbing the Sargent Mountain North Ridge Trail an hour and a half earlier I had wondered why the cosmos had called me out on such a hike. The landscape was bleak and dreary beneath a lid of gray clouds. What was my mission? Why was I here? When I heard the music of the vireo peal from that spruce, I knew I had been called out to witness that one event. The entire hike coalesced around that nugget of joy. Waiting quietly to make sure the bird had flown away unseen, after five minutes I completed my jump and regained the trail that had been blocked lower down by a cascade of ice. Reaching the small cairn marking Gilmore Peak's summit at 1,036 feet, I recognized the vireo's song as the anthem of that place. Surrounded by spruce woods, the peak looks over Bald Peak and Parkman Mountain to the west and the Hadlock Ponds to the south-southwest. Gilmore's summit ridge has not been denuded by cairn builders but is sprinkled with pebbles, cobbles, and boulders much as the glacier must have left it. Not made over for human comfort or convenience, it is very much an Acadian kind of

west. They went west; I went east. The only other person I met was a lone cyclist in full racing regalia who was leaning into the horseshoe bend where the Around-Mountain Carriage Road crosses Sargent Brook. Both surprised to meet someone there, we had time only to exchange quick hellos before he was gone.

From the former St. James Church on Route 198, the start of the Giant Slide Trail—one of Acadia's truly great hikes—is a little off-putting because of the battery of signs warning hikers not to stray off the trail onto private land. The Park Service has its sign, the owners of the former church theirs, and four other property owners theirs. In no uncertain terms the hiker is told:

PRIVATE DRIVE
PRIVATE PROPERTY
POSTED, PEDESTRIANS ONLY
KEEP OUT, NO TRESPASSING
DO NOT ENTER

Even the portable toilet by the former church had its sign:

POSTED
NO TRESPASSING
KEEP OUT

The message was clear, but I felt somehow unwelcome on a route that had served as a public way for over a hundred years. A more positive approach would be to make sure the trail was clearly marked so that hikers would not

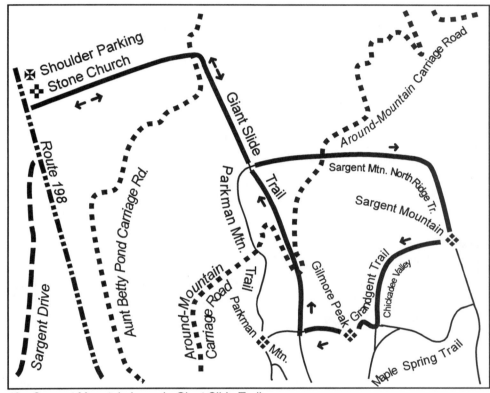

40—Sargent Mountain loop via Giant Slide Trail.

place, fitting habitat for a passing warbling vireo whose song reflects its virtue and true character.

I heard wood frogs quacking like ducks on both sides of Giant Slide Road near the start of the hike. I saw a leaping shadow in the saddle between Parkman Mountain and Gilmore Peak, a form that must have been a red squirrel though I saw it only briefly out of the corner of my eye. Bending down to look at blades of marginal wood fern, I found my nose six inches away from a minute spider aerialist bouncing up and down on a strand of thin silk. Horse scats marked the stretch of the Giant Slide Trail between St. James Church and the Aunt Betty Pond Carriage Road. Snowshoe hare pellets marked the rest of the loop here and there. Scattered cone scales hinted at red squirrel activity, and deep punctures in dead and living trees told of the pileated woodpecker's appetite for carpenter ants. Three hikers caught up with me at the Giant Slide where the Sargent Mountain North Ridge and Parkman Mountain trails head respectively east and

wander off out of uncertainty. How defensive we become when we own a piece of land. It brings out our fear of being intruded upon by strangers. Signs and fences go up as soon as we sign the deed. Think what Mount Desert Island would be without the park—a warren of barricaded acres defended with leers, signs, fences, and shotguns. Would the warbling vireo sing in such a place? Not without the owners' permission. We want no such racket here. No untoward displays of cosmic joy and celebration. The so-called right-use movement has it wrong. Earth is not meant to be divvied up among the fearful and defensive. Private property rights are a dangerous fiction. We cannot rightly control what we did not make and do not understand. Earth owns us, we are its creatures. It is as foolish to think we can own an acre of land as it would be to own our parents or the clouds that bring rain. I am thankful for state and national parks that remind us how beautiful our habitat is, and how lucky we are to share it for the brief span we are allowed. Earth welcomes our visit as long as we do not spoil the landscape or its inhabitants as we pass by. Who among us has ever posted a sign, **WELCOME EARTHLINGS!** I am glad the federal government had the wisdom to set Acadia aside for the benefit of spruce trees and warbling vireos, and for those who care about such things.

PUBLIC WAY, ENTER HERE!

After running the gauntlet of no trespassing signs, my route took me through mixed woods to the Aunt Betty Pond Carriage Road, then up the valley of Sargent Brook as far as the trail crossing by the Giant Slide, a huge slab of granite let slip from the Parkman side of the valley. From there I took the Sargent Mountain North Ridge Trail to the 1,373-foot summit, where I picked up the Grandgent Trail leading to the upper end of the Giant Slide Trail in the saddle between Parkman Mountain and Gilmore Peak, passing through what I call Chickadee Valley and over Gilmore Peak on the way. I followed the Giant Slide Trail from the saddle back to the former church on Route 198. Including the climbs to Sargent Mountain and Gilmore Peak, the route rises (and falls) a total of 1,424 feet in elevation in a distance of 5.6 miles, 2.4 miles to the summit of Sargent and 3.2

The rocky bed of Sargent Brook.

miles back. I took a little less than five-and-a-half hours to make the loop, and could probably do it in about three hours if I didn't take pictures and make notes.

The hike was about *being there.* Being in the valleys of Sargent and Hadlock brooks, being on the summits of Sargent Mountain and Gilmore Peak. I went from ecodomain to ecodomain, rocky stream valley to subalpine summit, to rocky stream valley, to a lesser summit, to a saddle between summits, and back through a rocky stream valley. Each domain was unlike the others, a place unto itself. Each brought out a different side of my nature: my icy valley side; my exposed, subalpine side; my sheltered, saddle-between-peaks side. I tried to be where I was at all times. To be who I was in each place. *Being there* is an art. It takes close observation, empathy, and openness. It requires moving with the land. Moving with the water flowing in and over the land. Moving with the plants that rise from the land and the

water running through it. Moving with the creatures that rise from the plants. *Being there* is a matter of entering into the dynamics of Earth and of the cosmos. We can do it because we are designed to do it. We are not meant to stand apart as rugged individuals always the same but to get with the program the universe is engaged in here and now. We are creatures of that program. It gives meaning to our lives. Born and bred of cosmic particles, we are here to do the work they lay out for us. If the warbling vireo is driven by whizzing electrons, so am I. As electrons go, so do we all. We go with the flow of the terrain and the waters, the flow of plants and animals, the flow of electrons and life. *Being there* means being alive where you are, fully alive, open to the forces around and within you, seeking resonance between the two. Finding that resonance, you have arrived. You are there. You are where you are. You are part of the scene. When the vireo sings, he sings of you and for you. When you sing, you sing *of* and *for* the vireo.

Private property loses its meaning when you are *there.* Keep-out signs are put up by people unsure of themselves because they are not where they think they are. They miss the resonance, so are afraid. They are intruders themselves, and know that they are. They don't own what they claim to own, and fear others will take it from them by resonating with the land before they do. *Being there* is not a matter of putting up fences and signs. It is a matter of opening to the place where you are, of giving yourself to the Earth so that you belong there as much as earthworms and robins do. The word human means Earthling (one of the soil or of the Earth) but we act as if we were visiting from outer space, taking what we want now, then moving on—the consequences be damned. We think of ourselves as sojourners making a temporary stop between stages of our journey to heaven, not recognizing that this is heaven where we are. *Being there* means finding heaven here on Earth. Look no farther, heaven is where the warbling vireo sings. *Being there* means letting the place where we are nurture us with its own cosmic juice. Fulfillment, no respecter of fences and signs, is here for the taking.

It was quite a hike. I knew I would be pushing the envelope of possibility by hiking the Giant Slide Trail this early in the season. I expected ice and that is what I found. But the ice only made the valley of Sargent Brook that much wilder and more exciting. Both going up and coming down I had to watch every step, but that was my way of working with the valley—of finding resonance with that place. Stones and roots protruded from the ice, providing solid if irregular footing. The brook itself was magnificent, a series of alternating plunges and pools, sometimes frozen over, sometimes splashing in the open. The rough and ready Giant Slide Trail makes the Gorge Trail with its well-laid steps seem tame and genteel. These steps are placed where they fell naturally from the cliffs or where the stream put them, not where the Village Improvement Society laid them out. You cannot hike the Giant Slide Trail without suiting your stride to the land. This valley has not been tamed or broken to the boot. It is what it is, a jumble of broken rocks orchestrating the fall of water and of hikers' feet. It is an excellent place to develop your skill in being where you are. Ice heightens the challenge: if you misstep you risk far more than appearing awkward in the eyes of the world.

The valley of Sargent Brook is full of boulders, cliffs, ferns, mosses, trees, and the sound of water inventing new ways to keep gravity satisfied. The brook is a Kamasutra of water on the make, water wholly dedicated to suiting itself to the rhythm of the valley, its current partner. From the union of water and rock life springs upward in every crevice. I found white ice covering much of the valley floor, but it effectively brought out the green that persists through the year. Wintergreen and goldthread leaves gleamed all along the brook as if never buried by snow. Northern white cedars are not daunted by winter any more than rock-cap ferns or feather moss are. Spruces, balsam firs, white pines, and hemlocks looked much the same now as they would in mid-June. The ice was not a curse but a blessing for in melting it helped the brook do what it does best. Ice was an integral part of the life of the valley, not an intruder but a welcome guest.

Coming to the Giant Slide itself, I peered beneath it to see if I could squeeze through the tunnel on my way down from the summit. The whole crossing area was frozen over. The tunnel was filled with two to three feet of ice. I wasn't sure there would be room for the ice and for me in that narrow space. As way opens, I told myself. If I couldn't get through I would go around.

It was hard enough getting out of the valley, the north ridge trail being a river of gleaming ice. I used a fallen tree as a bridge, then crept along the edge of the ice until it gave out on top of the bank. I met nine other flows of ice in the trail, some easily passable, others forcing me to climb above the glistening knobs where they seeped from the soil. If going around was called for, that is what I did. I was into the

music of the place, the rhythm and melody of the land. At one point a ruffed grouse took off ahead of me and sailed into the trees, adding its note to the song of the mountain.

The north ridge trail follows a curious route to the summit. After climbing out of the valley of Sargent Brook, it heads not for the summit but east, crossing the Around-Mountain Carriage Road, then rounding the ridge for a stretch before starting up, making a longer hike than neces-

The Giant Slide encased in ice.

sary for no apparent reason. The trail was laid out to connect with two other trails—the Aunt Betty's Pond Path and Chasm Brook Trail—both of which have faded back into the landscape, leaving the north ridge trail stuck with its dogleg route. From the former trail junction near Fern Spring on Chasm Brook, the trail heads south for the summit along a remnant of the old Aunt Betty's Pond route. The trail itself has no outstanding features other than the view to the north over Gilmore Bog and Aunt Betty Pond, Youngs and McFarland hills, with Lead Mountain on the Washington County line perched like a pair of giant limpets on the horizon over the saddle between the two hills. Looking westnorthwest over the head of Somes Sound, Blue Hill looks less like a limpet than a snail creeping south.

From the dogleg, the north ridge trail crosses through two small basins feeding tributaries of Chasm Brook, then heads up the raw granite ridge through a field of glacially deposited stones. Geckyracies, I thought, a word I learned from my son Michael when he was two. At Christmastime he kept going to the kitchen and asking for geckyracies. Geckyracies? No one could figure what he meant. Later when a plate of Christmas cookies was put on the table, he pointed and said, "Geckyracies!" It finally dawned on us that that was his word for *decorations,* the colored sprinkles we had put on the cookies. From now on my technical term for stones sprinkled across the Acadian landscape by the last glacier will be geckyracies. The north ridge of Sargent Mountain has a fine display illustrating exactly what I mean.

It is always a thrill to reach the cairn at the summit of Sargent Mountain. Standing next to it as you scan the horizon, you know you have reached your goal. You are *there*. No summit in Acadia is more satisfying. Cadillac's has been spoiled with gift shop and parking lot; Pemetic's is hard to define; Western Mountain's two peaks are closed-in with trees; Champlain and Dorr are open at the top, but Cadillac cuts off the view to the west. The cairn on Sargent marks the top of the world. Cadillac doesn't hog the view. You spin on your heel and see exactly where you are on this Earth. The summit is so other-worldly you are forced to adopt a new and larger perspective in order to incorporate it into your list of places been and seen. No matter what time of year you hike it, Sargent Mountain enlarges your experience, making you a bigger person. The winds I have met on Sargent are like no other winds I have known. From the southwest in summer, northwest in winter, they bring news of faraway places and foreign climes. Earth winds, they try your Earthling mettle to see what you are made of and how you measure up. To be becalmed on Sargent Mountain is to know the blessing of peace on Earth. No Matterhorn or Denali, on a more modest scale Sargent Mountain is where you must go if you want to stand at the center of Acadia so you can truly say you have been there.

I saw no soaring vultures this time on Sargent, no birds at all. No blooming flowers. The husks of mountain sandwort trembled at my feet, reminding me how they quiver with life in full bloom. These had had their day; it was hard to believe others would take their place. There was nothing spring-like about the summit. Cloud lichens seemed aptly placed, anchored against drifting off with their scudding cousins by thickets of stunted lambkill no more than four-to-six inches high. Arching tufts of yellow grass (sedge, actually) pranced nervously in the wind like terriers tied to a tree. *Being there* meant picking up the vibrations of the place, not battling the wind but letting it have its way. The summit cairn offered some shelter if you were willing to be pinned down, which I wasn't. I tasted the near and far view in every direction,

Sargent Mountain north ridge from the north ridge trail.

then took the Grandgent Trail down toward the west.

Where the trail starts dipping into Chickadee Valley between Sargent and Gilmore Peak, the view to the west opens up over Parkman Mountain and Bald Peak, with the Hadlock Ponds in the south-southwest. The transition between summit ridge and sheltered woods below is dramatic. A few red spruce and Northern white cedar have ventured out of the valley onto the exposed slope, rising tentatively into the wind, then dying back, their leaders pointing in the direction they thought they could go. Perhaps they were stymied by windblown ice in winter, a shortage of water in summer. Either way, few of them made it into the open. Their branches spread out close to the ground, but their vertical growth was checked by forces they could not overcome. Reduced to bushes with higher aspirations, they did the best they could with what they had where they were. Determined to break free of the crowd, they paid the price demanded by the summit ridge.

Dipping into the woods below, the Grandgent Trail drops steeply through woods of spruce, fir, and yellow birch. It is the quickest way to the top, and the quickest way down. Leading into Chickadee Valley, the trail passes through the headwaters of the northern branch of Hadlock Brook. This is one of my favorite places in the park because it shows nature at work turning ample carbon dioxide and water into plants native to the northern hardwood-spruce forest bioregion. Every place in Acadia does that, but in Chickadee Valley the process goes on largely unaffected by people, and is particularly dramatic because of the terrain. Great cliffs tumble down from Sargent on the east and Gilmore Peak on the west, forming a basin that has filled with plant and mineral detritus fallen over thousands of years. This, I imagine, is the way Acadia is meant to be, ungentrified by stone steps and carriage roads. Trees thrive in the valley, making good use of the shelter and nutrients the mountains provide. When they die, they lean against the cliffs, slowly giving their bodies for the advancement of their descendants. On this hike I found the cliffs and valley covered with melting ice, the rocks white and dripping, unseen rivers running under the ice beneath my feet.

An icy, wet, and wild place, it brought out the icy, wet,

and wild side of myself. Here was Maine during the glacier's retreat. This is how it was when caribou, wolves, and cata- mounts reclaimed their native haunts after having been banished by a change in temperature of a few degrees. Now they are exiles again, banished by human decree. But they live on in spirit, and when we are gone, they will reclaim what is theirs by prior right. Chickadee Valley gives a glimpse of the past, the present, and the future at once. What happens here is right for this place. The rhythms are those of the Earth, the rhythms that even ban- ishment under threat of death cannot destroy or deny. The name I have given that minor basin does not convey the power I feel when I am there. Wildcat Valley is more like it, but that name has been taken. Chickadees are there now, so that's what I call it. This time through I saw a robin calling nobly from the top of a spruce, chirping and chinking over his domain, announcing his presence to the universe at large. If I can't have catamounts, I will settle for robins and chickadees. All of us are ephemeral. Once woolly mammoths were here, now we are here; soon, like them, we will be gone. Our roads and gift shops will be gone. Our **KEEP OUT** signs will be gone. The rhythms of Earth will remain until the sun cools and implodes, then only the rhythms of electrons will remain, the rhythms of pulsars and galaxies, the rhythms of a slowing and cooling universe until everything we thought we knew is gone and all memory is gone. For now we are here. This is our one chance at being in the universe. I would rather spend what time I can in Chickadee Valley on the western slope of Sar- gent Mountain than most other places I can name. There the busy hum of men is a mere whisper in the distance. The songs of robins and warbling vireos are not lost in the whine of machines. There the truly important work of the universe is accomplished: the sun shines, winds blow, ice turns to water, trees grow, birds sing, night falls, and life goes on.

The Grandgent Trail continues out of the valley to the summit of Gilmore Peak, but the way was blocked by ice so I bushwhacked straight upslope through the woods, coming to the tree where the vireo sang. Crossing through splendid fields of geckyracies on the summit, the trail goes on to dip into the valley of Sargent Brook. The descent is pretty much a freefall in the company of rocks, but it is short and gets you to the valley without delay. There the Grandgent Trail ends. I picked up the Giant Slide Trail and headed north for St. James Church 2.4 miles away. Sargent Brook rises in that narrow saddle, fed by seepage from both sides of the valley. It starts out as a small stream winding slowly between moss- grown banks beneath deciduous trees, giving no hint of the tumultuous plunge that lies ahead. This was a kinder, gentler place than the valley below. There was some ice in the upper valley, but it was so open to the sun that it couldn't last. The

real ice began in the narrower and shadier middle valley where rays from the sun had less of an effect. The Around- Mountain Carriage Road marks the limit of the upper valley of Sargent Brook. From there the middle valley is steeper and rockier, and on this hike much icier.

The trail runs next to the carriage road for a way while the brook crosses under the carriage road through a culvert, trail and brook going their separate ways for a time. The trail then

Gilmore and Bald peaks and the Hadlock Ponds from the Grandgent Trail.

angles downslope to rejoin the brook in its narrow, rocky run for Somes Sound. That stretch where the trail runs next to the brook down to the Giant Slide at the crossing below had very much the feel of Chickadee Valley. The trail passes through a narrow, wet, and wild canyon where undaunted vegetation turned the valley green despite the ice. Great frozen seeps lined the Sargent Mountain side of the val- ley—literal walls of ice. Much of the brook and its valley were frozen solid by rippled blue-gray cascades. Boulders torn from the cliffs had lain there long enough to sprout gardens of rock-cap fern and moss. Northern white cedars love that kind of place, sprouting like pillars seemingly rooted in the ice itself. The trail was hard to follow in many places because it went its own way under the ice, letting those of us above fend for ourselves. Figuring the general direction the trail took was easy, given the valley was so narrow, but following along the ice took fancy footwork braced against trees, roots, and stones to avoid slipping on sloping ice. Soon the valley leveled off for a way, and foot- ing got easier. Approaching a large boulder, I was caught by surprise to see and hear a ruffed grouse rocket from behind it when I was no more than eight feet away. It was like seeing a rock take to wing. A part of the valley just rose up and flew. Bird or rock, they seemed to share equally in the life of that place.

The upper end of the Giant Slide was flooded with ice. I let myself down gently upon the surface, then skated into the cave beneath the slide. The throat ahead narrowed to a narrow triangle about nine inches wide and two feet high, too small even for my narrow frame. That settled that, there was no way to follow the trail beneath the slide. If you can't go through, go around. The whole area was so frozen I had no trouble skirting the slide by walking out over the brook. In a

Headwaters of Sargent Brook.

week or two it would be harder to manage the detour without getting wet. Late May or early June is a good time to start thinking about hiking the Giant Slide Trail. Blackflies can be handled by applying the dope of your choice, but ice is ice no matter how you smell.

Ice made it harder to retrace my steps from the crossing down the valley than it had been coming up by the same route. I went slowly, concentrating on where to place each step, not paying as much attention to my surroundings as I had before. The low arch down from the trail crossing was hard to squeeze through both ways, the ground beneath it being covered with slick ice. It was a wicked tight spot. I had bursitis in the right shoulder where the strap of my camera bag rests, which made ducking through that passage a memorable experience. Delivery on the far side both times made me feel born again. Lower down the valley, when the brook turned west for Somes Sound, I was sorry to see and hear it

go. I had gotten used to its ways and felt bereft to be left on my own.

I had seen two streamside plants starting to leaf out in the upper valley, one a gangly bush with pink, powdery terminal buds that looked like tiny hands clasped together in prayer, the other a low plant with two drooping, purple, alternate sawtooth leaves hoisting on a thin stalk a pair of miniature leaves that looked like a bird in flight. I had no idea what

Feather moss and rock-cap fern in the valley of Sargent Brook.

either of them was called, but the names were not important. They were opening to the place they were rooted in, being there in their own way in their own time. I empathized with them and tried to be true to my own roots while sharing their personal space.

While editing my write-up of this hike, I came to grips with the burst of song I had heard on Gilmore Peak by playing bird song tapes of all the possible singers that might have been passing through the park on April 23rd. No, it hadn't been a robin, a purple finch or winter wren, a ruby-crowned kinglet or rose-breasted grosbeak. When I came to the song of the warbling vireo I was transfixed exactly as I had been when climbing out of Chickadee Valley. That was the one; I had not a doubt. So warbling vireo is the name I have given here to the shade that shouted that jubilant noise.

41—FEATHERBED LOOP via POTHOLE TRAIL

From Canon Brook Parking on Route 3
To the Featherbed, and back
   Up by Canon Brook Trail, Dorr Mountain South
     Ridge Trail extension, and Pothole Trail
   Down by Canon Brook Trail

5.0 miles, April 30, 1997

The Pothole Trail is named for the small pits carved out by swirling waterborne gravel in the sloping granite flank of the south ridge of Cadillac Mountain. The potholes themselves are small, shallow, and unremarkable except for a couple to the side of the trail that are large enough to tempt overheated travelers to take off their boots and soak their feet. The trail originally tied into the Cadillac Mountain South Ridge Trail well south of Dike Peak; I wonder if there might be deeper potholes on the old route than are now found on the new. A silvered wooden post held up by a pile of rocks marks where the trail divides at one of the upper ledges where potholes are found today. A more conspicuous landmark along the trail is the Old Man and Old Woman, a pair of ten-foot-high boulders (actually one boulder split in two), one leaning against the other. Like Pulpit Rock on the Gorge Trail, this stony couple is hard to show clearly in photographs because nearby trees block the view from every angle.

But potholes and boulders are incidental to the Pothole Trail. The three times I have hiked it I felt transported to a foreign land where I walked among alien beings notable for their dignity and strong character. The pitch pines of Acadia grow where almost no other tree can take root. Along the Pothole Trail they rise from the granite like bristles of the mountain itself. Their character is stony, their dignity an expression of metamorphic rock. Traversing the sloping habitat that directs runoff into the cracks from which they rise, I feel there isn't another human within a thousand miles. I might as well be on one of Jupiter's moons. Human-

ity? What am I to it, or is it to me! In the days of the rusticators the Pothole Trail may have given direct access to Cadillac Mountain from the village of Otter Creek, but it has fallen into disuse. A relic of forgotten days, the pitch pines have taken it back and now call it their own.

Not shown on most maps, the trail is still there on the ground, though off the beaten path. A dedicated crew of trail phantoms flags the route to its starting point, and maintains

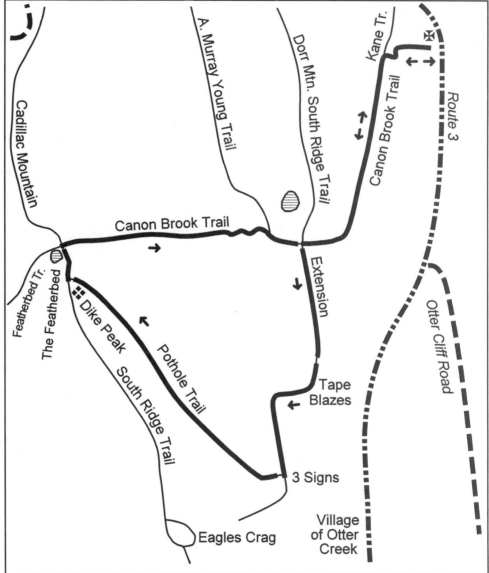

41—Featherbed via Pothole Trail.

the small cairns that mark the windings of the trail across the slope among the wizened pines. The trick to hiking the Pothole Trail is in finding where it starts. I have groped my way through the cedar swamp lying west of the village of Otter Creek, but do not recommend that soggy approach. It is easier to follow the (currently) dark blue flagging from where the Dorr Mountain South Ridge Trail extension spans

Otter Creek near the swimming hole west of Route 3. Though not shown on recent maps, the extension continues unmarked south past the Canon Brook Trail, coming to Otter Creek in less than half a mile. It passes first through birch and popple woods, then through a stand of mixed birch and spruce. Here you can witness for yourself the resprucing of Acadia fifty years after the 1947 fire. It was the fire that invited the sun-loving birch to replace the shade-loving spruce, and now it is the birch themselves that invite the young spruce to thrive in their shade. Otter Creek is ten feet wide where the extension overtakes it, but a series of boulders serves as a bridge leading hikers across with dry feet. The creek immediately downstream is worth exploring as it slides dramatically across sloping ledges into the village swimming hole.

The route to the Pothole Trail starts on the south side of the crossing, though there is no evidence of any trail at that point. Follow a small stream that runs into the creek, and in fifty feet you will find two small red arrows nailed at eye level to a cedar tree. From there you are on your own. If you are not used to finding your way through the woods using minimal clues, you should forget trying to reach the Pothole Trail. From the two red arrows, the way runs roughly south across the small stream (which may be dry in summer) through open woods. The only

The Pothole Trail follows cairns across ledges.

signs are a few cut stems and branches here and there. It is a virtual trail, a trail that exists only in your head. But that's where it counts. Imagine South Sea Islanders navigating by wave diffraction and the stars to islands they have never seen.

You soon come to an oldfield growing in with popple; this is where the blue flagging starts. If leaves are off the trees, you may see the gable of a white house to the east. From the clearing, follow those dark blue ribbons around to the southwest, keeping just inside the woods. Downed trees may block your way, so go around them; the route is not well maintained. A few remnants of orange flagging augment the blue. Soon you come to a woods road that actually looks and feels like a trail. The road heads more or less west toward the south ridge of Cadillac. The way is apt to be wet; follow the puddles. There are only a few bits of flagging along the road.

Near the ridge the way leaves the road and turns south. From that turn it is marked by small piles of two or three stones. The route wanders, but heads generally south parallel to the ridge. The stone piles are within eyeshot of each other. If you get lost, go back to the last stones and look around. When you come to three signs (**POTHOLES TRAIL, TO CANYON BROOK TRAIL, EAGLE'S CRAG FOOT**) on a maple tree a foot in diameter, you know you have arrived at the base of the Pothole Trail. The new base, not the old. The original base intersects the route you have been following farther south. The new base leads to a shortcut that joins the trail west of the three signs. On a six-inch maple is an older sign that reads simply, **POTHOLE**.

Standing by the signs surrounded by woods, you look in every direction. What trail, where? Again on faith, you head for the slope to the west. The trail becomes evident as you go, but never very evident. Look for bent twigs, cut branches, bare spots on mossy ledges. Follow the lowly cairns. You will soon come to a trail marked with more serious cairns that traverses the slope at an angle. Head northwest, not southeast. You have found the genuine article, the Pothole Trail of old.

But don't cast your hard-won navigational skills aside at that point; you will need them in keeping to the trail. The rule is: follow the cairns. If you come to a point where you don't see a pile of stones ahead, go back to the last pile and look around. The trail often turns abruptly one way or another. The track is subtle. Go slowly and let the cairns guide you. They continue all the way to the north slope of Dike Peak above the Featherbed. The last hundred feet are unmarked to prevent unwary hikers from wandering onto the Pothole Trail by mistake. The upper section seems more like a rabbit run than a trail, but follow it anyway. Rabbits don't build cairns. Besides, there aren't any rabbits in Acadia, only hares.

The upper reaches of the Pothole Trail look east over the Champlain-Gorham ridge, with the Beehive and Halfway Mountain as blips in the middle. In places you can look down into the blue waters of the Bowl. Schoodic Head rises beyond the Beehive, and Petit Manan Light stands blinking on its island beyond that. To the north, the trail looks onto the broad summit ridge of Cadillac Mountain with its two south-reaching ridges embracing a great stony basin which feeds the headwaters of Canon Brook. To the south, Baker Island is visible at some points, and the eastern end of Little Cranberry Island.

The virtue of the Pothole Trail is the sense it gives of a typically Acadian landscape that goes largely unheralded, so seems like a foreign land. The mechanics of that landscape are extremely simple: sloping granite ledges crossed by fractures or joints and peppered with glacial stones from gravel to boulders. Water flows across the slope wetting the joints, which in spring and fall are spread by ice, creating more pronounced fractures which widen and deepen over the years. The fractures capture particles of rock, which in that region pass for soil. That is all pitch pines need to take root—a narrow crack that fills with water now and again. Life springs from the side of the mountain like Athena from the brow of Zeus. Lichens drape the wettest slopes and add color to the driest. The resulting landscape is stark and luxuriant at the same time. It is a garden for those who can thrive in such a place. There is a spaciousness about the landscape stemming from the sparseness of suitable habitat for trees and plants. Wind and sunlight are the gardeners, not shade and damp. Thin soil has built up over the years in

A pothole on the Pothole Trail.

places where streaming water hasn't washed it away. Lamb-kill, blueberry, and huckleberry have taken root, intermixed with cloud and reindeer lichen. Mountain cranberry thrives in such a place, wherever it can get a good grip. The result is like a garden on the moon out of a Doctor Doolittle book. You see it but can't quite believe it. It is the landscape of Nirvana or Shangri-la, one of Acadia's many faces.

The biggest surprise I got on the Pothole Trail came when I wandered from a landscape dominated by pitch pines to one with much the same character without a pitch pine in sight. On Dike Peak the Pothole Trail is ruled by jack pines instead. The two trees may look similar at a glance, but pitch pine needles are longer and come in clumps of three while jack pine needles look like a cross between spruce and fir needles and come in clumps of two. Though they both thrive in the same harsh locale, their domains appear to be mutually

exclusive, I don't know why. Jack pines are relatively scarce in Acadia, growing primarily on Dike Peak and across Frenchman Bay on the Schoodic Peninsula. Bushy, almost bristly trees, they have a standoffish charm like porcupines and armadillos. They don't make very good pets, but they are worth taking the trouble to acquaint on familiar terms.

The Pothole Trail ends on the slope between Dike Peak and the Featherbed, that saddlebound wetland which seems so out of place at a 1,000-foot elevation on the south ridge of Cadillac Mountain. When I came out on the south ridge trail, a lone crow glided over my head toward Dike Peak, which it circled only three to five feet above the rock, rounding it twice as if looking for a place to land, then sailed past the peak and out of sight. I sped by the Featherbed, hearing no frogs, seeing no shoots tentatively poking above the cold water. I had been on the trail just short of four hours by then and wanted to hike the Canon Brook Trail before it was completely shaded by the ridge, so down I went without waiting for further signs of life.

The Canon Brook Trail runs for 1.8 miles between the Featherbed and a gravel pulloff on Route 3. It used to be called the Canyon (Cañon) Brook Trail, but the ñ lost its tilde in some map revision, and the trail assumed its current name by default. Accented or unaccented, the trail is terrific, one of Acadia's best. Particularly during spring when runoff is heavy, or anytime immediately following a rain. It is terrific even when the ledges are dry and the brook is reduced to a trickle. Where the Pothole Trail scales the ridge at an angle, the Canon Brook Trail runs straight up the slope between the Featherbed and Otter Creek, twining in and around the brook as it spills over naked granite. From the Featherbed the trail starts out through woods at an easy rate of descent over a treadway of laid rock. Passing a small wetland south of the trail, it soon comes out at the top of a slope of bare ledge resembling the site of a landslide. From there the trail shows its true character. The brook takes its name from a box-like canyon that tries to capture it midslope, but lets it go again—the original have-a-heart trap. The brook dug out the canyon in the first place by gradually chipping away a block of granite forty-five feet long, nine feet wide, and ten to fourteen feet deep. The brook cascades over broken ledge for twenty-five feet before plunging into the gulf—creating the best show of white water in the park. Canon Brook is not large by any standard, but its abrupt fall over pink granite makes it seem larger than life, spunkier, and more antic. I have seen it roar like a locomotive through the canyon; on this hike it breezed through like a deer. In August you wonder what all the fuss is about, there being no trace of a brook of any size.

Canon Brook is unusual in not having a channel or a valley for much of its run. It has a basin higher up, and a valley lower down near Otter Creek, but its midsection runs free over a granite spillway, steered not by any bank but by invisible fluid dynamics. Eventually the brook will carve its own channel, enlarging on the canyon it has already started, digging into the ledge a few fractions of an inch in a hundred years. Preparing the groundwork, like a lashing cable the brook has scraped the ridge free of soil and (except for lichen) vegetation, creating a bed of smooth granite to play on. It careens over the granite, diverted by subtle rises and falls where the rock flexes its muscle, flowing north, then south, then north, south, north—unable to make up its mind which way to go. A tributary falls into a twenty-foot pool on the southern edge of the bare swath, creating an idyllic spot for foot bathers and skinny-dippers who like their water cold.

Pool on the Canon Brook Trail.

A beaver tried to dam the outlet of the pool a few years ago, but not a trace of that project remains. At the base of the slope a fan of boulders spreads beneath the steepest plunge, showing the true width of the brook in full flood. The trail winds on stone steps through the boulders, a route that in early April requires waders or a wet suit. Sensuous ledge, still pool, whitewater canyon—the Canon Brook Trail is worth the trip at any time of year when it is free of ice. Ice turns the trail into a bobsled run without walls, a different challenge for a different breed of hiker.

From where Canon Brook flows into Otter Creek and the A. Murray Young Trail starts up to the Notch, the Canon Brook Trail takes an easy stroll around the south ridge of Dorr Mountain, then dips into the valley of Beaver Brook, following the brook north toward (but never reaching) the Tarn. At a signpost 0.7 mile south of the Dorr Mountain Ladder Trail, the Canon Brook Trail turns from the Kane Trail and heads east, crossing a former beaver dam over the brook, then winding along a graveled pathway through popple and birch to the parking area on Route 3, 0.4 mile south of the Tarn.

Often stopping to take photographs and notes along the way, I figure the five-mile loop took me almost six hours to complete. Starting at an elevation of 220 feet on Route 3, the route dips to 140 feet along Beaver Brook, then rises to 220 feet again on the south ridge of Dorr Mountain, falls to 140 feet at Otter Creek, then climbs to 1,030 feet on Dike Peak above the Featherbed, for a total rise and fall of 1,050 feet by the time I got back to my car. I figure the Pothole Trail rises 830 feet from the three signs, and the Canon Brook Trail rises 860 from Otter Creek to the Featherbed. The temperature was 55° Fahrenheit when I started at 1:00 p.m., 45° when I got back to my car shortly before 7:00.

I designed this hike as a loop that would take me along Canon Brook while it still carried its share of meltwater. I came to several large patches of ice in the woods along the brook, but with temperatures in the 50s they would be gone in a week. Soon Acadia's streams would be powered not by melting snow and ice but by seepage and recent rain. The winter of 1996–97 was history. The thirteen birds I heard or saw on this hike confirmed that opinion. But for now the three streams I came to were running with more water than usual. Beaver Brook was spread wide across its valley, aided by the three beaver dams I saw from the trail, probably abetted by others. Otter Creek splashed over the ledges into the village swimming hole with youthful abandon, its waters still too icy to appeal to the earliest of early-bird swimmers. And Canon Brook put on a good show of white water cascading into its canyon, doing its bit to sculpt a valley yet to come. It was a great hike for running water, the theme of my spring hikes, and for ledges deflecting sky-water into valleys below, rousing Acadia's slopes to green wakefulness. I had only one brook hike to go, the Deer Brook Trail up Sargent Mountain, which I was saving for the penultimate hike in this series.

Two woodpeckers drummed on snags along Beaver Brook as I passed, reminding me of the man outside Belfast who put out a sign in front of his place, **WOMAN WANTED**. That's what the banging on trees is all about, bringing the sexes together. I heard a subtler form of the same message seven times as I was coming down the Canon Brook Trail, a soft whumping in the distance from no apparent direction, tempo quickly building, then dying away. Male ruffed grouse were beating their wings, inviting females to their secret strutting grounds. Sex was in the air. I heard the sound near the Featherbed and all along the trail, representing at least two different birds, perhaps more. I also heard robins, chickadees, a pileated woodpecker, crows, and a song sparrow. From the Dorr Mountain South Ridge Trail extension I saw a large dark hawk dive before the wind into Beaver Brook valley. Chickadees and a golden-crowned kinglet darted above my head. Near Otter Creek I saw a flicker land in the topmost branches of an aspen. On the Pothole Trail two juncos flew into the trees ahead of me. On the Canon Brook Trail where the roar of Otter Creek drowned every sound, I looked up for no reason and saw a pair of yellow-rumped warblers gleaning the branches of a red-budded maple. Near the end of the hike two wood ducks took off from Beaver Brook and shot down the valley. I heard spring peepers in

Canon Brook plunges into its canyon.

a wetland not far from Route 3 and saw water striders skating on Beaver Brook and Otter Creek. Small insects were everywhere, undoubtedly having food and sex on their tiny minds. My way was not exactly strewn with hare pellets, but I saw a dozen or so scattered along the loop. The one fox scat I came across lay by a cairn on the Pothole Trail.

No such list of sightings and soundings can capture the sense of excitement I drew from the air. Flying birds, leaping waters, insects flexing their wings and legs—Acadia was on the move and on the make. If not yet pregnant, the air was potent and fertile with creatures declaring their availability to the world at large. Winter tracks had been replaced by spring wiles and tricks. The cosmic force was stirring in Acadia's veins, ready to work its charms on flesh and blood, pith and sap. Those not susceptible were not fully alive. A free-floating thrill was adrift on the wind, to be downloaded

by any and all who wished to join in. I felt that thrill along Beaver Brook, among the pines on the Pothole Trail, and in ogling the waters of Canon Brook. Zap! Like Dr. Frankenstein's dummy I felt a charge of electrons surge through my circuits. Ready for anything, I was wired for empathy with the lust-driven world.

Cosmic lust. Yes, that's what spring feels like. A craving for all that is colorful, shapely, and beautiful. That is, healthy and full of bounce. None of us would be here if our ancestors had been blind and deaf to that urge. None of our children would be alive if we could simply switch off our hearing aid and ignore the vernal uproar around us whenever it strikes. Ecosystems are groups of organisms responding in individual ways to a common call. Bioregions are large-scale expressions of that same cosmic cry. What else can we mean by divinity than that which compels us to act in the name of the highest cause of all, the further unfolding of universal creativity? Don't miss the next episode. That is what we are all about, what spring is all about, what Acadia is all about. Keep up the rhythms of life. Each of us is like a juggler focused on the Indian clubs looping overhead. Easy does it. Don't fumble, don't skip a beat. The rhythm is what matters. All that matters. Open yourself to it. Don't think of anything else. Life is an instant in the limelight; when the beam shines on you, trust the rhythm and nothing else. When the beam moves on, your part has ended; let the clubs fall in a heap, other will pick them up and keep the rhythm alive.

Instead of whirling our clubs in the air, some of us break the rhythm of life and try to make a profit by selling clubs to others, or by hoarding them against the day when clubs become scarce—as if Indian clubs were an end in themselves and not a means toward living a rhythmical, creative life. I don't know how we get into our rut of amassing as much wealth and as many possessions as we can, but the practice becomes such a burden that it keeps us from celebrating our own divinity and participating in the rhythm of universal creativity. Comfort, security, and luxury are dead ends that stifle cosmic beauty and excitement. They are meant to fend off whatever the future may bring by embalming the past.

They kill the rhythm. Wine is meant to be drunk, not stored in a cellar; Indian clubs are meant to fly, not lie in neat rows. Behind the shield of wealth there is emptiness. Life, as responsiveness to the flow of cosmic creativity, requires a light touch and quick response. Even in this day of electronic cash transfers, wealth is ponderous and slow moving, a sink that absorbs energy instead of freeing it for the advancement of the living and the unborn. Take the sun as a model. It burns its fuel as fast as it can, radiating energy to those who can reap and enjoy it. Wealth and possessions are dead energy, black holes that suck the zip and the zap out of life. Acadia comes to life in the spring because of a joyous sharing of sunshine, water, and air. Their benefit is in their use, not their storage; their freedom, not their capture. Spring is a release from the bondage of winter, a resurgence of youth and hope. I learned that from the whispering wings of a ruffed grouse I overheard on the Canon Brook Trail. I share it here for the benefit of bankers and brokers who aren't aware such a language exists. Forget comfort. Travel light and keep your eyes and ears open. Let the rhythm of life flow into your body. Earth and the cosmos will supply the fulfillment you seek.

Except for the pitch and jack pines on the Pothole Trail, most of the woods I passed through on this hike were in a state of transition, recovering from either the 1947 fire or a bout of short-term human stewardship. Popple (quaking and large-toothed aspen) lined the trail, mixed here and there with birch, beech, maple, and occasional oak. Hemlock and Northern white cedar prospered along streams, and red spruce was starting to make a comeback where it could. White pines stood above the common herd, reminders of the glory of these woods in former days. In the understory striped maple buds were splitting open, giving nascent leaves an early dose of sunlight. Blueberry twigs were in full bud. Partridgeberry leaves greened some upland spots, goldthread did the same for many lowlands. I saw patches of ground pine and ground cedar. I looked forward to finding mayflower in bloom where Canon Brook flows into Otter Creek, but found only white buds and no blossoms. That was the only patch of mayflower I saw on the loop. The previous Sunday I had gone up Kurt Diederich's Climb at the north end of the Tarn in search of mayflowers and found bumblebees hovering over open white blossoms all along the upper stretch of the trail. The blooms were eight to ten days later than usual this year because of a cold March and lingering ice.

I saw a great deal more, but those are the highlights. Green shoots were poking up among last year's leaves all along the trail. The revolution had begun.

❦

42—AROUND LOWER HADLOCK POND

From the pullout on Hadlock Pond Road
To the far side of the pond, and back
   Counterclockwise around the pond by the
    Hadlock Path

1.3 miles, May 7, 1997

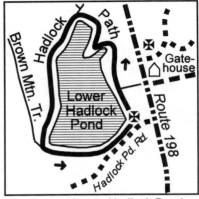

42—Around Lower Hadlock Pond.

It was snowing on top of Cadillac Mountain when I got up, and on toward evening it snowed across the whole of Mount Desert Island. In between it rained much of the day. The temperature rose from the low 30s to low 40s, then crept down again. A brisk wind blew damp air into every crevice on the island and under every overhang. There was no escaping the weather. It was a perfect day for watching water descend on Acadia, and for watching Acadia's response. Some people avoid hiking in wet weather, but there is no better time to see a bioregion in action doing what it does best—welcoming the elixir of life. Hiking only on dry days promotes the false impression that life proceeds on its own with no help from above. Not true. Skywater is the first parent of us all. The genius of a bioregion is the reception, storage, and timed release of water so that it is available to green Earthlings through their growing season. Solar-powered plants use water and air to store energy as sugar and starch, which they share with the rest of us so that Earthlings of all colors can turn their food back into energy, allowing them to keep up the rhythm of life. Indirectly we are all solar powered, driven by a cosmic process enabled by water. Without water there would be no photosynthesis, no algae or green plants, no eaters of plants, no eaters of eaters of plants, no labor, no human economy, no bioregions, no life as we know it. Some life would still cluster in the mud, in hot springs, around thermal vents a mile deep in the ocean, but Acadia and our kind of life would die without water. Rainy days are good days to go hiking because they invite us to get out and experience firsthand the element that brings life to us and brings us to life.

The Hadlock Path circles Lower Hadlock Pond, sometimes passing a foot from the water's edge, more often keeping a screen of trees ten to thirty-feet wide between it and the pond. The way is paved with stones and roots which trap water on damp days, making the going swampy in places. It is a route I hike not so much to see the small pond as to see the life hugging its margin, a standing-room-only crowd of tall trees. White pines and Northern white cedars give the shoreline its characteristic texture and color. Oxidized and lichen-clad granite crops out here and there, notably near the small parking area and along the foot of Norumbega Mountain whose wooded slopes rise above the pond to the north. The brick block of the Northeast Harbor Water Company pump house sits on the dam in the southwest corner of the pond. A cluster of three pink vacation homes dominates the near view in the southeast, but blends in with the trees at a distance. Most of the eastern half of the shoreline falls within Acadia National Park while the western half is owned by the Town of Mount Desert for protection of its public water supply. The path is less than a mile and a half long and can be easily hiked in under an hour if you are out for exercise more than to be in a particular place on Earth. I took three hours to round the pond, stopping every few feet to look and listen.

The first thing I noticed was tree swallows swooping across the pond in every direction, dipping down to the silver waves, rising steeply a few feet above them, staying always in a thin fly zone above the center of the pond. There must have been more than twenty-five swallows in that squadron, though counting them was like counting molecules bouncing around in Brownian motion. They were there every time I got a clear view of the pond; they were there when I came and there when I left, never seeming to take a break. I didn't see one insect on my loop of the pond, but there was something there for those swallows which I couldn't see. A lot of somethings, judging by the commotion. Enough to make such a mass expenditure of energy worth it to the birds. At the bottom of every dive and the apex of every climb, bird and something came together and flew on as one. I remembered reading that fishing fleets in the Pacific spend far more energy reaching their fishing grounds and catching fish than they reap from the salmon they actually catch, resulting in a net loss of energy as a result of their efforts. Any species or ecosystem operating at such a loss would quickly go out of business. But in the human world we don't put our true gains and losses on the same balance sheet, so we fool ourselves into thinking Earth's resources are free for the taking, and that we always come out ahead. The swallows in the airspace over Lower Hadlock Pond knew better than that. Their understanding of economics was based on practice, not theory. The somethings they took surely gave them more energy than they spent in the taking, the wind perhaps providing the loft that made the math work out.

Another squadron of birds accompanied me around the edge of the pond, a dozen or more yellow-rumped warblers feeding at the water's edge or in the screen of trees between me and the shore. Normally stem and branch gleaners, the

birds in this flock often foraged in the carpet of fallen needles beneath shoreline pines and cedars. I couldn't tell if it was the same group of birds, but they stayed with me throughout the hike, always flying counterclockwise around the shore. If it wasn't the same group of birds, then there were hundreds of yellow-rumped warblers on Lower Hadlock that day. They were beautiful to look at with their white throats and bright yellow crowns, flanks, and rumps that

Hadlock Path bridge over nameless brook.

gleamed when they flew. Again, there must have been myriad somethings in the duff and on branches of bushes overhanging the shore, somethings I couldn't see but the warblers could. Unlike the swallows, they may have been gleaning berries that had clung through the winter, fattening up for the breeding season ahead, making a pit stop before continuing north. I took it as a visitation by angels, the first in a wave that crests in mid-May. Why make up fabulous beings when we have them in their breeding plumage on the wing? The Sumerians started the whole idea of angels in seeing planets moving among the fixed stars as messengers conveying the will of the gods. Yellow-rumped warblers bring the same news if only we will receive it as such, revealing the will of the cosmic force that plays itself out in their lives and ours. Some regard bird watching as an idle pastime, but others know it as a way of staying in touch with the powers that rule us as Earthlings and determine our every act. I was glad to share the gentle company of the warblers on my walk, and they seemed not to be bothered by mine.

What I took to be two hermit thrushes (though they might have been veeries), one as round as a baseball, kept ahead of me for several hundred yards, scooting across the ground more than flying branch to branch. They would perch as if carved of wood, then dart for something they could see and I couldn't, perching and darting on legs so thin they seemed to float over the ground, moving separately but staying together, making me think of them as a mated pair. Their color was exactly that of the ground beneath them, the rufous tan of fallen pine and cedar needles. They were in their element, the very stuff of which they were made. That is the nature of habitats: we ingest them and express their most basic characteristics, taking on their flavor and coloring, becoming their inhabitants so that we have them and they have us in a rhythmical give-and-take between a place and the natives who call it their home.

On the northeast a narrow point of land juts into the pond, separating a major and a minor cove where major and minor streams spill in one final fling. I don't have a name for the minor stream, but the major one is Hadlock Brook which rises on the western slope of Sargent Mountain and enters salt water at the mouth of Somes Sound, feeding the two Hadlock Ponds on the way. Looking along the shore of the major cove from the point toward the Hadlock Brook inlet, I saw a white duck swimming toward me with its eyes and bill underwater the way a loon spies on prey from the surface. Fifty yards from me, it lifted its neck now and then, showing the green head and thin red bill of a male common merganser. It had red feet, too, which I knew were busy paddling. Cruising within six feet of the shore, it showed

Hadlock Brook plunges toward Lower Hadlock Pond.

no fear of any hunter who may have been crouched like me behind a tree letting it come at its own pace. When it got opposite me no more than ten feet away it looked up and saw me—zoom, it was airborne and flew off low over the pond, spiraling back to take a look at what had startled it. Later I saw two ducks in the distance but couldn't make out what they were other than that they didn't look like common mergansers.

Several gulls flew high over the pond without landing, but the most impressive bird I saw was an osprey which I heard crying shrilly overhead before I saw it perched in a nearby snag. It saw me too and took off, flying with strong beats of its wings, circling around again and again, like the merganser wanting to make sure of its foe. The somethings it hungered for were in the pond, brown trout stocked by the Maine Department of Inland Fisheries and Wildlife for the convenience of anglers and ospreys alike, whichever gets to them

first. Too big a bird to burn fuel just flying around on the chance something would turn up, the osprey perched in a snag overlooking the pond, batting its eyes instead of beating its wings. Having scared it off, I gawked at the great bird, admiring the power and control of its flight, the most beautiful display I witnessed all day.

When the osprey had flown off, I continued my walk, meeting it again in a few hundred yards where it had perched in another tree to continue its search for something to eat. I regretted scaring it off a second time, making it burn more calories for no reason, raising its hunger to a higher notch. We well-meaning gawkers do more harm than we care to admit, making our prey work all the harder to do what it does best without our intervening in its affairs. Shorelands are particularly useful habitats for a great many species which use the border between land and water to good effect. Shorelands, too, are where we blaze our trails and build our vacation and retirement homes, taking what we want from those who need it to survive. No loon will ever breed on Lower Hadlock Pond or Jordan Pond because our trails make it so easy for us to walk in on them when they most require to be off by themselves. How would we react to finding our bedrooms listed on a tour of scenic places open to the public at all hours? Perhaps we should close our ponds to human traffic from April through mid-July, just as we close the Precipice Trail, and more recently the Jordan Cliffs Trail, most of the summer to give peregrine falcons enough lebensraum to make a comeback in the park. Who was here first, after all? Who is the true native, the true owner? Who needs shoreland to survive—to reproduce or re-create—not merely to recreate? The Park Service has the two-pronged mission of protecting its holdings while promoting their enjoyment by the public. Those prongs sometimes get twisted together, producing a utensil that doesn't work for either mission. As a frequent user of the park, I own my part in the conflict. Where ospreys, mergansers, and loons are concerned, the enemy looks and acts like me.

I don't have to have complete freedom to enjoy the park when I want. It is a privilege to visit Acadia, not a constitutional right. The rule of law often does more to protect the big guy than the little because it's the big guy who makes the law. Pillars in the old rotunda of our nation's capitol are wound with symbols depicting cotton and tobacco, so who is surprised at the congressional influence of the cotton and tobacco lobbies? Peregrines have clout because we say they are endangered, but what about mergansers and ospreys who have trouble feeding and breeding because of people like me? In what capitol are their emblems intertwined? Who enacts laws favoring them? In the context of our growing Earth consciousness, that is not a rhetorical question. Who speaks for those without a voice in human affairs? Only at the last gasp do we step in like St. George and slay the dragon that looks so much like us. Human law is a subset of a higher law protecting the self-interest of Earthlings of every hue and feather. If that law requires us to back off, so be it. Justice is not an issue in our eyes alone. As we judge, so are we judged. By mergansers and ospreys who, like us, are entitled to equality under the law.

Would that osprey be surprised to learn it had triggered such a train of thought? Probably not. More likely it would cry, "What took you so long!"

Cone scales and cores lined the Hadlock Path on many stones, stumps, and fallen trees. I saw two of the scalers on a slope above the path, one of them hurtling over the ground,

Lower Hadlock Pond from the inlet of Hadlock Brook.

stopping, hurtling back the way it had come; the other chattering on the branch of a tree overhead. It was a scene out of a rodent production of *Romeo and Juliet*. I forgave the female lead for overplaying her part; she was too young to have learned to temper her performance. Red squirrels, like hermit thrushes, take their coloring from the local terrain. They are what they eat: spruce cones on legs.

Two ravens carried on a conversation while I was making my rounds, one sounding anxious to my ears, the other confident and reassuring. I didn't see either of them, but their dialogue, like the squirrels', added local color to my hike.

In various states of recovery from human use and abuse, plants line the shore of the pond where sunlight and water are readily available. In addition to Northern white cedar and white pine, I noticed balsam fir, red spruce, hemlock, and red pine. The eastern rim of the pond lies on the remains of a glacial delta where sand, gravel, and clay were laid down in

the sea. That deposit has been heavily mined for sand and gravel, and is now growing back to popple and birch, sunloving trees that start the woods on the road to recovery. Lesser (in size, not merit) plants included such Acadia standbys as wintergreen, lambkill, hair-cap moss, sphagnum moss, pincushion moss, bazzania, reindeer lichen, spotted lungwort lichen, and rock tripe. I saw several shaded patches of mayflower on the point, white flower buds showing between the leathery leaves but none yet in bloom. In sunnier locations in the park the blooms are already going by. Furled Canada May ruby leaves poked up all along the path. I looked for shadbush which often flowers this time of year, but didn't find it in bloom.

The special feature of this hike was water: water channeled into the pond by perennial and intermittent streams; water seeping from underground reservoirs in sandy soil; water collecting in puddles between roots and rocks; water falling from the sky. Every pond is the hub of its watershed, the bull's-eye at which the local terrain aims the water flowing through it. Water often isn't evident on the rocky ridges dividing one Acadian watershed from another. Plants that thrive on such dry divides are those with a greater need for sunlight than water, like the three pines: pitch, red, and jack. Ridges are quick to send most of the water that falls on them downward into the valleys on both sides. Top to bottom, soil grows deeper as slopes descend into valleys, and more readily holds water. At ground zero around the edge of a pond, water is generally abundant through the growing season, providing habitat for plants having greater need for water than sunlight such as red spruce, hemlock, sugar maple, and beech. The northern shore of a pond has the best of both worlds because it has plenty of water and gets an added dose of sunlight from reflection off the water. Competition for space is keen along any northern shore, a variety of species thriving there if they don't get crowded out by taller or pushier neighbors.

In rounding the pond, the Hadlock Path runs through a lush evergreen habitat that people and many species of animals find particularly inviting. The trail may not offer the same excitement as those that scale the peaks, but it has a drama of its own stemming from the combination of open water and thick woods. You are as likely to see mergansers, loons, and ospreys, which love the water, as you are warblers, which love the trees. This path and the loop around Jordan Pond are Acadia's outstanding examples of woodland trails encircling a body of fresh water. The Kane, Eagle Lake, and Long (Great) Pond trails run next to their respective ponds for a way without completing the circle.

Hadlock Brook was running swiftly after twelve hours of rain, providing an added bit of drama at the inlet where it drops twenty-some feet in its last dash for the pond. The brook flows innocently out of the woods then, after passing under the path's arched corduroy bridge, plunges in a series of noisy cascades over exposed granite ledges—to disappear without scream or kick into the maw of the waiting pond. The transition from running to still water is one of the most abrupt changes in nature, yet streams accomplish it with consummate grace, just as they instantly recover their former selves at the outlet on the far side. Water seems to be endlessly agreeable, adapting without fuss to whatever circumstances it is in. From running swiftly in a shallow course, it abruptly takes on a new dimension in fulfilling the depths of a pond, undergoing a personality change in the process. Tree-shaded streams are cooler and contain more oxygen than pond water, offering habitat to algae, insects, and fish that thrive under those conditions. Open to the sun, ponds offer a different range of habitats stratified top-to-bottom, favored by a different company of beings. I have never been an angler, so know little about stream or pond ecology. These days we often become entranced by events in outer space, when many of us know next to nothing about what goes on in streams, ponds, oceans, or even the ground beneath our feet where fellow Earthlings play out their lives. Does it make any sense to go looking for extraterrestrial life when we don't recognize most of our close neighbors on sight? In the future some higher race will sum up humanity in a paragraph or two, concluding we were more concerned with make-believe than the world around us. They will cite the empty hours we spent watching films, videos, and TV instead of reaching out to our companions, taking more interest in life on Mars than on the Earth. A walk along the Hadlock Path is a great way to make a start at contacting a few of the terrestrial wonders we know almost nothing about.

The level of Lower Hadlock Pond has been raised fifteen feet or more by the water company dam at the outlet in the southwest corner. Shoreline trees extend to the western end of the dam, so it is surprising to find yourself suddenly face-to-face with a brick pump house seemingly built in the middle of the woods. The path crosses the dam, then continues on the gravel road that runs along the south shore of the pond. The spell of the place is broken by these improvements and the power line overhead. Dam and road give good views of Norumbega Mountain to the north and Sargent Mountain to the northeast with its outriding companions: Parkman Mountain, Bald and Gilmore peaks, and the long ridge of Cedar Swamp Mountain. But the last short leg of my hike along the road was pretty much of a loss, which I minimized by finishing as quickly as I could.

Several other trails radiate from the Hadlock Path, leading to other worlds and other wonders. The Brown Mountain Trail up Norumbega Mountain starts at the western end of the dam. The Upper Hadlock Trail starts at the corduroy bridge over Hadlock Brook near the inlet and rounds Upper Hadlock Pond, the western leg running closer to the base of Norumbega Mountain than the upper pond (from which it is separated by Route 198). North of the pink houses a sign points toward Brown Mountain Gatehouse, the trail itself now ending at Route 198 opposite Gatehouse Road (it used to continue on to Forest Hill Cemetery and the connector to the Asticou Trail). And from the gravel road south of Lower Hadlock Pond a trail leads to the village of Northeast Harbor.

I had held this hike, the shortest in this series, in reserve for the week I moved from my apartment at park headquarters on McFarland Hill to my summer quarters at Harden Farm near the base of Kebo Mountain. I wanted to move without breaking the weekly rhythm of working, hiking, and writing I had kept to over the past several months. It was a frazzling week and my mind was at sixes and sevens, but my piles of papers were with me in my new digs at least, even if I couldn't put my hands on specific pages right away.

❦

43—AROUND JORDAN POND

From the boat ramp parking area off the loop road
To the north end of Jordan Pond, and back
   Clockwise around the pond by the Jordan Pond
    West and East Side trails

            3.0 miles, May 14, 1997

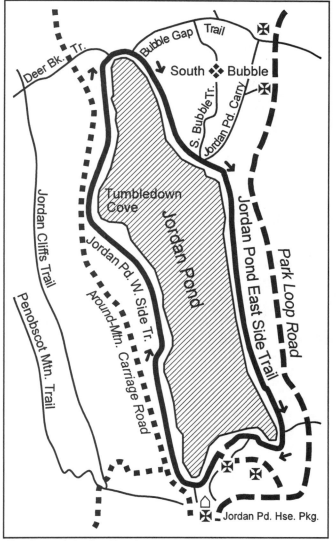

43—Around Jordan Pond.

On this hike I parked at the boat ramp parking area, walked west around Jordan Pond to the outlet, north on the Jordan Pond West Side Trail to the north end, then south on the Jordan Pond East Side Trail back to the boat ramp. I thought I was making a loop around the pond, but it turned out to be something else again.

Here it was almost mid-May and the seasons were stuck in their course, suspended halfway between winter and spring. Poplar leaves were showing the same green they showed last week; birches and alders were still on hold. The temperature wasn't cold, but it wasn't warm either, the thermometer generally ranging in the middle 40s and 50s. It rained every other day, and the days themselves were partly cloudy, partly sunny. Whatever goddess was in charge could not make up her mind. Maybe she was new on the job, doing the best she could to cope with a steep learning curve. The last ice was lurking in the shade of valleys and boulders but didn't look like it could hold out much longer. Ponds were open; streamflow was backing off. But you couldn't call it

Bogwalk on Jordan Pond West Side Trail.

spring. Not yet. Only the earliest warblers had arrived; the great yellow horde was yet to come. There were dandelions in the lawn at Harden Farm, and forsythia was golden yellow in front of the Congregational Church in Bar Harbor, but spring is more than a touch of yellow here and there, more than a tentative chirp from the top of a bare birch. Spring was teetering as if it could fall either way, back as well as ahead. There was no commitment in the air, no dedication, no sense of a sprint for the finish. If Acadia was into spring at all it was a maybe, perhaps, sort of, if-I-feel-like-it kind of spring. Fooling-around spring. Hemi-demi-semi spring. A rehearsal, perhaps, but the real thing was yet to come.

The day of my hike around Jordan Pond started with rain, then looked like it might clear. I drove to the boat ramp parking area under partly cloudy skies, which cleared when I reached the pond, but clouded up again as I walked the west side trail. When I got to the north end of the pond the sky turned dark and a few sprinkles fell. Then as I walked the east side trail it began to clear and the sun came out again, only to disappear behind thickening clouds. I drove home with my windshield wipers on. The wind was brisk from the south, raising whitecaps on the pond; higher up the clouds streamed over Jordan Ridge from the west. Even the wind couldn't make up its mind which way to blow.

What I am describing is the reluctant coming of spring to coastal Maine. Every year it digs in its heels and has to be dragged kicking and screaming over the land. The Gulf of Maine holds its winter chill well into June, and as the Gulf goes, so goes the coast. In fall it is just the opposite, the Gulf holding its heat, sharing it with the land, keeping winter at the gates until the sun is so low the fight isn't worth it. May is no merry month on the coast of Maine. It is a trial that builds character. Local chambers of commerce keep trying to lure tourists to the coast in May so they can get the commercial season off to an early start. Lately they have begun singing the praises of Memorial Day. If you succumb to the patter, don't forget to pack earmuffs and mittens. It is good to remember that the danger of frost hereabouts does not pass locally until June first.

The good news is, I didn't meet any blackflies or mosquitoes lusting after my flesh. The air was alive with kinder, gentler

South Bubble from Tumbledown Cove.

insects, though, and the tough guys couldn't be far behind. I had seen two mourning cloak butterflies on a walk earlier in the week. Insect eaters were beginning to arrive. I saw a male yellow-rumped warbler singing from the top of a birch over Jordan Stream. He was insistent, I'll give him that, if not very melodious. In the spruce woods south of the Tumbledown beneath the Jordan Cliffs I saw a black-and-white warbler probing up, down, and around the stem of a birch. From a distance he seemed to be a bird of infinite curiosity, but I knew his quest was driven more by a hearty appetite for insects and their eggs than a quest for knowledge. In bushes along the shore I kept seeing a sprightly, wren-like bird rise up, then quickly dive to the ground. Through binoculars I saw it was a common yellowthroat, the male masked with a black domino which set off the yellow of its breast. Compared to its pert agility, I saw myself as a slow and lumbering giant.

Herring and black-backed gulls kept up a steady flow of traffic to and from the middle of the pond. While there they busily ducked and splashed as if sprucing up for some important event. I guessed they were washing salt from their feathers. There weren't very many at one time, no more than fifteen or twenty. Most of their kin had left for their offshore breeding islands and wouldn't be back till July. The ones on the pond were probably juveniles not ready to assume life's responsibilities. By the boat ramp two black ducks dabbled in the shallows, and another pair did the same in the lagoon at the north end of the pond near a beaver lodge. I heard crows several times at different stages of my hike, their call giving voice to a landscape that in places looked stark and sere instead of on the verge of renewal.

Looking up the west slope of South Bubble from the east side trail, I saw four turkey vultures circling on the updraft coming off the pond. They slowly drifted north along the ridge, a fifth vulture straggling behind. They looked headless to me, like drones programmed to circle and drift without input from any sense of purposeful navigation. The five were joined by three more from North Bubble, the gang of eight then wandering mindlessly across to the slopes of Sargent Mountain where I lost them in the shadows. They looked like I felt—aimless, going through the motions, without cause, without hope. That syndrome is called cabin fever, and most folks in Maine suffer from it between March and the so-called arrival of spring, spring sometimes not putting in an appearance at all, winter sublimating directly into summer at some indeterminate point without passing through any transitional phase in between.

I heard many old friends cry from the offing as I rounded the pond: blue jays, chickadees, robins, hermit thrushes, and a flicker. Others left silent clues to their presence. Several piles of cone scales told of red squirrels eating their lunch. The northern end of the pond was strewn with beaver litter, felled birch poles lying every which way at the base of South Bubble, gnawed branches and twigs cast up all around the shore. The lodge itself was a good example of Acadian vernacular architecture. Woven of interlacing branches, it stood like a domed temple in its lagoon beneath the craggy cliffs of North Bubble, a subject worthy of a spread in the *National Geographic*. I was in the middle of taking what I was sure was just that sort of picture when the pesky breeze coming off the pond blew the cap from my head into the lagoon. I watched it sail like a coracle toward the black ducks, then went back to framing my shot of the lodge backed by the cliff. Click. With that done, I set about retrieving my cap. Looking for a tool to extend my reach, I picked up a five-foot branch stripped and trimmed by the beaver, and used that to fish the cap from the lagoon. I swung the dripping cap in my hand for half an hour until it was dry enough to put on.

It being the right time of year, I peered into the many pools along the west side trail looking for eggs of salamanders and frogs. In one pool I found a knobby mass of blue-white jelly floating just below the surface. Ten inches across, it looked like it had once sheltered a host of eggs, but they must have hatched in recent days, releasing tadpoles into the pool. Water seeped into the pool from a bank of sphagnum moss and drained by a trickle on the opposite side into the pond. I found smaller masses in nearby pools, eggs still intact. Tied to grass stalks rising through the water, these masses comprised about twenty-five clear jelly spheres less than half an inch across, each with a small kernel of life at the center. I guessed they were wood frog eggs, but wasn't sure.

West side trail winds across the Tumbledown.

In one short stretch along the east side trail I came to several patches of early everlasting (pussytoes) with packed white flower buds looking ready to pop open. I bent down over one patch for a closer look—and found my nose a few inches from a garter snake coiled among the plants at the edge of a smooth rock. The snake didn't move a muscle but seemed to transport itself by the power of its will, performing a lateral arabesque literally beneath my nose. One instant it was there, the next it was gone. It didn't bother to unwind its graceful knot but merely let the knot flow out along its body into the shelter beneath the rock.

Where the Tumbledown, that great talus slope at the base of the Jordan Cliffs, plunges into the pond, I saw the bodies of two small fish floating side-by-side at the shoreline, one an inch long, the other three inches, each with one eye looking up in a fixed stare. Seeing them, I was shocked. Not because they were dead, but because I saw them as so strange. They confronted me with a world beneath the surface of Jordan Pond about which my ignorance was colossal. I assumed it was as rich and intricate as the world above which it had taken me a lifetime to know on speaking terms. I have fish a ways back in my own family line, yet have turned my back on them as if they contributed nothing to my birth. Those black pupils looking up from the pond might well have accused me of familial neglect. If evolution can be put in reverse, my karma surely calls for me to come back as a fish.

But that is a fantasy. Entropy cannot be taken back. The universe is a one-way street. It is the fish who are reborn in my guise; the reverse runs against the grain of time. We are what our ancestors have made us. They live in us just as we will live in our children and their children's children for generations to come. My crime is in paying so little attention to my ancestry. Not only are ancient fish alive in me, but the cosmic particles of the Big Bang are in my flesh and bones. I carry on for them and for every stage of human evolution. The universe is always now, past and future latent in this particular instant. Tomorrow my dead eye will look up at all who come after me as if to see how they will spend their inheritance. Looking into such an eye, we see a black hole, a mystery that can tell us nothing about itself. It reminds us to live as fully and deliberately as we can while the universal spark shines in our eyes. When it dies, our possibilities fizzle out. We become so many dead fish floating between two worlds, one eye staring blindly into the future, the other into the hidden depths of the past. Now is the life in between, the life of possibility. Nothing else matters. To be alive is the sole gift. Budding flower, snake, and I are current facets of universal being. We are that we are. That is the one truth, the one mystery from which everything flows.

Such is the challenge I took from seeing two dead fish floating in Jordan Pond. Looking into those upturned eyes, I wondered if I was worthy of that unblinking gaze. I wasn't on a casual day hike after all but on my lap of the relay of the cosmic soul. No trial run; this was my one chance to live a particular day in the life of the universe. That is the sense I had later when looking into the eyes of the garter snake nestled among the low leaves of the early everlasting. The same sense with which I watched the vultures soaring overhead and the common yellowthroats darting among bushes along the shore. We were on the same journey, living out the day we had been given on the strength of our and our ancestors' openness to the universe living through our being, our senses, and our acts. On every hike I make in Acadia, some encounter reminds me to live in that state of openness. This time it was the dead fish. It doesn't take much to remind me that my soul is part of Acadia's soul, Acadia's soul is part of the Earth's soul, and Earth's soul is part of the universal soul. Nested like babushka dolls, we wrestle each possibility on our level of being. That is what the cosmos demands, and what we are pledged to deliver.

After passing the fish I came across several leatherleaf plants in full bloom among the great boulders dropped from the Jordan Cliffs toward the pond. Branches of the low plant arched over the water with a single row of delicate white bells hanging from each branch. Reminding me of blueberry bells, the flowers were about a quarter of an inch long, those farthest out on a branch looking like hanging urns or miniature hot-air balloons. The evergreen leaves were dusted with tiny white dots. A member of the heath family, leatherleaf is a bog plant that grows at higher latitudes around the globe. I imagined people in Scotland and Siberia finding it in bloom on their daily walk. It was the only bloom I saw on this hike.

The two plants I saw on the verge of blooming were early everlasting and hobblebush along the east side trail. I recognized the cupped hobblebush leaves as later stages of the ones I had seen along Sargent Brook three weeks ago which reminded me of praying hands. Strongly ribbed on the underside, these leaves came out in pairs, each looking now like a cowrie shell. The radial flower buds rose between pairs of leaves, tightly wound still, but looking ready to burst open in a day or two. Shad blossoms were in much the same state, all promise and no performance. Lance-sharp beech buds seemed ready to unfurl into green leaves any moment, and miter-like buds of striped maple gave the same impression. Red maples along the east side of the pond seemed stuck in a state of eternal bloom. Spruce and fir were lagging behind, giving no hint that this season was different from any other. A few fern scrolls were lifting out of the ruins of last year's growth, but I saw them only in one place along the east side trail, the general uprising of ferns not having truly begun.

Where birch, beech, and maple trees were notable along the east side trail, Northern white cedar was the tree of trees on the west side trail. The two opposite shores struck me as entirely different, the east being dominated by deciduous trees giving an open feel to the landscape, while the west was closed in with cedar and spruce the whole length of the

pond. The fire of 1947 burned as far as the south slope of South Bubble on the east, but left the west side relatively untouched. That explains why there are so many birches on the slopes of the Bubbles, but not why there are so few cedars south of the burn on the east side of the pond. The fire also accounts for the beaver lodge being where it is, in a lagoon surrounded by wall-to-wall birch, one of the beaver's favorite foods. The birches fed my eyes as well, their trunks gleaming beneath an overcast sky.

Spruce, birch, and North Bubble at the north end of Jordan Pond.

What is it about birches we find so attractive? They thrive on sites flooded with sunlight and having ample moisture and nutrients. Perhaps the white trunks flag areas where we are apt to do well ourselves. But birch is a fleeting species, a pioneer that settles an area, then gives way to others like spruce that move in and stay for the long term. We often reverse the normal pattern of succession, cutting everything but the birch, which we plant our houses among. Perhaps those white stems are a sign of recovery after fire in areas where soils are rich in ash. We are drawn to such places where undergrowth has been burned and life is on the rebound. As nomads, we would do well by moving on to groves of white birch. We say beauty is in the eye of the beholder, but it lies deeper than that. Beauty is a glint of survival in a world where life is the exception, not the rule. It is an invitation we ignore at our peril. We receive it at the core of our being, not the surface. Beauty appeals to the eye of the soul, not the eye that squints in the mirror. Every one of my hikes is a walk into beauty. Birches are an aspect of that beauty, along with spruces, Northern white cedars, and the other miracles I meet on my journey. In the end, beauty is recognition of a miracle shrouded in mystery. The mystery beneath the surface draws us as much as the miracle we can perceive. The question directs us not outward but inward: what is it about birches we find so attractive?

Walking north on the west side trail, I could see the Bubbles only now and then through gaps in the cedar hedge along the pond. I had a sense the cedars were playing tag with the Bubbles, the trees being "it" most of the time, the Bubbles being tagged now and then. From the south end of the pond the Bubbles look rounded, smooth, and symmetrical. As I went along the western shore, I saw them more and more from the side, their neat symmetry getting stretched into a long ridge running to the north. At every opening I had to get used to a new perspective until in the cove where the Tumbledown falls into the pond I stood opposite South Bubble and saw it fully from the side, where it reminded me of a bold headland reaching into the sea, which at one time it had been. Both Bubbles are built up in tiers of rugged yet crumbling granite. Looking at them up close without leaves covering their cliffs, I was reminded of the line from *Trial by Jury:* "She may very well pass for forty-three in the dusk with the light behind her." The standard view of the Bubbles from the south end of the pond flatters them, so they conform to a romantic, tea-and-popovers view of nature. A walk around the pond quickly sets the record straight.

Even though the long ridge of Pemetic Mountain is much higher than the Bubbles, it is generally upstaged by the lesser ridge as seen from the west side trail. This is partly due to Pemetic remaining relatively unchanged while the Bubbles change dramatically as seen from different outlooks along the trail. The west slope of Pemetic was clad in deciduous gray along the pond, coniferous green higher up. Jordan Ridge gave the opposite effect as seen from the east side trail, being granite gray above and coniferous green below. It was late afternoon by the time I started down the east side trail, what light there was coming from behind the ridge, casting its craggy face in shadow. In raking sunlight Jordan Ridge is a dramatic sight; backlighting steals much of its character.

Along with the trees and views being very different on the east and west sides of the pond, the trails themselves are like night and day. The Jordan Pond East Side Trail provides solid footing for the most part, only occasionally passing over spots that hold water and get boggy after a rain. The east side trail passes through two talus slopes, one fallen from Pemetic, the other from South Bubble, but neither slope is difficult to cross. The Youth Conservation Corps (YCC) improved the trail through the South Bubble talus slope several years ago, putting down a series of solid steps and a stretch of gravel. A number of cribwork steps help hikers across places where runoff streams off Pemetic, and a bogwalk provides a similar service at the northern end of the trail.

The Jordan Pond West Side Trail is a much different story. It is raw and wild by comparison with the trail on the opposite side. Where the ground it passes over isn't wet it is rooty, and where it isn't rooty it is full of stones. A wooden sign at the start of the trail gives fair warning: **CAUTION,**

TRAIL BECOMES DIFFICULT. The pond is ringed with boulders, Northern white cedars taking root in those on the west side, stabilizing them like a levee protecting the lower ground behind it. That lower ground is wet for much of the way. That's where I found the amphibian egg masses in a series of pools. A long bogwalk made of split logs takes hikers over the wettest, rootiest ground. It is tempting to step off the bogwalk to peer under the cedars in order to get a

Jordan Pond East Side Trail below Pemetic Mountain.

view of the pond, but signs at both ends of the walk ask hikers not to submit to that temptation:

> **LAKESIDE ECOSYSTEMS ARE**
> **FRAGILE AND EASILY DAMAGED**
> **PLEASE HELP US PRESERVE**
> **THIS AREA BY STAYING ON**
> **BOARDWALK**
> **THANK YOU**

Where stretches of higher ground make the bogwalks unnecessary, the west side trail passes over the roots of shoreline trees, the roots doing the work of a bogwalk at considerable risk to themselves from wear and tear caused by thousands of boots treading on them every summer and fall. It would be better for the trees if the bogwalk continued over those rooty stretches as well, but it would be a big job for the park to install the length of walk necessary to finish the job.

Over halfway to the north end the west side trail turns inland and passes through spruce woods with tall poles rising sixty and seventy feet overhead, the ground around them thick with saplings. That is where I gawked at the black-and-white warbler gleaning tidbits hidden in the bark of a birch. In short order the trail passes over a small stream which empties into the pond, its bed strewn with boulders fallen from the cliffs above. Then the trail skirts the shore of Tumbledown Cove through a talus slope with boulders twelve feet tall, others half that size. Here, the trail keeps within a few feet of the pond. This is where I saw the dead fish and the blooming leatherleaf. Rock-cap fern, rock tripe, and a variety of crusty lichens add touches of color and texture, turning the Tumbledown into a rock garden au naturel. The cove opens onto a profile view of South Bubble. It is worth taking the time to enjoy this section of trail without hurrying.

North of the Tumbledown, bluebead leaves were rising directly out of the soil, uncoiling as they rose, but their yellow blooms would not appear for another two or three weeks. Here the west side trail continues behind a screen of Northern white cedar until it crosses Deer Brook running out of the valley between Penobscot and Sargent mountains. Farther along, another stream comes in from the wetland between Sargent and North Bubble. This stream empties into the beaver lodge lagoon, then flows under the impressive YCC bridge into the pond. It is approximately a mile and a half to the south end of the pond from here by either the east or west side trail.

Together with six or seven intermittent streams draining the flank of Pemetic Mountain, two other streams of some consequence flow into the pond along the east side trail, one draining the valley between South Bubble and Pemetic along which the Jordan Pond Canoe Carry runs, the other draining the wetland in the southeastern corner of the pond. This second stream is bridged by an impressive ninety-foot row of stone steps placed by the YCC in 1983. The cedars in the wetland have been trimmed to a uniform height by browsing deer able to stretch their necks so high and no higher.

The trail continues along the south end of the pond, connecting the east and west side trails. This section looks across to the familiar aspect of the Bubbles in all their sensuous symmetry. A fine granite seat on the shore faces the view, its small plaque reading:

IN GRATEFUL LOVING MEMORY OF
SARAH ELIZA SIGOURNEY CUSHING
WIFE OF EDWARD TUCKERMAN
1832–1915
SHE DEARLY LOVED THIS SPOT

The brimming pond had risen to the base of the seat, so Sarah Eliza would have gotten her feet wet if she were there on the day I made this hike. I pictured her standing on the shore looking over the pond a hundred years ago, as others had stood there for thousands of years before that. Yes, there is magic in that place which bonds viewers to the view, creating a scenic habitat where people know they rightly belong. Beauty is the voice of the universe calling us to our senses, telling us we will thrive if we devote ourselves to its service. I sat on the granite seat and looked over the pond. Under dark clouds, the pond itself reflected the deep greens of shoreline trees and golds of lowering sunlight reflected through Southwest Pass at the far end, with every shade of

Youth Conservation Corps bridge, north end of Jordan Pond.

gray rippling on the waves surrounding the patches of color. The view included the invisible space above the pond as well as the slopes and woods surrounding it. The spirit of Sarah Eliza put her hand on my shoulder, and together we enjoyed a moment of silence before going our separate ways.

The outlet of Jordan Pond flows into Jordan Stream, which in turn empties into (Little) Long Pond and Bracy Cove. The Jordan Stream Trail runs along the stream between Jordan Pond House and Cobblestone Bridge, then in derelict form on to (Little) Long Pond and, by private carriage road, to Bracy Cove. The trail is worth hiking in springtime when the stream is running full-tilt, at least as far as Cobblestone Bridge just beyond the park boundary. Faced with smooth stones, the bridge is one of the most unusual in the joint public-and-private system of carriage roads established by John D. Rockefeller, Jr. before the Second World War. A much smaller carriage road bridge crosses Jordan Stream near the outlet of Jordan Pond. The west side trail starts at the western end of that bridge.

Hearing again the rush of water over the spillway at the

outlet while enjoying Sarah Eliza's view, I muttered "Full circle" to myself, then quickly took it back. I was almost six hours older than when I started, and had a new outlook on Jordan Pond. I had communed with dead fish; seen amphibian eggs, a living serpent, leatherleaf in bloom; and was up-to-date on the progress of spring in these parts. I was a different person than I had been when I parked my car, more in tune now with Acadia and its universe than I had been before the hike. Trails lead us on spiral journeys, not loops. They do not take us back to our beginnings but to wholly new places where we never expected to be—to new beginnings, not ends. If we were the same after a hike as before, what would that say about our openness to experiences along the way? No, we are changed by our journeys. We go into nature to expand our vision, not stay the same. That is why places like Acadia call to us, and why we heed the call, as we do by the millions every year. We only come full circle when we are stuck on a treadmill and cannot get off. That's what cabin fever feels like. The only cure is to wake up to the beauty around us so we can live up to it by growing out of our former selves. Then, before we know it, spring will be here.

Cribwork steps on the Bubble Gap Trail.

44—SARGENT MOUNTAIN via DEER BROOK

From Bubble Rock parking area on the loop road
To Sargent Mountain, and back
    Up by Bubble Gap Trail, Deer Brook Trail, and
        Jordan Cliffs Trail extension
    Down by Sargent Mountain South Ridge,
        Deer Brook, and Jordan Pond East Side trails,
        and Jordan Pond Canoe Carry
                4.6 miles, May 21, 1997

In the order in which I made these sixty hikes, this was my eighth and final trip to the summit of Sargent Mountain. I had made two hikes in fall, one in winter, two in summer, and now this was the third I had made this spring. You might get the idea that Sargent is my favorite destination in Acadia. The trail I am on is generally my favorite, but the record speaks for itself: in this series I have hiked Sargent Mountain more often than any other peak. Cadillac has its West Face and Canon Brook trails, Pemetic its Ravine Trail, Western Mountain its Perpendicular Trail; but the Sargent massif has the greatest variety of superior trails: Jordan Cliffs, Amphitheater, Hadlock Brook, Maple Spring, Giant Slide, Grandgent, among several others. Cadillac's summit has been degraded by more foot traffic than its fragile landscape can bear, while Sargent's summit ridge still offers an otherworldly experience that wakes me up and makes me appreciate the wonders of our home planet apart from what people have done to improve it.

Yes, I am happy to be on any trail leading to Sargent. I have thought a great deal about why that should be. Contrary to the fact that I am a writer, and that symbols (money, words, numbers, statistics, images) are the basis of modern American culture, I appreciate the immediate, nonverbal quality of my trail experience as I head for or away from the summit. When I lived alone on a thirty-acre island for over two-and-a-half years, I often talked to myself and came to realize that the thoughts I expressed existed whole and entire in preverbal form before I opened my mouth. Everything I muttered was redundant because my words reflected experiences consummated a fraction of a second earlier. And the words themselves never did justice to the richness of those experiences. They were tokens but not the experiences themselves. I thought of what I said or wrote as a shadow of my inner life but not the substance. The substance was too personal to convey. Experience lies beyond words because it takes place as myriad neural exchanges in the ineffable language of the body itself.

Except for a few weathered trail signs, nothing on Sargent Mountain addresses me indirectly through symbols. When Sargent speaks, it speaks to the nonverbal core of my experience, which I think of as my soul. Its soul and my soul connect without mediation or intervention. That is what I call true communion.

The closest thing to such communion we have in our culture is provided by music, a medium that moves many of us because of its sensuous immediacy. But music is a form of communion between people, not between people and the natural world. We depend on the pool of disciplined behaviors available in our social groups, but beyond that on the patterns and flow of organized energy in the world around us. If our groups do not respond to the native rhythms of the Earth, they will perish by separation from the source of energy itself. It is the music of the sun, air, water, and plants that sustains us. The music of wind, rain, and the seasons. If we are insensitive to that music, we have grown deaf to the anthem of planet Earth. The trails on Sargent Mountain lead me back to the rhythms and melodies of the natural world, to the music our people and their ancestors have been dancing to for over four million years. Sargent Mountain offers it as immediate experience without intervening concepts, symbols, or corporate agendas.

We seldom learn to appreciate those outdoor melodies during our formal education. Schools have largely lost sight of them, substituting the words of men for the native, non-verbal music of the soul. We have become enamored of ourselves, not the settings in nature from which we draw our inspiration and strength. Alexander Pope's assertion still commands us: "The proper study of mankind is man." Sargent Mountain brings me to my senses. Literally to my senses. To the skilled perceptions that inform me about the land where I live and on which my life depends. On Sargent my soul responds to the music of a mountain, the song of Acadia, my home on this Earth. If I do not respond to that song, my soul is out of touch with the source of its nurture. When that happens, life is at risk. That is why I go back again and again to the mountain that reawakens me to the music, not of the spheres, but of the Earth and its star, the song of the one sphere where I have risen briefly to awareness and whose native rhythms have shaped every aspect of my being and my soul. I am a minute reflection of the Earth soul, one spark reflecting the brilliance of the sun.

Passing along valleys and ridges of Sargent Mountain, I know where I am without being told. Words are extraneous. I navigate by affinity with the land, not by some rigid system of coordinates imposed upon it. The eight stories I tell of Sargent Mountain are about connecting with the life of the Earth through the season as expressed in the music of this place. I hike to the anthem of Acadia, which rings with more intensity on Sargent than in many of the more accessible places in the park.

This 4.6-mile hike was made up of portions of six different trails. Parking at the Bubble Rock parking area on the Park Loop Road below South Bubble, I took what I call the

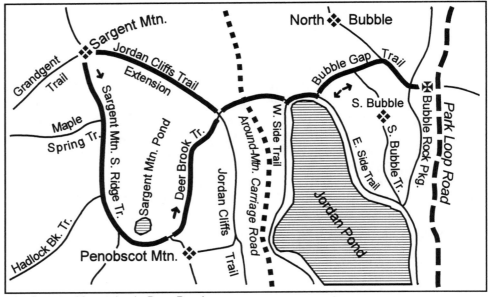

44—Sargent Mountain via Deer Brook.

Bubble Gap Trail connecting the parking area with the north shore of Jordan Pond by way of the gap between North and South Bubble. Passing by the beaver lagoon at the end of the pond, I picked up the Deer Brook Trail that runs up the valley between Sargent and Penobscot mountains, going as far as the intersection with the Jordan Cliffs Trail, which I followed up Sargent to the summit. From there I took the Sargent Mountain South Ridge Trail to Sargent Mountain Pond, where I stopped to admire the reflection of shoreline trees, and then on to the upper end of the Deer Brook Trail in the wooded gap where the Amphitheater on the west gives way to the valley of Deer Brook on the east. I took the Deer Brook Trail down to Jordan Pond. Following the Jordan Pond East Side Trail to the intersection with the Jordan Pond Canoe Carry, I turned along the carry to get back to the parking area six hours and twenty minutes after I started out. Counting the 180-foot rise to Bubble Gap from the parking area, the 1,098-foot rise to Sargent's summit from the pond, and the final 175-foot rise along the canoe carry, the loop rose and fell a total of 1,453 feet, equal to Sargent's elevation above sea level with another 80 feet thrown in for good measure. The temperature was 64° Fahrenheit when I started out, but felt a good deal cooler than that in wind and rain on the summit.

My goal was to follow Deer Brook from its rise in the valley between Sargent and Penobscot to its outlet into Jordan Pond. This was the last of the streamside hikes I had planned for this spring. Rain having fallen almost every day for two weeks, Deer Brook was no disappointment. I heard it rushing toward the pond as soon as I reached Bubble Gap. Not running full tilt, it was demonstrating how fast it could carry water off the slopes as a matter of course. It is due to that speed that Jordan Pond is listed as the clearest pond in Maine. Bill Gawley in the Natural Resources Division at the park tells me the average transparency readings for Jordan Pond over the past five years is forty-seven feet (the depth at which he can see a suspended object from the surface), with a maximum reading of sixty-six feet. Water feeding the pond doesn't sit around long enough to pick up a load of minerals and nutrients. As a result there is very little mineral or organic material in the water column to cloud the pond. Deer Brook was Exhibit A of the dynamics responsible for that outstanding clarity.

Falling steeply between the two mountains, the valley of Deer Brook is a rough-and-ready kind of place. Soil particles are typically the size of cobbles and boulders. Granite ledge lies a few inches below the organic matter covering the surface. A steep cliff on the Sargent Mountain side rises out of talus at its base. Start to finish, the brook flows over a jagged tumble of rock, which it makes no effort to do quietly. Valley woods are a mix of deciduous and evergreen trees including spruce, hemlock, white pine, red and striped maple, white and yellow birch, American beech, and red oak. Spring and late fall are the best times to appreciate the true character of Deer Brook and its valley because summer leaves screen out much of its unkempt nature and lack of refinement.

The Deer Brook Trail shares the character of the valley and its brook. The treadway is not made of carefully placed stones but is laid by the same forces that rule the landscape as a whole. It is made of jagged rocks and twisted roots. Wear on the section of trail below the cliffs trail crossing has led to severe erosion, soil particles doing what they do naturally when swept by torrents fed by a series of downpours. Above the crossing the trail is just as rocky but has more soil between the rocks to even the surface.

The valley of Deer Brook is so shaded, I came across a forty-foot section of the upper brook still covered by six inches of ice. One moment I was walking along on last October's leaves, the next I was gazing at ice from the intervening winter, while overhead yellow birch buds were set to release their charge of spring green. What season was it supposed to be, anyway? There is a wild defiance of convention in the valley that tests the readiness and grit of all who settle there and all who pass through.

The most notable settler I heard at first, then saw, was the black-throated blue warbler that was drawn to the middle stories of yellow birch which thrive in the valley of Deer Brook. The sound of the brook drowned out almost all bird

calls there may have been, but the black-throated blues were so close I could hear the five to seven scratchy bursts of their song through the general din. I saw two males flitting through the birches, and saw several more as I passed along the extension of the Jordan Cliffs Trail rising up the steep slope of the valley on the Sargent Mountain side. At one level I could look across into the branches of birches rooted lower down and get a good view of those restless blue, black,

Eagle Lake and Conners Nubble from Jordan Cliffs Trail extension.

and white sprites darting after insects which shared their living space.

On the way down from Bubble Gap toward Jordan Pond, I had seen other warblers: a black-throated green and two—make that three, no, four black-and-white warblers gleaning among the birches lining that rocky slope. Blackflies had arrived en masse, and the warblers had taken their cue. With so much food on the wing there was no reason to stay away any longer. I saw three common yellowthroats near the beaver lagoon at the north end of the pond. One hopped onto a stone island a few feet away from me and gave me a good look at his striking costume before darting back into the bushes. I also saw a black duck swimming in the lagoon, and a crow and a song sparrow nearby. Some sort of sandpiper flitted over the pond with deep-dipping strokes of its wings, crying a shrill weep, weep, weep, weep. I heard a whippoorwill and two woodpeckers half a mile across the water. On the way up to Bubble Gap I saw a robin posed nobly on a stone in the woods, looking as wild and keen as any creature in the park. Every bird is at its best this time of year. For comic relief, two hairy woodpeckers flew over my head in the last fifty feet of this hike, landing on gnarly beeches, emitting a series of raucous shrieks as they postured this way and that, looking like a pair of clowns sent to lighten up the serious work of ushering in spring. Blackflies kept up with me during much of the hike, but didn't seem hungry enough to strike, merely bouncing off my skin where soon they would draw blood.

Spring had arrived the previous Sunday, May 18th, a warm, sunny, windy day that brought relief after seven weeks of cool, rainy days. That is the day the late warblers arrived. Spring in Acadia starts in the warmer, lowland sections and slowly creeps up the slopes to summit ridges. On this hike I saw red maple flowers still in full bloom, shadbush abruptly exploding with white blossoms, violets nestled quietly along the trail around Jordan Pond, twin pale-yellow bells of American fly honeysuckle along the Deer Brook Trail, and hobblebush blooms looking like bridal wreaths with eight pale yellow flowers around the edge. Ungainly though it may be, hobblebush is one of the outstanding shrubs in the park, the first to leaf out in spring and the first to bloom. Waving large rounded, toothed leaves all summer which glow with color in fall, it bears bright red berries well into winter. Hobblebush grows along streams and in damp woods everywhere in the park, so is hard to miss at any season. The name comes from its habit of spreading by drooping the ends of its branches to the ground where they take root and sprout, creating a tangle of loops which hobble passing bipeds with big feet.

A badly eroded section of the Deer Brook Trail.

I saw mayflower leaves but no blooms, sarsaparilla flower buds on stalks rising under bronzy new leaves, and early everlasting (pussytoes) flower buds drooping along the Jordan Pond East Side Trail where I saw the garter snake last week. Canada May ruby flower buds were forming, and starflower leaves were up with no sign of blooms. A plant with tight-packed purple flower buds at the end of its stalks was about to bloom; I thought it might be red-berried elder but wasn't sure. Leaf buds of striped maple lifted up like tapers in hundreds of candelabra all through the understory along Deer Brook. Around Jordan Pond, white pine candles stood upright at the end of each branch. Other new arrivals I noticed included arching leaves of Solomon's seal, bristly clumps of mountain sandwort leaves on Sargent's summit ridge, a few new wine-leaf cinquefoil leaves in cracks along the ridge, blueberry leaf buds just beginning to open, and

bluebead lily leaves in wet areas around the pond. Mosses shone brilliant green with new growth. The soft domes of pincushion moss were particularly lush. Last week, fern scrolls were two to six inches high; this week they were six to ten. Only a few plants looked untouched by spring: mountain cranberry, partridgeberry, wintergreen, lambkill, and juniper. They weren't yet caught up in the wave of new growth.

Acadia's bursting forth was made possible by one of the coolest, rainiest springs I could remember, with the urging of an occasional glimpse of the sun. As on most days in April and May this year, the weather during this hike was unstable at best. A few sprinkles fell against my windshield while I drove to the parking area, as they fell again while I was driving home. I reached Sargent's summit under cloudy skies, then watched passing showers fall to the east on Eagle Lake and the west on the far side of Somes Sound. The summit was ringed by fast-moving low clouds except over the ocean where the islands south of Mount Desert Island—from Baker in the east to Placentia in the west—shone brightly in the blue waters of the Gulf of Maine.

While I was descending along the south ridge trail, a weeping dark-blue cloud came up from behind and gave the mountain a brief soaking. I was stopped in my tracks by the fresh smell of rain. How could I have forgotten that scent so it came to me as a surprise? After the cloud had passed over Cadillac to the east, the sun came out for a spell and cast a rainbow over Jordan Pond from Penobscot to Pemetic mountains. It was a broad, sweeping arch of color suspended in the air, violet on the inside, surrounded by concentric rings of blue, green, yellow, and orange. I looked for red on the outside, but couldn't make it out. Rain fell again when I got down to the pond, then stopped as quickly as it had begun. The sun came out and built a new rainbow, this time over South Bubble. The day was the epitome of spring. Acadia responded with new greenery and finery on every slope.

The trails that took me into the middle of this Acadian spring made for a fine hike. The Bubble Gap Trail rises by a series of cribwork steps through beech and birch woods to the saddle between the Bubbles, then falls steeply through birch woods over a slope of smooth boulders to the edge of Jordan Pond. Among birches beneath the cliffs of North Bubble I saw charred stumps of great trees blackened by the 1947 fire, reminders of what had once been, and would be again in a hundred years. Rounding the north end of the pond, I saw where during the past week the beaver had gnawed at the base of the handsome Northern white cedar near the end of the YCC bridge. Past the bridge the Deer Brook Trail follows along the brook to its rise in the dip between Sargent and Penobscot mountains, giving an intimate view of rugged terrain just now returning to life. The lower section of the trail passes below the Deer Brook Bridge on the Around-Mountain Carriage Road, a structure rising as impressively as a granite cliff higher up. The Sargent Mountain South Ridge Trail spans one of Acadia's most unspoiled subalpine habitats, and is a joy to walk along at any season. I have been there when every twig was coated with ice, when every branch lay beneath three feet of snow, when blueberry leaves were bright red, and when orange wood lilies bloomed beside the trail. Unlike similar areas on Cadillac, people have generally kept to the trail by following the row of meandering cairns, giving orange grass and mountain sandwort a chance to grow in the gravel pans which the trail makers have taken pains to avoid. Surprisingly, there are wetlands on the south ridge, pools supporting cotton grass and other hardy sedges. The east and west side trails around Jordan Pond offer upland views, water views, and views of the transitional riparian zone in between. The Jordan Pond Canoe Carry takes hikers on a gradual half-mile incline through birch, maple, and beech woods with a talus slope on one hand and a rocky streambed on the other.

The one trail I haven't mentioned is the extension of the Jordan Cliffs Trail running from Deer Brook straight for the summit of Sargent Mountain. This section had temporarily been closed the week before my hike due to unsafe conditions resulting from severe erosion. I had asked Trails Foreman Don Beal for the details, and he said melting snow had raised havoc with a section of trail at the upper end of the talus slope, but that I could get around that part with no problem. When I came to the sign reading, **Trail CLOSED: _Unsafe Conditions!_** I ducked under the strings suspending it in the middle of the trail and went on. The extension rises quickly up a talus slope which seems to have been a dumping ground for glacial boulders. No steps have been put down as a concession to human legwork; the boulders themselves are the trail. I soon came to a swath where the great stones had given way to water plunging from the cliffs above. The treadway was unstable there, so I went around that section and regained the trail above the worst damage. The route then winds along the base of terraced cliffs

through oak woods, rising here and there up the slope where footing is possible along a dike or other manageable slope. The trail comes out on the broad eastern ridge of the mountain, which it traverses at an easy grade through lambkill and a landscape strewn with stones of all sizes. The predominant lichen along that stretch was luminous with bright chlorophyll which painted the slope iridescent green. After passing through a stretch of krummholz, trees stunted and blasted by

A spring shower approaches the summit of Sargent Mountain.

particles of windblown ice, the trail climbs the final ridge and comes out at the great cairn marking the summit.

For years I have thought of this route up Sargent Mountain as hardly fit for human use because of the severe erosion caused by water following in hikers' footsteps. I hiked it this time primarily to complete my sampling of the various ways to reach the summit. Perhaps it was the reverse psychology worked by the trail's being closed, but I thoroughly enjoyed the extension and faulted myself for not hiking it more often. The black-throated blue warblers drew my attention this time to the yellow birches rising from the talus slope, and once in a treeful mood, I enjoyed the company of the hardy red oaks higher along the cliffs. The view toward Jordan Pond and the Bubbles backed by Pemetic Mountain provides an unusual perspective on how things fit together in that part of Acadia as seen from the higher slopes. From the broad eastern ridge the view opens up to the north and east, Conners Nubble against Eagle Lake in the foreground, with Frenchman Bay and the Black (Gouldsboro) Hills as a backdrop. I now rank the Jordan Cliffs Trail extension as a rewarding way for determined hikers to reach the summit. It is no Sunday jaunt, but it makes a great hike any day of the week once the trail is free of ice.

In addition to the greening of Acadia, another sign of spring was the increased number of fellow hikers I met along the trail. On most of my hikes since March I had had the trail pretty much to myself, but this time I met fifteen people on four different routes into the park. Right away I met four young men coming down from South Bubble.

"Hi, how's it going?" the first one greeted me.

"Fine," I said, not yet really into my hike.

They seemed to be in a rush to get back to their car, so we left our exchange at that. I met two groups rounding Jordan Pond, one on my way to the summit, the other on my way back. The first was a couple from California. The man was full of questions, perhaps triggered by the sight of my binoculars and the notebook and pencil tied around my neck.

"What's that tree?" he asked, looking over my shoulder.

"A red maple," I said.

Satisfied with my answers to that and three or four similar questions, he and his wife continued on their way. Later I was overtaken by two young women on the Jordan Pond East Side Trail. I heard their excited talk behind me and stood aside to let them pass.

"You're going faster than I am," I said.

They both laughed, then said, "Thank you," as they went by. They wore shorts and had knapsacks and sturdy hiking boots, which put them in the class of serious hikers. I was pleased by their musical thank-yous, which for some reason surprised me.

Wetlands on Sargent's summit ridge.

On the way up the Jordan Cliffs Trail extension I met a lone hiker coming down, he apparently as unabashed by the trail closing as I was. He had reached Sargent by the Bald Peak Trail, having gotten to the trailhead on in-line skates from Blackwoods Campground. He had his skates in his pack. I asked if he were German because of his faint accent, and he said yes, he came from Cologne. We talked about possible ways he could get back to Blackwoods before dark by various combinations of hiking and skating. He had a worn and creased park map, which I ripped neatly in two while trying to straighten out the folds.

On my way down the Deer Brook Trail two young men with boots and knapsacks overtook me while I was admiring the rocky junction of the two forks of the upper brook. I had seen the hikers along the south ridge trail, but they had been off to one side and we hadn't spoken.

"How's your hike going?" I asked.

"Awesome," the first one said. Then he said it again: "Awesome."

"Were you there for the storm?" he asked me.

I told him I was, and had seen the rainbow.

"Awesome," he said.

A three-awesome hike is like four-star brandy, something to make a connoisseur sit up and take notice.

I met a foursome on the Jordan Pond Canoe Carry, a young woman in the lead followed by a young man in a Hancock Lumber cap, tailed by another couple with pink and peeling noses and cheeks.

"Does this path go to the rock?" the lead woman asked.

"No," I said, "it goes to the pond."

Turning to her companions she said, "We took the wrong turn."

"I want to go to the rock," said the second young man.

I told them they could reach the top of South Bubble either way, from the pond or by going back the way they had come. They decided to go back.

"Thank you for saving us some steps," the lead woman said.

Three awesomes and three thank-yous in one day! I decided the younger generation was no more lost than my own had been during its coming-of-age. Some part of the future would be determined by people with social skills who loved Acadia. The prospect buoyed me up as I ended my hike.

45—FOUR TRAILS on ISLE AU HAUT

From the town dock on Isle au Haut
To Western Head, and back
   South by Duck Harbor and Western Head trails
   North by Cliff, Duck Harbor Mountain, and
     Duck Harbor trails

13.5 miles, May 27, 1997

The rocky upper valley of Deer Brook.

The three main premises on which I am basing these sixty essays are:

- Every inch of Acadia National Park teems with plant and animal life.
- To experience Acadia requires acquainting that life in selected areas of the park.
- Acadia's hiking trails give immediate access to the park's living wonders.

I started writing up my hikes in late August 1993 after seeing many visitors leave the park with slight understanding of or appreciation for the workings of Acadia's spectacular terrain. Most visitors "do" Ocean Drive, Jordan Pond House, and the top of Cadillac Mountain in their cars. Many walk or bike a section of the carriage roads. Others may attend one or two guided ranger programs. Almost everyone goes shopping and eats out. But of the millions who visit the park every year, how many take with them a deeper understanding of Acadia as a spectacular habitat where nonhuman beings thrive because it offers them the specific range of conditions their survival requires?

In a sense I wrote these essays to counter the hoodwinking of the American public by aggressive commercial forces that would have us believe we cannot experience nature without buying a particular brand of bicycle or four-wheel-drive vehicle. Instead of taking us into nature, these machines assure that we keep nature at a distance, experiencing primarily the jounce of the road with our seats firmly planted and our gloved hands gripping plastic and steel. We can whiz through Acadia on roads and carriage roads, but how are we changed by the experience? What have we taken in? What are we more alive to than we were back home before we set out? With wheels interceding between us and the Earth, we can go faster perhaps, but do we go better?

My answer is no. We go best on two legs alternately planted on the Earth. For two reasons: the rhythm of walking wakes us up, and our minds work best at two miles an hour, not twenty or sixty. When we speed we grow detached from where we are and our thoughts turn to foreign concerns. When we slow down to an amble we plant our feet firmly here, here, and here, prompting our thoughts to take root where we are, not some other place. The secret to enjoying Acadia is being there wide awake. The secret to being there is walking on the Earth where we are. On the Earth, not

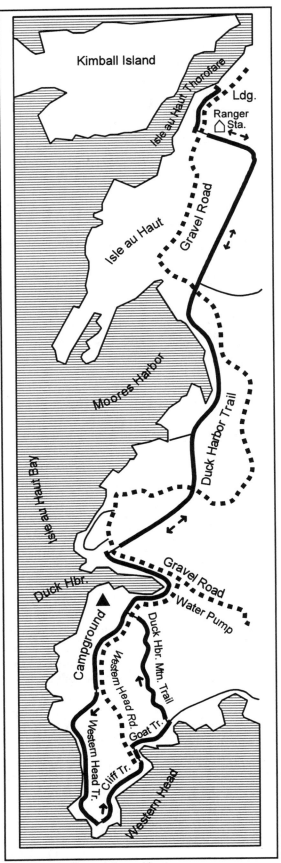

45—Four trails on Isle au Haut.

skimming across it. Awake, not asleep. What we get back follows directly from what we put out. Contrary to the way we were treated in school, the best way to stretch our minds is to stretch our legs. Seated, we grow dull. Aristotle kept his pupils on the go because he understood the vital connection between moving the body and getting the mind off its drachma. Medieval students walked to-and-fro in their cloisters while they disputed the great questions of their age. Now we sit on our duffs and wait for the world and its issues to come to us on their own. We segregate music, art, athletics, and academic subjects as if physical exertion, rhythm, visual stimulation, and learning had nothing to do with one another. What we overlook is if we don't actively engage the world, it will pass us right by. We are what we give ourselves to. Holding back, we end up with nothing. The sage on her mountaintop did not alight from the clouds but got there the hard way by climbing the longest and steepest trail; that's why she is so wise. More than Acadia, these essays are about reaching for experience day-by-day. If readers put off going into the world until they get to Bar Harbor, I will have failed. Acadia is where I live, so that's where I hike. Those who live elsewhere have the choice of coming to Acadia if they can swing it or going into nature where they are (even Manhattan Island will do in a pinch). The point is to get out and engage the world with your muscles and senses. Now is the time; this is the place. Earth is waiting; life is waiting; the flesh and the spirit are waiting. Let's go!

For the last of my spring hikes I adopted the attitude, if Isle au Haut will not come to me, I must go to Isle au Haut. I had never been there, and time was running out. I had meant to go a week earlier but couldn't fit my plans to the off-season ferry schedule. The day after Memorial Day I took annual leave and drove to Stonington, caught the 7:00 a.m. mailboat, hiked almost without stopping for nine hours, got the 5:00 p.m. boat back, and was in Bar Harbor a little after 7:00 that evening. It was a whirlwind trip, the kind I warn against, but was enough to whet my appetite for a longer, less hectic stay. Mount Desert Island, where most of Acadia National Park is located, is connected to the mainland by the Thompson Island Bridge, so doesn't seem all that insular. Six miles out in the Gulf of Maine south of Deer Isle, Isle au Haut, with no bridge, seems very insular indeed. You can't get there by car, and there is no point taking a bike because park rangers discourage the use of mountain bikes on the one gravel service road. The only way to get around is on foot. Isle au Haut is a back-to-basics kind of place where experience is heightened because you have to do everything for yourself, making sure that you put out the most and get the most back.

There are eleven hiking trails covering a distance of eighteen miles in the park section of Isle au Haut, the island itself being some six miles long and three miles wide. I hiked four of those trails covering seven miles, adding almost three miles on connecting roads and about four miles retracing my steps back to the boat landing for a total hike of thirteen-and-a-half miles. I went much faster than I usually do when taking notes and photographs, and do not suggest that anyone should try to follow my example. I kept wanting to dawdle and gawk, but pushed myself to cover the trails I wanted to do and still get back for the last boat. I was out to taste the trails, not savor them. A better way to see Isle au Haut would be to reserve one of the five lean-tos in Duck Harbor Campground between mid-June and early September when the mailboat makes a stop at the mouth of Duck Harbor, saving campers a five-mile hike from and to the town landing. Unlike reservations for Blackwoods or Seawall campgrounds on Mount Desert Island, Isle au Haut campground reservations are handled only by mail. Reservation information is detailed in the park's Isle au Haut brochure, which you can have sent to you by calling the park's information line, (207) 288-3338. Off-season the ferry currently costs $10.00 each way; during the season the fare goes up to $12.00; parking costs $4.00 a day at the Isle au Haut Company dock in Stonington.

The four trails I hiked were:

Woods along the Duck Harbor Trail.

- Duck Harbor Trail between the ranger station in town and Duck Harbor (3.8 miles)
- Western Head Trail off Western Head Road (1.3 miles)
- Cliff Trail back to Western Head Road (0.7 mile)
- Duck Harbor Mountain Trail between Squeaker Cove and Western Head Road (1.2 miles).

I also walked sections of the grassy Western Head Road and the Goat Trail between the road and Squeaker Cove where I picked up the Duck Harbor Mountain Trail. Except for graveled or grassy sections of road, island trails cross rocky, rooty, or boggy ground where footing is always an issue. Sturdy boots with a good tread are a must for hiking comfort and security. Isle au Haut is not for the faint of heart or frail of limb. Experienced hikers will take it in their stride, but casual vacationers should prepare themselves for something more than a lark.

The Duck Harbor Trail is the main link between the town of Isle au Haut and the campground on the south side of Duck Harbor. It runs parallel to the ridge of high ground in the center of the island (Isle au Haut, the name Samuel Champlain gave it in 1604, means High Island), the trail alternately crossing fingers of that ridge reaching westward toward the shore, and the dips between the fingers. The trail is through woods the whole way, largely red and white spruce and yellow birch in low areas, with pitch pines on rocky ridges, some measuring eighteen inches in diameter.

Several small streams flow in the dips between ridges, Eli's Creek for example making a last fast plunge over rocks into salt water. The middle portion of the trail runs along the eastern shore of Moores Harbor, giving hikers a sense of having water music at their elbow and the whiff of brine and seawrack in their nostrils. The best views are of the woods themselves, with a few open vistas across the open harbor to the west. Near the ranger station in town the trail crosses thin soil underlaid by off-white volcanic rock; along Moores Harbor and almost to Duck Harbor it crosses over the local gray granite.

The Western Head Trail takes hikers along the western shore of one of the two prongs of land reaching south into the Gulf of Maine. After leading down to the shore through coastal woods, the trail weaves along the shoreline, alternately running out onto cobble beaches, then rising over or ducking behind the headlands that frame the beaches. The trail crosses outcrops of pale volcanic rock, some impressively veined with dark stripes. Views include the rollercoaster silhouette of the Camden Hills on the horizon over Vinalhaven Island and, southwest, extend to Seal Island, Wooden Ball Island, Ragged Island, and Matinicus. The granite lighthouse on Saddleback Ledge stands to the west at the mouth of Isle au Haut Bay. Light House Service and, later, Coast Guard personnel regarded Saddleback as the hardest landing in the region, steep shoreline cliffs forcing them while the light station was manned to land by swinging in a harness or breeches buoy suspended from a swinging boom. Now automated and run on solar power, Saddleback Light is tended by the sixty-foot tug *Tackle* out of Rockland. To service the light, work crews carefully choose a calm day and approach the ledge in a work punt, getting close enough to clamber onto the ledge.

The Cliff Trail runs along the eastern side of Western Head, and is named for two sections of cliff that rise steeply above the waves. Coming out of the woods midway between the two cliffs, the trail gives dramatic views north and south. Like the Western Head Trail, the Cliff Trail has its ups and downs, hikers having to earn their views if they round the head west-to-east. Coming the other way from the end of Western Head Road, hikers can attain views of the cliffs with much less effort, almost stumbling across them when the trail has barely begun. The cliffs are volcanic in nature, containing rock fragments and ash which settled after being hurled aloft by ancient eruptions 400–600 million years ago when the island or subcontinent Avalonia collided with the continent we now call North America.

The Duck Harbor Mountain Trail is of a different complexion altogether. Rising to the modest elevation of 314 feet, it has enough ups and downs to add considerably to that figure, making it seem higher than it is. The summit is much nearer to the north end of the trail than the south, the approach from Squeaker Cove in the south covering almost a mile of rocky, uneven ground. On this trail I came up against what I call "the Isle au Haut assumption": that angling rocky slopes of thirty to forty-five degrees are to be considered the norm while in the rest of Acadia they might be regarded as extreme. For a minor peak Duck Harbor Mountain offers a major scramble on which hikers have no choice but to become intimate with volcanic rock. Views from the top (actually a series of tops) open over the trees to the horizon except in the northwest where the median ridge blocks sight of Mount Desert Island. The way is marked by low cairns and blue blazes painted on trees. I found the trail better marked for hikers heading south than north; in several places I saw no hint where the trail might go and had to circle to pick up the next cairn or blaze. I pictured the angling ledges of Duck Harbor Mountain to be slick when wet from rain or fog, and thought I would stick to lower trails under those conditions. The route is tricky enough when dry.

The heart of my Isle au Haut excursion was the alternation between walking in deep woods and then coming out on exposed rocky shores. Each aspect heightened my appreciation of the other. On the remarkable and almost unprecedented clear spring day I spent on the island, the shore was invariably warm and bright, the woods cool and shaded. A few clouds accented the potent blue of the sky at midday, but they quickly dispersed. I started out dressed for the 37° it was when I got up, then removed layer after layer until I got down to a T-shirt at one o'clock on Duck Harbor Mountain, the temperature surely approaching 70° on the open slopes. No other trail or combination of trails in Acadia has the blend of woods and shore that Isle au Haut offers. Sections of the Ocean Path on Mount Desert Island are similar, and of the Wonderland and Ship Harbor Nature trails, but the combination of cliffs, cobble beaches, woods, wetlands, and peaks on Isle au Haut is unique in my Acadian experience. Where Mount Desert often feels more like a headland than an island, Isle au Haut pretends to be nothing but what it is, and offers the quintessential island experience. That picture may sound romantic if only fair weather such as I had is in-

View from the Western Head Trail.

cluded, but, too, room must be made for howling winter gales and weeks of thick fog. Only 70 people live on the island year-round, mostly fishermen and their families; in summer that slim population soars to 300 when the island's seasonal residents migrate north. The Isle au Haut section of the park is officially open mid-June to mid-October, the four fairest months of the year.

Starry white goldthread was the flower of the day when I made this hike, subtly suggesting how much of Isle au Haut is made up of wetlands. Strawberry plants and violets were in bloom, along with blueberry plants in sunnier spots. Shadbush was the showiest of them all, white blossoms gleaming through open woods. I think of shad as a spindly, shrubby plant, but on the northern shore of Duck Harbor I saw one shad at least fifty feet tall with a trunk over twelve inches thick. In full bloom, it was the grandest sight I saw all day. The most surprising plant I saw, however, was skunk cabbage, which I had never found in the park even though it is included in the Wild Gardens of Acadia at Sieur de Mont Spring. [I have since seen it along Wonderland Fire Road.] On this last of my spring hikes I found the mother lode of skunk cabbage, which happens to be a wetland directly behind the ranger station on Isle au Haut, with enough specimens to satisfy even my thirty-year quest to view a single skunk cabbage plant within the bounds of Acadia. Edgar

Wherry places the plant at Seawall, but I have somehow missed it there. This time I saw hundreds of plants leafing out which, backlit by the sun, glowed with verdant light. I laughed when I saw them, partly in surprise, partly at the overkill, partly at myself for ever supposing skunk cabbages were rare in the park.

The spring woods of Isle au Haut are full of ferns, mosses, bazzanias, lichens, horsetails, and other low plants of damp places which add a layer of green beneath the canopy. Where fogs are frequent, trees near the shore are often hung with old-man's-beard. Bunchberry, raspberry, and beach pea leaves were coming out in their respective habitats. The island seemed lush and bursting with life.

Wind and salt air had a dramatic effect on trees within fifty to a hundred yards of the shore, shaping them, stunting them, toppling them over. The island was ringed with what in places resembled a combat zone, a no man's land looking like stereoscopic views from the First World War, blasted stems falling every which way, great roots grasping at the salt air, straggly undergrowth struggling to maintain an uncertain hold. In the interior the woods were thick enough to stave off the attack, but on the exposed fringe near the shore wind-driven salt air had the upper hand, forcing trees to bend and break before its superior might. When we dream of being shipwrecked on a lonely island, this is the part we leave out because it is too much like the chaos we wish to escape. But from the rubble new life was rising, particularly insects and birds.

Volcanic rock with dark striations, Western Head Trail.

On my return along the Duck Harbor Trail I saw a flicker land on the branch of a silver snag, then fly to another snag, then to an oblong hole near the broken top of a third snag, diving into the hole, then quickly springing forth and flying off. Immediately another flicker flew in from the opposite direction and, following much the same routine, dove into the hole. No man's land makes perfect flicker habitat. And hermit thrush habitat. I saw several of the lyrical tail-waggers gleaning insects among the carnage behind the shore. One flew up from the trail three feet in front of me and flew to a nearby branch. I have read that these birds are thought of as shy, but they have a brazen streak that makes them seem fearless on occasion. Who can explain what Clark Kent does in that phone booth to so completely remake his persona? Hermit thrushes have the same magic in real life.

Other insect eaters I saw included six common grackles in a shrub near the ranger station; three juncos singing in the sprucetops, seen from below with their white fronts gleaming in the sun appearing very unlike the dull little bird that makes its living so close to the ground; a white-throated sparrow; two yellow-rumped warblers, one on the shore gleaning insects among the seawrack; and three common yellowthroats, one alternately shushing and singing as if gripped by some kind of approach-avoidance crisis. The most spectacular insect-eater I saw was a scarlet tanager eyeing the shore from the tip of a branch at the edge of the trail ten feet ahead. By its gaudy plumage I spotted it right away as an illegal immigrant from South America. It might as well have been Carmen Miranda herself, or Eva Peron, perched on that branch. But this one was not singing. It took me a while to get over the shock of seeing that velvet red-bodied, black-winged-and-tailed apparition so close; I think of tanagers as being seventy feet away in the treetops. After thirty seconds the bird swept down to the shore and gulped an insect, then sat for three or four minutes on a piece of driftwood before it struck again. When it flew into the woods after that, I continued my slow progress toward the town landing, ready for just about anything.

The first bird I saw on the island was a ruby-throated hummingbird at the ranger station. Then I saw two crows. In a narrow cove on Western Head I saw two male and four female eider swimming toward open water. In Duck Harbor I saw three guillemots diving on the incoming tide. Great and double-crested cormorants dove all around the shore, and more black-backed and herring gulls flew over than I cared to count. Normally eagles make a striking impression, but the immature one I saw atop a boulder on a ledge out in Moores Harbor looked haggard—not hawk-like but weary and wimpy. I guessed it was worn out from the hunt. I had seen other young eagles look like that during their first winter while trying to pick up the prowess that seems to come so naturally to adults. Between forays they stood around awkwardly on the ice, looking skyward as if dinner would descend magically from above as it had when they were in the nest. This one looked wistful in that same way, hoping against all hope that a fish or a duck was in the mail and would arrive any time.

Along the trail I saw cone scales left by red squirrels, a great many hare pellets on Duck Harbor Mountain, tufts of hair shed by white-tailed deer adjusting to the season, and a set of deer prints in the mud. While refilling my water bottle from the hand pump at the head of Duck Harbor I looked over at a glistening red squirrel nibbling a spruce cone on a stump. Walking along the grassy roadway to reach the Western Head Trail, I looked up to see a white-tailed doe looking back at me. In no hurry, she walked, then trotted with grace into the shade of the woods. I have seen many deer in Acadia over the years, but that was the only one I met during this series of sixty hikes. Having become crepuscular (twilight) feeders for their own safety, they are more apt to be seen on the fringes of night than in bold sunlight like this one. There are coyotes and raccoons on Isle au Haut, but I saw no sign of either one. I heard red-breasted nuthatches, hermit thrushes, robins, crows, and ravens. Six spring azure butterflies crossed my path, but not one blackfly or mosquito.

View south from the Cliff Trail.

The one other mammal I met included fellow hikers on the trail, of which I came across thirteen, and the park ranger who met us at the landing. Seven hikers were coming along the Duck Harbor Trail from the campground, aiming to make the noon boat. They all carried huge packs which must have been almost as heavy on the way out as when they arrived, the park requiring campers to carry out their own trash. I asked two boys how long they had camped; one said four days, the other five, precipitating a discussion which settled on four-and-a-half as the correct answer. I asked a lone woman overtopped by a bulky pack how her stay had been.

"Fabulous!" she said.

"Did you see many warblers?" I asked,

"Maybe, maybe not," she said, "I don't know my birds."

"I'm sure you did," I said, not wanting to suggest she might be inadequate in any way.

I met two young men hiking solo, one in red pants, the other carrying a Nikon at the ready. Two couples, one from New York, the other Baltimore, came over with me on the seven o'clock mailboat and returned when I did on the five o'clock boat. Between boats I never saw them on the trail, each group making a day of it on its own, Isle au Haut being big enough to swallow us without a trace.

Wayne Barter, the park ranger, met us at the dock and told us how to get to the ranger station where he'd join us in a few minutes to get us pointed in the right direction. He gave out maps of the island and answered our questions. Wayne is among the last of Acadia's old-time rangers who handle a variety of duties—resource management, interpretation, law enforcement, maintenance, and administration—while the rest of the park staff has specialized assignments within one park division or another. I joined the Park Service to save trees, but the only time I get near a tree is when I hike on my own. My duty station in the planning office is in front of a computer screen where I have yet to see anything as common in Acadia as a shadbush or junco. The Park Service is full of idealistic types like Wayne and myself, enthusiasts who work hard and love their jobs—without medical or retirement benefits because they aren't allowed to work more than half-time (or full-time for half a year, which comes to the same thing), feeling themselves lucky to hold two such positions at different parks, without benefits at either one though they truly work full-time for the same employer, the U.S. Government. President Clinton was shocked to hear of a long-time Park Service employee in California who gave his all to his work, and then died with nothing to show for his lifetime effort. The President vowed to change the system, but nothing has changed. Idealists often make the crucial error of confounding their personal goals with the goals of the institutions they serve. I remember once attending the Iowa State Fair in Des Moines, watching the judging of baby beeves lovingly raised by members of the Four-H Club, then seeing those same animals crowded into chutes and onto trucks by men with electric prods and taken off to the stock yard to be turned into Grade-A cuts of meat, leaving boys and girls who had never thought the whole thing through in tears.

On the mainland I had mapped out my hike without truly knowing the terrain I would be up against. I wanted to do the

Western Head and Cliff trails, and the Duck Harbor Mountain Trail if I could squeeze it in. To reach any of them from the landing I had to take the Duck Harbor Trail twice. Could I manage all that between first and last boats? I figured I would see where I was on the trail at twelve-thirty when half the day was done, and revise my plan if I had to. As it worked out I had finished the Cliff Trail at twelve-thirty, which exceeded my hope that I would at least reach the tip

View northeast from the Cliff Trail.

of Western Head. I figured I had time to do the mountain trail, with a leisurely return stroll along the Duck Harbor Trail before five o'clock.

Walking along the Goat Trail to pick up the mountain trail, I found myself feeling very accomplished. I was sure I would be able to do all that I had wanted and still make the last boat. But my satisfaction was larger than that: I would finish the last of my sixty hikes, a project I had been working on for almost four years. Not wanting to count my chickadees before they hatched, I kept myself under tight control, but glee kept bursting through my seams. Like the Little Engine Who Could, I had made it up the steep grade and was about to coast down the far side. Whooee, my whistle shrieked, whooee, whooee! It is amazing to set about doing something, to do it, and then have it done. Except for drawing maps, editing text, choosing photographs, doing an index, and the hundred-and-one tasks required to produce a

book, I was home free. That's how it felt, anyway. The rest was follow-through, something I could handle with inbred New Engand discipline jogged by a few deft reminders. High Island was true to its name in ways I had never anticipated.

Hiking the trails of Isle au Haut is an invigorating experience because it is so elemental. You walk among the ever-present elements of rock, water, air, and energy—energy of the waves and of the sun. And that other element, which must be an element because we cannot account for its origin except by fable or myth—life. These days we read of great snowballs pelting the Earth from outer space, bringing water from above instead of below through the throats of volcanoes. Perhaps life rides as a stowaway on that cometary ice, a gift to our planet from the solar system, the Milky Way, the universe itself. Our ancestry is far more wonderful than we dare imagine. The coming-together of air, rock, water, energy, and life on Isle au Haut creates a diversity of being that has absolute integrity because it is true to that particular place. Isle au Haut is as Isle au Haut does; Isle au Haut does as the elements command. In that sense I experienced the island as more than just a spinoff of the mainland, as a miniature planet run on its own time according to its own rules—an island not merely in the Gulf of Maine but in the universe, an island pelted by the very forces of creation. This last of my spring hikes was no less than a cosmic experience.

Waiting at the town landing for the five o'clock ferry, I wrote down the names of fishing boats moored in the harbor. As I expected, there were names honoring women—*Donna S.*, *Geneva Sue*, *Linette A. II*, and *Mabelle Louise*—along with an assortment of others that spoke more to qualities the fishermen themselves might possess: *Handsome*, *Islander*, *Last Minute*, *Pegasus*, *Sea Ranger*, *Shock Wave*, *Surething*. Naming a boat is no casual act. It reflects a projection of the namer's true psyche, something valued or cherished, or an image meant as a symbol to live up to. *Surething* and *Last Minute* can be counted on to come through in the end; *Shock Wave*, *Sea Ranger*, and *Pegasus* tell of men aspiring to strength and decisive action; *Handsome* refers to inner comeliness of character, much as *Islander* speaks of a person shaped by the elements. Each of those boats spoke to me in its own voice, addressing appropriate parts of myself. When the mailboat came around Kimball Island into the thorofare, I saw it bore the name *Mink*, as sleek and feisty a critter as ever went to sea. All of us have a streak of mink in us, or we wouldn't survive. All of us are handsome in our own ways, all of us make shock waves, all of us dream of flying or ranging across the sea, all of us get things done sooner or later, and all of us are islands of humanity, shaped by the lives we lead.

Myself, I'm a hiker taking step after step, always looking forward to meeting what's around the next bend or over the next summit. I may cover the same ground more than once, but the trip is never the same because I have changed and the ground has chanced since last I came by, so the journey is always exciting, always new, always challenging.

Since birth I have had celiac disease, a genetic condition marked by an inability to digest gluten (the protein that binds flour together), turning wheat, barley, rye, and oats into toxic substances before which my gut makes a strategic retreat and against which my immune system mounts a frontal assault. When I ingest even a trace of gluten, my primary symptom for nine years has been a fiendish, burning itch that feels like slivers of broken glass lodged in my muscles and skin, the result of my immune system attacking my own flesh. In addition to gluten, I am also intolerant of milk, soy products, vinegar, grain alcohol, and canola oil, along with a host of food additives, which rules out much of the modern American diet. Though I have had the disease since birth, I never knew it until recently. I have walked in the dark all my life, putting one foot in front of the other, never able to explain to myself why I felt or behaved as I did. My character has been formed by living with an agonizing mystery. Now the mystery stands revealed, and I sense I am a whole person with, not a disability, but a unique form of personal integrity. My body and temperament are those of a hunter-gatherer displaced from his native habitat and set down in a time and place favoring pizza, pasta, doughnuts, sticky buns, bagels, croissants, and other products made with industrial-strength gluten. Had I been born where corn, rice, or potatoes were staple foods, I might never have exhibited the sensitivity to gluten that has colored almost every meal I have eaten until the past few months. I have long been on a quest for a better life, and now that life is at hand.

The feeling of satisfaction that flooded over me on High Island rose from satisfaction at being able to complete my hike, yes, and probably being able to finish this series of essays, yes, and far more fundamentally learning what kind of man I am. I am Last Minute, I am Islander, I am Shock Wave, I am Handsome, I am Sea Ranger, I am Pegasus, I am Surething. Some part of me is Donna S., Geneva Sue, Linette A, and Mabelle Louise. My own boat, a thirteen-foot peapod, is the *Aurora B.*, named for the northern lights that flood the sky when solar particles stream through the northern portion of Earth's magnetic field. Aurora was the Roman personification of the dawn. That is a fitting emblem for my life, for I have taken every day as a gift, moving much as I hike from gift to gift, hermit thrush to scarlet tanager, to hummingbird, to guillemot, to eagle, to junco, to yellowthroat, and on and on. Miracle to miracle. Dawn to dawn.

Leaf buds on a white spruce.

Wood lilies on Sargent Mountain in August.

ACADIA
THE SOUL
OF A
NATIONAL PARK

✦

Book Four
SUMMER

✪

CONTENTS—SUMMER HIKES

INTRODUCTION—SUMMER 240

46 BEECH MOUNTAIN LOOP 241
From Echo Lake parking area
To Beech Mountain summit, and back
    Up by Beech Cliff Ladder Trail and
      (Outer) Beech Mountain Trail
    Back by Beech Mountain South Ridge and
      Valley trails, Beech Mountain Notch and
      Lurvey Spring roads
                  4.0 miles, June 6, 1996

**47 PARKMAN MOUNTAIN &
BALD PEAK LOOP 246**
From Norumbega Mountain parking area
To Parkman Mountain, Bald Peak, and back
    Up by Parkman Mountain Trail
    Down by Bald Peak Trail
                  2.0 miles, June 12, 1996

48 CADILLAC MOUNTAIN 249
From Route 3 near Blackwoods Campground
To Cadillac Mountain summit, and on to
      Park Loop Road overlooking Bar Harbor
    Up by Cadillac Mountain South Ridge Trail
    Down by Cadillac Mountain North Ridge Trail
                  6.0 miles, June 20, 1996

49 SCHOODIC HEAD & ANVIL LOOP 255
From Blueberry Hill parking area
To Schoodic Head, the Anvil, and back
    Up by "Alder Path" and Schoodic Head Trail
    Down by Anvil Trail
                  2.6 miles, June 27, 1996

50 DORR MOUNTAIN LOOP 259
From Great Meadow
To Dorr Mountain summit, and back
    Up by Spring Road, and Jesup and
      Dorr Mountain East Face trails
    Down by Dorr Mountain North Ridge
      and Kebo Mountain trails
                  4.8 miles, July 3, 1996

To Jonathan

Who followed a track

he alone could see

and found it was

his life

51 ACADIA MOUNTAIN LOOP 265
From Acadia Mountain parking area
To Acadia Mountain summit, and back
 Up by west end of Acadia Mountain Trail
 Back by east end of Acadia Mountain Trail
 and Man o' War Brook Fire Road
3.0 miles, July 11, 1996

52 PEMETIC MOUNTAIN LOOP 269
From Bubble Rock parking area
To Pemetic Mountain summit, and back
 Up by Pemetic Mountain (Ravine) Trail
 Down by Pemetic Mountain South Ridge,
 west end of Pond, and Jordan Pond East Side
 trails; and Jordan Pond Canoe Carry
3.6 miles, July 17, 1996

53 NORUMBEGA MOUNTAIN LOOP 275
From Norumbega Mountain parking area
To Norumbega Mountain summit and
 Lower Hadlock Pond, and back
 Up by Norumbega Mountain (Goat) Trail
 Down by Brown Mountain Trail, Hadlock Path,
 and Upper Hadlock Trail
3.3 miles, July 24, 1996

54 CHAMPLAIN & GORHAM MOUNTAINS 280
From parking area at north end of the Tarn
To Champlain Mountain summit, the Bowl,
 Gorham Mountain summit, and Fabbri
 parking area
 Up by Beachcroft Trail, continue on Champlain
 Mountain South Ridge, Bowl, and north end
 of Gorham Mountain trails
 Down by south end of Gorham Mountain Trail
5.0 miles, July 28, 1996

55 PENOBSCOT & SARGENT MTNS. LOOP 286
From Jordan Pond House
To Penobscot Mountain summit, Sargent Mountain
 Pond, and Sargent Mountain summit, and back
 Up by Jordan Cliffs Trail, connector to Penobscot
 summit, and Sargent Mtn. South Ridge Trail
 Down by Sargent Mountain South Ridge and
 Penobscot Mountain trails
5.6 miles, August 3, 1996

**56 ST. SAUVEUR MOUNTAIN &
VALLEY PEAK LOOP 292**
From Acadia Mountain parking area
To St. Sauveur Mountain, Valley Peak, and back
 Up by St. Sauveur Mountain Trail
 Back by Valley Peak and Valley Cove trails,
 Valley Cove and Man o' War Brook fire roads
4.5 miles, August 10, 1996

57 WESTERN MOUNTAIN LOOP 297
From Long Pond pumping station
To Mansell Mountain, Knight Nubble,
 Bernard Mountain, and back
 Up by Perpendicular and Western Mountain
 Ridge trails
 Down by Western Mountain South Face Trail,
 Western Mtn. Truck Rd., and Cold Brook Trail
4.5 miles, August 16, 1996

58 CADILLAC MOUNTAIN LOOP 304
From Bubble Pond parking area
To Cadillac Mountain summit, Featherbed, and back
 Up by Cadillac Mountain West Face Trail
 Down by Cadillac Mountain South Ridge and
 Featherbed trails, Boyd Road, and
 carriage road along Bubble Pond
4.3 miles, August 23, 1996

**59 SARGENT MOUNTAIN via HADLOCK BROOK
& MAPLE SPRING TRAILS 309**
From Norumbega Mountain parking area
To Sargent Mountain summit, and back
 Up by Hadlock Brook and
 Sargent Mountain South Ridge trails
 Down by Grandgent and Maple Spring trails
4.1 miles, August 29, 1996

**60 THE BUBBLES &
CONNERS NUBBLE LOOP 314**
From Bubble Rock parking area
To the Bubbles, Conners Nubble, and back
 Up by south end of Jordan Pond Canoe Carry;
 and South and North Bubble trails
 Down by North Bubble, Conners Nubble, and
 Eagle Lake trails; and north end of Jordan Pond
 Canoe Carry
4.5 miles, September 6, 1996

INTRODUCTION—SUMMER

The trails of Acadia National Park invite us to become reacquainted with the natural world. They bring us face-to-face with shorelines, streams, ponds, wetlands, summits, ridges, cliffs, talus slopes, dikes, woods, and other features of our environment. We hike these trails to connect with nature, our other self which, for months and years at a stretch, we sometimes neglect as if it had nothing to do with us. We come to Acadia to redeem that connection, to become natural beings again, celebrating the basic roles air and sunlight play in our lives, along with water and soil, friends, family, and loved ones, and the myriad Earthlings who enable us to live. There is no better way to heal ourselves than by hiking the trails of Acadia where every plant, bird, and stone we meet extends us into nature, and nature into us, restoring the connection that, once severed, leads to gloom and ill health.

These essays describe fifteen summer hikes in Acadia's high season, June through August, 1996. Here I explore some of the more popular trails in the park, the ridge trails tending generally north and south, at a season when visitors are most likely to be out and about. I meet those visitors as I would any other species of wildlife, hoping to learn what draws them to Acadia, and what they find once they are here. From the 561 hikers I met on the trail I learn that Acadia is particularly attractive to families and couples seeking to enjoy natural experiences together. Acadia's main attraction is its accessible, outdoor wholesomeness. It challenges people of all ages in ways that are particularly meaningful when shared with families, loved ones, and friends. Who hikes Acadia? Those looking to share natural experience, and those seeking to deepen their relationships in, and with, nature.

As for nature itself, there is a lot of it around Acadia in the summer months. With so much to do and see, no wonder migrating flocks of tourists stop over for days and weeks at a time. On these summer hikes I saw eighty-five flowering and fruiting plants that I could identify, and many others that I couldn't. I saw fourteen flowering plants on my first hike on June 6th, including rose-purple rhodora, saxifrage (stonebreaker), blueberry, and pink lady's slipper. On my last summer hike three months later I saw beechdrops, asters, and goldenrod. On other hikes I saw wood lilies, golden heather, mountain sandwort, partridgeberry, twinflower, and rattlesnake plantain. The entire length of my summer journey was lined with blossoms. I also saw a variety of birds, including (taking one bird from each hike) a black-throated blue warbler, junco, ruffed grouse, flicker, hermit thrush, kestrel, bald eagle, loon, white-throated sparrow, raven, osprey, yellow-rumped warbler, cedar waxwing, hairy woodpecker, and a Tennessee warbler. A bird—any bird—in its native habitat is worth a hundred birds depicted in a guidebook. *Being there* is the secret of Acadia's trails;

they take you to the leading edge of ongoing creation. What you do once you are there is up to you.

Keeping track of plants and wildlife I saw as the season progressed, I made lists of typical species I met along the trail. Here are my proposals for species typifying Acadia in the summer months.

Summer Birds	Junco & Yellow-rumped Warbler
Summer Mammal	Red Squirrel
Summer Amphibian	Green Frog
Summer Reptile	Garter Snake
Summer Insect	Dragonfly
Summer Trees	Red Spruce & Pitch Pine
Summer Flowers	Lambkill, Wine-leaf Cinquefoil, & Bush Honeysuckle
Summer Fruit	Blueberry
Summer Ferns	Rock-cap & Cinnamon Fern
Summer Rock	Cadillac Mountain Granite
Summer Motto	"This is what we came for!"

Steve Perrin
Bar Harbor
Summer 1996

Blueberry blossoms on Cadillac Mountain north ridge.

46—BEECH MOUNTAIN LOOP

From Echo Lake parking area
To Beech Mountain summit, and back
  Up by Beech Cliff Ladder Trail and
    (Outer) Beech Mountain Trail
  Back by Beech Mountain South Ridge and
    Valley trails, Beech Mountain Notch and
    Lurvey Spring roads

4.0 miles, June 6, 1996

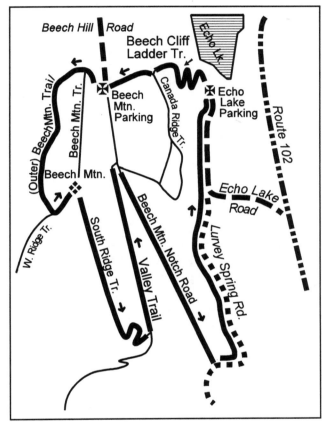

46—Beech Mountain loop.

Picture the hulking naturalist on an Acadian mountain ridge, hunkered down, peering back and forth through bifocals between wildflower guide and puzzling bloom on its midget stem, unable to describe what he thinks he sees in terms the guide will accept, guide holding back the sought-after name until the description is more precise, blackflies looking on at first, then mobbing, then going in for the kill, the naturalist hitting back between swings of attention between book and bloom, bloom and book, blackflies persisting, book resisting, bloom bobbing in the wind, naturalist sticking it out for twenty minutes, then, no wiser than before, fleeing for his life.

No wonder it took me over seven hours to hike Beech Mountain from the south end of Echo Lake: summer had overtaken Acadia, and the entire park was greening and blossoming at once. The last hike I had written up was on Sargent Mountain in March when summer was only an icy blur in the eye of a late-winter storm. Now Acadia's soil had carried that blur to term, birthing myriad leaves, blossoms, and blackflies without favor or prejudice. I was out to acquaint the entire crop. The loop was a little over four miles long, but strewn as it was with leafing-blooming-biting life, it took me seven hours to complete.

I chose my route to fit as many summer landscapes into one hike as I could: deciduous and coniferous woods, mountain ridges, cliffs, valleys, and lakes. Actually, I made a loop within a loop, or two loops in a loose figure-eight centered on the parking area at the end of Beech Hill Road. Either loop would make a splendid hike on its own, but to celebrate summer's arrival I wanted it all, so did both.

The first loop comprised four legs: Beech Cliff Ladder Trail from Echo Lake Beach, connector to Beech Mountain parking area, the old road from Beech Mountain Notch toward Southwest Harbor, and the Lurvey Spring Road back to the parking area at Echo Lake. The second loop comprised three more legs: (Outer) Beech Mountain Trail from Beech Mountain parking area to the fire tower at the summit, Beech Mountain South Ridge Trail, and the Valley Trail back to the parking area in the notch. Either loop samples Acadia at its best; spliced together, they make a superb hike. Not one you do once to check off your life list. You will want to come back every year, more likely every season.

The old road connecting Southwest Harbor to Beech Mountain Notch—a southern extension of Beech Hill Road—is not generally shown on modern maps, but it is there on the ground, following the same track it took two hundred years ago and, according to Ralph Stanley, thousands of years before that as an Indian path. Ralph knew a man who bounced a Model-T Ford up that road in the 1920s, but it hasn't borne much traffic for a hundred years or so. It was built in the early 1800s for ox carts and wagons, linking Southwest Harbor to the rest of Mount Desert Island. Though neither marked nor maintained as a trail, the old road is easy to follow once you get onto it. In winter it is an icy chute, and in warmer months can be wet and slick, but if you like to picture early settlers goading oxen through the wilderness, such ghosts are yours for the imagining along what is now a scenic walk through woods on an easy grade. A broad dike runs down the old road for several hundred feet where bedrock is still exposed. Vegetation is taking hold again, sphagnum moss and ground cover creeping in from the sides, forming a kind of linear wetland, but the road is still a respectable path over gravel or bedrock down to Lurvey Spring Road. The easiest way to find it is to head south from Beech Mountain parking area to the trailhead where the Valley Trail splits west for Long Pond, and the Canada Ridge Trail splits east. Take the east fork for a few feet past the trailhead, but where the trail proper turns left across a split-log bridge, continue on in the same direction you have been heading, and you will soon see that you are on the old roadway already.

I got a late start on this hike because I thought I might be able to outwit the bugs who were waiting for me. I realized my plodding hiking style played right into the wings of those who lusted for my blood. After a wet spring, blackflies and mosquitoes were out in force. They seem to go for hikers in dark clothes. All my hiking hats and shirts were dark. Hesitant to volunteer as a sacrificial victim, I waited for stores to open to buy the palest hat and polo shirt I could find. Properly suited up, smeared with herbal bug juice, I arrived at Echo Lake parking area at ten o'clock on a cloudless summer day. In recent weeks morning temperatures had hovered in the 40s and 50s; by 8:00 a.m. my thermometer had already climbed to 70°. Aside from a park-maintenance-crew truck, there wasn't a car in the Echo Lake lot.

If for the next seven hours I was in a land where the blackfly was the national insect, I was also in a land where black chokeberry was the national flower, and the national bird was the black-throated blue warbler. Except when puzzling over the blossom on the ridge, I hardly noticed the bugs. As long as I kept moving, they jockeyed for position, but seldom struck. They were like street kids tagging after me more out of curiosity than hostility. But when I stopped, they would have seized my wristwatch and wallet in a second if I had let them. That darting, whirling cloud around my head had the collective appetite of a grizzly bear; it was as fascinated by me as I was fascinated by Acadia's greening flesh.

The instant I was away from Echo Lake parking area, I was in my green and blossoming element. In the cool shade of beeches and birches, there were starflowers, Canada May ruby (a.k.a. Canada bead ruby, Canada mayflower, wild lily-of-the-valley), and acres of wild sarsaparilla leaves screening down-to-earth flowers resembling exploding fireworks or, by a less percussive image, dandelions gone to seed. That would have been enough, but I went on to find thirteen other plants in bloom, including bunchberry dogwood, Solomon's seal, saxifrage ("stone breaker" because its roots pry into hairline cracks), bluebead (an early lily with yellow flow-

Cliff and shelf, Beech Cliff Ladder Trail.

ers), blueberry (plants covered with delicate white bells), wine-leaf cinquefoil, pink lady's slipper, black chokeberry, buttercup, rhodora, and violet. And the mystery bloom I found next to a boulder on the south ridge of Beech Mountain, which in the quiet of my room after the hike I discovered to be pale corydalis—little pink hot-dogs with mustard faces painted on one end, skewered on a toothpick stem through the middle. I remembered seeing it here and there in the park, but never knew its name.

As colorful or strange as they all were, the flower that took the day was black chokeberry, which was at its peak on Beech Mountain. For much of the way the trail was lined with it, and it ran in every sunlit crack along the ridge. The ten thousand blooms drew bumblebees that surfed their pink-and-white crests wave after wave. There is a branch of psychology that heals the psyche with the aura of flowers in bloom. The technical term is "gardening." Hiking does the same with wildflowers. If blackflies symbolize the ills of the world, then their power is nothing compared to the healing aura of black chokeberry the first week in June.

The first week in June. That is where Acadia was on this hike, at that precise point in Earth's orbit around the sun. The quarter days dividing the seasons are cardinal points on the sun's compass rose, and we take them by turn on our annual swing around our favorite star. We think of seasons as stretches of time, but they are also sweeps in space. On the summer solstice, Earth tips its northern pole inward toward the center of its orbit, bowing to the source of goodness and life. On the winter solstice, Earth tips its northern pole outward away from the sun toward Nirvana, the emptiness of space. At the equinoxes, the poles are at right angles to the sun, tangent to Earth's orbit, moving toward the summer quadrant in spring, winter quadrant in fall. With each new day we are one degree farther along on our path. Every week we move to a new solar address. With fourteen degrees to go till the summer solstice, black chokeberry ruled Acadia's ridges, blackflies its running waters, black-throated blue warblers its deepest woods. A week (seven degrees) earlier, rhodora and blueberry held sway, and a month (twenty-eight degrees) before that, mayflower, as the first thrushes and warblers flew in from their wintering grounds. Next week, Solomon's seal and goldthread will have their day, then hawkweed, blackberry, and so on as summer progresses. Hiking through the seasons, I wend a trail around the compass of the sun. My goal is to make it all the way around in sixty hikes. To witness the marvels setting each week off from every other. To be awake to Acadia through a full cycle in its lifetime, and mine.

The Beech Cliff Ladder and Valley trails are both good for viewing ferns. I am drawn to damp, ferny glens under cliffs, though I can't put a name to every fern I see. Rock-cap fern is easy to spot because it grows right where its name suggests, on top of boulders. Bearing spores midway along its blade, interrupted fern looks . . . well, interrupted. Christmas fern has bladelets shaped like Christmas stockings. Marginal wood fern is the only fern I know with spore cases around the edges of the underside of each bladelet. Flat, three-bladed bracken is so common almost everywhere in Acadia, it is a fern that needs no introduction. Oak fern is harder, looking like a smaller, more delicate version of bracken. Fine as old lace, with a scaly stalk, spinulose wood fern is one of Acadia's great beauties. Small and slender, New York fern tapers both fore and aft like a dory or peapod. I saw all of these on my hike, and several others I couldn't identify. Every blade was busy uncurling from its fiddlehead or crozier. These were adolescent ferns. A week earlier I would have found many of them still in early childhood.

Top of Beech Cliff Ladder Trail.

What is the point of identifying plants in the wild? Is it a hobby, a harmless way of wasting time, like collecting matchbook covers or paperweights? I do it to sharpen my eyesight. The more plants I recognize, the more I see. At first, all ferns look alike. But starting with the easiest to distinguish—like rock-cap or interrupted ferns—I compare the next fern I notice with those and see how it is different. I look it up in a fern finder till I can put a name to its unique bundle of characteristics, then go on to the next, and the next. As a young man, I hiked to reach the summit as fast as possible, and to get back the same way. I didn't know anything about the landscape I raced through. Acadia was just a

place to stretch my legs. I imposed my will upon it instead of asking what it had to offer. Over the years I have become less concerned with goals, more open to events along the way. Not being familiar with those events, I bought guides to birds, wildflowers, ferns, and trees. Carrying them on the trail, I searched for names to give those who whispered to me as I passed by. The more names I learned, the richer my experience grew—not because naming is wisdom or power, but because naming is a way of making new friends and of reacquainting old ones. Now I am on familiar terms with much of the regional landscape, and hike among friends every time I go out. When I learn a new species, I enrich myself, adding another dimension to my world. Now Acadia is a place where I can be fully myself in the company of friends and true peers. I have grown into Acadia as it has grown into me. Like a trailside fern released from its tight-wound former self, I have opened to sunlight, wind, and rain, leafing out in my own way.

At 839 feet, the summit of Beech Mountain rises 720 feet above the Echo Lake parking area where I began my loop. The ladder trail covers the first 415 feet of that distance in getting to the top of Beech Cliff. Packing beech woods, talus slopes, cribwork traverses, cliffs, four iron ladders (of ten, eighteen, fourteen, and fifteen rungs), and a great variety of trees and plants into a mere half mile, it is one of my favorite trails. Rising up the slope and cliff by ten switchbacking traverses, it hoists you into the air as easily as an escalator. The trail is as solid and user-friendly as any in the park, worth checking out to see how a trail can be built. Along the way I noticed striped maple leaves already five inches across, pendant rows of Solomon's seal in first bloom, a great many ferns and lichens, poison ivy, saxifrage rosettes and white flowers growing out of damp cliffs, yellow clintonia (bluebead lily—the flower is yellow, the berry deep blue), a few bunchberry dogwood blooms, and one lady's slipper (deep pink) guarding the approach to the first ladder. I saw one junco in the woods. The showpiece of the trail is at the upper end where it runs along the base of a 50-foot vertical cliff, then scales (with the help of three ladders) a notch in the cliff to reach the top, where I came squinting into direct sunlight for the first time on my hike.

On the ladder trail I neither saw nor heard the peregrine falcons nesting on the face of the cliff. I did hear Tarzan yodel for Jane three times from the brink of Acadia Mountain across the lake, and met seven fellow hikers, the only people I saw for the rest of my trek. The first couple caught up with me on the trail, but they weren't actually hikers.

"The beach?" he asked with a soft German accent.

"This trail goes to the cliff," I said.

"Cliff, oh no!" he said.

I showed them the way to the beach.

I met a hiker in jump boots farther on, his clothing uniformly as dark as mine was light.

"Have you seen anything interesting on your hike?" I asked him.

"It's pretty up there, but nothing stands out," he said.

I asked the next hiker, a young man who rapidly overtook me, the same question.

Beech Mountain fire tower.

"*Everything* is interesting!" he said, "we don't have this at home."

"Where is home?" I asked.

"Holland. Everything is flat. Tulips and daffodils. This is beautiful!"

By the time I came out into the sun at the top of the cliff, Holland was saying good-bye to three people who had come over from Beech Mountain parking area. He had a bright green Frisbee in his hand, which he had not had on the way up. I asked the three what they had seen.

"Lady's slippers, trilliums, and a frog," they said.

They went off, and I had the brink of the cliff to myself. A seaplane buzzed low over the beach and headed up the lake. The sound of hammering rose from Echo Lake Camp on the far shore. As the dark hiker had said, it was pretty up there. Cinquefoil was blooming where I sat, and the mountains across the lake—Acadia and St. Sauveur nearby, with Sargent, Penobscot, and Cadillac farther off—rippled with waves of new green. With only a few cumulus clouds against the blue, the day was what my friend Gene Franck would call "a beauty day."

It was slightly downhill to the Beech Mountain parking area from the top of Beech Cliff, through tall mixed and evergreen woods the whole way. That section of trail was well-worn, spreading out six or seven feet wide in places. Bunchberry was further along here than on the shaded ladder trail. I saw several mossy patches of goldthread, and a lot of starflower and Canada May ruby. At one point I was stopped by a small spider going hand-over-hand across a

silken tightrope strung across the trail between two trees fifteen feet apart.

"How do you *do* that?" I asked, but she was too busy to reply. I meant, string the line between trees. I have watched a great many spiders spin their webs once the anchor line was up, but I've never seen one cast that first crucial strand itself.

From the Beech Mountain parking area, I took the scenic route to the fire tower, winding counterclockwise around the western side of Beech Mountain overlooking Long Pond and Mansell Mountain. The trail quickly opened up onto sunny granite ledge covered with blueberry (gone by) and black chokeberry (in full swing). Two pale lady's slippers rose Nessie-like from a sea of white flowers. I heard a flicker and a raven, then saw a yellow-rumped warbler alternately hawking insects and singing from the top of a spruce. Two tiger swallowtail butterflies came lilting down the trail, and several spring azures wandered by. Sheep laurel (lambkill) looked less bedraggled than in winter, its leaves being not so droopy and more green. Rhodora still flaunted its luminous purple blooms, though they were past their prime, downy leaves now pushing beyond last year's seed pods, which were dry and open-mouthed. On the upslope side, I came to the largest spread of club moss (ground pine) I had seen in the park, two species (staghorn and tree) tipped with new growth covering nearly a thousand square feet. I found a fallen nest by the side of the trail, a two-inch cup woven from grass, birchbark, and spruce needles. Several dragonflies and bumblebees darted past, and, as always, blackflies hovered near.

From where the west ridge trail branches off for Long Pond, the trail makes a short, steep, rocky rush for the summit, which I reached three-and-a-half hours after setting out from Echo Lake. West, south, and east, the view abruptly opens onto mountains, islands, and blue sky. A bumblebee, junco, and I had the vista to ourselves, the three of us turning our backs to the fire tower—the most grim and commanding structure in the park. Functional as a virus, and just as ugly. We didn't give it a second look. Through binoculars, I took a census of boats in Bass and Southwest harbors: forty-four and seventy-one, respectively. Four white sails cut among the green islands.

No sign points to the south ridge trail, but the ridge is obvious, so the trail is easy to find. Anchored at the steel fire tower, the trail winds through scrubby, brackeny terrain, then dips down to connect with the Valley Trail on its way from Long Pond to Beech Mountain parking area. Black chokeberry blooms filled every crack, turning my hike into a festive occasion. I met more tiger swallowtail and spring azure butterflies, more pink lady's slippers, more club moss. Reindeer and cloud lichen added texture and soft colors to the route. Ridge soils were thin, so trees were not as tall as those growing lower down the slope. While I was listening to a chickadee, a cigarette boat roared to life on Long Pond and raced away, either self-destructing or getting beyond earshot in a matter of seconds. In the same category of local distractions, the trail offers great views of the Southwest Harbor transfer station, the Quiet Side's eyesore equivalent of Jackson Lab. Near the end of the ridge I saw something white among blueberry bushes a few feet off the trail—the pelvis of a small deer, with three vertebrae attached. How slight and slim-hipped it must have been. Now of interest only to flies and ants, and the occasional hiker. Then I came to the puzzling pink and yellow blooms clumped in a group of five behind a boulder, the only place I saw them in seven hours of peering right and left. Why only there? Chance, perhaps, though site conditions must have something to do with it. My wildflower guide says that pale corydalis, a member of the poppy family, likes rocky clearings and is common throughout the Alleghenies. There is anecdotal evidence that it incites the Acadian blackfly to bloodlust and mayhem.

At the south end of the ridge, the trail takes an abrupt turn to the east and, by a stepped series of switchbacks, drops through the best woods on Beech Mountain to join the Valley Trail, which runs north and south at the base of the ridge. When I say "best" woods I mean the most beautiful, health-giving, and sacred woods on Beech Mountain.

Steps on Beech Mountain South Ridge Trail.

I defy the most ardent ridgerunner to race through them unmoved. As in any feat of magic, you can watch everything that happens, and yet not explain the effect. Here are graceful evergreens rising from a steep slope, luminous beds of sphagnum moss, masses of rock-cap fern, great colonies of lichen, choirs of sapling spruce, boulders, cliffs, sunlight slanting through trees, needles everywhere, and a trail winding through it all, descending by granite steps in runs of three, six, or ten—and yet the collective event in experience is every bit as inexplicable as it is astounding.

The Valley Trail heads straight toward Beech Mountain parking area on an easy grade for 0.8 mile. It was no anticlimax to the trail I'd just come down. I had crossed the same ground last December, but with ferns and new leaves sprouting everywhere, warblers darting overhead, and no ice, it seemed a new trail to me. Here was goldthread, wood sorrel, club moss, an eighteen-inch beech unscarred by disease, a

small brook, and another draining away from steep cliffs. In the midsection of a yellow birch, a small warbler made forays out and back, out and back, uttering an insistent series of notes more like an insect than a bird. Dark above, white below, white wing patch—a black-throated blue warbler hawking its lunch. Now I knew exactly where I was: in deep woods. A woman at a gathering I had attended the night before had said, "I am often afraid in the city, but never in the woods." In urban areas, people under stress have become the true danger, replacing cougars and wolves as public enemies. I stand with the woman and the warbler: we trust deep woods. Deep woods are where we belong.

Rising gently, the Valley Trail winds among huge boulders fallen from the cliff. I remembered a hike in August 1982 when I first took my son Jesse and his friend Sam on the Valley Trail from the pumping station at Long Pond. The boulders, and the caves beneath and between them, made a big impression on all of us. I am glad that is the kind of image I remember. I have boulders in my head. I mean to lug them to the grave.

At the upper end of the Valley Trail where the Canada Ridge Trail splits off, there is no sign for the old Southwest Harbor Road; you have to know it is there or you will miss it. I made a U-turn at the trailhead and went straight into the trees—and there was the road, or at least a track heading south. I'm not big on old roads, but this one has been so reclaimed by surrounding woods and ground cover, it serves as an honorary trail (I call it the Beech Mountain Notch Trail), connecting to Lurvey Spring Road, which connects to Echo Lake parking area, providing a way of turning a hike up Beech Cliff Ladder Trail into a satisfying loop. I saw partridgeberry, wintergreen, mountain cranberry, goldthread, wild strawberry, starflower, ferns—my kind of traffic.

❂

47—PARKMAN MOUNTAIN & BALD PEAK LOOP

From Norumbega Mountain parking area
To Parkman Mountain, Bald Peak, and back
  Up by Parkman Mountain Trail
  Down by Bald Peak Trail

2.5 miles, June 12, 1996

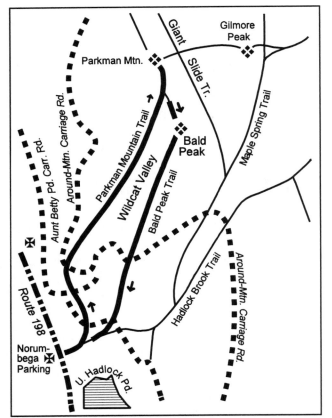

47—Parkman Mountain & Bald Peak loop.

and Gilmore peaks by a well-marked network of trails including the Hadlock Brook, Maple Spring, Birch Spring, Parkman Mountain, and Bald Peak trails. It is easy to overlook the Norumbega parking area, but keep it in mind for July and August when you find your intended startup point overflowing with cars.

The circuit of Parkman Mountain and Bald Peak has long been one of my favorite hikes, though I can't put my finger on the reason why. Of course, every hike I take is my favorite at the time, largely because it is vivid in my experience. But even as months and memories pass away, a loop up Parkman and Bald Peak lures me with a kind of fatal attraction. It is a classic hike, one I can count on to take me to Acadia's heart every time. I always do it the same way—up Parkman, down Bald Peak. It is a hike for all season because maples, birches, and beeches keep changing the color scheme, along with blueberry and huckleberry bushes which turn red in the fall. The view of Bald Peak across Wildcat Valley is one of the highlights on the way up; views from the two summits are great all around; the cairn-to-cairn descent over Bald Peak's granite ledges into Wildcat Valley with its chortling brook is a joy when the going is dry and free of ice. The landscape varies from valley woods to open ledges, offering a wide variety of plants and habitats. I often see hawks scouting the slopes and rising on the wind. When I close my inner eye, my experience focuses on the feel of the trail underfoot—smooth and granite firm. What can I say? It attracts me and makes me feel good. More accurately, I make myself feel good when I am there. It is a beautiful trail. Something drives me to experience that beauty again and again.

The trail was alive and opened onto a landscape of life, as every trail in Acadia does this time of year. Blackflies and mosquitoes hit me as soon as I crossed the highway and got into the woods. Several sizes of brown moths fluttered at the edge of my vision. I saw two damselflies and two dragonflies; a mourning cloak, four tiger swallowtail, and five spring azure butterflies. Ants, ants, ants crawled wherever I looked. Yellow jackets seemed about to rent a condominium in the cairn on top of Bald Peak. A small frog squirmed into the muck at the bottom of a slow-draining pool, which made up the bulk of its froggy universe. I heard one robin, and spent several minutes trying to see who had been calling to me from the treetops, without success. I did see two juncos, one with a caterpillar in its beak, in different snags. Two turkey vultures soared overhead, one up Wildcat Valley, the other around Parkman's flank. Rocking on brittle-looking wings, they seemed fragile somehow, unlike eagles and hawks. As for wildlife (charismatic mammals), I smelled fox scent a couple of times (once mixed with balsam fir where a vista had been cleared) and saw the first red squirrel I had seen in almost four months. I was part of the scene, too, since much of the wildlife seemed to hunger for my flesh.

I met a man and woman coming down from Sargent

I got off work at noon, ate lunch, and had four hours until I had to get ready for a meeting I was going to that evening; where could I hike in four hours? At my note-scrawling rate of travel, I was looking for a hike not much over two miles long. The only one that short on my list of proposed summer hikes was a loop of Parkman Mountain and Bald Peak from Route 198. I got to the Norumbega Mountain parking area a little after one, and was back before five, making the two-and-a-half-mile loop in three hours and forty minutes. The temperature was 83°, the vertical climb to the 974-foot summit of Bald Peak about 730 feet.

Unlike Sieur de Monts Spring or the pumping station at Long Pond, the parking area where the Goat Trail starts up Norumbega Mountain does not spring to mind as a major trailhead offering a wide variety of hikes. But just by crossing to the east side of Route 198, you can reach Sargent, Penobscot, Cedar Swamp, or Parkman mountains, and Bald

Mountain, a slight pink woman being walked by a large black dog on a carriage road, and a large blue man with spectacular orange eyes. The couple had seen three "ferks."

"Three foxes?" I asked, surprised.

"Three frogs," the woman corrected me.

The slight pink woman had seen lady's slippers, and the large blue man what he thought might have been an immature bald eagle soaring over Bald Peak.

"Could it have been a turkey vulture?" I asked him, having seen one not long before.

"It could have been an albatross," he said, "I didn't bring my prescription shades with me."

All in all, it was an extremely peaceful hike. Acadia and its passengers were on an even keel. Including me. Images of inner peace began floating into my mind. The landscape entered me and came out as words.

Peace is striped maple leaves dancing in still woods.

Peace is red spruce buds casting off their swaddling sheaths.

Peace is the granite slope of Wildcat Valley rising to Bald Peak.

Peace is a frog diving into the pond at the center of its universe.

The second week in June, a week before the solstice, mine was a sunny, green, and blossoming universe. The Parkman Mountain Trail started out in cool woods with sarsaparilla, starflower, mountain cranberry, and Canada May ruby in various stages of bloom. It quickly reached more open terrain where bracken, juniper, blueberry, huckleberry, black chokeberry, bunchberry, and sheep laurel took over. Striped maple keys hung in four-inch chains, the tree having set fruit weeks ago. Reproduce early and often, was its message. Red maples in Wildcat Valley were dark with similar fruit.

Peace is fitting easily into place where you most want to be.

The Parkman Mountain Trail crosses three carriage roads early in its career. Near the third (the Around-Mountain) carriage road, a thick spread of mountain sandwort—all blossom and no leaf—trembled in the light onshore breeze. A plant of mountain ridges, it seemed out of its element so low on the slope. I didn't see any higher up where I might have expected to find it. I came to a scattered group of four lady's slippers near the trail, more purple than pink. I have seen bumblebees slip through the purple curtain into the

sanctum, then climb out the top covered with pollen. How do they know to do that? Clearly, the flower beckons to them. Behind every great bloom there is a pollinator it trusts with its life. Later, I came to a lady's slipper of a different color—brown—that looked to have lost the bloom of youth yet was in full flower. Reproduce, it advised, but be quick about it. A true remnant was the single rhodora blossom I saw on a twiggy bush. Its day had come and gone. As on

Cinnamon fern on Parkman Mountain Trail.

Beech Mountain the week before, black chokeberry blooms ruled the slopes, but they were looking peaked, a few petals having fallen off. Too late, too late. Huckleberry blooms were just coming on, their swollen buds reminding me of mosquitos fat with blood.

Past the third carriage road, the trail gradually rises through woods and open ledges, then winds more steeply over sculpted granite ramps and ledges on the brink of Wildcat Valley. Except for a few soggy spots, the trail is solid underfoot. Twice it dips into dark woods, then scrambles up a granite wall into daylight again. It is a scaled-down synopsis of more strenuous mountain hikes, short and to the point.

It took me two hours to reach the Parkman Mountain summit cairn; half an hour crossing from Parkman to Bald Peak; and about an hour coming down, first on open ledge, then along the stream in Wildcat Valley. Wildcat Valley, what a great name. Like Catamount Hill, Mermaid Ledge, and Cape Porpoise. Someone met a wildcat there, sometime, or thought she did. A name handed down from wilder, more animated days. Otter Creek, Seal Cove, Bass Harbor, Eagles Crag, Fawn Pond, Bear Island—names commemorating our former greatness. Lest we forget.

Parkman doesn't look much like a mountain until you get to the top, where the vista says it all. There is Norumbega close in the west, then Acadia and St. Sauveur across Somes

Sound, Beech on the far side of Echo Lake, and Mansell and Bernard mountains on the far side of Long Pond. Gilmore Peak arcs like a dolphin to the east, backed by Sargent like a whale. Beyond Sargent the day of my hike, thunderclouds punched up into the blue like clenched fists. Thirty-three feet higher than Parkman, Bald Peak anchors the southern horizon. There is water, too—the Hadlock Ponds, Somes Sound, Western Way, and the Gulf of Maine. Parkman is one of those middling peaks from which Acadia looks so grand. Like Bald Peak, it puts the surrounding landscape in proper perspective.

Peace is a fleet of thunderheads sailing on the far horizon beyond Sargent Mountain.

Bald Peak seemed to exist in a climate zone all its own. Blueberry was still in full bloom on the rise out of Wildcat Valley, as was a trailside nest of six bluebead lilies (yellow clintonia). Wine-leaf cinquefoil added its white blossom, single and longer stemmed than the chokeberry blooms. On the north side of the peak, a mountain ash tree looked like a painting of white clouds spread against a darkening sky. One blooming blackberry bush clawed at my pants on my way down the peak's sunnier side.

Lady's slipper along Parkman Mountain Trail.

Peace is a crow in no hurry gliding from Bald Peak to Norumbega over Brown Mountain Notch.

From the top of Bald Peak I saw another crow sail off Northeast Harbor. The view from there includes Cedar Swamp Mountain falling away in three swells toward the south. Two rivers of pale deciduous leaves ran up the slope of Sargent Mountain's south ridge amid darker evergreens. In March I had been lost in a snowstorm trying to find the trail to Birch Spring up one of those rivers. Eventually I got to the ridge, and the trail running along it. Standing on the brink of the Amphitheater, what a grand view I had had of Penobscot Mountain through blowing snow like old Leviathan coursing through spindrift! This time Penobscot looked more serene, like the limb of a coppery moon rising over Sargent's south ridge.

Peace is sitting in warm sunlight on Bald Peak, remembering being lost in a winter storm three months before.

I had the two summits to myself. One other person would have felt like a crowd. I had seen a summary of the park's carriage-road-use study in which respondents generally felt comfortable with as many as seventeen people in view. Seventeen people! That's more like the Bronx than Acadia.

Peace is being in Acadia when you could be in the Bronx.

That's why people come here; why they leave the Bronx in the Bronx. Acadia is full up with bugs, birds, and blossoms already; people are extraneous. Even worse, they are opaque. When you can't see the park for visitors and their pets, the park is no longer a park—it's a zoo. Is that where we're headed? Is that, in fact, the best of all possible futures?

Peace is savoring what you have today because tomorrow it will be gone.

Coming down the Bald Peak Trail, I met another junco on a snag, this one singing without a caterpillar in its beak.

Peace is listening to a junco sing, not caring that you don't know the words, or it isn't much of a tune.

The Bald Peak Trail heads for Upper Hadlock Pond from the summit down across one granite terrace after another, a shorter ridge trail than some, but in the same league with those on Champlain, Dorr, Cadillac, Pemetic, Sargent, and Penobscot. With firm footing through open terrain looking onto wooded slopes, ponds, and marine waters beneath a blue sky, such trails offer the hiker a characteristically Acadian experience. Seek no further—you are there! Shorter and steeper than most ridge trails in Acadia, the Bald Peak Trail compresses the effect, heightening it, making it all the more remarkable. Plunging to the Around-Mountain Carriage Road, it doesn't stop there but continues into Wildcat Valley where it follows the stream across the lower carriage road almost to Upper Hadlock Pond. The wooded valley adds another dimension to the trail, complementing the feeling of looking onto nature from above with the feeling of being in its midst. There is sufficient soil lower down to hold some of the water rushing off the peak, turning the landscape into a garden of ferns and tall trees. The Bald Peak Trail is a tale of two Acadias.

Just after crossing the lower carriage road, the trail meets the Hadlock Brook Trail, which leads to the trailhead oppo-

Summit of Bald Peak backed by Gilmore Peak and Sargent Mountain.

site the Norumbega Mountain parking area. Walking that last stretch, I felt I was coming out of a trance. At some point I became aware that those sounds I had been hearing were cars rushing by on Route 198. Cars! What did they have to do with anything? Where was I, anyway? Then it all came back.

Peace is bringing Acadia with you in the eye of your eye when you come to the end of the trail.

❂

48—CADILLAC MOUNTAIN

From Route 3 Near Blackwoods Campground
To Cadillac Mountain summit, and on to the
Park Loop Road overlooking Bar Harbor
Up by Cadillac Mountain South Ridge Trail
Down by Cadillac Mountain North Ridge Trail
6.0 miles, June 20, 1996

The first day of summer. At 9:24 p.m. Earth would tip its northern pole to the sun, producing the longest day in the Northern Hemisphere, and the shortest night. The sun would rise and set today at the northern limit of its yearly sweep along the horizon. How could I tip my pole to the sun in a show of empathy with the season? What hike would I take? A hike to the north, not a loop. On Acadia's highest peak. Cadillac Mountain from south to north. At noon I would line up with the radius between Earth and its star, my tether to the source of all being, all knowing, and all good. It is not every day I can hike the axis of life itself.

If the sun is in its glory on the summer solstice, what about the other quarter days that mark the seasons? What rules the winter solstice, the equinoxes in fall and spring? In December when the sun is low, northwest winds scrub the air of haze and grime, bringing short, clear days and long, starry nights. Of the four ancient elements, air gains supremacy on the winter solstice, bringing snow and cold to the northern world. In fall when plants and trees build

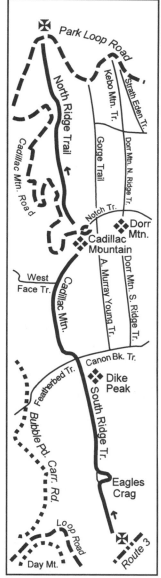

48—Cadillac Mountain hike.

soil with their leaves, earth comes into its own as the ruling element. In spring when roots are bathed in moisture, water rules. One by one through the seasons, the elements rise and fall in orderly succession. Sun, soil, air, and water. Essential ingredients of life, but not life itself. They make life possible, but do not ignite it. Life has an essence of its own passed generation to generation in chromosomes and coils-upon-coils-upon-coils of DNA. Life—the collective ability to eat, drink, breathe, excrete, grow, rest, move, repair, defend, perceive, imagine, communicate, and reproduce—is a spiritual (Latin *spirare*, to breathe) element that depends on the other four to become viable, but is different and distinct. Life is the mystery of mysteries, the melody running through a sequence of individual notes. The solar year celebrates life running through the seasons, life made possible by the ruling elements, but transcending them as music transcends its separate auditory components. Where life arose, where it is going, why it is here—nobody knows. Our task is to sing joyfully in close harmony with those around us and, when we can't keep up the melody, to let others carry it on without us.

In my case, I sing the living trails of Acadia. If I didn't find joy in nature, I wouldn't be me. On the summer solstice, I celebrate the sun's energy which, added to soil, air, and water, sustains the ongoing mystery of my and every being. Each hike I make is an event in the life of one member of the universe. I can at least tell the story of that day, even if I can never explain it.

It was 60° when I left my apartment at Harden Farm off Kebo Street in Bar Harbor. I parked at the overlook on the Park Loop Road across from the trailhead for the Cadillac Mountain North Ridge Trail. It was foggy, and the overlook overlooked not Bar Harbor at all but the creamy inside of a giant marshmallow covering all of Frenchman Bay. My son Ken and his wife, Linda, drove me 6.3 miles to the trailhead for the Cadillac Mountain South Ridge Trail on Route 3 near the entrance to Blackwoods Campground. My route was up and over Cadillac by way of Eagles Crag, Dike Peak, and the Featherbed. The south ridge trail rises 1,340 feet in 3.7 miles (which includes a side trip to the crag), the north ridge trail descends 1,240 feet in 2.2 miles. Including a 0.1-mile circuit of the summit parking area to tally license plates, I figure the hike covered an even 6.0 miles.

What did I see? First of all, plants, life that receives energy directly from the sun. This was their day of days. Near roads at the start and end of my hike, and at the summit parking area, I saw plants that thrive where people and their machines have disturbed the soil, all in full bloom: red clover, buttercup, hawkweed, cow vetch, and daisy. None of these are native plants. They are all from Away, brought by early settlers from Europe. Field dwellers, they shun the woods.

Scattered along the trails themselves, I met huckleberry with small white blossoms hanging like miniature hot-air balloons; a few blueberries still in flower, especially in shady areas higher up; one sarsaparilla plant in bloom out of hundreds near the two trailheads; Canada May ruby and starflower universally gone by; bunchberry in bloom higher up,

gone by lower down; wine-leaf cinquefoil blooming on open ledges everywhere I looked, a few lower leaves here and there colored a rich claret; eight lady's slippers ranging from deep pink to white; sheep laurel (lambkill) in pink bud on lower slopes, blooming near the summit; three-inch mountain sandwort blooming with white petals radiating from yellow and green centers on gravelly areas on the south ridge; a few black chokeberry blooms determined to last

Pitch pine, Cadillac Mountain south ridge.

through the solstice; yellow bush honeysuckle blossoms just bursting out; witherod buds turning from hard little kernels to sprays of delicate white flowers; and in a narrow basin on Dike Peak, cotton grass waving in the wind.

The sun had an amazing effect on plant life along the trail. The whole mountain was in bloom. And what wasn't blooming was greening, fruiting, swelling, spreading. Blueberries on a few plants looked ready to be picked in a week or so. Mushrooms sprouted in damp woods. Ferns, too, including rock-cap, cinnamon, interrupted, New York, and bracken. Lichens covered every square inch of the mountain's flesh that wasn't otherwise spoken for: reindeer, cloud, rock tripe, and map, among a variety of crusty species in black, and pale and bright green. Sweet fern, a bayberry cousin, bore peacenik burrs (looking like burdocks, they wouldn't hurt a soul), and scented the air with the spice of the solstice. Juniper sprayed along the open slopes as the seasonal wreath.

Both up and down, the trail passed through living landscapes expressing the influence of climate, soil, and conflagration in a variety of ways. Only the first mile was through what I would call real woods—tall woods, old woods, woods full of blowdowns and snags. Here were red spruce, balsam fir, white pine, mountain maple, red maple, and yellow birch growing back after having been cut some seventy years ago, not a primeval forest in any sense, but respectable modern-day woods. In places the trail was strewn with red maple keys. Here I heard crows, blue jays, hermit thrushes, and saw a yellow-rumped warbler and female ruffed grouse. The grouse twined stiffly through the undergrowth, making a soft cup-cup-cupping sound. I suspected she had a brood nearby and was warning it to be still. If she had been free to fly, she would have flown.

North of Eagles Crag, about a mile from Route 3, the landscape became noticeably diminished. There were no more tall trees for the rest of the hike. Scrubby gray birch and pitch pine took over, surrounded by low shrubs. The terrain opened to the sky. There were red spruce here and there, but no big ones. Mountain ash appeared, covered with sprays of white blooms, in turn covered with sprays of flying insects. From where the crag loop rejoins it, the south ridge trail passes through ledgy terrain with little soil to speak of all the way to the summit ridge. Compared to the woods I had just left, the change was abrupt. What had happened here? When I got back to my apartment, I checked a map showing the extent of the 1947 fire and, sure enough, the burn had ended exactly where the tall trees stop and the scrub begins. Sparing a small area of woods at the summit, the fire had burned

Cotton grass in wetland on Dike Peak.

the next five miles of trail north of Eagles Crag. The north ridge trail runs inside the burn for all but a tenth of a mile near the summit. It passes through woods that have been in transition for almost fifty years. Fifty years sounds like a long time, but as woods go, it barely sees trees through adolescence. Maine trees can get turned into pulp two or three times in that span without ever reaching maturity. Though spared by the fire, red and white spruce on the summit of Cadillac Mountain are exposed to often lethal climate extremes reducing them to caricatures of the trees they might have been. Nipped by wind, cold, and drought, summit trees are often twisted and dwarfed, with naked spires still pointing toward their youthful aspirations.

Calamity builds character because it demands character in those who survive. Those who don't have it leave few descendants and are quickly forgotten. Those with the right stuff have the scene to themselves. Witness the "barren"

ledges of Acadia which, at closer look, blossom with life. Where black chokeberry had ruled the slopes of Beech Mountain two weeks ago, wine-leaf cinquefoil held sway on Cadillac on the solstice. Every crack was filled with spunky white blooms rising above compound leaves with three narrow, toothed leaflets. For its needs, here was sun enough, and air. Water and soil were harder to come by. Where a few grains of soil clung in cracks in the granite, that was all the invitation cinquefoil needed; it put down root and claimed squatters' rights. Mountain sandwort did the same in shallow pans of mud and gravel, blossoming among hikers' footsteps. Pale juniper fringed much of the trail, and lichen decked the treadway itself.

Pitch pine, with its inverse needs for sunlight (high) and water (low), is a ridgeline tree, but on the south slope of Dike Peak it yields its scant hold to jack pine, a species more well known at Schoodic Point. Jack pine is said to set seed only after a fire, so my guess is the fire of 1947 gave it the chance of a lifetime. Now it sits in stoic self-denial, praying for another holocaust.

The so-called Featherbed is an anomaly on the ridge, a wetland setting off the barren slope like the moon of yang in the night of yin. The ridge dips from Dike Peak into a basin that, in profile, looks like a bluefish bite in the back of a pogy. Here water collects, forming an oasis supporting alien beings. Frogs. Green frogs, judging by the chorus of slack-strung banjo notes from all sides. The tempo was slow, sixteen to the minute, yet heartfelt and spontaneous. How did the first frog get here, or the second who became its mate? It is as likely they fell from the moon as climbed a wall of rock. Mystery, as I said. Wherry says the Featherbed was named for the cotton grass that thrived there, though I didn't see any in flower in the Featherbed itself.* My guess is that the Featherbed has moved, the name we now give the oasis in the dip in the ridge having formerly been applied to the narrow wetland higher up on Dike Peak where cotton grass thrives today. Labels on a 1941 trail map seem to support that conjecture.

---

*Edgar T. Wherry, *Wild Flowers of Mount Desert Island, Maine*. N.p.: Garden Club of Mount Desert, 1928.

Dike Peak on the south ridge trail (just south of, and overlooking, the Featherbed) is in a class by itself. I have gawked at dikes all over the park, puny little veins of gray stone a few inches wide, when I could have made one trip to Dike Peak and seen Acadia's finest display. You want dikes, here are dikes—six-foot dikes, fifteen-foot dikes, dikes twenty-four feet wide! Enough dikes for a lifetime. Here is a chapter in Acadia's geological history writ large in bold type. When the subcontinent now referred to as "Avalonia" collided in slow motion with "North America" some 400–600 million years ago, molten rock welled up from the depths, forming the pluton (rock bubble) of course-grained Cadillac Mountain granite. When it hardened, the pluton could no longer flow under stress from the ongoing collision, so it cracked at joints running north-and-south. Molten rock forced its way upward into these joints and, cooling more quickly than the granite, formed fine-grained seams of basalt or diabase. Where these seams break the surface, they show up as linear dikes of blue-gray or black rock. Map lichen often colonize the smooth surface of dikes, painting them battleship gray. Hiking beyond Dike Peak, you can follow that same broad river of gray with your eyes as it flows down Cadillac on a small ridge east of the trail, and meet it (or its twin) again at the horseshoe turn on the Cadillac Mountain Road, and again opposite the first Eagle Lake overlook.

At 1,082 feet, Dike Peak is one of Acadia's 1,000-foot summits. I have never heard of anyone going out of his way to check it off his list of summits attained, but I don't think you can claim to have "done" Acadia until you have ogled the jack pines and dikes in this part of the park. In addition to the south ridge trail from north or south, you can reach the peak by the Featherbed Trail from Hunters Brook or the Canon Brook Trail from Route 3 south of Sieur de Monts Spring, approaching the Featherbed from west or east.

From the Featherbed, the south ridge trail rises by a short, steep stretch up onto the western of two south ridges leading to Cadillac's summit. The way seemed barren at first, like a landscape on the moon, but blossoming life persisted in pans and cracks, and lichens parti-colored the landscape in soft hues and tones. Winds whipping across the ridge have held the growth of spruce and shrubs to three feet or less. I found fewer sprays of mountain sandwort than I expected, assuming the rest had been trampled through the years. The ridge is broad and inviting, making it difficult to keep hikers to a single track. Designer cairns keep springing up, erected more in fits of sculptural recreation than from any desire to help hikers on their way. In keeping with the place, I met three turkey vultures soaring on the updraft from Bubble Pond, gliding with equal ease up and down the ridge. Increasing road kills and perhaps warmer temperatures have

brought them to Maine in recent years. This threesome was trying to put a good face on their visit by acting wild and free, but they couldn't fool me. Like many today, they like their food fast by the roadside.

The summit woods of Cadillac Mountain were spared by the 1947 fire, so they are older than the size of individual trees might suggest. Twisted trunks, gnarled branches, and silver spires hint at the true age of the stand, and the hard-

The Featherbed (foreground), Dike Peak (rear left), Day Mtn. (rear right).

ships it has endured. Red and white spruce predominate. Pink-budded sheep laurel (lambkill) lined the trail; it was blooming lower down, but not here, not yet. Bunchberry still bloomed at the summit while it had already had its day below. Even a few black chokeberry blooms hung on. The trail parallels the road across the summit ridge, but standing in thick, muffling woods, from time to time I enjoyed the illusion that there was no traffic on the mountain aside from myself. The trail dips into a gully, crosses a fire road, then rises over stepped granite to the highest point in the park. Here I saw a man and woman urging a lumbering box kite into the air. I stood on the benchmark punched with the elevation, 1,530 feet, to be able to say I had hiked to the top. It had taken me five hours and fifteen minutes to hike all but 190 of those vertical feet. No, I hadn't truly hiked Cadillac because I hadn't started at sea level, but I had made it 88% of the way.

Moving away from the benchmark, I met hawkweed and daisy, water tank and radio antenna, gift shop and parking area—the long arm of human culture stretching deep into the park. I tallied license plates to see where folks had come from, then headed down the north ridge trail.

I met forty-seven people on the trail, thirty-nine on the way up, all but two of whom overtook me on the trail as I scrutinized some vital detail in the middle distance. I did an informal survey of the size of hiking groups, counting two groups of four, one group of three, seventeen groups of two, and two solos. The solos were both men, one a runner, the other an athletic type who climbed Pemetic in the interim before catching up to me the second time. Twenty were female, twenty-seven male. Of the pairs, fourteen were mixed, two were female, one male. Two of the males were children under ten. I wished them all a happy solstice, and got the general response, Oh, is it today? Sample replies include:

"What can I say?—another in a string of beautiful days."

"That's right! What a great way to celebrate!"

"Ooh, it's so hot!"

"You mean it's today? We'll have plenty of daylight to get back."

"So today's the day—well begun, I'd say."

Fifteen hikers passed me twice, on their way up and down. One of them wished me happy solstice at our second meeting. I thanked him and said I was right where I wanted to be, and could not be happier.

The sun came out when I reached Eagles Crag, and stayed out, though Frenchman Bay was socked-in the whole day, and whale-watch cruises out of Bar Harbor were canceled. When it got its act together, the first day of summer came on as it should, warm, clear, with a cooling breeze. Several spectacular vistas opened up, beginning with the view east from Eagles Crag looking out on Gorham and Champlain mountains, the Beehive, and Huguenot Head across the valley of Otter Creek and Beaver Brook. Higher up the ridge, Pemetic Mountain dominates the view to the west; then, near the summit, Pemetic fades back and Sargent, Penobscot, and the Bubbles come into view. Approaching Cadillac from the south, the hiker walks into the mountain's central mass which dominates the skyline to the north in three humps, like a giant taking a siesta. The Porcupine Islands are a main feature of the view from the north ridge trail, but they were taking a siesta, too, beneath a cool blanket of fog.

I didn't count people at the summit, there were too many, most of them streaming toward or away from the gift shop. I did a geographical survey instead to see where they came from. Of fifty-nine cars, here is a state-by-state breakdown:

Massachusetts—13 cars, Maine—10, Pennsylvania—6, New York—5, Michigan—4, New Jersey—3; 2 cars each from Florida, Georgia, Illinois; and 1 car each from Alabama, Arizona, Connecticut, Maryland, New Hampshire, North Carolina, North Dakota, Tennessee, Texas, Vermont, Wisconsin, and Ontario.

There were several panting dogs looking for shade at the

summit. I met only two dogs on the trail, neither on leashes, both looking hot. I saw four scats all day, two containing hare fur which had passed through a canid's digestive tract during the winter, and two more recent specimens—one of which looked skunky, the other foxy (perhaps).

It had been relatively dry for a week, so I wasn't surprised to see only one slug happily nibbling away at its mushroom couch. I saw ants by the thousand, over thirty

Bald and Long Porcupine islands, with Stave Island (left rear).

dragonflies, more mosquitoes than I could count (most of them in the lower woods), assorted flies and moths, nine spring azure butterflies, four tiger swallowtails, one mourning cloak, and two white admirals doing sprightly loop-the-loops together.

I heard hermit thrushes, a hairy woodpecker, several white-throated sparrows, three crows, blue jays, and numerous birds I couldn't identify by ear. I also heard the moan-moan-moaning of a foghorn in Frenchman Bay, two great cannonades of thunder early on, and noon signals from Seal Harbor and Otter Creek. When I heard the noon sirens as I was admiring the jack pines on Dike Peak, I made note of my shadow which, the sun bearing down almost from the zenith, was as short as it gets at this latitude—about two-and-a-half feet.

I saw crows, blue jays, three turkey vultures, and a white-throated sparrow, as well as a yellow-rumped warbler, ruffed grouse, cedar waxwing, three juncos, many gulls soaring over Blue Hill Overlook, two robins, and a smallish brown hawk climbing a spiral trail of its own, then sliding along Cadillac's west ridge gradually down, down, down until it dipped below the trees, never once flapping in the four minutes I watched it. From a distance, singing in the top of its spruce, the whitethroat looked like your ordinary little brown bird, but through binoculars it was a shaman in full dress and yellow paint ready to heal the world, or at least bring rain to parched fields. The waxwing was as powerful a figure, its crest looking like a raised visor or a shield. Even the robins looked good to my eyes, having the noble bearing of true thrushes, not the easiness of suburban pets.

Just as legislatures take it upon themselves to designate state birds, trees, and flowers, I thought I could play that game, too, filling the standard categories with species met along the trail. That might be a shorthand way of getting across the outstanding features of a hike. On the Cadillac Mountain south and north ridge trails on the summer solstice, 1996, by the authority duly invested in me, I do hereby proclaim the following designations:

Hike Bird	White-throated Sparrow
Hike Insect	Dragonfly
Hike Flower	Wine-leaf Cinquefoil
Hike Mammal	Fellow Hikers
Hike Amphibian	Green Frog
Hike Tree	Jack Pine
Hike Fruit	Maple Key
Hike Mollusk	Slug
Hike Motto	"Have a nice solstice."

Starting down from the summit at 2:25 p.m., I found the north ridge trail a sobering anticlimax to all that had gone before. Traffic on the mountain road was visible or audible a good part of the way, plastic pipes and metal cables kept cropping up to dull the effect of walking in the woods, the view was toward Bar Harbor featuring neatly groomed Kebo Valley Golf Course in the foreground, trailside vegetation was still fighting its way back after the fire almost fifty years ago, and the trail itself seemed put together by a committee of twenty-three who settled disagreement by each taking a section and doing what they wanted with it. Parts of the trail probably go back a long way—hundreds if not thousands of years—but now it is a hodgepodge without a plan or strategy for getting from A to B. One carefully laid run of fifty-six stone steps, followed by forty-seven more, placed somewhere in the middle of the trail for no reason that I could see, made the rest of the trail seem shabby and untended. Footing is difficult in places where the treadway crosses rubbly stretches of cobbles and broken rock. I met nine hikers on the north ridge trail, compared to thirty-seven on the south ridge trail, so I judged it wasn't used that much as a thoroughfare.

The summer solstice marks the start of peak visitation at Acadia National Park. School was out and flocks of migrant vacationers were striding the slopes. Last week I had met four hikers on Parkman Mountain, this week sixty-two on Cadillac (counting the fifteen I met a second time on their return, but not the herd that reached the summit by car). From now till Labor Day, I would have plenty of company on my hikes. Even so, I won't feel crowded. Sixty-two

hikers in seven hours and forty minutes averages out to about one hiker every seven or eight minutes, a more comfortable ratio than I would find on the carriage roads, not to mention the streets of Bar Harbor.

✪

Mountain cranberry and reindeer lichen.

49—SCHOODIC HEAD & ANVIL LOOP

From Blueberry Hill parking area
To Schoodic Head, the Anvil, and back
   Up by "Alder Path" and Schoodic Head Trail
   Back by Anvil Trail

                  2.6 miles, June 27, 1996

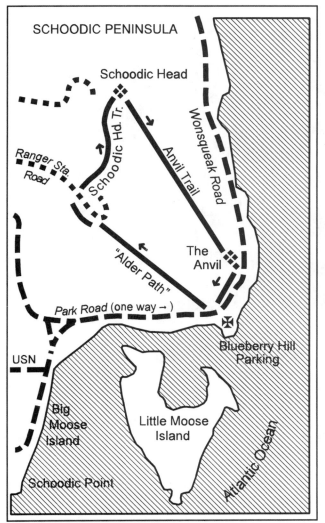

49—Schoodic Head & Anvil loop.

The quickest way to introduce my hike the last week in June on Schoodic Peninsula is to proclaim its emblems right at the start:

Hike Bird	American Bald Eagle
Hike Insect	Mosquito
Hike Flower	Golden Heather
Hike Mammal	Porcupine
Hike Reptile	Garter Snake
Hike Tree	Jack Pine
Hike Fruit	Spruce Cone
Hike Motto	"Short and sweet."

Was it worth the 96-mile, over-two-hour round trip from Bar Harbor? Absolutely. Making a circuit of Schoodic Head and the Anvil from Blueberry Hill parking area is a gem of a hike. Only 2.6 miles long, the loop takes you exactly where you want to go—to the heart of natural beauty and mystery.

The loop is made up of three sections: what I call the Alder Path, a straight and level walk to Ranger Station Road (0.7 mile); the Schoodic Head Trail from the road to the 440-foot summit (0.9 mile); and the Anvil Trail between Schoodic Head and the Wonsqueak Road across the Anvil, a 190-foot wooded, granite dome southeast of the head (1.0 mile). Each section offers excitement and challenge in its own way. On the Alder Path I met a silent garter snake and even more silent porcupine. On the Schoodic Head Trail I met two flying eagles and two blooming clumps of golden heather. On the Anvil Trail I met a flicker at her nest and a black-throated green warbler calling the faithful to prayer from its spruce minaret. Too, there were other trailside miracles of blooming and flying life.

Summer seemed delayed by two or three weeks at Schoodic Point, perhaps because it juts so deeply into the cooler Gulf of Maine. Bunchberry dogwood was still in bloom on Schoodic Head, along with starflower and Canada May ruby in shady woods. Sarsaparilla was in full flower, while it had passed its prime on Mount Desert Island a week ago. I had seen sheep laurel blooming on Cadillac the week before; most plants on Schoodic had yet to come into bud. Out of thousands, the one exception was a single plant burst into pink flower on the south-facing ledges of Schoodic Head. A Polly Wardwell plant. In ninth grade, Polly Wardwell came into bloom in pink sweaters, Venus on the half-shell among the rest of us starfish and clams. My eyes burned when I looked at her, so I kept to my geography book. She soon took up with an older man, left school, and moved over the horizon to someplace like Cazenovia. I hadn't seen her since, but there she was on Schoodic Head, fresh as a flower, not a day over fifteen.

To reach Blueberry Hill parking area, it is almost a fifty-mile drive from Bar Harbor by way of Route 1 through Hancock and Sullivan, south on Route 186 in Gouldsboro to Winter Harbor, then south again on the Moore Road to the Schoodic Point Section of Acadia National Park. Where the road forks, giving a choice between **NAVAL SECURITY GROUP ACTIVITIES** and **WONSQUEAK**, go **WONSQUEAK** (left) about half a mile to the parking area overlooking Schoodic and Little Moose islands. When I got there, the National Park Service himself was mowing the grass, cigarette dangling from grimaced lips, massive frame riding a Bolens mower the size of a router, taming the wilderness pass after snarling pass. Despite the noise, the view kept baiting me with gulls, eiders, guillemots, cormorants, crows, and restless waves. Through binoculars, I saw hundreds of gulls on Schoodic Island, one of their offshore breeding grounds. Like Ulysses upon hearing the Sirens' song, I steeled my nerves and held my course away from the view into the bushes on the other side of Wonsqueak Road.

Just getting out of the parking area, I saw rugosa roses in bloom; white and red clover; yellow hawkweed; bluets; blackberry; lesser stitchwort (starry blooms trying to make up for an unprepossessing name); purple cow vetch, like kids of a certain age, climbing on everything; daisies; wine-leaf cinquefoil; and fifty blue flag iris in a drainage ditch. Across the road two wooden signs [since replaced by a trailhead] pointed into the alders: **RANGER STATION .6 MI.; SCHOODIC HEAD TRAIL .7 MI.** At 8:45 a.m. I was on the trail again.

At 8:46 a.m. I was rummaging through my fanny pack looking for mosquito dope. It had rained every day since the solstice, and still pools of water were everywhere. Conditions were perfect for mosquitoes to multiply by spontaneous combustion, or however it is they reproduce. The Alder Path led immediately to a horde of lurking insects hungry for red meat. I was prepared in an abstract way, but not that prepared. They had me pinned to the ground before I knew I was dinner for ten thousand guests. Whipping out my vial of Bygone Bugs (rosemary, eucalyptus, sweet birch, and peppermint in an oil base), I defended myself as best I could. The bugs backed off, but shadowed me the whole hike, making forays into my ears and down my neck to see if one or two could slip by. Knowing their strategy was to sacrifice thousands for a single success, I played it their way, accounting for as many as I could. They claimed victory for the four or five that eluded me, but I came through largely unscathed, the contest adding a certain bite to my adventures.

The Alder Path is a straight and narrow extension of Ranger Station Road coming in from the west near Pond Island. Road and path run parallel to the wetland separating Big Moose Island from the peninsula proper, and probably once provided access to East Pond Cove and Little Moose Island from Winter Harbor. With a road now leading to the Naval installation and the Schoodic Point parking area on Big Moose Island, the swampy extension of the original road has reverted to a path unlike any other in the park that I know of. Now lined with alder, pin cherry, and mountain ash, it offers a closeup view of the gradual transition from swampy to upland habitats. Here I saw white blackberry and yellow dwarf cinquefoil in bloom much of the way, with showy patches of yellow rattle, Canada May ruby, yellow and orange hawkweed, bunchberry, sarsaparilla (not that showy), and pink bells of mountain cranberry trailing along the ground. Wild raisin (witherod) was in bud, but hadn't opened yet. I also saw several old apple trees, great fountains of cinnamon ferns, and two bright orange amanita mushrooms, first of what I am sure will be a bumper crop,

given the rain we have had. The Alder Path passes through a few wooded stretches with spruce, birch, Northern white cedar, red maple, and jack pine, but it is the more open, shrubby areas that give the path its flavor.

Shortly after my first encounter with mosquitoes in the wettest part of the path, I saw a garter snake wind into the undergrowth a few feet ahead. I wanted to study its markings, but couldn't find it again. Moths and butterflies also

Schoodic Peninsula and Schoodic Head from Champlain Mountain.

animated the landscape, as did ants, spiders, spittlebugs, flies, bees, wasps, cormorants and gulls flying overhead, a blue jay, and crows shouting from the slopes of Schoodic Head. I found one downy grouse feather resting lightly in a bush. Stopping to look at pin cherries, I smelled something dead. Eying the undergrowth, I saw a mass of quills in the scrub eight feet from the path. Something had gotten past those barbed spears to subdue the inner porcupine now rotting underneath. It had gone to porcupine glory—not to some hokey heaven, but back to the damp soil from which it had come.

I heard a truck go by ahead, then came to a solar-powered weather station. At the gravel road, a small sign pointed between overarching birches to **SCHOODIC HEAD TRAIL.** A tenth of a mile farther on, a similar sign pointed up the slope into the woods. It would be easy to miss that small sign. Last winter, Acadia's trails foreman made sturdy trailheads for the Schoodic section of the park; in a few weeks they would replace the inconspicuous signs I followed on this hike.

The Schoodic Head Trail runs almost a mile through dense woods to the highest point on Schoodic Peninsula, rising some 390 feet at a generally easy grade. In one place it leads up a steeper ravine, followed by a rocky defile, but those sections are short. The footing is rocky and rooty in places, but firm on upper ledges where it levels off. The trail is marked with bird silhouettes, galvanized metal cutouts painted red, which have become scratched and faded over the years. The bottom two silhouettes have been refurbished; don't be surprised if you meet a yellow bird with eyelashes and blue eyes.

The trail rises through gnarled woods and mossy cliffs, terrain to please the most ardent seeker of wilderness. This is the real Acadia, Maine as it was in beginning times before men of any color vied with cougar and wolf for the role of top predator. The trail takes you back to days before even hunting and gathering were respectable occupations. People may still pass through, but they know immediately they do not belong in such a place. Nature spirits are likely to show up in unfamiliar guise. Their frame of reference is not only prehistoric but prehuman. Prehominid, pre-wisdom itself. Here is the seat of creative energy fed directly by sunlight, soil, water, and air. In other words, here is a sacred site, a world of pure spirit because it is wholly of the living Earth. There used to be a lot of such sites around, but they are becoming scarce. Those who revere these places and hike to discover them will find sanctuary during the time they spend on the Schoodic Head Trail. As I did, they might encounter one of the local wood spirits, hearing it mimic the sharp, squeaky call of a black-backed woodpecker—*pic, pic, pic*—never glimpsing the form it actually took.

Cleft in the ledge, Anvil Trail.

Where the trail levels off on the upper ledges and soil becomes thin, jack pines take over the terrain, maintaining the twisted, wild look of the place. The ledges run with sheep laurel, one plant as I have mentioned standing radiant in full, if precocious, bloom. In an inconspicuous corner, two clumps of heather turned sunlight, air, and water into gold. Views open up to the west, from nearby islands—Mark with its lighthouse, Ned, Turtle, Spectacle, Heron—out to Egg Rock (with its lighthouse) and Ironbound Island in the middle of Frenchman Bay, to the Porcupines beyond and, in the background, the receding ridges of Champlain, Dorr, and Cadillac mountains on Maine's largest island, Mount Desert. Through binoculars I could see where a rockfall had coursed two-thirds of the way down the Precipice, leaving a scar of pale granite against dark. South of Mount Desert, Baker,

Little Cranberry, and the Duck Islands formed a variation on the constellation I was familiar with.

Lowering my binoculars, I saw two dark birds circling half a mile away over West Pond Cove near Pond Island. A pair of adult bald eagles in full dress. They circled around each other, rose to my level, then came straight toward Schoodic Head, and me on my ledge, passing a hundred and fifty feet over our respective domes. When they were gone, I wondered what was going on back at the nest, assuming they were a mated pair. Junior would not be likely to fledge till mid-July; who was minding the nursery on Hog Island or Gouldsboro Point, wherever it was they called home? Maybe they had had an off year and were free to go cruising all day. Some people get tired of hearing about certain high-profile species of wildlife—snail darters, spotted owls, eagles, and others of their threatened or endangered ilk—but when it comes to sparking a thrill in the gut, eagles do a good job every time, no matter how jaded we have become. Not because they are the national bird, but because it is always a thrill to see so much skill and hard work performed with such consummate grace. Why else do we watch the Olympics? But there is no need to wait four years; competitions in nature are run year-round, every minute, every day.

Continuing on, I soon got to the top, arriving at 11:35. Through binoculars, I saw another adult eagle downeast from where I stood as I was ogling the radio towers in Cutler. I wasn't out looking for eagles; they appeared because my path intersected their daily rounds. Put yourself in certain spots, and the world reveals itself. That is what I mean by sacred places. Revelatory places. Schoodic Head has the magic.

Spruce Point on the far side of Wonsqueak Harbor to the east appeared wooded and unsettled. Across Prospect Harbor, large houses lined the shore of Cranberry Point, much developed since Louise Dickinson Rich wrote of her sojourn there. Off its point, Petit Manan Island looked too puny to support so tall a light tower. Part of Petit Manan National Wildlife Refuge, the island supports a large colony of terns which hatches its young in late June. So much protein in such a small place draws a fan club of hungry gulls and hawks. It is a lively time of year on Petit Manan Island, but the only suggestion of life I could see through binoculars was a periodic glint of warning from the tower.

The sky had been largely overcast in the morning but was now half-and-half, cumulus clouds beginning to spread against a background of blue over the mainland. Turning onto the Anvil Trail, I headed into a high glare that cleared as I went. The temperature jumped from cool to warm to hot. A hermit thrush sang somewhere in dark woods. The trail wound through twisted jack pines and huckleberry bushes about to bloom. Looking scary and untrustworthy, large inch-and-a-half wasps with orange abdomens hung over the huckleberry. Tiger swallowtails wandered across the ledges. The trail dipped into spruce woods, then returned to the ledges, opening now and then toward the dark wooded slopes of the Anvil ahead backed by pale green Schoodic Island and the shimmering gulf beyond. When the noon siren sounded from Prospect Harbor, I estimated my shadow to be thirty-two inches long, give or take. If I remember, I'll measure it again at noon on the winter solstice.

Stretching toward the Anvil, the trail drops 240 feet in elevation, much of it in one precipitous plunge down a crumbling rocky pitch. This is the only bad part of the trail because footing becomes unsure. Shards of rock slip and slide as you tread on them, in a place you would not want to fall. Sound footing can be found, but you have to pay attention and stay on the trail. The good news is, the trail dips into thick woods with that stirring, primeval feel. The rocky slope is the entrance to another sacred grove, guarded this time of year by vigilant mosquitoes. Ferns line the trail. The local spirit appeared to me in the form of an aged white scat filled with crunched bones and curved orange teeth. Passing a snag, I saw a flicker dart from a hole twenty-five feet overhead. I backed up forty feet and waited for the bird to return. Four minutes later, through binoculars, I saw it (or its mate) grasp the rim of the hole and flip itself inside in one motion with a great show of yellow under the tail feathers. Just then a man and a woman—the only people I saw on the trail all day—came hiking toward me from the Anvil, so I left my perch and went on to avoid making a disturbance near the nest.

Approaching the Anvil, the trail winds through ledgy

Twinflower along the Anvil Trail.

terrain peopled by stunted jack pines often only three to four feet tall. Huckleberry is thick beneath the pines, and sheep laurel beneath the huckleberry. The spot reminded me of the walk across Great Wass Island where, too, jack pine rules the ledges. Here was another aging scat, large, containing leaves and hair. Then the trail enters dark open woods of spruce and fir, and the treadway changes from granite to soft needles. Dipping slightly, it approaches the Anvil proper, then scales it by a series of wooded ledges. Rock-cap fern lines the short, rocky ascent. The site was as sacred as any I had come to on this hike, as beautiful and untouched. I resisted the temptation to give a name to the presence I felt in that place. Typically, when we confront a mystery, we give it a name, a voice, a form, a mind with motives and desires. We personify it, turning it into something we can understand. That is, we deify it, creating a god to meet our personal needs. Deity is mystery personified. Not so much to bring it to life as to help us to know who we are when we encounter it so we can respond in familiar ways. I prefer to stop short of deifying what I do not understand, to hold it in awareness in and for itself. That way I can give it the awe, wonder, and respect it deserves as a phenomenon without my tinkering with it. Holding back the drive to make it familiar by making it human, I meet it on its terms, not mine. If I can hold off trying to explain it long enough, curiosity often leads to admiration, which opens onto beauty and—if I hold off long enough—to love. I need more to love the Earth than understand it. Understanding reduces it to my level; love raises me from where I am to where I want to be. By welcoming mystery along the trail, I open myself to the continuing creativity of the universe, of which the natural world around me is at the forefront. Opening my awareness to it, I feel that creativity flow through me as I participate in it myself.

A sign on top of the Anvil points to **OVERLOOK**. A short spur trail through woods leads to an open ledge on the lip of a sixty-foot drop. In the immediate foreground, purple spruce cones hung from the ends of treetop branches at eye level. In the distance, the Precipice rises on Mount Desert Island across Frenchman Bay. Big Moose Island and the Navy base have the middle ground to themselves. Schoodic Head fills the view to the northwest. Every place that isn't sky or salt water is trees and more trees. This hiking loop does not peter out; it keeps going to the last.

The trail winds through sparse jack pine and spruce woods on top of the Anvil. I saw spring azure butterflies, dragonflies, another awesome wasp, more golden heather, and a junco trilling from the top of a spruce. Just past where I saw the junco, the trail begins its descent of the rocky south face, coming first to a great cleft eighty feet long, seven feet deep, and from one- to seven-feet wide—a gash in the granite. Native Australians would sing the history of such a place when they came to it on their walkabout: Junco Gap they would call it, a place of great healing power. Past the gap, I saw in another sprucetop a black-throated green warbler quietly singing as if to itself, but reaching the ears of an alien species nonetheless. Talk about gaps! In *The Songlines,* Chatwin relates that Aborigines exchange songs when they meet at a water hole. Barter is secondary. They cannot own the land, but they can own the songs they sing of the land. Songs are the hard currency of their trade. I thanked the warbler for his offering, and for my part of the bargain whistled a phrase from "This Land is Your Land."

Coming down off the Anvil among fern-topped boulders, I passed plants browsed by hares, blooming Canada May ruby, starflower in mint condition, and a three-foot patch of twinflower looking like pairs of old-fashioned glass lampshades, pink outside, deep purple within. Passing sprays of juniper, I came to the end of the trail at Wonsqueak Road at 1:25 p.m. There was so much to see, I took another twenty minutes getting to my car just down the road. Eider were drifting and flying, daisies waving, vetch clinging, wine-leaf cinquefoil bobbing. I took my time, reluctant to let the hike end. There were six other cars next to mine, four from Maine, one from Massachusetts, one from Pennsylvania—the same threesome that headed the list on Cadillac last week. Taking one last look as I started my car, I saw two guillemots scooting across the waves. Averting my gaze, I headed for home.

✺

50—DORR & KEBO MOUNTAINS LOOP

From Great Meadow
To Dorr Mountain summit, and back
   Up by Jesup and Dorr Mountain East Face trails
   Down by Dorr Mountain North Ridge
     and Kebo Mountain trails

4.8 miles, July 3, 1996

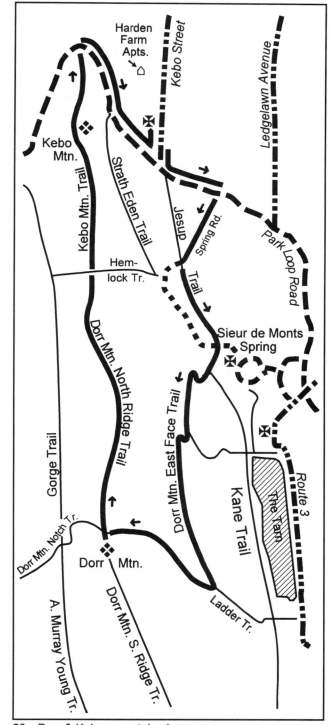

50—Dorr & Kebo mountains loop.

I do not hike in freezing rain, downpours, or thunderstorms. A low-pressure area was heading for Maine with thunderstorms and heavy rain predicted for July 4th. I made my Independence Day hike a day early, having only to deal with dense fog. Getting a chilly reception over the Gulf of Maine, warm air ahead of the approaching low cooled, forming banks of fog that smothered the coast. When I reached the top of Dorr Mountain, visibility was so bad I had trouble finding the summit cairn, a massive pile of stones heaped higher than my head. Beaded with small drops, my glasses looked like insect eyes. I felt like a bug dropped in a vanilla milkshake. Under the circumstances, what could I do but enjoy myself?

I started and ended at my apartment in the park's Harden Farm housing unit set between Kebo Mountain and the golf course. There was no need to start my car. Times and distances for different legs of the hike include:

Spring Road and Jesup Trail across Great Meadow
    (1.0 mile from Harden Farm; 1.5 hours),
Dorr Mountain East Face Trail to the summit
    (1.5 miles; 2.0 hours),
Dorr Mountain North Ridge Trail across Kebo Mountain
    (1.8 miles; 2.0 hours), and
Kebo Mountain trailhead to Harden Farm
    (0.5 mile; 0.25 hour).

Put together, the various legs made a 4.8-mile hike. With half an hour spent cruising around Sieur de Monts Spring, it took me almost six-and-a-half hours to make the loop at my bookish, write-it-all-down pace.

The rise from the Sieur de Monts springhouse (90 feet above sea level) to Dorr's summit (1,270 feet) is some 1,180 feet. The north ridge trail drops 980 feet to a low of 290 feet, then gains another 117 feet in reaching Kebo's 407-foot hump.

On Dorr and Kebo mountains there were no views to be seen other than miniature landscapes along the trail. But noises came through the fog with sound-bite clarity: ten hermit thrushes warming up their fifes; a wicha-wicha bird caroling its anthem again and again—*wicha-wicha, wicha-wicha, wicha-whee;* a parade of cars on Route 3 in the Gorge; a foghorn blaring twice every thirty seconds; boat horns blaring back, dueling with the foghorn and with each other; and from Kebo Valley, the soft *whik* of golf balls lofted into the fog (and perhaps down the fairway).

I gathered that many people I met on the trail hiked mainly for the view. When I asked if they had seen anything interesting, they replied with one voice that there was nothing to be seen. Yet I did meet forty-three hikers on my way up Dorr Mountain. Why did they hike on such a foggy day? I can't answer for them, but they were all in a hiking mode. Having come to Acadia on vacation, the occasion called for a hike. Perhaps they did it for exercise, more likely for

adventure. Like golf balls sent into the white unknown, they were driven by a powerful force. The urge to *do* something, to move, to get out of the car, to see something new. Every hiker seemed to be having a good time. When I asked how the hike was going, some were jubilant. "Great hike!" "What a day!" They seemed proud to be doing something exceptional, which is how I always feel when I hike. Our ancestors lived in nature for over three million years before in-

Steps on the Dorr Mountain East Face (Emery) Trail.

venting offices, schools, and halls of entertainment. Despite the way we lead our lives, we belong outdoors on the trail. That is what we are made for. Look at our legs, our stride, our arms that swing in time with our gait. Given our history, sitting in front of television screens and computer monitors is truly exceptional. Who feels comfortable preparing a child to lead such a life, much less leading it herself? Our bodies might as well end at the buttocks. Through genetic engineering we could sprout digits on our abdomens, and have modems wired to our vocal cords. Why go hiking in the fog? Because if we don't, we will lose the fog, as most of us have lost the starry night.

I asked most everyone I met on the trail one or two questions: Have you seen anything interesting? or, How is your hike going? The answers were variations on a theme.

"Nothing special, but it's pretty."

"Can't see much."

"Nothing but fog."

"Just clouds, lots of clouds."

"Foggy, but it's a nice hike."

"It's a bit too much with the slippery rock."

One couple said they never made it to the top, but didn't mind because they had reached other summits on other hikes.

A man hurrying down with a young boy said, "We don't

Dorr Mountain summit cairn.

want to leave the rest of the family down there too long."

Two young women told me they had seen a snake hole. I asked how they knew it was a snake hole. "It was awfully small," one of them said.

One mother seized upon me (notebook and pencil dangling from my neck) as an object lesson. Addressing her three young daughters she said, "Look, girls, you should write down what you see on our trip." I told them I thought it was enough to make the hike and, when they had children of their own, to take them for hikes as their parents had taken them.

One boy said, "You're almost there." I thanked him for the encouragement.

I met a woman with an infant snuggled to her breast, and later a man coming very slowly down the trail. I asked how his hike was going. He said, "Good. I'm slow because I'm diabetic. Last year on this trail I went into insulin shock." I asked if he wanted help. "No, I'm pacing myself. My wife is with me—you probably just met her with the baby." We talked for several minutes. He came from Scotland, Connecticut, and had climbed Dorr several times. He found it interesting that there was a trail from Dorr to the summit of Cadillac; he hadn't known that before. Some day he hoped to move to Mount Desert Island.

The last man I met was reaching the summit just as I was

starting down. His hair and T-shirt were drenched.

"Slippery. Not a very nice day," he said.

I didn't meet a soul on the north ridge trail, suggesting that even during months of peak visitation it is possible to find solitude in Acadia. At Sieur de Monts Spring, I found solitude at the George Dorr memorial next to the nature center. A green stone plaque set in a boulder bears this inscription:

> IN MEMORY OF
> GEORGE BUCKNAM DORR
> 1853–1944
> GENTLEMAN SCHOLAR
> LOVER OF NATURE
> FATHER OF THIS
> NATIONAL PARK
> STEADFAST IN HIS ZEAL
> TO MAKE THE BEAUTIES
> OF THIS ISLAND
> AVAILABLE TO ALL.

I think of George Dorr as the man who not only engineered the founding of Acadia National Park and served as its first superintendent, but who, in 1911, had the vision and savvy to protect the entire watersheds of Jordan Pond and Eagle Lake. He hoped to protect every watershed on Mount Desert Island, but the state legislature didn't go along with him on that. My meditation on George Dorr was cut short by a catbird landing at my feet. It carried a large insect in its beak, which, though it looked like a sacrificial offering, I did not assume was meant to honor either Mr. Dorr or myself. More likely the bird had a nest in thick bushes near the plaque and was trying to distract me before I found it. I took the hint and turned away.

With the Abbe Museum, nature center, and Wild Gardens of Acadia—three must-see attractions—in the vicinity, as well as trailheads in every direction, there were more people in the Sieur de Monts Spring area than I could cope with. I settled for a tally of the 44 license plates in the parking lot:

Maine—11, Massachusetts—8, New York—6, Connecticut—5; 2 each from Florida, Indiana, and Maryland; and 1 each from Idaho, New Hampshire, Pennsylvania, Rhode Island, Virginia, U.S. Government, Nova Scotia, and Quebec.

Many of the blooming plants I saw were not native to the area either, or to the continent for that matter, particularly those along roads near the golf course. Yellow and orange hawkweed are alien species, as are daisy, clover (yellow, white, and red), buttercup, stitchwort, common St. Johnswort, sheep sorrel, smooth hawksbeard, and yarrow. Before reaching the Spring Road (formerly the road to the spring, now a gravel path across Great Meadow), I saw more aliens than natives in bloom. The five natives I did recognize were whorled loosestrife with yellow stars pointing to the horizon in four directions, yellow rattle, bluets (a.k.a. Quaker ladies or innocence), blackberry, and shinleaf pyrola looking shiny and new. Crossing Great Meadow on sections of the Spring Road and Jesup Trail, I saw several other native species in bloom: pink and white spires of meadowsweet just bursting open, tiny marsh bedstraw, common cinquefoil, yellow cow

Pitch pines in the fog, Dorr Mountain.

lily (spatterdock) with golf-ball-size flower buds, and a single blue flag iris. A patch of sensitive fern marked the beginning of the Spring Road where it turns off the loop road. On Dorr Mountain I saw great stretches of lambkill (sheep laurel) in pink bloom, wine-leaf cinquefoil running along cracks in the granite, yellow bush honeysuckle everywhere I looked except the actual summit, mountain sandwort, staghorn sumac, witherod (wild raisin), and the last two bunchberry plants I expected to see blooming this year. Blueberry and huckleberry fruit were swelling and ripening. Why hike in the fog? One reason is to encourage trailside flowers to bloom in our awareness.

I heard a robin and a woodpecker as I was starting out from Harden Farm, saw gulls and chickadees, and a great many sheet webs spread like drying handkerchiefs along the way. I saw two swamp sparrows in Great Meadow, one singing on a dead branch, the other gleaning insects among the grass. A male common yellowthroat came within a few feet of me, looking like a masked highwayman as it snatched insects among alders and gray birches along the trail. A green frog twanged its one-string harp as I passed. On the ferny, birchy Jesup Trail I heard a hermit thrush in the offing and saw a female redstart overhead in a maple crown. At Sieur de Monts Spring I watched a catbird pluck waterstriders from the stream rising near the springhouse, probably the same bird that distracted me at the Dorr memorial. On the Dorr Mountain East Face Trail I heard another robin and two more hermit thrushes, saw a mourning dove, and

found a fox scat on a coping stone overlooking the Gorge. Two sixteenth-inch spiders huddled at the centers of their respective four-inch orb webs, but the one small brown moth I saw was nowhere near those traps. I heard the wicha-wicha bird on the north ridge trail, and three more hermit thrushes. A chipmunk ran stone-to-stone ahead of me in oak woods on Kebo Mountain. I smelled fox scent near a cairn, and found a leaf-filled scat. Sheet webs covered the ground under pitch pines and oaks. In one fifty-square-foot area I counted twenty-seven webs. Like innkeepers, the resident spiders waited expectantly in their entranceways, but business was slow. They caught fog droplets and little else. At the end of the hike I came across one slug in the Park Loop Road, and found deer prints in the mud near my apartment.

To represent all that life in a single coat of arms, I would include the following devices:

Hike Bird	Hermit Thrush
Hike Spider	Sheet-web Weaver
Hike Flower	Bush Honeysuckle
Hike Mammal	Eastern Chipmunk
Hike Amphibian	Green Frog
Hike Tree	Pitch Pine
Hike Fern	Royal Fern
Hike Motto	"Rising fogs prevail."

Each principal leg of the hike told a different story in woods, water, and rock. On the first leg across Great Meadow from the loop road to Sieur de Monts Spring on sections of the Spring Road and Jesup Trail, there were no rocks to speak of, but plenty of water and woods. Passing through an extensive wetland, the trail is close to water the whole way. Here the Spring Road is a birch- and alder-lined ridge of filled land running across the meadow with water on both sides. This is duck and blackbird country, where you are apt to see a variety of birds—kingbirds, wood ducks, yellowthroats, yellow warblers, great blue herons, tree swallows, among many others. From where the Spring Road and Jesup Trail cross, the Jesup Trail runs over slightly higher ground on the edge of the meadow through open birch and maple woods. This is one of the most beautiful sections of trail in the park, made possible by a split-cedar bogwalk in some seventy-eight sections that keeps your feet dry under all but the wettest conditions. The trail is lined with spectacular ferns—including royal, cinnamon, and long beech—which, combined with slender trees on both sides, the wildlife they support, and the walkway itself, make for a great (if short and level) hike.

The Dorr Mountain East Face Trail (or Emery Trail) is the primary route to the summit from the Sieur de Monts Spring area. With solid granite steps held in place by coping stones, and stone culverts carrying runoff beneath the treadway, it is a classic Acadian trail, providing solid footing for the hiker while protecting both soil and vegetation. At least for the first 700-foot rise in elevation, to a little past where the ladder trail comes in. From there to the top, the treadway is whatever material is underfoot—mainly sloping ledge or stony soil— which does little to protect hikers from slipping, or thin soils from eroding. In several places the trail has cut a fifteen-inch rut into the soil, creating a streambed inviting water to wash away more soil every time it rains. It looks like the trailmakers ran out of steam at the 700-foot level, or outran their supply lines. Up to that point, the trail is spectacular; after that, it is less than mediocre (though the terrain it passes through is as spectacular as ever).

The lower part of the east face trail makes excellent use of local materials and terrain in rising at a brisk rate up the slope. Stepped all the way, it winds across ledges by a series of switchbacks, and scales a talus slope by an impressive run of steps mined from the slope itself. The trail winds through narrow clefts in the ledge, providing intimate views of the geometry of granite bedrock. Attaining the rim of the east face, the trail hugs the top of the cliff in a long gradual traverse through birch, oak, and pitch pine, then rises more directly toward the summit through pitch pine woods. At first the upper section mimics the ladder trail by following the base of a fifteen-to-twenty-five-foot cliff, then it crosses increasingly broad, sloping ledges alternating with patches of thin, stony soil. Cairns mark the trail, but designer cairns erected by visitors are sometimes misleading. In places the trail does not seem to be marked at all, so you have to trust your internal guidance system to interpret what signs there are. The east face trail attains the summit ridge at a cairn marking the start of the Dorr Mountain Notch Trail which leads to the summit of Cadillac Mountain. The actual summit of Dorr is a short walk south of that crossing through stunted pitch pines and open ledges. Why hike in the fog? There is no better way to focus your attention on the trail instead of the beckoning view.

The Dorr Mountain North Ridge Trail descends gradually over the glacial ramp smoothed by ice streaming from the Laurentian Highlands twenty-some millennia ago. Footing is solid through pitch pine woods, which grow taller as the trail descends. The trail is less worn than the east face trail, and less eroded. Blooming sheep laurel, meadowsweet, and bush honeysuckle added touches of pink and yellow to the trailside. Abruptly oak, birch, and popple mix with the pitch pines. Charred stumps of large trees cut after the 1947 fire crouch like old tombstones in spindly woods. Smooth cobbles and boulders take over the treadway, making for hard traveling. As the trail drops more steeply, white pine and hemlock appear. Then oak takes over, and lichen-clad boulders crowd the stumps. The woods are less than fifty years old, but crusty boulders make the landscape seem ancient. I shadowed a wheezing hermit thrush for several hundred feet without glimpsing it once. Except for runoff, the north ridge trail is dry, meeting running water only once where the trail bottoms out in the saddle between Dorr and Kebo.

Crossing the Hemlock Trail, the north ridge trail continues on over the three humps of Kebo Mountain. The boulder field continues, too, and the hard traveling. In a few spots, lack of a worn path makes the trail difficult to follow. Rising up a stony slope through oak woods, the trail quickly reaches the first hump in a stand of slender birches topped by two windswept white pines. Here I heard three hermit thrushes caroling independently—a concert of three anar-

Pitch pine cone and needles, Dorr Mountain.

chists. The effect was spirited if ungoverned, an anthem for Independence Day. Moving right along, the trail drops slightly, then winds through beech, birch, and oak woods to rise up a bouldery slope to the granite ledges of Kebo's middle hump, where the boulder field ends and pitch pines predominate. Approaching the hump, I watched a chipmunk hopping boulder-to-boulder ahead of me, the first and only non-primate mammal I met in over six hours. If I had blinked, I would have missed it.

Visitors who come to Acadia for the wildlife are apt to be disappointed. A chipmunk? Take me to your moose and deer, your bear and fox! Hiking every week in the park, I have gone months without seeing more than red squirrels and perhaps a porcupine. With troops of people on the trail, and unleashed dogs bounding either side, we have created a zone of domesticity whose chief occupant is ourselves. Acadia has been taken over as recreational habitat for primates. What we see when we come here is primarily ourselves and our pets. To see other species, the best strategy is to go somewhere unaccompanied and sit still for an hour or two or three, giving the natives a chance to emerge when they feel comfortable. I felt lucky to see a chipmunk when our territories overlapped. Wild animals have learned they will live longer if they stay out of our way. On Kebo I saw a bird dart into the distance at my approach, leaving a pine branch gently swaying. To most native inhabitants, I am anathema. I study the runes of swaying branches to find out if I have any neighbors at all.

Spread with pitch pine needles, the Kebo Mountain Trail takes on a special quality as it passes over the middle and northern humps. The landscape gets down to basics—granite ledge, pitch pine, blueberry, and huckleberry. Misty sheet

The Jesup Trail north of Sieur de Monts Spring.

webs covered the ground, glowing like galaxies spread through space. A universe unto itself, Kebo is one of the lesser peaks that strengthens the character of the park. It used to bear a lot of hiking traffic from Bar Harbor, but now cut off by the golf course and private houselots, it is isolated and relatively untrodden. On clear days it offers views of the Porcupine Islands and Great Meadow, but you do not hike Kebo for the view. You go there to share in the integrity of a place that thrives on hard times. With its spare but hardy landscape, it is the kind of place James Agee, author of *Let Us Now Praise Famous Men,* might have written about, and his collaborator, Walker Evans, photographed. There is no unequal distribution of wealth on Kebo, no division between the haves and have-nots. It is a bare-bones kind of place with a beauty all its own favoring clear ideas and bold perceptions.

Coming off Kebo's granite ramp, the trail dips sharply

into mixed woods to end abruptly at the loop road just short of the golf course. I walked along the road a ways, then cut through birch and popple woods to my apartment at Harden Farm. Deer prints reminded me whose woods they really were.

Walks on foggy days clear my head. On Dorr Mountain, I saw that we celebrate our independence while it is our dependence on the natural world we should remember because it makes us who we are. We landed on these shores free men (some of us), assuming the right to take what we wanted, to amass and distribute wealth, to multiply without limit—collectively ravishing what we thought was a "new world," but was in fact the same old world that had cared for us all along. Severing political ties to Europe, we asserted our freedoms and handed ourselves a tablet of inalienable rights, while we would have done better to mind the allegiances and responsibilities binding us to our one green Earth. The Constitution was written by men of property to defend what they claimed to own. Our nation is founded on the myth that men can own—even if piecemeal—the world. To own is to rule; to rule is to control; to control is to destroy. When it came to self-rule, we got it wrong. We took, but gave nothing back, not even awe and respect to the source of our good fortune. We sold our birthright to inherit the Earth for wealth in this lifetime. We forgot about the context that makes life possible, our earthly environment. Is that something to mark with fireworks and parades? Better we go for a walk in the fog and commune with wicha-wicha birds and all they represent. That sets off fireworks in the mind, which is where they belong.

✸

51—ACADIA MOUNTAIN LOOP

From Acadia Mountain parking area
To Acadia Mountain summit, and back
  Up by west end of Acadia Mountain Trail
  Back by east end of Acadia Mountain Trail
    and Man o' War Brook Fire Road

3.0 miles, July 11, 1996

I met five spirit guides on my Acadia Mountain hike, one for each section of the trail. A hermit thrush in the path just off Route 102 told me things would get better away from the noisy highway. When the din of traffic followed me up the Acadia Mountain Trail, a yellow-rumped warbler plucking worms said to keep going, I was on the right track. A junco on the ridge leading toward Somes Sound said, "What noise, where?" On the way down to Man o' War Brook, a sharp-shinned hawk shooing three turkey vultures from the airspace above its nest demonstrated that challenge is the mother of skill and grace. And a wood frog by the fire road reminded me that the good life is lived close to the earth.

The spirit guides helped me rise above the commotions and alarms of daily life in a summer resort. Waves of infernal combustion engines migrate to Mount Desert Island from every corner of the continent in July and August—cars, trucks, buses, motorcycles, and recreational vehicles of all sorts. Streaming through narrow mountain valleys, they raise a collective ruckus sounding off valley walls, producing a discordant drone that fills the woods. Hikes near routes 3, 198, and 102 on Mount Desert Island can be noisy, subtle calls of warblers and thrushes going unheard in the din. Opening myself to nature, I opened myself to unnature as well. Amplified by a brisk west wind, traffic noise on this hike seemed particularly bad. It followed me until I passed the summit and headed along the ridge toward Somes Sound. Feeling oppressed by the roar, I turned surly and took a long time getting into the hike. Even on the ridge, a chainsaw screamed from Hall Quarry like brawling cats, breaking the spell of the place. Excessive horsepower taunted me from Somes Sound, too, where cruisers and speedboats scratched dagger-sharp wakes. The hulking *Excellence* from Washington, D.C., hove up the sound, a private water hotel with jet ski on deck. These distractions were not enough to ruin the hike, but I had to work hard to maintain my focus. Sometimes I got stung: where I saw a white mushroom lodged on a pitch pine branch, I thought some squirrel had stashed it for lunch. When I got closer I found no mushroom but a wad of toilet paper. The sharp-shinned hawk advised me to stop grum-

bling and get on with my hike.

The loop up Acadia Mountain and back by the fire road is about three miles long. I took six hours and fifteen minutes to go the distance, but spent as much time sitting on granite ledges peering at the surrounding scene as actually walking. From the Acadia Mountain parking area on Route 102, the trail rises 500 feet to the 681-foot "summit" (the peak has several summits at roughly the same elevation),

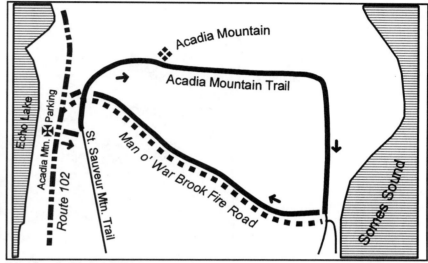

51—Acadia Mountain loop.

then drops to sea level at the overlook where Man o' War Brook sprays onto the shore. My thermometer read 68° when I left my apartment a little before eight, and 80° when I got back at two-thirty. The day was clear and breezy, with more sunshine than I'd seen in two weeks. Mine was the only car in the parking area when I set out, but there were twenty-three other cars at the end of the hike, ten from Maine, three each from Massachusetts and New York, with single cars from Alabama, Connecticut, Louisiana, Maryland, Vermont, Virginia, and Quebec. I met forty-nine other hikers on the trail, and saw two dozen more in the distance. I met only one solo hiker in six hours; most people were traveling in pairs and small family groups, the sexes hiking in about equal numbers.

Unlike most ridges in the park, Acadia Mountain runs east and west across the path of the glacier. The trail rises in about a mile to the summit ridge from Route 102, crosses the ridge and descends to Man o' War Brook in a second mile and, with a short side trip to view the falls, returns to the highway by way of the fire road in a final mile. Dividing each of the first two miles into two shorter sections, I thought of the hike in five distinct parts. Part one passed through woods from the parking area to where the trail crosses the fire road; part two rose up the wooded slope from the fire road to the summit; part three crossed the granite summit ridge west to east; part four descended steeply over granite terraces to the brook; and part five ran at a slight grade through mixed woods from the brook to the highway, largely along the fire road.

I was so distracted by traffic noise during the first part of the hike, I noticed only the most obvious features: a boulder that looked like a huge popover, a stand of red pine, sheep laurel in pink bloom, mosquitoes, a downy woodpecker showing four fledglings how to feed themselves (they wanting only to be fed), and a hermit thrush in the trail ahead. Crossing a stream draining the northwestern slope of St. Sauveur Mountain, the trail comes to the fire road, where the Acadia Mountain Trail begins.

The second part was longer and steeper, rising 440 feet in six-tenths of a mile over granite outcrops and ledges. Like wolves following a troika, traffic sounds pursued me up the slope. My main thought was to get away from that noise, so I went faster than I usually do. In passing I noticed large white pine, red pine with purple bark, striped maple, red oak, Northern white cedar, and, on the upper slopes, scrub oak and pitch pine. The scrub oak is unusual for Acadia in being far north of its usual range (the sandy barrens of New Jersey and points south), and in growing primarily on the south slopes of St. Sauveur and Acadia mountains. Sheep laurel was the only bloom I saw on this part of the hike. Juniper and kinnikinnick were covered with

Acadia Mountain Trail.

ripening berries. Morning sunlight glinted on strands of spider silk strung through the woods. I heard a hermit thrush twice, and saw two yellow-rumped warblers gleaning insects among the leaves. What struck me most about the warblers was their silence; they had what I wanted. On the ledges I saw several dragonflies, and watched a cormorant spiral higher and higher on a column of air as if it were a hawk, though its rubbery wings gave it away as a pretender. Views on the upper ledges opened onto Echo Lake lying blue and serene at the base of Beech Cliff, backed by Beech and Mansell mountains to the west, and the pale blue Camden Hills across Penobscot Bay.

At the summit, the view opened to the east onto Somes Sound and Norumbega Mountain, with Sargent, Penobscot, and Cadillac to the rear. Youngs and McFarland hills lay to the north, with Schoodic and the Black Hills across Frenchman Bay, and Lead Mountain in Township 28 on the hori-

zon. I perched for half an hour on top of the cliff overlooking the valley of Man o' War Brook and the north slope of St. Sauveur, watching for soaring hawks but seeing mainly soaring trees. It was a sparkling summer day, and the islands between Mount Desert and the Gulf shone chlorophyll green. Through binoculars I made out Mount Desert Rock with its light tower and dwelling floating like a ceremonial barge far at sea, though well below the horizon. I joined a couple that had passed me earlier on the trail, now sitting on granite cushions, binoculars poised, leaning into the view.

"Is this what you came for?" I asked.

"Sure is!" the woman said.

They wanted to see an osprey, but settled for looking at gulls following a lobster boat. I counted fourteen power boats and nineteen sails.

The third part of the hike wound along the summit ridge among pitch pine and scrub oak on a granite treadway smoothed by the glacier. Infant acorns no more than three-eighths-of-an-inch across flared like miniature bells. Here were a few cinquefoil blooms (white), sheep laurel (deep pink), and bush honeysuckle (yellow). Juniper, blueberry, and kinnikinnick were doing their thing, turning air and water into berries. Meeting two women scanning their surroundings through binoculars, their big dog firmly anchored to a rock, I asked if they were enjoying themselves.

"Absolutely!" one of them said.

I heard a crow and a hermit thrush call from the valley below, saw hornets dancing among clumps of pitch pine needles, three dozen brown moths floating in a puddle, a junco singing to the blue sky, a white admiral patrolling the wind. I counted seven dikes on Acadia Mountain, ranging from four inches wide to thirteen feet. But best of all I found silence. I felt as if a splinter had been tweezed from beneath my nail, a cinder removed from my eye, a stone shaken out of my shoe. It was *quiet*. QUIET! Quiet. Away from the road, nature recovered its voice. Acadia was its old self, and I was mine. That's when my senses fully opened and the hike truly began.

I perched at the eastern end of the summit ridge, this time for almost an hour, and asked the landscape what it held for me. It answered with the voice of a pileated woodpecker from the valley, and with the squeal of gulls on the sound. Seeing my binoculars, a couple asked me about the birds.

"What birds?"

"Those three big ones behind you."

Turning, I saw three turkey vultures surfing on the wind about a hundred and fifty feet from where I sat. They played in the vicinity for the next hour, making a pass along the ridge, then circling back over the valley, passes and circles in endless variation at different heights in different formations. Sometimes there were four, sometimes two or one, but usually the trio stuck together. Once one vulture swept down the valley at treetop level, acting for all the world like a marsh hawk, its shadow undulating as branches rose and fell away, but with its carrion-eating soul on an even keel. Riding the wind, the vultures flapped only now and then, a single downthrust in which their wingtips almost touched beneath them, then they locked again in their trademark dihedral, wings uplifted in a gesture that seemed to ask the audience to hold its applause.

Turkey vultures are newcomers to Acadia, coming up from the south to help crows and ravens clean up the mounting pile of bodies along our highways. I first saw them nine or ten years ago when they were a great rarity. Now they are regular visitors, often seen rocking along Acadia's ridges and cliffs

Kinnikinnick (bearberry).

on rising winds. They are not good at catching live prey, so feed largely on a diet of carrion. Acadia's bird list has recently been revised to acknowledge their presence from April through September. Perhaps they are harbingers of global warming, telling us something we don't want to hear.

However we feel about them, turkey vultures are magnificent fliers when the wind is up. I watched them for a long time, trying to figure out what they were doing on Acadia Mountain. Hunting? Playing? Performing some sort of ritual dance? Whatever they were up to, they were a powerful presence in the air, in a brittle kind of way. With a wingspan of almost six feet, they are an imposing bird. They don't build nests, so lay eggs in natural features of the landscape such as rocky outcrops and hollow trees. Do they breed on Mount Desert Island? If not now, someday they will. Think of it, the vultures of Acadia. And what effect do

they have on other birds? Certainly the two hawks I saw did not like having them so near.

Watching through binoculars, I followed a vulture over Somes Sound, then picked up a sharp-shinned hawk flying from Eagle Cliff on St. Sauveur to woods on the south face of Acadia Mountain, where it swooped down among the trees. Had it seen prey at that distance? Watching it pester the vultures later on, I decided it might have a nest in those woods.

A small rufous hawk with no evident patterning on its tail also put on a good show, acting like the peregrine's little cousin, which it was—an American kestrel. Climbing and diving on the wind, scurrying cliff-to-cliff, it made the turkey vultures seem like lumbering dinosaurs. It kept making cameo appearances, but disappeared as quickly as it came. I never saw where it went. I didn't see it hover as kestrels are wont to do over their prey, so was not sure what the acrobatics were all about. I ask nature questions, it replies with questions of its own.

By eleven o'clock when I started down toward Man o' War Brook on the fourth—and steepest—leg of my hike, more people were on the trail. When I asked if they were enjoying their hike, they spoke with one voice:

"Yup."

"Great day!"

"Great, isn't it!"

"Great day, finally."

"Best day in two weeks!"

A couple from Minneapolis said Acadia had the best day-hiking in the country. They were making plans to come back in the fall.

When I stood aside to let a couple coming up the trail get by, the man asked:

"Are you local?"

I said I thought so, "Here I am."

"Where can we get a good painting of this?"

"You mean the view?" I said, sweeping my hand toward Somes Sound and the islands.

"Everything, all of it," he said, looking west toward the cliffs. "We're on our honeymoon and want to remember what we've seen."

"It's so beautiful!" she said.

I said I didn't know where they could get a painting of

this exact vista, but suggested they buy a set of Acadia place mats so they could eat breakfast here every morning.

He told me they lived in Cincinnati, and had taken a trip to Hawaii last year.

"But this is prettier than Hawaii," he said.

I said I was on an extended honeymoon in Acadia myself, and had decided never to leave. They knew what I meant.

The eastern end of the Acadia Mountain Trail falls (or

Flying Mountain, Valley Peak, and Valley Cove from Acadia Mountain Trail.

rises) by a series of stepped ledges covered with juniper, kinnikinnick, pitch pine, and oak. Several unofficial spur trails branch off to outcrops overlooking the sound. The honeymooners were right, it is a pretty trail, one of the most beautiful in the park. It has views of woods, mountains, islands, cliffs, the sound, and open sky. Here, too, the elements that shaped Acadia are on display or, more accurately, their handiwork is. The granite is beautiful in its own right, having been roughed out by the glacier, and patiently finished by millennia of fine chipping by water, wind, and ice. Yes, you know you are in Acadia on this trail, but you have to earn your own passage. Up or down, these terraces will stretch even the longest legs, and make you think where to place your next step.

Abruptly, the trail dips into a stand of Northern white cedar, levels off on a mat of twisted roots, and comes to

Man o' War Brook, spanned by cross-planks nailed between two poles. Fed by weeks of rain collected in the wooded swamp between Acadia and St. Sauveur mountains, the brook ran clear and cold, looking more like April than July. A couple coming the other way joined me in the middle of the bridge.

"Last water you'll see on the trail," I told them.

"Our canteens are full," the man said, "we won't need it."

"I didn't mean for drinking," I said, "more for cooling."

"Been drinking it all my life," he said, "I'm immune."

"You play the odds," I said. "I never touch it myself."

"You got him there," the woman said, "he's a risk taker."

"Life's a lot of fun if you go at it right," he said.

They went up the mountain, I began the fifth part of my hike, turning down the spur trail to the shore over almost sixty steps that had the look of CCC handiwork to take a look at the falls where the brook drops into the sound. Barnacles! Mussels! What strange creatures to meet along the trail. The tide was out far enough to let me scramble over the rocks to view the falls, which fanned out into several good trickles before spraying on the shore.

Up from the brook, the trail comes to a crossing:

VALLEY PEAK 1.2 MI.; ST. SAUVEUR MTN. .8 MI. [south]
VALLEY COVE 1.0 MI.; FLYING MTN. 1.3 MI. [east]
MAN O' WAR TRUCK RD. .1 MI. [west]
ACADIA MTN. .7 MI. [north, the way I had come].

I turned west and shortly came to the Robinsons' dooryard with its wayward apple trees, blooming vetch (purple), buttercup (yellow), yarrow (white), hawkweed (yellow), and common heal-all (blue). Acadia Mountain is shown on old maps as Robinson Mountain. The family undoubtedly drank from the brook in their day, and did their best to clear the stony land. They would be amazed by the parade of summer visitors now passing through their yard. The house is long gone, with the site marked only by the ending of the road, a few stones and apple trees, and *H. Robinson* or *The Hermitage* on dusty maps. Standing in the turnaround, I got a strong whiff of fox scent that reminded me I am never as alone as I might think I am.

Being low in the valley, the Man o' War Brook Fire Road was much wetter than the slope I had just come down. I saw several sorts of fern—bracken, sensitive, interrupted, and oak. But the true story of the terrain was told by trees rising above the road—cedar, fir, white pine, red and white spruce, maple, birch, and a great many snags. Tall, mixed woods, beloved by turkey vultures, sharp-shinned hawks, and wayfarers looking for new worlds. Having crossed the valley of Man o' War Brook side-to-side, end-to-end many times studying it as a representative watershed, I knew the terrain as well as I knew any in Acadia, but in my muscles and in my bones, not in words. I have walked where the Robinsons walked and shared some of the sights they knew, which is like walking into an old photograph much as Alice went through the looking glass. Most of what we see is a reflection of the world we make for ourselves; other worlds exist beyond the mirror, but the trick is in getting there. First we have to escape the traffic we take so for granted on the highways of life. We need guides to show us the way, guides who live back of other mirrors and lead other lives. If we walk where they walk and look where they look, perhaps we can glimpse some of the images that make up their life experience. We spend the first half of our lives building a world for ourselves, and the second half trying to transcend what we have built, knowing it is not the world we want. Behind every mirror, nature is the encompassing limit of all our worlds, the ultimate world which, if we try hard enough, and live long enough, we finally discover is the one we have been in all along. People keep pointing somewhere else, but heaven is where we are born.

I came to a long patch of twinflower on the edge of the fire road, mostly gone by but a few still in bloom. Sunlight through trees shone on a scattering of club moss, which I wanted to photograph. Bending to get a closer look, I startled a wood frog, which took a small hop, then sat looking into the middle distance while I crouched above it studying its folds, speckles, warm brown skin, and black eye shadows. I wanted to know what *it* saw, what the world looked like to a wood frog. On second thought, maybe I knew enough already about my own folds, speckles, and shadows. I wasn't ready for that much transcendence. Stepping back, I left the frog behind its mirror, contemplating a world of its own.

To summarize my hike up Acadia Mountain:

Hike Amphibian	Wood Frog
Hike Bird	Turkey Vulture
Hike Tree	Scrub Oak
Hike Flower	Sheep Laurel
Hike Fruit	Kinnikinnick Berry
Hike Motto	"Better than Hawaii."

Nearing Route 102, I came out from behind the mirror I had slipped into on the mountain and heard the drone of traffic loud as ever. In fact I even got into my own car and drove into the stream of whizzing metal, adding my four-cylinder growl and rubberized whine to the symphony of civilized beings. Now other wayfarers faced the challenge of fleeing from the noise *I* made. Where I had been helped by thrush, warbler, sparrow, hawk, and frog, I knew they would find spirit guides of their own and have a great hike.

❁

52—PEMETIC MOUNTAIN LOOP
From Bubble Rock parking area
To Pemetic Mountain summit, and back
  Up by Pemetic Mountain (Ravine) Trail
  Down by Pemetic Mountain South Ridge,
    west end of Pond, and Jordan Pond East Side
    trails; and Jordan Pond Canoe Carry
              3.6 miles, July 17, 1996

Hiking the Olympian heights and terraces of Pemetic Mountain, I gave myself to a trail meditation along these lines:

The Olympic games start Friday in Atlanta. Originally honoring the Olympian Zeus, Greek god of weather and the bright sky, the games are now a multi-billion-dollar commercial enterprise honoring corporate profits and national pride. Athletes from nearly 200 countries will strive for gold medals, honoring Zeus with a view of their backsides as they race down the course. Times are hard for the old gods. Sky, earth, and nature have lost their sanctity. Zeus, once the cloudgatherer, raingiver, thunderer, and chief of the Olympians, is now a homeless and discredited relic. He is a has-been, like his consort the earth goddess who, quickened by rain, bore all living things in her loamy womb. It was she who gave us grain, cattle, culture, and ourselves. Now she is a bag lady on the streets, gleaning refuse and crumbs for a living. Religion has lost its central focus on nature, weather, and the living earth. The old sky and earth gods get no respect. The faithful have lowered their gaze from luminous and fruitful nature gods to national and corporate overlords demanding their money *and* their life. The games, now held for lesser purposes, give us a mirror image of our impoverished beliefs.

That may not seem a very Acadian line of thought, but hiking through some of the most dramatic and beautiful terrain in the park, I felt I was walking on Mount Olympus itself in the realm of the true gods. With Cadillac Mountain on the east, the massive ridge of Penobscot and Sargent on the west, the Jordan Cliffs, Jordan Pond, and the Bubbles in the foreground, I walked in a timeless world half-green, half-granite, as if I were following in Zeus's footsteps as he gathered swirling clouds about him and hurled lightning to herald the coming rain. In fact, on the summit I was overtaken by dark clouds from the northwest, and it did shower for fifteen minutes. But then the sky cleared again, and I watched five turkey vultures circle overhead, until they drifted off toward Sargent, leaving one vulture circling the summit. But, no, it didn't look like a vulture. Through binoculars I saw it was a bald eagle, probably the reason the vultures had taken off. Come to pick Prometheus's liver, no doubt, as punishment for giving fire to humankind against Zeus's express order.

You can't expect thoughts on the trail to be politically correct. Acadia has a mind of its own which affects all who stray from their accustomed ways. On the mountain you think mountainous thoughts. The terms in which you think are drawn from the terrain you pass through. I had vultures and eagles on the brain, granite and scrubby trees, rain and thunder. My mind became one with Acadia's. In *Hidden Heart of the Cosmos*,[*] Brian Swimme says, "each person lives in the center of the cosmos," and, "the actual origin of the universe is where you live your life." If Albert Einstein had universal thoughts when he drew up his theory of special relativity, all of us think universally when we place ourselves at the center of our creativity. We can think small, but we can also think big and think for Earth, for stars, for systems of stars. Surrendering to the will of Acadia is a step in the right direction, out and away from self toward the cosmic mind.

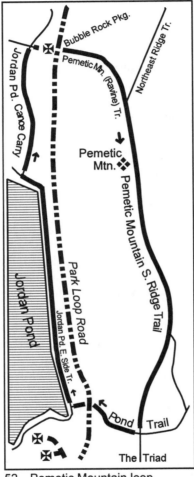

52—Pemetic Mountain loop.

I don't hold any more with new age thinking than with old age thinking, but I do believe that as the old gods die out we have an opportunity to ask the universe what it intends for us as creators of the now. When I listen closely, I hear a voice telling me to break free of the cultural cocoon my society would weave around me, to dwell in the natural world consciously and deliberately, to experience the diversity and integrity of that world, and to revere it as a miracle without equal or substitute.

Openness to natural experience, wonder, awe, respect, and reverence—these are the tools of universal creativity. Everywhere I go, I find sacred ground, ground that should

not be profaned for the sake of glory, power, or wealth because its sanctity and its beauty, once destroyed, are lost forever. Who are we to ruin what we cannot replace, to spoil one square inch of the universe? As creators, our job is to replenish and improve the Earth, not ravish it. In nature, that goes without saying—every species leaves the world a better place because its descendants depend on that progression. With us, teeming hominids that we are, we act as if now were forever, and we breed, hoard wealth, and sap Earth's resources for our personal *dis*tinction at the cost of others' *ex*tinction. We are far better at destruction than creation because destruction—like hammering on a watch when we were kids—takes little control and less thought.

Are these the reflections of a wayfarer ambling the trails of Acadia? Of one wayfarer, yes. I own them as part of my experience on Pemetic Mountain. My heaven contains no natural-born deities, only projections I have placed there myself. Voices come to me out of the blue of the sky and white of the cloud, voices from the mysteries that I have personified so I can talk to my own reflection, much as a ventriloquist talks to his dummy. Hiking is not all outward and upward; it is inward and downward as well. Behind every scene is the persona of the hiker with her stock ideas, images, expectations, perceptions, aspirations, memories, emotions, intuitions, behaviors, grasp of situations, and spiritual strivings. Each of us sees the world from a limited range of perspectives, one at a time. There are no impartial observers, selfless scientists or judges, no hikers wholly open to the landscape around them. We are who we are, product of our heritage and experience. On Pemetic I was a child of my times, seeker of natural truth, believer in continuing revelation—which I would have you believe even as I describe encounters with deities I installed on Olympus myself.

A hike into Acadia is a hike into the universe, and the hiker is left to sort out the consequences on her own. You set out for a place you thought you knew—and end up on Mount Olympus. Hiking up the Jordan Pond Canoe Carry near the end of my loop, I met a woman coming the other way. She had set out from Jordan Pond House for the Jordan Cliffs, but missed the trail and ended up on the south ridge of Penobscot Mountain. Looking for the other end of the cliffs trail, she had followed Deer Brook down to the pond, then taken the Bubble Gap Trail to the top of South Bubble. I met her coming down from there. She had a map with her, but it didn't seem to match the terrain where she found herself. I pointed out where she was.

"This is not where I meant to go," she said.

"Life is like that," I said.

"Sure is," she said. "So much for maps."

She told me she was a cultural anthropologist from California who had been planning to visit Acadia for twenty years. She had recently hiked the Half Dome Trail in Yosemite, which she had found very exciting.

---

[*]Brian Swimme, *Hidden Heart of the Cosmos*. Maryknoll, NY: Orbis Books, 1996.

"This is different," she said.

"How?" I asked.

"More serene. That's why I hike—for serenity."

I told her that for someone who hadn't been where she thought she was for most of the day, she didn't seem upset.

"You set out for one place and end up someplace else, what's wrong with that? You have to keep moving."

As one who had set out for Pemetic and found Olympus, I knew what she meant. We continued our hikes, she toward the pond, I up the carry.

The loop I made included five trails, or sections of trails. Starting at the Bubble Rock parking area on the loop road, I took the Pemetic Mountain (Ravine) Trail to the summit (0.6 mile), the Pemetic Mountain South Ridge Trail down (1.4 miles), the Pond Trail to Jordan Pond (0.3 mile), the Jordan Pond East Side Trail to the foot of South Bubble (0.8 mile), and the Jordan Pond Canoe Carry back to the parking area (0.5 mile), for a total of about 3.6 miles in 5 hours and 45 minutes. The rise in elevation from the parking area to the summit is 790 feet, the drop from the summit to Jordan Pond 963 feet, with a final rise along the carry of another 173 feet. I started at 1:00 p.m. and was back by 6:45 p.m. on a beautiful summer day, the temperature peaking in the low 80s.

With the vacation season at its height, I was surprised to meet only sixteen people on the trail. All but one were having a good time. I talked with several of them at some length, exchanging trail adventures and information. A couple coming down the Pemetic Mountain Trail as I was starting out told me it was sunny, breezy, and cool on top. They had come over the Triad from Jordan Pond House.

"I'd rather come down this trail than go up," the woman said, referring to the steep and stony slope.

My own preference is just the opposite. When it comes to Acadia's steeper trails—Cadillac Mountain West Face, Norumbega (Goat) Trail, Grandgent—I find it easier and less jarring going up than coming down. On this hike I had deliberately chosen my direction so I would go up the Pemetic Mountain (Ravine) Trail, more to enjoy its rugged features than to get to the top in a hurry.

Nearing the summit, I met two men and a woman starting

Ladder out of ravine, Pemetic Mountain (Ravine) Trail.

down. I asked if they had seen anything interesting.

"Just look around you," one of the men said, "the views are great in every direction!"

I did look around, and they were. The view west from Pemetic's upper ledges is one of the most scenic in the park. And most dramatic. Cliffs rise starkly above the glistening pond toward massive ridges supporting the sky itself. The landscape is Olympian, like I said. From the summit and all down the south ridge, islands spread across the near Gulf—Baker, the Ducks, the Cranberries, Sutton, Bear, Greening, Great and Little Gott, Placentia, and many others. Here is Acadia at its best, worthy of the weightiest adjective you can come up with, including "awesome" and beyond.

Through binoculars, I saw eighteen people on South Bubble, two on North Bubble, and three on the Bubble Ridge Trail, but I didn't meet a soul on Pemetic's summit or south ridge while I was there. The next hiker I met was well down the slope. He was hiking Pemetic by default. He said he was looking for the shortest way back to Bubble Pond where his car was parked, and figured the shortest way went over the top of Pemetic Mountain.

"How much more of a climb is it?" he asked.

"A lot more," I told him. "You have the option of turning back and taking an easier route."

"One doesn't turn back in these situations," he said.

"How will you feel about that tomorrow?"

"Terrible. My legs are stiff already," he said.

"You can still turn back," I said.

"Thanks, I'll keep going."

I met a woman and two girls on the Jordan Pond East Side Trail. Had they seen anything interesting?

Not moving her lips, one girl murmured, "Mm-hmm," the rising two-note affirmation as old as human speech.

"Gulls, I guess," the woman said. "At Otter Point this morning we saw seals and—what do you call them?—dolphins; the girls got a big kick out of that."

I also met two men and a woman coming back from South Bubble. One of the men said they'd had a beautiful day.

"Tired," the woman said.

"You'll sleep well tonight," I said.

"Yes, we will," she said.

"Better than taking a pill," I said.

"Well, I'm not sure about that," she said, knowingly wagging her finger at me.

I asked another pair how their hike was going.

"Great, so far," the man said, reserving judgment on things to come.

I wanted to ask if he were a lawyer, but held my tongue.

Each part of the loop has a character of its own. The Pemetic Mountain (Ravine) Trail rises steeply through rocky woods. The south ridge trail spans the top of the world. The Pond Trail descends gradually through ranks of noble trees. The Jordan Pond East Side Trail combines the magic of fresh air, the pond, lush vegetation, and a double dose of sunlight into a single spell enlivening every sense. And the canoe carry rising slowly through beech woods seems to exist in a time zone apart from any scheduled events in the civilized world. I hiked slowly because I had to keep adjusting to the different worlds I entered along the trail. Each had its own idioms and customs. Hiking takes me to one border crossing after another; I am constantly fumbling for my passport or looking up phrases in an unfamiliar tongue.

The Pemetic Mountain (Ravine) Trail scrambles through boulders much of the way, first gradually through small ones, then more steeply among big ones, then steeper still on granite cliffs. The trail makers used a number of techniques to help hikers up the slope—stone steps, wooden railings, ladders, and cribwork. It is not a trail to undertake lightly without sturdy footwear and a sense of adventure. Passing through woods of spruce, cedar, ash, birch, and maple, it rises quickly from the loop road to its main attraction about a third of the way up. A simple post offers a choice between two routes, **RAVINE** to the left or **LEDGE** to the right. I went **RAVINE**. I always go **RAVINE**. Swinging to the left, I found myself walking up a streambed into a narrow canyon with walls canted sharply to the north, a seven-rung wooden ladder mounting boulders blocking the upper end eighty feet ahead. Four days earlier a worn-out Hurricane Bertha had crossed the Gulf of Maine, sluicing a downpour on Acadia all day. Remnants of that storm were still running off the slopes of Pemetic, making for a splashy hike. The walls of the ravine grow higher the deeper in you go. Near the ladder, the right wall extends directly overhead. Scaling the ladder, you come to a second ravine, shorter than the first, but with walls between ten and twenty feet high, and another cedar ladder leading out the far end. This section of trail teaches you what it feels like to walk inside a mountain. You climb the second ladder a changed person,

more appreciative of Acadia's sacred recesses than you were back at the signpost offering a choice of routes. The trail continues less steeply over a stony treadway which includes a flight of forty-nine cribwork steps. Coming to smooth, open ledges overlooking the Bubbles and the cliffs to the west, you know you are near the top, having risen much more quickly than you expected to.

The Olympian heights of Pemetic Mountain were decked

View of the Bubbles and Sargent Mountain from Pemetic Mountain.

with swirling, bright green juniper and cedar, wine-leaf cinquefoil, blueberry, and waving sprays of mountain sandwort, all making it seem a festive kind of place. I came to two patches of fully ripe blueberries on the south ridge, plucking the first ripe fruit of the season at 3:13 p.m. on July 17, 1996, a moment to commemorate—at least until the second handful a few seconds later. I knew the gods ate well, but never realized till then *how* well. Finest kind!

Fair-weather cumulus clouds floated over the summit, with a darker wall of blue-gray advancing from the northwest. I sat on a granite knob overlooking the stand of red spruce growing in a sheltered dip, asking, "Who lives in this place?" Two sulphur butterflies came dancing out of the trees, and a junco landed on a nearby ledge—that's who. The big show was the five vultures floating on the updraft for twenty-minutes, whirling and tumbling around an invisible center that drifted along the mountain ridge. Wheeling higher and higher, they headed off toward Sargent, and a lone bald eagle took their place.

I cannot describe the state of mind I was in by that time. The ravine on the way up had been a gateway to the summit, a border crossing into a higher and better world. There was no traffic here, no hype, no hard or soft sell. This was no canned show on the tube, no hyperlink in cyberspace. It was happening now, both in the world and in my experience.

Without sponsors, producers, editors, or technicians of any sort. This was the ultimate in high tech—the real thing in real time! I was up there with the gods, breathing the air, eating the berries, watching the pageant of life. It grew dark and began to rain, but that was part of the drama of the place. Every plant and animal needs water, so there can't be a show without rain. I heard thunder in the northeast and southwest, but it was a rumble off in the wings, part of the special effects, as the nine dikes I crossed, ranging in width from four inches to sixteen feet, were part of the scenery. The rain was over in fifteen minutes, the sky cleared, the sun returned. In the warmth and the wind, I was dry in a few minutes.

All together, these Olympian events produced a profound effect, confirming that I had made the right hike on the right day. I had no doubt I stood at the center of the universe, with access to universal insights and trains of thought. Never in fifteen billion years of history had this exact sequence of events taken place in the awareness of any being. The universe was doing its creative thing; I was at the center, joined to myriad centers around me, together setting the stage for what was to follow, and what after that. Moment after moment, Earth lives its life in the cumulative awareness of its inhabitants. While all eyes were turning to Atlanta to see the same thing on the same screen with instant replays and commercials, I turned to Olympus to watch a onetime procession of events worthy of Zeus himself. One thing I know about gods is that they see with their own eyes and hear with their own ears. If you let others do your seeing for you, you give away the power to make your world and live your own life.

Passing several further checkpoints, I descended from the heights to amble through tall, open woods on a downhill section of the Pond Trail winding through the gap between Pemetic Mountain and its sidekick, the Triad, to the south. Here was a great forest as it should be, standing tall before storms, not bowing to chainsaws and chippers. To cut a living forest is to destroy it. What grows back in succession is a wimpy imitation requiring at least a hundred years to mature. Every so-called "harvest" is a setback for soil, fungi, wildlife, ground cover, and certainly the trees themselves.

Mountain sandwort, south ridge, Pemetic Mountain.

You can tell at a glance. Beauty is our intuitive gauge to the health of our surroundings. What is naturally beautiful is sound; what is unsightly is unsound. It took us two million years to learn to make that assessment. Turning fiber into corporate profits, in two hundred years we have forgotten what we knew. Walking along the Pond Trail above Jordan Pond, I recalled the old learning.

I have already mentioned the magic to be found on the east side of Jordan Pond. Hurricane Bertha had left the trail full of puddles, so the going was wet underfoot. But the landscape was as vibrant and green as the trail was mucky and brown. Looking from a wooded shore upon cliffs and clouds rising on the far side of the pond, what more could I want? The same elements I found on Olympus were here as well, the sunlight doubled by its reflection. The trail follows the shoreline among cedars, spruces, maples, alders, witch hazel, and ferns. Photosynthesis may be only two percent efficient, but that's good enough for plants to power the Earth. Add sunlight to water and air—poof, out comes Acadia.

I ended the hike with a stroll through luminous beech woods along the southern leg of the Jordan Pond Canoe Carry, where I met the California woman who found Acadia more serene than Yosemite. On that day and that trail, Acadia was serenity itself, but that didn't tell the whole story. Like the rest of us, Acadia's temperament is unpredictable. It has its wild and tempestuous side as well. If it didn't, we would neither recognize nor value its serenity. Zeus was hurling no thunderbolts, but that didn't mean he wasn't charging them up for tomorrow. Serenity is where we find it. We usually recognize it after the fact when we have moved beyond it and look back with regret at having lost it. I suspect Yosemite, being closer to her home, was closer to the jolts and tensions of the California woman's daily life than Acadia, which she knew only while on vacation. The serenity she found here was at a psychic as well as physical remove from her home experience. Getting lost in Acadia wasn't a trauma for her but an opportunity to free herself from her concerns. She was a free spirit when I met her, the picture of serenity, and I am happy to accept her at face value, as I accept beech trees and running brooks.

Except for winterberry, meadowsweet, lambkill, and mountain sandwort, I saw few flowers on this loop. Early bloomers were busy setting fruit; late bloomers were taking a last deep breath before going for the gold. The seasonal plot was shifting from blossoms to berries—cranberries, huckleberries, blueberries, bunchberries, blackberries, among others. Hawkweed, speedwell, and buttercup grew where the trail crosses the loop road. Selfheal grew in the

season, but as every camper knows, so far this year has been an exception. Hurricane Bertha was one in a series of storms.

The name "Zeus" shares a common origin with "deity," "divine," "Jove," "Jupiter," "July," "journey," and "sojourn." It is no accident my hike took me to Mount Olympus. Religion is meant to help us tie our activities to appropriate seasons of the year. If we sow or harvest our grain

Terraced landscape, Pemetic Mountain south ridge.

Beech woods along Jordan Pond Canoe Carry.

trail in a few places. I saw one rose on the south ridge. Compared to others I had met on recent hikes, this one had lost the bloom of youth. Summer mushrooms were coming into their own; I counted thirty-four by the side of the trail.

As for wildlife, I saw two yellow-rumped warblers catching insects along the Pemetic Mountain (Ravine) Trail, a junco, an eagle, gulls, and five turkey vultures on the summit and south ridge, and a common merganser with one russet duckling spotted with white on a rock in Jordan Pond. The sulphur was the butterfly of the day, flitting along every section of trail. A few mosquitoes found me in the woods, but the wind was too much for them out in the open. Minnows nudged in the shallows of the pond. I heard hermit thrushes, robins, crows, white-throated sparrows, among many calls I didn't know. Where the south ridge trail enters spruce woods and starts dipping toward the Triad, I found a single fox scat by a cairn. I didn't see any chipmunks, squirrels, or dogs.

There was more water on Pemetic than I expected. For much of its length, the Pemetic Mountain (Ravine) Trail follows the same stream it joins in passing through the ravine. Drainage from a wetland in the middle of the south ridge created a loud gurgle. Near the loop road, the Pond Trail bridges a small stream fed by runoff from the ridge. Jordan Pond was brimming with recent rain. Every culvert across the east side trail was trickling, and the stream by Jordan Pond Canoe Carry rushed with a greater flow than I had ever seen in July. July and August are Acadia's dry

too late or early, we will not have bread to last the winter. We need sky fathers and earth mothers to tie us to cycles of sunlight and moisture, migrations of birds and animals, the blooming and fruiting of plants. Acadia is a wonderful place to rediscover divinity. Zeus, for all his thunder, lightning, and amorous ways, is one means of addressing the reproductive cycles that engender all life. He and other Olympians offer an intuitive grasp of nature in terms we can all understand and connect with. Our deepest wisdom is recorded in the antics of the gods in every culture—the old gods, not the new. For guidance in making moral decisions or returning to family values, set out on one of Acadia's trails with your partner and children to see where it leads. The gods you need will appear, in your heart if not before your eyes.

❂

53—NORUMBEGA MOUNTAIN LOOP

From Norumbega Mountain parking area
To Norumbega Mountain summit, Lower Hadlock
   Pond, and back
  Up by Norumbega Mountain (Goat) Trail
  Down by Brown Mountain Trail, Hadlock Path,
   and Upper Hadlock Trail

3.3 miles, July 24, 1996

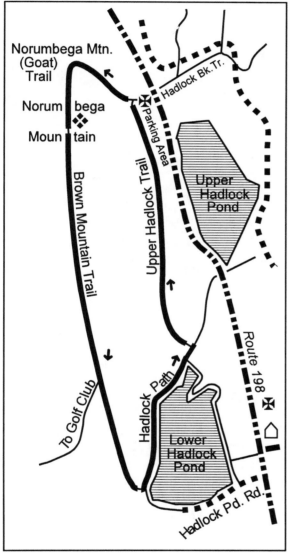

53—Norumbega Mountain loop.

Near the end of this hike, I saw a small square piece of paper lying on a bed of scale moss fifteen feet off the trail. Thinking it might contain a clue that would help me in my lifelong quest to unravel the mysteries of the universe, I picked it up. It was a receipt from Don's Shop 'n Save in Bar Harbor, dated July 23, for seven items: five pounds of potatoes, two pounds of onions, vinegar, oil, salt, bread, and coffee. Pretty basic stuff. The kind of receipt a mountain man like Jere-

miah Johnson would have left behind, or some hermit eking out his forty days in the wilderness. A John Muir receipt would have been even simpler: oatmeal and tea. Lumberjacks lived on beans and bread. On the trail, you don't need a lot of variety in your diet. The woods will fill you up. I came back from this hike with more than I took in. My own receipt included two loons, three black-throated green warblers, a red squirrel, ten wildflowers in bloom, eight ferns, five kinds of ripening berries, 275 mushrooms, and more spider webs than I could have carried in two plastic bags.

Many of the things I brought back from Norumbega Mountain and Lower Hadlock Pond were ineffable and could not be itemized. I had the strong sense of a hidden presence in the woods, a presence behind or underneath such conspicuous things as mushrooms and webs, which are outward and visible signs of the inner workings of nature. Beneath every one of the mushrooms I counted along the trail lay an underground web of pale threads spreading outward through the soil, gathering nutrients and water which they shared with the roots of trees, helping the woods to regrow after having been cut in earlier days. Two webs actually, male and female which, twining underground, gave rise to the colorful spore-producing caps and parasols I saw on the surface. Behind every spider web crouched a talented weaver; behind every weaver stretched a saga of trial and success as old as life itself. Walking through woods in the modern town of Mount Desert, I was at the forefront of ongoing creation. All around me I felt life pressing ahead, driven by the same force that created electrons, atoms, stars, galaxies, supernovas, planets, and every form of plant and animal life. No, that force is not a kind of god. Gods are means of taming nature by personifying it with human qualities. They are not the force behind anything, but effects of our deepest fears and desires projected outward by an anxious imagination. The force behind the expansion and evolution of the universe—on Earth as elsewhere—is a mystery that has no name, language, temperament, thoughts, or compassion. It certainly has no foresight or sense of design. It is a shove from the rear without purpose or aim. It is pure and simple opportunity. How we respond to that opportunity is up to us. We can depict the mystery as the collective source of all that is, but we cannot describe it. It is not ours to beg favors of or even praise. It simply is, giving us the possibility of responding while we are alive. The presence I felt on my hike was the inner and spiritual grace of universal creation made evident in the living diversity and integrity of the place where I walked.

I saw two loons swimming and diving in Lower Hadlock Pond. The nearer one floated sixty feet off shore, a distance my ten-power binoculars cut to a seeming six feet! I could see every band and speckle, and the depth of its garnet eye. The black dagger of its bill fused with its sleek but massive head to shape a missile no fish would ever forget. It floated so low in the water that the base of its neck was awash in the pond, making it look like two creatures in one, half-bird, half-serpent. Peering face-down into the pond, it hoisted both wings upward in a lazy stretch without flexing the primaries, then stowed them neatly on its back. Spreading every feather, it reached its left wing back along the water, showing how grand a bird it was. When it dove, it slid easily downward to merge with its native element. Taking to the air, loons clearly go against their better judgment: they flap and stomp to tell the world how hard it is. The two birds I saw were content to stay in the pond. Watching them, I sensed the force that shaped their bodies and their lives. If something works, that force gives the worker a chance to do it better and better, again and again. Loons are on Hadlock Pond not by design but by persistence and success. Trial and success have shaped the contours and feathers of the loon, as they have shaped the forms and features of the rest of us.

Over the pond and over the mountain, the sky was hung with clouds and mist. Light rain fell throughout the hike. Trees and mossy cliffs drip-drip-dripped. Every juniper branch bore beads of water. Puddles formed in granite basins. When I reached the top, Norumbega's summit was a green island in an infinite fog. Two hundred feet shore-to-shore, that island rose like Ararat—the only island in the world. Lower down I had a pallid glimpse of Parkman, Bald Peak, and the flank of Cedar Swamp, but Sargent and Penobscot mountains were whited out.

While I was down on my knees eying small white and yellow flowers growing in a sandy pan, a hiker with a German accent said, "Not much to see up here," and steered into the mist. That depends on where you look, I thought, and on what you are looking for. We hike more in our heads than over the ground, seeing what we expect to see and little else. The words we speak on the trail refer more to our inner journeys than to the outer world. Acadia is not a place so much as a set of mind. For those who pass quickly, it is merely an extension of places they have been before and brought with them in habits and patterns of mental life. Language lulls us into believing that, because we use similar words, we mean similar things in the same world of reference. Not so. Every child begins the world again, and language again, matching outer sounds to inner events. We mean what we mean on the inside, not the outside. No wonder nations, races, religions, ethnic and political groups, men and women, the aged and the young have such trouble understanding one another. Each of us lives in a different world of private experience with a unique vocabulary and field of reference. Mind-set is everything because it is all we have. In any medium, understanding is the exception, not the rule. To achieve it, we must share similar experiences, and view them in similar ways. Which takes careful speaking and careful listening, in an atmosphere of respect for the life experience of the other. It is more usual that, like the German hiker and I, we pass in the mists of personal assumptions and expectations, he absorbed in his train of thought, I in mine, two worlds given opportunity for making contact, but keeping on as before.

I met only seven hikers in five-and-a-half hours on Norumbega Mountain, two couples and three solos. I was

Cloud lichen on Norumbega Mountain.

stopped in my tracks fifteen feet past the trailhead at the start of the Goat Trail when a trim woman headed in no-nonsense fashion up the trail. Everything about her was trim and deliberate—her gear, her clothing, her features, her movements. In contrast, I felt unkempt and disarrayed, my gear and clothing slung loosely about my lanky frame.

"Hi," she said crisply.

"Hi," I said, and that was all there was to that.

My encounter with the last people I saw on the trail was very similar. Standing off the trail by the falls where Hadlock Brook rushes dramatically into Lower Hadlock Pond, I was musing about the loons I had been watching five minutes before when a couple came by, also trim—both of them—I noted, while I felt spacy and at sixes and sevens.

"Hi," I said, caught unaware by their brisk approach.

"Hi," the trim woman said, and they were gone.

One man came up the Brown Mountain Trail while I was heading down. He told me he was renting a house toward the village for a month and, rain or no rain, was making the most of his stay. He caught up with me a few minutes later on his return.

"I stopped for a few blueberry sessions," he said, smiling.

The first couple I met was coming down the Goat Trail as I was going up. The way was steep and slippery, so they were taking their time.

"Is this the Goat Trail?" the man asked.

I said it was.

"That's where we were going," he said, "but we got turned around and went around the pond."

"Are you Michigan?" I asked, having seen three cars in the parking area below (Massachusetts, California, Michigan), thinking they looked like Michigan.

"Yes," he said, "you must have seen our car."

I couldn't figure how they had started up the Goat Trail and yet taken the turn for Lower Hadlock Pond instead, going their intended route in reverse. With navigational skills like that, they were lucky to end up where they started, particularly in the fog. We hike in our heads, as I said, and it is easy for heads to get turned around.

The misty three-and-a-third-mile loop I made on Norumbega Mountain joined four trails into one five-and-a-half-hour hike. The steep Norumbega Mountain (Goat) Trail leads from the parking area on Route 198 above Upper Hadlock Pond to the summit (0.5 mile); the Brown Mountain Trail runs from the summit to Lower Hadlock Pond (1.2 miles); the Hadlock Path goes around the west side of the pond (0.5 mile) to connect with the Upper Hadlock Trail, which follows along the base of the mountain back to the parking area (1.1 miles). Lower Hadlock

Twining pitch pines, Brown Mountain Trail.

Pond has an elevation of 190 feet; the parking area, 280 feet; the summit, 862 feet; for a climb up and down of 672 feet, with a few extra dips and rises thrown in for good measure. The sky was overcast with a variable ceiling as low as 400 feet. The temperature was 62° Fahrenheit. On the outside it might have been dark and damp, but on the inside it was as bright and dry as the hiker's spirits.

My way was strewn not with fog but with flowers. Lamb-kill with its spring-loaded stamens still bloomed, shining like pink beacons in clearings and on open ledges. A few white blackberry blossoms still clung to thorny stems. Yellow stars of whorled loosestrife gleamed here and there on the Hadlock Path, where I also found one last pair of twinflower blooming in damp woods. In a wetland near the summit, large cranberry was in flower, petals peeled back in a show of pink. White-and-yellow cow wheat blooms rose among several patches of blueberries on the Brown Mountain Trail.

Pairs of four-pointed partridgeberry stars shone white in one spot on the Hadlock Path. And though all the mushrooms I saw might have prepared me, I was surprised to find a group of four Indian pipes on the Upper Hadlock Trail, each a different height from a half inch to two inches tall, gleaming with pale translucence against a bank of bright green scale moss (liverwort or bazzania). When the German hiker passed me, I was gawking at a patch of orange grass on the upper ridge, a miniature constellation of bright yellow stars on two-inch, leafless stems growing out of glacial sand. What looked like mountain sandwort shared the same pan except, instead of radiating white petals, its blooms formed five-pointed bells or trumpets. A cousin, perhaps, or variant form.

I often wonder why we pay so much attention to flowers. Why, when they are so tangential to our daily concerns, do we find them attractive? If we ate protein from their pollen or drank sugar from their nectar it would make sense to be drawn to them for utilitarian reasons. But wildflowers, which live in such different worlds from ours—what are we to them or they to us? Why did Lawrence Newcomb (among many others) go to the trouble of compiling a wildflower guide? The two answers I can offer hinge on the survival advantage flowers might give us: they tell us the landscape has sufficient moisture, sunlight, and nutrients to support their—and perhaps our—growth; and they help us identify specific plants which might provide food, medicine, fiber, or other benefits. Attracted by their color, shape, or scent, we bend to notice them, inviting them into our worlds of conscious awareness, where we name and classify them. From mayflower in spring to witch hazel in fall, we admire flowers through the seasons, noting their locations and ways of life. Too, we feel a spiritual affinity with flowers, using them to decorate our holy places and ceremonies. Instead of asking what we should do *with* them, I will ask what we would do *without* them. Imagine a life without flowers. Without the insects and animals that depend on flowers for their livelihoods. A life without trees, without birds, without sexual reproduction in the kingdom of plants, without beauty, without love. I might as well ask what sort of life we would lead if we felt no attraction for one another. Flowers and loved ones are in the same category; life without them is unthinkable. That simple thought experiment leads to the conclusion that life without flowers is death of the natural world as we know it, and the cultural world along with it.

Last week I saw thirty-four mushrooms on my Pemetic loop; this week eight times as many on Norumbega. Colorful or drab, each cap affirmed that soil heat and moisture were right for mushroom reproduction. Billions and billions of spores were in the air, landing on damp soil, starting new underground colonies. Life is not all flowers and loons. The fungi are waiting. Waiting for plants that make sugar from water and air. Waiting for those who eat plants. Waiting for those who prey on those who eat plants. The fungi are out there, waiting for us all. Ready to take us back where we started, to return us to the soil from which we came. Mushrooms are the bone sweepers of Acadia, the caste that completes the life cycle, tidying up after this generation, preparing the ground for the next. Without them, as without flowers, this landscape would not exist. Like yin and yang, life and death are complementary, each giving meaning to the other. The future springs from our remains. We are born to die, to decay, to make way for others. Our death is their good fortune. In them we are born again. That is the truth and the mystery behind some of our principal spiritual beliefs. In nature, resurrection is the rule, not the exception. For millennia we have celebrated the rising of grain from damp soil as personified by Persephone, Attis, Adonis, Osiris, Tammuz, Marduke, Jesus, and others, each revised to suit the idiom of a particular time and place. Joy out of sorrow, hope out of despair, beauty out of ruin, stability out of instability, new life out of old, all made possible by the sacred union of the sky father and earth mother—that is the universal message behind the diverse rites and symbols of our many creeds. Strange, we cannot see through the trappings to the common origin of our faiths. Stranger still that we deny the birth of the spirit in the reproductive pageant of the natural world. We mistake our symbols for that which they represent, worshipping icons instead of the miracle that engendered them. Acadia in July is as much a lesson in theology as basic ecology. Every hike is a stage in a spiritual journey. If we hike often enough through the seasons, we begin to see Acadia in a new light as the cradle of human imagination, understanding, and awe. If it weren't for flowers, for fungi, for all that Acadia is, we wouldn't be here. Why else do we have natural and national parks if not to get back in synchrony with all they preserve and represent?

To extend that thought one more step, from the spiritual to the economic realm, think of the basic processes on which life depends. First, photosynthesis, by which plants and algae produce the food we eat. Then respiration, by which we convert that food to energy in every cell in our bodies. Then paid labor, by which we receive symbolic value for the orderly work we do with that energy. And finally, the human economy, by which we relate to one another on the basis of the value we command because of the useful work we contribute to our society. Which way does wealth flow, top-down or bottom-up? From the economy to nature, or from nature to the economy? It is hard to believe we see more

Brown Mountain Trail.

than one answer. Remove the human economy, nature still exists; remove nature, the economy crashes. Putting first things first, photosynthesis is the most important process on Earth. The view from Wall Street is upside-down because Wall Street is so isolated from Acadia. If brokers were hikers they'd get it right, and add a depletion index to their economic indicators. As modern religions are distanced from the original content of their symbols, so economists forget the fundamental processes to which they owe their lives. I would start by bringing them by the busload to Norumbega Mountain on foggy days in July to round out their education. Economic theory would never be the same after that.

Economists were not among the wildlife I met on my loop. I heard chickadees, hermit thrushes, crows, a kingfisher by the pond, and saw four tufts of tan-and-white hair by the side of the trail. Spider webs were everywhere, mostly sheet webs and bowl-and-doily webs. I met one slug, one green worm dangling on a strand of silk, one red squirrel gleaning tidbits among fallen needles. On the Goat Trail I saw a seagull, a junco with two fledglings, three black-throated green warblers, and a sparrow gobbling a blueberry. The loons on Lower Hadlock were the highlight of the hike. Watching fellow predators at work, I felt reassured that Acadia was in good order top-to-bottom. If loons, hawks, or foxes were to vanish, I'd look for trouble down below.

Speaking of the bottom, I also saw six or seven plasmodial slime molds, bright yellow splotches gleaming like crystallized sulfur against the general green of pincushion mosses and bazzania. Were they animal, vegetable, or mineral? None of the above. A primitive form of life, they feed on bacteria and yeasts on the forest floor, moving at a slow ooze place-to-place. Lacking personality and charisma, these humble predators are not written up in the guidebooks, but like fungi (to which they are unrelated) they have a certain colorful appeal and are remarkable when seen in damp woods. I doubt the romance of slime molds will ever be written, but they are an older race of Earthling than our own, and as our elders deserve at least both passing notice and respect.

Like many hiking loops in Acadia, this loop winds between two worlds, upper and lower, both equally damp on the day of my hike. The Goat Trail starts in the lower world of mixed woods, then quickly rises over rocks and roots to open ledges populated by pitch pine, juniper, huckleberry, blueberry, and a variety of lichen. Generally this upper world is a drier, sunnier, windier place than the shaded woods, opening onto vistas of parallel ridges on Mount Desert Island and lesser islands spread like stepping stones to the horizon. Shrunk by the fog, my view was no less spectacular, looking upon a landscape of granite and wizened pines receding into shifting mists. The weather added a dramatic element of its own, forcing attention onto the foreground, adding a sense of mystery to the beyond. Those who looked for distant views were struck blind; those who suffered myopia were blessed with new sight.

The upper world of Norumbega Mountain extends for about a mile along a ridge running north and south on the eastern side of Somes Sound. Similar to ridges on Champlain and Dorr mountains, this world offers a glimpse of terrain where rainfall equals that in other parts of Acadia, but there is almost no soil to hold moisture for later use, so vegetation is limited to species needing little water and a great deal of sunlight. Enter the pitch pine and its faithful companions to create a landscape which, though spare, is as beautiful as any in Acadia. With my attention focused on nearby plants and trees, I moved through the landscape as through a dream, distant forms rising ahead of me out of nothing, then taking on substance and character as I drew near, to fade behind me into nothing again. As the genius of a watershed is the timed release of moisture through the growing season, the genius of this upper world was the serial revelation of a landscape in slow motion. One scene led to another, each unique, yet joined by a common cast and plot. The landscape didn't emerge in time so much as it created time by means of successive apparitions. The universe was coming into being before my eyes, now giving way to now, giving way to now. Had I stopped moving, time would have stopped. I would have rooted in a crack and become as gnarled and twisted as the pines. Hiking in Acadia means merging with the landscape to become one with the natural world. Living apart as we do, we lose the knack. Recovering it is one of life's great discoveries.

Heading south from the summit, the Brown Mountain

Bridge over Hadlock Brook above Lower Hadlock Pond.

Trail (Norumbega was called Brown Mountain before George Dorr tweaked the names to make them worthy of a national park) leads down a gradual slope into the lower world of damp woods and tall trees. Here pitch pines cannot compete, so eventually give way to spruce, fir, cedar, maple, beech, and red and white pine. What struck me most about this lower world was the luminous green mat of bazzania covering the forest floor, here and there accented by ferns and patches of low plants. The mists were not daunted by the woods, so crept in here as well, creating an effect similar to the one above, a landscape of tall poles growing paler with distance. The descent is not steady but proceeds by a series of broad terraces between granite slopes, pitch pine thriving on the drier ledges, then alternating with stands of thirstier species where soil is thicker. People often hike this trail for views of islands to the south, but it also offers splendid views of Acadia's trees and woods themselves, giving an immediate sense of where you are instead of where you are not.

The Brown Mountain Trail descends to the south shore of Lower Hadlock Pond, where it meets the Hadlock Path which circles the pond. I turned north and followed around the west side of the pond to the falls where Hadlock Brook makes its entry, the path keeping to the woods the whole way. The two loons showed as black silhouettes against pale mists shrouding the far shore. They were the highlight, but the woods themselves held their own, offering large white pines, rich ground cover, and a variety of ferns including long beech, oak, bracken, interrupted, royal, New York, spinulose wood, and rock-cap. Wet roots can be slippery, so this trail called for cautious footwork in places, as did the following stretch of the Upper Hadlock Trail connecting to the Norumbega Mountain parking area. The wettest spots on both trails are spanned by corduroy bridges or poles laid over the mud. The best bridge on the loop is the arched corduroy span across the brook on the Hadlock Path. It had been rebuilt this year, so was once again as sturdy as it was graceful. Below the bridge, the brook spreads to a width of twenty-five feet; above, it races through a gap between a rock and a hard place only eighteen inches wide. It hardly seems like the same brook in both places, but adaptability is any brook's middle name. I followed along Hadlock Brook for a short distance, then turned left along a section of the Upper Hadlock Trail to complete the loop.

In a sense this last leg was the best leg of the entire hike, which I hadn't expected because earlier legs had been wonderful. No, the treadway, rooty and soggy in places, wasn't that great, and it was as damp down below as it had been on top. Having been cut earlier this century, the woods were no virgin forest, and only now were showing signs of recovery. But the terrain all along the base of Norumbega Mountain is spectacular nonetheless, largely because, with plenty of water flowing off the mountain, conditions are right for growth. Bazzania blankets the duff, making the landscape into a green garden. Ferns and ground cover flourish. Wetlands thrive at the base of the cliffs. And the cliffs themselves are alive with great trees rising from sprawling networks of roots. I kept catching my breath in silent exclamations of awe and amazement at the living wealth of these surroundings. The difference between the upper world and this one was the difference between spare and lush, tactful and effusive, Doric and Corinthian. I was reminded of hikes along the Valley Trail on Beech Mountain and the abandoned trail at the base of Canada Cliff. The island may be named for its barren mountains, but only because Champlain knew nothing of its fertile valleys. They, too, are Acadia.

What have I left out? Berries were ripening everywhere—bunchberry, Canada May ruby, blueberry, huckleberry, juniper. I stepped over nine dikes ranging in width from four inches to six feet. Did I mention mosquitoes? They were one of the few insects I saw. I didn't see a single butterfly. It was a great hike every step of the way. I'd do it again tomorrow if I didn't have to stay indoors and write.

❂

54—CHAMPLAIN & GORHAM MOUNTAINS

From parking area at north end of the Tarn
To Champlain Mountain summit, the Bowl, and
    Gorham Mountain summit
  Up by Beachcroft Trail, continue on Champlain
    Mountain South Ridge, Bowl, and north end of
    Gorham Mountain trails
Down by south end of Gorham Mountain Trail
5.0 miles, July 28, 1996

Beachcroft Trail on Huguenot Head.

Acadia is more than a resort at the end of a road; it is a natural community—a living bioregion—made up of interlocking neighborhoods and their inhabitants. Wherever we go in the park, we are in one neighborhood or another and are sure to come across plants and animals whose lifestyles are suited to that particular place. We visit Rome to discover its citizens in their natural habitat, and we come to Acadia for the same reason, though we all approach it our own way. Some bring folding chairs and set up on granite ledges by the sea; some lie in the shade and read a book; some go swimming, sailing, or shopping; many go biking on the carriage roads; and others go hiking. Whatever our approach, wherever we go in the park, we open ourselves to Acadia and expect it to work the magic for which we have come. If we are lucky, it opens doors we never knew were closed, onto scenes we never dreamt or imagined.

Hiking up Champlain Mountain by the Beachcroft Trail and down by the south ridge trail to the Bowl, then over Gorham Mountain by the Bowl and Gorham Mountain trails

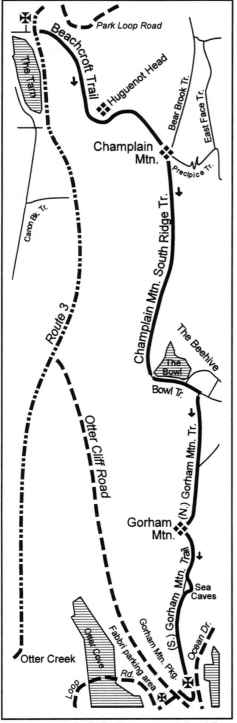

54—Champlain & Gorham mountains hike.

in a five-mile ridgewalk, I heard a bullfrog in the Tarn and a green frog in the Bowl, a song sparrow, two white-throated sparrows, several juncos, and four hermit thrushes. I saw damselflies, dragonflies, an orange-and-black pearl crescent

butterfly, one fox scat wound with tan hair, gulls, three juncos, two crows, a turkey vulture, four peregrine falcons, an immature bald eagle, and 129 people along the trail. Through binoculars I saw 39 sails on salt water, 3 people on the summit of Dorr Mountain, 99 on Cadillac, 68 at Thunder Hole waiting for the big splash that never came, 15 dipping in the Bowl, and 189 taking the cure at Sand Beach. Every one of us had a share of the magic on that rare sunny day between the prevailing rains of July 1996.

Unlike most of my hikes, this one did not end up where it began. It was a straight shot from Huguenot Head near Sieur de Monts Spring to the Fabbri parking area on Otter Point. I parked at Fabbri and my partner drove me in her car to the Beachcroft trailhead on Route 3 at the north end of the Tarn. From there I did the five-mile hike in six hours and fifteen minutes. Starting at an elevation of 100 feet, the Beachcroft Trail rises 958 feet to the summit of Champlain at 1,058 feet. The south ridge trail drops 643 feet to the Bowl, then the Bowl and Gorham Mountain trails dip another 115 feet before rising 225 feet to Gorham's summit at 525 feet. The Fabbri parking area is 465 feet down from there at an elevation of 60 feet. Which is a complicated way of saying the route climbs 1,183 feet and descends 1,223 feet all told, ending 40 feet lower than it began. The temperature ranged between 70° and 80° Fahrenheit. It was a perfect summer day with cumulus clouds endlessly combing through a sea of blue. I didn't take a lunch because a darker sea of blue ran along the trail from beginning to end; like every hiker I met, I accepted Acadia's generous offer and ate handfuls of blueberries along the way.

The section of the Beachcroft Trail winding up Huguenot Head above the Tarn is one of the wonders of Acadia. Rising gradually by a series of eighteen switchbacks, it turns what looks to be a daunting cliffside scramble into an easy stroll. The treadway is solid on well-laid blocks of granite taken from the mountain itself. Many of the park's trails are at their best while crossing talus slopes which provided ample materials worthy of the trailmakers' craft. Higher up where talus is scarce, many trails are not laid at all but seem cut like cow paths by passing traffic through thin soil, or mount bare and sometimes slippery ledges without ado. That is the story of the Beachcroft Trail, which takes the hiker up Huguenot Head in fine style, but then abandons her to the raw slopes of Champlain if she wants to press on to the top. Skirting the summit of Huguenot Head, the trail dips slightly in the wooded saddle between the two mountains, then the slope increases and the scramble begins. In places the upper trail is not well marked. It has to go up, but the route is indeterminate. Several times I followed my intuition and eventually came to a cairn or the rare blue blaze. There is no danger of getting lost; simply head upslope and you will soon reach the summit. The view across the Tarn to the east face of Dorr Mountain is worth the 1.2-mile hike, even on a trail with a split personality. And coming up the west side of the mountain, you experience the summit view as a fresh revelation. Suddenly you are on top of the world with all Frenchman Bay at your feet and the Down East coast stretching beyond Schoodic Peninsula across the bay. You can see more islands than you can count, and five lighthouses—Egg Rock, Mark Island, and Petit Manan to the east; Baker Island and Mount Desert Rock to the south.

The Beachcroft Trail starts off with thirty-one gray (nonnative) granite steps rising from Route 3. There were so many flowers on that first slope, it took me twenty minutes to reach the top step. I was stopped in my tracks by the first goldenrod I had seen, which tried to tell me summer had reached maturity and fall was on its way, but I wasn't listening. St. Johnswort was still holding forth from Midsummer Day, looking a little ragged if truth be told. Mullein was just coming into bloom, tall spikes sparkling with bright yellow. A wild rose gleamed in the grass, looking pale next to the unabashed color of Deptford pinks on their gangly stalks. Two kinds of vetch lined the steps, purple cow vetch and showier pink-and-white crown vetch. But best of all, where the upper steps entered mixed woods, the trail was lined with wintergreen, one or two white lanterns hanging from every sprig. Don't try to tell me the season is getting on; this is high summer, the glory of the year. Higher up the Beachcroft Trail I saw hawkweed, meadowsweet, bush honeysuckle, and wine-leaf cinquefoil in bloom, and deep blue-violet harebell (bluebell) in sprightly clusters on damp cliffs. Too, I saw one purple aster in the woods, which tried to second goldenrod's motion that summer was winding down, but I chose not to bring the issue to a vote.

Except for yellow-and-white mountain sandwort and pink lambkill blossoms on the ridges, and a few yellow swampcandles near the outlet of the Bowl, once I passed Huguenot Head the rest of the hike was almost flowerless. From Champlain to Gorham Mountain, lichens, cinquefoil, and pitch pine softened the granite ridge. Plants that bloomed earlier were now putting their energy into producing fruit: juniper, sarsaparilla, kinnikinnick, bunchberry, huckleberry, and the berry of the day—blueberry, which was at its peak. Most splotchy bird droppings had a lavender tint. I saw milling gangs of seagulls swoop down on the slopes to get their share of fruit.

For the most part, the Champlain Mountain South Ridge Trail is an easy walk down the backbone of Mount Desert Island's easternmost ridge. Exposed to the elements, pitch pine and granite lend Spartan character to the terrain. The ridge dips in the middle into a small protected pocket where spruce, oak, and gray birch mix with resident pitch pine. The trail drops steeply in one stretch where the ridge shifts to a lower level, but that drop is quickly passed. On a clear day,

the horizon spans the Gulf of Maine in a lazy arc south and east. The vista is expansive, inviting hikers to take a larger world view that places daily concerns against a background of sky, clouds, and ocean. To the west, the south ridge of Cadillac runs a parallel course, hiding much of Acadia except for Dorr and Day mountains. South, the Bowl and Beehive come into view over the dropping ridge, with Gorham Mountain and Otter Point beyond, and Sand Beach and

Porcupine Islands and Frenchman Bay from Champlain Mountain.

Great Head to the east. Mountain ponds are always likened to jewels; the Bowl deserves that comparison with the rest, glistening with reflected clouds and sky in its green setting among the trees. Approaching the pond, the trail winds through gray birch, popple, and oak, to come out below two beaver dams at the outlet. Recent rains had filled the pond, and the stream draining toward Otter Creek was rushing to keep up.

Crossing the stream on granite stepping stones, I picked up the Bowl Trail which rounds the south shore of the pond through spruce woods before dropping toward Sand Beach. Red clusters of bunchberry lined the damp trail, a bogwalk in eighteen sections of split cedar keeping hikers' boots from the worst of the muck, and the soft muck from the worst of hikers' boots. On the small ledge where the Beehive Trail reaches the pond, toe-dippers and swimmers gathered in a gleeful cluster to see how many bodies could cram together on one rock before one of them fell overboard. Tree swallows seemed to be having just as much fun sweeping through the airspace above the pond.

Heading away from the pond, the Bowl Trail first rises over a series of waterbars through birch and maple woods, then descends into cool beech woods toward the junction with the Gorham Mountain Trail. At the junction I left the Bowl Trail and turned south around Halfway Mountain through birch, popple, and maple woods along the wettest and stoniest section of my hike. The trail drops 115 feet below the Bowl then, at a sign for **SAND BEACH PARKING**, starts rising toward Gorham's summit. At first the trail was not much of a trail, being more of a rocky streambed running with water, but soon it came out on dry granite overlooking Sand Beach and the Beehive in profile, to scale Gorham in short order. Coming to an impressive cliff, the kind trail-makers cannot resist, the trail runs along the base for a short distance, then resumes its climb, the views getting better and better. As seen from the summit of Gorham Mountain, Champlain, Dorr, and Cadillac line up for their portrait, posing as grand massifs rather than the humble glacial hills they often seem. Only 525 feet above sea level, Gorham is another of Acadia's middling peaks offering spectacular views. Here the base of the mountain is literally sea level, Frenchman Bay adding another dimension to the panorama from the top, just as Somes Sound expands the view from Acadia and St. Sauveur mountains. The evening before, my partner and I had hiked up Gorham for a picnic after the rain, and had been met at the summit by the first rainbow either of us had seen in over a year. On one winter hike I had met a dark spirit on the summit, a raven that waited till we were thirty feet apart to lift off its boulder, hang motionless in the wind, then glide without stirring a feather across the valley of Otter Creek, leaving me in charge of the summit. This time I met eight campers from Montreal having a gallicking time being out after three days of rain.

South from the summit, the Gorham Mountain Trail continues the gradual descent along the ridge, dropping steeply in only one place, to reach the loop road in just under a mile. It offers a choice of routes, one sticking to the ridge, the other dropping down to the base of cliffs once washed by the tide before the coast recovered from its ducking by the glacier, cliffs now 200 feet above sea level. These sculpted granite stacks rising in the middle of the woods add to a dramatic landscape that challenges our dream of nature's timelessness. The cliff trail rejoins the ridge trail by another stack sheltering a bronze plaque to one of Acadia's pioneers:

1857/1909
WALDRON BATES
IN
MEMORIAM
MCMX
PATHMAKER

The plaque features representations of two directional arrows made from forked twigs, one of the earliest means of marking trails. I met a park ranger about to give her Waldron

Bates spiel to the twenty-five hikers she had in tow, so I skedaddled—not because I wasn't interested in her message, but because I wasn't ready to cope with such a crowd. I soon reached the Gorham Mountain parking area and walked along the Ocean Path for a ways till I took Otter Cliff Road back to Fabbri where I had parked my car.

That's a bare rundown of the route my body took on this hike. What it leaves out is the experiential adventure that

Summiteers, Champlain Mountain.

evolved as I went along. That adventure was based on my inner responses to the places, scenes, plants, animals, and people that sparked my living awareness. It was not the flowers that held me on those first thirty-one steps so much as my reaction upon seeing them. They did not hold me; I held myself. As I lived it on the inside, the hike was a continuous dialogue between my personal outlook and the inlook of the trail. Yes, the trail looks into each hiker, asking, "Is anybody home?" It offers us the opportunity to be who we are in that place. The question is, what are we going to do about it? Who are we, anyway, now that we are here? The trail is not the hike. The trail is the opportunity for us to *make* a hike. To make it not merely by moving our legs but by moving our inner awareness through the world of possible experience. Since each of our awarenesses is keyed differently, each of us makes a different hike as our bodies move along the same trail.

So what hike did I make? My experience unfolded in a series of episodes that gripped my attention. There was the episode of seeing the flowers by the steps. The episode of not wanting to see the aster. The episode of switchbacking higher and higher along the Beachcroft Trail. The episode of scrambling on the upper trail toward the summit. The episode of seeing a turkey vulture over the shoulder of a young woman from France. The episode of gawking at two peregrine falcons directly overhead dancing with each other and with the wind. The episode of overhearing the summit debate whether those were falcons or immature eagles. The episode of talking with a couple from Pennsylvania while watching a falcon tangle with an eagle in the air behind them. And many, many more episodes, each distinct, each unique, each an engagement between one passing mote and the universe of possibility through which it floated. The hike was a series of engagements daring my awareness to grapple with the novel opportunities Acadia offered moment-by-moment.

Each episode had a temporal depth to it, a way of fitting into a matrix of similar episodes on other occasions. Seeing the vulture and the falcon-eagle affair over the shoulders of other hikers, I remembered making my first hike up Schoodic Mountain with my family when I was eight, climbing through the wind up a ladder that bowed with my weight into the fire tower on the summit, talking with the ranger standing over his plane table with its map centered on where we were, the ranger never taking his eyes off the horizon, looking not at us but over our shoulders for plumes of smoke, my child self wondering if he was trying to impress us with his watchfulness, if he would go back to his book when we left. Hearing whitethroats and song sparrows, I remembered hearing them other times, other places. Watching a man taking a picture of a woman, she removing her glasses and holding them behind her back, I flashed on others who had done the same in my former life as a photographer twenty-five years earlier. Hiking down Champlain's spine, I remembered hiking the other way in the snow with three friends last Thanksgiving, and hiking solo in February, seeing hare and fox prints in the trail and a pair of snow buntings at the summit. Rounding the Bowl on the bogwalk, I remembered wading through four-foot drifts of fine powder blown off the pond onto the trail just there. Cued by a sense of being where I had been before, the raven and rainbow on Gorham entered from the wings of memory to further the action of my experience as it developed according to a plot wholly unknown to me.

Released by some inner connection, layer upon layer of memory came back as my hike progressed, creating a kind of virtual space rich with hyperlinks to other events in other days. Building a life means building a coherent landscape of experience from many layers of data, a process somewhat similar to assembling a map in a geographic information system (GIS) on a computer. Exploring Acadia, I discover the wealth of images making me who I am in my world. The moral of that discovery is: the more we hike, the richer our hikes become. Acadia is built up over time in our experience. To the first-time visitor and the old hand the park is two different places in two different worlds. None of us can

ever know the park as it *is;* we have only our experience *of* it, which can grow through the years, layer added upon layer, till the range of possibilities we have fulfilled represents a fair sample of what Acadia has to offer. As two hawks seen soaring at eye level, falcons and eagles can look alike until we accrue enough life experience to tell them apart.

I am deliberately hiking Acadia's major peaks this sum-

The Bowl, the Beehive, and Gorham Mtn. from Champlain south ridge.

mer to meet as many park visitors on the trail as I can. These fellow travelers make up a major part of my trail experience, at least on sunny days. While standing on the steps at the start of the Beachcroft Trail, I was overtaken by a couple I had met two weeks before on the Pemetic Mountain Trail. They had been to Fundy National Park in the meantime, and were back in Acadia to pick up where they had left off. With thirty-five-foot tides and stark cliffs, New Brunswick was dramatic, they said, but they had come to love Acadia, and wanted to see as much of it as they could.

The first couple I met coming down the trail did not look as happy. The woman told me the rocks were slippery up above. The man coming behind her stopped to leash their dog, then set him free again when they were past. I wasn't sure if he thought the dog was a danger to me or I a danger to the dog.

I met the woman from France twice, she overtaking me on the Beachcroft Trail, then I coming up to her while she was taking a picture. Not sure what she was focusing on, I asked what she saw.

"The sea," she said.

I told her the view was even better from the summit. She said she had been here two weeks and loved every minute, hiking and biking every day, rain or no rain. As we talked, I saw the taut V wings of a turkey vulture farther along the slope, but by the time she could turn, the bird had veered behind the cliff.

"See you at the top," she said as she went on.

I didn't see her, but I met two groups at the summit, parties of three and five, both watching the falcons, debating what kind of birds they were.

"Bald eagles," a man said, "you can see their white heads."

"I've been vindicated!" a second man said.

"Look at those narrow wings; falcons for sure," a third man said.

Two schools of thought, two different birds. I sided with the falconers, but didn't butt in.

On the south ridge trail, I asked a boy how his hike was going.

"Pretty good," he said.

"Nice day," said another boy farther on.

I agreed.

"Seen any falcons?" he asked.

I said I had seen four, two adults at the summit and two immatures diving on a young eagle over the Precipice half an hour ago. He told me about seeing two pods of whales from his uncle's boat, or maybe the same pod twice, he couldn't tell. His name was Ben, a triplet, seven years old, going into third grade. His family stopped for lunch on a lower ledge, but Ben, the vanguard, ate his sandwich where he was. Usually I speak first when I meet fellow hikers, but it was Ben who engaged me in a ten-minute conversation. He wanted to know what I had seen, and to tell me what he had seen. He balanced his entire world on the tip of his tongue, and shared it readily with me, as I, struggling to keep up, did my best to share mine with him.

A couple off the trail was collecting handfuls of blueberries in plastic sandwich bags. They were silent at their work; I didn't interrupt them.

Near the low point between the Bowl and Gorham Mountain, I met four women in single file, also silent. I asked the last if she had seen anything interesting on her hike.

"Umm . . . no," she said, resting her hand on the trunk of a birch while she thought. "Great views, though," she added.

A boy catching up with a woman who had stopped to wait for him said, "I just couldn't walk by those berries!"

After the eight French-speaking hikers from Montreal had headed back toward Sand Beach, a solo man arrived at the summit of Gorham Mountain. He lived on Long Island and said he and his family came to Acadia every year the last week in July. Things were changing at home, he told me. A fifty-store mall was under construction in what till now had been a largely rural area. It must have been in both our minds, but neither of us mentioned TWA Flight 800 that had gone down off Long Island July 17.

Like a frisky mountain goat bounding down the mountain, a man dashed by on a steep section of trail. A woman came behind him at a more leisurely pace.

"He runs, I take my time," she said with a smile.

"What waits down below? I asked.

"Our food," she said, "we're hungry!"

By the sea-eroded cliffs, I met another couple coming toward me.

"Nice day for a walk," I said.

"Beauty day!" the man said, reminding me of my friend Gene Franck, who often used that expression when we worked together in the 60s. The same Gene Franck who, in situations now referred to as worst-case scenarios, would say, "jelly-side down," the image referring to a piece of bread fallen on the floor.

The Olympics are going full-bore in Atlanta these days, the world hanging on every event to watch physical prowess stretched to the limit and beyond. World records and gold-medal performances define the envelope of the possible within which we go about our daily tasks. Most of us stay well within the center of that envelope, coming nowhere near the records our species is capable of setting. I don't follow the Olympics. They have become too commercial and nationalistic to capture my interest, and I have only an idle curiosity about how fast or high or far human bodies can propel themselves through space. I view speed with suspicion. A century ago, I would have been one of those shaking their heads as a Stanley Steamer raced by at fifteen miles an hour. I watch bikers speed through the park on carriage roads and wonder what they take with them when they leave. What do they know of Acadia they didn't know before? How has their experience grown richer and more delightful? I speak as one hit by a speeding biker who chose to turn toward me rather than run into a dog leash stretched tight across the road by a family pet. I own my prejudice. Perhaps I overlook the spiritual side to going fast, but I am convinced Acadia reveals its secrets to those who take their time and look about them. The man racing to his dinner will tiredly sit down by himself; the woman strolling in later, refreshed, will bring Acadia as her guest.

What I brought back from this hike was a sense of being alive in the place I love most, and of being in the company of others exploring it their own way. I had been to Rome and knew more of its citizens than I had known before. What I gave up in speed I made up for in wonder, enjoyment, and a sense of spiritual connection. I set no records, but records require a finish line; mine is an ongoing quest. The only finish I recognize is the last, the ultimate summit offering no views and no means of descent. I will get there sooner or later. I see no reason to rush.

❂

55—PENOBSCOT & SARGENT MOUNTAINS LOOP

From Jordan Pond House
To Penobscot Mountain summit, Sargent Mountain
    Pond, Sargent Mountain summit, and back
    Up by Jordan Cliffs Trail, connector to Penobscot
      summit, and Sargent Mountain South Ridge Trail
    Down by Sargent Mountain South Ridge and
      Penobscot Mountain trails
               5.6 miles, August 3, 1996

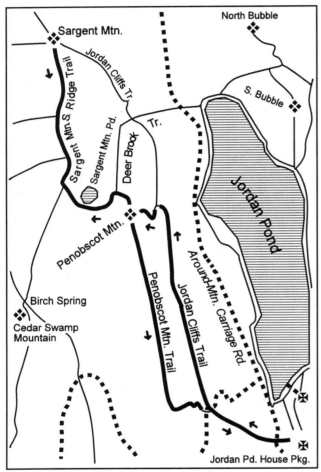

55—Penobscot & Sargent mountains loop.

When we talk about the world, we are talking about the world of inner experience, the only world we know, which is very different from any notion of an objective, outside world. That outer world remains a mystery, even when we observe it, because we cannot know it without changing it through the process of observation. Once observed, it is given life by the workings of awareness, which transform it into a wholly new creation. Molecules in the air become smells; energy patterns given off by other molecules become flowers or voices; changing patterns of energy become time, space, or the plot of a drama. The world *as it is* is a fiction beyond reach of our dreams. *Reality* is right up there with *truth*, *justice,* and *Nirvana* in a mental domain of ideals sealed with seven-thousand-times-seven-thousand seals. All we can know is the world we make for ourselves from the cosmic stuff coming at us from every direction. The world we make because we are the leading edge of universal creation, direct descendants of the Big Bang, galactic formation, supernova explosions, stellar radiation, and the evolution of life on Earth—heirs to the genetic fortune our ancestors passed to us when we were conceived.

So when I talk about seeing wood lilies on the south ridge of Sargent Mountain, I am describing an episode in my personal experience, not an event in a factual world. I know this because other hikers I met walked by the lilies without looking at them, while I stopped in my tracks and could hardly believe my eyes. There I was on hands and knees at the edge of the trail bending over the most beautiful flower I had ever seen in Acadia, and yet others kept to their itineraries as if the flower did not exist. And it did not exist—for them—because it never entered their awareness. Different hikers, different worlds, different Acadias. A lot of people were spending time those days watching the Olympics in Atlanta; I hadn't watched one event. The Olympics are not part of my world, just as the blooming of wood lilies will never make it to prime time TV. Yet both are spectacular, world-class events. We watch the Olympics not so much because we want to see them but because a lot of *other people* want us to see them. Sporting events are now tools of national and corporate policy. They are staged to draw our attention to ideas and products others want us to consume. Since nobody has figured out a way to capitalize on wood lilies, they are left to their amateur ways with no corporate promoters or sponsors.

And yet which is the greater achievement, winning the 200-meter dash or blooming on a mountain ridge? The race is wholly arbitrary: why not 153 meters, or 202? The meter was supposed to have been one ten-millionth of the distance from the equator to the North Pole along the Paris meridian, but the French got it wrong, so it is a wholly meaningless unit of measurement. What does it mean to go an arbitrary distance faster than anyone else? Does that make the winner superior? Many people think so, even though they won't think of the race for another four years. No, the hype is the thing, the grabbing of mass attention for a few seconds—long enough to sell millions of dollars worth of advertising. Olympic athletes are paid performers in a worldwide promotion. "Going for the gold" has become the moral philosophy of our age.

Meanwhile, back on the slopes of Sargent Mountain the wood lily blooms, not at a price, not as a gimmick, but as a revelation of life's inner beauty and creativity. Here rising among blueberry bushes like torches lining the trail are erect, orange, six-pointed miracles with golden throats speckled deep red. Blooming just above the berries, petals and sepals forming perfect stars two inches across, they are radiant in a cosmic, not a worldly, sense. I saw the first one and stopped, then saw four others farther on in an open constellation. Spread widely across the broad ridge, thirty must have been within easy sight from the trail as I walked along. A few were deeper in color, more crimson than orange. The ridge has one of the harshest climates in the park, moderated by no sheltering cliffs or trees. It is wholly exposed to wind, storm, cold, and heat. The odds against the lilies surviving in that place must be daunting. Yet there they were reaching for the zenith in full glory, proof that the site had exactly the conditions they needed to grow, blossom, and reproduce. On the day of my hike, they were perfect. I hiked up the next day with my partner to show her what I had seen, and by then many of them were dry and pale. Enough were still in full bloom to give her an idea what I was talking about, but the effect was diminished. Blooming in only one other section of the park that I know of, the lilies showed themselves to those with eyes to see in the right place at the right time. The irony was that I had deliberately kept away from Sargent Mountain in July and August for twenty years, preferring less traveled ways during the season of peak visitation. How many times have fear and loathing held me back when

Stepped log bridge, Jordan Cliffs Trail.

I had the opportunity to witness similar revelations of cosmic beauty?

When I told another woman about my experience a day later, she said, "We have much to learn from the wood lily."

The price I paid to see the lilies was meeting dogs on the trail. Panting dogs whose companions (not owners—I don't think you can own another spirit) carried no water, roaming dogs, barking dogs, snarling dogs. Wood lilies are native to Acadia; dogs are not. The park puts a lot of effort into eradicating purple loosestrife, an invasive species, from its wetlands, but does nothing to keep dogs, another invasive species, from its trails. The problem is not the dogs themselves but their companions who take them everywhere as members of the family. People are so heavily invested in their pets that separation becomes a problem. I saw one dog snap at a passing hiker, and heard another bark every five seconds while its companions enjoyed a picnic above Sar-

gent Mountain Pond. Dogs, being dogs, break the spell of Acadia, which is what I hike to discover. Being territorial and possessive, they draw attention to themselves and their companions, distracting me from the natural wonders I came to see. I have heard dogs defended as being cousins of the wolf, but they are so removed from their wild state that the family connection has long been severed. Like cats and gerbils, they are a domestic species, bred to the hearth rug and the bowl. Except on search and rescue missions, dogs have no place in national parks. My suggestion is that parks license kennels outside their boundaries to care for pets at a reasonable cost while people go hiking. There's a market nobody has opened up yet. Go to it, America, do your thing. Care for your parks and your pets both at the same time.

There are no easy routes up Sargent and Penobscot mountains. To reach the summits, you have to commit yourself to hiking in earnest. No matter what trail you take, your feet, ankles, and knees will be put to the test. Do not go lightly up the trail without well-fitting boots, heavy socks, water, and a clear sense where you are going. If you are not in good physical shape, stick to the carriage roads, or take a walk along the east side of Jordan Pond. I met one stocky hiker bent double on the trail because he couldn't breathe fast enough to supply his muscles with oxygen. He was an emergency waiting to happen, an emergency that would put a lot of other people at risk.

There are at least ten routes to the Sargent–Penobscot ridge, with many other variations. In order of increasing hazard and difficulty I tentatively rank them as follows:

1. Sargent Mountain South Ridge Trail from Asticou by way of Cedar Swamp Mountain
2. Penobscot Mountain Trail from Jordan Pond House
3. Amphitheater Trail from the Around-Mountain Carriage Road to the Sargent Mountain South Ridge Trail at Birch Spring
4. Jordan Cliffs Trail via connector to Penobscot Mountain summit from Jordan Pond House
5. Hadlock Brook Trail from Norumbega Mountain parking area

6. Giant Slide and Sargent Mountain North Ridge trails from the stone church on Route 198
7. Maple Spring Trail off the Hadlock Brook Trail from Norumbega Mountain parking area
8. Deer Brook Trail to the notch between Sargent and Penobscot mountains from the north end of Jordan Pond (badly eroded much of the way)
9. Giant Slide and Grandgent trails from the stone church on Route 198, and
10. Jordan Cliffs Trail to Sargent Mountain summit by way of Deer Brook from Jordan Pond House (from brook to summit, another badly eroded trail).

Almost all of these routes are steep in places and cross stretches of broken rock and smooth cobbles, requiring hikers to attend to their footing. And, each in its own way, all are wonderful because they take you to the heart of Acadia, the mile-long stretch between the summits of Sargent and Penobscot along a trail dipping to the edge of Sargent Mountain Pond, one of Acadia's smallest and most secluded oases. Anywhere along that stretch you know you are in a place apart. A place where law and order are determined by climate, terrain, and native species finding a foothold in one remote corner of the universe. On this hike, the wood lily and blueberry were first citizens on the ridge, along with wine-leaf cinquefoil, cotton grass, meadowsweet, and mountain sandwort. In the shaded glen where the Deer Brook Trail labors up from the east, damp-loving scale moss, lichens, and ferns thrived beneath sheltering trees. By the pond, white water lilies and yellow cow lilies (spatterdock) shone from the far shore. A black duck cruised among the grasses, and a robin—showiest of our thrushes—looked out from the branches of a white birch. A green frog twanged its one note. A father and son swam in the pond, which they told me must be 70° at the surface, cooler a few inches down. On my return, six women squatted in deep conversation on the shore, drying in the sun after swimming. Like bathers by Matisse, they belonged to the scene as naturally as lily or frog, adding a murmuring liveliness to their idyllic surroundings.

A raven strutting around Sargent's summit cairn struck a sterner note. I watched it fly along the slope, then land twenty feet from the cairn. It stayed there the fifteen minutes I was on top. Circling the cairn, walking, hopping, and flapping, it was active the whole time, seeming to have some agenda I could not figure out. The bird added a shadowy presence to the summit which, with its massive cairn looking like the grave mound of a kingly burial, was steeped in mystery already. It is easy to dismiss encounters in nature as accidental, but I choose to view them as opportunities for further learning. The question was not what was the raven there to teach me, but what was I there to learn from the raven? I would have to figure that out for myself, asking what I needed to know, then finding a way to read the signs

for an answer. The art of augury is in framing our questions very carefully, then in reading some sort of answer in the signs we receive. That is how nature instructs us through wood lilies and ravens—by inciting our curiosity, then leaving us to come up with our own answers.

What I learned on the mountain was that discovery is everything. When someone teaches you something, they are out to control your mind. When you discover something by

Northern end of the Jordan Cliffs Trail.

reading the signs yourself, you set yourself free. Teaching has to do with knowledge imposed from outside, learning with knowledge from the inside welling up. Science is more about ways of sharing human insight than it is about universal truth. "Come over here and look from where I am looking," the scientist says, "and see if you don't see what I see." The best science (or philosophy, theology, or any other discipline) can aim for is consensus among like-minded discoverers. By standardizing terminology, equipment, and procedures, it calibrates its practitioners to share similar outlooks and draw similar conclusions. But nature does not reveal its ways through rules laid upon it from outside. Nature is as nature does. Natural beings ourselves, our job is to *be* ourselves, to use our particular gifts in discovering the world around us so we can contribute effectively to its smooth operation. If we will surrender to their silence, wood lilies and ravens become master teachers. The trick to learning is in looking and listening with patience, awe, and humility. Instead of explaining things, we should experience them deeply inside and make them part of ourselves. Then we will discover what it is we have to learn from them.

Starting at 8:00 in the morning, I hiked from Jordan Pond House to the top of Penobscot by way of the Jordan Cliffs, then went on to the top of Sargent, and returned by the Penobscot Mountain Trail, reaching the pond house again at 3:35 p.m. The route was about 5.6 miles long, rising 1,113 feet from a low of 260 feet at the west branch of Jordan Stream to Sargent's 1,373-foot summit. The sky was hazy, but the sun shone brightly all day, the temperature ranging between 70° and 80° Fahrenheit. It was the perfect day to make the perfect hike up the perfect mountain.

I met 83 fellow hikers scattered at intervals along the trail, which never seemed crowded. I asked many of them how their hike was going, and replies ranged from "good" to "great!" One couple sent mixed messages, he saying "good," she saying "great!"

"You are having a better time than he is," I said to the woman.

"He has the trick knee," she said, "not me."

Later, another woman replied, "Great, but it's not finished yet."

"A work in progress," her partner said.

Just below the summit of Penobscot, another woman said, "OK, but we want to get to the top."

"Of Penobscot?" I asked. "If that's your goal, it's within easy reach."

"That's enough for today," she said.

I met a young woman hiking solo as I was coming down the Penobscot Mountain Trail. She said she had planned to go to work but had taken the day off because she hadn't been out all summer. She passed me again on her way down.

"You're fast," I told her.

"By yourself you can go as fast as you want," she said.

I thought about that, realizing that I speed up when I am with others on the trail, going faster than I normally would because my inclination is to stop and look at everything.

Studying the summit cairn, a woman from Mississippi had a lot of questions about the rocks on Penobscot Mountain, which led to a long discussion about glaciers. They don't have glaciers in Mississippi. She wanted to know the life history of every stone. She had a high level of curiosity, but would have learned more if she had asked the stones instead of me.

While we were standing there, a party of six came up single file from the Jordan Cliffs Trail. They were glad to get to the top.

"Ha!" said the first.

"Hallelujah!" said the second.

"Yea!" said the third.

"Neat!" said the fourth.

"Wow!" said the fifth.

"Lunchtime!" said the sixth.

Seeing a Cornell T-shirt, I asked the wearer if he had gone to Cornell. No, but his son had graduated from there six years ago. We talked about upstate New York where both of us had grown up, and he ended up telling me about the weather in Belgium this summer.

Sargent Mountain Pond.

"Forty days of rain," he said. Then he said it again.

The first three people I talked to passed me at the north end of the Jordan Cliffs. I had heard their voices behind me for five or ten minutes. They were a family from Atlanta.

"Escaping the Olympics," the woman said.

"This is my favorite trail," the daughter said, "next to the Precipice."

I had stopped to watch a pine siskin gathering nesting material in the trail ahead. She had a full grassy mustache by the time she flew off.

"Some women don't know when to quit," the woman from Atlanta said.

The man from Atlanta told me about a bird that nested in a plastic cup in a tree in their front yard.

I saw two hermit thrushes on the Jordan Cliffs Trail, and heard several others. I saw one turkey vulture rocking along Sargent's south ridge. The most conspicuous birds were flocks of gulls loafing near the south end of Penobscot. Some were still wading through the bushes gulping blueberries, but most of them were standing flat-footed with that look gulls have when they are full but wouldn't turn down another morsel if it were offered. They try to look disengaged, but follow every move you make. Gulls eat a great variety of foods, from garbage to blueberries. When they stand about like that, I think they might be suffering some sort of gastric distress. Their hangout ledges are covered with chalky blue poop this time of year, which the next rain washes off.

I also saw dragonflies, blue damselflies, a sulphur butterfly, grasshoppers, bees, and a hundred flies swarming on the wooden signpost rising out of the cairn on Sargent's summit.

Berries were everywhere. Blueberries, huckleberries, black chokeberries, Canada May rubies, bunchberries, juniper berries, and Solomon's seal berries dangling like green grapes.

One or two pink lambkill blossoms caught my eye, but they were rare exceptions. This was August. It was goldenrod's turn to bloom. And flat-topped aster's. Meadowsweet hung on, along with yarrow and a few roses. Pale trumpets of tall rattlesnake root were just coming on, every bit as prepossessing as their name. Harebell was at its height, cracks in the Jordan Cliffs sprouting graceful stalks hung with blue bells. At one point along the cliffs trail I saw a cluster of them waving in the corner of my eye, trying to get my attention, but I was busy scrambling up a nine-foot cliff. I thanked them for calling and said I couldn't come to the phone right now, but if they wanted to leave a message I'd get back to them.

Wood lilies, Sargent Mountain south ridge.

Just then a seaplane flew south between the Bubbles and the cliffs at an altitude no more than 150 feet above the pond. It banked sharply with a roar and flew off above the canoe carry between the Bubbles and Pemetic Mountain. The noise echoed from the cliffs, but what surprised me most was how far below me the plane had flown. Shades of Grand Canyon.

The mushroom militia was everywhere along the trail, making their move to take over Acadia at last. "Comes the revolution," nothing; the revolution was here. Some mushrooms looked like flapjacks, some round tins of cornbread, some funnels, others the familiar parasols. Pink colonies of coral fungi looked like miniature cities on Mars. Every clump was a different color, from deep red to bright yellow, glistening white to carbon black. Wherever I stopped along the Jordan Cliffs Trail, I could see a dozen or more from where I stood.

The Jordan Cliffs Trail. I agree with the young woman from Atlanta: it is one of my favorites, too. It is one thing to gawk at the cliffs from the far side of Jordan Pond, but to put your body where your eyes are looking and actually go

there is an entirely different experience. The big surprise is how green the cliffs are, how full of life. I saw a greater variety of blooms and berries on the cliffs trail than anywhere else on my hike. And a greater variety of trees. The trail starts out in mixed woods of spruce, pine, cedar, birch, and maple. Then that variety is winnowed down to oak and cedar; and then to cedar for the most part on the steeper slopes. If they were stripped away, the true nature of the trail would stand revealed; but hiking through woods most of the way, the hiker is often unaware of the drop-off veiled by the trees. As I said, we live in inner worlds at a remove from the cosmic drama around us. Sheltered by dim awareness, we head into territory where angels hold back. If we knew what we were getting into every time, we would sit on the sidelines sucking our thumbs. We would never have children, for instance, or build a house. But blessed with half-sight as we are, we blithely push on into the bright future we paint for ourselves. We scramble along cliffsides as if that is where we belong. The Jordan Cliffs Trail is remarkable not only in spanning the cliffs but in coaxing us to go along, and in getting us across once we are there. At either end the park posts a warning sign:

CAUTION: TRAIL STEEP
WITH EXPOSED CLIFFS
AND FIXED IRON RUNGS.

That notice reminds us we are on our own. Which we are anyway, no matter where we go. Think of the contagious diseases we might be exposed to at Jordan Pond House, yet there is no sign to alert us. OK, we get the message—under our own recognizance. We accept full responsibility. Let's get on with the hike.

Despite the warning, for the most part the trail is not steep. From the south, it rises gradually along a granite ridge, cuts across several stretches of talus, offering a pleasant walk through Acadia's woods while approaching the cliffs. Early on, there are no views to speak of. Perhaps you notice Jordan Ridge rising to the west, but that seems to have no more to do with you than the distant hulk of Pemetic to the east sensed here and there through the trees. Then you come to a prospect onto the Bubbles across the pond, and you are surprised how high you are. From there the trail actually goes down for a ways, then up, then down again. The trail is marked with two sets of painted blazes: red and blue. The park has found blue to be more visible, so uses that exclusively. Yearning for the good old days, trail phantoms stick to red, inadvertently cluttering the trail. Dueling blazes. Dueling mind-sets. Collision of inner worlds. In other places it is common to mark different trails with different colors. Seeing the dual marks, some hikers might think there were two different trails along the cliffs. In fact there is only one official trail which is redundantly marked.

Crossing a talus slope, the trail comes at last to a mossy cliff, but this is sheltered among trees and seems to have no connection to the Jordan Cliffs. A subtle harbinger, nothing more. But the cliff is there to stay. The trail rises by a flight of thirteen granite steps along the cliff, coming out beneath a wall of rock twenty-five feet high. The real thing. You have arrived! Harebells hung up and down the wall the day of my hike, decking it as if for the arrival of a presidential candidate, or a beauty queen. But no, I was the only traveler. I chose to believe it was for me. Rising on more steps, the trail angles upward, soon coming to the first open outlook unscreened by trees. How high you are! The landscape drops abruptly, then recedes in layers—from steep plunge, to a wooded shelf below, backed by the pond, then dark Pemetic rising on the far side, topped by bright sky. I heard a strange, rhythmic sound like the bow of a boat cutting through small waves—but there was no boat on the pond. Then I pictured a runner plying the graveled surface of the carriage road through the woods below, and I knew that was the sound I heard. Rounding a bend, I saw near-vertical cliffs ahead. In the foreground, asters, goldenrod, harebell, meadowsweet, and yellow shrubby cinquefoil bloomed by the trail. Bees and dragonflies patrolled the airspace above them. Distant views give no hint of the color you will find up close. These are no *monts-désert*, as Champlain put it in September 1604, but *monts-de-vivre*, mountains of life.

From here on, the trailmakers used a variety of techniques to help hikers navigate the cliffs. With iron rods, they pinned logs along narrow, sloping shelves to hold stones laid down to level the treadway. The first two logs run seventeen feet across an otherwise impassable stretch. Later on I came to shorter runs of seven, nine, and six feet using the same device. The only problem was the logs looked old and not that strong. Would they hold my extra weight? Deciding not to press the issue, I stepped on solid granite where I could, using the reinforcements to steady myself. Those logs need replacing in the near future, for hikers' peace of mind if nothing else.

Past the first retaining log, the trail enters cool oak and cedar woods, rising over broken rock past outcrops sprouting with rock tripe. Then it crosses a steep cliff on an open shelf four to five feet wide. Peering over the edge, I looked straight down on a talus slope surprisingly far below. Looking up, I saw water streaming toward me over sheer cliffs cloaked in dark, velvety moss. The water formed a pool in the trail, then continued its plunge toward the pond. With no trees to filter the truth, I could believe these were the real McCoy—the Jordan Cliffs. Crossing another pinned log, the

Sargent Mountain summit cairn; Western Mountain in distance.

trail enters cedar woods thriving on water dripping from above. The treadway gets rootier and rockier but, sheltered under the trees, it seems safer than the open cliffside stretch a few paces back. A large boulder looms ahead, the trail crossing over the top of it with help from single iron rungs for hand and foot. Running at the base of a cliff rising thirty feet amid the cedars, the trail drops seven feet, cedar roots giving hikers a helping hand. Then the *pièce de résistance* of the trailmaker's craft, a seventeen-foot log bridge across a narrow gap in the cliff. Supported by an X-brace in the middle, the single log slants down across the gap, with thirteen steps cut into it to improve the footing. Even with handrails on either side, the bridge doesn't look all that trustworthy. It, too, will soon need replacing. Even so, because it is made of local materials and is tailored to its setting, it is the perfect bridge for the site. Bar none, it is the best bridge in Acadia. A real mind sticker, a bridge you will never forget. On a hike in late fall I came this far to find the bridge coated with ice; turning back, I felt glad to have caught sight of an old friend.

Past the bridge, the trail drops fifty feet, switchbacking over carefully laid cribwork steps. An iron handrail offers help across a sloping shelf. Here was a clump of maple leaves turned bright red at the end of a branch. What did they know that I didn't? I crossed an eighteen-inch shelf onto the boldest part of the trail. Two more sustaining logs offer footing under cliffs rising fifty feet straight up. This is where you become a true believer. These *are* the Jordan Cliffs, and you *are* right out there on them. A hand rung helps you up a six-foot wall, then four more rungs and two handrails get you up another fifteen feet, where you scale a nine-foot wall on stones wedged in a crevice. This is where I got a call from the harebells, and the seaplane roared by below. Distractions, distractions, when I was trying to concentrate.

The view from the open cliffs is straight down to Jordan Pond, across to the Bubbles, up to Pemetic across the valley, and to Cadillac beyond. I could see campers and RVs on the Cadillac Mountain Road, their inmates scanning Acadia from a distance while I was out there hanging on the cliffs. I didn't feel superior, but I felt blessed in knowing the park the way I do.

Coming up from the south, the Jordan Cliffs Trail builds to a climax that is absolutely granitic. From that rocky high, it is a short scramble to the oak at the end of the cliffs where the trail turns into the woods one last time. Maps show the cliffs trail dropping into the valley of Deer Brook, then rising steeply to the summit of Sargent Mountain. I consider the cliffs trail to end at the oak. From there I took the connector to the summit of Penobscot, and headed for Sargent by way of the mountain pond and the wood-lily barrens.

When I got down to Jordan Pond House at the end of my hike, I saw 103 people being served at outdoor tables, and 38 more serving themselves from blueberry bushes by the pond. There were 63 cars from 15 states and 3 provinces of Canada in the parking lot, with that many again parked on both sides of the loop road, not including the overflow and boat ramp parking lots. High summer in Acadia. Why would anyone want to be anywhere else?

❂

56—ST. SAUVEUR MOUNTAIN & VALLEY PEAK LOOP

From Acadia Mountain parking area
To St. Sauveur Mountain, Valley Peak, and back
Up by St. Sauveur Mountain Trail
Back by Valley Peak and Valley Cove trails,
Valley Cove and Man o' War Brook fire roads
4.5 miles, August 10, 1996

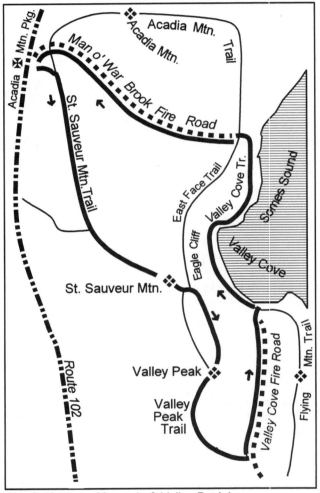

56—St. Sauveur Mountain & Valley Peak loop.

"Where are we headed?" the woman asked.

Bingo! I thought to myself, that's what we'd all like to know. The elderly man and his daughter had taken a wrong turn. I met them coming down the St. Sauveur Mountain Trail shortly after eight o'clock as I was heading up; they were looking for the top of Eagle Cliff, which meant they had to turn around and go the other way.

"Have you seen any eagles?" the man asked.

"On other hikes," I told him, "not on St. Sauveur, not today."

"Have you seen any ospreys?"

I gave the same answer. The hikers had been on Mount

Desert Island five days and hadn't seen the hawks they had expected. They thought they might see some at Eagle Cliff.

"What's that white flower?" the woman asked, "I don't see any here, but it's all along the trail. With a yellow tip."

Binoculars and notepad must have made me look like some kind of oracle. I told her cow wheat was the only white and yellow flower I had seen. I am always glad to talk with hikers about what they see along the trail. We had a good talk, settling the major issues of the day. I wanted them to go ahead of me so I could amble at my usual speed, but they said they were slow hikers, so I went on.

Having a poor memory, I wanted to write down what we had talked about, but I couldn't stop because they were hot on my heels. I scribbled as I went. I thought I would soon outdistance them, but I kept hearing the sharp tink of the man's stick against granite, so went faster and faster. Tink, tink, tink. Between tinks I heard heavy breathing. The man seemed bent on keeping up with me. I was right, they were faster than I was. Not willing to play hare to his greyhound, I stopped and made some notes.

Osprey poised in flight.

"Have you seen any warblers?" the man asked, catching up with me. "We thought they'd be getting ready to migrate, but we haven't seen or heard any, not one."

This was my kind of hiker. We discussed the warbler issue at some length, drawing no conclusions. Our business finished, I went ahead, this time without pursuit.

We met twice more, once as I was leaving a note saying, "cow wheat" next to a thick scattering of the plant, and again on top of Eagle Cliff just down from the 679-foot summit of St. Sauveur Mountain.

"This is what we came for," the man said.

The three of us peered through binoculars, seeing only gulls. A little past nine o'clock, the day was as still as dawn, warmth from the sun just now stirring up a gentle breeze. After ten minutes we went our separate ways, they to go sailing, I to continue my loop.

Two trails connect Eagle Cliff with Valley Peak. I took the lower trail, the one toward the edge of the cliff. It dips down through great sweeps of juniper into mixed woods where I saw a midnight-blue fox scat. Reaching a bare patch of ledge I looked back at Eagle Cliff—and there was a splendid osprey bearing a fish in its talons floating on the gentle updraft rising from Valley Cove. Not one osprey, two

ospreys, one fifty feet above the other, both clutching fish. With that extra weight to carry, they had waited for the updraft to give them a lift up the 650-foot wall. The overcast had burned off while I was heading for Valley Peak, sunlight warming the air column next to the granite, getting the elevator off to a slow start. Both birds wound up a gradual incline, tracing a great circular stairway in the air. Even without binoculars, I could see their pale undersides, shaded wrists, and as they spiraled toward me, gleaming white crowns. They performed their graceful maneuvers together like partners in a slow dance, seemingly mindful of each other, the distance between them only enhancing their bond. Well above the summit, they went off to their respective nests, the first crossing Somes Sound toward the flank of Norumbega Mountain, the second heading south-southeast toward Manset and Seawall Pond. As I swung around to watch one then the other, I picked up the strong scent of fox.

Scanning the cliff through binoculars, I soon saw another osprey almost brushing against the granite. It rose easily on flexed wings, circling out, then rounding in to sweep the cliff with outstretched primaries. Round and round it went, higher and higher. Below it, another followed in its wake. Neither had a fish. The dance continued in slow motion. Around and up, around and up, adagio, always adagio. "Have you seen any ospreys?" the man had asked. He left ten minutes too soon. Maybe he looked back like I did, but the trees would have blocked his view. His timing was off by a whisker. To be in the right place at the right time to find what you are looking for, hike early and hike often. In hindsight, I saw that the ospreys had waited in a holding pattern below, or had perched until the sun came out and the wind had risen enough to help them scale the cliff. It was no accident they were there when I saw them; my being there to see them was the accident.

The upper osprey glided north above the sound while its partner continued the slow circle dance alone, round, and round, and round. No, not alone. A turkey vulture coasted along the cliff, then took up the spiral, rising beneath the osprey, the two forming another visual pair, one on flat wings, the other with wings in a slight dihedral. I paired them in my mind as I might pair strangers walking near each other on the sidewalk in front of me. The thermal was their link, not any direct relationship. Two big birds sharing the same strategy for gaining altitude. Both depended on strong winds and thermals to maintain their lifestyles. Without air currents, how big would such raptors be? No larger than a gull, perhaps, or a crow. Think of vultures on Jupiter coasting on two-hundred-mile-an-hour winds, birds with wingspans of twenty or thirty feet. Wouldn't mission control be surprised to have the next planetary probe send back signals from the gizzard of a giant Jovian condor.

While watching the osprey-vulture duet through binoculars, I saw another bird fly across my field of view—flap-flap-flap-glide—a sharp-shinned hawk that needed no assistance from the wind to go where it wanted, when it wanted. Lowering my binoculars to watch the dancers and the sharpie at the same time, I saw another osprey taking the elevator up the cliff. That made five ospreys in six or seven minutes. The sharpie disappeared as fast as it had come. Then another turkey vulture rode over from Acadia Mountain and entered the thermal, making a foursome with vulture number one and the two ospreys, all spiraling at once in the same column of air above the cliff, all spinning the same direction, all rising with similar grace. Five ospreys, two turkey vultures, and a sharp-shinned hawk. Change that order to *three* turkey vultures—another had entered the thermal from somewhere, so there were now two ospreys and three vultures ascending in great rounds to the top of the sky. There I was on Valley

Eagle Cliff rising above Valley Cove.

Peak, every moment adding to my sense of universal creation, every second revealing the lively inner workings of Acadia. Two low-flying jets thundered over Eastern Way, banked, and shot off over Western Way, stealing the show for ten seconds, but they didn't have the stamina to keep it up. A petty annoyance, nothing more. Nobody has ever asked me if I have seen any jets. If I have, I am not likely to remember. One man in trunks on deck, a hulking yacht (I guessed it was a hundred-and-twenty-feet long) wallowed from behind Flying Mountain, with a Zodiac and two jet skis performing aquatic arabesques in its wake. A waterbug drifting from behind a rock, nothing more.

Every instant in the universe is different from every other instant. Valley Peak is as good a place as any to watch the passing procession. In March I wrote about falling snow revealing hidden patterns of moving air, giving rise to the sensation of walking through the mind of God. The circling birds I had seen kindled a similar thought. Spiraling upward in my experience, the ospreys and vultures revealed currents in the air that reflected currents in my mind. My awareness orchestrated those moving shapes into a coherent event. The coming together of those nine birds (including the sharpie) at Eagle Cliff was pure happenstance. Independently doing their own thing, they coalesced in a mind hungry for mean-

ingful patterns and relationships. It was not God's mind I witnessed but the workings of my own.

God is that which complements our feeble awareness, completing it, making us whole. She works from the inside, not by some trickle-down magic laid on from above, but by insights welling up from the core of our being. The source of those insights is our life experience, our inclination or temperament, and the collective successes of our ancestors passed to us in our genetic inheritance. God is the ineffable mystery within that makes us who we are. Personified, projected outward, she becomes the creator, law giver, exemplar, protector, sovereign, lover, judge—giver of whatever we are too weak to get for ourselves.

Taking a positive view of humanity, Quakers often cite George Fox's phrase, "that of God in every one," by which they mean to address the goodness and virtue residing in every soul. That notion has become a truism among Friends, a cornerstone of their faith. Yet like so many truths, it is also an enigma in that it dresses a universal mystery as an accomplished fact. Is God a great flame igniting a small spark in each breast? Or is she the collective brightness of those singular sparks taken together? How does that work? How does that of God enter into me, and how do I enter into God? What is the relation between part and whole, whole and part? How does my paltry experience of the universe relate to the universe in its entirety? Our traditional attack on the problem is to work from the outside in, from the whole to the part, from God to ourselves, from divine principle to specific example. But if we take the view that wholes are constructions built of their various parts, we have to work the other way, starting with our own experience and working out from there. The Quaker saying then gets turned on its head: *that of every one in God.* God becomes the collective sum of our individual notions and experiences of divinity. Together, we create God, not the other way around. Which—given that gods follow in the footsteps of particular men and women, take form in particular languages and dialects, and die with the civilizations espousing them—makes a certain amount of sense. We freely export God to the larger world, then struggle to get her back.

What I saw from Valley Peak was not evidence of the mind of God, but a direct revelation of my personal need to discover order in the universe. That order appeared to me as a parade of stately birds spiraling above Eagle Cliff. Standing at the center of a granite ledge surrounded by trees, I felt a profound sense of reverence for all that I was privileged to witness. I knew I was watching a unique event, a sequence never to be repeated in the history of the universe. Similar events would take place, but never one exactly like this. I stood at the forefront of universal creation, and the remarkable thing was that I knew it. The universe was expanding before my eyes, and incorporating my awareness in the process. Such is life: a succession of universal events unfolding in the minds of those who take part. The sharpie brought its awareness, the vultures theirs, the ospreys theirs, I mine. Each of us was at the forefront of an instant of universal unfolding built of remnants of

Valley Cove Trail at the base of Eagle Cliff.

former instants back through the evolution of our respective species to the formation of the solar system from remnants of supernovas, galaxies, hydrogen atoms, and electrons. As Brian Swimme puts it in *Hidden Heart of the Cosmos,* "The center of the cosmos is each event in the cosmos. Each person lives in the center of the cosmos. . . ; the actual origin of the universe is where you live your life." He is not resorting to hyperbole. The universe is alive and well in us. We make it what it is at this moment. When we die, others will fill our place on the front line of creation.

What I am grappling with here is the sense of reverence I felt on Valley Peak. That, not God, was the issue of my experience. We import God to answer to our reverence, but that is a stopgap measure we fall back on when our experience leaps ahead of our imagination and understanding. Reverence does not give us access to the divine but to something far more grand—the unfolding of the universe itself.

To that, and to ourselves as creatures of that unfolding. Reverence points two ways at once: to the aspect of the universe which is revered, and to the subject experiencing a sense of awe and gracious humility. Reverence incorporates both in one event, uniting the inner world of awareness with its setting in all-encompassing mystery. There were the ospreys, the vultures, the sharpie, the granite cliff, the air, the trees—and there was me. Perhaps I was the only witness.

I was as much a participant in the flow of events as the others. I was grateful to have seen what I saw. The feeling I felt was love, the highest form of reverence. We love what we cannot do without. It is our way of opening to what we value most so that we become a part of it and it of us. That is what the man meant when he asked if I had seen any ospreys. He had his values straight. He was looking to take part in the life of Acadia, to declare himself to the universe, and have it declare itself to him. At least he had a sense of the possible; he missed it by minutes. The older we get, the deeper we wonder at our few gifts, the clearer our needs become. Acadia is the place some of us meet the universe face-to-face. Here God is alive and well, not outside us only, or only inside, but in the interaction between us as partners in the universal dance that joins us all in a single celebration of the possible come to life in a moment of beauty.

Which is a long-winded way of saying I had a great hike. Besides the wonders I have mentioned, I saw tracks of deer and woodchuck, holes drilled by sapsucker and chiseled by pileated woodpecker. I heard mourning doves, crows, and hermit thrushes; saw a junco and hundreds of gulls; and met spiders, ants, grasshoppers, mosquitoes, damselflies, and dragonflies. I also met twenty-four people, including two men at the base of Eagle Cliff on the Valley Cove Trail who asked me how to get back to the St. Sauveur Mountain parking area.

"The shortest route would be to bore straight through this cliff," I said, "either that or go around."

They debated whether to retrace their steps or take the Valley Peak Trail from the fire road, both ways being about equally long. They opted to go ahead, not back.

On the St. Sauveur Mountain and Valley Peak trails, the

flowers I saw included meadowsweet, goldenrod, cow wheat, wintergreen, mountain sandwort, and only two wine-leaf cinquefoil blooms. Yellow wood sorrel bloomed along the Valley Cove Fire Road, with yellow hawkweed and tall buttercup. The section of the Valley Cove Trail around the cove itself was a veritable garden. Herb Robert edged the trail, every plant showing one or two pink blossoms. Three asters—large-leaved, flat-topped, whorled—stood here and there. Tall rattlesnake root looked pale and ungainly in patches of goldenrod exploding like fireworks. A few harebells added a touch of blue to the cliff, and sundrops a touch of yellow at their base. The one clump of Indian pipes added no color at all beyond a glow of pink translucence. Shriveling poison ivy leaves caught my eye as if they were blooming. A patch of blue-bead hoisted potent-blue berries on tall stems for all to admire and the wary to forgo; one of my guides lists them as "somewhat poisonous." St. Johnswort bloomed at the turnaround on the Man o' War Brook Fire Road.

Scrub or bear oak stood out as the most unusual deciduous tree, red pine as the most notable conifer. Pitch pine dominated the gradual ascent to the summit of St. Sauveur Mountain, with Northern white cedar, white pine, red spruce, and various maples filling in the gaps where the soil was thick enough. Red oak replaced the scrub oak on the lower end of the Valley Peak Trail. Along Somes Sound where glacial soil deposits are thicker than elsewhere on the loop, a variety of trees gave a sense of thriving mixed woods. Here ash, beech (one big one with no bark disease that I could see), and yellow birch added texture to the landscape. The cluster of six oaks fallen asunder on the edge of the trail (you now have to duck under two of the trunks) was an object lesson in true grit. Two of them had leafed out and were bearing acorns while lying in a prone position. You are not down until you are down, and even then you may not be licked, so you might as well keep trying.

I took six-and-a-half hours to go the four-and-a-half miles composing this loop. The low point was the tide line in Valley Cove where I stepped off the trail to take a picture of Eagle Cliff. The high point was the summit of St. Sauveur 679 feet above. Valley Peak, a spur on the south end of St. Sauveur, rises 520 feet above the cove. The temperature ranged comfortably between 68° and 78° Fahrenheit. All in all, I felt I had discovered the perfect loop. Not too long or too short, too steep or too easy, with solid footing ninety-nine percent of the way (except for a few jumbled places around the edge of the cove), the trail is one of the quickest ways I know to get the full flavor of Acadia in a single morning or afternoon hike. No, you won't see the same aerial display I did, and I won't see it again, either. But

something else will be happening on the leading edge of creation, and all we can do is give ourselves to it, whatever it is, which is true of every hike we can make.

One thing I hadn't expected was the upsurge of memory from the last time I had hiked along Valley Cove on February 22nd of this year. That was the time I watched a missile of ice shoot down the cliff and land in the trail a few yards ahead of me, smashing into shards of shrapnel which

Herb Robert blooming along the Valley Cove Trail.

sprayed across the slope (see Hike 28). The closer I approached the spot this time, the clearer the image got. I was not hiking in the here-and-now so much as the there-and-then. My experience had turned the site into a shrine of personal remembrance. Where there had been snow and ice six months ago, harebell and herb Robert bloomed now. The universe shows different faces at different seasons. If we turn toward them without prejudice, our experience grows richer than we expect. Until we meet the face that speaks our name and calls us beyond ourselves, which is why we have names in the first place, to be singled out.

I saw eleven dikes on this loop, ranging in width from two inches to fifteen feet. Volunteers from the Appalachian Mountain Club summer camp on Echo Lake had been digging dips and ditches along the Valley Peak Trail, trying to prevent the trail from becoming a drainage channel every time it rained. I could smell the fresh earth, making me think I had just missed the trail crew by a day at most. I could see the recruiting poster: "Vacation in Acadia—dig a ditch!" That is the spirit that kept the Civilian Conservation Corps going in the '30s and '40s, though that was no vacation but a matter of survival for a generation of young men who went on to fight in World War II. Whatever you do, put your heart into it. That is the law of universal success, the one law governing oaks, hawks, hikers, and vacationers alike.

Mine had been the one car in the Acadia Mountain parking area at eight o'clock; when I got back at two-thirty, there were forty-seven others spilling onto both sides of the highway: a third from Maine; a third from Massachusetts, Connecticut, and New York; and another third from eight other states and the province of Quebec. At three passengers per car, some 150 people had converged on that spot. Was it happenstance we were all there together, or were we all out searching for the same thing? Without taking an exit poll, I guessed we were trying after our fashion to connect with the universe we lived in, looking to rouse a sense of reverence that would help us sort our values and keep them straight. I silently wished my fellow wayfarers well in their quests, got in my car, and drove off.

❁

Steve Perrin on Western Mountain.   (Photo: Carole Beal)

57—WESTERN MOUNTAIN LOOP

From Long Pond pumping station
To Mansell Mountain, Knight Nubble,
    Bernard Mountain, and back
    Up by Perpendicular and Western Mountain
        Ridge trails
    Down by Western Mountain South Face Trail,
        Western Mountain Truck Road, and
        Cold Brook Trail

4.5 miles, August 16, 1996

Rungs and ladder on the Perpendicular Trail.

On my loop up the Perpendicular Trail, across the ridge of Western Mountain from Mansell to Bernard, and down the Western Mountain South Face Trail back to the to the pumping station via the Cold Brook Trail, I met eight groups of hikers. The largest, a group of sixteen, was made up of this summer's Youth Conservation Corps, their leaders, and members of the park's trail maintenance crew. They had hiked to the top of Bernard Mountain on their lunch break, and were going back to work on the Western Trail coming up from Pine Hill. The seven other groups were couples and families. All but one were engaged in lively conversations. The silent exception was a man carrying a toddler papoose-style on his back. The others were all talking, talking, their tongues working as hard as their legs. I heard them coming,

I heard them going. Standing aside to let them pass, I noticed they generally fixed their eyes a few feet in front of their feet, seldom looking to either side.

Hiking solo and silently for the most part, I realized how different my trail experience must be from theirs. I cannot gawk and talk at the same time. To write about my trail adventures, I have to give myself to the trail, which means going alone, taking the trail as my only companion. It engages me, but not in my native tongue. It speaks its own language, which I struggle to learn as I go. My job is to give Acadia a fair hearing in my experience, then to translate that experience into words which others will read their own way.

What is the difference between hiking in a group and hiking solo—single, unaccompanied, alone? It is hard for our minds to grasp the meaning of separateness, the nature of things by themselves. Unique events and singularities are almost beyond comprehension. There is nothing we can compare them to. We think in terms of classes of things, categories, repeatable events. A class of one is no class at all. It is something waiting to be grouped with something else—to be made plural, coupled, included as part of a whole. Nothing exists by itself. Relationship is all. All is relationship. Plato labored over the problem of the one and the many, the difference between one thing and more than one. Here is a thing all by itself; it is what it is. Put it with another thing, it becomes party to a relationship, which is something else again. No longer an independent whole by itself, its nature now depends on its connectedness to something beyond itself. Man and wife. Mother and child. Teacher and student. Labor and management.

In school we learn that $1 + 1 = 2$, but that simple formula speaks a mystery the greatest minds do not understand. There is a distance and a tension between individual things that must be included in the notion of plurality. A couple exists in relationship. The relationship is what makes it a couple. Yet the relationship is not part of either one by itself. It is something else. The mystical plus sign is everything. That is where the magic is hidden.

Language, love, and beauty live in the plus sign, the space between partners in relationship, and between pluralities. The plus sign makes room for science, religion, government, and art, which are not disciplines in themselves so much as systems of relationship within society. The plus sign gives ideas a place to grow. A couple hiking along a trail includes two people and the space between them: between parent and child, husband and wife, friend and friend, lover and lover. World literature is devoted to describing such spaces. We live in the plus sign. It holds every relationship we can know, and the possibility of every relationship

beyond that. The toddler carried in the frame on his father's back lives in that space. The boy asking his father at the top of the Perpendicular Trail, "If you jumped off the world and fell, would you fall forever?" lives in that space. The NYNEX doctor on a "bike and hike day" with his companion lives in that space. The man from Quebec who said, "We speak so many languages, we don't know what culture we belong to," lives in that space. The plus sign (the

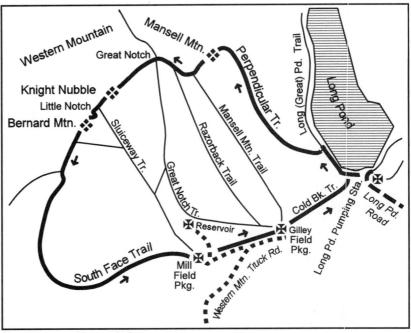

57—Western Mountain loop.

possibility and actuality of relationship) moves with them as they hike. When Mainers talk about folks being from Away, that is what they mean: those people bring Away with them tucked in the space between them. The space they bring with them gets in the way of their experience because it comes between their senses and their surroundings. When we look out at a vista, we see what the plus signs we carry in our packs let us see.

Ideally, hiking solo means to leave relationship behind. To go forth as an independent mote in the universe open to events as they occur. Of course that ideal state can never be. Every act of perception requires reaching out from some sort of preexisting mind-set. But it is possible to hold mind-sets in abeyance, to see what comes up and then to surrender to the moment as it emerges in awareness. Going alone makes it easier to hike with an open mind. To give attention to the landscape. To engage that landscape in dialogue asking, listening, reframing the question. What is that pink flower? That fish in the shallows? Why is the landscape like this? Why do only these few plants grow here? Making Acadia our hiking companion, we establish a growing relationship with it. It is, after all, the place where we are. Our street address in the universe. If not there, where are we? People drive all the way to Mount Desert Island yet may leave without seeing it if their mind won't let them get free from Away. When our minds and bodies are in different places, we are lost.

The wonder of hiking with a companion is that both people can enrich their relationship by being together in similar landscapes at the same time. Letting the landscape be the plus sign that unites them, couples can grow in new ways in new places, sharing new experiences, letting their relationship grow beyond what it was before they set out. One of the secrets of sustaining a relationship is to let it grow in new ways. This takes trust that the new ways will not threaten what has been attained, but will add new dimensions to it. I have seen American military personnel stationed in Europe in peacetime be so fearful of their new surroundings that they locked themselves in an enclave and never went abroad. That's how I see hikers lost in trail conversations. They are not where they think they are.

For people hiking in groups, *being there* is the secret. Being together in relationship as who they are, where they are. Not as who they *were* somewhere else; who they *are,* together, here, right now. One of the plus signs, the elements of relationship, is the location where the relationship comes into being. Relationships don't exist in a vacuum; they are situated where the participants are as they relate to one another. The setting is part of the relationship. Not in an incidental way, but fundamentally and substantially. Location shapes what happens, becoming part of events as each participant and witness experiences them. Events are an expression of the landscape where they come into being in awareness. People take in their surroundings, becoming partners with trees, plants, birds, water, sky, and other natural elements. Acadia becomes more that just a place to visit; it becomes a place to be and to live—a habitat. An address in the universe where people can reach out and be touched.

Love is one of the greatest mysteries in any relationship. We know people become attracted to each other in such a way that acquaintance blossoms into friendship and, when desire conquers fear, into the more intimate stages of love. We do not know what starts the progression, or sustains its development. Why these two people out of millions? Why now? Why here? We come up with star-crossed love and fatal attractions, but those are metaphors, not explanations. My hunch is that place draws people together. Lovers are active expression of their place on Earth. They stand somewhere, rising from ancient roots, living proof that their lineage is successful, and they are ready to commit themselves to the continuation of their lines into the future. Love flows not from the heart but from the Earth. From the springs of beauty, health, promise, and success. When two

people come together as particular expressions of Earth's bounty and ongoing creativity, they lay the foundation of the future, not just for themselves or their habitats, but for the next stage in the unfolding of the great universal adventure. Without the dimension of place, couples represent only themselves as motes entangled in air. The word "casual," as in casual encounters, casual conversation, and casual sex, hints at the missing element of commitment to place. If this

The Perpendicular Trail winds up Mansell Mountain.

commitment is not part of a relationship, the coming together of two people is an accident of two desires rubbing against each other for fleeting gratification. Partners who endure represent more than themselves. They are Earth embracing Earth, place embracing place, life embracing life.

Which seems a heavy trip to lay on hikers out for a little fun on Western Mountain. You can't be in love all the time, anymore than you can be profound. Profundity is what many are trying to escape. Enough, already! Relax! But what I see is people working hard to hold onto Away because that is where they know who they are. They are driven by forces pursuing them from other contexts. Away is alive and well right here. It takes a lot of effort to import it and lay it on top of Acadia. My point is that opening to where you are takes less work, and is more gratifying at the same time. Many visitors work harder than they need to when they go on vacation. They put a lot of energy into preserving the status quo instead of discovering themselves in a new place. Hiking means moving ahead into the unknown. Some of the hikers I see are doing jumping jacks in place. When they leave, they haven't *been* anywhere. If you haven't been anywhere, the question is, can you claim to have been at all?

The problem is we don't know how to let go of the old routine. We take it with us everywhere we go, thinking it is the only routine there is. Habit, William James would say.

Once we tame a world, we want it to stay that way. But where's the excitement in that? The fun, the challenge, the adventure? If we come back from a hike the same as when we left, what have we accomplished? How have we grown?

My own advice would be to say nothing on the trail that does not spring from experiencing the landscape itself. Use the hike to expand a relationship, not tie it down. Grow into the space Acadia offers. Become larger together. Fall in love

Beech Mountain and Long Pond from Mansell Mountain overlook.

again, with the landscape and with each other. Let the past rest in peace. Transcend it. Go where you have never been. Discover who you can be in this place. Discover who your companions can be. Instead of being strangers in a strange land, go native. Learn about local ecosystems. Find out what plants grow here, what animals and birds, what insects, what fish, what mosses and ferns. Learn about granite and glaciers, peat bogs, the fire of 1947. Hike in Acadia, not in Away. Put your mind where your feet are—you will be amazed how rich life can be on the trails of Acadia. You will discover life forms you never saw before, and never knew existed. You will develop respect for native flora and fauna, species that have found ways to survive not only Maine winters but Maine summers to boot. In short, by actually being in Acadia while you are here, you will take Acadia with you when you leave. It will be woven into the fabric of your life, yours to take home, not because you bought it, but because you opened to it and invited it in.

When I have been inactive for a few days, I sometimes go out on a trail for exercise. When I do, I move right along, zip, zip, zip, paying attention to the treadway ahead so I don't slip or fall. I see almost nothing along the trail. Ask me if I see anything interesting, I have to admit, no, nothing interesting at all. And when I go with a companion, I sometimes get carried away by our conversation, with the same

result. In either case I suffer a kind of trail blindness, an affliction that disconnects my awareness from my senses so that I lose my bearings and can't say much about the trail I am on. I don't call that hiking. Hiking takes my full attention in the here-and-now. Being alert to my surroundings is the main issue. I have to be proactive, looking and listening, sniffing and reaching out. The landscape is wild in the sense it does not come to us of its own free will. We have to lasso it, bridle it, corral it, break it to saddle and bit. Not by altering its natural inclinations, but those of our own awareness. Directing our attention toward it, the landscape will stand still and let us approach. It will be there for us. The question is, will we be there for it? The silent father with his papoose was there on the Perpendicular Trail. "What a great trail—fantastic!" he said with a grin as he passed. The last entry in the log in Great Notch recorded a similar sentiment:

8/16 Love the Perpendicular Trail—
seeing fog below me.
This is the best!
Bob Fox

I started out at 7:30 a.m. from the pumping station at the south end of Long Pond, the landscape shrouded in thick fog. Not thick like pea soup so much as tofu, yogurt, sour cream. I knew the view by heart—Mansell Mountain west, Beech Mountain east, the two green slopes divided by the intervening waters of the largest pond on the island. None of that was visible. Acadia had shrunk to the size of a pearl, and I was inside, peering out through translucent mists. Shaped like a crescent moon, the pond was a window onto an alien landscape where six-inch fish floated in the air and pipewort was the only tree. The spell was broken by three workers who drove away from the pumping station in their trucks as if it were a normal working day in a normal world. When they had left, the spell descended again and I started around the pond to the foot of the Perpendicular Trail. Cobwebs beaded with drops hung from every tree and bush. Fog hides, but it also reveals. Seldom do we realize how many of our neighbors have eight legs. Each with its wizened concierge, delicate orbs, sheets, and tangled nets formed a world of antimatter coexistent with our own, a world we ordinarily deny until shown the fleeting proof which, like our dreams, we soon forget. My guess is that the missing matter that keeps the universe from blowing apart is distributed among spider webs hung between the stars.

Later, from the overlook at the top of the trail, I was startled to look down on the fog and see snow-covered trees rising through the mist. Then I blinked and the landscape did a figure-ground flip. The white trees became bright sky reflected from the surface of the pond between dark silhouettes of upside-down cedar and spruce. Beech Mountain rose a dark massif above swirling clouds. East across the island, every valley was flooded with mist. Gradually, the white flood receded as I watched. I saw a dove land on Sargent, pluck an olive branch, and fly off toward the Gulf of Maine.

Beyond spiders and fish, I also saw flies, dragonflies, moths, grasshoppers, a wood frog, two yellow-rumped warblers, a junco just out of the nest, a flicker on a spruce branch, and a hairy woodpecker on a red maple. I often heard crows and red-breasted nuthatches, but never saw them. Cone scales hinted at red squirrels, browsed twigs and a single pellet at snowshoe hares, but I didn't see them either. I heard a dog bark from somewhere near Seal Cove Road, and the beep-beep-beep of backing trucks from the Southwest Harbor transfer station.

Goldenrod, meadowsweet, and hawkweed bloomed by the pumping station. Spindly pipewort (hatpins) stuck up from the edge of the pond. One tall stalk of yarrow waved on the bank of Cold Brook. Asters (whorled, large-leaved, and flat-topped) lined the start of the Perpendicular Trail, with pink blossoms of herb Robert in the treadway itself. One sweet pepperbush was coming into bloom higher up. I didn't see any flowers on the ridge of Western Mountain or on the south face trail. Wintergreen and cow wheat bloomed by the side of the Western Mountain Truck Road between Mill and Gilley fields.

In many places along the trail, berries were more evident than flowers. Showy red-orange bunchberries cropped up everywhere, as decorative as any bloom. I saw one clump of red raspberries in a sunny spot on the Perpendicular Trail. Blueberries were common, but the best had been picked. I saw a few pale green partridgeberries, mottled Canada May rubies, and black chokeberries.

Several low plants covered the ground in patches without sign of fruit from their earlier blossoming. In Little Notch, wood sorrel was rampant where I had come across it in full bloom on earlier hikes in other years. Dark green cinquefoil ran in cracks along the ridge. Goldthread leaves ran along mossy sections of the ridge and south face trails, more than I had seen on any other trail in the park. I also saw two small patches of twinflower. Bazzania (scale moss) was common on the ridge, producing a tended, lawn-like effect beneath the spruce. Pale green pincushion moss grew where the soil was too dry for most other plants. Ferns were common, though I couldn't identify all that I saw. I count on a twenty percent error when I put a name to a fern. It is beyond me to keep so many intricate fine points in my head. I believe in trial and error, making a stab, then adjusting it when I find I am wrong. Successive approximations to the truth, gradually zeroing in, that's my method. To be right, I have first to be doubtful or wrong. What it takes is brashness and humility at

the same time in a kind of seesaw balance. Sometimes brashness is up, more often humility. I will say I saw sensitive fern, rock-cap fern, hayscented fern by the lake view at the top of the Perpendicular Trail, marginal wood fern, spinulose wood fern, spreading wood fern, and bracken.

Aside from its remarkable trails, the distinguishing characteristic of Western Mountain is not its views or open ledges so much as its woods. You experience them in two

Goldthread and hair-cap moss.

ways, from outside and inside. Outside the woods, you look onto them from a perch on one of the three peaks—Mansell, Knight Nubble, Bernard—seeing spires of dark green spruce ranked across the opposite slope. Here in the upper world of light and wind you sit among billions of needles capturing sunlight, turning air and water into food for themselves and the masses of roots toiling in the earth below. These are trees on parade, generic trees all looking alike, none standing out from the rest. It is easy to take them for granted, to dismiss them as nothing out of the ordinary. Such is the world we live in. There are trees; what else would you expect? Pretty, of course, but nothing special. That is the outsider's view.

Inside the woods, walking among the stems that hold that greenery aloft, you discover an entirely different scene. Every tree has a distinct personality. Look at the bark on this one, the branches on that, the way that one over there splits in two. How tall they are, how slender, how graceful. Except for lichens and mosses, there is little greenery here. We think of them as evergreens, but spruce drop their older needles in the fall, slowly building up the moisture-holding duff on the forest floor. The pervading color is tan or brown, not green. Here the needles and fallen twigs do a different kind of work, adding organic matter to the soil, building for years and generations ahead. The ridge trail on Western Mountain winds among many such stems, some thin and close together, others thicker and more widely spaced, all stretching between damp soil and bright sky, raising the roof of our homeland, the living skin of planet Earth that shelters, feeds, and protects us every day of our lives.

If plants had not invented vascular systems and woody stems, think how thin that skin would be, on the order of lichens, mosses, and bazzania—a few inches at most. Tiny plants would cling to any soil where moisture rose to the surface. Season after season, Earth would be dry with little shade. Insects would lurk in the shadows, but there would be no large charismatic mammals—certainly no hominids. Without trees, we would not be here at all. Comparable to the amniotic egg and the mammalian womb, the woody stem is one of nature's greatest inventions. It pushed up the ceiling of Earth's habitable zone, creating a moderate climate, an ample supply of plant and animal food, and living space for lumbering creatures like us. We belong more to the densely wooded slopes of Western Mountain than the granite ridges of Sargent or Penobscot. We may have passed out of the woods to the open savannas a long time ago, but our roots are in damp woodland soil, and our dreams still rise to the green canopy overhead.

There are two kinds of trails on Western Mountain, trails I will say are improved or unimproved. The Long (Great) Pond and Perpendicular trails are in the first class; the rest largely belong in the second. By improved trails I mean trails with built treadways that take hikers across difficult terrain while at the same time protecting plants and thin soils against wear and tear from tromping boots. The Beachcroft Trail up Huguenot Head is an improved trail, as are Kurt Diederich's Climb and the ladder and east face trails on Dorr Mountain. Crossing talus slopes where blocks of stone could be cut with relative ease, these trails are examples of Acadia's finest, providing solid footing on difficult slopes.

The Perpendicular Trail on Mansell Mountain is the finest of the fine. It rises steeply up a talus slope to Mansell's south ridge, then follows the ridge and a narrow ravine to the summit, passing through mixed woods much of the way, past granite outcrops and cliffs. Both the trail and its landscape are beautiful. The best section is a mounting series of six switchbacks built with sustaining and retaining walls of stone mined from the talus. A stairway fit to join heaven and Earth. The name of the trail does not do it justice, making it sound too stern and too steep. The route is more serpentine than perpendicular. Rebuilt by the Civilian Conservation Corps (CCC) in the '30s when labor cost five dollars a month (plus three squares a day and a roof overhead) and trails were built rather than merely blazed through the woods, the Perpendicular Trail is a period showpiece that is a national treasure sixty years later. When the hiker

with papoose said, "Fantastic!" he meant it. We can hardly imagine a time when manual labor was approached with such craftsmanship and dignity. The trail is truly an improvement, heightening both the landscape and the hiker's experience.

The Western Mountain ridge and south face trails, on the other hand, allow passage without benefiting the landscape. The ridge trail joins summit to summit in straightforward

Mansell Mountain from the south shore of Long Pond.

fashion, while at the same time cutting into tenuous layers of soil, promoting erosion, undoing thousands of years of natural improvement. Where the trail is difficult, hikers have stepped aside in search of easier ups and downs, widening the spread of the trail, narrowing the spread of trailside vegetation. If hikers are spoiled by Acadia's best trails, the park gets spoiled by its worst. Unimproved trails take hikers where they want to go, but at a cost in wear and tear on what they have come to see. Should the park pave the trails as the circuit on Cadillac's summit was paved? Should it lay bogwalks over every foot of soft ground? How about spreading a plastic carpet, or ten thousand tons of gravel? Or closing worn trails for a thousand years so they can rebuild on their own? I can't think of any way of making unimproved trails any better without expending the same kind of labor that went into constructing the Perpendicular Trail. Everything else is a stopgap measure, as unsightly as it is cheap. Given the cutting-back of appropriations, our parks will necessarily degrade as usage increases. The future is clear: more hikers, more tromping boots, more impacts, more degradation of national treasures. Solidly built in the first place, improved trails will survive with regular seasonal maintenance. Opened up without thought to the cumulative impact of thousands of footsteps, unimproved trails will eventually scar the landscape, degrading it year by year.

Why not charge hikers a dollar for every hike, and put the money collected in a trail maintenance fund? What is a hike worth? What is a fantastic hike worth? The problem there is collecting the funds. I am sure most people would be willing to pay as they go, but it would cost more to put toll collectors (or iron rangers) at trailheads or summits than it would be worth. Imposing a fee on trail use, and making sure every park user paid it in advance might work, even if it meant going against the grain of tradition. If you stay for two days, that would be two dollars a person; stay a week, seven dollars. Why not? Sounds reasonable to me. Is this series of sixty hikes worth sixty dollars to me? A bargain at ten times that price. The park would have to hold up its end by hiring a trail crew that could keep up with the work. Recently the crew has been cut, and cut again, even as visitation goes up. Is that logical? Prudent? When the gas gauge is on empty, the car rolls to a stop. If Congress won't put up the money, the people have to bypass Washington and do it directly. Pay as you go is the wave of the future. For the sake of Acadia's trails, I hope it comes soon.

Having said that, I have to add that the ridge of Western Mountain is a great place to hike. The woods and ground cover are worth the effort. You won't find them in malls or on TV. You have to go where they are. The ridge is serrated with ups and downs, the hiker having to scramble in a few spots, but there is no other trail like it in the park. And the south face trail curving around from Bernard's summit in a long sweep through mixed woods down to Mill Field and the Western Mountain Truck Road is a pleasant amble in its own right. That is where I saw the wood frog, flicker, and woodpecker, and heard a gaggle of nuthatches. Most birds broadcast on AM (amplitude modulation) frequencies; nuthatches are on FM (frequency modulation) because that is how they talk—by changing the frequency with which they repeat their single note instead of creating a melody by varying the pitch. Goldthread lines the trail in many places, the little wetland plant with yellow roots that Indians used against toothaches. I think the trail should be renamed the Goldthread Trail. There are three old signposts along the way, their messages having fallen or rotted away. One was by a spring. The others seemed nowhere in particular. I asked what needed noting at such a place, but could think of nothing words could add.

I took six hours and twenty minutes to complete the four-and-a-half-mile loop. I climbed some 1,360 feet, all told, though not in one stretch. Mansell's summit is 889 feet above the pumping station. From there I went down to Great Notch (640 feet), up to Knight Nubble (930 feet), down to Little Notch (890 feet), and up again to Bernard at 1,071 feet. The temperature was 57° Fahrenheit when I started out,

86° when I got back. Above the fog it was warm and hazy. I started out wearing my Gore-Tex parka over a long-sleeved shirt. Out of the fog I got down to a T-shirt. I don't remember seeing a mosquito the whole way, which would be a first for these summer hikes. Maybe I am so used to them that they don't register on my radar screen anymore.

There are several overlooks along the trail. The first is at the upper end of the Perpendicular Trail. That is where I saw

Beech, Mansell, and Bernard mountains at the south end of Long Pond.

the snowy trees. Another is where the Razorback Trail heads off the ridge toward Gilley Field. That one overlooks Great Notch and the green flanks of Knight Nubble and Bernard Mountain. The nubble has a comparable overlook facing the other way. Bernard has an overlook facing north over Long Pond and west over Blue Hill Bay. Except for those, the rest of the route offers underlooks beneath the canopy above.

Back at Long Pond, the fog had lifted and I could see three sails at the far end, a canoe, and a kayak just setting out from the boat ramp. Fifty gulls floated out on the water, with more coming down in waves as I watched. There were twenty-one cars besides my own in the parking area, representing nine states, the District of Columbia, and two provinces of Canada. The occupants had made it this far; had they gone the rest of the way to Acadia? Had they found what they were looking for, or were they stuck in Away, unable to extricate themselves from attitudes and affairs they brought with them? Many of them were on holiday. Holy day. Healing, making-whole day. What is it that completes us and gives us what we need to make us whole? Fresh air, clean water, sunlight, good food, exercise, rest, and loving companionship. They had come to the right place.

✪

58—CADILLAC MOUNTAIN LOOP

From Bubble Pond parking area
To Cadillac Mountain summit, Featherbed, and back
  Up by Cadillac Mountain West Face Trail
  Back by Cadillac Mountain South Ridge and
    Featherbed trails, Boyd Road, and
    carriage road along Bubble Pond
                4.3 miles, August 23, 1996

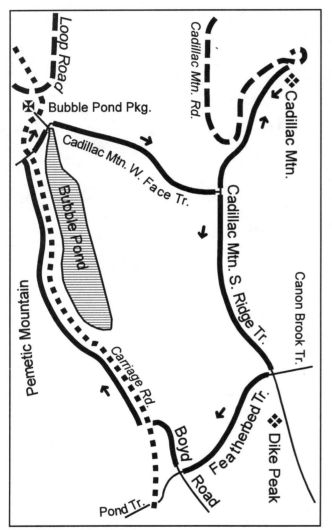

58—Cadillac Mountain loop.

I had been waiting all summer for this one. Every hike I take is my favorite hike at the time, but my favorite of all favorites is the West Face Trail up Cadillac from the north end of Bubble Pond. It is the ultimate unimproved trail, a trail *au naturel* without rungs, handrails, steps, or retaining walls. The treadway is Cadillac Mountain granite most of the way, in broken fragments, boulders, or sweeping ledges. What you see is what you get. No flair, no frills. You want to go up—the trail goes up. Starting straight off on glacial cobbles, it graduates to boulders, then takes you through cedar woods

to the base of a terraced cliff. Throw your hiking stick away; you will need both hands on this one. Past the cliff you cross a granite slope smoothed by the glacier, then a wooded shelf with soil only inches thick. Up a river of cobbles and boulders among oak, beech, cedar, yellow birch, white pine, and maple. Another cliff, then a river of larger boulders flowing in slow motion.

At that point I was stopped in my tracks by the smell of

White pine against fog, Cadillac Mtn. West Face Trail.

pine pitch oozing from a cut branch. Right up there with mayflower blooms, fox, and balsam fir, Acadia has no better scent. Higher, higher. Views opened across the pond—or would have opened if fog were not pouring in from the south. Pemetic was but a fable shrouded in mist. Above unseen North Bubble, Sargent's long summit ridge raced like a canoe on white water. Up, up. Cedar roots splayed across granite. Boulders were crusted with gray lichens. Luminous green mats of sphagnum moss edged cliffs dark with alpine moss where living waters flowed from the sky. Pitch pines mixed with the cedars. More outlooks, more vistas of swirling emptiness. The void is closer than we know. Can't think about that. Scrambled across terraced ledges. Cedars and pitch pine; pitch pines and cedar. No iron rungs here. Roots to grab when you need a lift. Granite underfoot, best of all possible treadways.

The slope opened up. Huckleberry bushes. Cinquefoil

running in cracks. Why not name trails for their plants? The Cinquefoil Trail; Black Chokeberry Trail; Lambkill Trail; Mountain Sandwort Trail; Northern White Cedar Trail; Pitch Pine Trail. Hikers would get to know at least one plant a day. Get to know; grow intimate with; regard as brothers and sisters. In a week or a season, how many connections would that be? If our family does not grow every day, are we paying attention? . . . Cry of a blue jay farther along the slope. I hear you, I hear you, little sister. Yes, it could be the Blue Jay Trail. Peace.

Heading south along the granite slope, the trail is buttressed by trees, with frequent vistas in between. The view is spectacular. Breathtaking. Acadian. Like a fan dancer, the less the shifting mists reveal, the more enticing the view becomes. On a clear day, Pemetic's evergreen wooded slopes would rise across the pond, with Bubble Ridge behind, and Sargent and Penobscot back of that. Eagle Lake, too, would open to the north. Charms merely suggested by the teasing fog.

The Juniper Trail. Sweet Pepperbush Trail. Keeping on, the treadway follows sinuous shelves across ledge after sloping ledge. Then it angles more directly up the slope, reaching higher and higher. I don't believe in racial memory, but I felt I belonged where I was. Why else would a profound sense of

Cadillac Mountain West Face Trail.

gladness and well-being descend on me in such a place? My people had been here before or, if not here, in places like this. Rocky, wooded places where they thrived in sunlight and storm alike. They wanted me to know, so encoded a message in my genes. G-mail. Looking over the green valley of Bubble Pond, I did not want to be anywhere else. I got the message. No, I am not a mighty hunter scanning the hills for ibex or mammoth. I eat vegieburgers and chicken which, as far as I am concerned, come from the grocery store. Survival addresses us in different ways at different times. In our tree shrew phase, we got turned on by scurrying insects. As great apes, we were into fiber and fruit. Now it's burgers and sorbet. G-mail isn't that fast. There's a lag in delivery. We bake our nuggets of wisdom in fortune cookies and send them on. Fifty thousand years from now, my descendants, instead of getting depressed, will get a thrill when they push a loaded cart down the aisle of the local food distribution

center. "This is where I belong," they will cry, "this is my destiny!" But we are not there yet. My genetic fortune says, "Find happiness on the west face trail."

Out in the open, lichens get more adventurous. They break their gray habit and experiment with different shades, textures, patterns, and colors. On the upper sections of the west face trail, granite is painted with map lichen in battleship gray, splotches in dark and middle gray, concentric rings in pale green, and speckles in fluorescent green. Sun, storm, and granite make a great exterior decorating team. No surface is left untouched. Every ledge and boulder sparkles with color. The trail itself is alive.

Tall rattlesnake root bloomed beside the trail. That plant, now the flared white trumpets were opening, was at last coming into its own. The droopy flower buds look sickly at first, but when they bloom they shine with good health. Ha! the Tall Rattlesnake Root Trail. Rising higher and higher, the trail makes a rush straight up the slope toward the crest of the ridge. False alarm. It turns south again and follows along the slope among cedar woods. Shallow striations mark the way, blazed in granite by the glacial surveyor who laid out the trail.

After two hours of hiking, I saw Sargent and Penobscot emerge from behind the mist. The day was warming up. I was grateful for the gusty wind off the Gulf. Once the power behind the fog, it now brought cool refreshment. Crossing a stretch of broken rock, the trail comes out on broad sloping ledges, tricky to cross in wet weather. I have hiked this trail in the rain when every step had to be staked out in a search for the least bad among a poor selection of choices. It is wonderful how our eyes find footholds when they have to in terrain that looks uniformly smooth at first. Fixing on a small area, we find subtle pockets and grooves big enough for heel or toe. I avoided the west face in July because the trail was streaming wet the whole month. August had done a great job drying it out. Conditions were perfect.

Ending its southerly run, the trail makes a final dash for the top of the ridge. Marked by cairns, it heads straight up the slope. Trailside trees get shorter and shorter as soil thins and water becomes scarcer. At eleven o'clock, I reached the south (or west) ridge trail where the west face trail leaves off. Seeing a group of ten hikers gathered around the sign at the junction, I realized I hadn't met another hiker in two-and-a-half hours. It is still possible to hike Acadia in high season and not see a soul. The group was a field biology class from a community college outside Philadelphia. I asked what they had found exciting.

"Great year for fungi!" said one.

"Peat bogs!" said another.

The teacher asked if I could help him identify a flower he was uncertain of. It turned out to be orange grass (pineweed, a member of the St. Johnswort family), whose minute yellow stars were in full bloom in pans along the ridge. Many plants were sere and brown, but in a few damp spots they gleamed like tiny suns. I hadn't seen them in bloom since my foggy hike on Norumbega a month ago. Here it was again, an old friend. The Orange Grass Trail.

My loop was to take me south along the ridge to the Feather-bed, where I would return to Bubble Pond by way of the Featherbed Trail (westerly extension of the Canon Brook Trail) and the headwaters of Hunters Brook. Having come as far as I had, I decided to detour to the summit to see what berries and blossoms I could see. August is berry month in Acadia. Between the west face trail and the summit I saw huckleberry, juniper, blueberry, raspberry, blackberry, mountain ash, black chokeberry, pin cherry, wild raisin (witherod), mountain cranberry, bunchberry, and wintergreen. Not bad for mountains that are named for their barren appearance. Downy goldenrod and flat-topped aster bloomed within fifteen feet of the benchmark at the summit, most elevated flowers on the East Coast.

Walking down the fire road back of the gift shop toward the summit parking area, I met a couple on bicycles riding up. The man was singing, "Georgia, Georgia on my mind." I saw forty-six people standing about, and seventy-one cars. Four states accounted for seventy-five percent of the cars: Maine, Massachusetts, New York, and Pennsylvania. Nine other states were represented, and the province of Quebec. A huge bus from Maryland pulled up while I was there. The passengers got out, went to the gift shop for ten minutes, got back on the bus, and drove off.

Pemetic Mountain rising beyond Bubble Pond.

I like the south ridge of Cadillac for the same reason I like the south ridge of Sargent: the dramatic, other-worldly landscape. These are no-nonsense, subalpine habitats with few places to hide. Granite below, the wind and stars above, plants here forgo the luxuries of deep soils and sheltering canopies. They live on what they have, out in the open, exposed to extremes of heat and cold, wet and dry. The halfhearted need not apply. Everything extraneous shaved by climate's keen razor, there is a kind of integrity here, a unity that defines the landscape as a place apart from the wooded slopes and valleys below. Trails are marked by cairns, sturdy heaps of glacial stones whose shape and shadow guide hikers through dim light, fog, and storm. Made of local materials, simply built, cairns fit in such a landscape, sharing the integrity of the place.

The first hint that not every hiker respected that integrity to equal degree was a smiley face ten feet in diameter made of cobbles near the upper end of the west face trail. While the sentiment might have been apt, the concrete expression seemed out of place in that setting. The scale was too grand, the medium inappropriate. Every stone hefted from its natural place leaves soil particles less protected from wind and rain. The habitat is disarranged, its hardy plants made more vulnerable. If such symbols have a place on bumper stickers and third-grade blackboards, this one was definitely out of place. Instead of making me happy it made me sad.

That was only the beginning. The whole sweep of the south ridge to the brink of the Featherbed—almost three-quarters of a mile—had been decorated with stone sculptures and designer cairns. Littered would be a better word. In every age, each person struggles to express herself in meaningful terms. Advancing age to age, the collective results of such struggles are viewed as progress, when often they are simply random doodles or experiments. These were doodles writ large in the flesh of Cadillac Mountain. Cairns or doodles, it does make a difference. I speak as one who has been misled in snow and fog by false cairns. Not only do such playful works clutter the landscape, they make it unsafe, promote erosion, and threaten native plants. Cairns and blazes have the useful aim of keeping people on the trail, a good place for them to be, considering the damage they can do to soils and vegetation. Bah, humbug! I am not out to dampen anyone's holiday, but I do wish visitors would channel their excess energy and inventiveness in less destructive ways. We are an exuberant and irrepressible race that finds it hard to let well enough alone. What we require is the discipline to turn our restless tweakings and fiddlings into creative acts that harmonize with our natural surroundings. Why not learn about a landscape first before we start rearranging it? That would be the environmental approach.

The fog dissipated by noon, but then a bank of dark blue clouds began rolling in from the northwest, threatening rain. Not having heard mention of rain on the forecast I listened to before setting out, I didn't have rain gear with me, so hiked faster than I usually do to keep ahead of the clouds. Which was just as well since I found the rearranged landscape on the ridge so upsetting. The clouds caught me at the Featherbed where I got psyched to be soaked, but they passed out to sea after nothing more than a sprinkle. The sky grew lighter, and that was that.

The way up and the way down on this loop couldn't have been more different. The trail west from the Featherbed into the valley of Hunters Brook is just as steep as the west face trail, but it is much shorter. The

Sloping ledge on Cadillac Mountain West Face Trail.

treadway is broken rock and laid steps rather than broad stretches of ledge. It passes through mixed woods the whole way. Tom St. Germain calls it the Featherbed Trail; others call it the Pond Trail or an extension of the Canon Brook Trail. To me it was the Smaller Purple Fringed Orchis Trail because I passed three plants of that species which had just gone by. Lower down it became the Trillium Trail because I found a bright red trillium berry sitting Buddha-like atop three narrow sepals and three broad, interconnected leaves.

In the wetland at the bottom of the trail I found tracks of mink and raccoon, and in a nearby spruce, actually saw two red squirrels, the first I had seen in almost three months. The wetland catches water streaming down Cadillac on the east and Pemetic on the west, forming the wellspring of Hunters Brook. It was a birdy place when I came by, but other than a robin, I wasn't sure what I was looking at darting there in the distance. I had seen gulls, four cedar waxwings, and two

ravens on the ridge, and heard chickadees and blue jays on the west face trail. Dragonflies, mosquitoes, grasshoppers, and water striders respectively flew, hopped, and strode in places along the loop.

From the wetland, the trail turns south toward the gap between Pemetic and the Triad. Rather than take the long way round, I picked up the grassy Boyd Road about twenty-five feet east of the last section of bogwalk, which took me through beech, maple, and yellow birch woods in five minutes to the carriage road west of Bubble Pond. This was a ferny stretch with clumps of cinnamon, long beech, New York, sensitive, Christmas, interrupted, and royal ferns along the wayside. I saw twenty bikers on the carriage road, some actually riding, others soaking their feet in Bubble Pond. One little girl riding by was so distracted by the pond that she fell off her bike, but didn't hurt herself. A couple was eating a picnic lunch on top of a large rock.

"Want a fig newton?" the man asked.

I thanked him, but declined.

Pipewort, water parsnip, and yellow cow lily bloomed in the pond. Other flowers I had seen included: hawkweed; meadowsweet; slender and downy goldenrod; large-leaved, whorled, and flat-topped aster; sweet pepperbush; tall rattlesnake root; mountain sandwort; orange grass; cow wheat; yarrow; bush honeysuckle (only two flowers in bloom, one yellow, one red); cotton grass in the Featherbed; steeplebush at the head of Hunters Brook; and heal-all. Purple fringed orchis had come and gone, but I missed it. In varying degrees of ripeness, earlier blooms were now bearing fruit: blackberry, raspberry, huckleberry, juniper, black chokeberry, blueberry, lambkill, mountain ash, pin cherry, mountain cranberry, wild raisin, bunchberry, mountain holly, wintergreen, trillium, Canada May ruby, and hobblebush. I also saw bright yellow and orange slime molds, and a destroying angel mushroom (the Destroying Angel Trail?). I hadn't set out to look for blooms and berries, but there they were: Acadia self-disclosed in her native tongue. Why do we name mountains after men (Champlain, Gorham, Dorr, Cadillac, McFarland, Young, Sargent, Parkman, Mansell, Bernard, to name a few) when we could name them after the fruit they produce? Who wouldn't hike up

Cherry Mountain, Blackberry Mountain, Cranberry Mountain, Blueberry Mountain? Men come and go but berries, like mountains, endure. To quote Ecclesiastes on the matter:

Vanity of vanities, saith the Preacher, vanity of vanities; all is vanity.

What profit hath a man of all his labour which he taketh under the sun?

One generation passeth away, and another generation cometh: but the earth abideth for ever.

Islands south of Mount Desert Island from Cadillac Mountain south ridge: (near) portions of Little and Great Cranberry Islands, Sutton Island; (far) Great and Little Duck Islands; (right foreground) Crowninshield Point, Seal Harbor.

When I got back, there were thirty cars in the parking area. They came from Connecticut, Maine, and Massachusetts, five other states, and Quebec. I had covered 4.3 miles in a little under six hours, climbing 1,194 feet from pond to summit. The temperature was in the 60s for the most part, rising briefly into the mid-70s before the rain cloud came over. Smiley face notwithstanding, a wonderful hike.

As I started my car, a family approached the pickup next to me with fishing poles in hand.

"Don't steal my pillow!" yelled one child.

"Don't steal mine either!" yelled another.

As I drove off, the woman in charge had the last word:

"Get in, shut up, and stay off the fishin' poles!" she yelled.

Back in the land of law and order, I realized the mountain had left me to my hike without yelling at me once. I had gone where I wanted to go, done what I wanted to do. If I hadn't made my own rules, I had been in full sympathy with those that applied. Perhaps it takes a lifetime to learn to act appropriately. Nature is a patient guide, forgiving error after error. Now I want to stay on the trail and off the plants as if it were my own rule, as if desecration of nature were somehow a violation of myself. Violation of any part disturbs the integrity of the whole. Integrity means untouched, unaf-

flicted, healthy, sound, entire. Beyond pillows and fishing poles, the circle of our concern grows wider as we age, from self, to possessions, to other selves and theirs, to all imaginable selves and what they care for. In the end, we count stones, flowers, birds, and the stars above as members of our families, not to order around but to love and defend.

Red fox of Acadia.

59—SARGENT MOUNTAIN via HADLOCK BROOK & MAPLE SPRING TRAILS

From Norumbega Mountain parking area
To Sargent Mountain summit, and back
Up by Hadlock Brook and
Sargent Mountain South Ridge trails
Down by Grandgent and Maple Spring trails

4.1 miles, August 29, 1996

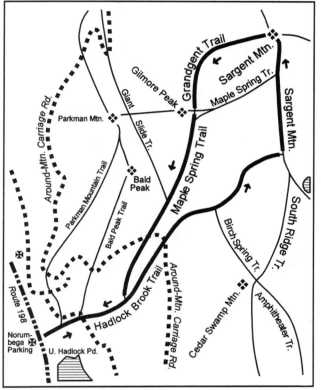

59—Sargent Mountain loop.

I hiked this hike on Thursday, then took off on Friday for Fundy National Park in New Brunswick for Labor Day weekend before writing it up. When I got back, my head was full of Fundy, not Acadia. In many respects the two parks are alike. Both feature hilly, maritime forests and vegetation that thrives in damp climates. Both have myriad lakes and streams, miles of hiking trails, and tidal shores. Acadia has its carriage roads, Fundy its golf course. Aside from 42-foot tides, what Fundy has that Acadia lacks is real rivers. The Point Wolfe and Upper Salmon rivers, with their many tributaries and waterfalls, are worth the drive from Bar Harbor and the hikes into their valleys. Acadia has brooks or streams, not rivers. In August, month of least rain, many run almost dry, while Fundy's rivers plunge pool to pool. Having hiked a loop from Fundy's Forks Trail along the scenic Broad River to Laverty Falls on Laverty Brook, how was I to write about Acadia's trickling Hadlock Brook?

Hadlock Brook, after all, was the reason I had chosen the route I took. Up the south fork, down the north, giving an inside view of the watershed of Upper Hadlock Pond bottom-to-top, top-to-bottom. I parked at the Norumbega Mountain parking area at 12:40 p.m., hiked 1,103 vertical feet to Sargent's 1,373-foot summit and back by a 4.1-mile loop, reaching my car again four hours and forty minutes later at 5:20 p.m. The sky was hazy the whole time, the temperature comfortably lodged in the upper 70s.

What can I say? Even seen in retrospect through the mists of Fundy's falls and rivers, it was a glorious hike. Any hike up Sargent Mountain is bound to be memorable. This one, by one of the most direct routes you can take to the top, was along water a good part of the way. No, there were no Atlantic salmon turning in deep pools, but there were water striders on every quiet surface, insects that take walking on water as a matter of course. There were grasshoppers clicking their way along the slopes, insects that defy gravity to walk through the air. The usual crew of flies hung around the wooden sign rising out of the summit cairn, flies which, having scaled Sargent because it is there, seem to have become summit bums with nowhere else to go. Perhaps it is an ego thing, the flies investing their identity in their accomplishments. Resting on their laurels now, they will cling to glory in the grave sooner than they know.

Every plume of goldenrod, every aster blazing like a white or purple sun, was host to creatures stranger than we imagine in the depths of space. Microbes on Mars are rudimentary compared to these, our six-legged neighbors. I know a bumblebee when I see one, but the rest were so fantastic I think I might have dreamt them. If I have any lives left to spiral through, I hope I come back as an entomologist or, better yet, as an insect pollinator so I can acquaint this blooming-buzzing universe from the inside as part of the loop. Our crops and flowers depend on creatures we do not recognize face-to-face. That's nature, we say, as if it all happened automatically without billions of tiny selves devoting their lives to making our old familiar world bloom and bear fruit.

Damselflies and dragonflies patrolled the slopes, preying on their smaller cousins, limiting populations, making way for the best and the brightest, devouring the dull and the slowest. And the unluckiest. Natural selection at work right here in Acadia. We think of nature as run by design, but more accurately it is run by default. Winners live to reproduce, extending the possibilities encoded in their genes. They weren't designed to win, they just happened to avoid the dead end that counts as defeat. Luck, chance, accident, happenstance, serendipity—whatever you call it, we all need a big dose of good fortune if we are to lead any kind of life. Being strong, clever, and influential is not enough. Being rich, gifted, and promising is not enough. Being beautiful, charming, and well-connected is not enough. There is no formula that always works, no elixir, no magic. We make it if we make it; we don't if we don't. Success is what is left after everything else falls by the wayside. That is universal law. The order we find around us stems from that: from what has worked till now. Design-after-the-fact. Twenty-twenty hindsight design. Which is no guarantee the same thing will work next week or next year. Earth is littered with the bones of species and civilization trimmed by the razor of expedience. Dead species and dead civilizations, every one of which had a covenant with its ancestors or its creator. When they died, their ancestors and gods died with them, as ours will die with us. The living are the living, period. Not by design, not by destiny, not by supremacy—but because they are alive. Tomorrow, everything will change. Comes the big hurricane, the tiny virus, the asteroid—who knows? Beyond hope, hard work, and luck lies the void where all of us, including the most arrogant, end up. I know. I heard it on Sargent Mountain from a dragonfly. Even dragonflies succumb to spiders, storms, and hawking birds.

I heard crows and red-breasted nuthatches, and saw five berry-blue scats which, being the right size and shape, I took to be signs of fox. Sargent Mountain is a special place in fox geography. Perhaps that is where the Ur fox touched down when canines descended from the stars in beginning times. Sargent may well be their sacred mountain, the locus of their origin. My hike to the summit on snowshoes in early January taught me that (see Hike 21). With over three feet of snow on the slopes, the temperature well below zero, I found fox prints everywhere on Sargent's broad, snowy back. If I had surveyed the ridge in a grid at three-foot intervals, every square would have been crossed by tracks. Not rows here and there—every square. Foxes were there for a reason. Something had drawn them there. Food, most likely. Or sex. Or religion. Maybe they had been trapped by a blizzard. All I know is they had been where I had not expected them. When I meet signs of fox on Sargent Mountain, I try to fit them to a mythology that is largely incomplete. I do know that foxes and humans often share the same trails, and when my route was buried by drifting snow, fox tracks showed me the way. Even in summer, the fox is present in my experience on Sargent Mountain.

Experience, mythology—same thing. It is all we know of the world. Calling it a mythology allows for my personal contribution to the world scheme as I construe it. In *Personal Knowledge**, Polanyi calls it the tacit component, what we know without knowing how we know it. Beauty is the clincher. If a thing is beautiful, we know it is true. What is

beauty? Intuition is our sole authority on that. Trust me, it says. Yes, our world view is a matter of trust. Fox prints in the snow are beautiful. I trust them implicitly. Fox scats, ditto. I believe, I believe. What does understanding have to do with it?

I didn't see any foxes or signs of foxes on the summit this time; I saw four ravens. They lifted off when I was fifty feet away, hung on the west wind like black holes ten feet in the

Rattlesnake plantain near Hadlock Brook Trail.

air, then floated a hundred feet to a ridge where they set gracefully down and continued their business. Adolph, Rudolf, Doc, and Henry. I have remembered that foursome for fifty years, ever since getting a haircut in Billings, Montana, giving the barber a ten-dollar bill, getting nine silver dollars in change. He got a phone call while I was in the barber chair, about a poker game. He said, "Poker, sure. Call Adolph, Rudolf, Doc, and Henry." There they were on Sargent Mountain, still at it after all those years.

That is episodic memory, a unique event you remember because of its emotional charge. Like what you were doing when Kennedy was shot; or where you were when you first learned to whistle or ride a bike. Semantic memory is different, a slow buildup over years of repetition, unique features falling away, only the core concept remaining: ravens; mountains; trees; plants; frogs; snakes. Empty categories waiting to be fleshed out by concrete, episodic experience: those ravens getting set for a poker game; Sargent Mountain in the snow on January 4, 1996; that twisted Northern white cedar with bare, silvery limbs; the withered mountain sandwort next to that boot print over there; that milk-chocolate-colored spring peeper scrambling into a clump of bunchberry; that maritime garter snake sunning in the trail. When emotion incarnates a latent concept, experience happens.

That's what a hike is for me, a series of possibilities

*Michael Polanyi, *Personal Knowledge: Towards a Post-Critical Philosophy*. Chicago: University of Chicago Press, 1958.

brought to life as mythological events by my motivated passing here and there. When I open myself to Acadia, I lay my mythology on the line and wait. Ravens happen; foxes happen; striders happen; asters and goldenrod happen. Acadia happens. Awareness happens. I happen. Beyond that, the void where nothing happens, ever.

Three frogs and a snake hopped or slid through my experience on this hike. The first was a spring peeper about an

Sargent Mountain summit.

inch long for whom the edge of the trail must have seemed a great cliff. A tree frog, the peeper was in the Hadlock Brook Trail when I saw it, its pale tan skin mimicking the color of dry soil. Its markings looked like some sort of harness on its back. With mighty effort it scrambled out of the trail into shelter beneath a bunchberry forest, where I let it collect itself.

The next frog was a green frog about the same size as the peeper. It was on the bank of the northern branch of Hadlock Brook where the Grandgent Trail crosses toward Gilmore Peak. Smaller than most green frogs I see, it must have been a young one just graduated from the tadpole stage. It was a mottled greeny-brown with conspicuous light-colored folds of skin like seams on its back.

The third was an adult green frog near the Pulpit on the same branch. I saw it squatting in a pool with just its eyes out of water. I made a note of it; when I looked back it was

gone. There were striders in the pool, which I thought the frog must have been hunting when I disturbed it.

The garter snake was sunning itself in the Hadlock Brook Trail as I neared the end of my loop. Twenty inches long, it seemed to lack the typical bold rows of dark spots on its back, the entire back looking uniformly black between three pale stripes. I thought it might have been a ribbon snake, but it would have been well out of its normal range. It didn't fit my image of either garter snake or maritime garter snake, but I couldn't think what else it could be. I will call it a maritime garter snake because of the missing spots, though by rights it should have had two stripes, not three.

As I went along, I was aware of scanning both sides of the trail for plants and signs of life. I looked five feet to the right, five feet to the left, five to ten feet ahead. What do I know of Acadia? A mere ribbon twelve to fifteen-feet wide along trails here and there throughout the park. To gain a sense of the whole I would stop from time to time and look deeper into the woods on either hand. The ribbon of my awareness is more like a knotted string. Even so, of the thousands of acres I have passed through I know very little. Acadia largely escapes me. I have seen a few frogs and snakes out of how many? Tokens, that is what my mythology is made of. The rest is extrapolation and imagination. Even in the narrow band I scrutinize, I miss much that is before my eyes. To see three frogs, I probably overlooked twenty. That is why I go back again and again. Hiking twice a week as I regularly do, that makes about 100 hikes in one year. If each hike averages four miles, and I scan a strip fifteen feet wide as I go, I figure I cover less than a fiftieth of the park in a year. If I should add up everything I see on those hikes, and multiply that by fifty, I would get a better idea of the richness the park offers, but that estimate would be nowhere near complete because of all I miss as I go. A mote in the wilderness. Well, then, three frogs and a snake at least. I can work my way up from there.

In addition to mayflower, goldthread, wine-leaf cinquefoil, lambkill, and tree club moss, the plants I saw were:

Blooms

large-leaved aster	whorled aster
flat-topped aster	downy goldenrod
slender goldenrod	large-leaved goldenrod
tall rattlesnake root	Indian pipes
rattlesnake plantain	meadowsweet
witherod	mountain sandwort

Berries

black crowberry	black chokeberry
huckleberry	blueberry
mountain cranberry	hobblebush
bunchberry	mountain holly
wintergreen	juniper
partridgeberry	Canada May ruby

Ferns

bracken	Christmas fern
cinnamon fern	interrupted fern
long beech fern	spinulose wood fern
spreading wood fern	rock-cap fern

How tall is tall rattlesnake root? The tallest I saw was about four-and-a-half feet, the shortest ten inches or so. The

View from upper end of Grandgent Trail: Gilmore and Bald peaks, Hadlock Ponds, Norumbega Mountain.

root was reputedly useful in combating snakebite, hence the name. The other rattlesnake on my list was a real find, though I take no credit for it. Don Curley alerted me to a patch of rattlesnake plantain about to bloom, so I went thirty feet out of my way to see if I could find it. I did. The lowest buds on the ten-inch stalks were open, with the rest yet to come. But the small white blossoms are not the thing with this orchid. They are upstaged by the rosette of blue-green leaves at the base of the stalk, each leaf delicately veined in white, creating a lacy effect. The plants are so handsome, people have trouble leaving them where they are. They mysteriously disappear from their natural settings. Leaves patterned like snakeskin, the plant was once thought useful against snakebite. Mythology here, too, as everywhere.

Where wood lilies had bloomed on a hike earlier in the month, tall rattlesnake root, downy goldenrod, and flat-topped aster had replaced them on Sargent's south ridge. How fast the seasons change. Hiking the same route two weeks apart results in two different hikes. Every plant has its day, then retires to turn blooms into fruit. Heavy bunches of red hobblebush berries lined both branches of Hadlock Brook, adding a festive note to the shaded streams. More subtly, tiny partridgeberries were just forming four-horned red fruit from the ovaries of twin blooms on the female

plants. I noticed one Canada May ruby with a tinge of rose, only now starting to live up to its name. Mountain cranberries near the summit were unabashedly red, looking plumper than I remembered seeing them. On the matter of berries, Fundy National Park demands to be recognized. I have never seen such splendid fields of bunchberry as I did everywhere along its trails. Ferns and ground cover are the park's forte, its trees having been cut for lumber earlier in the century. In another fifty years Fundy's trees will be magnificent again; right now, bunchberry steals the show. With clumps of orange-red berries dangling everywhere I went, I couldn't help smiling at the fecundity of the place, just as twins and triplets make me smile.

I met nine adults and six children on this loop, fewer people than I expected on a sunny August day. With school and Labor Day so close, I think many visitors had already left for home. The one solo man who passed me was heading for the Amphitheater Trail by way of Birch Spring from Hadlock Brook. I got lost on the way to Birch Spring in March, but that was in a snowstorm, so held my tongue. The other four parties I met were family groups. On the south ridge at the top of the Hadlock Brook Trail, a silent father responded to my greeting by lifting his right forearm horizontally in brief salute, a gesture as old as humankind itself. Referring to the ridge, one woman said,

"It's so wide; what makes it so wide?"

"It's as the glacier left it," I told her.

"This is my favorite mountain," the man with her said, sidestepping the issue of its shape.

The last man I met carried four collapsible metal walking sticks in his pack, one for each member of the family.

I didn't meet a soul on the way down the Grandgent and Maple Spring trails. I take that back. Who am I to assume frogs and snakes don't have souls? Or grasshoppers, or slender goldenrod for that matter? The forty-inch-in-diameter white pine downstream from Hemlock Bridge looked like it might well have a soul. What am I looking for if not the soul of Acadia? By which I mean the integrating factor that unifies its diverse parts into a single entity. Every plant and animal in Acadia is part of Acadia, contributing to the whole; ergo, every plant and animal in Acadia shares in Acadia's soul. Certainly humans possess no invisible seal of divinity that singles them out from all other beings. By the divine, what can we mean but the whole of the imaginable universe? Divinity marks us as members of that family. That's what the soul is, our badge of membership in the family of all families. If we have souls, so do the members of other species. Mythology again, my version of the truth.

The trails making up this loop are unimproved trails. They are more worn tracks through the woods than treadways laid down to protect the innocent. Except for the stretch along the south ridge where every step falls on solid granite, they are apt to be stony and rooty. In places they are steep. And again, except for the ridge, they are not heavily traveled. Jordan Pond House is commonly thought to be the staging area for a hike up Sargent, not the Norumbega Mountain parking area overlooking Upper Hadlock Pond. But the hike from Norumbega is shorter, more direct, more protected, and follows mountain streams a good part of the

Sargent Mountain and Upper Hadlock Pond.

way. The bad news is the footing, which requires careful stepping and good boots. Being in good physical shape also helps.

The route is fairly straightforward, though there are several intersections that might lead you astray. Off the Hadlock Brook Trail, which starts on the east side of Route 198, signs indicate turnoffs for the **PARKMAN MOUNTAIN TRAIL** (left), the **BALD PEAK TRAIL** (left), the **MAPLE SPRING TRAIL** (left), and, above Waterfall Bridge, for **BIRCH SPRING** (right). The Hadlock Brook Trail starts out nearly level, then rises gradually to Waterfall Bridge, then somewhat more steeply along the southern branch of the brook, and more steeply still as it rises rapidly up the granite flank of Sargent Mountain, until it connects with the south ridge trail, which leads to the summit at an easy grade.

Coming down, I picked up the Grandgent Trail at the summit, which heads west and quickly enters spruce and yellow birch woods for a rapid descent into what I call Chickadee Valley where the northern branch of Hadlock Brook gets its start. From there, the trail links up with the Maple Spring Trail, which follows the brook almost to Upper Hadlock Pond where a junction with the Hadlock Brook Trail leads back to the parking area on Route 198. For some reason the park has painted over the trail markers on the two connectors between the Grandgent Trail and the Maple Spring Trail, leaving the hiker to follow the well-worn route along the stream without additional guidance. If you find yourself scaling Gilmore Peak out of Chickadee

Valley, you are following the Grandgent, not the connector heading for the Maple Spring Trail. Follow the brook out of the valley, and you will be right on course.

The Maple Spring Trail passes through a rocky defile above Hemlock Bridge that is one of the park's sacred places. When you come to a signpost pointing north to the **GIANT SLIDE TRAIL**, you are at the upper end of the defile. Swing around the guardian rock, and you will find yourself in a rocky gorge no wider than the brook. Descending, the trail winds around several impressive cliffs, passes the Pulpit (one of MDI's three stone pulpits that I know of), then straightens out and runs beneath the bridge, entering a lower gorge farther on. The descent from the summit by the Grandgent and Maple Spring trails to the junction with the Hadlock Brook Trail is one of the most beautiful routes in Acadia. I say that as a man who has recently hiked along the Broad River in Fundy National Park. Acadia's streams may not be impressively large, but beauty is more a function of scale and proportion than absolute size. I strongly recommend hiking down from the summit of Sargent Mountain along the northern branch of Hadlock Brook. You will need good boots and reliable knees, but the trip will repay you for every step you take.

Jordan Pond Canoe Carry.

60—BUBBLES & CONNERS NUBBLE LOOP

From Bubble Rock parking area
To the Bubbles, Conners Nubble, and back
Up by south end of Jordan Pond Canoe Carry;
and South and North Bubble trails
Down by North Bubble, Conners Nubble, and
Eagle Lake trails; and north end of
Jordan Pond Canoe Carry
4.5 miles, September 6, 1996

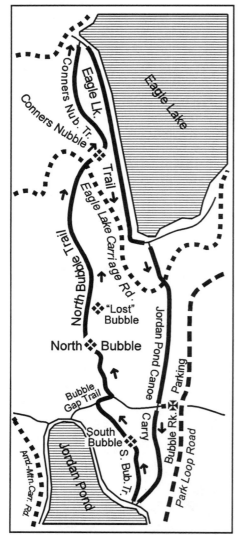

60—Bubbles & Conners Nubble loop.

Pivoting in bright sunlight on the summit of South Bubble, I scanned the peaks around me through binoculars looking for other hikers out in the park on a perfect, late-summer day. North Bubble—no one. Sargent and Penobscot—ditto. Pemetic—ditto. Cadillac—ditto, not even a car or RV. The summer of 1996 was over. The public had gone back to school and back to work, leaving Acadia National Park to its

own devices. I was on the last of fifteen hikes in the summer portion of my project to explore the trails of Acadia through the four seasons. I would go on hiking after this, but privately, off the record. For me hiking is more than recreation—it is a way of life. It is how I keep tabs on the present state of the universe. With everyone else back at her work station, someone has to do it. My duty is clear. Who will count Acadia's mushrooms, or make lists of its ferns, flowers, and fruit if I don't?

That may sound facetious, but I am not trying to be funny. By taking nature for granted, we have gotten ourselves in deep trouble. In 1915, the owner of the Point Wolfe sawmill in New Brunswick boasted his timber supply was inexhaustible; it ran out in 1921. In 1996, transnational wood products corporations in Maine say their forests will go on forever. They paint themselves as good stewards—while their machines and stockholders grow hungrier year by year. In this century we have found that there are limits on how much of the Earth we can consume or despoil. To ignore those limits is to risk endangering ourselves and spoiling our children's inheritance. The Point Wolfe sawmill is gone, its holdings now growing back as a national park. The Maine Woods are falling fast. When they are gone, the crash will shake every life in the state. It makes sense to check on local plants and wildlife before that to learn what we stand to lose.

For my part, I feel called to take the pulse of my natural surroundings. A firm believer in preventive medicine, I am not interested in watching a fatal disease take its course. I want to understand how nature works in my region, and to recognize a healthy wetland or forest when I see one. Then when change comes along, I will be able to tell if it falls within tolerable limits, or is a warning of serious trouble ahead. Most people won't know the difference, even though their livelihoods depend on it. So it is up to us pulse takers to make our rounds and report any suspicious activity we might see. The position doesn't pay anything to speak of, but I can not imagine a more rewarding job than patrolling the creative edge of the universe.

On this hike my rounds took me from the Bubble Rock parking area on the Park Loop Road to Jordan Pond by the Jordan Pond Canoe Carry, up the South Bubble Trail, across to North Bubble, then by the long glacial ridge across Lost Bubble to Conners Nubble and the shore of Eagle Lake, and then back to the parking area again by the Eagle Lake Trail and the northern half of Jordan Pond Canoe Carry. I went slowly, taking seven hours to hike that four-and-a-half-mile loop, largely because there was so much to see. Summer may have ended in the workaday world, but Acadia's berries had unfinished ripening to do, and a great many blossoms were still in their prime. There was no wind to speak of to cool the summery temperature, which hung in the low 80s. The hike was a series of ups and downs between the two ponds, for a total rise and fall of 1,080 feet.

The peaks along Bubble Ridge are well under 1,000 feet in elevation (South Bubble 768 feet, North Bubble 872 feet, Lost Bubble 825 feet, Conners Nubble 588 feet), but the view from each one is spectacular. With Penobscot and Sargent mountains to the west, Pemetic and Cadillac to the east, Eagle Lake and the Black (Gouldsboro) Hills to the north, and Jordan Pond and the islands off MDI to the south, the landscape rolls with wooded slopes and valleys in every direction, the ridge trail running straight through the heart of Acadia. Ambling along, you are in the middle of it all—bays, wetlands, ponds, woods, slopes, cliffs, peaks, and sky. This is what I came for. To get back to my earthly roots, my living connection with the universe.

I thought a lot about that on this hike, about my relationship to the whole of Acadia and the great beyond. Most of life is taken up dealing with details. Endless details. It is hard to put them together to get the big picture. We focus on one step at a time: on fixing dinner, eating what we have prepared, washing the dishes, putting them away, getting ready for the next meal. One thing after another, detail, detail, detail. What does it all mean? How does what I am doing right now fit into the whole? Is there a whole to fit into?—that is the question. Is there more to life than a seemingly endless series of now events?

Is there a universe, for instance, or only an infinite array of minutia buzzing off in every direction—what William James called a teeming multiverse? Does Acadia exist, or is it only a trick of the mind, a fiction made by adding every step of every hike into a mythological locale? I know where I am right now. Is it fair to lump that with other wheres and other nows to create a continuous domain in time and space? Or are time and space illusions in experience, artifacts of consciousness projected onto a jumble of disparate motes and particles having little to do with one another? How can a multiplicity of consciousness ever add up to a whole?

Look at that twig on the ground. How does it relate to the boulder over there, or to anything else? I relate the twig and the boulder in my mind, but that doesn't mean they are related in themselves. Twig doesn't know boulder is there, and vice versa. They don't seem to affect each other in the slightest way. Perhaps they did at one time, twig shading boulder or boulder sharing minerals with twig. But now only my free-roaming consciousness puts them together. Who am I to join them, when in fact they are separate and distinct?

On this loop between the two ponds, in addition to eighty-seven mushrooms, I met the following residents of Acadia:

Blooms

heath aster	whorled aster
flat-topped aster	large-leaved aster
large-leaved goldenrod	hairy goldenrod
slender goldenrod	yellow wood sorrel
beechdrops (many)	meadowsweet (one)

Berries

Solomon's seal	Canada May ruby
starflower	wintergreen
partridgeberry	bunchberry
blueberry	mountain cranberry
huckleberry	black chokeberry
mountain ash	mountain holly
wild raisin	pin cherry

Ferns

spinulose wood fern	spreading wood fern
marginal wood fern	rock-cap fern
bracken	New York fern
cinnamon fern	long beech fern
sensitive fern	Christmas fern

More lists yet! Put the separate entries together, what do they add up to? Do they collectively say anything about Acadia? In a certain place on a certain day in a certain season in a certain year, these plants were present. Do they represent random events, or do they contribute to a portrait of a place on the Maine coast in early September?

All are products of photosynthesis, so the list demonstrates that there was enough carbon dioxide, water, and sunlight in the park to support that process in a variety of species. Water, being the limiting resource, had evidently been available to plant roots during the growing season. Mycorrhizal fungi were on the job gathering moisture and nutrients. The local climate looks to have been within the normal range. Oxygen and water are byproducts of photosynthesis; these plants have done their bit to contribute oxygen and water vapor to the air. The variety of berries suggests conditions favored fertilization and the setting of fruit, crucial stages in the reproductive cycle. There is a good chance the same plants will be present next year. And animals that eat their leaves, sap, or fruit will be present, too. Ferns grow under a canopy that maintains cool temperatures and high humidity; it looks like that canopy has been in good working order up to now. Seen in that light, the lists are diagnostic tests probing the well-being of Acadia. The leaves, blooms, and fruit of such plants speak to concerns on a broader scale. No wonder we rejoice in flowers and fruit; our livelihoods depend on them directly, and on the resources and conditions they represent.

Maybe Acadia isn't a figment of my imagination. Maybe I am the figment, and Acadia is the imaginer. I am just a drifting mote after all, another wanderer passing through. Like a meter reader crossing yard after yard, I can't call this my turf. I am not a native, not like many of the plants on my lists. I do not own any of this; it owns me. It gives me place to plant my feet, to roam and gawk. My eyes are the eyes of Acadia, my tongue is its tongue. I do not dream Acadia, it dreams what I am. I will die, but it will go on, dreaming other wanderers, other makers of lists. Here on the cusp of the twenty-first century is a piece of planet Earth in good working order, a piece that hints beyond itself at the marvels of the modern universe.

The universe is the creative source of everything, not merely the passive setting for the human parade. My history is the history of the universe. My roots go deep through a hundred thousand generations of hominids, through billions of generations of primates, tree shrews, amphibians, fish, and one-celled life; through the evolution of the solar system, the birth of the sun, explosions of supernovas; formation of galaxies, stars, gas, and dust; through the forging of hydrogen atoms, electrons, particles, and energy itself. I am a microevent in the great cosmic unfolding, an entry in the catalog of all possible Earth happenings.

Bubble Rock.

At the same time, I am the product of a billion billion chance encounters, an accident too rare to predict. My father was walking from Hanover, New Hampshire, to Nova Scotia when he met my mother in Sullivan, Maine. Far from being star-crossed lovers, my parents met because my father's friend had a classmate who lived along the way, and that classmate had a sister. A few years later, I was born at eight o'clock in the morning, after the night nurses had gone off duty, before the day shift was on. The doctor handed my father a wad of cotton and bottle of chloroform and said, "Here, give her this." Which he did, pouring a shot of chloroform into her eye. Shazam! I was on the world scene. Every generation has similar stories, back to the beginning. Accident culminating in accident, one after another for thirteen billion years.

And, too, every one of our pedigrees lists success after success. Our ancestors were winners, every one. They lived long enough to reproduce. Maybe some of them were not very nice people, very nice tree shrews, or very nice stellar explosions, but they managed to get the job done. They led to the next stage, the next, and the next. Here we are, the current crop, proof of our forebears' prowess and blue ribbons all the way back. One slip anywhere along the line, and we would not be here. Most other lines never panned out. They fell by the wayside, unable to cope with the circumstances they were born into, if they were born at all. More species have dead-ended than gone on, way more. We are

the rare exceptions. Not because we are better, but because we had better luck. Things might have turned out differently. The asteroid that blotted out the dinosaurs might have missed the Earth; mammals might not have amounted to more than gleaners of crumbs between the toes of great lizards. But the asteroid did hit, dinosaurs were stuck in prehistory, and mammals won the day. True grit, orneriness, and luck saw us through, time after billions of times.

So here we are, motes at the leading edge of universal creation, ready to carry on, screw up, or get zapped, whichever. Being here now, we are the sowers of tomorrow. Earth is our garden. The seeds we plant today will sprout the possibilities of tomorrow. Do we know what we are doing? Do we have any idea of the responsibility we bear? Do we care what happens? Stay tuned. Coming episodes will tell all.

Meanwhile, back in Acadia, I hike with a conscience because I hike for Earth and the universe. I feel a spiritual imperative in every cell of my body. Be humble, it says, but do your best. Be true to the strugglers and seekers who got you where you are. Be true to the accidents that let you slip by. Hold up your end. Prepare the way for those yet to come. Build on the past. Keep joy and possibility alive. Why else are we here? I take that imperative seriously. As do we all, more or less. For now, I do what I can. Acadia is far more than the sum of my steps, but that is the best I can do. I sense the wholeness and wholesomeness of the place, the health, the soul, the divinity, the integrity around me. As a sample of the universe in its present condition, it is doing well. The beauty surrounding me tells me that, backed up by my lists.

I heard flickers and crows on this hike, and loons. I watched one loon in Eagle Lake splash and roll over again and again, flashing its white belly as if it were trying to attract a mate in April. It made a great show of itself, half-running on, half-swimming under the water. What was it doing? There was one boat on the lake, a collapsible affair from which two men were fishing. I thought the loon must have been performing for them, trying to distract them from something it didn't want them to see. I had seen two loons at first, but one of them had gone off. Who knows what it was doing? Loons are crazy, everybody knows that. Crazy like a fox. Speaking of which, I came across four blue scats in the trail, each filled with leaves, black berries, and seeds. Sowing the seeds of the future, that is our job. Everyone's job. I crossed a great many drainage channels along the Jordan Pond Canoe Carry, every one with pools left from Hurricane Edouard which had passed by earlier in the week, each pool full of striders twitching here and there, casting shadows like four-leaf clovers on the bottom from the dimples their legs pressed in the surface. Ants, thousands of ants, on granite ridges, in shaded valleys, all along the slopes. Crickets warming up for their fall concert. Grasshoppers like mechanical toys made in Taiwan, clicking as they unwound. Add sunlight to granite: snap-crackle-pop bugs livened up the air. I saw a robin near the summit of South Bubble, two ravens on Sargent (through binoculars), a Tennessee warbler gleaning insects in birch and popple near Conners Nubble, and several swarms of ant-like insects dancing with Brownian motion in the sprucetops, their flightpaths framing geodesic domes in the air. I saw four frogs: a green frog in Jordan Pond, and pickerel frogs in three sizes near Eagle Lake. Each of them took one leap to avoid me, then sat while I studied it in detail. One frog hit my pants leg when my stride intercepted its leap, but it rebounded with another kick against my shin, which carried it out of harm's way. I also heard two red squirrels south of Eagle Lake where I had come across their cousins three years ago when I hiked the same loop going the other way (see Hike 5). That time I had seen three peregrine falcons, which I watched for this time, thinking they might be migrating, but without success.

I met twenty-four people traveling in twelve couples, one male, one female, ten mixed. The kids had gone back to school. These were all adults, or near adults. They were a hardy and energetic crew, giving me a warm sense of comradeship along the trail. The first overtook me early on, the woman talking to me breathlessly over her shoulder:

"This is our last day. We're cramming in all we can, running up every trail we've missed."

They were heading down the carry toward the South Bubble Trail. Three couples rounding Jordan Pond passed me as I scanned for loons at the intersection of the carry with the east side trail. I met no one on either of the Bubbles. I came onto two men sitting in the North Bubble Trail north of Lost Bubble. Facing north, they had a map spread over their knees.

"Is that Somes Sound beyond the lake?" one of them asked me.

I told him it was the northern reach of Frenchman Bay.

"Then I'm completely turned around," he said.

They had taken a wrong turn from the Bubble Rock parking area and ended up approaching North Bubble from the north instead of the south.

"Do you go around the park looking for lost souls?" the other man asked.

"No," I said, "but anyone looking at a map is unsure about something, so I always ask if I can help."

I met a couple with an unleashed bulldog on the Eagle Lake Trail. The woman warned me it was a rocky trail.

"You have to watch your ankles," she said.

She meant the stones might trip me up, but I was more worried about her dog.

Two young women hiking together told me about seeing

Mountain ash on North Bubble Trail.

a great big turtle sunning on a rock in the lake.

I had a long talk with a couple from Toronto who had discovered Acadia in 1985 and been back six or seven times since. We leapfrogged each other on the Eagle Lake Trail, they stopping to rearrange their gear, I stopping to watch loons and take notes. I found them again eating lunch on a flat rock on the shore of the lake. They didn't like the heat of summer, so came as late as they could, leaving their bikes at home because they saw more of the park if they walked. I had asked if they were Canadian, which surprised them; they didn't feel their accent was that obvious. I told them anyone who said "aboot" for about might as well wear a maple leaf flag around his neck.

The hike began and ended in beech woods along the canoe carry, said to be one of the oldest trails in the park. A number of trees toward the Jordan Pond end were free of the bark disease that scars so many of the park's beeches. They seemed somewhat resistant either to the scale insect that punctures the trees' outer skin, or to the fungus that invades the wound, spreads, and kills the bark. Leafless, parasitic, purple-striped beechdrops sprouted beneath many of the trees, feeding on their roots. Most of my route had been burned in the 1947 fire, so birches lined much of the way. Northern white cedars grew along the Eagle Lake Trail and in the drainage northwest of Pemetic Mountain. Seen from Lost Bubble (my name for the first granite outcrop north of North Bubble), the slopes of Pemetic and Cadillac were patterned with dense stands of deciduous and coniferous trees. Here it was almost fall, and Acadia was still lush and green.

The trails that led me through the landscape between the two ponds were as varied as the terrain. I took the canoe carry connecting Eagle Lake and Jordan Pond in two sections, first from the apex in the middle, heading over stones and roots down to Jordan Pond; then, later, picking up the carry again on the last leg of the hike, rising from Eagle Lake over eleven sets of stepping stones, twenty-eight sections of bogwalk, and four small plank bridges to high ground and the parking area again. Both sections of the carry cross wet ground, the southern section paralleling the stony channel draining the slopes of South Bubble and Pemetic toward Jordan Pond, the northern section draining the northwestern slope of Pemetic toward Eagle Lake. Ferns and tall trees rise from the damp soil, making the carry an outstanding lowland trail end-to-end.

The South Bubble Trail rising from Jordan Pond to the summit of South Bubble is a wholly different kind of trail, steeper, rockier, more open, a trail that dramatizes the transition from shoreline woods to granite ridge. It crosses through smooth boulders heaped by the glacier and rough ones fallen from higher cliffs. A lot of work has been put into refining the trail, but even so it gives a rough-and-ready impression. The trail is short, only four-tenths of a mile long, rising almost 500 feet at a fairly steep grade. In a few places gravel eroding into the trail acts like ball bearings, particularly on wet days, making the going slipperier than it looks. Footing is better going up this route than coming down. [The South Bubble Trail was repaired in 1997.] At the top, views open over the pond onto Jordan Ridge, Penobscot and Sargent mountains, and the islands to the south. And there is always Bubble Rock, the most famous glacial erratic boulder in the park, smoothed by the tumbling action of the glacier, then

Conners Nubble from south shore of Eagle Lake.

plunked down on top of a cliff when the glacier receded, providing a focus for people like me—gawkers who marvel at nature's whims and tricks.

The trail connecting the summits of North and South Bubble bears a lot of foot traffic, so has been carefully tended by the park and the Youth Conservation Corps over the years. Cribwork, stone steps, and waterbars have been put in place, partly to ease the way for hikers, partly to direct running water away from the treadway. From South Bubble the trail dips 170 feet to the North Bubble Trail (coming up from the Bubble Rock parking area), then rises 270 feet over terraced ledges to the 872-foot summit of North Bubble, where the views are even more impressive due to the 100-foot gain in elevation. Here is another of those magical places in the park offering superb views in many directions, in this case west, south, and east. Salt water, fresh water, islands, cliffs, woods, peaks—you can have it all from North Bubble.

The North Bubble Trail continues north from the summit over the long granite ridge terminating in the northernmost Bubble, Conners Nubble, which overlooks Eagle Lake. I call this the Bubble Ridge Trail, which crosses "Lost Bubble," an unnamed blip of granite giving views east, north, and west, complementing the North Bubble vista. The North Bubble Trail drops 422 feet to the Eagle Lake Carriage Road, rises 138 feet to Conners Nubble—another magical spot with vistas in all directions—then eases down 314 feet to the level of Eagle Lake.

Following the shoreline, the Eagle Lake Trail wends among great blocks of talus resting in their tumble from cliffs above to lake below. It is a stony trail, paved with boulders much of the way, but being near water, a wonderful trail through lush woods featuring a variety of trees, ferns, fungi, lichens, and other vegetation. The lake trail meets the canoe carry at the south end of the lake, a little over half a mile from the Bubble Rock parking area.

All in all, the loop is an Acadian classic comprising woods, cliffs, talus slopes, ridges, summits, lakeshores, and stirring vistas within a single hike. I found it a mentally challenging hike because, as my last hike of the season, I kept asking myself if I had gone out looking for the real Acadia and missed it somehow, letting it slip away into a maze of details. Is this it? I kept asking myself—this bunch of mountain ash berries, these birches, that loon, those cliffs over there? I couldn't reconcile all the parts with the whole, the whole with its myriad parts. Where was Acadia? The real Acadia? Or was it elusive, a figment I could only clasp in serial form, but not all at once? My wandering meditation was one question after another with no answers in between.

Close-up, the landscape was filled with details in complex relationships; at a distance, it looked simpler and more of a piece. Which was the real Acadia, the landscape as seen from inside or outside? I kept shifting between the two perspectives, walking surrounded by woods where I could see 500 cobbles and boulders, stems of 500 trees, with 50,000 leaves overhead; or looking onto the woods from above where I could see a variegated sweep of green culminating in granite cliffs and ridges. Snapshots and postcards usually show the sweep of the landscape, emphasizing vistas taken in at a glance. Hiking through the landscape, my eyes presented me with a moving picture that changed with every step. What we sacrifice in the larger view is resolution of fine detail, while in the closeup the overview is lost. Experience tells me that every section of the park is as rich and varied as any other. Complexity is the rule. If those same sections look simple at a distance, that is a trick of the eye abetted by a mind looking to grasp the landscape without working too hard. Looking down at the canoe carry from Lost Bubble, then hiking along it, I saw how inadequate my first impression had been. Simplicity is an illusion. The more we probe any landscape, the more complex it becomes. If something appears simple, we aren't looking closely enough. Get into the details. Break it down into its parts. Analyze, analyze, analyze. But there comes a point when we have to step back to see how those parts connect together to make larger and larger wholes. To get the big picture. The bigger picture. The biggest picture of all. Synthesize, synthesize, synthesize.

We go back and forth, taking the universe apart, putting it together again, vacillating between subatomic particles and the oneness of it all. The universe remains what it is, a cascading onrush of energy. But we can't make up our minds how to look at it. In moments of innocence we say it is transparently simple, harmony on a cosmic scale. But in cannier moments we see it in all its diverse parts, an entity so complex only one part can be engaged at a time, completely filling our consciousness. The universe does not change; we change. We keep looking at it in different ways by varying our perspective, seeing generally, then particularly; abstractly, then concretely; inductively, then deductively; intellectually, then sensually—trying all the while to fit the world of petty facts to the world of grand meanings and ideas. That is the nature of experience, to keep shuffling our possibilities in novel ways or, by a better image, to keep

juggling them, tossing as many as we can in the air at once. As jugglers of perspectives, we are fascinated by the visions that, like so many Indian clubs, float before our eyes, while, at the same time, it is our own skill that makes them fly.

Taking hike after hike, I juggle my view of Acadia, always looking at it in new ways from different points of view. The park is not contained in the leaf of the rattlesnake plantain any more than in the view from North Bubble. It is

Water striders and their shadows, Jordan Pond Canoe Carry.

both, and much more besides. It includes everything I have said about it in these essays, and everything I have left out. It includes everything other hikers have experienced, other bikers, other equestrians, other paddlers, other wheelchair rollers, other travelers of every sort—other birds, other mammals, other fish, other reptiles and amphibians, other insects, other spiders, other algae, other bacteria—everything other motes of any kind have experienced from any and every perspective. Acadia is vivid and true for each of us in different ways at different times. Add those views together with all imaginable past and present views—there, now, that is Acadia! That is juggling! That is an inkling of what the leading edge of universal creation is like.

Just thinking about what I have missed makes me humble. I bow before the vast splendor of my ignorance. It makes me who I am, complementing my tiny wisdom, urging me to take other hikes. Embracing the possibility of that which I have yet to experience, I discover two things: my many ties to a world I can never know, and a spiritual sense of awe before the mystery of my relationship with that hidden world. I can juggle only so much at one time before

Indian clubs spill in every directions and I fall in a heap beneath them. Bonk! The universe won't let me get too good a grasp on it. The more I try, the faster I have to move, the less sure my grip becomes, the more certain I am to fail. At a certain point details have to be clumped together in larger units to keep them from spilling. The more we experience, the more we have to clump single events into generalities so we won't lose what we have worked so hard to gain.

There is my experience and there is my ignorance—that reduces the universe to only two parts. That's as far as I can go. From that split rises my spirituality like a jinni from a lamp. I know what I know, but my existence depends just as much on what I don't know. We talk a lot about freedom, liberty, and independence in this country, but who among us can claim to be free in any true sense? Our lives depend on luck, fresh air, clean water, sunlight, wholesome food, family, friends, loved ones, social groups and institutions, other species of plants and animals, and our unique genetic heritage back to earliest days, and before that into times not calibrated in years, days, hours, seconds, or any other units we have heard of. Thinking about what I don't know and yet depend upon because it makes me who I am, I am humble, grateful, awestruck, and mystified. Knowing it is there for certain but I can never grasp it in detail gives rise to a deep sense of spirituality that springs from within and without at once, joining me to everything else without spelling out the means of that connection. Hiking the trails of Acadia I am accompanied by that spirit as a presence that keeps me sane by preventing me from thinking too much of myself. A mote passing by, that is all I am, yet I am tied to every other mote and together we make a multiverse that, seen the right way, becomes a universe, of which we are all on the leading edge.

Viewing myself as a member of the August Order of Contemporary Motes, I see that I share responsibility for what we are to accomplish in preparing the way for the next generation of motes who are to partake in the next leading edge. I try to live so that the next generation will be able to view the universe in its own way in its own time, and the same for generations after that as far as I can imagine them. Make way for asters and goldenrod, grasshoppers, crickets, pickerel frogs, and loons! See they get the chance they deserve. The human record isn't that great. We seem to destroy most of what we touch. The beauty we claim to create is derived from the beauty around us that we had no part in creating. The part of universal creation we like best is our personal selves. Everything else is expendable—other people, other races, other species. "Me, me, me, me!" is our cry. What we forget is the mystery that completes us and makes us whole—all of nature—as if it were somehow beneath us. Which it truly is, supporting us, holding us in the light. Hiking the living trails of Acadia puts me in touch with what I am not, with all that makes me possible, with my companions on the journey of life. I don't find them written up in the newspaper or their affairs covered on TV. We focus on politics, business, education, the military, sports—everywhere but on the source of our good fortune, on the spiritual force that makes it possible for us to take part in creating a better world for coming generations of Earthlings and universelings. Hiking grounds me, reminding me that life is an ongoing event, not a thing. An opportunity, not an accomplishment. The universe never rests. Onward! is its motto. Get moving, it tells us, get out and about. Walk in love and beauty always, and cherish those who go with you, for without them you lie down alone.

✪

Hikers on the Beachcroft Trail, Huguenot Head.

INDEX

Acadia National Park
  (note: most entries in this
  index refer to aspects of
  Acadia National Park)
  carriage roads (see Roads)
  carriage-road-use study 248
  crowd control 123
  federally funded exercise yard
    for pets 118
  firing range 98, 100
  the heart of 34, 58, 111, 122,
    204, 246, 288, 315
  Isle au Haut section 229–236
  more than a resort at the end
    of a road 280
  an ongoing event 145
  protection 36
  resprucing of 208
  Schoodic Point section
    255–259
  sex ratio of hikers in 18, 265
  world image of 123
Acorns 57–59, 66, 67, 296
Amphibian(s)
  eggs 219, 221
    wood frog 219
  frogs 16, 24, 196, 244, 246,
    247, 251, 310–312, 317
    bullfrog 281
    green frog 15, 251, 254,
      262, 281, 288, 311, 317
    pickerel frog 317, 320
    spring peeper 211, 310,
      311
    wood frog 201, 265, 269,
      300, 303
Amphitheater (see Valleys)
Appalachian Mountain Club
  (AMC) 43, 111, 296
  Echo Lake Camp 244, 296

Balloon(s) 23, 57, 60, 130
Beach
  ancient 178
  cobble 144, 231
  Echo Lake 43
  Hunters 96, 99
  Sand 79, 80, 180–182,
    281–283
  seawall 144
Bedrock
  Bar Harbor formation 180,
    181
  gabbro 180, 181
  granite 8, 22, 66, 79, 85, 142,
    144, 180, 181, 210, 231,
    252, 263, 304
  crumbling 69, 132, 221
  granite plutons 40, 252
  shatter zone 79, 180, 181
  volcanic 142, 155, 231, 232

Benchmark, Cadillac Mtn. 69,
  134, 136, 252, 306
Berries 16, 301, 306
  ash, mountain 306, 307, 315,
    317, 319
  blackberry 306, 307
  bluebead 296
  blueberry 8, 250, 262, 266,
    272, 274, 276, 278,
    280–282, 285, 289, 290,
    292, 301, 307, 311, 315
  bunchberry 274, 280, 282,
    290, 301, 306, 307, 311,
    312, 315
  Canada May ruby 280, 307,
    311, 312, 315
  cherry, pin 306, 307, 315
  chokeberry, black 306, 307,
    311, 315
  cranberry, mountain 306, 307,
    311, 312, 315
  hobblebush 312
  holly, mountain 41, 307
  huckleberry 262, 280, 282,
    306, 307, 311, 315
  juniper 266, 280, 282, 290,
    306, 307, 311
  partridgeberry 138, 311, 312,
    315
  raspberry 301
  sarsaparilla 282
  sheep laurel 307
  Solomon's seal 290, 315
  starflower 315
  trillium, red 307
  winterberry 40
  wintergreen 306, 307, 311,
    315
  witherod 250, 256, 307
Berry Finder 15
Berry month, August is 306
Bicycle path 61
Binoculars 80, 82, 83, 129, 137,
  142, 144, 180, 196–199, 218,
  254, 255, 257, 258, 266, 267,
  269, 271, 275, 281, 293, 294,
  314, 317
Bioregion 161, 168–171, 185,
  204, 211, 212, 280
  b. at work 168
Birds
  blue jay 15, 30, 32, 33, 37,
    38, 41, 42, 44, 57, 66, 67,
    92, 95, 163, 196, 199, 200,
    218, 251, 253, 256, 305,
    307
  bunting, snow 284
  Canada goose 187
  catbird 261, 262
  chickadee 15, 30, 33, 42, 44,
    47, 52, 57, 66, 67, 70, 72,
    82, 92, 95, 102, 103, 109,
    110, 113, 118, 129, 134,

Birds/chickadee (continued)
  137, 140, 161, 163, 173,
  193, 197–200, 211, 218,
  244, 262, 278, 307
cormorant 255, 256, 266
  double-crested 78, 233
  great 77, 143, 233
condor, giant Jovian 294
crow 12, 15, 19, 20, 30, 33,
  35, 38, 47, 52, 57, 67, 70,
  77, 92, 95, 113, 115, 126,
  129, 130, 137, 144, 161,
  172, 173, 175, 177, 180,
  182, 187, 197, 199, 211,
  218, 225, 233, 234, 248,
  251, 253, 255, 256, 266,
  274, 278, 281, 295, 301,
  310, 316
dove, mourning 144, 161,
  175, 177, 199, 200, 262,
  295
ducks 24, 25, 28, 64, 77, 126
  black 82, 144, 199, 218,
    219, 225, 288
  bufflehead 57, 61, 144, 145
  eider 77, 80, 128, 144, 145,
    180, 182, 233, 255, 259
  goldeneye 144
  harlequin 79
  merganser 215
    common 79, 145, 214,
      274
    red-breasted 137, 141
  oldsquaw 77, 137, 140,
    145
  wood 199, 211
finch, purple 147
flicker 28, 211, 218, 233,
  244, 255, 258, 300, 303,
  316
gannet 79
grackle 233
grebe, red-necked 77
grosbeak, pine 53, 56
grouse, ruffed 107, 198, 200,
  203, 205, 211, 251, 253
guillemot 77, 145, 180, 233,
  255, 259
gull 12, 38, 67, 82, 83, 129,
  144, 180, 214, 253, 255,
  256, 258, 262, 266, 267,
  274, 278, 282, 289, 290,
  293, 295, 303, 307
  black-backed 218, 233
  herring 77, 218, 233
hawks 24, 211, 246, 253,
  258, 284, 293
  eagle, American bald 33,
    34, 144, 164, 173, 233,
    255, 257, 269, 272, 274,
    281, 284, 285
  kestrel 24, 27, 28, 267
  marsh 25, 199

Birds/hawks (continued)
  osprey 11–13, 18, 32, 214,
    215, 293, 294
  peregrine falcon 21, 23, 62,
    129, 136, 137, 180, 214,
    215, 244, 267, 281, 283,
    317
  red-tailed hawk 70
  sharp-shinned hawk 33, 37,
    265, 267, 294
heron, great blue 199
hummingbird 233
junco 8, 38, 188, 196, 199,
  211, 233, 243, 244, 246,
  248, 259, 265, 266, 272,
  274, 278, 281, 295, 300
kingfisher 278
kinglet, golden-crowned 70,
  211
loon, common 19, 20, 128,
  137, 140, 141, 145, 180,
  275, 276, 278, 279, 316,
  317, 319, 320
nuthatch, red-breasted 30, 47,
  52, 102, 137, 140, 161, 187,
  190, 200, 234
owl (see Wildlife signs) 132
phoebe 197, 199
raven 53, 82, 98, 118, 121,
  161, 172, 175, 177, 193,
  197, 200, 215, 234, 244,
  267, 283, 288, 307, 310,
  317
redstart 262
sandpiper 225
siskin, pine 289
somebird 30, 47, 53
sparrows 38, 278
  song 196, 199, 211, 225,
    281, 284
  swamp 262
  white-throated 196, 199,
    233, 253, 274, 281, 284
swallow, tree 213, 282
tanager, scarlet 233
tern 257, 258
thrushes 242, 254, 269, 288
  hermit thrush 197, 199,
    213, 214, 218, 233, 234,
    251, 253, 258, 260, 262,
    263, 265, 266, 274, 278,
    281, 289, 295
  robin 19, 23, 38, 47, 50, 52,
    79, 180, 187, 191, 193,
    197–200, 205, 211, 218,
    225, 234, 246, 253, 254,
    262, 274, 288, 307, 317
vireo, warbling 200–202, 205
vulture, turkey 191, 197, 199,
  218, 220, 246, 247, 252,
  253, 267–270, 272, 274,
  281, 283, 284, 289,
  293–295

Birds (continued)
warblers 180, 217, 225, 226,
242, 245, 259, 265, 269,
293
black-and-white 218, 222,
225
black-throated blue 225,
227, 242, 245
black-throated green 225,
255, 259, 275, 278
confusing fall 32
palm 198, 199
Tennessee 317
yellow 262
yellow-rumped 211, 213,
218, 233, 244, 251, 253,
265, 266, 274, 300
waxwing, cedar 253, 254, 307
whippoorwill 225
wicha-wicha bird 260, 262
woodpecker 15, 30, 134,
160, 211, 225, 262, 303
black-backed 257
downy 53, 57, 82, 92, 95,
118, 196–199, 266
hairy 15, 17, 19, 20, 47, 50,
53, 71, 82, 92, 94, 102,
107, 109–111, 118, 129,
130, 187, 190, 198, 199,
225, 226, 253, 300
pileated 8, 11, 12, 15, 18,
126, 173, 199, 211, 266
sapsucker (see Wildlife
signs)
wren 38
winter 188
year-round birds 30
yellowthroat, common 218,
220, 225, 233
Blazes (see also Cairns) 306
arrows, red 208
ax 45
bird silhouette 50, 109, 257
blue 8, 9, 31, 32, 63, 67, 71,
99, 104, 125, 148, 182, 232,
281, 291
diamond 50, 102, 109, 148,
189
orange 125
red 9, 103, 182, 291
tape (see Flagging)
Boats and vessels (see also
Vehicles) 11, 244, 265, 266,
316
Aurora B. 42, 236
Beagle 148
Bluenose ferry 63
cigarette boat 5, 244
cruise ship 31
Excellence 265
fishing 56, 81, 131, 143, 266,
316
Grand Design 143

Boats (continued)
Isle au Haut
fishing 235, 236
mailboat 230, 231, 235, 236
Queen Elizabeth II, 11
Sunset 13
tug Tackle 231
yacht, hulking 294
Bogwalks 36, 41, 140, 188,
221, 262, 282, 284, 307, 318
Bones 139, 188, 193, 245, 258
Boulders 9, 16, 18, 20, 30, 33,
34, 41, 63, 85, 99, 140, 144,
154, 155, 172, 177, 189, 197,
203, 205, 207, 210, 220–222,
227, 245, 259, 261, 263, 266,
272, 291, 304, 315, 318, 319
boulder that looked like a
popover 266
Bubble Rock 318
Buddha 17, 197
glacial erratic 9, 85, 91, 112,
154, 318
Old Man and Old Woman
207
Bridges
Adams Brook Br. 153, 156
Asticou Trail br. 125, 188
Beehive Trail br. 129
carriage road bridges 119
Amphitheater Br. 119–122,
146, 147, 186, 188
Chasm Brook Br. 24, 26,
119, 120
Cliffside Br. 120–122, 177
Cobblestone Br. 222
Day Mtn.–Triad Br. 175,
177
Deer Brook Br. 120, 227
Hadlock Brook Br. 101,
102, 146, 147, 188
Hemlock Br. 100–103, 120,
312, 313
Jordan Stream Br. 223
Little Harbor Brook Br.
186, 188
Stanley Brook Br. 159, 161
Waterfall Br. 102, 118–120,
146–148, 168, 171, 313
West Branch Br. 8, 120
corduroy bridge 216
Great Brook br. 6, 109, 111
Hadlock Path br. 279, 280
Jordan Cliffs Trail br. 10, 291
Long Pond Trail bridges 112
Thompson Island Br. 230
YCC bridge 41, 222, 227
stone bridge 41, 222
Brooks (see Streams)
Buds 44, 126, 129
beech 220
birch 225
blueberry 212, 226

Buds (continued)
Canada May ruby 226
candles, white pine 226
with donkey ears 174
elder, red-berried 226
everlasting, early 219, 220,
226
hobblebush 220
huckleberry 247
lily, cow 262
maple, striped 212, 220, 226
mayflower 198, 215
pink, powdery 206
plantain, rattlesnake 312
pussy willow 143
rattlesnake root, tall 305
sarsaparilla 226
shad 220
sheep laurel 250, 255
spruce, red 247
witherod 250
Buildings
Abbe Museum 261
Asticou Inn 192
Asticou Map House 87, 89,
192, 194
Brown Mtn. Gatehouse 77,
116, 146, 216
fishing shack 158
gift shop, Cadillac Mtn. 253
the Herimitage 139, 268
High Seas 62, 64, 67, 129
Jordan Pond House 10, 120,
158–160, 229, 287–290,
292, 313
dormitory 159, 160
nature center 261
pink vacation homes 213, 216
pump house 213, 216
St. James Church (stone
church) 205, 288
stable, private 159
Summit House 69, 134
the Tool Barn 163
Wildwood Stable 177
Buoys
bell 80, 88
lobster 12
Bushwhack 99, 102, 103, 148,
163, 167, 175–178

Cairns 66, 94, 104–106, 131,
148, 172, 188, 189, 192, 263,
274, 305–307
a cairn for the ages 188
designer cairns 69, 252, 263,
306, 307
Duck Harbor Mtn. 232
Sargent Mtn. n. ridge 27
summit cairns
Dorr Mtn. 60, 69, 260, 261
McFarland Hill 94
Parkman Mtn. 247

Cairns/summit (continued)
Penobscot Mtn. 289
Sargent Mtn. 36, 105, 168,
170, 171, 204, 227, 288,
290, 291, 309
the Triad 177
Campgrounds
Blackwoods 173, 228, 250
Duck Harbor 230
Seawall 143, 156, 157
Canyon of Canon Brook 71,
209, 210
Cemetery, Forest Hill 88, 190,
192, 193, 216
the Chasm of Chasm Brook 26
Civilian Conservation Corps
(CCC) 13, 58, 86, 296
the Cleft (Day Mtn.) 177, 178
Cliffs 10, 34, 243–245, 257,
263, 266, 272, 276, 280, 283,
302, 304, 313, 318, 319
Beech Cliff 42, 43, 180, 243,
244, 266
Beech Mtn. 82, 85
Bubble, North 227
Canada Cliff 43, 46
Cedar Swamp Mtn. 121, 148
Champlain Mtn. 127
Chickadee Valley 204
crumbling 69, 197, 221
Dorr Mtn. 16, 58, 59, 199
Eagle Cliff 12–14, 136–138,
141, 267, 292–296
Eagles Crag 250, 251, 253
Eliot Mtn. 125
Jordan Cliffs 9, 41, 121,
218–220, 269–271,
287–292
Otter Cliff 80
Pemetic Mtn. 30, 31
the Precipice 62, 63, 67, 128,
180, 257, 259, 285
Sargent Brook 203
Sargent Mtn. 225
Clothing 76–78, 101, 242, 244,
276
caps 39, 156, 219, 228
face mask 104
Comet Hale-Bopp 170
Cones, spruce 255, 258
Cone scales 12, 82, 175, 193,
218, 234, 301
spruce 156, 172, 183, 215
white pine 8
Contrail 98, 99
Coves and harbors
Bass Harbor 142
Bennet Cove 142, 144
Bracy Cove 125, 144, 222
Duck Harbor 231, 233
Emery Cove 96
Fernald Cove 14
Hulls Cove 166

Coves (continued)
Little Harbor 125, 126
Monument Cove 79
Moores Harbor 231, 233
Newport Cove 79, 128, 180–182
Pond Cove
East 256
West 257
Prospect Harbor 257
Raccoon Cove 69
Salisbury Cove 96
Seal Cove 115
Seal Harbor 96, 157–160
Ship Harbor 142, 145
Squeaker Cove 232
Tumbledown Cove 221, 222
Valley Cove 12, 13, 136–138, 140, 141, 293, 294, 296
Wonsqueak Harbor 257
Cribwork 22, 41, 43, 221, 227, 243, 272, 291, 318
Culverts 61, 139, 154, 205, 262, 274
Cyclists 8, 21, 26, 30, 36, 201, 285, 307

Dikes 9, 22, 23, 25, 27, 29, 31, 36, 43, 50, 57, 68, 70, 72, 131, 132, 135, 140, 241, 252, 266, 273, 280, 296
Don's Shop 'n Save in Bar Harbor 275

Ecosystem 211, 213, 221, 300
Ecozoic Era 155
Equinox (see Quarter days)
Erosion (see also Trail erosion) 8, 56, 60, 69, 72, 227, 263, 288, 302, 306, 318
Eyesores and distractions
Jackson Laboratory 61, 66, 128, 132, 245
Southwest Harbor transfer station 53, 82, 245, 301

Fabbri picnic area 77, 281, 283
Ferns (see Plants)
Fever
cabin 154, 218, 223
spring 200
Films
The Fly 60
Incredible Voyage 122
of my hike 108
Fire of 1947, 20, 22, 23, 25, 31, 130, 165, 208, 212, 220, 227, 251, 252, 254, 263, 300, 318
Fire roads (see Roads)
Fire towers
Beech Mtn. 9, 44, 82, 85, 86, 241, 244
Schoodic Mtn. 284

Fish 25, 219, 293, 300
Atlantic salmon 309
brown trout 214
dead 219, 220, 222
minnows 15, 16, 24, 25, 274
Flagging (see also Blazes) 207, 208
Flowers (see also Plants)
ash, mountain 248, 251
aster 15, 30, 40, 282, 291, 296, 301, 309, 311, 320
flat-topped 8, 19, 290, 296, 301, 307, 311, 312, 315
heath 315
large-leaved 296, 301, 311, 315
purple 7, 16, 19, 282
whorled 296, 301, 307, 311, 315
bedstraw, marsh 262
beechdrops 315, 317
blackberry 243, 248, 256, 262, 277
bluebead (yellow clintonia) 242, 243, 248
blueberry 232, 242, 248, 250
blue flag 256, 262
bluets 256, 262
bunchberry dogwood 242, 243, 247, 250, 252, 256, 262
buttercup 242, 250, 262, 268, 274
tall 296
Canada May ruby 242, 244, 247, 255, 256, 259
chokeberry, black 242, 244, 247, 248, 250–252
cinquefoil
common 262
dwarf 256
shrubby 291
wine-leaf 242, 244, 248, 251, 254, 256, 259, 262, 266, 272, 282, 288, 296
clover
red 250, 256, 261
white 256, 261
yellow 261
corydalis, pale 241, 242, 245
cotton grass 250, 251, 288, 307
cow lily 262, 288, 307
cow wheat 277, 293, 295, 301, 307
cranberry
large 277
mountain 247, 256
daisy 250, 252, 256, 259, 261
dandelion 217
everlasting, early 219, 220
forsythia 217
gerardia, purple 16

Flowers (continued)
goldenrod 7, 8, 15, 42, 282, 290, 291, 295, 296, 301, 309, 311, 320
downy 306, 307, 311, 312
hairy 315
large-leaved 311, 315
slender 307, 311, 312, 315
goldthread 232, 243
harebell 14, 282, 290–292, 296
hawksbeard 261
hawkweed 243, 250, 252, 274, 282, 301, 307
orange 256, 261
yellow 256, 261, 268, 296
heather, golden 255, 257, 259
herb Robert 14, 42, 43, 296, 301
hobblebush 220, 226
honeysuckle
American fly 226
bush 250, 262, 263, 266, 282, 307
huckleberry 247, 250
Indian pipe 277, 296, 311
lady's slipper 242–244, 247, 248, 250
leatherleaf 220, 222
lily, wood 286–290, 312
loosestrife
purple 287
whorled 262, 277
maple, red 220, 226
mayflower 187, 199, 212, 242, 277, 304
meadowsweet 262, 263, 274, 282, 288, 290, 291, 295, 301, 307, 311, 315
mullein 282
orange grass 277, 306, 307
orchis, smaller purple fringed 307
parsnip, water 307
partridgeberry 277
pepperbush, sweet 301, 307
pink, Deptford 282
pipewort 300, 301, 307
plantain, rattlesnake 310–312
pyrola, shinleaf 262
rattlesnake root, tall 290, 296, 305, 307, 311, 312
rhodora 242, 244, 247
rose 274, 282, 290
rugosa 256
St. Johnswort 261, 282, 296
sandwort, mountain 9, 32, 247, 250–252, 262, 272–274, 277, 282, 288, 295, 307, 311
sarsaparilla 242, 247, 250, 256
saxifrage 242, 243

Flowers (continued)
selfheal 268, 274, 307
shad 220, 226, 232
sheep laurel (lambkill) 247, 250, 255, 257, 262, 263, 266, 269, 274, 277, 282, 290
skunk cabbage 232
Solomon's seal 242, 243
sorrel, sheep 261
sorrel, wood 51
yellow 296, 315
speedwell 274
starflower 242, 244, 245, 247, 250, 255, 259
stitchwort 261
strawberry 232
sumac, staghorn 262
sundrops 296
swamp candles 282
trillium 244
twinflower 258, 259, 269, 277
vetch
cow 250, 256, 259, 268, 282
crown 282
violet 226, 232, 242
water lily 288
winterberry 274
wintergreen 282, 301
witherod 250, 262, 311
witch hazel 58, 95, 104
yarrow 261, 268, 290, 301, 307
Flowers, imagine a life without 277
Fog 8, 11, 12, 14, 140, 233, 250, 253, 260–264, 276–279, 300, 303–307
Foghorn 57, 64, 88, 135, 253, 260
Frenchman Bay 66, 70, 79, 105, 131, 135, 180, 181, 187, 227, 250, 253, 257, 259, 266, 282, 283, 317
Frogs (see Amphibians)
Fundy National Park 284, 309, 312–314
Fungi (mushrooms) 250, 256, 274, 275, 278, 279, 290, 306, 315, 318
amanita 32, 33, 36, 256
destroying angel 307
bracket 160
coral 290
mushroom militia 290
mycorrhizal 98, 315
witches butter 12, 41

Gardening 242
Gates
Brown Mountain 88, 91, 92,

Gates/Brown Mtn. (continued)
100–102, 119, 190–192, 194
Cadillac Mtn. entrance 133
Jordan Pond 160
Giant Slide 34, 37, 201–205
Glacial deposits 159, 176, 215
delta 159
end moraine 159
Glacier 29, 32, 66, 85, 96, 99, 120, 130, 136, 142, 159, 161, 168, 177, 178, 180, 201, 205, 263, 264, 282, 283, 317
Gorge above Hemlock Br. 101, 120, 312, 313
Gravel pits 100, 159, 215
Great Snake Flat 72
Gulf of Maine 31, 106, 115, 152, 218, 226, 230, 235, 255, 260, 272, 282

Habitats 52, 65, 214–216, 229, 233, 256, 299
Hancock County Trustees of Reservations 23
Hershey's chocolates 21
Hiking 17, 40, 53, 110, 131, 146, 229, 230, 243, 250, 260, 267, 269, 270, 272, 279, 280, 297–300, 311, 313, 314, 320
"best day-hiking in the country" 267
carriage road 119
winter 76, 83, 92, 101, 127, 128, 138, 153, 284
Hiking alone 118, 122, 265, 297, 298, 300
Hiking groups 253, 297–300
Hiking with a companion 298–300
Horseshoe (see Wetlands)
Hurricane 79
Bertha 272–274
Edouard 317

Ice 70, 84, 138, 153, 154, 177, 196, 203, 205, 206
noisy 131
organ-pipe 135
pond 82, 115, 121
stream 125
trail 71, 83, 84, 110, 124, 127, 128, 130, 138–140, 160, 172, 181, 188, 191–193, 195, 196, 203, 205, 210
Ice creepers 116, 124, 127, 141, 160, 172, 191–193
Ice crystal 52, 84, 85, 110
Ice elephants 120
Icefalls 70, 82, 109, 127, 128
Icicles 43, 52, 55, 56, 82, 84, 117, 120

Ideas
1 + 1 = 2, 298
Acadia
A. happens 311
A. is vivid and true in different ways 319
A. largely escapes me 311
A. reveals its secrets to those who take time 285
inner workings of A. 294
looking for the real A. 319
the soul of A. 312
the spell of A. 287
the well-being of A. 315
accident culminating in accident 316
the American dream 166
analysis/synthesis 319
angel messengers 98, 165, 213
augury 288
awareness 44, 89, 91, 110, 118, 258, 273, 277, 283, 284, 286, 290, 294, 295, 298–300
mote of 114
Away 299
hike in Acadia, not in A. 300
people from A. 298
beauty 17, 42, 48, 83, 84, 107, 111, 124, 174, 175, 184, 192, 195, 198, 220, 222, 223, 255, 258, 270, 273, 277, 287, 298, 310, 313, 316, 320
being alone 170
being there xv, 202, 204, 240, 298, 299
Big Bang 155, 191, 219
boulders in my head 245
the Bubbies 158
Buddha 11, 17, 197
the busy hum of men 205
channelization 120, 123
character 49, 61, 251
cherish those who go with you 320
childhood images 27
cliff dweller 46
commercial forces, aggressive 229
commitment, element of 299
communion 45
concern, circle of our 308
conscience, I hike with a 316
consciousness, higher order of 162
consensus among like-minded discoverers 288
consumption 202
Constitution, U.S. 170, 264
cosmic force 211, 213

Ideas (continued)
cosmic mind 270
cosmic soul 219
creation, universal 77, 110, 130, 147, 161, 184, 235, 258, 270, 273, 286, 294, 295, 314, 316, 319, 320
creativity 193, 194, 211, 270, 286, 299, 307
dance, the great 165
deity is mystery personified 258
democracy 154
design-after-the-fact 309
details 20, 88, 186, 315, 319, 320
details/generalities 52, 108, 109, 315
different hikers, worlds, Acadias 286
dirigo 10, 114
discovery 288, 300
divinity 211, 274, 294, 312
Earth
divinity of 87
rhythms of 224
voice of 189
Earth brothers and sisters 89, 162, 171
Earthspeak 162
economics 278
economy, human 278
element(s) 235, 268, 273, 299
ancient 249, 250
my green and blossoming 242
spiritual 250
endurance 49
events are an expression of the landscape where they come into being 299
evolution 60, 77, 90, 316
experience 223, 230, 235, 246, 248, 269, 270, 276, 283, 284, 286, 294–298, 301, 310, 315, 319, 320
coil of 146, 147
fireworks in the mind 264
first one out after a snow-storm 88, 158
flow xvii, xviii, 32
flow, go with the 130
flowers 277
forgetfulness 110
fortune, good 309
geckyracies 203–205
genius 161
genius of a watershed 279
getting around 178
g-mail 305
G/god(s) 87, 91, 98, 184, 258, 269, 270, 272–275, 294, 295, 310

Ideas/G/god(s) (continued)
out of a machine 164
storm and weather 146, 269, 274
that of everyone in 294
"going for the gold" 286
gravity 71, 129, 203
habit 299
half-sight, blessed with 290
happiness 200
Hawaii, prettier than 268
heaven 55, 184, 202, 269, 270
heaven is where the warbling vireo sings 202
Heaven's Gate 184, 185
heroes 11
hike early and hike often 293
home 6, 12, 46, 76, 83, 122, 138, 169, 214, 223, 224, 273, 283, 300, 301
homeland 4, 191
horizon 81
how I fritter my life 110
how we see the world 158
human imagination, cradle of 278
humanus 155
humus 26, 27
I am dissatisfied, therefore I eat 202
idealists 234
ideals, mental domain of 286
independence 264, 320
Independence Day 264
the inlook of the trail 283
integrity 89, 97, 122, 132, 264, 270, 275, 306, 308, 312, 316
island universes 15
islands of life 59
journeys, spiral 223
joy out of sorrow 278
as we judge so are we judged 215
judgment 81, 83, 106, 114, 153
language 276
laying on of hands 90
Las Vegas 158
learning 288, 289
life 249, 250, 270, 273–278, 284, 286, 295, 300, 315, 320
l. and death are complementary 278
building a l. 284
context of l. 264
elixir of l. 212
new l. out of old 278
rhythm(s) of l. 211, 212
life of possibility 219
life on the edge 79, 80
life's fundamentals 191

Ideas (continued)
live and let live 171
looking *for* 40
lost, when our minds and bodies are in different places, we are l. 298
love 136, 161, 200, 258, 277, 278, 295, 298–300, 320
"don't l. the messenger" 164, 166
fall in l. again 300
flows not from the heart but from the Earth 299
luck, chance, accident 309
machines 102
memory, episodic/semantic 310
metaphor 147, 158
root 47–49, 84
metaphysics 13
microdialogues 156
mind-set 276, 298
miracles 44, 58, 109, 115, 220, 221
miracle to miracle 236
mobility 12, 25, 122
moral journey 81
Motes, the August Order of Contemporary 320
Mount Olympus 269–274
mystery 220, 250, 255, 258, 275, 278, 279, 286, 288, 294, 295, 298, 319, 320
living with a 236
mystery within, ineffable 294
mythology 40, 310–312, 315
natural selection 309
natural world, reproductive pageant of 278
nature xiv, xv, 240, 309
n. is the encompassing limit 269
n., our true story teller 191
n., the ultimate world 269
n. is as n. does 288
n.'s local idiom 169
navigation 88, 112, 128, 146, 178, 224
none of us can ever know the park as it is 284
now, the only time it ever is 167
Ockham's razor 194
oldsquaw-in-the-woodsism 140
Olympian heights 269, 272
Olympians 269, 274
Olympus 269, 270, 274
the one and the many 298
openness 220
opportunity 275, 276, 283,

Ideas/opportunity (continued)
287, 320
oral history worth writing down 161
order 169, 184, 295, 310
origin of matter and life 13, 29, 114
other worlds beyond the mirror 269
ownership 50, 170, 171, 191, 202
paradise 22, 33, 115
parts and wholes 319
pathways of earthly inquiry 59
patterns 183, 184, 224
pay as you go 302, 303
peace 247–249
perception of the woods 114
perfect hike up the perfect mountain 289
peripatetic line of thought 89
Persephone, Attis, Adonis, Osiris, Tammuz, Marduke, Jesus 278
perspective 61, 270, 319
outside/inside 301, 319
place draws people together 299
plurality 298
plus sign 298
pollinator, behind every great bloom there is a 247
possessions 212
possibilities, juggling 319
possibility 109, 110, 283–285, 295, 298, 309, 310, 316, 319, 320
possible, envelope of the 285
the Presence 87, 102–105, 114, 122, 141, 161, 162, 166, 183, 275, 288, 320
primate recreational habitat 263
pronouncements 110
property, private 170, 191, 201, 202
proud sons and daughters of the third planet 191
put your mind where your feet are 300
raven, what was I there to learn from the? 288
reality, conjunct 170
recycling 17
relationship
elements of r. 299
is everything 298
the space between partners in r. 298
religion 123, 269, 274, 276, 278, 298, 310
resonance 17

Ideas (continued)
responsibility 171
reverence 110, 295, 297
revolution 212
comes the 154
right-use movement 201
rootedness 11
roots 47, 48
roots of our being 155
rule of law 215
sacred marriage 146, 278
salvation 192
satisfaction 235, 236
savage 54
science 288
seeing *as* 158
separateness 298
serenity 271, 273
Shangri-la 46
the shapers of my beliefs 165
silence 30, 70, 109, 110, 158, 176, 184, 266, 288
simplicity/complexity 52, 108, 319
Sky-Father and Earth-Mother 123, 146, 269, 274, 278
sky gods and earth goddesses 164
the song I would sing 200
soul 131, 220, 223, 224
source of Acadian life 141
spermatozoa, shadowy 70, 71, 131
spirare 250
spirit 277, 283
birth of 278
canine 287
Earth 147
spirit guide 106, 265, 269
spiritual awe 319
spiritual beliefs 278
spiritual connection 285
spiritual experience 132
spiritual focus 147
spiritual imperative 316
spirituality 146, 320
spiritual journey 278
style 169
success 296, 309, 316
the Sumerians 98, 165, 213
supreme being 147
symbols 223, 224
systems and countersystems 81
terrain
extraordinarily ordinary 94
personalized 172
thought, preverbal 189, 223
tortoise and hare 156
traffic, din of 265, 266, 269
transcendence 269
transitions 30, 32, 104, 143, 212, 251, 318

Ideas (continued)
tree falling in the woods 89
trial and success 276
truth 110, 111
successive approximations to 301
unity, variety, gravity 33
unity with the powers that be 131, 136
unity with the woods 114
universal language of Earthlings 184
universe
our address in the u. 298, 299
blossoming of the u. 110
children of the u. 155, 162, 191
a hike into Acadia is a hike into the u. 270
a mote in the u. 298
my history is the history of the u. 316
navel of the u. 168
universum 155
unnature 265
untamed youth meets the abominable snowman 196
vacuum, nature abhors a 81
water and life 6, 48, 59, 114, 120, 123, 130, 161, 168, 185, 202, 203, 205, 210, 212, 215, 273
water, the limiting resource 315
"as way opens" 94, 203
wealth 212
flow of 278
we are what we give ourselves to 230
the weather in Belgium 289
we belong outdoors on the trail 260
we make the worlds we believe in 184
wheels interceding between us and the Earth 229
why I hike 130
why not name trails for their plants? 305
wildflowers 277
women, influence of 18
wood lily, we have much to learn from the 287
woods, back to the 114
woody stems 301, 302
the world
as it is 286
every child begins the w. again 276
I changed the w.; therefore I am 189
"if you jumped off the w.

Ideas/world (continued)
and fell, would you fall forever?" 298
I left the w. as I found it; therefore I am 189
a w. beneath the surface of Jordan Pond 219
wreaths, laurel 157
writing 54, 110, 119, 177, 178, 223
Zeus 269, 270, 273, 274
zone of domesticity 263
Insects 57, 137, 161, 175, 180, 188, 196, 197, 199, 211, 218, 233, 251, 256, 261, 262, 266, 274, 277, 280, 302, 305, 309, 317
ants 6, 12, 246, 253, 256, 295, 317
bees 19, 256, 290, 291
blackflies 225, 226, 241, 242, 244–246
bumblebees 212, 242, 244, 247, 309
butterflies 256
mourning cloak 218, 246, 253
pearl crescent 281
spring azure 234, 244, 246, 253, 259
sulphur 272, 274, 290
tiger swallowtail 244, 246, 253, 258
white admiral 253, 266
caterpillar 13, 246, 248
crickets 8, 10, 11, 15, 17–20, 22, 31, 33, 36, 38, 317, 320
damselflies 25, 246, 281, 290, 295, 309
dragonflies 15–17, 19, 20, 24, 25, 244, 246, 253, 254, 259, 266, 281, 290, 291, 295, 300, 307, 309, 310
dream bugs 11
flies 42, 44, 60, 253, 256, 290, 300, 309
gnat, last of summer 67
grasshoppers 11, 15, 290, 295, 300, 307, 309, 312, 317, 320
hornet 266
mosquitoes 14, 242, 246, 247, 253, 256, 258, 266, 274, 280, 295, 303, 307
moths 42, 44, 196, 246, 253, 256, 261, 262, 266, 300
our six-legged neighbors 309
snap-crackle-pop bugs 317
springtails (snow fleas) 161, 175, 177, 188
water striders 12, 15, 24, 25, 27, 34, 196, 211, 317
wasps 16, 256, 258, 259

Insects (continued)
yellow jackets 246
Iron 140
handholds 23, 62, 64, 65, 127, 129, 292
pinned logs 291
rungs 9, 62–65, 127, 129, 292
Islands
Avalonia 232, 252
Baker Is. 47, 106, 121, 171, 182, 197, 209, 226, 257, 271, 282
Bartlett Is. 105
Bear Is. 31, 47, 124, 125, 247, 271
Black Is. 171
Bunkers Ledge 193
Cranberry Islands 142, 177, 271
Great 11, 44, 47, 106, 143, 171, 308
Little 47, 106, 121, 125, 142, 171, 209, 257, 308
Deer Isle 230
Duck Islands 56, 106, 177, 257, 271
Great 35, 45, 143, 171, 308
Little 143, 171, 308
Egg Rock 61, 64, 70, 131, 135, 181, 257, 282
in Frenchman Bay 257
Gott Is., Great 143, 171, 271
Gott Is., Little 171, 271
Great Wass Is. 258
Greening Is. 11, 12, 31, 44, 47, 271
Hardwood Is. 27
Heron Is. 257
High Is. (see Isle au Haut)
Ironbound Is. 61, 128, 131, 135, 257
Isle au Haut 8, 79, 171, 177, 230–236
Jordan Is. 61, 135
Kimball Is. 235
Long Is. 27, 105, 171
Long Ledge 143, 144
Mark Is. 257, 282
Matinicus Is. 231
Moose Islands
Big 78, 256, 258
Little 255, 256
Mount Desert Island (MDI) 4, 6, 7, 11, 17, 29, 48, 77, 79, 80, 87, 91, 96, 108, 112, 114, 122, 130, 134, 139, 152, 153, 159, 170, 179, 181, 186, 192, 198, 199, 201, 212, 230, 232, 241, 251, 255, 257, 258, 261, 265, 267, 279, 280, 282, 292, 293, 298
Mount Desert Rock 35, 45,

Islands/M.D. Rock (continued)
266, 282
Ned Is. 257
Old Soaker 180
Petit Manan Is. 208, 257, 258, 282
Placentia Is. 50, 143, 226, 271
Pond Is. 256, 257
Porcupine Islands 61, 64, 66, 128, 131, 135, 181, 253, 264, 282
Bald 15, 70, 253
Bar 135
Long 253
Ragged Is. 231
Saddleback Ledge 231, 232
Schoodic Is. 255, 258
Seal Is. 231
south of MDI 29, 47, 106, 171, 226, 257, 266, 271, 279, 308, 315, 318
Spectacle Is. 257
Stave Is. 61, 135, 253
Sutton Is. 47, 106, 125, 171, 177, 271, 308
Swans Is. 143, 171
Thompson Is. 230
Thrumcap 66, 70, 129, 131
Turtle Is. 257
Vinalhaven Is. 231
Wooden Ball Is. 231
Isle au Haut Bay 231

Keys, maple
red 251
striped 247

Labels 54
Ladders, trail 42–44, 58, 62, 64, 131, 243, 271, 272
Landscape 91, 107, 114, 152, 243, 246–251, 260, 264, 266, 271, 273, 278, 279, 283, 291, 298–300, 306, 307, 315, 319
Acadian 204
cultural 132
fitting into the 105
fluid 32
forested 85
Olympian 271
ornamental 124
summer 241
tiered 36
Landscape drama 40
Landscape integrity 89
Landscape mosaic 59, 67
Landscape ritual song and dance 41
Landscape sounds 126
Leaves 58
ash 25
aspen (popple) 50, 66, 196,

Leaves/aspen (continued)
217
beach pea 233
beech 42, 44, 86, 147
birch 13, 66
bluebead 222
blueberry 227
bunchberry 39
cedar 33, 39, 58, 85, 88, 154
deciduous 248
elder 26
fall foliage 4, 13, 19, 26, 30–37, 39, 40, 44
first spring 206
hobblebush 220
huckleberry 35, 36, 50
maple 19, 33, 34, 196, 291
striped 39, 66, 212, 243, 247
needles
evergreen 42, 301
fir 88
hemlock 58, 88
pine 32, 33, 58, 82, 84
pitch 263, 264, 266
spruce 53, 55, 58, 244, 301
oak 44, 50, 57, 66, 196
plantain, rattlesnake 312
sheep laurel 50, 58
starflower 39
sumac 23
tumbling 32
yellow 34, 41
License plates 67, 72, 78, 253, 259, 261, 265, 277, 292, 297, 303, 307, 309
Lichens 5, 6, 13, 20, 26, 29, 30, 34, 43, 49, 54, 58, 59, 63, 72, 85, 91, 98, 143, 147, 172, 182, 222, 227, 233, 243, 245, 250–252, 263, 279, 282, 288, 301, 304, 305, 318
cloud 12, 204, 244, 250
gray 43, 188
green 8, 91, 98
lungwort, spotted 154, 160, 172, 174, 215
map 31, 250, 252, 305
old-man's-beard 233
reindeer 12, 49, 128, 139, 154, 172, 182, 193, 197, 215, 244, 250
rock tripe 40, 112, 138, 215, 222, 250
shield 20, 139, 182
Lighthouses 65
Baker Island 45, 282
Bear Island 45
Egg Rock 57, 61, 181, 257, 282
Mark Island 257, 282
Mt. Desert Rock 35, 282
Petit Manan 257, 282

Lighthouses (continued)
  Saddleback Ledge 231
Literature cited
  Berry Finder 15
  Bible
    Ecclesiastes 308
    Psalm 18, 146
  Colby's *Atlas of Hancock
    County, Maine* 98
  "The Dead" 146
  *Flora of Mount Desert Island,
    Maine* 159
  *The Geology of Mount Desert
    Island* 80
  *Golden Guide to Acadia
    National Park* 155
  Hidden Heart of the Cosmos
    270, 295
  *Let Us Now Praise Famous
    Men* 264
  Mr. Rockefeller's Roads 122
  *Newcomb's Wildflower
    Guide* 277
  Personal Knowledge 310
  Romeo and Juliet 215
  Shelley's "Ozimandias" 194
  The Songlines 40, 259
  Trails of History 27, 58, 62,
    132
  Trial by Jury 221
  Walden 148
  *Wild Flowers of Mount
    Desert Island, Maine* 159

Mammals (see also Scats;
  Tracks, Wildlife signs)
  bat 24, 28, 57
  beaver 15, 17, 24, 28, 38, 40,
    41, 57, 70, 93, 118, 121,
    129, 130, 132, 163, 164,
    166, 180, 183, 199, 210,
    218, 220, 222, 227, 282
  canids (see coyote; dog; fox)
  chipmunk, Eastern 11, 13, 19,
    23, 57, 59, 196, 199, 262
  coyote 7, 15, 17, 24, 53, 56,
    99, 113, 114, 118, 129, 130,
    132, 156, 161, 180, 183
  deer, white-tailed 13, 19, 20,
    24, 27, 38, 41, 42, 45, 78,
    87, 92–95, 97, 102, 107,
    109, 111, 113, 118, 129,
    134, 137, 139, 140, 156,
    165, 171, 175, 176, 180,
    185, 187, 193, 196, 199,
    222, 234, 262, 264, 295
  dog 19, 20, 32, 78, 113, 118,
    126, 139, 144, 165, 185,
    285, 287
    anchored 266
    barking 287, 301
    beagle 15, 16
    black, large 246, 247

Mammals/dog (continued)
    black Lab 118
    Bonzo 69
    Bowser 53
    bulldog 317
    dachshund 195
    panting 253, 287
    Raven 35, 36
    shaggy 196
    unleashed 30, 33, 35, 36,
      78, 253, 263, 284, 317
    Weimaraner 72
  dolphin 271
  fox, red 6, 19, 22, 42, 47, 82,
    87, 91–94, 98, 103, 105,
    106, 109–111, 113, 118,
    122, 126, 129–131,
    134–137, 147, 161,
    163–165, 171, 175–177,
    185, 187, 188, 191, 193,
    211, 246, 262, 268, 274,
    281, 293, 310, 317
    arctic kingdom of 105
  hare, snowshoe 38, 57, 72,
    91–93, 98, 106, 107, 109,
    111, 113, 129, 131, 134,
    136, 137, 145, 156, 161,
    165, 171, 175, 176, 180,
    185, 187, 188, 193, 201,
    211, 233, 259, 284, 301
  horse 8, 118, 156, 201
  mink 307
  moose 109, 112
  mouse 87, 98, 102, 104, 107,
    109–111, 180, 183
  muskrat 24
  porcupine 24, 28, 103, 109,
    111, 165, 255, 256
  raccoon 185, 187, 307
  seal, harbor 180, 271
  shrew 87, 99, 102–104, 107,
    126, 137, 139
    pygmy 99
  skunk 47, 253
  squirrel 8, 12, 24, 25, 87, 91,
    92, 107, 109, 131, 136, 161,
    175, 185, 265
    gray 32, 33
    red 11, 15, 19, 20, 28, 32,
      33, 38, 42, 44, 50, 53,
      55–57, 59, 61, 66, 70, 77,
      98, 110, 111, 113, 126,
      129, 134, 156, 161, 165,
      175, 180, 183, 187, 193,
      201, 215, 234, 246, 263,
      275, 278, 307, 317
  vole, meadow 126, 137, 139,
    156, 161, 171, 175, 187
  weasel 102, 180, 183, 185
    ermine 102, 126, 187
  woodchuck 137, 140
Maps
  Colby 139

Maps (continued)
  DeLorme 87
  experiential 122
  first path 159
  Isle au Haut 234
  Phillips 44, 87
Marine and intertidal life
  barnacle 268
  dulse 143
  kelp 143
  lobster 137
  mussel 79, 137, 143, 145,
    180, 268
  periwinkle 80, 144, 145
  rockweed 80, 143, 144
  sea urchin 143, 180
  sponge 143
Millwheel 182
Mollusk (see also Marine and
  intertidal life)
  slug 253, 254, 262, 278
Moon 10, 27, 28, 34, 170
Mountains and hills
  Acadia Mtn. 244, 265–267,
    269, 294
  the Anvil 255
  Bald Peak 103, 121, 122, 148,
    246–249
  Beech Mtn. 83, 85, 241, 242,
    245, 247, 251, 280, 300
  the Beehive 127, 129, 130,
    181, 282–284
  Brown (Norumbega) Mtn.
    279
  Bubble(s) 90, 158, 220–222,
    314–320
    Lost 19, 22, 314, 315, 318
    North 19, 22, 218, 219,
      224, 314, 315, 318
    South 19, 22, 218, 220,
      222, 224, 226, 314, 315,
      318
  Cadillac Mtn. 68, 69, 71, 72,
    133–136, 212, 229,
    249–254, 269, 304–307
  Cedar Swamp Mtn. 87,
    100–102, 106, 120, 122,
    186–188, 287
  Champlain Mtn. 62–67, 127,
    128, 130–132, 281, 282
  Conners Nubble 19, 20, 314,
    315, 318
  Day Mtn. 173, 176–179, 282
  Dike Peak 207, 208, 250–253
  Dorr Mtn. 57–61, 69, 70, 187,
    195, 196, 198, 200, 260,
    262, 264
  Duck Harbor Mtn. 232, 234
  Eliot Mtn. 87, 92, 121, 125,
    186, 188, 192–194
  Enoch Mtn. 130
  Flying Mtn. 14
  Gilmore Peak 35, 36, 100,

Mountains/Gilmore (continued)
    104, 200–202, 205
  Gorham Mtn. 281–283
  Halfway Mtn. 282
  Hio Hill 153, 154
  Huguenot Head 199, 281,
    282, 302
  Kebo Mtn. 196, 216, 260,
    262–264
  Lead Mtn. 21, 69, 121, 203,
    266
  McFarland Hill 28, 92–95,
    167
  Mitchell Hill 126
  Mt. Katahdin 9, 69
  Mt. Monadnock 23, 101
  Mt. Rushmore 158
  Norumbega Mtn. 102, 122,
    213, 216
  Paradise Hill 166
  Parkman Mtn. 104, 121,
    246–248
  Passadumkeag Ridge 9
  Pemetic Mtn. 8, 29–32, 158,
    221, 222, 269–274,
    290–292, 306, 307, 318
  Penobscot Mtn. 7–10, 120,
    121, 148, 186, 188, 224
  Pine Hill 111, 113, 115, 116,
    297
  Robinson Mtn. 268
  St. Sauveur Mtn. 11, 12, 137,
    139, 265–268, 283, 292,
    293, 296
  Sargent Mtn. 24–28, 33–37,
    100, 104–106, 120, 122,
    152, 168–173, 204, 205,
    214, 223, 224, 227, 241,
    246, 248, 286–288, 309,
    310, 313
  Schoodic Head 255–257, 259
  Schoodic Mtn. 284
  the Triad 30, 99, 176, 177,
    179, 273, 274, 307
  Valley Peak 11, 292–296
  Western Mtn. 5, 6, 47, 49, 51,
    53, 108, 111, 112, 115,
    188, 297–303
    Bernard Mtn. 51–56, 297,
      301, 303
    Knight Nubble 51, 56, 301,
      303
    Mansell Mtn. 5, 6, 47–51,
      108, 110, 297, 300–303
  Youngs Hill 94, 167
Mushrooms (see Fungi)
Music 63, 126, 189, 224
  the anthem of Acadia 224
  flowing water 189
  mountain 189, 224
  of the place 203
  of the warbling vireo
    200–202

Music (continued)
Symphonic Poem for Two Legs 68
water 141, 231

Naval Security Group 255
Noon signals 17, 32, 57, 71, 131, 253, 258
Notches and gaps 56
Beech Mtn. Notch 86, 241
Brown Mtn. Notch 168, 248
Bubble Gap 224, 225, 227
Great Notch 7, 47, 51, 56, 108, 109, 115
Little Notch 51, 54–56, 301
the Notch 16, 18, 69, 195–197, 210

Olympics 154, 257, 269, 285, 286, 289

Parking areas (see also Trailheads)
Acadia Mtn. 138, 265, 292, 296
Beech Mtn. 44, 82, 84–86, 241, 244, 245
Blueberry Hill 255, 256
Brown Mtn. Gate 86, 116, 145, 190
Bubble Pond 29, 304, 308
Bubble Rock 19, 23, 39, 223, 224, 271, 314, 317, 318
Cadillac Mtn. Summit 68, 69, 135, 250, 252, 306
Echo Lake 42, 43, 45, 46, 241–243, 245
Fabbri picnic area 77, 281, 283
Gorham Mtn. 283
Great Head 181–183
Jordan Pond House 158, 160
Long Pond (pumping station) 5–7, 47, 48, 50–52, 54, 56, 82, 83, 108–111, 245, 246, 297, 300, 301, 303
Lower Hadlock Pd. 213
Norumbega Mtn. 168, 246, 249, 275, 277, 280, 287, 288, 309, 313
Precipice 62, 128, 129
St. Sauveur Mtn. 295
Sand Beach 129, 130, 179, 181
Schoodic Point 256
Ship Harbor 142
Sieur de Monts Spring 15, 194–196, 199, 261
the Tarn (Beachcroft) 281
Valley Cove 11, 14, 137
People (see also Plaques)
Adolph, Rudolph, Doc, and Henry 310

People (continued)
Agee, James 264
Alice 269
Aristotle 230
Atlas, Charles 124
Barter, Wayne 234
Bates, Waldron 24, 27, 28, 58–60, 62, 67, 159, 283
Beal, Don 227
Berry, Thomas 155
Birchard, Bruce 91
Botts, Alexander 103
Boyd, R. 98
Braque and Picasso 61
Brunnow, Rudolph 62, 64–67, 132
Caesar 33
Cartier, Jacques 154
Champlain, Samuel 29, 231, 280, 291, 307
Chatwin, Bruce 40, 259
Clinton, President 234
Clinton, Hillary 54
Curley, Don 312
Damon, Sheldon Leroy 191
Dickinson, Emily 69, 156
Dominick, Liz 50
Dorr, George 23, 60, 61, 199, 261, 262, 279
Einstein, Albert 270
Evans, Walker 264
Fox, Bob 300
Fox, George 294
Franck, Gene 244, 285
Francklyn, Lilian Endicott 18, 195, 198
Gaudi, Antonio 102
Gawley, Bill 225
Gros, Ohio 153
hikers, fellow 38, 39, 234, 240, 244, 252–254, 261, 265, 267, 271, 276, 284, 285, 289, 297
Ben 285
bundled 78
couples 39, 267, 276, 299, 317
eating a picnic lunch 307
English 39
from Toronto 317
cultural anthropologist 270
elderly man and his daughter 292, 293
family from Atlanta 289
family with fishing poles 308
family groups 59, 312
field biology class 306
five youths 195, 196
lone hiker from Cologne 228
lone hiker seeking three companions 118

People/hikers (continued)
man, diabetic 261
man and woman with box kite 252
man from Long Island 285
man from Quebec 298
man making tracks 104
man not called Stanley 13
man taking a picture of a woman 284
man with German accent 228, 276
man with orange eyes 247
men and boys 35, 36
Michigan 277
newlyweds 267
Pam, Mike, and Leah Rae 111
party of six 289
silent father with papoose 300, 302
six characters 36
skiers 86, 91, 107, 147, 164
tailgate foursome 11
toe-dippers and swimmers 282, 288
trim woman 276
trim couple 276
two boys on three-wheeler 164, 165
two women 39
woman, pink 246, 247
woman from Mississippi 289
woman on a horse 156
woman on steps 8
woman raised in ice-free Tallahassee 128
woman who said, "Look at that yellow!" 40
woman with binocs 39
young woman from France 283, 284
Icarus 105
James, William 54, 299, 315
Jaques, Herbert 159
Johnson, Jeremiah 275
Johnson, Samuel 82
Joyce, James 146
Kant, Immanuel 91
Kennedy, President 310
Kent, Clark 233
leaf peepers 44
Merleau-Ponty, Marcel 169, 170, 173
Miranda, Carmen 233
Muir, John 275
my parents iii, xvi, 316
my sons
Jesse 150, 245
Ken 2, 250
Michael 74, 203
my stepson, Jonathan 238

People (continued)
the National Park Service himself 255
Newcomb, Lawrence 277
Olson, Charles 28
Peron, Eva 233
Plato 34, 298
Polanyi, Michael 310
Pope, Alexander 224
Porter, Eliot 26
Pyle, Robert 139
Price, Vincent 60
Prometheus 269, 270
Rand, Edward L. 159
Rich, Louise Dickenson 257
Roberts, Ann Rockefeller 122
Robinson family 139, 140, 268, 269
Rockefeller, J.D., Jr. 22, 119, 122, 135, 223
Roosevelt, Teddy 15
Russell, Jane 122
St. Germain, Tom 58, 132, 307
Shakespeare 156
Smith, Adam 166
snowmobilers 134
Stanley, Ralph 153, 241
Stanley, Thomas 13
street thug 158
striding biped 156
Swimme, Brian 83, 155, 270, 295
tall, lanky 17
Tarzan and Jane 244
Thoreau, H. D. 6, 84, 105
Thornton, Mrs. Seth 153
Tuckerman, Frederick G. 40
Ulysses 255
Vadar, Darth 129, 131
Wardwell, Polly 255
Wherry, Edgar T. 159, 232, 251
Whitehead, Alfred North 94
Young, Andrew Murray 198
People spoor 185
beer can 138, 153, 157
cigarette butts 22, 47, 56
pistachio nut hulls 47
plastic diaper 7
Petit Manan National Wildlife Refuge 257
Photosynthesis 30, 98, 123, 161, 168, 204, 212, 273, 278, 301, 315
Plants (see also Berries; Buds; Flowers; Leaves; Trees)
arrowhead 16, 19
aster 15, 30, 40, 282, 291, 296, 301, 309, 311, 320
flat-topped 8, 19, 290, 296, 301, 307, 311, 312, 315
heath 315

Plants/aster (continued)
    large-leaved 296, 301, 311, 315
    purple 7, 16, 19, 282
    whorled 296, 301, 307, 311, 315
bayonet rush 19
bazzania (see liverwort)
beach pea 233
beechdrops 187, 315, 317
blackberry 243, 248, 256, 262, 277, 306, 307
bluebead lily 222, 226, 242, 243, 248, 296
blueberry 29, 31, 36, 49, 65, 72, 86, 128, 138, 139, 156, 169, 226, 232, 244–248, 250, 264, 272, 277, 279, 286, 288, 306
blue flag 256, 262
bluets 256, 262
bunchberry dogwood 43, 78, 143, 233, 242–244, 247, 252, 255, 262, 310, 311
bur reed 16
buttercup 242, 250, 261, 268, 274
    tall 296
Canada May ruby 215, 226, 242, 244, 245, 247, 250, 255, 256, 259, 280, 307, 311, 312, 315
chokeberry, black 8, 22, 29, 31, 242, 244, 247, 248, 250–252, 306, 307, 311, 315
cinquefoil 8, 31, 49, 86, 226
    common 262
    dwarf 256
    shrubby 291
    wine-leaf 22, 29, 58, 272, 282, 301, 305, 311
clover
    red 250, 256, 261
    white 256, 261
    yellow 261
club moss (ground pine, ground cedar) 47, 66, 138, 160, 212, 244, 269, 311
corydalis, pale 241, 242, 245
cow wheat 277, 293, 295, 301, 307
cranberry
    large 277
    mountain 52, 126, 128, 153, 160, 178, 192, 197, 226, 245, 247, 254, 256, 306, 307, 311, 312, 315
crowberry, black 32, 78
daisy 250, 252, 256, 259, 261
elder, red-berried 226
everlasting, early 226
ferns 6, 13, 16, 20, 26, 28,

Plants/ferns (continued)
    30, 34, 61, 63, 85, 143, 187, 198, 203, 220, 233, 243, 245, 249, 258, 262, 268, 273, 275, 279, 280, 288, 300, 301, 307, 312, 314, 315, 318
    beech, long 262, 279, 307, 312, 315
    bracken 8, 47, 58, 78, 128, 154, 250, 268, 279, 301, 312, 315
    Christmas 42, 43, 58, 178, 243, 308, 312, 315
    cinnamon 30, 247, 250, 256, 262, 307, 312, 315
    hayscented 301
    interrupted 30, 243, 250, 268, 279, 308, 312
    New York 6, 243, 250, 279, 307, 315
    oak 243, 268, 279
    rock-cap 8, 40, 42, 46, 58, 67, 82, 86, 112, 122, 138, 203, 205, 222, 243, 245, 250, 258, 259, 280, 301, 312, 315
    royal 30, 262, 279, 308
    sensitive 262, 268, 301, 308, 315
    sweet (not a true fern) 250
    wood ferns 42, 46, 52, 56, 67, 86, 122, 197
        marginal 42, 58, 138, 141, 243, 301, 315
        spinulose 138, 243, 280, 301, 312, 315
        spreading 301, 312, 315
fireweed 78
goldenrod 7, 8, 15, 42, 78, 282, 290, 291, 295, 296, 301, 309, 311, 320
    downy 306, 307, 311, 312
    hairy 315
    large-leaved 311, 315
    slender 307, 311, 312, 315
goldthread 37, 52, 154, 192, 203, 212, 232, 243–245, 301, 303, 311
grass 78, 121
    cotton 36, 227, 250, 251, 288, 307
    orange 227, 277, 306, 307
harebell 282, 290–292, 296
hawkweed 243, 250, 252, 274, 282, 301, 307
    orange 256, 261
    yellow 256, 261, 268, 296
heather, golden 255, 257, 259
herb Robert 14, 42, 43, 296, 301
hobblebush 220, 226, 312
holly, mountain 41, 307

Plants (continued)
    horsetail 233
    huckleberry 31, 36, 42–44, 165, 169, 246, 247, 258, 264, 279, 305
    Indian pipe 277, 296, 311
    juniper 14, 29, 31, 42, 43, 49, 58, 70, 72, 86, 138, 193, 226, 247, 250, 259, 266, 268, 272, 276, 279, 293
    kinnikinnick 52, 58, 64, 67, 86, 128, 129, 132
    lady's slipper 242–244, 247, 248, 250
    lichens (see Lichens)
    lily, wood 169, 227, 286–290, 312
    liverwort (scale moss, bazzania) 6, 11, 25, 30, 46, 52, 54, 55, 63, 67, 72, 160, 215, 233, 275, 277, 279, 280, 288, 301
    mayflower 42, 45, 58, 61, 67, 187, 191, 215, 226, 242, 277, 304, 311
    meadowsweet 282, 288, 290, 291, 295, 301, 307, 311, 315
    moss 6, 11, 26, 34, 54, 56, 58, 59, 61, 63, 67, 72, 85, 86, 143, 154, 187, 203, 205, 233
        feather 154, 197, 203
        hair-cap 128, 154, 160, 174, 191, 197, 215
        pincushion 55, 154, 182, 191, 215, 226
        sphagnum 7, 36, 55, 58, 115, 122, 143, 154, 174, 175, 192, 215, 219, 241, 245, 304
    mullein 122, 282
    orchis, smaller purple fringed 307
    parsnip, water 307
    partridgeberry 138, 187, 193, 212, 226, 245, 277, 311, 312, 315
    pepperbush, sweet 301, 307
    pickerelweed 16, 19
    pink, Deptford 282
    pipewort 300, 301, 307
    plantain, rattlesnake 310–312
    poison ivy 78, 243, 296
    raspberry 233, 301
    rattle, yellow 256, 262
    rattlesnake root, tall 290, 296, 305, 307, 311, 312
    rhodora 242, 244, 247
    rose 274, 282, 290
        rugosa 143, 256
    sandwort, mountain 29, 204, 226, 227, 247, 250–252,

Plants/sandwort (continued)
    262, 272–274, 277, 282, 288, 295, 307, 310, 311
    sarsaparilla 226, 242, 247, 250, 256, 282
    saxifrage 138, 242, 243
    scale moss (see liverwort)
    sedge (see also grass) 36, 204, 227
    selfheal 268, 274, 307
    shad 232
    sheep laurel (lambkill) 44, 65, 72, 78, 86, 143, 147, 153, 165, 169, 172, 179, 182, 204, 215, 226, 244, 250, 252, 257, 258, 311
    skunk cabbage 232, 233
    Solomon's seal 226, 242, 243, 290, 315
    sorrel, sheep 261
    sorrel, wood 51, 245, 301
        yellow 296, 315
    speedwell 274
    starflower 226, 242, 244, 245, 247, 250, 255, 259, 315
    strawberry 245
    sundrops 296
    swamp candles 282
    trillium 244, 307
    twinflower 258, 259, 269, 277, 301
    vetch
        cow 250, 256, 259, 268, 282
        crown 282
    violet 226, 232, 242
    water lily 288
    winterberry 40, 274
    wintergreen 52, 55, 58, 67, 86, 128, 138, 154, 160, 172, 191, 203, 215, 226, 245, 282, 301, 302, 306, 307, 311, 315
    witch hazel 58, 95, 104, 273, 277
    witherod 250, 256, 262, 306, 307, 311
    yarrow 261, 268, 290, 301, 307
Plants, symbolic
    cotton and tobacco 215
Plaques, memorial
    Allen, Joseph 40
    Bates, Waldron 283
    Cushing, Sarah Eliza Sigourney 222
    Dorr, George B. 261, 262
    Fabbri, Alessandro 78, 81
    Francklyn, Lilian 18, 195, 198
    Jesup, Morris & Maria 199
    Kane, John Innes 199
    Mather, Stephen Tyng 69

Plaques (continued)
  Rand, Edward Lothrop 159
  Rockefeller, John D., Jr. 78, 79
  Satterlee, Louisa P. 78, 182
  Young, A. Murray 17, 198
Points, peninsulas, heads, and necks
  heads and headlands
    granite 142, 144
    Great Head 180–184, 282
    Western Head 231, 232, 234, 235
  neck, Northern; Southern 115
  Peninsula, Schoodic 255–257, 259
  points
    Cranberry 257
    Otter 77–81
    Schoodic 187, 251, 255
    Spruce 257
Ponds and lakes 216
  Aunt Betty Pond 24, 28, 96, 121
  beaver 64, 71, 163–166, 198
  Beaver Dam Pool/Pond 61, 129
  the Bowl 127–130, 281–285
  Breakneck Ponds 92
    Lower 165, 167
    Upper 95, 164, 165, 167
  Bubble Pond 29, 30, 32, 96, 252, 271, 304–306
  Duck Pond 112–115
  Eagle Lake 19, 96, 135, 195, 226, 314–318
  Echo Lake 42, 82, 85, 139, 241, 247, 266, 296
  the Featherbed 71, 72, 211, 250–252, 307, 308
  frozen ponds 82, 115, 163
  Hadlock Ponds 188, 214
    Lower 212–216, 275–279
    Upper 82, 102, 168, 194, 216, 277, 309, 312, 313
  Halfmoon Pond 165–167
  Hodgdon Pond 112–115
  Jordan Pond 8, 9, 19, 23, 38, 87, 90, 96, 118, 121, 157–159, 214, 216–228, 269, 271–274, 290–292, 314, 317, 318
  Lake Wood 96
  (Little) Long Pond 124–126, 188, 222
  Long (Great) Pond 5, 51, 82, 85, 86, 108, 112–115, 241, 244, 245, 248, 300–303
  the Reservoir 52, 54, 109
  Sargent Mtn. Pond 89, 186, 224, 287–289, 292
  Seal Cove Pond 54, 114, 115
  Seawall Pond 293

Ponds (continued)
  Somesville Mill Pond 82
  the Tarn 15, 16, 57, 61, 194, 198, 199, 212
  Witch Hole Pond 164–166
  Wizard Pond (Black Mtn.) 55
Pretty Marsh picnic area 112
Potholes 207
the Pulpit 311, 313
Pulpit Rock 18, 197, 207

Quakers 73, 91, 94, 122, 134, 294
Quarter days 95, 242, 249
  equinox 242, 249
    fall 25, 30
    spring 146, 168, 179
  solstice
    summer 242, 247, 249–251, 253, 254
    winter 92, 95, 192, 242, 249, 258
the Quiet Side 115

Railroad, Cadillac Mtn. 69, 134
Rain 21–23, 48, 67, 77, 112, 113, 116, 127, 128, 137, 138, 212, 217, 218, 224, 226, 256, 260, 269, 272, 273, 276, 282, 283, 307
  forty days of 289
Rainbow 11, 22, 226, 283, 284
Rainy days 212
Reptiles
  turtle 317
  garter snake 219, 220, 255, 256, 311
Ridge(s) 265, 267, 279
  Acadia Mtn. ridge 265, 266
  Bubble ridge 20, 22, 314, 315, 318
  Cadillac Mtn.
    east ridge 72
    south ridge 207–209, 250–253, 305–308
    west ridge 252
  Canada Ridge 42, 44
  Champlain Mtn. s. ridge 282, 284
  Dorr Mtn. s. ridge 70, 210
  Gorham Mtn. ridge 283
  Jordan Ridge 8, 119, 158, 218, 221, 271, 290
  median ridge 232
  Norumbega Mtn. ridge 279
  Pemetic Mtn. s. ridge 29, 271, 272, 274
  Sargent Mtn. s. ridge 286–288, 290, 304, 312
  Sargent–Penobscot ridge, ten routes to 287
  Western Mtn. ridge 297, 301–303

Roads
  Beech Hill Rd. 82, 84, 86, 241
  Beech Mtn. Notch Rd. (see trails)
  Boyd Rd. (see trails)
  Breakneck Rd. 92, 95, 163–165, 167
  Cadillac Mtn. Rd. 8, 112, 133–136, 197, 252, 254, 292
  carriage roads 30, 87, 101, 119, 120, 123, 124, 146, 186, 223, 229, 247–249, 254, 280, 285, 287, 291, 309
    Around-Mountain 8, 28, 34, 36, 102, 107, 116–123, 125, 146, 177, 186, 201, 203, 205, 227, 247, 248, 287
    Aunt Betty Pond 25, 33, 201, 202
    Barr/Redfield hills 159
    Bubble Pd.–Jordan Pd. 176, 307
    Day Mtn. loop 159, 176, 178
    demonstration mile 8
    Eagle Lake 20, 21, 133, 318
    Paradise Hill 163
    private carriage roads 124
    Seven Sisters 28
    Witch Hole Pond 163, 166
  Eagle Lake Rd. 92, 163, 167
  Fernald Point Rd. 138, 141
  fire roads
    Cadillac summit 69, 306
    Long Pond 111–116
    Man o' War Bk. 137, 138, 265, 266, 268, 269, 296
    Valley Cove 11, 14, 137, 138, 141, 295, 296
    Wonderland 142–144, 232
  Gatehouse Rd. 88, 190, 216
  Giant Slide Rd. 201
  Hadlock Pond Rd. 212
  Hio Rd. 153–158, 160
  Long Pond Rd. 54
  Lurvey Spring Rd. 45, 86, 241, 245
  Moore Rd. (Schoodic) 255
  Ocean Drive 78–80, 229
  Otter Cliff Rd. 283
  Park Loop Rd. 179, 250, 314
  Ranger Station Rd. (Schoodic) 255, 256
  Route 1, 255
  Route 3, 124–126, 163, 185, 186, 199, 208, 211, 250–252, 260, 265, 281
  Route 102, 112, 138, 153,

Roads/Route 102 (continued)
  265, 269
  Route 186, 255
  Route 198, 168, 190, 201, 202, 216, 265, 277, 288, 313
  Schooner Head Rd. 181
  Sea Cliff Drive 99
  Seal Cove Rd. 301
  Seawall Rd. 143
  Stanley Brook Rd. 158, 159
  truck roads
    Kebo Mtn. 196
    Western Mtn. 47, 48, 54, 110, 111, 301
  Western Head Rd. (Isle au Haut) 231, 232
  Wonsqueak Rd. 255, 256, 259
Roots 47, 221
Runoff 117, 119, 120, 174

Sacred sites 110, 270, 272
  the Anvil 258
  Beech Cliff 43
  Canada Cliff 46
  Chasm Brook 26
  the Horseshoe 132
  Maple Spring Tr. 313
  Pulpit Rock 18
  Sargent Mtn. 168
  Schoodic Head 257
  spiritual heart of Acadia 111
Scats 70, 193, 253, 258, 262
  bird droppings 282, 290
  canine 137, 141
  coyote 7, 17, 53, 56, 99, 113, 118, 156
  dog 118
    poodle 8
  fox 6, 19, 22, 42, 47, 82, 106, 118, 188, 211, 262, 274, 281, 293, 310, 317
  horse 8, 118, 156, 201
  mystery 47
  pellets
    deer 13, 24, 27, 42, 45, 193
    hare 38, 107, 137, 145, 193, 201, 211, 233, 301
    porcupine 103
    skunk 47, 253
Scent
  balsam fir 246
  brine and seawrack 231
  earthy 128
  fallen leaves 17
  fox 164, 188, 191, 246, 262, 268, 293
  patchouli 61
  pine pitch 304
  rain 226
  sweet fern 250
  wood smoke 131

Sea smoke 105
the Seaside shuffle 160
Season(s) 242, 243, 249, 250,
    277, 278, 296, 312, 314, 315
  changing 30, 217, 218, 225,
    312
  fall 2, 25, 44, 58, 218, 249,
    277, 282, 291, 301
  a hike for all seasons 246
  peak visitation 78, 254, 271,
    287, 306
  spring 117, 128, 131, 152,
    153, 157, 160, 163, 166,
    173, 179, 180, 186, 187,
    191–198, 200, 211, 217,
    223, 226, 242, 249, 277
  mud season 118
  summer 218, 240–243, 249,
    250, 253–255, 282, 314
  winter 4, 41, 42, 57, 58, 66,
    68–70, 76–78, 83, 85–87,
    92, 93, 95, 100, 102, 103,
    106, 109, 111–114, 117,
    120, 124, 127, 128, 135,
    138, 142, 144, 146, 153,
    154, 157, 163, 173, 174,
    191, 195, 196, 200, 217
  elements 106
  northern 138
  spirit of 146
the seasonal plot 274
Seawall 232
Seawrack (sea spoor) 143, 144,
    233
Seeps 68, 94, 123, 140, 205,
    219
  frozen 84, 140, 172, 203, 205
Shadows 8, 66, 109, 110, 121,
    131, 253, 258
  water-strider 317, 319
  Thirsty Fiber 8
Shorelands 214
Signposts
  on Asticou Trail 87
  Eliot Mtn. summit 193
  on Hadlock Brook Tr. 313
  foot of Man o' War Bk. Fire
    Road 268
  No. 1, 166
  No. 2, 166
  No. 10, 25, 28, 121
  No. 11, 25
  No. 14, 8, 121
  No. 19, 117, 119, 120, 122
  No. 21, 121
  Sargent Mtn. summit 290
Sign(s)
  for Birch Spring 148
  carriage road rules 160
  caution 290
  danger chlorine 50
  lakeside ecosystems 221
  Long Pond Fire Rd. 113

Signs (continued)
  no trespassing 201, 202
  photo opportunity 122
  Precipice warning 63, 65
  public water supply 39
  woman wanted 211
  wrong way 80
Slime mold 279, 307
Snow 77, 86–88, 146, 169,
    172, 179, 183, 212
  blizzard 100, 108, 179, 182
  blowing 104, 106
  bones 90, 91, 147
  drifts 105, 106, 110, 146
  glare 93
  headgear 89
  line 81
  magnetism 90
  shadows 106
  vane 89, 182
Snowflake 95, 147
Snowshoes 92, 93, 101, 107,
    112, 113, 116, 117, 121, 134,
    146, 163, 174, 176–179
Soil 26, 31, 41, 49, 58, 59, 67,
    176, 193, 199, 215, 220, 225,
    244, 248–251, 256, 257, 263,
    273, 278, 296, 301, 302,
    304–307
Solstice (see Quarter days)
Somes Sound 12, 33, 34, 137,
    139, 140, 205, 206, 214, 226,
    265–267, 279, 283, 293, 296
Spiders 6, 16, 40, 201, 244,
    256, 262, 275, 278, 295, 300
  orb weaving 15
  sheet-web weaving 262, 278
Spider webs 53, 244, 262, 266,
    275, 278, 300
Springs 94
  Birch Spring 101, 102, 106,
    146, 148, 185, 186, 188,
    287, 312, 313
  Fern Spring 203
  Maple Spring 36, 172
  Sieur de Monts Spring 15, 16,
    60, 94, 196–199, 232, 252,
    260–262
Stars 10
Stems 48, 147, 174
Steps 46, 50, 51, 55, 58, 61,
    66, 132, 140, 141, 210, 245,
    254, 260, 262, 263, 268, 272,
    282, 283, 291, 307, 318
  cribwork 272, 291
Streams and brooks 48, 123,
    216, 222
  Adams Brook 143, 153
  Beaver Brook 199, 210, 211
  Breakneck Brook 163, 166
  Canon Brook 15, 68, 72, 197,
    209, 210
  Chasm Brook 24, 25, 28, 119,

Streams/Chasm Bk. (continued)
    120, 203
  Cold Brook 48, 52, 110, 301
  Cromwell Brook 15
  Deer Brook 38, 118–120,
    222, 224, 227, 270, 288
  Eli's Creek 231
  ghost brook 140
  Great Brook 6, 109
  Hadlock Brook 119, 147,
    168, 172, 173, 214, 216,
    276, 279, 280, 309, 312
  north branch 35, 100, 103,
    120, 204, 309, 311, 313
  south branch 36, 120, 309
  Hodgdon Brook 115
  Hunters Brook 96, 98–100,
    125, 174–179, 252, 306
  Jordan Stream 120, 158, 218,
    222, 223, 289
  Kebo Brook 15, 18, 195–197
  Little Harbor Brook 119, 120,
    124–126, 146, 185–188
  Man o' War Brook 12, 265,
    268
  Marshall Brook 48, 54, 109,
    111
  Meadow Brook 129
  Old Mill Brook 96
  Otter Creek 15, 17, 197, 198,
    208, 209, 211, 282
  River Fleete 48
  Sargent Brook 33, 37, 121,
    200, 201, 203, 205, 206
  Seven Sisters Brook 28
  Stanley Brook 96, 159, 161
  Union River 9
Supercontinents (Gondwana,
    Laurasia, Pangaea) 155
Summits
  Acadia Mtn. 265, 266
  Bald Pk. 249
  Beech Mtn. 86, 243
  Bernard Mtn. 55, 303
  Bubble
    North 22, 318
    South 22, 23, 314, 317, 318
  Cadillac Mtn. 68, 69, 134,
    136, 204, 223, 251–254,
    263, 306
  Champlain Mtn. 66, 131, 204,
    281–285
  Conners Nubble 21
  Dike Peak 252
  Dorr Mtn. 60, 204, 260–263,
    281
  Eliot Mtn. 191
  Gilmore Peak 201
  Gorham Mtn. 281, 283, 285
  Mansell Mtn. 7, 302, 303
  McFarland Hill 93
  Norumbega Mtn. 276, 277,
    279

Summits (continued)
  Parkman Mtn. 35, 247
  Pemetic Mtn. 32, 204, 269,
    271, 272, 274
  Penobscot Mtn. 287–289, 292
  St. Sauveur Mtn. 293, 296
  Sargent Mtn. 28, 100, 102,
    204, 223, 224, 226,
    287–292, 309–313
  ultimate 285
  Western Mtn. 204, 302

Talus 8, 10, 13, 16, 18, 22, 23,
    42, 63, 66, 69, 85, 103, 112,
    119, 132, 137, 140, 141, 199,
    219, 221, 222, 225, 227, 243,
    263, 281, 290, 291, 298, 302,
    318
  the Tumbledown 40, 119,
    121, 218, 219, 221, 222
Tectonic plates 32, 40, 80, 142,
    155, 181, 232, 252
Thunder Hole 79, 281
Time warp 13
Toilets 20
Tracks (see also Mammals;
    Scats; Wildlife signs) 97
  beaver 180, 183
  coyote 99, 113, 114, 118,
    156, 161, 180
  crow 165, 180
  deer, white-tailed 19, 20, 78,
    87, 92, 94, 95, 97, 102, 107,
    109, 113, 118, 134, 137,
    139, 156, 165, 171, 175,
    176, 180, 185, 187, 196,
    199, 234, 262, 264, 295
  dog 19, 20, 118, 126, 139,
    144, 165, 185
  fox 82, 87, 91–94, 98, 103,
    105, 106, 109–111, 113,
    118, 122, 126, 129–131,
    134–137, 147, 161,
    163–165, 171, 175–177,
    185, 187, 193
  front-end loader 92
  grouse, ruffed 107, 129, 171,
    175, 180, 183, 185, 187
  hare, snowshoe 91, 92, 98,
    106, 107, 109, 111, 113,
    129, 131, 134, 136, 156,
    161, 165, 171, 175, 176,
    180, 185, 187, 284
  horse 144
  mink 307
  mouse 87, 98, 102, 104, 107,
    109–111, 180
  moose 109, 112
  muskrat 185, 187
  mystery 134
  people 126, 139, 185, 193
    crampon 129
    skate blade 129

Tracks/people (continued)
  ski 86, 105, 111, 139, 185
  snowmobile 92, 113, 115, 134
  snowshoe 93, 94, 104, 139
  porcupine 103, 109, 111, 165
  raccoon 185, 187, 307
  robin 180, 187
  shrew 87, 99, 102–104, 107, 126
  squirrel 87, 91, 92, 107, 109, 131, 136, 161, 175, 185
    red 98, 110, 113, 126, 129, 134, 156, 165, 180, 187
  vole 126, 156, 161, 171, 187
  weasel 102, 180, 185
    ermine 102, 126, 187
  woodchuck 137
Trail blindness 300
Trail dialogue 7, 156
Trail erosion 8, 14, 56, 58, 60, 67, 131, 225, 227, 263, 302
  the cumulative impact of thousands of footsteps 302
Trailheads (see also Parking areas) xix, 256, 302
  Acadia Mtn. parking 138, 265, 292, 296
  on Around-Mtn. Carr. Rd. 122
  Beehive 129
  Beachcroft Trail 281
  Blueberry Hill 256
  Bubble Rock parking 19, 23, 39, 223, 224, 271, 314, 317
  Cadillac Mtn.
    N. Ridge Tr. 250
    S. Ridge Tr. 250
  Champlain Mtn. E. Face 132
  Gilley Field 54, 56, 108–111, 301
  Great Head 181
  Jordan Pond House 158, 160
  Mill Field 51, 54, 301
  Norumbega Mountain 168, 246, 249
  pumping station 5–7, 47, 48, 50–52, 54, 56, 82, 83, 108–111, 245, 246, 297, 300, 301, 303
  Sieur de Monts Spring 15, 194–196, 199, 261
  the Tarn (Beachcroft) 281
  Valley Tr. 245
Trail memories 89, 90, 172, 173, 284, 296
Trail mishaps 101, 105
  bolt of ice 141, 296
  last hike 153
  losing the trail 51, 103, 104, 111, 148, 172, 179, 182
  Mt. Monadnock 101
  running over squirrel 38

Trail mishaps (continued)
  terra incognita 146, 148
  venery; vagary; villainy! 35
Trail phantoms 28, 182, 207, 291
Trails xix–xxi
  Acadia Mtn. Tr. 265, 266, 268
  Alder Path (Schoodic) 255, 256
  Amphitheater Tr. 146–148, 186–189, 287, 312
  A. Murray Young Tr. 15, 17, 195, 197, 198, 210
  Anvil Tr. (Schoodic) 255
  Asticou Tr. 86–89, 124–126, 146, 185–188, 190, 192
  Aunt Betty's Pond Path 203
  Bald Peak Tr. 168, 228, 246–249, 313
  Beachcroft Tr. 66, 281–284, 302
  Bear Brook Tr. 66, 90, 127–129, 131
  Beech Cliff Ladder Tr. 42, 43, 241, 243, 245
  Beech Mtn. trails
    Beech Mtn. Tr. 85, 86
    Notch Tr. 241, 245
    (Outer) Beech Mtn. Tr. 241, 244
    S. Ridge Tr. 241, 244, 245
    W. Ridge Tr. 82, 84–86, 244
  Beehive Tr. 129, 282
  Birch Spring Tr. 147, 168
  Bowl Tr. 129, 281–283
  Boyd Road 96–100, 176, 307
  Breakneck Road 92, 95
  Brown Mtn. Tr. 216, 276–279
  Bubble trails
    North Bubble Tr. 21, 317, 318
    Bubble Ridge Tr. 19, 21, 315, 318
    South Bubble Tr. 23, 314, 317, 318
  Bubble Gap Tr. 224, 227
  Cadillac Mtn. trails (see also Canon Brook Tr.; Featherbed Tr.; Pothole Tr.)
    E. Ridge Tr. 68, 72
    N. Ridge Tr. 250–254
    S. Ridge Tr. 68, 207, 249–252, 254, 306
    W. Face Tr. 223, 271, 304–307
    W. Ridge Tr. (see also S. Ridge Tr.) 306
  Canada Ridge Tr. 44, 241, 245
  Canon Brook Tr. 17, 68, 70, 71, 187, 195, 198, 199,

Trails/Canon Bk. (continued)
  208–212, 223, 252
  Cedar Swamp Mtn. Tr. 186–188
  Champlain Mtn. trails (see also Beachcroft Tr.; Bear Brook Tr.; Precipice Tr.)
    E. Face Tr. 64, 66, 67, 127, 132
    S. Ridge Tr. 130, 131, 281, 282, 284
  Chasm Brook Tr. 24–28
  Cliff Tr. (Isle au Haut) 231, 232, 234, 235
  Cold Brook Tr. 47, 50, 51, 53, 54, 108–110, 297
  Conners Nubble Tr. 21
  Day Mtn. Tr. 177
  Deer Brook Tr. 38, 39, 224, 225, 227, 228, 288
  Dorr Mtn. trails (see also Kurt Diederich's Climb)
    E. Face (Emery) Tr. 57, 59, 60, 260, 262, 302
    promenade 58, 61
    Ladder Tr. 57–60, 127, 199, 210, 302
    extension 59
    N. Ridge Tr. 196, 260–263
    Notch Tr. 60, 68, 69, 197, 261, 263
    S. Ridge Tr. 58, 59, 68, 70, 198
    extension 207, 208, 211
  Duck Harbor Tr. (Isle au Haut) 231, 233–235
  Duck Harbor Mtn. Tr. (Isle au Haut) 231, 232, 234, 235
  Eagle Lake Tr. 19, 20, 216, 314, 317, 318
  Eliot Mtn. Tr. 87, 186, 192
  everytrail concept 44
  Featherbed Tr. 252, 306–308
  Flying Mtn. Tr. 13, 14, 137
  Forest Hill Cemetery–Asticou Tr. connector 88, 190, 192, 193, 216
  Giant Slide Tr. 33, 34, 36, 103, 187, 195, 201–203, 205, 206, 223, 288
  Goat Tr. (Isle au Haut) 231, 235
  Gorge Tr. 15, 18, 187, 195–197, 199, 203, 207
  Gorham Mtn. Tr. 281–283, 285
  Grandgent Tr. 33, 35, 36, 100–105, 202, 204, 205, 223, 288
  Great Head Tr. 179–184
  Great Notch Tr. 51, 52, 54, 108, 109, 111
  Hadlock Brook Tr. 87, 101,

Trails/Hadlock Bk. (continued)
  102, 147, 148, 168–173, 187, 223, 287, 288, 311–313
  Hadlock Path 212–216
  Hadlock Trail, Upper 216
  Half Dome Tr. (Yosemite) 270
  Hemlock Tr. 18, 195, 196, 263
  Hio Road 153–158
  Homans Tr. 46
  Hunters Brook Tr. 97–99, 173, 175, 176, 187
  Jesup Tr. 15, 195, 199, 260, 262, 264
  Jordan Cliffs Tr. 9, 214, 223–225, 227, 228, 287–292
    connector to Penobscot summit 292
  Jordan Pond trails
    Canoe Carry 19, 20, 23, 222, 224, 227, 228, 270–274, 314, 317–319
    East Side Tr. 41, 217–222, 224, 226, 227, 271, 272
    Nature Tr. 7
    West Side Tr. 41, 217–223, 227
  Jordan Stream Tr. 222
  Kane Tr. 16, 195, 199, 210, 216
  Kebo Mtn. Tr. 196, 263, 264
  Kurt Diederich's Climb 57, 61, 199, 212, 302
  Little Harbor Brook Tr. 87, 89, 123–126, 185–189
  Long (Great) Pond Tr. 5, 6, 83, 108, 111, 115, 216, 302
  Mansell Mtn. Tr. 47, 49, 50, 54
  Maple Spring Tr. 33, 36, 100, 103, 120, 168, 223, 288, 312, 313
  McFarland Hill Tr. 93
  Norumbega Mtn. (Goat) Tr. 277
  Ocean Path 77–80, 130, 232, 283
  Paradise Hill Tr. 166
  Parkman Mtn. Tr. 33, 34, 168, 201, 246, 247, 313
  Pemetic Mtn. trails
    Goat Tr. 59
    N.E. Ridge Tr. 31, 32
    Ravine Tr. 32, 223, 271, 272
    S. Ridge Tr. 30, 271, 272, 274
    W. Cliff Tr. 31
  Penobscot Mtn. Tr. 8
  Perpendicular Tr. 7, 42, 223,

Trails/Perpendicular (cont.)
297–303
Pond Tr. 30, 271–274
Pothole Tr. 207–209, 211,
212
Precipice Tr. 42, 62–65, 67,
128, 214, 289
Razorback Tr. 47, 49, 51, 54,
111
St. Sauveur Mtn. Tr. 292, 295
East Face Tr. 12
Sargent Mtn. trails (see also
Deer Brook Tr.; Giant Slide
Tr.; Grandgent Tr.; Hadlock
Brook Tr.; Jordan Cliffs
Tr.; Maple Spring Tr.)
N. Ridge Tr. 24, 200–203,
288
S. Ridge Tr. 33, 36, 87,
100, 102, 106, 148, 168,
186, 224, 227, 287, 313
Schoodic Head Tr. 255–257
Seaside Tr. 157–161
Ship Harbor Nature Tr. 142,
143, 232
Sluiceway Tr. 51, 54–56, 111
Spring Road 18, 195, 196,
260, 262
Spring Tr. 51, 55
Squeaker Cove Tr. (Isle au
Haut) 231
Triad Tr. 177
Upper Hadlock Tr. 102
Valley Tr. 82, 83, 85, 86, 241,
243–245, 280
Valley Cove Tr. 137, 295,
296
Valley Peak Tr. 11, 138, 197,
295, 296
Western Tr. 111, 115, 297
Western Head Tr. (Isle au
Haut) 231–235
Western Mtn. trails (see also
Great Notch, Long Pond,
Mansell Mtn., Perpen-
dicular , Razorback, Sluice-
way, and Western trails)
Ridge Tr. 51, 55, 111, 297,
301–303
S. Face Tr. 297, 301–303
Trails, improved and unim-
proved 302, 312
Trails, ladder
Beech Cliff Ladder Tr. 42, 43,
241, 243–245
Beehive Tr. 129, 282
Dorr Mtn. Ladder Tr. 57–60,
127, 199, 210, 263, 302
Jordan Cliffs Tr. 9, 214,
223–225, 227, 228,
287–292
Pemetic Mtn. (Ravine) Tr. 32,
223, 271, 272

Trails/ladder (continued)
Perpendicular Tr. 7, 42, 223,
297–303
Precipice Tr. 42, 62–65, 67,
128, 214, 289
Trees (see also Flowers; Plants;
Woods) 53, 233
alder 16, 27, 93, 95, 105, 143,
154, 165, 198, 217, 256,
262, 273
apple 139, 182, 256, 262
ash 13, 25, 138, 165, 174,
187
mountain 16, 27, 36, 248,
251, 256, 306, 307, 315,
317, 319
beech, American 15, 20, 30,
32, 42, 58, 59, 71, 94, 129,
165, 168, 178, 212, 215,
220, 225, 227, 242, 245,
272, 273, 282, 307, 317
birch 6, 12, 14, 16, 23, 30,
32, 54, 58, 66, 69, 71, 85,
94, 109, 111, 114, 121,
128–132, 138, 154, 159,
168, 174, 180, 182, 190,
196, 197, 199, 208, 212,
215, 217, 218, 220–222,
227, 242, 246, 256, 262,
263, 268, 272, 282, 285,
290, 317–319
gray 31, 34, 36, 39, 66, 94,
129, 165, 251, 262, 282
white 8, 95, 165, 187, 197,
220, 225, 288
yellow 15, 16, 35, 56, 95,
96, 109, 139, 147, 178,
187, 197, 204, 225, 227,
231, 245, 250, 296, 304,
307, 313
cartoon trees 8
cedar 11, 20, 25, 30–32, 34,
36, 43–45, 54, 59, 60, 72,
78, 97, 107, 112, 115, 121,
126, 137–140, 155, 158,
174, 208, 221, 268, 272,
273, 279, 290, 291, 304
arbor vitae 155
Northern white 7, 15, 40,
42, 49, 70, 86, 87, 93, 95,
97, 109, 114, 139, 154,
165, 168, 172, 187, 193,
197, 203–205, 212, 213,
215, 220–222, 227, 256,
266, 268, 296, 310, 318
tree of life 155
cherry, pin 16, 256, 306, 315
coniferous (evergreen) 50, 88,
94, 109, 147, 225, 248, 301
deciduous 205, 225, 248, 296,
318
elder 27
fir, balsam 13, 15, 94, 138,

Trees/fir (continued)
143, 154, 159, 165, 174,
187, 198, 203, 204, 215,
220, 250, 258
hemlock, Eastern 6, 18, 20,
23, 25, 30, 34, 42, 45, 66,
85, 93, 95, 97, 103, 132,
138, 165, 174, 196, 198,
203, 212, 215, 225, 263
krummholtz 227
maple 6, 12, 14, 20, 23, 27,
30, 34, 36, 39, 115, 138,
154, 159, 165, 168, 174,
187, 208, 211, 220, 227
mountain 6, 8, 15, 114
red 15, 33, 36, 56, 225,
228
striped 6, 8, 12, 15, 30, 32,
47, 129, 225, 266
sugar 15, 30, 35, 215
oak 13, 16, 58, 59, 64–67, 70,
94, 138, 140, 165, 212, 268,
282, 290–292, 304
red 9, 139, 225, 227, 266,
296
scrub (bear) 11, 266, 269,
296
pine 45, 55, 67, 98, 114, 115,
138, 174, 279, 290
jack 209, 212, 215,
251–253
pitch 11, 15, 45, 59, 60,
65–67, 70, 78, 129, 131,
132, 143, 165, 180–182,
207, 209, 212, 215, 231,
251, 262–266, 268, 277,
279, 282, 296, 304
red 11, 15, 86, 147, 165,
166, 197, 215, 266, 296
white 11, 13, 15, 32, 42, 45,
54, 71, 95, 97, 102, 131,
139, 147, 154, 159, 161,
165, 166, 168, 187, 197,
203, 212, 213, 215, 225,
250, 263, 266, 268, 279,
296, 304, 312
popple (aspen) 53, 71, 85,
107, 114, 131, 165, 180,
182, 196, 208, 211, 212,
215, 263, 264, 282, 317
shadbush 220
snags 97, 98, 114, 126, 138,
147, 156, 165–167, 175,
199, 214, 233, 250, 268
spruce 6, 11, 20, 30–32, 34,
36, 44, 45, 55, 66, 69, 78,
82, 85, 95, 97, 98, 102, 103,
109, 114, 116, 121, 131,
132, 134, 135, 138, 143,
147, 158, 160, 165, 168,
174, 178, 182, 187, 190,
194, 197, 202–205, 207,
220, 225, 244, 245, 252,

Trees/spruce (continued)
253, 255, 256, 258, 259,
273, 279, 282, 290, 300,
301, 307
red 15, 16, 48, 68, 95, 126,
154, 159, 161, 168, 175,
180, 198, 204, 212, 215,
231, 247, 250–252, 268,
272, 296
white 68, 79, 180, 182, 231,
251, 252, 268
Stephen Hawking tree 45
sumac 16, 129, 262
tamarack 113, 114, 165
TWA Flight 800, 285

Valleys 186, 215
the Amphitheater 106, 125,
148, 186, 188, 224, 248
Beaver Brook 16, 198, 210,
211
Beaver Hollow 197, 198
Breakneck Brook 166
Bubble Pond 30, 31, 305
Canada Hollow 42, 86
Canon Brook 60
Chickadee 35, 36, 100–105,
200, 202, 204, 205, 313
Deer Brook 135, 224, 292
Great Brook 111
Green Mtn. Gorge 197
Hunters Brook 30, 31, 99,
307
Jordan Pond 31, 121
Jordan Stream 87, 121
Kebo Brook 16, 195, 196,
260
layered 121
Little Harbor Brook 87, 88,
126, 146, 186
Man o' War Brook 139,
266–269
Otter Creek 60, 129, 130,
253, 283
Sargent Brook 33, 34, 36,
104, 121, 200, 202, 205
Southwest Pass 222
Wildcat Valley 205, 246–248
Vehicles
jets, low-flying 294
machines 102
mower, Bolens 255
seaplane 244, 290, 292
skates, in-line 228
ski-trail grooming machine
102
snowmobiles 112, 134, 153
Stanley Steamer 285
Views from 260
Acadia Mtn. Tr. 266–268
the Anvil 259
Around-Mtn. Carr. Rd. 121,
122

Views from (continued)
Asticou Tr. 88
Bald Peak 246, 248
Bear Brook Tr. 131, 132
Beech Cliff 43, 44, 244
Beech Mtn. 83, 86, 244
the Beehive 128, 130
Bernard Mtn. 55, 56
Blueberry Hill 255
Brown Mtn. Tr. 279
the Bubbles 19, 22, 315, 318, 319
Cadillac Mtn. N. Ridge Tr. 253, 254
Cadillac Mtn. Rd. 135
Cadillac Mtn. S. Ridge Tr. 253
Cadillac Mtn. W. Face Tr. 304, 305
Cedar Swamp Mtn. 106, 107, 188
Champlain Mtn. 128, 131, 281, 282
Cliffside Bridge 121
Cliff Tr. (Isle au Haut) 232
Conners Nubble 21, 318
Day Mtn. 177
Dorr Mtn. E. Face 61
Duck Harbor Mtn. (Isle au Haut) 232
Duck Harbor Tr. (Isle au Haut) 231
Eagle Cliff 12
Eagles Crag 253
Eliot Mtn. 193
Gilmore Peak 35, 201
Gorham Mtn. Tr. 283
Grandgent Tr. 104, 105, 204, 312
Great Head 179–181
Hadlock Brook Tr. 309
Halfmoon Pond 167
Hemlock Bridge 120
Jordan Cliffs Tr. 291, 292
Jordan Cliffs Tr. extension 227
Jordan Pond 158, 222, 227
Kebo Mtn. Tr. 264
Knight Nubble 56
lesser peaks 19, 21
Little Harbor Brook Tr. 125
(Little) Long Pond 125
Long Pond parking 300
Mansell Mtn. Tr. 47
Maple Spring Tr. 36
McFarland Hill 93
Norumbega Mtn. Tr. 279
the Notch 197
Parkman Mtn. Tr. 34, 246–248
Pemetic Mtn. 32, 271, 272
Penobscot Mtn. 8, 9
Precipice Tr. 63, 64

Views from (continued)
Razorback Tr. 47
Sargent Mtn. 105, 171
Sargent Mtn. N. Ridge 27, 203
Schoodic Head Tr. 257
the Triad 177
Valley Peak 11
Westerm Head Tr. 231
Western Mtn. 303
Witch Hole Pd. 164, 166
Volcanoes 142, 155, 232

Water 6, 47, 48, 55, 59, 60, 114, 117–119, 123, 215
running and still 216
Water bars 48
Waterfalls 117, 141, 198
Chasm Falls 26, 120
frozen 71
Hadlock Falls 102, 147, 168
Watersheds 114, 215
Aunt Betty Pond 24
Eagle Lake 23, 261
genius of a 279
Hadlock Ponds 168, 169, 309
Hodgdon Pond 115
Kebo Brook 15
Jordan Pond 23, 261
Jordan Stream 91
Little Harbor Brook 91, 185
Man o' War Brook 269
miniature 51
north facing 15
visible 85
Wetlands 241, 251, 256, 262, 268, 274, 277, 280, 287, 307
alder swamp 181, 182
Bass Harbor Marsh 48, 143, 153
below Precipice 65
Big Heath 142, 143, 153
cedar swamps 114, 115, 154, 207
draining to Witch Hole Pond 166
Gilmore Bog 24, 28
Great Meadow 131, 196, 199, 260, 262, 264
the Horseshoe 66, 127, 128, 132
Hunters Brook 307
Isle au Haut 232, 233
Jordan Pond, north of 121
Jordan Pond, southeast of 41, 222
on legs 6
Maple Spring Tr. 36
Norumbega Mtn. 277, 280
Pemetic Mtn. 274
Sand Beach Marsh 129, 180
Schoodic Peninsula 256

Wetlands (continued)
scrub-shrub swamp 154
sphagnum bog 56
vernal pool 196
Wild-deer-ness 20
Wildflowers (see Flowers) 242, 243, 275, 277
Wild Gardens of Acadia 232, 261
Wildlife signs (see also Mammals; Scats; Tracks) 180, 183, 184
ants 98, 201
bark beetle 86
beaver 15, 38, 41, 93, 132, 183, 218, 227
beaver dam 17, 164, 166, 199, 210, 282
beaver lodge 17, 40, 57, 70, 118, 121, 129, 130, 163, 164, 166, 180, 183, 199, 218, 220, 222
bird 93
chickadee 86, 147
coyote 15, 24, 183
crow 183
deer 38, 41, 93, 129, 137, 140, 234
feathers 12, 19, 42, 180
grouse 47, 256
junco 17
flicker 15
fox 93
grouse, ruffed 183
hare, snowshoe 57, 72, 93, 129, 156, 188, 259, 301
insect tunnels 67, 147, 171
junco 15
lichen dust 111, 114, 147
mouse 183
nests 86, 93, 118, 128, 132, 165, 244
deer 109, 111
flicker 233, 258
sparrow's 72
wasps' 15
owl pellet 129, 132, 180, 183
robin 183
shrew 137, 139
squirrel 25
squirrel, red 15, 57, 156, 175, 183, 193
vole 137, 139, 172, 175
weasel 183
woodpecker 147, 175
pileated 13, 17, 19, 38, 42, 57, 82, 86, 93, 97, 137, 156, 188, 193, 201, 295
sapsucker holes 8, 15, 17, 24, 38, 86, 93, 295
Wind 18, 22, 29, 31, 32, 34, 100, 101, 104, 106, 111, 121, 142, 145, 146, 166, 176, 180,

Wind (continued)
181, 183, 191, 193, 204, 218, 224, 233
equinoctial 30
"Window on the sea" 79, 80
Wonderland 142
Woods (see also Trees) 161, 246, 247, 250–252, 256–259, 264–266, 279, 280, 290, 301, 303, 318, 319
beech 16, 21, 177, 227, 243, 263, 272–274, 282, 307, 317
best 53, 245
birch 93, 179, 199, 227, 262–264, 272, 282, 307, 313
birch and maple 262, 282
cedar 13, 291, 304, 305
coniferous (evergreen) 7, 58, 87, 139, 161, 166, 178, 179, 186, 244
deciduous 58, 71, 178, 179, 186, 196
Eliot Mtn. 192
golden 40
Maine 97, 98, 114, 314
mixed 30, 48, 50, 168, 169, 187, 266, 268, 279, 282, 290, 293, 296, 302, 307
"mossy and moosey" 6
oak 93, 94, 139, 196, 227, 262, 263
old and decadent 11
old-growth 55, 97, 192
open 189
pitch pine 58, 129, 263
primal 161
private 124, 125
real 250
self-employed 5, 47
self-governing 124
serious 54
spring 233
spruce 50, 72, 191–193, 204, 218, 222, 258, 274, 282
old-growth 51, 52, 55
spruce and birch 181
unending 114
wet 6, 138, 250, 277, 279
Western Mtn. 53
winter 109
Worm, green 278

Youth Conservation Corps (YCC) 221, 297, 318